Racism, Colonialism, and Indigeneity in Canada

Racism, Colonialism, and Indigeneity in Canada

A READER

EDITED BY

Martin J. Cannon & Lina Sunseri

With foreword by Brendan Hokowhitu

THIRD EDITION

OXFORD
UNIVERSITY PRESS

Oxford University Press is a department of the University of Oxford.
It furthers the University's objective of excellence in research, scholarship,
and education by publishing worldwide. Oxford is a registered trade mark
of Oxford University Press in the UK and in certain other countries.

Published in Canada by Oxford University Press
8 Sampson Mews, Suite 204, Don Mills, Ontario M3C 0H5 Canada

www.oupcanada.com

Library of Congress Cataloging-in-Publication Data
Names: Cannon, Martin J., editor. | Sunseri, Lina, editor.
Title: Racism, colonialism, and indigeneity in Canada : a reader / edited
by Martin J. Cannon, Lina Sunseri.
Description: Third edition. | Ontario, Canada : Oxford University Press,
[2024] | Includes bibliographical references.
Identifiers: LCCN 2023032635 (print) | LCCN 2023032636 (ebook) | ISBN
9780199039920 (softcover) | ISBN 9780190167714 (epub)
Subjects: LCSH: Indigenous peoples—Canada—Social conditions. | Indigenous
peoples—Canada—Government relations. | Racism—Canada. | Canada—Race
relations.
Classification: LCC E78.C2 R25 2024 (print) | LCC E78.C2 (ebook) | DDC
305.800971—dc23/eng/20230713
LC record available at https://lccn.loc.gov/2023032635
LC ebook record available at https://lccn.loc.gov/2023032636

Oxford University Press is committed to our environment.
This book is printed on Forest Stewardship Council® certified paper
and comes from responsible sources.

Printed by Marquis, Canada

Contents

Foreword

Disciplinary Cogency

Brendan Hokowhitu

Although I have only had the opportunity to meet Dr. Cannon once at the 8th Annual Native American and Indigenous Studies Association conference held in Honolulu, Hawaii in 2016, I have met with Dr. Sunseri a few times. I first met her at a graduate gathering in about 2000 during which time we were both in the throes of completing our PhDs. Back then, access to Indigenous writings was limited to critical Indigenous studies writings written by Indigenous scholars. This was a major source of conversation between us and, as with other burgeoning youngish Indigenous graduate students, we were crying out for material that could at least provide a scaffold for our PhDs. Fortunately, Linda Tuhiwai Smith's seminal text, *Decolonising Methodologies* (1999), was available to us. Yet, it is fair to say that as a canonical field critical Indigenous studies did not exist before 2006. Prior to that, its genesis had been *ad hoc*, with the amorphous concept of "Indigenous Studies" arising out of the ashes of anthropology and area studies departments in Canada and elsewhere. Edited collections did exist that concentrated on localized Indigenous issues; however, they were typically edited and authored by primarily white people.

The creation of various iterations of Native studies departments and programs in unsettler countries from the 1970s through to the 2000s meant also the possibility, at least, existed for the conception of a global Indigenous studies. However, these units were strongholds for local Indigenous knowledges, while critical Indigenous Studies per seas a broader disciplinary concept was viewed as auxiliary to localized core curricula. Typically, Indigenous studies units have historically developed as subdivisions of other disciplines such as anthropology with their own established canons, particularly in Aotearoa. In Aotearoa, Māori Studies departments began being established in the 1970s, growing out of anthropology and, thus, had foci on the "preservation" of culture and language. While in the United States and Canada, prior to 2006, the standard was programs without a disciplinary home and tethered together in piecemeal fashion. These programs were taught by scholars with home departments such as History, English, Women's Studies, Geography, Anthropology, Political Science and Law. Indigenous Studies, thus, lacked any semblance of a coherent genealogy from which it could build on, in large part because it had borrowed multilaterally from various disciplines, while trying to account for a diverse range of Indigenous contexts.

This is not to say, however, that local departments necessarily lacked a coherent genealogy within their own distinct context. Yet, the broader genealogical incongruence and orphan-like history meant that in 2000 the likelihood of a cogent critical Indigenous studies discipline emerging was unlikely. At the time, it was hopefully pointed out by Tuhiwai Smith that "the movement has developed a shared international language or discourse which enables indigenous activists to talk to each other across their cultural differences."[1] Yet, in Aotearoa at the time the appetite amongst

---

1. L. T. Smith, *Decolonising Methodologies* (New York: Zed Books).

Māori Studies staff at least was limited because of the weight given to the ontological importance of local contexts, languages, and cultures. Moreover, while we may have hoped for ubiquitous theorization that could abet all Indigenous peoples in their resistance, as Smith also pointed out, "the strength of the movement is to be found in the examples of how communities have mobilised locally, the grassroots development. It is at the local level that indigenous cultures and the cultures of resistance have been born and nurtured over generations."[2]

Since then, however, critical Indigenous studies has boomed with the groundwork being laid by our activist ancestors in the 1970s and 1980s in particular, and, henceforward, the soil was fertile for the flourishing of courses, programs, Departments, Schools, research institutes, and even Faculties of Native, Aboriginal, First Nations, Hawaiian, Sami, Māori, and Indigenous Studies. I refer to the year 2006 above as a notable date because it was the year of the first meeting of the Native American and Indigenous Studies Association (NAISA) in Oklahoma, although it wasn't until the gathering in Minneapolis in 2009 that the Association was officially instated. The gathering at Oklahoma was a landmark event in relation to the proliferation of critical Indigenous studies as a discipline. Indeed, at least three of the authors in this collection were at that meeting, as was I. I relate this short disciplinary history to locate my trajectory with one of the editors, and to recount that the academic world we live in now, for Indigenous scholars, is incredibly different to what Lina and I experienced as Indigenous PhD students in the late 1990s and early 2000s. The first edition of this edited collection was published in 2011, which is remarkable to consider given the dearth of scholarship at that time, and that Smith's seminal text was only published 12 years prior.

Coming at possibly the height of critical Indigenous studies (so far) the third edition of this edited collection brings together some of the leading Indigenous and non-Indigenous scholars and writers not only in Canada but worldwide. Broken into fifteen parts and 30 individual chapters the collection offers comprehensive coverage of the most pressing issues and fundamental pillars to critical Indigenous studies in Canada and globally. I relate this back to the short disciplinary genealogy I offer because the collection's taxonomy speaks to the fundamental conceptual underpinnings of what is now a cogent and flourishing discipline because of this intellectual stability. It could even be said that this collection adds weight to the argument that the tenets of a universal critical Indigenous studies have concretized. This stabilization has largely emerged because of Indigenous academic leadership and specifically those ground-breaking Indigenous scholars who oversaw the formation of NAISA; Warrior, O'Brien, Lomawaima, Kauanui, and others. This emergence also occurred because of the inevitable impulsion to produce internationally recognised scholarship within western academia, which indeed has compelled many indigenous scholars and writers to theorise their local contexts within frameworks that enable dialogue across colonial contexts. Nevertheless, all the authors in this edited collection write with a confidence that, taken as a whole, I can only interpret as a sign that critical Indigenous studies has come of age in Canada and globally.

Undergirded by concepts such as nation building, heteropatriarchy, gendered violence, displacement, marginality, health, and resistance, the authors produce a collection where locally indigenised truths are tabled for analyses that goes beyond "discovery" or "conclusion" to a collective Indigenous realm of resistance, ensconced within a multiplicity of Indigenous subjectivities. These disciplinary underpinnings are markers of resistance that scholarly Indigenous self-determination movements and activism are now anchored by. I revel in the new breed of Indigenous scholars that many of the authors in this collection have supervised and mentored, who are now assertively

---

2. Ibid.

comfortable talking about these topics in safe academic spaces. Indeed, scholarly resistance via these key concepts has, to some extent, led to a new way of Indigenous being nurtured by what is fast becoming a conventionalised critical Indigenous studies. While the collection in no way forgets the disciplinary ancestors of these stabilizing concepts (because they are indeed present throughout this collection), nonetheless land, language, and culture no longer hold the Indigenous studies limelight that they once held.

The uniqueness of each chapter and each area of analyses does not belie an oppositional collective identity focused on eradicating the social inequalities of colonisation or to breaking down the binary of the racialized indigenous Other and western Self. Rather, as a collective determined by issues of indigenous existentialism it is indigenous situatedness that is emphasized, including embodied notions of place and culture that dismiss attempts to locate Indigenous people as "Canadian." The collection's transcultural indigenous union is underpinned by difference and contradictions. Although constrained by the limiting notions of the nation "Canada" and "race," nonetheless the authors' situated fluidity in what it means to be "indigenous" and what it means to resist the nation state and racist discourse speaks to how critical Indigenous studies, as a cogent discipline, can speak and narrate together in discord.

I lived in Canada during a time which seemed to me to be pivotal in its history. I arrived at the University of Alberta just as Idle No More reared its beautiful head and returned to Aotearoa as Canada's Truth and Reconciliation Commission released its action plan. Since then, I have never been far from Canada's Indigenous political landscape due to the ever presence of social media and because of the ingenious ways Indigenous people and youth employ it to mobilise and radicalize. Other events since I left Canada have occurred more locally with Ihumātao in Aotearoa and Mauna Kea in Hawai'i. The ubiquitousness of the struggles that we face as Indigenous peoples is highlighted by this collection as I instantly comprehend a common language even though it refers to a context that is not my own. With the global sharing of Indigenous resistances through academic texts and social media, coherent communities of international resistance and support have formed, meaning the further emergence of new Indigenous ontologies and community identities. Although focused on the nation of Canada, the collection speaks to the possibilities of an Indigenous movement where the need for "Canada" will be no longer.

All Our Relations

Acknowledgements

This anthology of writings stems from conversations we have had about them as scholarly works, and in general, since meeting each other as graduate students at York University in the mid-1990s. Faced with the formidable responsibility of teaching courses concerning social justice, Indigenous peoples, and racism, we have incorporated these writings in our classes and discussions, and we have spoken about them with friends, family, colleagues, students, and, sometimes, the authors themselves. In each case, we feel they contain instructive insights, indispensable to those wishing to explore and combat racism and colonialism in Canada.

As colleagues and friends, we share much in common as Indigenous peoples. We are both Haudenosaunee—our fathers English and Italian respectively. We also share in our experience of post-secondary education wherein, as students of the Sociology of Race and Ethnic Relations, it seemed at times that racism and colonialism—and their impact on Indigenous peoples—did not fare centrally enough. The inspiration for this book thus emerged, at least in part, out of our undergraduate frustrations. We hope this anthology—and pedagogical components—will work toward fostering change within the academy, and for younger generations of Indigenous and non-Indigenous peoples.

There are many people to be acknowledged for the realization of this book. We especially wish to extend our gratitude to Oxford University Press for their diligence and enthusiasm at every stage of the publication process. We wish to thank Mariah Fleetham, Emma Guttman-Moy, and Isabelle Shi for helping us to realize the third edition of *Racism, Colonialism, and Indigeneity in Canada*. Jessey Coffey, Ian Gibson, Jodi Lewchuk, Jennifer Mueller, Darcy Pepper, Nancy Reilly, and Jennifer Wallace helped us to realize the first and second editions of the book.

Several colleagues and friends have supported and challenged us over the years and also need to be acknowledged. We are grateful to Beverley Jacobs (Mohawk) and the late Trish Monture (Mohawk). Martin wishes to acknowledge colleagues, including Susan Hill (University of Toronto) and Rinaldo Walcott (University of Toronto). Lina wishes to acknowledge her colleagues at Brescia, Western University, in particular Lisa Jakubowski. While we are both responsible for the articles, openers, and pedagogical material we have included in this book, these individuals have in some way supported us and shaped our ideas and thinking.

We wish to acknowledge students who have assisted us in realizing this third edition, including Morgan Mannella (Henvey Inlet First Nation) and Heather Watts (Mohawk, Six Nations of the Grand River), both of whom provided invaluable research assistance.

We also thank friends and family for loving and supporting us over the many years. Martin wishes to thank his parents Gord Cannon and the late Alva Cannon (4 Sept 1938–10 Nov 2021), and his immediate and extended family. Lina wishes to thank her parents and immediate and extended family.

But most importantly, we want to give our thanks to the Creator, Sky Woman, and All Our Relations for nurturing us and providing us with daily gifts.

About the Cover Art

Jeff Thomas

I was born and raised in the city of Buffalo. New York and I are also a member of the Six Nations of The Grand River Territory in southern, Ontario. I began my career as a photographer in 1980 and my first subject was the old and abandoned area of downtown Buffalo; a vibrant place I had seen as a kid. But a point came in 1984, when I wanted to inject my work with an Indigenous perspective, and my first step was making street portraits of my son Bear. The second phase began when I started posing plastic Indian figures in locations that interested me. The new series has the concurrent meaning of addressing cultural absences and cultural stereotyping. The series "Indian on Tour" began in 1999 and is still a part of my practice.

Not Disappearing

An Introduction to the Text

Our third edition of *Racism, Colonialism, and Indigeneity in Canada* follows on the heels of several significant developments and events in Canada. Following from the publication of our second edition in 2018, we provide a brief overview of some of these developments in Chapter 15 of this volume, including the resurgent and historic Land Back initiative aimed at recuperating economic control and territory across Turtle Island (landback.org); the Wet'suwet'en defending their land from the Coastal GasLink pipeline project (unistoten.camp); the insistence by Mi'kmaq lobster fishers of their sovereign right to fish without interferences by non-Indigenous peoples and Fisheries and Oceans Canada (CBC News, 12 July 2022a); Red Dress Day (lilreddressproject.ca), and the Every Child Matters movements marked by the now yearly *Orange Shirt Day* and other initiatives aimed at creating and rejuvenating "meaningful reconciliation in Canada" (National Centre for Truth and Reconciliation). At every turn, Indigenous resistance, and more accurately, refusal to consent to settler colonialism's eliminatory logic (Simpson, 2016: 238), has been steadfast since 2018. Moreover, it has increasingly become "grassroots Indigenous, Black Lives Matter, and non-Indigenous Canadians" showing up and in solidarity and to make it clear that "there is no room for social injustice in a just Canada" (Macleans, 15 Sept 2020).

A great deal has taken place as well following Canada's Truth and Reconciliation Commission (TRC), who in 2015, shortly before the release of our second edition, released its final report listing 94 "calls to action" necessary to repair the harm imposed by Indian Residential Schools (IRS). As colleagues, we were deeply troubled to learn of unmarked graves being reported at the site of former residential schools across the country in 2021 (CBC News, 27 May 2021f), followed by a visit to Canada in summer 2022 by the Bishop of Rome, Pope Francis, who in delivering an apology for the evils of IRS and the Catholic Church's role in them (Global News, 5 August 2022), stopped short of denouncing the Doctrine of Discovery and other papal bulls used still today to dispossess Indigenous peoples of land and to further the colonial project.

In 2022, as in 2018 when our last volume was released, the importance and urgency of apprehending the structure (and not event) of racism and settler colonialism cannot be underestimated. It is necessary to implement the *United Nations Declaration on the Rights of Indigenous Peoples* (The Canadian Press, 30 September 2022), and not just pay lip service to reconciliation in the current *Framework for the Implementation of Indigenous Rights* (Canadian Bar Association, 30 September 2022). We also echo the concerns of others, including the CBC in its "Beyond 94" website (https://newsinteractives.cbc.ca/longform-single/beyond-94), and The Yellowhead Institute (https://yellowheadinstitute.org/trc/), that there is still much to be done to reverse and repair the damage done, both past and presently, in settler colonial and post TRC Canada.

The violence enacted on Indigenous communities via IRS is far from being a matter of the historical past. In fact, Cindy Blackstock (2007) has argued that IRS, while they may have closed their doors, have morphed into child welfare practices. Canadian courts have agreed with Blackstock, and the Canadian human rights tribunal, in issuing a recent judgment that argues Canada discriminates against children on reserves, especially because "on-reserve child welfare receives up to 38% less funding than elsewhere." Within the last few years, survivors of the Sixties Scoop have obtained a $700 million settlement, and an Agreement in Principle has also been reached to compensate First Nations communities for the government's failure to fairly and adequately fund children and family services in reserves (CBC News, 1 February 2021d). Combined, these issues point to a set of critical issues in need of reconciliation in Canada; notably, the need to acknowledge that Settler colonialism is what Patrick Wolfe (2006) has referred to as a "structure" and not "event" that remains in place today; and also, the need for a set of theoretical perspectives written by Indigenous scholars in particular that address the past and present history of Settler colonial wrongdoing.

The range of theoretical perspectives written by and about Indigenous North Americans on race and Settler colonialism is vast in scope. This book could not possibly capture all of these voices. We do not apologize for including classical writings by now deceased scholars who we believe paved the way in both Native and also Critical Indigenous Studies for more contemporary scholarship to ensue. We recognize that our book is focused on Canada and that a book addressing comparatively the United States and Canada (and also internationally) would be a different book altogether, but definitely one we would like to explore as scholars in the near future. Our third edition also seeks to include a greater breadth of writing about the Canadian landscape and geography, including western and northern Canada as well as the prairies. We do not purport that our book can cover everything or even all of these things. Instead, in this updated volume, we seek to provide an initial overview of perspectives, as well as some of the issues, themes, and concerns that have been raised when it comes to addressing matters of Settler colonialism and Indigeneity. Some of these perspectives draw attention to the structural and interpersonal impacts of racism on the lives of our peoples and nations. Others draw attention to the obligations of Indigenous peoples and Settlers where understanding, acknowledging, and taking responsibility for systemic colonial injustices is concerned. Of course, we recognize that "empire may create settlers but that not all settlers are shaped universally by empire" (Veracini, 2010: 4).

Indeed, and as Roxanne Dunbar-Ortiz (2021: 50) has already written:

> Settlers are founders of political orders and carry their sovereignty with them., whereas immigrants face a political order that is already constituted. Immigrants can certainly be co-opted within settler-colonial societies, and often are, but they do not enjoy inherent rights and are characterized by a defining lack of sovereign entitlement . . . policies based on exclusion make the new immigrant's life precarious, particularly for immigrants of color entering a racial order that renders them suspect already, so they may not want to know the reality or that they have a choice and that by default they become settlers.

Walia (2103) also writes of "appellants facing a political order that is already constituted" (Veracini, 2010: 3). Some migrants, she writes, are:

> Indigenous to their own lands, but often displaced due to Orientalist crusading and corporate plundering . . . thrown into capitalism's pool of labor and, in a cruel twist, violently inserted into the political economy of genocide: *stolen labor on stolen land*. (ibid: 126, emphasis in original)

We invite a critical engagement with the question of "who, under what conditions, inherits the power to represent or enact settler colonialism" (Saranillio, 2013: 283). These are recognizably complex questions of settlement and citizenship, the latter being a concept finding its early roots in whiteness, a domain from which Black and other racialized peoples were excluded from historically in not being conceived of as human (Maynard, 2019: 127; McKittrick, 2015).

The literature concerning Indigenous-settler relations speaks to the promise of realizing a new set of possibilities still being articulated. We hope that our third edition, like prior editions, might foster further alliances and collaborative relationships where building relations of co-resistance between Indigenous, Black, migrant, and racialized peoples is concerned. It is important to consider as part of this process, as Haunani-Kay Trask (2006: 9) once wrote that "the color of violence is the color of white over black, white over brown, white over red, white over yellow," and also that, "the bloody extermination of Native peoples, the enslavement of forcibly transported peoples, and the continuing oppression of dark-skinned peoples" shows that genocide and settlement work in tandem with slavery and anti-black racism both historically and in the settler colonial present. We would like to suggest also that early nation-to-nation agreements represent an important set of organizing principles where realizing the shared responsibility to address colonial injustice is concerned, and toward a renewal and rejuvenation of Settler–Indigenous relations.

Turtle Island is a word that is commonly used by Indigenous peoples to refer to North America. For Haudenosaunee(sometimes called the Six Nations or Iroquois) our story of creation describes how this land came to be. Our elders tell us that before this earth was created, there was only water and water beings. There also existed the sky world and sky beings. One day, Sky Woman fell from this world and brought with her the medicines: the corn, squash, beans, tobacco, and strawberries that sustain us. The water beings laid Sky Woman and her medicines upon a turtle's back and Mother Earth was created. This version of the creation story, albeit shortened for our purposes here, has been told in slightly different ways. Our Elders have kept these teachings alive, even when forbidden by racist, colonial, and genocidal legislation (Posluns, 2007) and we give Yawa:ko (thanks) for their ongoing resistance.

We take the maintenance of our traditional stories seriously. We recognize that as we move toward decolonizing and Indigenizing the academy, it is important to engage with Indigenous communities and invite Indigenous Elders and culture keepers to share their stories and knowledge in the classrooms. This must be done collaboratively and respectfully and by following the cultural protocols of the specific communities from where any guest is coming. Things to consider would be the giving of offerings like tobacco, providing a fair honorarium, and having a space for smudging if this is to be practiced. Ultimately, one should consult with community members and seek advice from any Indigenous services or programs that their academic institution might have in place, so to ensure that these learning experiences are conducted in a culturally safe and ethical way (see Western University's policy on such matters, as an example for consideration.; available at https://indigenous.uwo.ca/initiatives/docs/working-indigenous-community.pdf)

We are also concerned with the memory of historic treaties made on a nation-to-nation basis between our ancestors and the newcomers to Turtle Island. We believe these agreements hold original instructions and are key to showing how Indigenous and non-Indigenous peoples alike might address colonial injustice and racism. The Two-Row Wampum or Guswentah in particular is an agreement that is familiar to us as Haudenosaunee scholars. A historic wampum—a beaded belt embroidered from freshwater shells—serves to formalize or "certify" original nation-to-nation agreements. Wampum are of great significance to our ancestors because they function to formalize agreements and, as Patricia Monture-Angus (1999: 36–7) has explained, were neither easily forgotten nor destroyed.

The Two-Row Wampum dates to 1613 and is represented on a beaded belt which contains two purple beaded lines against a white backdrop. As Williams and Nelson (1995: 3) have described, "The two row wampum . . . symbolizes the river of life on which the Crown's sailing ship and the Haudenosaunee canoe both travel." The three white rows are recognized as symbolizing an everlasting "peace, friendship, and respect between the two nations" (quoted in Johnston, 1986: 32; also see Monture-Angus, 1999: 37). Peace, friendship, and respect—as represented by the three white rows—embody the basis upon which we are "bounded together" and also interdependent (Mackey, 2016: 135; Hill, 2008: 30; and Turner, 2006: 45). The metaphor of the European vessel and Confederacy canoe functions to characterize two distinct jurisdictions which were ordained in 1664 to coexist independently (Borrows, 1997: 164–5). Originally exchanged with Dutch traders, and subsequently the British Crown, the Two-Row Wampum belt speaks of separate jurisdictions. As Johnston (1986: 11) writes:

> The two were to go exist as independent entities, each respecting the autonomy of the other. The two rows of purple wampum, representing the two governments, run parallel, never crossing. The two vessels travel together, as allies, but neither nation tries to steer the other's vessel. In the relationship envisioned by the Two Row Wampum, neither government has the authority to legislate for the other.

In the twenty-first century, the Two-Row Wampum continues to be of tremendous significance. For the Six Nations Confederacy, the Guswentah establishes an historic relationship with the British Crown as an independent nation and also as allies. Moreover, the Two-Row Wampum embodies the principle of separate jurisdictions. This is something that other Indigenous scholars on Turtle Island have highlighted in their work. For example, Lynn Gehl (2014) reminds all Canadians that the original spirit of the Royal Proclamation of 1763 and the 1764 Treaty at Niagara were both intended to enable Algonquin Anishinaabeg to live as sovereign nations practising mino-pimadiziwin (the good life). Leanne Simpson (2008, and in this volume) also talks about the treaties made among ourselves as nations, including Gdoo-naaganinaa, our Dish With One Spoon, intended to provide Haudenosaunee and Anishinabe with a means of realizing separate jurisdictions within a shared territory. From this perspective, racism and Settler colonialism—in seeking as they do to disrupt and restrict the lives of Indigenous peoples ranging from issues of land administration to the ability for us to determine our own peoples—constitutes a British "foot" in the Haudenosaunee canoe.

Although we use racism here to mean a violation of original principles set out in original nation-to-nation agreements, racism has been and can be defined academically in several different ways. Henry and Tator (2006: 5) define racism as a set of "assumptions, attitudes, beliefs, and behaviours of individuals as well as to the institutional policies, process, and practices that flow from those understandings." Combined, racism refers to societal disadvantages experienced by a people or group. Racism can be further divided into the forms it takes in society, including individual, systemic, and structural racism (ibid., 350–2).

Individual racism stems from an individual's conscious and/or personal prejudice (ibid., 350). It refers to outward and overt attitudes of intolerance or bigotry. Systemic racism refers to policies and practices that result in the exclusion of individuals, or that work to effect considerable disadvantages on a specific group. Systemic racism can be both institutional and structural; the former referring to "racial discrimination that derives from individuals carrying out the dictates of others who are prejudiced or of a prejudiced society" (ibid., 352). Lastly, structural racism refers to inequalities that are "rooted in the system-wide operation of a society" (ibid., 352). They refer to practices that "exclude substantial numbers . . . of particular groups from significant participation in major social institutions" (ibid., 352).

Racism is not always obvious, overt, or even impolite. Indeed, Henry and Tator have focused on racism as it is effected in liberal and democratic societies like Canada. They define democratic racism as "any set of justificatory arguments and mechanisms that permit individuals to maintain racist beliefs while championing democratic values" (ibid., 19). It is through 12 popular discourses that racism is structured and effected, including the discourse of denial, political correctness, colour-blindness, equal opportunity, blaming the victim, white victimization, reverse racism, binary polarization, moral panic, multiculturalism, liberal tolerance, and the discourse of national identity (for a detailed discussion, see Henry and Tator, 2006).

We take these academic definitions of racism seriously, but as discussed, we argue that within an Indigenous context racist ideologies and practices violate ancient principles set out in the Two-Row Wampum, among other original agreements made between Indigenous and Settler populations. The treaties and original principles between Indigenous and newcomer populations have not been fully respected, but the spirit of this relationship—however wounded it has become—cannot be so easily broken. Indeed, it is our objective to first revisit the original principles and to remind all future generations, Indigenous or otherwise, of its terms.

Each author in this collection is re-telling the story of "settlement" (read colonization) through Indigenous eyes, hearts, minds, and souls and in the process has never forgotten, metaphorically speaking, that historic treaty principles were originally meant to guide us in our relationship with one another. The one party has always acted accordingly with respect to original principles and intention of the original agreements, and throughout the centuries has reminded the colonizer to keep its foot out of its canoe—in short to respect the autonomy of Indigenous peoples as we have respected Settler colonists. The voices in this collection will vary somewhat because of the multiplicity of our experiences, but we feel that we share a commitment to restore the original balance upon which the two entities ought to be travelling. We believe that in order to restore balance, each side needs to follow treaty principles and to know of the historical forces that upset them and brought about much disruption on Turtle Island. Once that happens, then healing can begin and a new peaceful and just journey retaken.

The word "Haudenosaunee," or People of the Longhouse, is one that we use to describe our individual sense of identity and well-being. And while we might be just as comfortable with using words like "Ukwehuwé" (the Original People), "Onyota'a:ka" (People of the Standing Stone), or even "Six Nations," we resist the concept of "Indian" to describe our collective identity. Naming is a powerful act of self-determination; in naming ourselves Haudenosaunee we are explicitly connecting ourselves to the League of the Six Nations, (re)claiming our connections with the past, present, and future peoples who make up that League wherever they or their spirits might reside in Turtle Island.

We are bound together as Haudenosaunee through kinship and clan affiliation and have an interdependent responsibility that therefore guides our every thought and act. As Monture (2008: 156) writes:

> [O]ne must understand something of the person's tribal tradition as this grounds who they are, as well as the symbols and styles they will use . . . my name grounds me in the gift of words Creator gave me. It is both identity and direction. It is strength and responsibility. It is this location, as Mohawk citizen and woman, which guides the way I see the patterns that in turn ground my understanding of who I am and what I know.

Both of us are positioned as Ukwehuwé, Onyota'a:ka, and Turtle Clan. Not all Haudenosaunee are Longhouse or possess traditional names. "Yeliwi:saks" is the spiritual name belonging to Lina assigned to her by her clan mother, which translates as "She Is Gathering Stories/Knowledge." Through the naming, she carries the responsibility of gathering stories and sharing the power of these words with others. Naming ourselves Onyota'a:ka is a powerful act of decolonization as it (re)juvenates our national identity, and tells the rest of the world that we were and are nations and are calling on others to see and treat us as such. The history of governing ourselves dates back many centuries before the arrival of ha dih nyoh (white settler).

This book stems in part from our individual and collective sense of resistance to the term "Indian," as it is one that embodies the historic and contemporary violation of Guswentah among other original agreements made between Settler and Indigenous populations, and the autonomous right of Indigenous nations to determine their own citizenry. "Indian" embodies the very first act of colonial injustice and we believe that neither decolonization nor self-determination can be realized unless we challenge this history that institutionalized Indianness. We agree with other Ukwehuwé scholars in seeing the act of self-determination to begin first with the Self (Monture, 1999). We also agree with Indigenous scholars who speak of their own nationhood and resist foreign impositions that require the terms "Aboriginal," "First Nations," and "Indian" to be used when describing Indigenous people (Alfred, 2005). We must begin to (re)identify ourselves as Indigenous nations based on our own individual peoplehood and kinship organization (Andersen, 2014, and in this volume).

Indigenous peoples became Indians under a legal classification that did not distinguish between their linguistic and cultural differences or between the multiplicity of Indigenous nations at the time. People became Indians so that the state could delimit the occupation of lands to Indians alone. It was through these sorting out of lands that the concretization of race as a social construct took place in Canada. Prior to colonization, Indigenous peoples defined themselves as distinct nations with their own socio-economic and political systems. Under Settler colonialism, the Canadian State treated all Indigenous nations as one "Indian race"; their oneness constructed by virtue of otherness. This process coincided with the conceptualization of Turtle Island as "terra nullius," a land imagined as empty and unoccupied. Property was therefore equated with whiteness (Harris, 1993); a process that allowed the colonizer to dispossess Indigenous nations of their lands.

Another motive for instituting the *Indian Act* was to protect Indians from outside land encroachments (Tobias, 1983). Early Indian policies sought to encourage the gradual civilization of the Indians through enfranchisement (ibid., 42). Enfranchisement aimed to assimilate the Indians of Canada. The premise of the legislation was simple: upon meeting certain criteria, men who were literate, free of debt, and of good moral character could (along with their "dependents") give up legal *Indian Act* status and become ordinary Canadians with all the according rights and privileges (ibid., 42) The title and premise of enfranchisement law reveals its racist underpinnings: one could not be a "civilized person" without giving up their Indian status. This is how racial categories were institutionalized. The first group to be racialized in Canada were the Indigenous peoples.

The *Indian Act* held the potential to reorganize Indigenous kinship structures, in particular those that were both matrilocal and matrilineal prior to contact. Kinship structures were based on the clan system, where descent was passed through the women's line. This stood in opposition to the patrilineal registration criteria of the *Indian Act*. If one considers that in Canada, and in most of Europe, women were not considered persons but merely the property of men, the *Indian Act* clearly devalued females and the powers they enjoyed in some Indigenous nations. The process of establishing the category "Indian" was therefore also informed by patriarchal understandings. What this history suggests to us is that the colonial enterprise of racism is inseparable from (hetero)sexism and patriarchy, as has been argued by many Indigenous scholars (see Anderson, 2000; Cannon, 2019; Green, 2007; Lawrence, 2004; Monture, 1995; Smith, 2005, 2006; Sunseri, 2000, 2011).

Patriarchy has been defined as:

[H]ierarchical relations between men and women, manifested in familial and social structures alike, in a descending order from an authoritarian—if oftentimes benevolent—male head, to male dominance in personal, political, cultural and social life, and to patriarchal families where the law of the father prevails. (Code, 2000: 378)

Patriarchy invaded our nations, transforming what was largely egalitarianism into an imbalanced set of gender relations. Jacobs (2014) defines patriarchy as none other than an attack on Indigenous womanhood following from colonization that has enabled a continued violence to be enacted on the bodies of Indigenous women. In this book, we wish to investigate these and other ideological transformations of race and gender, as well as the interlocking ways in which patriarchal notions were reaffirmed through Indian policy and other broader sets of social relations.

The *Indian Act* entrenches a set of legalized parameters involving lands. As Wotherspoon and Satzewich (1993) have pointed out, the *Indian Act* provided for the appropriation of Indigenous territories and the accumulation of capital. "The land was acquired [through] the forcible and relentless dispossession of Indigenous peoples, the theft of their territories, and the implementation of legislation and policies designed to affect their total disappearance as peoples" (Lawrence, 2002: 23). As such, "any theorizing of race must go beyond simple cultural politics [and] acknowledge the centrality of broader political and economic developments" (Anderson quoted in Wallis and Fleras, 2009: xv). The history of capitalist relations is therefore inseparable from the emergence of race as a social construct in North America. Having said that, Canada has tried to erase its historical record. It is through storytelling that we might hope to reveal and redress the hidden dimensions of political economy. As Monture (2008: 156) notes, storytelling traditions are very common in our Indigenous nations, and "through our stories we learn who we are. These stories teach about identity and responsibility." Through the stories we gather by writers in this book, we openly name the *Indian Act* and all other sociopolitical structures imposed by the Canadian State as imperialist projects.

The *Indian Act* imposed an "elected" band council system of governance upon Indigenous nations. These councils were empowered to make bylaws and, upon approval of the Superintendent of Indian Affairs, to deal with all other concerns. An elective system of governance remained a choice for Indigenous nations in Canada until an amendment in 1895. After this time, the government delegated itself the authority to depose both chiefs and councillors of bands not following an elected system (Tobias, 1983: 46–7; *Indian Act* [S.C. 1895, c.35, s.3] reprinted in Venne, 1981: 141). It is important to acknowledge that the *Indian Act* represented an imposition to already established, hereditary forms of government. We see this as a blatant act of colonialism. In seeking to replace traditional governance with an elective model, the belief in European political superiority and higher civilization became institutionalized. These ways of thinking are not confined to the past: an example of ongoing beliefs about European superiority takes place whenever the contributions of Indigenous peoples are said to have offered nothing to the building of North American civilization (*The Globe & Mail*, 25 October 2008).

We want to suggest that the *Indian Act* and other policies represent the very first instance of racialized thinking and institutionalized racism in Canada. We also want to examine how an Indian/white colour line is established and constructed under Settler colonialism. The processes that continue today to uphold, maintain, and reproduce a set of racialized ways of thinking were put into place over 150 years ago. By Settler colonialism, we are referring to the process whereby Indigenous peoples were dispossessed of their lands through a series of genocidal acts, including the imposition of racial hierarchy through Indian status distinctions. Whiteness itself became constructed as the superior racial category and consequently white supremacy has become legitimatized and normalized (Razack, 2002).

The category of Indian is by no means a neutral one. It is a category established by Europeans to refer to Indigenous difference. These distinctions are inherent to processes of racialization and Settler colonialism. Kauanui (2008: 194) has written of the way in which taxonomies of race and blood quantum thinking are tied to theft of lands and the legal extinguishment of Indigenous peoples (see also Palmater, 2011). The legal extinguishment of Indians continues today in Canada, as shown in the *McIvor* case (Cannon, 2014). Lina Sunseri (2011: 83) writes of the link between racialization and Settler colonialism as follows:

> The process whereby social relations between people became structured by attributing significant meaning to human biological and physical characteristics is referred to as racialization. This process helped to categorize colonized peoples as "races" that were "naturally different" from the colonizers. Of course, this categorization was never neutral but was closely linked to the formation of the unequal social and economic power relations inherent to colonialism.

Issues of race are not easily introduced into conversations about the self-determination of Indigenous peoples. We recognize that dialogues about racism and Settler colonialism are challenging and can trigger difficult and uncomfortable emotions in any setting where these occur, including our classrooms. However, these conversations are necessary; readers and classroom participants need to be taken out of their comfort zone for transformative learning to be able to occur. Instructors, of course, need to set guidelines for such sensitive discussions, as well as provide space for debriefing and guide students to additional resources outside of the classroom.

The construction of Indigenous difference takes place through processes of racialization and additional sets of discursive practices. Edward Said (1979) referred to an "Orientalist" discourse, a Western construction of the Orient seen as essentially "different" and inferior to the "West." When Indians are represented as the Other in their own lands, they are seen in contrast to the colonizer. Within the binary framework of Self and Other, the outcomes provide for injustice. Indigenous peoples are pathologized as genetically inferior and deviant, while the Western Self becomes the progressive, modern, and civilized subject (Sunseri, 2007). It also provides the ideological justification for the ongoing dispossession of lands, the accompanying attack on sovereignty, and the maintenance of cultural imperialism required for the furthering of capitalist exploitation.

Indeed, as Rob Porter (1999: 158), a Seneca scholar, suggests, transforming conceptions of separate political status into matters of race works ultimately to erode the status of Indigenous peoples as citizens of separate sovereigns. He writes:

> Even though Indigenous society is rooted in a sovereignty separate and apart from American sovereignty, Indians today appear to be suggesting that they should be treated in the same way as such racial minority groups as African Americans and Asian Americans. . . . While it certainly is the case that Indians have long been thought to be of a different "race," protestations solely along racial lines can only serve to undermine the perception that Indian nations have a political existence separate and apart from that of the United States. (ibid., 154)

It is incumbent upon us as Ukwehuwé to think seriously about the issues raised by Porter. In contemplating our own Haudenosaunee existence, we acknowledge that original nation-to-nation agreements were made at the time of contact with Settler colonists, including Guswentah or Two-Row Wampum. These wampum do not make reference to Ukwehuwé as races of people, but rather sovereign nations whose inherent rights were granted by the Creator, or as Augie Fleras has put it, nations who "share the sovereignty of Canada through multiple and overlapping jurisdictions" (2009: 78). We also feel that before a timeless and unbroken assertion of sovereignty can be fully realized, it will be necessary to acknowledge that colonial injustice, racism, and sexism are inextricably linked, historically, and even still today.

To begin to think about the interconnections we are describing, it is important to revisit Canada's *Indian Act*, and more specifically, Indian status distinctions. The *Indian Act* exemplifies the institutionalized racism and patriarchy that has characterized colonial dominance. Indian status is the process whereby Indigenous nations became Indians for state administrative purposes. It refers to a set of practices, beliefs, and ways of thinking that made—and continue to make—Indianness compulsory. In order to restore our status as Indigenous nations, indeed as separate political entities, it will be important to think about these historic processes, and as the Indigenous Bar Association (2010, 2017) once put it, to move citizenship and jurisdiction over the inherent right to self-definition to where it properly belongs and that is with First Nations governments. In this book, we want to suggest that asserting our political status as Indigenous nations is impossible without challenging histories of racialization.

We are not suggesting that the *Indian Act* is everything when it comes to determining Indigenous identities. Indeed, many Ukwehuwé prefer to talk of identity and citizenship—as we have in this Introduction—in nation-specific terms. But even as we assert our nation-based identities—indeed even as we know who it is that we are—the *Indian Act* continues to define who is and who is not an Indian in Canada (Cannon, 2008: 15). The act of exogamous, "out-marriage" was no means a neutral one for over 135 years from 1850–1985 (and beyond), because under earlier provisions the Indian Act worked to disenfranchise the children and grandchildren of women who married non-Indians before 1985. These individuals are a prior class of "involuntarily enfranchised" Indians—their loss of legal entitlements was brought on by their parent's choice to marry non-Indians (ibid.).

The matter of sexist discrimination under the *Indian* Act was raised at both the Superior Court and Court of Appeal levels in British Columbia in what is known as the *McIvor* case. The justices have all agreed unanimously: the treatment for Indian women and their children who claim Indian descent through them is unequal to that afforded to Indian men and their descendants (*McIvor v. Canada, Registrar, Indian and Northern Affairs*, 2007 BCSC 827 at 236). In recognizing that the grandchildren of *Indian women* were being treated differently than the grandchildren of *Indian men*, the *McIvor* case set the way for changes to federal Indian policy. It is now possible for the grandchildren of Indian women to be federally recognized as Indians (Cannon, 2014).

The history of S 6(2) of the *Indian Act* shows how pervasive the impact of sexism has been on the lives of Indigenous peoples (ibid). Of course sexism is not the only issue involved. Race and racism can also be used to describe historic injustices imposed by the *Indian Act*. The process whereby Indigenous nations became status Indians for state administrative purposes involves deeply racialized thinking. The issue itself is one that even our courts have been unable to address and acknowledge, even in progressive BC Court of Appeal judgments like the *McIvor* case. The case itself shows how intractable the institutionalized racism that characterizes the colonial present has become. The category "Indian" literally disappears below the surface of progressive politics and the law. Furthermore, in order to resist the category, we must appropriate and affirm its use. Bonita Lawrence describes the paradox we are highlighting. As she writes: "Legal categories . . . shape peoples' lives. They set the terms that individuals and communities must utilize even in resisting these categories" (2004: 230). In 2017 the Canadian Senate finally passed an amendment to Bill S-3 to eliminate all existing sexist discriminations, and in August 2019 promised that it would proceed to remove any remaining sexist inequalities in the Act, and to extend Indian Status to those prevented from it because of the 1951 cut-off rule. However, as Senators Lovelace and Francis recently pointed out, the restoration of Indian Status to those women who had lost it and to their children has shown little progress, due to systemic barriers such as backlogs and a complicated and inaccessible registration process (see Part Seven in this volume for further discussion; see also Lovelace and Francis, 2022).

We concur with Robert Porter that being awarded racial minority status cannot be understood as the central issue facing Indigenous peoples today. Having said that, we feel it is important to raise as a matter of political scrutiny and critical reflection the process through which we became racialized as Indians in Canada. This thinking does not start with adopting racial minority status but in revisiting Indianness itself. If the very first act of historical and colonial injustice involved the renaming of our diverse nations, then the urgency of dismantling racialized regimes cannot be underestimated or denied. If it is true that histories of racialization have made racism so intractable, so institutionalized, then we cannot be truly free of colonial domination if the racism directed at our nations remains intact.

In saying that we are nations and citizens of Indigenous nations, we are not only opposing the *Indian Act* and other racialized processes but we are also opposing an identity-making process that was—and is still today—key to the building of Canada as a nation (Thobani, 2007). We also want to encourage and further current discussions, as noted above, about the way in which Black, migrant, and racialized populations are invited into racialized, nation state, and border imperialist ways of thinking about citizenship and belonging (Walia, 2013; Sehdev, 2011; Phung, 2011; Madden, 2009; Lawrence and Amadahy, 2009). In that sense, this book is as much about white supremacy as it is about race, Settler colonialism, and Indigeneity. By refusing the category "Indian," we are asking all Canadians to think about how identity legislation plays a part in creating colonial settlements, and indeed lands for the taking. We are saying that our territories extend far beyond the identity classification schemes used to define them as "reserve-based lands." We want white and non-white Settler populations to think of themselves in relationship to Indigenous nations and not just the Canadian nation-state (Palmater, 2011; Thobani, 2007). We are asserting our political status as separate political entities, but we are simultaneously challenging the racialization and sexism that comprises Settler colonialism.

In contemplating the current Canadian political landscape, we draw attention to the RCAP and TRC "Calls to Action." Recommendations in both reports are not being addressed. Also, we stand by for the federal government of Canada to address the matter of settler colonialism and land back, especially in Canadian settler colonial law (Canadian Bar Association, 30 September 2022). It is necessary to address the matter of colonial reparations, including a return to original treaty and nation-to-nation principles. Both in general and in light of recent developments, we want readers of the third edition to consider the following: What sort of relationship do people want or see themselves as having with Indigenous nations? How are Canadians complicit in ongoing Settler colonialism? What is the responsibility of all Canadians to address historic wrongs? What sorts of symbolic and material work goes into the dispossession of lands, including the urban spaces we have occupied and have always been a part of? In addition to providing an overview of the writings of Indigenous peoples on and about race and Settler colonialism, it is our hope that our third edition of RCIC might again contribute to a further course of decolonizing, land back, anticolonial action, and settler-Indigenous relationships building and rejuvenation.

Organization of the Book

As surely as racism is not disappearing in North America, neither are Indigenous peoples. We offer only a glimpse of the work that is being done to understand the interconnections between race, racialization, racism, sexism, and colonialism over the past centuries. In outlining the resistance to these systems of inequality, the book draws from multiple theoretical frameworks and crosses disciplinary boundaries. This is inevitable, if not desirable: many standpoints, views, identities, and backgrounds make up Indigenous knowledge and scholarship, and our experience is shaped by where we are located within communities, the academy, and mainstream society. These differences are sources of strength because the authors in this collection offer their own gifts, their own ways of knowing and being Indigenous on Turtle Island. Each is focused on specific themes, issues, and questions that offer a unique set of perspectives about race, racism, sexism, colonialism, and decolonization.

We open the book with a review of some central theoretical foundations in Part One. How are we to think about and engage with questions of colonial dominance, racism, and Indigenous resurgence? In Chapter 1, Arthur Manuel addresses this question by centering land. He reminds the reader of an imperialist mindset that stands in the way of lands stewardship and protection. His chapter provides readers with a look at the ideological basis and underpinnings of racism and settler colonialism (e.g., the doctrine of discovery and terra nullius) that has sought to erase the territorial, political, and cultural autonomy of Indigenous peoples, a colonial way of thinking in need of our unwavering scrutiny, interrogation, and apprehension.

In Chapter 2, Leanne Simpson provides a context for understanding how it is that relations of "peace, mutual respect and mutual benefit" between nations (Settler and Indigenous) might be rejuvenated in accordance with traditional principles contained in early diplomatic and treaty relationships. She reminds us, as does Manuel, that we ought to look inward and at ancient principles rather than the status quo or Eurocentric worldviews where "resurgence, re-creation, and decolonizing" relationships is concerned.

Part Two of this book consists of two chapters outlining the history of nation-building in Canada and the construction of a racialized Indian Other. In Chapter 3, Deborah Doxtator shows how the idea of Indian was created using labels such as ferocious, drunkards, and primitive, and through stereotypical symbols like tepees, totem poles, and face paint. These symbols persist in the colonial imagination and have little to do with the actual people of the past or present. Doxtator shows how "Indians" have been portrayed in history textbooks: either as tools, as threats, as allies; nevertheless always secondary to the official heroes and builders of the nation. Colonialism is hardly ever taken up seriously in history textbooks; instead it is conceptualized as "settlement," as something that "just happened." In this way, we concur with Doxtator: the mythology of the "two founding nations" and the disappearing Indian endures within the minds of most Canadians. It is no wonder Indigenous youth feel alienated by the educational system. How are they able to see themselves reflected in textbooks if the history of their ancestors is not honestly represented?

Thomas King picks up on this review by Doxtator. In Chapter 4, he is concerned with the Indian that exists in the Settler imagination. The imaginary itself requires that Indigenous peoples always be disappearing in order to make possible, among other things, the recovery and recuperation of Settler sovereignty and lands dispossession. Much has been invested in a representation of Indigenous peoples, from popular culture to theatrics, in order to rid the state of "the inconvenient Indian."

Part Three of the book looks at how Indigenous territories and notions of peoplehood have been shaped by Settler colonialism. In Chapter 5, Bonita Lawrence challenges the dominant historical narratives of Canada and rewrites them. She examines the impact of racism and colonialism on Indigenous lands and communities in what is now called Eastern Canada. Although we cannot homogenize Indigenous experiences with colonialism, there are similar patterns that link them. In Chapter 6, Chris Andersen addresses the matter of nationhood, in particular state-based and European models that do little to centre matters of relationality and kinship organization. He emphasizes the importance of peoplehood, a concept that exists well beyond racialized categories imposed by the state, as well as some of the theoretical literature involving nationhood.

Part Four is new to our third edition. We wish to center the vastly understudied refusal by Indigenous peoples in both the United States and Canada to relinquish jurisdiction or accept the limitations imposed upon them by white settler borders and the perceived "gift" of United States or Canadian citizenship. In Part Four, we are concerned with the longest international border in the world, the US-Canada border as a site of geopolitical dominance, racism, and settler colonial regulation.

In an early and classical piece of writing, Clinton Rickard draws attention to these matters in Chapter 7 where he traces the Indian Defense League of America and his own work to assert the presence of Haudenosaunee existence that pre-dates the origin of either nation state. Rickard also highlights the Jay Treaty of 1794, which provides for the right of free passage established in the first historic instance of Indigenous-Settler contact. We are reminded of the way in which our nations well pre-date Canada and the United States as nation states.

Audra Simpson, in Chapter 8, further challenges an a-storying of history that would have us believe that our bodily movements are between and across the nation-states of Canada and the United States instead of our original homelands. She provides critical analysis of the refusal by Haudenosunee to consent to settler colonialism's eliminatory logic, and to accept the criminalization of economic activities termed by settlers as "smuggling" which misrepresents, mischaracterizes, and fails to recognize people as original occupants of land. Combined, the authors highlight the inherent nature of Indigenous sovereignty in terms of history and relationships.

Racism and colonialism have had a profound influence on Indigenous identities, including gender identities. Part Five is about how the ways in which we see our gender, how others perceive our gender to be, and how we treat each other, is all shaped by racism and settler colonialism which transformed gender relations from balanced to unequal heteropatriarchal ones. In Chapter 9, Lina Sunseri illustrates how the Canadian state's colonial laws and policies, such as the *Indian Act*'s definitions of Status Indians and the residential schooling system, negatively impacted Indigenous women's lives. While in pre-colonial times Indigenous women were regarded as "mothers of the nations" and held powerful decision-making authority in their communities, they began to experience marginalization, sexism, and patriarchy as a consequence of settler colonialism. As we move towards decolonization, we must remember that it is everyone's responsibility to reestablish gender equity in our nations, including reclaiming empowering notions of Indigenous womanhood and mothering.

However, as Pyle points out in Chapter 10, we must be careful that such reclaiming efforts do not "reproduce colonial heteropatriarchy and [affirm] essentialist so-called natural differences between men and women, and naturalizing and idealizing heterosexuality." Indeed, linking women's assumed biological characteristics with social roles can be disempowering for many individuals who do not identify exclusively, or at all, with womanhood or mothering. We must remember that there are diverse identifications and expressions of gender and sexuality, and that in many Indigenous traditional societies these were embraced. We need to ensure that all genders, including transgender, non-binary, and genderqueer people are valued and given respectful spaces in our Indigenous communities as we walk towards nation-building and a decolonized future and deconstruct cis-heteronormative notions rooted in settler colonialism.

Part Six addresses issues of gender violence affecting Indigenous women, by examining the interconnection between Settler colonialism, racism, sexism, and heteropatriarchy. Undoubtedly centuries of devaluation of Indigenous peoples in general, and of women in particular, has led to an attack on egalitarian gender relations, and an epidemic of gendered violence, as the reported Missing and Murdered Indigenous Women and Girls (MMIWG) cases illustrate.

Robyn Bourgeois, in Chapter 11, argues that Canada is a settler colonial state built upon the dispossession of lands and domination inflicted upon Indigenous peoples, particularly affecting Indigenous women. She points out that racist ideas of Indigenous women like that of the promiscuous "squaw," accompanied with discriminatory oppressive policies, led to women becoming marginalized in both their own communities and the broader Canadian society, and vulnerable to sexual objectification and violence. Racist colonial laws, negative stereotypes of Indigenous women are at the root of the epidemic of the MMIWG, an epidemic that for many decades had been ignored by the media, and not properly addressed by the Canadian justice system. It was not until few years ago that a commission report was finally concluded, which clearly linked this gendered violence to the historical settler colonialism impacting Indigenous peoples, and an action plan was recently released in 2021.

In Chapter 12, Alex Wilson examines how trans and Two-Spirit individuals are not always adequately included in discussions about Indigenous gendered violence, yet they tend to face higher rates of sexual and other forms of violence than heterosexual Indigenous women. In her chapter, Wilson discusses how colonial discourses and policies eventually replaced inclusive Indigenous notions of gender and sexuality with heterosexist ones, which led to homophobia and violent acts against trans and Two-Spirit Indigenous people. As Wilson argues, any future implementation of the recommended actions put forward by the MMIWG report must include a close analysis of the experiences of the LGBTQ2S+ communities, to ensure their needs and perspectives are fully heard and addressed.

Part Seven addresses issues of belonging, displacement, and the dismantling of traditional family life. The residential schooling system, the Sixties Scoop and other state policies and laws have demonstrably impacted traditional family relations. Many children were taken away from their biological families because the state intended to limit, if not altogether eliminate, the ability of Indigenous families to transmit Indigenous culture to the future generations. In Chapter 13, Lavell-Harvard and Anderson explore how the Canadian state and other Euro-Christian institutions like the churches directly targeted and attacked traditional Indigenous mothering practices. Given that Indigenous mothers held much influence in their nations, they were seen as a threat to the colonial project to assimilate Indigenous peoples into European belief systems. In a genocidal attempt by the state to get rid of the "Indian problem," children were appropriated and placed into white families. The intergenerational trauma of these experiences is still living with us today, and the TRC report revealed the ongoing negative impacts of such policies and the hard work that is ahead of us all to heal and rebuild our communities and a more just Canadian society.

Lynn Gehl in Chapter 14 addresses the matter of unstated paternity, an issue that has profoundly impacted Indigenous families, identity, and belonging. The *Indian Act* perpetuated patriarchal understandings by instituting the imperative that women had to state the paternity of children at the time of registration. She argues that the "negative presumption of unstated paternity"—the idea that one's father is not an Indian—had resulted in the displacement of numerous children from Indigenous nations. After decades of legal battles, this policy was scrapped, and in 2017 the Canadian Senate passed an amendment to the *Indian Act* to eliminate all remaining sexist discriminatory policies and extend Indian Status to those who had been impacted by such legislations.

Part Eight of the book explores Indigenous rights, citizenship, and nationalism through Indigenous perspectives. In Chapter 15, Bonita Lawrence examines contemporary self-government and comprehensive claims policy negotiations. She convincingly argues that these negotiations are still constraining Indigenous peoples, as the Canadian government ultimately still holds more power in the process, thereby limiting Indigenous rights of sovereignty, and often further reducing Indigenous lands. The current negotiations processes do not, then, correspond to the original principles of a nation-to-nation relationship between Indigenous nations and Canada.

In Chapter 16, Audra Simpson shows how Indigenous rights to self-determination are tied to sovereignty over matters of membership in Indigenous nations. Focusing on her own Kahnawà:ke Mohawk Nation, she explores the complexities and contentions surrounding discourses and practices of citizenship. In her chapter, she covers traditional criteria of membership, the impact of the *Indian Act* on "band" membership rules, the contentious "blood quantum" rule, as well as the various lived experiences of citizenship that exist in her community. All of these contemporary forms of citizenship, Simpson reminds us, are linked to colonialism, and are issues that the nation must confront as it proceeds to decolonize itself.

Part Nine of the book addresses Indigenous education from a perspective that centres critically anticolonial and reform-based efforts that forgo a culturalist line. In light of calls by Canada's Truth and Reconciliation Commission and the Canadian Association of Deans of Education to have all Canadians take responsibility for colonial injustices, we highlight authors who ask in particular how Settler populations might work to create programmatic and pedagogical initiatives and efforts aimed at Settler decolonizing, colonial reparations, and relationships rejuvenation.

In Chapter 17, Verna St Denis, a Cree/Métis scholar, revisits the usage of culture theory in Indigenous education and questions, the extent to which studying culture can disrupt unequal power relations that exist between Indigenous and Settler Canadians. She argues that the current focus on cultural difference and incommensurability does little to displace the unequal power relations that have arisen in Settler colonial society. This prevents all students—both Settler and Indigenous—from thinking critically about colonial realities and the strategies that might be used to repair them.

In Chapter 18, Martin Cannon is concerned with reform-based educational and programmatic initiatives centered on exposing and apprehending the violence of settler colonialism and law. He asks how schools might seek to ensure that all Canadians know about, consider, and challenge an investment in colonial dominance and complicity. He asks how it is possible to have teachers and learners think critically, and more importantly structurally, about the colonial injustice that surrounds us and what it might take to do something about it.

Transforming the educational system also means validating Indigenous knowledges, epistemologies and research methodologies, and provide them an equitable space in the academic institutions. The chapters in Part Ten highlight how, as part of the overall global colonial project, Indigenous knowledges and traditional research methodologies were considered inferior to that of Western ones, and researchers (almost always non-Indigenous) conducted their studies through their own colonial gaze with often damaging results for Indigenous communities. Decolonizing education is a promising endeavour where Indigenous own ways of knowing and research methodologies that best fit with Indigenous values and experiences, and meet the needs of Indigenous peoples, will finally be given their overdue validation.

In Chapter 19, Johnston, McGregor and Restoule outline what Indigenous research consists of. As they point out, Indigenous research is, above all, a relationship between the researchers and their community, the land, Creator, and all relations. The main purpose of Indigenous research is to contribute to the overall struggle of Indigenous sovereignty and to conduct research by following the principles of respect, responsibility, relevance, and reciprocity. In doing so, they can nurture healthy and equitable relationships with the research participants and the broader Indigenous communities.

In Chapter 20, Kathleen E. Absolon describes her own research project and demonstrates how she practiced the principles identified by Johnston, McGregor, and Restoule in Chapter 19. She ensured she followed proper cultural protocols, connected with the land throughout her research, and formed collaborative relationships with the research participants throughout the whole research process. In doing so, her research was indeed respectful, responsible, relevant, and reciprocal. Together, Chapters 19 and 20 provide practical guidelines that researchers can follow to ensure that their research with Indigenous communities is truly decolonizing, and part of the broader transformation needed in the educational systems.

Part Eleven of the book covers issues of violence and criminality as experienced by Indigenous peoples. In Chapter 21, Lisa Monchalin starts with an overview of the risk factors associated with the overrepresentation of Indigenous peoples in the criminal justice system. Monchalin links systemic inequities, settler colonialism, and institutional racism to this overrepresentation, showing how poor socioeconomic conditions are connected to the cycle of crime and violence impacting Indigenous peoples in Canadian society. She further argues that these risk factors should not be viewed as individual or cultural deficiencies, but as legacies of centuries of historical trauma resulted from settler colonialism. In order to break the cycle of violence, we need to deliver Indigenous-focused social programs and support systems that acknowledge and address the root causes of the risk factors. This would mean eliminating racist ideologies and practices that exist across all Canadian social institutions and removing systemic barriers that impede Indigenous peoples, especially the youth, from achieving their full potential.

In Chapter 22, Gina Starblanket and Dallas Hunt offer a critical analysis of the criminal case of Gerald Stanley, the man who shot Colten Boushie, an Indigenous youth, for trespassing on his property, and who was later acquitted by the court. As Starblanket and Hunt point out, throughout the case, racism as a likely mitigating factor was not considered during the proceedings. Such a denial of racism, as the reading reveals, is part of an overall settler narrative that has both dispossessed Indigenous peoples of their lands and treated them as wild, unruly, violent, leading to their criminalization and discrimination when they come in contact with the criminal justice system. In sum, the two chapters of Part Eleven show that in order to transform our justice systems, we need to stop the denial of racism, and remove the systemic root causes of the cycle of crime affecting Indigenous peoples.

Part Twelve is concerned with environmental racism. In this section new to our third edition, we wish to explore how humans might better coexist with our living and nonliving relatives in ways that are responsible and that work to eliminate harmful extractions and exploitation. In Chapter 23, Anne Spice illuminates Indigenous worldviews concerned with critical infrastructure (e.g., animals, rivers, mountains) and where they stand in relation to invasive fossil-fuel conceptions of infrastructure that threaten the world around us. She shows how Indigenous peoples draw from Indigenous feminism and worldviews to counter settler devastation on Indigenous lands.

Deborah McGregor similarly explores the role of Indigenous feminism in Chapter 24. She is concerned with Indigenous women and how, globally, they have been impacted negatively by harmful practices brought on by corporate capitalism and nation-states. She calls on global citizens and leaders to include a gendered analysis in any future environmental policies, outlining a series of legislative Declarations that seek to integrate traditional Indigenous knowledges, and a gendered analysis concerned with traditional governance, Indigenous knowledges, and poverty.

In Part Thirteen, we link poverty with colonial histories of dispossession and environmental degradation that has left many nations and communities in the economic margins of one of the wealthiest countries in the world. In Chapter 25, Pam Palmater discusses the Idle No More Movement that began in the fall of 2012 and took Canadians by surprise. This movement was initiated by four women who intended to make Canadians more aware of the negative impacts that Bill C-45 would have on our environment, in particular on Indigenous territories and peoples. As Palmater covers in the chapter, Idle No More was also effective in bringing awareness of the ongoing poor socio-economic conditions affecting Indigenous nations due to centuries of colonialism. Idle No More was a call for action to all Canadians to work together to end colonialism and improve the socioeconomic conditions of Indigenous communities.

Brian Calliou and Cynthia Wesley-Esquimaux, in Chapter 26, propose a wise practices model of Indigenous community development as an approach to improve the socioeconomic conditions of Indigenous communities. This approach would revitalize Indigenous traditional cultural principles and values, while building internal capacity to adapt to changes in Indigenous peoples' physical and social environments. This model would use appropriate tools and resources, and mobilize community members under ethical and effective leadership in order to achieve sustainable and equitable economic and social development, as well as revitalize Indigenous cultures, languages and protect our Mother Earth for the next generations.

In Part Fourteen, we explore problems involving racism and colonialism in Canada's health care system. We draw attention, in particular, to authors who are concerned with anticolonial approaches to health care services delivery. In Chapter 27, Simon Brascoupé and Catherine Waters point to a New Zealand–based scholarship concerning cultural safety, in turn showing a series of analytical gaps in the Canadian literature. As they suggest, cultural safety is useful in prompting critical questions about cultural difference, wellness, and the material and symbolic perception of Indigenous deficit and inferiority.

Janet Smylie and Billy Allan, in Chapter 28, call on culturally sensitive health care practitioners to address racism more purposefully by addressing and reconciling the scholarly epidemiological research illuminating the colonial determinants of health. They draw attention to health and wellness outcomes that are impacted by issues of poverty, environmental racism, and displacement brought on by Settler colonialism. They call on health care practitioners to research, understand, become activist minded about, and indeed remedy the factors producing disparate and negative health indicators.

We conclude the third edition of *Racism, Indigeneity, and Colonization in Canada* with Part Fifteen: Resistance. As the chapters in this part demonstrate, Indigenous peoples have never been "idle" in their efforts to resist colonial injustices. Rather, we have always lived accordingly to the principles of our traditional teachings and of the treaties and nation-to-nation agreements entered with Settler Canadians.

In Chapter 29, Jeff Corntassel and Cheryl Bryce point out that Indigenous acts of self-determination reflect Indigenous ways of acting responsibly toward land, people, and all of creation. Whenever Indigenous peoples are resisting colonial destructive policies and practices, we are revitalizing and protecting our Indigenous territories and ways of being. In so doing, we are maintaining a holistic relationship with all Creation, despite the barriers imposed on us by the colonial Canadian government or capitalist projects that threaten our territories.

In the last chapter of the book, Chapter 30, Arthur Manuel provides a further set of reflections about Indigenous resurgence and self-determination; however, he is intent on highlighting the power enforced legally by Canadian courts and the state to contain Indigenous resurgence and refusal. Manuel condemns the criminalization of Indigenous resistance, calling on Canada to relinquish its policy of court injunctions, a racist Doctrine of Discovery, and "self-government" policies based on extinguishment and "surrender and grant back." Manuel is focused on matters of jurisdiction, including domestic and legal orders that might affirm an inherent right to self-determination as peoples.

The intent of our book's third edition is to examine the interplay of racism and colonial forces and how these have shaped the lives of Indigenous peoples and their relations with Settler colonialists. Our aim is to provide insight into and dialogue into what can be done to address historic wrongdoings and envision an onging path forward, one where the founding principles of Settler-Indigenous relationships informed by a Two Row Wampum understanding of nation-to-nation building are honoured, understood, re-established, and rejuvenated.

Notes

1. The word "Haudenosaunee," meaning "People of the Longhouse" (a reference to the distinctive houses in which our ancestors once resided), may differ depending on the Six Nations person or community to whom one is speaking. For example, Taiaiake Alfred refers to his people (the people of Kahnawake Mohawk Nation) as "Rotinohshonni" (1995: 38; 1999: xi). Doxtator (1996) chose the word "Rotinonhsyonni." We use the word "Haudenosaunee" as it is one that is familiar to us, and also one that has been used by the Six Nations people in political dealings with the Canadian state (see Haudenosaunee Confederacy, 1983). Several words used henceforth in this book, including the words "Ukwehuwé" (the Original People) and "Onyota'a:ka" (People of the Standing Stone), are in Oneida (the language of both of our Indigenous ancestors), and we are grateful for the advice that has been provided to us in this regard by several Oneida speakers.

PART 1

Theoretical Foundations

Editor Introduction

We introduce the third edition of *Racism, Colonialism, and Indigeneity in Canada* with two perspectives offered by Indigenous scholars on matters of colonial dominance, **racism**, and Indigenous **resurgence**. The articles we have selected provide a way of thinking about racism as a continually evolving and postcolonizing process that is informed by—and indeed inseparable from—early colonial precedents. We highlight an Indigenous perspective concerning precolonial political diplomacy which explores the meaning of treaty and an unbroken assertion of sovereignty. The readings provide a glimpse of the kinds of assumptions and understandings that are too often negated by some academic scholarship, contemporary knowledge production, racism, the colonial politics of recognition, as well as narratives of healing and reconciliation.

The late Arthur Manuel, a Secwepemc author and leader whose article we include as Chapter One of this third edition, writes of the imperialist mindset that works to alienate people—including *ha dih nyoh* (white Settler) and non-Indigenous peoples—from caring for and protecting land. For Manuel, racism is a way of thinking with an imperialist's mindset. Combating racism must therefore employ institutional analyses centred on the ideological basis and underpinnings of racism and Settler **colonialism**, including the **doctrine of discovery** that would have us believe that lands in Canada were *terra nullius*—empty or unoccupied—prior to the arrival of the first Europeans. It is the belief in this doctrine predicated on the erasure of Indigenous sovereignty, our legal, economic, kin-based, and political existence as peoples, and the declaration of lands as empty of unoccupied that requires our unwavering attention and scrutiny. As Leanne Simpson points out in Chapter 2 of this edition, we need to ask critical questions about sovereignty and nationhood, including at once acknowledging and honouring how it is that we relate to and are related to each other as Indigenous and Settler peoples in the first historic instance of what is currently called Canada. We must revisit and ask critical questions about taken-for-granted practices that foreclose historic questions about Settler colonialism such as capitalism, democracy, and a legal system based on the unilateral assertion of settler sovereignty and individual rights. These practices embody apparatuses of power now firmly entrenched into colonial consciousness and Settler common sense (Rifkin, 2014).

Imperialist ways of thinking are not easily dismantled. This is because they are continually enabled through social, political, and legal processes that fashion the Indian as Other within the racialized colonial imaginary. Indigenous nations continue to be consumed under the category "Indian"—a process that is exemplary of the material and ideological violence that erases colonial histories of dispossession, nation-to-nation agreements, and the diversity that exists among us as **Ukwehuwé** as defined in our introduction to the text as meaning The Original People (also Cannon, 2019). This way of thinking also eclipses the individual specificity of languages, worldviews, and political cultures of the original First Nations people, including the Nishnaabeg diplomacy described by Leanne Simpson. As Manuel suggests, Indianness, including Indian status, should also be regarded as an instrument of repression concerned historically and still today with our dispossession as peoples (ibid).

The reparation of colonial and racialized injustices will remain complicated so long as they are shaped by Eurocentric principles. Before Indigenous peoples can take their rightful place as partners in the founding of what is now called Canada—and before any real change can be realized in the areas of law, politics, and economics—the meaning of justice itself must be entirely reconceptualized. Colonial reparations must also be seen as a collective and shared responsibility—not a gift—of **white Settler society**. It will be necessary to decolonize our own ways of thinking as Indigenous peoples; that is, to think outside of the racialized categories and taken-for-granted processes that have been made available to use by the colonizer.

Meaningful change also requires that we think about knowledge production. Whose knowledge is valued and with what set of consequences? How have Indigenous knowledges been defined, addressed, incorporated, or assumed out of existence in courts, curricula, and other sites of power? What knowledges inform and structure legal and political outcomes? For Leanne Simpson, we need to be vigilant in asking these sorts of questions, starting not with the political status quo established by governments and Settler colonists, but rather relationally, and with respect granted toward the stories told by our own peoples and nations when it comes to visioning "peace, mutual respect, and mutual benefit." We share in Simpson's perspective along with other Indigenous scholars who suggest that the political landscape of Canada be transformed into one that fosters public education and Settler literacy about Indigenous peoples and political traditions, treaty-making, and mutual coexistence.

Amid ongoing calls for an anticolonial and decolonizing pedagogy, and an approach to public education that centres Indigenous histories and Settler colonialism, the articles we have selected address two major areas of theorization. First, both articles illuminate a colonial politics of recognition shaped by unchecked State racialization practices that have worked to create "unprecedented repression" for Indigenous peoples. However, and as Manuel suggests, "this repression did not extinguish resistance." The stalwart efforts of Indigenous peoples and nations over generations have worked twofold: to prevent the assimilationist goals of the Indian Act and other oppressive legislation from being realized; and also, to (re-)generate and maintain practices that are home to resurgences beyond the Canadian state and the refusal whatsoever to be recognized by the colonizer. We address resistance and resurgence in detail in Part Fifteen of this book, but for now, we highlight the importance in theory and in practice of highlighting the agency and refusal (A. Simpson, 2017) of Ukwehuwé that has always rejected the inevitability of lands dispossession, capitalism, and ecological destruction. While there are subtle nuances that exist between us as nations with respect to sovereignty and governance (see Andersen, this volume), we continue to exercise our sovereignty as Indigenous peoples and nations (Simpson, 2013; 2017; Sunseri, 2011). Indigenous sovereignty has never been relinquished. We acknowledge territoriality and all our relations.

Second, the articles we have selected also affirm that nation-to-nation agreements were bilateral at the time of colonial contact in what is now Canada, and that it is both the Crown's and Government of Canada's responsibility to sort out where it is that Settler Canadians fit in relation to existing treaty and nation-to-nation agreements (Borrows, 1997). Leanne Simpson highlights the relationship we are in with each other, respectively, as Indigenous peoples and as Indigenous people and Settlers. There is a need to provide for and to center Indigenous-Settler relationship-building and rejuvenation in Canada. As Manuel writes, "We welcome new alliances. And when we speak about reclaiming a measure of control over our lands, we obviously do not mean throwing Canadians off it and sending them back to countries they came from. . . ." These ways of thinking about our relationships must flourish and will require Settler Canadians to consider where it is that they fit with respect to historic wrongdoings and also Settler relations and responsibility.

The literature suggests that there is a conversation to be had in Canada, a renewal of dialogue, especially where Indigenous-Settler relations are concerned. Simon (2013: 136) wrote of the interpersonal and intercultural dimensions of Indigenous-Settler relationships in Canada, calling on "non-Indigenous peoples" to sort out where they "fit in relation to Aboriginal peoples" (see also Cannon, Chapter 18). Clearly—and in calling for these sorts of analyses and relationship-building—we are not suggesting that all migrants are Settlers, invested for that matter in state-based ways of knowing and citizenship (Thobani, 2007) or even a dyadic Indigenous/white Settler binary (King, 2016). Some Settlers are "appellants facing a political order that is already constituted" (Veracini, 2010: 3) or as South Asian activist and ally Harsha Walia (2013) has reminded us: stolen labor on stolen land. The literature suggests that Black, arrivant, and racialized populations do not share the same relationship to white supremacy, Canadian Settler colonialism, and also to Indigenous peoples (Phung, 2011; Saranillio, 2013; Sehdev, 2011). We invite readers to situate themselves in relation to land and to engage in discussions about relational sovereignty (Cannon, 2018; Monture, 1999: 36). This works to help people recognize that, as Lorenzo Veracinci (2010) has put it, Empire may create Settlers—but not all Settlers are shaped universally by Empire (also, Saranillio, 2013).

The articles we have selected focus on Indigenous peoples getting to know each other, our representation and demographics, the nature of our social conditions under Settler colonialism, and how it is that a dialogue between Indigenous and Settler peoples might best be rejuvenated. What we are suggesting in this book is to look inward at Settler culture and the ontology of Settler colonialism, and to think about how we might begin to rebuild Indigenous-Settler relations beyond constructions of the other. We are also asking that our respective nationhoods be given consideration, and where it is that all Settlers fit in relation to this history. The matter of relationship-building and rejuvenation is still relevant in light of recent developments concerning Canada's public apology and the Truth and Reconciliation Commission (TRC).

The TRC has already suggested, like the RCAP before it in 1996, that emphasis be placed on reparations and renewal, especially where Settler–Indigenous relationships and the rejuvenation of original nation-to-nation principles is concerned. The third edition of *Racism, Colonialism, and Indigeneity in Canada*—like the first and second editions—is focused on inviting a new and historically informed dialogue concerning histories of Settler colonialism and reparations. We recognize the importance of Indigenous and Settler dialogue—a reconfiguration of relationships in what is currently called Canada—about Indigenous-Settler relations and the history of Settler colonialism. The readings convey a relational sovereignty and set of anticolonial principles that need to inform and indeed shape next steps in a post-RCAP, postapology, and post-TRC Canada.

CHAPTER 1

The Lay of the Land

Arthur Manuel

There is no denying the beauty of the land. From the hills above Neskonlith . . . you can see the blue waters of the Shuswap lakes, the dry scrubland of the valley, and the cooler hills shaded by stands of ponderosa pines. Below, the South Thompson River empties from the lake and winds westward through the valley toward Kamloops, where it joins the North Thompson and flows to the Fraser and down to the sea.

This is British Columbia's Interior Plateau. The land my people have shared for thousands of years, and still share with our ancient neighbours. . . .

I drove up to the hills above Neskonlith on an afternoon in June 2012. I was just back from New York, where I was serving as the co-chair to the Global Indigenous Peoples Caucus at the United Nations' Permanent Forum on Indigenous Issues (UNPFII), and I was looking for a quiet place to think things over.

Somehow we had gotten our message through the clamour of states that make up the United Nations. We had condemned, as Indigenous peoples, the innocent-sounding doctrine of discovery, which was the tool—the legal fiction—Europeans used to claim our land for themselves. Even that claim rested on obvious mistruths. The Americas were first portrayed as *terra nullius* on European maps. But in almost all cases, Europeans were met, at times within minutes of their arrival, by Indigenous peoples. There was an attempt to get around this inconvenient fact by declaring us non-human, but this was difficult even for Europeans to sustain over time. The doctrine of discovery remained because it was a legal fig leaf they could use to cover naked thievery.

. . . The United Nations report had called this doctrine frankly racist and described it as no more legitimate than the slavery laws of the same era. . . . The Permanent Forum on Indigenous Issues' committee report attacked the ongoing efforts to extinguish our title to the land through force or one-sided negotiations as a continuing violation of international law.[1]

I would like to think that we live in a world where enlightenment—like the Permanent Forum statement on the doctrine of discovery—is a warm breeze spreading across the planet, and that with patience and good faith we will finally be warmed by the justice we have been so long denied. But I know that is not the case. At an earlier session of the UN, Canada, the United States, Australia, and New Zealand fought bitterly against the whole world to try to block the Declaration on the Rights

Unsettling Canada: A National Wake-up Call, second edition, Arthur Manuel and Grand Chief Ronald M. Derrickson, (Toronto: Between the Lines Press, 2021), pp. 1–12. Used with permission of the publisher.

1. United Nations Permanent Forum on Indigenous Issues, "Preliminary Study of the Impact on Indigenous Peoples of the International Legal Construct Known as the Doctrine of Discovery," New York, April 19–30, 2010.

of Indigenous Peoples (UNDRIP), which eventually passed in 2007 by a vote of 144 to 4, with Canada leading the charge of the rights deniers.[2]

Nothing we have ever gained has been given to us or surrendered without a fight. When circumstances forced the Europeans to make concessions, as was the case with the parts of the Royal Proclamation of 1763 that recognized Indigenous sovereignty, the next generation would take advantage of a resurgence in its strength to reverse the concessions and try to push us even further into poverty and dependence. . . .

Before we look at where we are today and where we are heading, it is important that we first look at how we arrived at this place. . . . Among the other Indigenous peoples in Canada and throughout the Americas, there are many variations, but there is one constant: the land was stolen from underneath us.

Europeans made their initial land claim on our Secwepemc lands in 1778 . . . According to the tenets of the doctrine of discovery, all that Europeans had to do to expropriate the lands in a region was to sail past a river mouth and make a claim to all of the lands in its watershed. Our lands, given to us by our Creator and inhabited by us for thousands of years, were transformed into a British "possession," not only without our consent and without our knowledge, but also without a single European setting foot on our territory.

In the early 1800s, European traders and advance men like Simon Fraser did begin to show up on our rivers. For the first fifty years, they were seen and treated as guests on our lands. We had more or less friendly relations. We traded with them, we shared food with them, and we often helped them on their journeys through our territory. On a personal level, we tolerated their eccentricities and they tolerated ours.

But gradually, the numbers of these uninvited guests began to increase, and they began to act less and less like guests and more and more as lords. It was a process that Indigenous peoples around the world have experienced. The strangers arrive and offer trade and friendship. The Indigenous population responds in kind. Gradually the strangers begin to take up more and more space and make more and more requests from their hosts, until finally they are not requesting at all. They are demanding. And they are backing their demands with garrisoned outposts.

In the case of the people of the Interior Plateau, we are fortunate to have a document from our ancestors that describes the precise pattern of usurpation. This declaration, which is known as the Laurier Memorial, was presented to Prime Minister Wilfrid Laurier on August 25, 1910, by the Interior chiefs when the prime minister was visiting Kamloops on an election campaign stop.[3]

It was prepared in the months before in mass meetings by our chiefs and people, who wanted to ensure that Canadians knew that we clearly remembered the betrayals of the previous century and that we demand redress in the current one. We called it a *memorial* because it represented, in a very precise way, our collective memories of our history with the settlers. . . .

The following are excerpts of what our chiefs told Laurier about their initial experience with Europeans:

> At first they looked only for gold. We knew the latter was our property, but as we did not use it much nor need it to live by we did not object to their searching for it. They told us, "Your country is rich and you will be made wealthy by our coming. We wish just to pass over your lands in quest of gold."
>
> Soon they saw the country was good and some of them made up their minds, to settle it. They commenced to take up pieces of land here and there. They told us they wanted only the use of these pieces of land for a few years, and then would hand them back to us in an improved condition;

2. Eric Hanson, "UN Declaration on the Rights of Indigenous Peoples," First Nations Studies Program at the University of British Columbia, indigenousfoundations.arts.ubc.ca.

3. "The Memorial to Sir Wilfrid Laurier," Shuswap Nation Tribal Council, shuswapnation.org.

meanwhile they would give us some of the products they raised for the loan of our land.

Thus they commenced to enter our "houses," or live on our "ranches." With us when a person enters our house he becomes our guest, and we must treat him hospitably as long as he shows no hostile intentions. At the same time we expect him to return to us equal treatment for what he receives.

It soon became apparent that the settlers were not offering equal treatment, and they were not planning to leave. On the contrary, their numbers were increasing. . . . The trickle of prospectors grew into a full-blown gold rush. With the unrest putting this new mining wealth at risk, James Douglas, the governor of the small colony on the coast, sent an emissary to meet with Chief Neskonlith to try to defuse the situation.

Chief Neskonlith, who was known as a tough and uncompromising leader, had been chosen to speak for the four bands around the Shuswap lakes. . . . Neskonlith was forceful with the colonial representative. He told him that the encroachments on our land had reached an intolerable level and we would not accept any more European settlement. The emissary understood that this was not a bluff. But he had no financial or other resources that he could offer a deal with. So he simply asked Chief Neskonlith what the necessary lands were for his people and the other three Secwepemc bands.

Neskonlith showed the essential area on the emissary's map. Together they marked out the territory for exclusive Secwepemc use; today, this area is known as the Neskonlith Douglas Reserve 1862. On this map, our land area totals almost a million acres; the emissary agreed this territory was for the exclusive use of our people. Chief Neskonlith then went out and staked the land where non-Secwepemc settlement was to be forbidden.

But as Indigenous peoples around the world have discovered, a deal is not a deal when it comes to settler governments. No restraint was placed on settlers moving onto our lands. In fact, colonial powers began to give away 160 acres of our land, free of charge, to each settler who applied. At the same time, in an astounding act of racism, the authorities

allocated only 20 acres for Indian families. Our forests were then handed over to the control of the lumber companies. Our million acres was gradually, without our consent or even notification, whittled down to barely seven thousand acres scattered in small strips across our territory. The Interior chiefs told Laurier in 1910 that they had been betrayed by the government.

[The settlers] have knocked down . . . the posts of all the Indian tribes. They say there are no lines, except what they make. They have taken possession of all the Indian country and claim it as their own. . . . They have stolen our lands and everything on them. . . .

After a time when they saw that our patience might get exhausted and that we might cause trouble if we thought all the land was to be occupied by whites they set aside many small reservations for us here and there over the country. This was their proposal not ours, and we never accepted these reservations as settlement for anything, nor did we sign any papers or make any treaties. . . . They thought we would be satisfied with this, but we never have been satisfied and never will be until we get our rights.

Bitter insult, the Interior chiefs told Laurier, was added to injury when the settlers not only invaded our territory, but also began to treat us as trespassers and bar us from the lands that had been ours since time immemorial. . . .

Indigenous peoples from around the world recognize this process of slow, lawless confiscation of their lands, with promises made and laws of protection enacted, then quickly broken as soon as the coalescence of forces again favours the settlers.

Non-Indigenous readers may be thinking—yes, terrible things went on in those days, but really, it's all ancient history. To you, I want to stress that this is not at all ancient history. The meeting with Laurier occurred in my own grandfather's time. When I was young, I hunted on Secwepemc lands with my father, and I remember being surprised to see how nervous he was that he would get caught by the authorities.

In recent years, my daughters have been arrested and sent to jail for protesting a new encroachment on Secwepemc lands. My people have been beaten, jailed, and shot at by the authorities simply for occupying our own lands.

And it is the loss of our land that has been the precise cause of our impoverishment. Indigenous lands today account for only 0.36 per cent of British Columbian territory. The settler share is the remaining 99.64 per cent. In Canada overall the percentage is even worse, with Indigenous peoples controlling only 0.2 per cent of the land and the settlers 99.8 per cent. With this distribution of the land, you don't have to have a doctorate in economics to understand who will be poor and who will be rich. And our poverty is crushing. Along with suffering all of the calamities of life that hit the poor with greater impact, our lives are seven years shorter than the lives of non-Indigenous Canadians. Our unemployment rates are four times higher. The resources to educate our children are only a third of what is spent on non-Indigenous Canadian children. Our youth commit suicide at a rate more than five times higher. We are living the effects of this dispossession every day of our lives, and we have been living this misery in Canada for almost 150 years.

What has been the response of the Canadian government when we protest the illegal seizure of our lands and the intentional impoverishment of our people? Generally, it has been to simply turn away. Until our voices become too loud to ignore; then false promises or outright repression come into play. This was the response after our chiefs made their determined plea to Laurier. First, silence from Canada. Then, after the First World War, when Indigenous veterans returned to their communities and began to insist on action on the land and on rights issues, the Dominion government responded with unprecedented repression. . . .

The government tried to separate activist veterans like Chief William Pierrish from the people by offering them citizenship—with the basic human rights afforded other Canadians—but only if they surrendered their Indian status. . . .

The Indian superintendent in the 1920s, Duncan Campbell Scott . . . called our people "a weird and waning race" and said: "I want to get rid of the Indian problem. Our object is to continue until there is not a single Indian in Canada that has not been absorbed."[4]

. . . Our reserves began to resemble the internment camps that were set up during the world wars for enemy aliens.

But this repression did not extinguish resistance. It merely drove it underground. Communities met at night with travelling activists like Andrew Paull, who kept the fight for Aboriginal title alive. Paull, a Skwxwu7mesh (Squamish) political organizer, had attended law school, and he was able to travel the country as the manager of an Indian lacrosse team. He founded the Allied Tribes of British Columbia in the 1920s and later founded a loose coalition he somewhat grandly called the North American Indian Brotherhood. Because of the restrictions of the day, both organizations existed mainly in his briefcase, but Paull, tirelessly criss-crossing the country to preach resistance, provided the light in this period of darkness.

. . . In the 1950s, when some of the more oppressive laws against our people were finally lifted, my father's generation began to build the national organization—the National Indian Brotherhood (NIB), forerunner of the Assembly of First Nations (AFN)—to take their fight to Ottawa and to Canadians. But first they had to find each other again. Organizing meant taking a collection at a local meeting, travelling long distances, and sleeping in their cars. . . . These men and women . . . led us back out of political wilderness and fought for our rights in the national and provincial capitals, in the courts, and when necessary, by demonstrating in the streets. The struggles of my parents' generation are . . . important . . . because we can learn from their successes and their failures. . . .

My generation has been able to build on the successes of our parents' generation, but we will also look at some of our missed chances and wrong turns. This history is still being written with our

---

4. Brian Titley, *A Narrow Vision: Duncan Campbell Scott and the Administration of Indian Affairs in Canada* (Toronto: University of Toronto Press, 1986), 50.

deeds; the story includes some tensions and conflicts within our movement. As we search for the path through the chaotic and often bruising world we all inhabit, we should not be afraid to disagree among ourselves. . . .

Before we embark on this journey, it is important to note that when we speak of rebuilding Indigenous societies and Indigenous economies, we are not seeking to join the multinationals on Wall Street or Bay Street as junior partners, but to win back the tools to build our own societies that are consistent with our culture and values. Our goal is not simply to replace Settlers Resource Inc. with Indigenous Resource Inc. Instead we are interested in building true Indigenous economies that begin and end with our unique relationship to the land. This is essential so we can be true not only to ourselves, but also to a future we share with all of the peoples of the world.

Our Indigenous view—which includes air, water, land, animals, and people in a continually sustaining circle—is increasingly seen by both scientists and citizens as the only way to a sustainable future. As Indigenous peoples, we must always keep in mind that taking care of Mother Earth is the most important contribution we can make. This is how we can support a new international economy that is not based on the outdated and environmentally unsound laissez-faire concepts of economics. In this endeavour, we can be an important ally of those growing forces—in Canadian society and internationally—that understand that for our collective survival on the planet, fundamental changes must be made. Mother Earth cannot simply be reduced to the industrial binary of profit and garbage.

We welcome the new alliances. And when we speak about reclaiming a measure of control over our lands, we obviously do not mean throwing Canadians off it and sending them back to the countries they came from—that is the land of *reductio ad absurdum* that some of those who refuse to acknowledge our title try to use against us. We know that for centuries Canadians have been here building their society, which, despite its failings, has become the envy of many in the world. All Canadians have acquired a basic human right to be here. We also know that Canada does not have the astronomical amount of money it would cost to pay us for the centuries of use of our lands. We are certainly asking for compensation for the illegal seizures, but those amounts we can discuss. And we can begin these more precise discussions with Grand Chief Ron Derrickson's Afterword to this book. At present, we are asking for the right to protect our Aboriginal title land, to have a say on any development on our lands, and when we find the land can be safely and sustainably developed, to be compensated for the wealth it generates.

. . . The land retains its power and its beauty. All we have to do is rethink our place on it. Simply by removing the shadow of the doctrine of discovery, you find a rich tapestry of peoples who need to sit down to speak to each other as equals and build a new mechanism to co-operate with each other, to satisfy each other's needs and aspirations in the modern world.

There is room on this land for all of us and there must also be, after centuries of struggle, room for justice for Indigenous peoples. That is all that we ask. And we will settle for nothing less.

CHAPTER 2

Looking after Gdoo-naaganinaa

Precolonial Nishnaabeg Diplomatic and Treaty Relationships

Leanne Simpson

It has long been known that Indigenous nations had their own processes for making and maintaining peaceful diplomatic relationships, such as **Gdoo-naaganinaa**,[5] with other Indigenous nations prior to colonization.[6] These "treaty processes" were grounded in the worldviews, language, knowledge systems, and political cultures of the nations involved, and they were governed by the common Indigenous ethics of justice, peace, respect, reciprocity, and accountability. Indigenous peoples understood these agreements in terms of relationship, and renewal processes were paramount in maintaining these international agreements. They also viewed treaties in terms of both rights and responsibilities, and they took their responsibilities in maintaining treaty relations seriously. Although these agreements were political in nature, viewed through the lens of Indigenous worldviews, values, and traditional political cultures, one can begin to appreciate that

these agreements were also sacred, made in the presence of the spiritual world and solemnized in ceremony. . . .

Harold Johnson, a Cree, explains traditional Cree conceptualizations of treaty relationships in his territory, Kiciwamanawak, in terms of relations and relationships. He writes that when the colonizers first came to his territory, Cree law applied, the foundation of which rests in the "maintenance of harmonious relations." He sees the treaty as an adoption ceremony, where the Cree adopted the settlers as family and took them in as relatives, inviting them to live in Kiciwamanawak and live by the laws of the Cree. . . .[7]

For the past decade, I have been interested in understanding how my ancestors, the Mississauga of the Nishnaabeg Nation,[8] understood and lived up to their responsibilities to the land, their families, their clans, and their nation and with neighboring nations. Through years of learning from our elders

Wicazo Sa Review 2008, published by University of Minnesota Press.

5. Gdoo-naaganinaa means "Our Dish" and refers to a pre-colonial treaty between the Nishnaabeg and the Haudenosaunee Confederacy. This is the inclusive form, as opposed to the ndoo-naaganinaa "our dish (but not yours)." Gdoo-naaganinaa is a symbol of our shared ecology and territory in southern Ontario.

6. For a more complete discussion see the *Final Report of the Royal Commission on Aboriginal Peoples,* vol. 1 (Ottawa, Ontario: Minister of Supply and Services, 1996), http://www.ainc-inac.gc.ca/ch/rcap/sg/sg11_e.html.

7. Harold Johnson, *Two Families: Treaties and Government* (Saskatoon, Saskatchewan: Purich Publishing, 2007), 27.

8. Dale Turner, *This Is Not a Peace Pipe: Towards a Critical Indigenous Philosophy* (Toronto, Ontario: University of Toronto Press, 2006), 8. This concept is known as treaty federalism in Canada.

and Nishnaabeg knowledge keepers, spending time on the land, and interpreting the academic literature through an Nishnaabeg lens, I have come to understand Nishnaabeg conceptualizations of treaties and treaty relationships . . . and these conceptualizations exist in stark contrast to the Eurocanadian view of treaties entrenched in the colonial legal system, the historical record, and often the contemporary academy.

In Canada, many Indigenous scholars have argued that the "Canadian state's political relationship with Aboriginal Peoples should be renewed with respect to the early treaties."[9] Although this is an important decolonizing strategy, the fact remains that Canadian politicians and scholars, as well as Canadians in general, have a poor understanding of Indigenous treaty-making traditions, Indigenous political traditions, and Indigenous cultures in general. For many, the idea that Indigenous nations had their own precolonial diplomatic relations and political cultures exists in sharp contrast to the racist stereotype of "savages wandering around in the bush" still prominent in mainstream Canadian culture.[10] For others, it is difficult to understand that although both Indigenous and European nations engaged in treaty making before contact with each other, the traditions, beliefs, and worldviews that defined concepts such as "treaties" were extremely different. This misunderstanding is further confounded by the fact that as time passed, the colonizers' view of treaties was entrenched in the Eurocanadian legal system and the academy, and that there are few written records of treaty agreements made in the early colonial period where Indigenous perspectives were most influential. Destabilizing and decolonizing the concept of "treaty" then becomes paramount to appreciate what our ancestors intended to happen when those very first agreements and relationships were established, and to explore the relevance of Indigenous views of "treaty" and "treaty relationships" in contemporary times.

The purpose of this paper is to begin to articulate Nishnaabeg cultural perspectives on our relationships within our territory, whether those relationships were with the land, with the animal nations that form the basis of our clan system, or with neighbouring Indigenous nations and confederacies. . . . I begin by discussing cultural contexts within which Nishnaabeg people maintained and nurtured relationships within their territory. I then discuss two examples of treaty relationships with the nonhuman world, concluding with a discussion of precolonial international treaty relationships with the Dakota Nation and the Haudenosaunee Confederacy. Although these perspectives are not new or unique to Nishnaabeg knowledge holders and our elders, they exist in contrast to mainstream academic literature regarding treaties.

Bimaadiziwin: Relationships as the Context for Nishnaabeg Treaty Making

Our ancestors knew that maintaining good relationships as individuals, in families, in clans, and in our nation and with other Indigenous nations and confederacies was the basis for lasting peace . . . Bimaadiziwin or "living the good life . . ."[11] is a way of ensuring human beings live in balance with the natural world, their family, their clan, and their nation and it is carried out through the Seven Grandfather teachings, embedded in the social and political structures of the Nishnaabeg. . . .

At the individual level, Nishnaabeg culture allowed for strong individual autonomy and freedom, while at the same time the needs of the collective were paramount. There was a belief that good governance and political relationships begin with individuals and how they relate to each other in families.

---

9. Turner, *This Is Not a Peace Pipe*, 3–38, and for a broader discussion on this imagery in Canadian culture generally see Daniel Frances, *The Imaginary Indian: The Image of the Indian in Canadian Culture* (Vancouver, British Columbia: Arsenal Pulp Press, 1992).

10. Lester-Irabinna Rigney, "Internationalization of an Indigenous Anticolonial Cultural Critique of Research Methodologies: A Guide to Indigenist Research Methodology and Its Principles," *Wicazo Sa Review* 14, no. 2 (Fall 1999): 109–122; Linda Tuhiwai Smith, *Decolonizing Methodologies: Research and Indigenous Peoples* (London: Zed Books, 1999); Kiera Ladner, "When Buffalo Speaks: Creating an AlterNative Understanding of Traditional Blackfoot Governance" (PhD dissertation, Department of Political Science, Carleton University, 2001), 37–38.

11. Ladner, "When Buffalo Speaks," 69–70.

Haudenosaunee academic Trish Monture explains a similar concept among the Haudenosaunee:

> As I have come to understand it, self-determination begins with looking at yourself and your family and deciding if and when you are living responsibly. Self-determination is principally, that is first and foremost, about relationships. Communities cannot be self-governing unless members of those communities are well and living in a responsible way.[12]

In a real sense for the Nishnaabeg, relating to one's immediate family, the land, the members of their clan, and their relations in the nonhuman world in a good way was the foundation of good governance in a collective sense. Promoting Bimaadiziwin in the affairs of the nations begins with practicing Bimaadiziwin in one's everyday life....

Nishnaabeg Doodem

Traditional Nishnaabeg political culture was based on our clan system. . . . Clans connected families to particular animal nations and territories, where relationships with those animal nations were formalized, ritualized, and nurtured.[13] Clan members held and continue to hold specific responsibilities in terms of taking care of a particular part of the territory, and specific clans hold particular responsibilities related to governance.[14] Individual clans had responsibilities to a particular geographic region of the territory, and their relationship with that region was a source of knowledge, spirituality, and sustenance. They also were required to maintain and nurture a special relationship with their clan animal....

Treaty Making with Animal Nations

In many instances, clan leaders negotiated particular agreements with animal nations or clans to promote Bimaadiziwin and balance with the region. In Mississauga territory,[15] for example, the people of the fish clans, who are the intellectuals of the nation, met with the fish nations[16] twice a year for thousands of years at Mnjikanming,[17] the small narrows between Lake Simcoe and Lake Couchiching. The fish nations and the fish clans gathered to talk, to tend to their treaty relationships, and to renew life just as the Gizhe-mnido[18] had instructed them. These were important gatherings because the fish nations sustained the Nishnaabeg Nation during times when other sources of food were scarce . . . Nishnaabeg people . . . only took as much as they needed and never wasted....

. . . Nishnaabeg scholar John Borrows retells one of our sacred stories in *Recovering Canada: The Resurgence of Indigenous Law*[19] and further illustrates the importance of these diplomatic agreements between human and animal nations. In a time long ago, all of the deer, moose, and caribou suddenly disappeared from the Nishnaabeg territory. When the people went looking for them, they discovered the

---

12. These are known to the Nishnaabeg as the Seven Grandfather teachings, see Eddie Benton Banai, *The Mishomis Book* (Hayward, Wis.: Red School House Publishing, 1988), 64.

13. This has somewhat changed in contemporary times. While many elders and knowledge holders acknowledge that there was/is a distinct territoriality to the clan system, with specific clans holding responsibilities to particular areas as also evidenced by Darlene Johnson ("Connecting People to Place: Great Lakes Aboriginal History in Cultural Context," report prepared for the Ipperwash Inquiry, 2004, http://www.ipperwashinquiry.ca/transcripts/pdf/P1_Tab_1.pdf) in the Eurocanadian historical record, there are now often many different clans present (and many people who do not know their clan affiliation at all) in a single reserve community. This is in part a result of the original colonial construction of our communities.

14. Located in the southeastern portion of Nishnaabeg territory.

15. To Western scientists different species of fish gather at this location in the spring and fall to migrate and spawn. To the Nishnaabeg, these are not just "species of fish," they are nations within their own right, with political structures unto their own. This reflects a different conceptualization of "nationalism" similar to the conceptualizations in Ladner's *Women and Blackfoot Nationalism*. To be clear, fish clans represent the Nishnaabeg people, fish nations are the actual species of fish.

16. Mnjikanming is located near Orillia, Ontario, Canada, and has a series of ancient fish weirs reminding us of this relationship.

17. Creator.

18. John Borrows, *Recovering Canada: The Resurgence of Indigenous Law* (Toronto, Ontario: University of Toronto Press, 2002), 16–20.

19. Ibid., 19. Borrows notes that there are many slightly different versions of this story in print and in our oral traditions.

animals had been captured by the crows. After some negotiation, the people learned that the crows were not holding the moose, deer, and caribou against their will. The animals had willingly left the territory because the Nishnaabeg were no longer respecting them. The Nishnaabeg had been wasting their meat and not treating their bodies with the proper reverence. The animals knew that the people could not live without them, and when the animal nations met in council, the chief deer outlined how the Nishnaabeg nation could make amends:

> Honour and respect our lives and our beings, in life and in death. Cease doing what offends our spirits. Do not waste our flesh. Preserve fields and forests for our homes. To show your commitment to these things and as a remembrance of the anguish you have brought upon us, always leave tobacco leaf from where you take us. Gifts are important to build our relationship once again.[20]

The Nishnaabeg agreed and the animals returned to their territory. Contemporary Nishnaabeg hunters still go through the many rituals outlined that day when they kill a deer or moose, a process that honors the relationships our people have with these animals and the agreement our ancestors made with the Hoof Clan to maintain the good life. Judy DaSilva, Nishnaabeg-kwe[21] from Asubpeechoseewagong Netum Anishinaabek (Grassy Narrows) in northwest Ontario explains how these teachings are still relevant in her community today:

> When a hunter kills a moose, there is a certain part of the moose that the hunter takes off, and leaves in the forest, and with that the hunter will say a few words to thank the moose for providing food for his family. . . . My brother said our grandmother told him

that you do not get an animal because you are a good hunter, but because the animal feels sorry for you and gives himself to you to feed your family. This is why when our people hunt, these thoughts are ingrained in their minds and their hearts and they have great respect for the animals they get.[22]

According to Nishnaabeg traditions, it is my understanding that our relationship with the moose nation, the deer nation, and the caribou nation is a treaty relationship like any other, and all the parties involved have both rights and responsibilities in terms of maintaining the agreement and the relationship between our nations. . . . [T]reaties are about maintaining peace through healthy collective relationships . . . and there are two common terms in the language that refer to agreements made between two nations: "Chi-debahk-(in)-Nee-Gay-Win," which refers to an open agreement with matters to be added to it, and "Bug-in-Ee-Gay," which relates to "letting it go."[23] It is my understanding that "Chi-debahk-(in)-Nee-Gay-Win" is not meant to be interpreted as an unfinished agreement, rather it is an agreement that is an ongoing reciprocal and dynamic relationship to be nurtured, maintained, and respected. Treaties made by the Nishnaabeg with colonial powers in Canada as late as the Robinson–Huron Treaty of 1850, according to the oral tradition of the Nishnaabeg, was to be "added to."[24] This type of agreement was absolutely necessary in negotiations between nations with different languages and in the times before the written word, but it should not be viewed as an archaic or obsolete form of political culture. Oral agreements based on relationship, negotiation, and understanding required plenty of maintenance and nurturing to ensure lasting peace. That maintenance required commitment and hard work, but also encouraged understanding another point of view and when done correctly can bring about a lasting peace for all involved.

20. Nishnaabeg women.

21. Interviewed for another project by Leanne Simpson, 31 March 2003. Judy DaSilva is a traditional knowledge holder and environmental activist.

22. James Morrison, *The Robinson Treaties of 1850: A Case Study*, prepared for the Royal Commission on Aboriginal Peoples (Ottawa, Ontario: Minister of Supply and Services, 1994). (Research reports from the Royal Commission on Aboriginal Peoples are available in digital form on "For Seven Generations: An Informational Legacy of the Royal Commission on Aboriginal Peoples [RCAP] CD-ROM," Libraxus.)

23. Ibid.

24. This is how Algonquin people are known in their language.

Nishnaabeg International Diplomacy

. . . The ethics of respect and reciprocity were reflected in international Nishnaabeg diplomatic relations through the process known as "waiting in the woods" or "waiting at the woods' edge." Omàmìwinini[25] scholar Paula Sherman explains: "[I]t would have been expected that upon leaving one's own territory to cross into someone else's territory, that an individual or a group would build a fire to announce that they were 'waiting in the woods.'"[26]

An Omàmìwinini delegation would have been sent out with a string of white wampum to welcome them to Omàmìwinini territory. Omàmìwinini would have prepared a feast for them, and gifts would have been exchanged. . . . Visitors to one's territory were to be treated with the utmost respect to promote peaceful diplomatic relations between nations. These relations were also formalized in treaties, and the following section discusses two examples of precolonial Nishnaabeg treaties with neighboring nations.

Our Drum and Our Dish: Treaty Making with Other Indigenous Nations

The Nishnaabeg Nation, in addition to living up to their treaty relationships with the nonhuman world, also made political agreements with their neighbouring nations. . . .

Gdoo-naaganinaa acknowledged that both the Nishnaabeg and the Haudenosaunee were eating out of the same dish through shared hunting territory and the ecological connections between their territories.[27] The dish represented the shared territory, although it is important to remember that sharing territory for hunting did not involve interfering with one another's sovereignty as nations. It represented harmony and interconnection, as both parties were to be responsible for taking care of the dish. . . . The Nishnaabeg Nation and the confederacy related to each other through the practice of Gdoo-naaganinaa, it was not just simply agreed upon, but practiced as part of the diplomatic relations between the Nishnaabeg Nation and the confederacy. All of the nations involved had particular responsibilities to live up to in order to enjoy the rights of the agreement. . . .

Nishnaabeg environmental ethics[28] dictated that individuals could only take as much as they needed, that they must share everything following Nishnaabeg redistribution of wealth customs, and no part of the animal could be wasted. . . . Nishnaabeg custom required decision makers to consider the impact of their decisions on all the plant and animal nations, in addition to the next seven generations of Nishnaabeg.

The Haudenosaunee refer to the treaty as the "Dish with One Spoon" and there is an associated wampum belt. . . .[29] [I]n the Haudenosaunee version there is one spoon not only to reinforce the idea of sharing and responsibility, but also to promote peace. There are no knives allowed around the dish so that no one gets hurt.[30] Again, Haudenosaunee people understood the treaty as a relationship with

25. Paula Sherman, "Indawendiwin: Spiritual Ecology as the Foundation of Omàmìwinini Relations." (PhD dissertation, Department of Indigenous Studies, Trent University, 2007), 207.

26. Ibid.

27. For a complete discussion see Leanne Simpson, "Traditional Ecological Knowledge: Insights, Issues and Implications." PhD dissertation, University of Manitoba, 1999.

28. The dish wampum belt is currently housed at the Royal Ontario Museum. For a Nishnaabeg historical telling of the meaning of the wampum belt see D. Johnson, "Connecting People to Place."

29. The purpose of this paper is to focus on discussing Nishnaabeg pre-colonial treaty-making processes. For discussions of the treaty from a Haudenosaunee perspective see Barbara Gray's "The Effects of the Fur Trade on Peace: A Haudenosaunee Woman's Perspective," in *Aboriginal People and the Fur Trade: Proceedings of the 8th North American Fur Trade Conferences*, Louise Johnson, ed. (Akwesasne, Mohawk Territory: Dollco Printing, 2001), n.p.; J.A. Gibson, "Concerning the League: The Iroquois League Tradition as Dictated in Onondaga," H. Woodbury, R. Henry, and H. Webster, eds, *Algonquian and Iroquoian Linguistics Memoir* 9 (1991); A.C. Parker, *Parker on the Iroquois: Iroquois Uses of Maize and Other Food Plants; the Code of Handsome Lake, the Seneca Prophet: The Constitution of the Five Nations* (New York: State University of New York, 1992).

30. For a complete discussion of Haudenosaunee land ethics see Susan Hill, "The Clay We Are Made of: An Examination of Haudenosaunee Land Tenure on the Grand River Territory" (PhD dissertation, Department of Indigenous Studies, Trent University, 2006); Susan Hill, "Traveling Down the River of Life Together in Peace and Friendship, Forever: Haudenosaunee Land Ethics and Treaty Agreements as the Basis for Restructuring the Relationship with the British Crown," Leanne Simpson, ed., *Lighting the Eighth Fire: The Liberation, Resurgence and Protection of Indigenous Nations* (Winnipeg, Manitoba: Arbeiter Ring, forthcoming).

both rights and responsibilities. Haudenosaunee land ethics also ensured the health of the shared territory for generations to come.[31]

Our Dish in Contemporary Times

At no time did the Haudenosaunee assume that their participation in the Dish with One Spoon treaty meant that they could fully colonize Nishnaabeg territory or assimilate Nishnaabeg people into Haudenosaunee culture. At no time did the Haudenosaunee assume that the Nishnaabeg intended to give up their sovereignty, independence, or nationhood. Both political entities assumed that they would share the territory, that they would both take care of their shared hunting grounds, and that they would remain separate, sovereign, self-determining, and independent nations. Similarly, the Nishnaabeg did not feel the need to "ask" or "negotiate" with the Haudenosaunee Confederacy for the "right" to "self-government. . . ." [B]oth parties knew they had a shared responsibility to take care of the territory, following their own culturally based environmental ethics to ensure that the plant and animal nations they were so dependent on them carried on in a healthy state in perpetuity. Both parties knew that they had to follow their own cultural protocols for renewing the relationship on a regular basis to promote peace, goodwill, and friendship among the Nishnaabeg and the Haudenosaunee. Both parties knew they had to follow the original instructions

passed down to them from their ancestors if peace was to be maintained.

Although Gdoo-naaganinaa is a living treaty with the Haudenosaunee, the Nishnaabeg understanding of it can give us great insight into Nishnaabeg traditions governing treaty making and their expectations in their early interactions with settler governments. . . . They expected Gdoo-naaganinaa would be taken care of so that their way of life could continue for the generations to come. They expected respect for their government, their sovereignty, and their nation. They expected a relationship of peace, mutual respect, and mutual benefit, and these were the same expectations the Nishnaabeg carried with them into the colonial period. . . .

Too often in contemporary times we are presented with a worldview that renders us incapable of visioning any alternatives to our present situation and relationship with colonial governments and settler states. Indigenist thinkers compel us to return to our own knowledge systems to find answers. For the Nishnaabeg people, Gdoo-naaganinaa does just that. It gives us an ancient template for realizing separate jurisdictions within a shared territory. It outlines the "rights" and "responsibilities" of both parties in the ongoing relationship, and it clearly demonstrates that our ancestors did not intend for our nations to be subsumed by the British crown or the Canadian state when they negotiated those original treaties. It is time to decolonize our relationships with our neighboring nations, and it is time to decolonize our relationship with the Canadian state.

---

31. Banai, *Mishomis Book*, 90–95.

PART 1

Additional Readings

Ashok, Mathur, Jonathan Dewar, and Mike DeGagné, eds. *Cultivating Canada: Reconciliation through the Lens of Cultural Diversity*. Ottawa: Aboriginal Healing Foundation Research Series, 2011.

Byrd, Jodi A. "Not Yet: Indigeneity, Antiblackness, and Anticolonial Liberation," pp. 309–324 in Moon Kie Jung and João H. Costa Vargas, eds, *Antiblackness*. Durham, NC: Duke University Press, 2021.

Craft, Aimee and Paulette Regan, eds. *Pathways of Reconciliation: Indigenous and Settler Approaches to Implementing the TRC's Calls to Action*. Winnipeg: University of Manitoba Press, 2020.

Maynard, Robyn and Leanne Betasamosake Simpson. "Towards Black and Indigenous Futures on Turtle Island: A Conversation," pp. 75–94 in Rodney Diverlus, Sandy Hudson, and Syrus Marcus Ware, eds, *Until we are Free: Reflections on Black Lives Matter in Canada*. Regina: University of Regina Press, 2020.

Monture, Patricia. *Thunder in My Soul: A Mohawk Woman Speaks*. Halifax: Fernwood Publishing, 1995.

————. *Journeying Forward: Dreaming First Nations Independence*. Halifax: Fernwood Publishing, 1999.

Vowell, Chelsea. *Indigenous Writes: A Guide to First Nations, Métis & Inuit Issues in Canada*. Winnipeg: Highwater Press, 2016.

Relevant Websites

David Suzuki Foundation
https://youtu.be/3sVg0Cvqh3k
https://youtu.be/UsyyYeVHGJ0
https://youtu.be/McVEgEA4qvg
A three-part video series entitled *Land Governance: Past, Present, and Future* was created by the David Suzuki Foundation, including other videos related to Indigenous Peoples' Land, Law, Governance, and Ecological Well-Being.

Ogimaa Mikana: Reclaiming/Renaming
http://ogimaamikana.tumblr.com/
This website documents an aesthetic endeavour to name, re-map, and re-assert an Indigenous presence in what is now called Toronto and the Province of Ontario.

Tribal Nations Maps
http://www.tribalnationsmaps.com
This website outlines the work of Aaron Carapella (Cherokee) who has created maps (available for purchase) illustrating the original territories and names of the Indigenous peoples of North America.

Royal Commission on Aboriginal Peoples (All Volumes)
https://www.bac-lac.gc.ca/eng/discover/aboriginal-heritage/royal-commission-aboriginal-peoples/Pages/final-report.aspx
The Royal Commission on Aboriginal Peoples (RCAP) was released in 1996 and consists of five volumes. While not an exhaustive source, it offers a great deal of information and history of the Indigenous peoples of Canada and their relationships with the Canadian State.

Yellowhead Institute
https://yellowheadinstitute.org/
The Yellowhead Institute is an Indigenous-led research centre producing policy perspectives intended to (re-)shape Indigenous governance, facilitate Indigenous-Settler alliances, research opportunities, government accountability, and public education.

Films

The Grandfather of All Treaties. Dir. Candace Maracle. Vtape, 2015.
The Re-naming of PKOLS. Dir. Steven Davies. Steven Davies, 2015.
The Disappearing Indian. Dir. Grant McLean. National Film Board of Canada, 1995.
The Other Side of the Ledger: An Indian View of the Hudson's Bay Company. Dir. Willie Dunn and Martin De Falco. National Film Board of Canada, 1972.
You Are on Indian Land. Dir. Mort Ransen. National Film Board of Canada, 1969.

Key Terms

- Colonialism
- Doctrine of Discovery
- Gdoo-naaganinaa
- Resurgence

- Racism
- Ukwehuwé
- White Settler society

Discussion Questions

1.   What would be involved in radically transforming the social, political, and economic relationship between Indigenous peoples and Canadians according to Arthur Manuel and how is this different than what is taking place right now?

2.   How does Leanne Betasamosake Simpson define Gdoo-naaganinaa? What is the significance of the "Dish with One Spoon" where political diplomacy and decolonizing relationships are concerned?

3.   What are the similarities and differences between the following terms: anticolonialism, postcolonizing, and decolonization?

4.   What sorts of public education would be at once transformative and decolonizing according to Manuel and Simpson and what sorts of information would they need to convey to all Canadians?

Activities

Take 10–20 minutes to reflect on what you have been taught about Indigenous and Canadian histories. Discuss your individual reflections as a class. What kinds of patterns and differences emerge? How do these lessons make you feel? How have they impacted on the way you think of yourself and the land on which you live?

Watch the 1955 National Film Board production *The Disappearing Indian* (written and directed by Grant McLean). What colonial tropes, Eurocentric knowledge, and assumptions are present in this film?

Nation-Building and the Deeply Racialized Other

Editor Introduction

In his book *Everything You Know about Indians Is Wrong*, Comanche curator Paul Chaat Smith asks Americans to think *seriously* about the **representation** of Indigenous peoples in the historic **colonial imaginary**. His concern is with **romanticism**, or the depiction of Indigenous peoples based on myths, **stereotypes**, and oversimplification. Romanticism has long constituted a distinct form of racism aimed at Indigenous peoples. As Chaat Smith writes, it is "a specialized vocabulary created by Euros for Indians" ensuring in turn "a status as strange, primitive and exotic" (2009: 17). In this chapter, we provide two articles written by Indigenous scholars on matters of race and representation.

The late Deborah Doxtator, a Mohawk scholar whose article we include in Chapter 3 of the text, wrote about the idea of Indianness in a still influential piece of classical theorization written some 30 years ago in 1992. In her view, the concept cannot be considered without addressing historic acts of racism and Settler colonial injustice. Indianness works in the colonial imaginary to construct Indigenous peoples as different and **Other**. Indians are believed to live in a world of long ago. They refuse to adopt modern conveniences. Their deficits enable and effect histories of dispossession. Defined as just so many teepees, headdresses, and totem poles, Indians are everything that civilization is not in the minds of Settler colonists. Indianness makes possible the idea that Indigenous peoples must always be disappearing, a belief that is central to and constitutive of the logic of genocide and land appropriation.

Histories of genocide are made possible through rigid assertions of difference between "real Indians" and Others. Without the difference produced through myths and stereotypes about "authentic" or "real Indians," Indigenous peoples cannot move past the primitivism that defines their culture, or become civilized, for that matter. They are of culture and not of mind (Cote-Meek, 2014: 141–145). Resistance is paradoxical. The refusal to perform Indianness only reaffirms the idea that they have all but disappeared. Romanticism makes possible the ongoing dispossession of Indigenous peoples. So long as Indians are incapable of being themselves, rendered invisible, or no longer living, the act of land appropriation and Settler emplacement ensues.

Romanticism makes possible a caricature of Indigenous identities. It forecloses the breadth of Indigenous identities that exist and are possible in modern contexts. It encourages an understanding of Indigeneity on narrow grounds, wherein some Indigenous people are believed to be more authentic than others. As Chaat Smith writes, "silence about our own complicated histories supports the colonizer's idea that the only real Indians are full blooded, from a reservation, speak their language, and practice the religion of their ancestors" (2009: 26). How do we explain this need for **authenticity**? What are modern practices of difference making, where are they located, and how do they operate in the contemporary world? These are just some of the questions being asked by Indigenous scholars about colonial representations of Indianness.

The politics of representation is as tied to normalized whiteness as it is to Indianness. In saying this, we are not suggesting the focus shift from Indigenous peoples to that of whiteness alone. Rather, we want to take seriously the meaning of Indianness in the minds of the colonizer. If the privilege of whiteness is to pass invisibly as the norm, then the difference that Indianness makes must be exposed. As Carol Schick and Cree/Métis scholar Verna St Denis wrote: "addressing racism means more than examining the experience of those who experience racism" (2005: 299). Challenging racism must also involve exposing the ways that "white men name and mark Others, thereby naming and marking themselves" (ibid.).

Naming and marking Others as different does not only involve racist beliefs about the inherent superiority and inferiority of individuals. Historically, the process of difference-making was gendered—often involving sexist and demeaning assumptions about Indigenous women. As Cree scholar Winona Stevenson wrote, stereotypes about Indigenous women were often used to create boundaries between Indigenous and white Settler populations (1999). Early missionaries wrote of Indigenous women as "licentious, squalid, and immoral" in order to justify the overall "savage wretchedness" of Indigenous life (ibid., 64), to rationalize Indigenous women's subjugation (ibid., 49), and notably, to justify European intervention and impose Victorian Eurocentric patriarchy and violence (also see Razack, 2002: 130). In the first historical instance of early Settler colonialism and still today, many of these understandings served to justify early colonial dominance and policies of exclusion.

Representations of Indianness are central to the construction of white Settler identities. The colonizer imagines himself as civilized and therefore rightly entitled to land (see Razack, 2015), but only insofar as he establishes himself in contrast with the mythical construction of savagism. The ideal woman construct discussed by Stevenson is inseparable from this process of upholding the binary between civility and savagism. As Stevenson suggests, missionary accounts are rife with examples of "exploited, overworked drudges, abused, misused, [and] dirty" (1999: 58). Put simply, the pinnacle of European womanhood would likely never have been constructed without colonial representations of Indigenous womanhood.

In order to justify the appropriation of Indian lands and emplace themselves, the colonizer has always had to prove the inferiority of Indigenous peoples. The rationale for these kinds of dispossession found their early ideological basis in colonial representations of Indianness and savagery. As Stevenson (1999: 64) who quotes the work of Sarah Carter (1997) shows, "expounding the righteous triumph of civilization over savagery" required "proving the inferiority of the Indian." These understandings enabled the transfer of Indian lands into the colonizers' hands, gave way to the statutory subjugation of Indigenous women, and have stood the test of time into the twenty-first century (Cannon, 2014). As Razack (2002) points out in her discussion of the murder of Pamela George, representations of Indian womanhood in particular still work today *to construct bodies that are violable with impunity.*

The challenge we face as Indigenous peoples today is very much dependent on the ability to claim a more vibrant and dynamic representation of our peoples. As Thomas King suggests in Chapter Four, the mission in particular remains complicated by practices that reproduce the "Dead Indian," which he defines as "the stereotypes and clichés that North America has conjured up out of experience and out of its collective imaginings and fears." It is this precise colonial imaginary that works to disappear both "Live" and "Legal" Indians—Indians who are required to "get out of the way" in order for the "counterfeit" to ensue. The conundrum, as King suggests, is even further complicated by a tendency on behalf of a Settler State to rid itself of the "Indian problem" and to constitute and recuperate its own Settler sovereignty at every turn.

Like Doxtator, Chaat Smith, and many other Indigenous artists and critical thinkers, Thomas King focuses on the task of reinventing ourselves as "Indians," and in the face of popular and scholarly representations that have relegated us to past domains. There is another story to be told in his estimation. They tell the story of contemporary Indians, including traditional symbols and meanings resituated in the present (Simpson, 1998: 52). They force us to "reflect on what . . . things meant, and what they now mean" (ibid., 52–3). The task of reinvention will remain as much urgent as it is difficult into the future. As Chaat Smith suggests, it will "require invention, not rewriting" (2009: 52). It may even require "a final break with a form that was never about us in the first place" (ibid.).

CHAPTER 3

"The Idea of Indianness" and Once Upon a Time

The Role of Indians in History

Deborah Doxtator

Just a little more than a hundred years ago school texts were describing Indians as being "ferocious and quarrelsome," "great gluttons," and "great drunkards" (Miles, 1870: xxii). How have attitudes towards Indian people changed? Do people still carry in their minds the idea, even if it goes unsaid, that Indian culture is "primitive" and incapable of survival in a twentieth-century environment? Are some people still looking for the disappearing Indian? What does "Indian" mean?

Teepees, headdresses, totem poles, birch bark canoes, face paint, fringes, buckskin, and tomahawks—when anyone sees images, drawings, or paintings of these things they immediately think of "*Indians*." They are symbols of "Indianness" that have become immediately recognizable to the public. To take it one step further, they are the symbols that the public uses in its definition of what an Indian is. To the average person, Indians, *real* Indians, in their purest form of "Indianness," live in a world of long ago where there are no high-rises, no snowmobiles, no colour television. They live in the woods or in places that are unknown called "Indian Reserves." The Indians that people know best are the ones they have read about in adventure stories as a child, cut out and pasted in school projects, read about in the newspaper. They may have "played Indian" as a game, or dressed up as an Indian for Halloween. To many people "Indians" are not real, any more than Bugs Bunny, Marilyn Monroe, or Anne of Green

Deborah Doxtator. "The Idea of Indianness and Once Upon a Time: The Role of Indians in History." In *Fluffs and Feathers: An Exhibit on the Symbols of Indianness: A Resource Guide*, Brantford: Woodland Cultural Centre (© 1992), p. 199.

Gables are real to them. So it is not surprising that when they do meet Indian people they have some very strange ideas about how "Indians" behave, live, and speak.

In their excitement at meeting this celebrity, this "Indian," people sometimes say foolish things, that if they thought about it, they would never ask anyone: "Is that your own hair?," "What is the significance of that design, is it sacred?," "Say something in *Indian*." Other Indian people have been asked whether or not their blood is red, or if feathers once grew out of their heads.

It is very difficult to discuss "Indianness" with any measure of neutrality. The emotions and experience of both parties in the relationship between "Indians" and "Whites" has been such that there is no easy way to discuss the facts. It is impossible to discuss the concept of "Indianness" without addressing racism and the injustices that have occurred. It is impossible to talk about "Indianness" without facing the uncomfortable reality of the dispossession of one people by another. . . .

"Indian" has meant so many things, both good and bad: from an idealized all-spiritual, environmentalist, to a "primitive" down-trodden welfare case. These popular images of "Indians" have very little to do with actual people. Instead they reflect the ideas that one culture has manufactured about another people. These images influence the concept of "Indianness" held by many people.

Definitions of "Indianness" have changed a little over the past four hundred years. In the seventeenth century, there were debates concerning whether or not Indians were animals or human beings. In the twentieth century, the debate about Indians has shifted to whether or not "Indians" are competent human beings, capable of running their own affairs. For decades, Indian children grew up being told that their culture was inferior, their religion was wrong, and their language useless.

The concept of "The Indian" as primitive, undeveloped, and inferior has a long history, that extends back into the sixteenth century (Dickason, 1984: 35). Ever since the two races first met, non-Indians have been trying to teach, convert, "improve" or otherwise change Indian peoples. The idea has persisted that, somehow, Indians are really just undeveloped human beings in desperate need of training in the proper way to live and make a living.

Academic disciplines still have great difficulty accepting Indian art, history, literature, music, and technology as art, history, literature, music, and technology without first placing it in an anthropological context. Museums continue to foster the view of Indians as "pre-historic." They have special galleries that focus on presenting something called "Native Culture" in ways that are perceived inappropriate for "Canadian culture." It is not particularly unusual for museums such as the National Museum of Civilization to display human remains from a native culture which have included skeletal remains in their archaeological exhibits. It is seen as being comparable to scientific displays of the skeleton of "Early Man." But it is not likely that the bones of Laura Secord will be installed in any museum exhibit in the near future. Indians, like the "Iron-Age" man, are seen as being separated from modern technological society by the fact that their technology, or rather perceived lack of it, makes them "primitives" or "wild-men," ancient ancestors that just don't exist anymore.

It has been difficult for industrial Canadian society to accept that non-industrial cultures are still viable. To Canadian society, Indian cultures are based firmly in the past, and Western culture has a tradition of repudiating the past as out-of-date and irrelevant to the present. Since the sixteenth century, "Indians" have been seen as representing an earlier, less civilized version of Europeans. They have, in the minds of Europeans and Canadians, come to symbolize human beings at an earlier, less complex stage of development.

This has meant that images of "Indians" created by Western society have emphasized their perception of Indian inferiority. In the nineteenth and early twentieth centuries "Indian" culture was either denounced as immoral or seen as having degenerated from a higher form of culture. To those who were inclined to see the world as a struggle between good and bad, God and the Devil, Indians were "pagans," devil worshippers. To those who accepted Darwin's theories of evolution, Indians were seen as halfway between men and beasts, simple people who needed to be eventually "raised" to the level of Western civilization through education and training. To those who saw the world in terms of a "golden past" against which everything in the present could never measure up, "Indians were simply no longer what they used to be" (Barbeau, 1923). No matter what the approach, all of these views concluded that Indian societies were ultimately inferior to Western societies.

Every culture creates images of how it sees itself and the rest of the world. Incidental to these images of self-definition are definitions of the "other." Canadian society through control over such tools as advertising, literature, history, and the entertainment media has the power to create images of other peoples and these images often operate as a form of social control. For example, images in the media of women as incompetent, physically inferior, and scatter-brained have justified why women should not hold executive positions in Canadian business. Racial stereotypes in television situation-comedies have justified why it is all right to deny other racial groups access to power and financial rewards. Indians as part of a different racial group have been subject to this type of "control" but also to a unique form of physiological warfare. Minority groups often endure discrimination but they never experience situations in which the discriminating group usurps their identity. The image of the "romantic Indian princess" was created for the benefit and imagination of Euro-Canadian, not for the benefit of Indian people. It uses symbols derived from Indian cultures and changes them so that they better suit the needs of Canadian society. Through use of the romantic images of "Indian princesses" and "Indian chiefs" non-Indian people can become "noble Indians" in their own minds. . . .

Once Upon a Time: The Role of Indians in History

In disposition the Savages were fierce, cruel and cunning. They seldom forgave an affront. They used to SCALP the enemies whom they had killed, and to torment those whom they had taken alive. . . . However, as the Indians were so cruel and bloodthirsty, we cannot but lament and condemn the practice of using their services in warfare. Those who used them were often unable to manage them. (Miles, 1870)

Eighteen days after setting out Davis handed over his charges to the personnel

at Fort Battle ford—from outside the buildings. Realizing from personal experience the effect of such close contact with over a thousand Indians, the personnel there suggested that before presenting his dispatches it might be well for Davis to strip to the skin, burn his clothing and take a bath. (Robins, 1948)

Interpretations of history can best be understood as a series of stories or myths. My generation grew up with the story of how North America was "discovered" by Christopher Columbus and of how civilization was "started" by the French. There were lots of statements in the textbooks about "virgin land," "uninhabited territories." Then suddenly into the picture came the Indians. Sometimes they were portrayed as tools, sometimes as threats, sometimes as allies. Indians were incidental because the story was not about them. They were just there—in the way.

I remember learning about Cartier, about Frontenac, about Brock, and feeling disappointed that the Indians always lost. When we studied the fur trade, the Indians were always doing foolish things, giving up all their valuable fur resources worth thousands of dollars for a few pots and pans, selling huge tracts of land for a handful of shiny beads. I didn't want to accept it, but there it was in print, in the textbook that never lied.

It wasn't until I went to University that I understood that what I had read, studied, and reiterated in my test answers was a type of story. It was somebody else's story about how Canada was settled, and it functioned as a justification and explanation for "the way things happened." This fall I discovered that the story still functions in this way. One of my tutorial students remarked to me that he felt it was unfair to blame the Canadian government for the reserve system and broken treaties because it was unintentional that the treaty promises were not kept, that no one had planned that the Cree in Saskatchewan would starve, that it "just happened."

The Canadian history textbook was sprinkled with references to the clash between "primitive and civilized societies." It stated that "despite their nomadic habits and their mixed blood the Métis were not savages," but "unsophisticated peoples." Métis people had "primitive nationalism"; Crees didn't advance to the battle, they "prowled" around neighbourhoods frightening townspeople. Riel himself was said to be filled with "primitive aggressiveness and hostility" (Francis et al., 1986). In the bulk of the reading, Indians still were in the periphery of the story, their part was still that of the obstacle, and source of conflict.

Historically, these stories about Indians being "primitive," violent, and generally incompetent at ṫḣḋ gȯvḋṙṅṁḋṅṫ jṵṡṫḋḋ two elements of Canadian Indian policy: non-Indian land settlement and non-Indian control over Indians. For example, it was easy for nineteenth and often twentieth century analysts to justify why Indians no longer should control the land. They simply didn't know how to use it "properly." They built no roads, no fences, raised no cattle, they were not "improving" the land with European technology. Regulations were passed in the Canadian Parliament to control Indians—where they could live, how they were governed, how they should make their living. In the years following the second Riel Rebellion, Indians in the west were not allowed to leave their reserves without the permission of the Indian agent. The government decided who was an Indian and who was not. During the nineteenth century, no other group in Canada was as closely regulated and controlled.

Why were Indian people so closely watched and regulated? Why has this regulation seemed understandable to the public? Why does the phrase "wild Indians" make the public feel uneasy if not frightened? Conflict between Indians fighting for their land and settlers fighting to take the land happened in the relatively recent past, only a hundred years ago. Or it may be, as some have argued, that Indians have always been viewed by historians and other scholars as being a submerged, frighteningly violent part of the Euro-North American psyche (Fielder, 1968).

Indians have always been viewed by Euro-North Americans in comparison with themselves. In the seventeenth century, Europeans believed that all of mankind was descended from Adam, the first man. Europeans also believed in a hierarchy of mankind. At the top of the hierarchy of societies, not surprisingly, were Europeans, and under them in development and "civilization" were all of the other peoples who were not Europeans.

From the beginning, Europeans had tried to set Indians into this order of peoples. The earliest perceptions of Indians were that they were more like the ancient Romans or Biblical Israelites than they were like Europeans. Lafitau, an early French "Indian" scholar went to great pains to demonstrate the similarity of North American customs and language to classical models. Early engravings of Indians often present them in poses and clothing that suggests a connection with ancient Greece or Rome. . . .

This tradition of presenting Indian individuals as classical figures has continued well into the twentieth century in the form of heraldry on coats of arms of Canadian cities (City of Toronto, City of Brantford), provinces (Newfoundland, Nova Scotia), and historical cultural organizations (Ontario Historical Society).

In establishing the hierarchy of societies, the major criteria for classification were industrial technology and material wealth—two accomplishments of which Europeans were very proud. When these criteria were applied to Indians, most Europeans came to the conclusion that "Indians" were also "savages." They lacked all the things that were necessary to be accepted as "civilized" and as Europeans. They had no printing presses, no books, no wine, no factories, no European style government, no Christianity, no guns, and "no polite conversations" (Dickason, 1984: 52). The associations of Indians with the European tradition of the "primitive" half-animal "wild man" were so strong that Indians were often depicted with long flowing beards and body hair even though explorers repeatedly remarked upon the fact that surprisingly, Indians were not very hairy and did not have beards.

To Cartier on the Gaspe coast in 1534, there was no doubt that the occupants of the new land were to be considered "wild" men:

> This people may well be called savage; for they are the sorriest folk there can be in the world and the whole lot of them had not anything above the value of five sous, their canoes and fishing nets excepted. . . . They have no other dwelling but their canoes which they turn upside down and sleep on the ground underneath. They eat their meat almost raw, only warming it a little on the coals and the same with their fish. (Hoffman, 1961: 135)

Described as being without houses, possessions, and comforts, the Indian nonetheless attracted some interest from those Europeans who were interested in changing materialistic European society. Like unfallen man, Adam, the Indians appeared to be very generous with their possessions and as some saw them, completely, "without evil and without guile" (Berkhofer, 1979: 11). This idyllic "Adam" side to the "savage" and "uncivilized" man was used to great effect by those who were dissatisfied with society and sought to reform it. They presented "Indians" in ways that directly criticized European society.

Peter Martyr's sixteenth century history of the conquest of the "New World" contrasted the "crafty deceitful" Europeans with the "Indians" who lived instead in a world of innocence, liberty, and ease uncorrupted by civilized ideas of property, greed, and luxury (Crane, 1952: 4). In Montaigne's "On Cannibals," Brazilian people were used to criticize French poverty and social inequality. He contrasted the aboriginal practices of cannibalism with the common European practice of torture and concluded "better to eat your dead enemy as do the Amerindians than to eat a man alive in the manner of the Europeans" (Dickason, 1984: 56). Similarly the women of France were chastened for their lack of affection for their children, scarcely waiting "the birth of their children to put them out to nursemaids," unlike "savage women" who breast-fed their own children with no ill physical effects (Jaenan, 1976: 33).

By the seventeenth century, Europeans had certain fixed ideas about what an Indian was supposed to look like. The "official costume" of Indians in European art was a feather skirt and upright headdress occasionally with some feathers at the wrists and ankles (Chiapelli, 1976: 504). The physical remoteness of Indians to Europeans made it possible to create representations of abstract "Indians" that bore no resemblance to reality. In a sixteenth century illustration depicting Amerigo Vespucci awakening "America" from the sleep in her hammock, America is represented as being a nude Indian woman. She is surrounded by European-looking animals in a forest scene; a spear is propped against a tree. These abstract depictions of Indians created a visual symbolic language that was immediately recognizable as "Indianness"; nudity, feathers, headdresses, bows and arrows. It was upon this system of symbols that nineteenth and twentieth century

symbolic language about "Indianness" was elaborated and developed.

Whenever Canadian and American society has found itself in competition with Indians over land and resources, the images generated about Indians by the non-Indian public are predictably negative. They are designed to create feelings of hate and anger. The newspaper engravings of the late nineteenth century provide ample examples of images of hate. "The Sentinel's Evening Visitors," depicting Indian women waiting to get a drink of the guard's whiskey, possibly in exchange for certain services, and the sketch entitled "Indian Loafers" both from Canadian newspapers, illustrate the feeling of disgust that the public was expected to share with the artist. Depictions of leering crazed Indians threatening women and children, riding demented through their camps crying for scalps, making off with stock animals and anything else that was portable, were common in newspapers of the 1870, and 1880s such as *The Graphic* and *The Illustrated War News*.

The pictorial story in these same newspapers of the Canadian and American participants in the wars with the Indians are strikingly heroic. Although an Indian may be depicted as scowling, demented, savage beyond all reason, the settler or the soldier is neat, calm, and in control. Although threatened, they appear as though they will never be defeated. This sense of the superiority, of "British cheer and pluck" in the Battle of Batoche was reflected in the newspaper coverage of the victory for the Canadian forces:

> The charge started at high noon by routing them out of the advanced pits. At 3:30 p.m. the enemy were totally routed, many having been killed and wounded, many more were prisoners in our hands and others had fled and were hiding in the surrounding bushes. Col. Williams said simply: "Men will you follow me?" The answer was drowned in a roar of cheering such as I never heard before. Over the bluff we went, yelling like mad. The Indians fired one volley and ran. Neither the Indians nor halfbreeds stood their ground. (*Winnipeg Free Press*, 13 May 1910)

References

Barbeau, Marus. 1923. *Indian Days in the Canadian Rockies*. Toronto: MacMillan.

Berkhofer, Robert. 1979. *The White Man's Indian*. New York: Vintage Books.

Chiapelli, Fred. 1976. *First Images of America*, Vol. 1. Berkeley: University of California.

Oruno, Ford. 1952. "The Noble Savage in America 1815–1860." Unpublished PhD Thesis, Yale University.

Dickason, Olive. 1984. *Myth of the Savage*. Calgary: University of Alberta Press.

Fielder, Leslie. 1968. *The Return of the Vanishing American*. Toronto: Stern and Day.

Francis, Douglas, et al., eds. 1986. *Readings in Canadian History: Post Confederation* (pp. 63–127). Toronto: Holt Rinehart and Winston of Canada, Ltd.

Hoffman, Bernard. 1961. *Cabot to Cartier*. Toronto: University of Toronto Press.

Jaenen, C.J. 1976. *Friend and Foe*. New York: Columbia University Press.

Miles, Henry. 1870. *The Child's History of Canada: For the Use of the Elementary Schools and of the Young Reader*. Montreal: Dawson Brothers.

Robins, John D., ed. 1940. "West by North" in *A Pocketful of Canada*, written for the Canadian Council of Education for Citizenship. Toronto: Collins.

Winnipeg Free Press. 1910. Friday, 13 May. Souvenir Reprint, Glenbow Archives.

CHAPTER 4

Too Heavy to Lift

Thomas King

Few looking at photos of mixed-bloods would be likely to say, "But they don't look like Irishmen."

—Louis Owens, *I Hear the Train*

Indians come in all sorts of social and historical configurations. North American popular culture is littered with savage, noble, and dying Indians, while in real life we have **Dead Indians**, Live Indians, and Legal Indians.

Dead Indians are, sometimes, just that. Dead Indians. But the Dead Indians I'm talking about are not the deceased sort. Nor are they all that inconvenient. They are the stereotypes and clichés that North America has conjured up out of experience and out of its collective imaginings and fears. North America has had a long association with Native people, but despite the history that the two groups have shared, North America no longer *sees* Indians. What it sees are war bonnets, beaded shirts, fringed deerskin dresses, loincloths, headbands, feathered lances, tomahawks, moccasins, face paint, and bone chokers. These bits of cultural debris—authentic and constructed—are what literary theorists like to call "signifiers," signs that create a "simulacrum," which Jean Baudrillard, the French sociologist and postmodern theorist, succinctly explained as something that "is never that which conceals the truth—it is the truth which conceals that there is none."

. . . For those of us who are not French theorists but who know the difference between a motor home and a single-wide trailer, a simulacrum is something that represents something that never existed. Or, in other words, the only truth of the thing is the lie itself. . . .

You can find Dead Indians everywhere. Rodeos, powwows, movies, television commercials. . . .

I probably sound testy, and I suppose part of me is. But I shouldn't be. After all, Dead Indians are the only antiquity that North America has. Europe has Greece and Rome. China has the powerful dynasties. Russia has the Cossacks. South and Central America have the Aztecs, the Incas, and the Maya.

North America has Dead Indians.

This is why Littlefeather didn't show up in a Dior gown, and why West and Campbell and Fontaine didn't arrive at their respective events in Brioni suits, Canali dress shirts, Zegni ties, and Salvatore Ferragamo shoes. Whatever cultural significance they may have for Native peoples, full feather headdresses and beaded buckskins are, first and foremost, White North America's signifiers of Indian authenticity. Their visual value at ceremonies in Los Angeles or Ottawa is—as the credit card people say—priceless. . . .

On the other hand, if you like the West and are the outdoors type, you can run out to Wyoming and pedal your bicycle over Dead Indian Pass, spend the evening at Dead Indian campground, and in the morning cycle across Dead Indian Meadows on your way to Dead Indian Peak. If you happen to be in California, you can hike Dead Indian Canyon. And if you're an angler, you can fish Dead Indian Creek in Oregon or Dead Indian Lake in Oklahoma, though the U.S. Board on Geographic Names recently voted to rename it Dead Warrior Lake.

Sometimes you can only watch and marvel at the ways in which the Dead Indian has been turned into products: Red Chief Sugar, Calumet Baking Soda, the Atlanta Braves, Big Chief Jerky, Grey Owl Wild Rice, Red Man Tobacco, the Chicago Blackhawks, Mutual of Omaha, Winnebago Motor Homes, Big Chief Tablet, Indian motorcycles, the Washington Redskins, American Spirit Cigarettes, Jeep Cherokee, the Cleveland Indians, and Tomahawk missiles. . . .

One of my favourite Dead Indian products is Land O' Lakes butter, which features an Indian Maiden in a buckskin dress on her knees holding a box of butter at bosom level. The wag who designed the box arranged it so that if you fold the box in a certain way, the Indian woman winds up *au naturel*, sporting naked breasts. Such a clever fellow. . . .

All of this pales by comparison with the contemporary entrepreneurs who have made a bull-market business out of Dead Indian culture and spirituality. . . . Folks such as Lynn Andrews, Mary Summer Rains, Jamie Samms, Don Le Vie, Jr., and Mary Elizabeth Marlow, just to mention some of the more prominent New Age spiritual CEOs, have manufactured fictional Dead Indian entities—Agnes Whistling Elk, Ruby Plenty Chiefs, No Eyes, Iron Thunderhorse, Barking Tree, and Max the crystal skull—who supposedly taught them the secrets of Native spirituality. They have created Dead Indian narratives that are an impossible mix of Taoism, Buddhism, Druidism, science fiction, and general nonsense, tied together with Dead Indian ceremony and sinew to give their product provenance and validity, along with a patina of exoticism. . . .

From the frequency with which Dead Indians appear in advertising, in the names of businesses, as icons for sports teams, as marketing devices for everything from cleaning products to underwear, and as stalking goats for New Age spiritual flimflam, you might think that Native people were a significant target for sales. We're not, of course. We don't buy this crap. At least not enough to support such a bustling market. But there's really no need to ask whom Dead Indians are aimed at, is there?

All of which brings us to Live Indians.

Among the many new things that Europeans had to deal with upon their arrival in the North American wilderness were Live Indians. Live Indians, from an Old World point of view, were an intriguing, perplexing, and annoying part of life in the New World. . . .

[T]he death of the Indian was a working part of North American mythology. This dying was not the fault of non-Natives. The demise of Indians was seen as a tenet of natural law, which favoured the strong and eliminated the weak.

George Catlin, who travelled around North America in the 1830s painting Live Indians, said of the tribes he visited that, "in a few years, perhaps, they will have entirely disappeared from the face of the earth, and all that will be remembered of them will be that they existed and were numbered among the barbarous tribes that once inhabited this vast Continent...." The American newspaperman Horace Greeley, on a trip west in 1859, was not quite as kind as Catlin . . . "The Indians are children . . .", "These people must die out—there is no help for them...."

Problem was, Live Indians didn't die out. They were supposed to, but they didn't. Since North America already had the Dead Indian, Live Indians were neither needed nor wanted. They were irrelevant, and as the nineteenth century rolled into the twentieth century, Live Indians were forgotten, safely stored away on reservations and reserves or scattered in the rural backwaters and cityscapes of Canada and the United States. Out of Sight, out of mind. Out of mind, out of Sight.

All Native people living in North America today are Live Indians. Vine Deloria, the Lakota scholar and writer, didn't use the term "Live Indians" when he wrote his famous 1969 manifesto *Custer Died for Your Sins.* Instead, he talked about Native people being "transparent." "Our foremost plight," said Deloria, "is our transparency. People can tell just by looking at us what we want, what should be done to help us, how we feel, and what a 'real' Indian is really like." Deloria might as well have said that Indians are invisible. North Americans certainly *see* contemporary Native people. They just don't *see* us as Indians.

When I was kicking around San Francisco, there was an Aboriginal photographer, a Mandan from the Fort Berthold reservation in South Dakota named Zig Jackson, who had a wonderful wit. For one of his photographic series, "Entering Zig's Indian Reservation," he took photographs of himself in a feathered headdress wandering the streets of San Francisco, riding cable cars and buses, looking in store windows. What he was after and what he was able to catch were the apprehensive and delighted reactions of non-Natives as they came face to face with their Dead Indian come to life.

Carlisle Indian Industrial School, an early residential school, took photographs of Indians when they first came to that institution and then photographed them after they had been "cleaned up," so that the world could see the civilizing effects of Christianity and education on Indians. Not to be outdone, the Mormon Church, or the Church of Jesus Christ of Latter-Day Saints (LDS), has for years maintained an impressive collection of photographs of Indian children, taken when the children were first brought into the church's Home Placement Program. This was a program in place from 1947 to 1996, through which Native families were encouraged to send their kids off-reservation to live with Mormon families, the expectation being that these children would have a greater chance at Success if they were raised and educated in White society. The purpose of the photographs was to track the change in the children's skin colour, from dark to light, from savagism to civilization....

When I lived in Salt Lake City, I was privileged to see some of the Church's Polaroids. Frankly, I couldn't see much of a difference between the "before" and "after" shots, but then I wasn't looking at the photographs through the lens of scripture.

In the late 1970s, I went to Acoma Pueblo and took the tour of the old village up on the mesa. One of the adobe houses had a television antenna fixed to the roof. . . . One of the women in the group, a woman in her late thirties from Ohio, was annoyed by the presence of the television set. This was supposed to be an authentic Indian village, she complained to the rest of the group. Real Indians, she told us, didn't have televisions. . . .

In order to maintain the cult and sanctity of the Dead Indian, North America has decided that Live Indians living today cannot be genuine Indians. This sentiment is a curious reworking of one of the cornerstones of Christianity, the idea of innocence and original sin. Dead Indians are Garden of Eden-variety Indians. Pure, Noble, Innocent. Perfectly authentic. Jean-Jacques Rousseau Indians. Not a feather out of place. Live Indians are fallen Indians, modern, contemporary copies, not authentic Indians at all, Indians by biological association only.

Many Native people have tried to counter this authenticity twaddle by insisting on tribal names—Blackfoot, Navajo, Mohawk, Seminole, Hoopa, Chickasaw, Mandan, Tuscarora, Pima, Omaha, Cree, Haida, Salish, Lakota, Mi'kmaq, Ho-Chunk—and while this is an excellent idea, it has been too much for North America to manage. As with the Dead Indian, North America has, for a very long time now, insisted on a collective noun for Live Indians—Indians, Aboriginals, First Nations, Natives, First Peoples—even though there are over 600 recognized nations in Canada and over 550 recognized nations in the United States. . . .

Dead Indians. Live Indians. You would think that these two Indians would be akin to matter and anti-matter, that it would be impossible for both of them to occupy the same space, but each year Live Indians and Dead Indians come together at powwows and ceremonies and art markets from Alberta to Arizona, Oklahoma to Ontario, the Northwest Territories to New Mexico. At the same time, with remarkable frequency, Live Indians cum Dead Indians show up at major North American social, artistic, and governmental events and galas to pose for the cameras and to gather up any political advantage that might be available. . . .

For Native people, the distinction between Dead Indians and Live Indians is almost impossible to maintain. But North America doesn't have this problem. All it has to do is hold the two Indians up to the light. Dead Indians are dignified, noble, silent, suitably garbed. And dead. Live Indians are invisible, unruly, disappointing. And breathing. One is a romantic reminder of a heroic but fictional past. The other is simply an unpleasant, contemporary surprise. . . .

Let's be clear, Live Indians dance at powwows. And when we dance, when we sing at the drum, when we perform ceremonies, we are not doing it for North America's entertainment. Where North America sees Dead Indians come to life, we see our families and our relations. We do these things to remind ourselves who we are, to remind ourselves where we come from, and to remind ourselves of our relationship with the earth. Mostly, though, we do these things because we enjoy them. And because they are important.

I know that this sort of rhetoric—"our relationship with the earth"—sounds worn out and corny, but that's not the fault of Native people. Phrases such as "Mother Earth," "in harmony with nature," and "seven generations" have been kidnapped by White North America and stripped of their power. Today, Mother Earth is a Canadian alternative rock band, a Memphis Slim song, an alternative-living magazine; and a short story by Isaac Asimov. . . . "Harmony with Nature" is a hypnosis session that you can download for only $12.95 and which will "gently guide you into a rapturous sense of connection to the whole of natural creation. . . ."

There's a "Seven Generations" company out of Burlington, Vermont, that sells "naturally safe and effective household products," while an outfit called "Hellfish Family" will sell you a T-shirt that has a crucifixion scene on the back with "Seven Generations" at the top and "You Are Not My Christ" at the bottom for $12.95. . . .

Dead Indians. Live Indians. In the end, it is an impossible tangle. Thank goodness there are Legal Indians.

Legal Indians are considerably more straightforward. Legal Indians are Live Indians, because only Live Indians can be Legal Indians, but not all Live Indians are Legal Indians.

Is that clear?

Legal Indians are those Indians who are recognized as being Indians by the Canadian and U.S. governments. Government Indians, if you like. In Canada, Legal Indians are officially known as "Status Indians," Indians who are registered with the federal government as Indians under the terms of the Indian Act.

According to the 2006 census, Canada had a population of about 565,000 Status Indians. . . . In the United States, federal "recognition," the American version of "Status," is granted to tribes rather than individuals, and in 2009, the government's Federal Register recognized some 564 tribes whose enrolled members were eligible for federal assistance. . . .

As I said, these numbers will never be accurate. But if they are close, it means that only about 40 percent of Live Indians in North America are Legal Indians. A few more than one in three. This is important because the only Indians that the governments of Canada and the United States have any interest in are the Legal ones.

"Interest," though, is probably is too positive a term, for while North America loves the Dead

Indian and ignores the Live Indian, North America *hates* the Legal Indian. Savagely. The Legal Indian was one of those errors in judgment that North America made and has been trying to correct for the last 150 years. . . .

[B]ecause of the treaties, Legal Indians are entitled to certain rights and privileges . . .—with the exception of certain First Nations bands in British Columbia and some executive order reservations in the States—Legal Indians are the only Indians who are eligible to receive them.

A great many people in North America believe that Canada and the United States, in a moment of inexplicable generosity, gave treaty rights to Native people as a gift. Of course, anyone familiar with the history of Indians in North America knows that Native people paid for every treaty right, and in some cases, paid more than once. The idea that either country gave First Nations something for free is horseshit.

Sorry. I should have been polite and said "anyone familiar with Native history knows that this is in error" or "knows that this is untrue," but . . ., as Sherman Alexie (Spokane-Coeur d'Alene) reminds us in his poem "How to Write the Great American Indian Novel," "real" Indians come from a horse culture.

In Canada, Legal Indians are defined by the Indian Act, a series of pronouncements and regulations, rights and prohibitions, originally struck in 1876, which has wound its snaky way along to the present day. The act itself does more than just define Legal Indians. It has been the main mechanism for controlling the lives and destinies of Legal Indians in Canada, and throughout the life of the act, amendments have been made to the original document to fine-tune this control. . . .

A 1905 amendment allowed the removal of Aboriginal people from reserves that were too close to White towns of more than 8,000 residents. . . .

Until at least 1968, Legal Indians could be "enfranchised," which simply meant that the government could take Status away from a Legal Indian, with or without consent, and replace it with Canadian citizenship. Technically, enfranchisement was proffered as a positive, entailing, among other benefits, the right to vote and drink. All you had to do was give up being a Legal Indian and become . . .

well, that was the question, wasn't it. Legal Indian women could be "enfranchised" if they married non-Native or non-Status men. If Legal Indians voted in a federal election, they would be "enfranchised." Get a university degree and you were automatically "enfranchised." If you served in the military, you were "enfranchised." If you were a clergyman or a lawyer, you were "enfranchised. . . ."

In the United States, Legal Indians are enrolled members of tribes that are federally recognized. That's the general rule. However, tribes control how their membership rolls are created and maintained, and eligibility for membership varies from nation to nation. Most base their membership on blood quantum. If you have enough Native blood in you, then you are eligible for enrollment, and, once enrolled, are a Legal Indian.

In Canada, loss of Status has been an individual matter, one Legal Indian at a time. A rather slow process. In the United States, where things reportedly move faster, the government, particularly in the 1950s, set about "enfranchising" entire tribes en masse. They started with the Menominee in Wisconsin and the Klamath in Oregon and, in the space of about ten years, they removed another 107 tribes from the federal registry. . . .

In 1969, the Canadian government tried to pull a homegrown Termination Act—the 1969 White Paper—out of its Parliamentary canal. In that year, Prime Minister Pierre Trudeau blithely intimated that there was no such thing as Indian entitlement to land or Native rights and suggested that it was in the best interests of First Nations people to give up their reserves and assimilate into Canadian society. The reaction was immediate and fierce. Almost every Indian organization came out against the plan. Whatever the problems were with the Indian Act and with the Department of Indian Affairs, Native people were sure that giving up their land and their treaty rights was not the answer. . . .

All North America dreams about is the Dead Indian. There's a good reason, of course. The Dead Indian is what North America wants to be. Which probably explains the creation and proliferation of Indian hobbyist clubs, social organizations that have sprung up in North America and around the world as well, where non-Indians can spend their leisure time and weekends pretending to be Dead Indians.

There are Indian clubs in Florida, Texas, California, Washington, Oregon, Idaho, New Mexico, and Arizona . . ., in Italy, in France, in Poland, in Hungary, and in most of the other eastern European and Scandinavian countries. . . .

I haven't found any clubs in Canada yet, but would guess there must be a couple hidden away here and there . . . while Woodcraft Indians and the Scouts made use of what they saw as Indian content in their structures and performances, neither was an "Indian club."

Indian clubs are magnets for non-Natives who want to transform themselves, just for a day or two, into Dead Indians. Folks who attend go to dance and sing and participate in pipe ceremonies and sweats. . . .

The one thing that you can say about Indian hobbyists is that they take their fantasies seriously.

Still, all of this dress-up, roleplaying silliness has as much to do with Indians as an Eskimo Pie has to do with the Inuit.

The irony is that these clubs and the sentiments they espouse would be better served if Live Indians and Legal Indians somehow disappeared, got out of the way. After all, there's nothing worse than having the original available when you're trying to sell the counterfeit.

Live Indians. Legal Indians.

If you listen carefully, you can almost hear North America cry out, in homage to Henry II and his feud with Thomas à Becket, "Who will rid me of these meddlesome Indians?"

And, as luck would have it, Canada and the United States are working on a solution.

PART 2

Additional Readings

Misko-Kìsikàwihkwè (Acoose, Janice). *Iskwewak Kah'Ki Yaw Ni Wahkomakanak: Neither Indian Princesses nor Easy Squaws*, 2nd Edition. Toronto: Women's Press, 2016.

Chaat Smith, Paul. *Everything You Know about Indians Is Wrong*. Minneapolis, MN: University of Minnesota Press, 2009.

Deloria, Philip J. *Indians in Unexpected Places*. Lawrence, KS: University Press of Kansas, 2004.

Duffek, Karen, and Tania Willard, eds. *Lawrence Paul Yuxweluptun: Unceded Territories*. Vancouver: The Museum of Anthropology at UBC Press, 2016.

Francis, Daniel. *The Imaginary Indian: The Image of the Indian in Canadian Culture*. Arsenal Pulp Press, 1992.

L'Hirondelle Hill, Gabrielle, and Sophie McCall, eds. *The Land We Are: Artists and Writers Unsettle the Politics of Reconciliation*. Winnipeg: Arbiter Ring Press, 2015.

Marubbio, M. Elise, and Eric L. Buffalohead. *Native Americans on Film: Conversations, Teaching, and Theory*. Baltimore, MD: The University of Press of Kentucky, 2013.

Singer, Beverly R. *Wiping the War Paint off the Lens: Native American Film and Video*. Minneapolis, MN: University of Minnesota Press, 2001.

Summary of the American Psychological Association Resolution Recommending Retirement of American Indian Mascots. Available online: https://www.apa.org/pi/oema/resources/indian-mascots

Relevant Websites

Zig Jackson Photography
http://www.risingbuffaloarts.com
Rising Buffalo (Zig Jackson) is a photographer of mixed Mandan, Hidatsa, and Arikara ancestry whose award-winning art and portraiture explores issues of cultural identity, representation, and appropriation across spaces marked as white/urban and Indian/reserve.

Adrian Stimson
www.adrianstimson.com
Adrian Stimson (Siksika) is an interdisplinary artist and Governor General's Award Winner whose extensive paintings, installations, and performances explore issues of landscape, identity, and Two-Spiritedness, often through a performance moniker, Buffalo Boy and The Shaman Exterminator.

Susan Blight
www.susanblight.com
Susan Blight is an Anishinaabe interdisciplinary artist, curator, and writer, exploring matters of identity and space and is co-founder with Hayden King (Anishinaabe) of the Ogimaa Mikana artists collective which works to reclaim and rename landmarks through public art and social practice.

The National Museum of the American Indian
http://www.nmai.si.edu
The National Museum of the American Indian is, as defined on their website: "the sixteenth museum of the Smithsonian Institution. It is the first national museum dedicated to the preservation, study, and exhibition of the life, languages, literature, history, and arts of Native Americans. Established by an act of Congress in 1989 (amendment in 1996), the museum works in collaboration with the Native peoples of the Western Hemisphere to protect and foster their cultures by reaffirming traditions and beliefs, encouraging contemporary artistic expression, and empowering the Indian voice."

Jeff Thomas
http://jeff-thomas.ca
Haudenosaunee artist, photographer, and curator Jeff Thomas explores the presence of Indigenous peoples in urban and contemporary spaces, the silences produced by photographic histories—including those produced by Edward S. Curtis—and seeks to engage both Indigenous and Settler populations in critical conversations about Indianness and the colonial imaginary.

Films

Aboriginality. Dir. Dominique Keller and Tom Jackson. National Film Board of Canada, 2008.
Couple in the Cage: A Guatinaui Odyssey. Dir. Coco Fusco and Paula Heredia. Third World Newsreel, 1993.
More than a Word. Dir. John and Kenn Little. Kanopy, Inc. 2017.
Reel Injun. Dir. Neil Diamond. National Film Board of Canada, 2009.
Shooting Indians: A Journey with Jeffrey Thomas, A Film by Ali Kazimi. Dir. Ali Kazimi. Peripheral Visions Film and Video Inc., 1997.

Key Terms

- Authenticity
- Colonial imaginary
- Dead Indians
- The Other
- Representation
- Romanticism
- Stereotype

Discussion Questions

1. What does Thomas King mean by "Dead Indians"? How do we explain the fascination historically with "Dead Indians"? Where do "Dead Indians" stand in relation to "Live Indians" and "Legal Indians"?

2. How do images of "Indians" created by Settler societies work to perpetuate racism and lands dispossession? How do they work to enable and benefit Settler colonialism? What

are the implications of the "Noble Savage" or renderings of Indigenous peoples as a "disappearing race"?

3. How do we explain the need for certainty about Indian difference? Where are these practices located and how do they operate in the contemporary world? What kinds of material consequences does keeping the racialized Other firmly intact have in legitimating and perpetuating Canadian Settler colonialism?

4. If Settler populations are complicit in producing colonial representations of Indianness, then what is the way forward in terms of provoking a more critical consciousness to disrupt them? What sorts of Settler consciousness are possible and/or already being realized?

Activities

Identify different representations of "Indians" in popular culture (e.g., Disney films, children's literature, "Cowboy and Indian" figurines, Halloween costumes, etc.). For whom and what do these representations serve?

Locate some local, provincial, state, or national sports teams that have "Indian" names or mascots. How are these altogether common and racist practices allowable? What does their persistence suggest?

How have representations of "Indians" been handled by regional media in your area over the last five years? How are the individuals and stories being portrayed? If you were to rework these representations differently, how would you do it, and why?

PART 3

Race, Territoriality, and Peoplehood

Editor Introduction

The idea of North America as a once vast, open wilderness, historically unoccupied and empty prior to the arrival of first white Settlers, is a powerful myth informing much of Canadian and American history. The early and sometimes forcible displacement of Indigenous peoples and territories rests on this fiction, furthered by an assumption that racism does not define the colonial past. "In order for Canada to have a viable national identity," writes Miqmaw scholar Bonita Lawrence, "the historical record of how the land was acquired must be erased." In this chapter, we provide two theoretical perspectives contesting this erasure, the future of nationhood shaped by territorial displacement, and a scholarship that defines the rewriting of lands in solely racialized terms.

The displacement of Indigenous peoples has a long history. The history varies regionally, but in many cases, though certainly not all, it involved the movement of people from traditional territories to lands created for them by the colonizer. From the mid-1800s, it was effected through colonial policy aimed at putting some Indigenous peoples on Indian reserves—originally meant to protect us and thought to provide us with the Eurocentric education and instruction necessary for our assimilation into an emerging capitalist economy. The idea was that reserves and other rural, remote, and economically marginalized lands were the only appropriate place for us as Indians. We use the word Indian deliberately in this case because it refers accurately to early race-based thinking about blood quantum and colonial legislative histories (i.e. the *Indian Act*) that still today does not recognize linguistic and cultural differences among Indigenous groups and First Nations (see Cannon, 2019). These and other kinds of symbolic violence persist even today.

Today, many Indigenous peoples live in cities. In 2016, only slightly less than half of the registered Indian population lived on reserves in Canada. The statistic is revealing of a choice by at least some Indigenous peoples to reject the economic marginalization of reserve life and move into urban contexts. Social scientists have spent countless hours documenting the experience of "Aboriginal peoples in cities." Much of this literature has focused on the cultural incommensurability of Indians and urban ways of life, including the social problems plaguing Indigenous populations when they arrive in cities. These analyses offer little, if any, insight into difference-making practices that have long characterized Settler colonialism.

In order to mark spaces as urban, Indigenous bodies are regulated. Historically, this took place through policy, including the reserve and pass system. Indians belonged on reserves and required the approval of Indian agents to leave them. Though the ability of the Indian agent to enforce the pass system was repealed in 1951 under amendments to Canada's *Indian Act*, today, the policing of Indigenous bodies is still as symbolic as it is material. It is accomplished through the invisibility of countless urban Indigenous peoples thought to be assimilated, or who, as the Cree politician Ovide Mercredi once put it, "blend effortlessly into the multicultural framework of Canadian society." It is also accomplished through over-policing, racial profiling, police brutality, and systemic racism as evidenced in Cree scholar Tasha Hubbard's 2004 and 2019 films *Two Worlds Colliding* and *nîpawistamâsowin: We Will Stand Up* about the freezing deaths of Indigenous men in Saskatoon, Saskatchewan and the murder of a young Cree man named Colten Boushie in Biggar, Saskatchewan.

The challenge we face as urban Indigenous peoples is as much a problem of poverty, inadequate housing, and ineffectual services delivery as it is a problem of exclusion and recognition. **Indigeneity and urbanity** are by no means incompatible to one another, nor do they stand in a dichotomous, either/or relation. The assumption is that we do not belong in cities. This prevents us from seeing that many of us as Indigenous peoples—we authors included—have lived in urban locations for generations. It negates the reality that many Canadian cities are situated on or near traditional Indigenous territories. It defies the historical reality that not all Indigenous peoples were placed on reserves. It prevents us from acknowledging exclusionary practices and from understanding the work that goes into providing the ongoing ideological justification for the displacement of our peoples.

The racism effected through difference-making and other spatial practices has not been experienced uniformly among all Indigenous peoples. For some Indigenous women, racism and sexism interlocked to separate them from communities and to erode their rights and influence within communities (Cannon, 2019). In Canada, the requirement that all women lose status as Indians—and therefore all birthrights and entitlements—upon marriage to non-Indian men contributed to their relocation to cities until the 1985 *Indian Act* amendments. Others came to cities because of federal and provincial/territorial laws that fell short of addressing the distribution of matrimonial real property upon dissolution of marriage (Bastien, 2008; Montour, 1987). This matter was not addressed by Canada until 2009. Canada did not even endeavour to address sexism in the *Indian Act* until 2010 under its *Gender Equity in Indian Registration Act* (see Part Five, this volume).

The rewriting of lands involved highly racialized ways of thinking employed by the State to define some Indigenous peoples as Indians and others as not. The effect was to leave some people without federal recognition, or to displace and remove them from the land altogether. Of course, the history of Indigenous peoples in Settler colonial Canada, as Chris Andersen (2014: 204) writes, "is not only irreducible to its relationship to Indianness but also obscured." He points to the danger of charting Indigenous landscapes and identities in solely racialized terms, such that these approaches "beggar the kinds of deep analysis that would accord **Métis peoplehood** an autonomous footing linked but in no way reducible to . . . . . Indianness" (ibid.). The sorting of lands may have been effected in part by Indianness in Canada, but the racialization of Indigenous peoples cannot be understood as a uniform process that legislatively impacted on "Métis," "half-breed," and "mixed-blood" peoples in the same ways.

Indigenous peoples find their ethnogenesis not in histories of racialization, but in a distinct constellation of land-based, historical, and precolonial relationships. Indeed, by working to complicate a "Métis as mixed" train of logic, Andersen (Chapter 6, this volume) favours a "people-to-people" based way of thinking about identity, nationhood, and events at once tied to and embodied in land. He centres a detailed analysis of land, the political economy surrounding it, and the events connecting people to lands, seeking to link histories of Settler colonialism, racialization, and lands **dispossession**. The process through which Indigenous peoples were impacted by Settler colonialism, accommodated, and in turn challenged colonial power requires greater historical understanding and appreciation. These sorts of understandings cannot happen without a more anticolonial and nuanced recounting of lands.

Bonita Lawrence provides another such way of recounting histories of Settler colonialism and lands, particularly as this relates to both land theft and dispossession. In Chapter 5, she rewrites histories of the land, challenging the normative and Eurocentric frameworks that have defined much of academic scholarship. As she suggests, some historians have written of dispossession in ways that prevent us from understanding the perspectives of Indigenous peoples experiencing and challenging its authority. Her chapter aims to "decolonize the history of Eastern Canada," dismantling in turn a number of myths that are crucial to Canadian **nation-building**, including the idea that Settler colonialism was a benign process, innocent of racism, genocide, and legislative hegemony.

CHAPTER 5

Rewriting Histories of the Land

Colonization and Indigenous Resistance in Eastern Canada

Bonita Lawrence

The claim to a national culture in the past does not only rehabilitate that nation and serve as a justification for the hope of a future national culture. In the sphere of socioaffective equilibrium, it is responsible for an important change in the native. Perhaps we have not sufficiently demonstrated that colonialism is not simply content to impose its rule upon the present and future of a dominated country. Colonialism is not merely satisfied with holding a people in its grip and emptying the native's brain of all form and content. By a kind of perverse logic, it turns to the past of an oppressed people, and distorts, disfigures, and destroys it.

—Frantz Fanon, *The Wretched of the Earth*

Canadian national identity is deeply rooted in the notion of Canada as a vast northern wilderness, the possession of which makes Canadians unique and "pure" of character. Because of this, and in order for Canada to have a viable national identity, the histories of

---

"Rewriting Histories of the Land: Colonization and Indigenous Resistance in Eastern Canada" by Bonita Lawrence in *Race, Space and the Law: Unmapping a White Settler Society*, Sherene H. Razack, ed. (Toronto: Between the Lines Press, 2002), pp. 21–46. Used with permission of the publisher.

Indigenous nations,[1] in all their diversity and longevity, must be erased. Furthermore, in order to maintain Canadians' self-image as a fundamentally "decent" people innocent of any wrongdoing, the historical record of how the land was acquired—the forcible and relentless dispossession of Indigenous peoples, the theft of their territories, and the implementation of legislation and policies designed to effect their total disappearance as peoples—must also be erased. It has therefore been crucial that the survivors of this process be silenced—that Native people be deliberately denied a voice within national discourses (LaRocque, 1993).

A crucial part of the silencing of Indigenous voices is the demand that Indigenous scholars attempting to write about their histories conform to academic discourses that have already staked a claim to expertise about our pasts—notably anthropology and history. For many Aboriginal scholars from Eastern Canada who seek information about the past, exploring the "seminal" works of contemporary non-Native "experts" is an exercise in alienation. It is impossible for Native people to see themselves in the unknown and unknowable shadowy figures portrayed on the peripheries of the white settlements of colonial Nova Scotia, New France, and Upper Canada, whose lives are deduced solely through archaeological evidence or the journals of those who sought to conquer, convert, defraud, or in any other way prosper off them. This results in the depiction of ancestors who resemble "stick figures"; noble savages, proud or wily, inevitably primitive. For the most part, Indigenous scholars engaged in academic writing about the past certainly have little interest in making the premises of such works central to their own writing—and yet the academic canon demands that they build their work on the back of these "authoritative" sources. We should be clear that contemporary white historians have often argued in defence of Aboriginal peoples, seeking to challenge the minor roles that Native people have

traditionally been consigned in the (discursively created) "historical record." What is never envisioned, however, is that Indigenous communities should be seen as final arbiters of their own histories.

What is the cost for Native peoples, when these academic disciplines "own" our pasts? First of all, colonization is normalized. "Native history" becomes accounts of specific intervals of "contact," accounts which neutralize processes of genocide, which never mention racism, and which do not take as part of their purview the devastating and ongoing implications of the policies and processes that are so neutrally described. A second problem, which primarily affects Aboriginal peoples in Eastern Canada, is the longevity of colonization and the fact that some Indigenous peoples are considered by non-Native academics to be virtually extinct, to exist only in the pages of historical texts. In such a context, the living descendants of the Aboriginal peoples of Eastern Canada are all too seldom viewed as those who should play central roles in any writing about the histories of their ancestors.

Most important, however, is the power that is lost when non-Native "experts" define Indigenous peoples' pasts—the power that inheres when oppressed peoples choose the tools that they need to help them understand themselves and their histories:

> The development of theories by Indigenous scholars which attempt to explain our existence in contemporary society (as opposed to the "traditional" society constructed under modernism) has only just begun. Not all these theories claim to be derived from some "pure" sense of what it means to be Indigenous, nor do they claim to be theories which have been developed in a vacuum separated from any association with civil and human rights movements, other nationalist struggles, or other theoretical approaches. What is claimed, however, is that new ways of theorizing

1. I have used a number of terms interchangeably to describe the subjects of this article. Generally, I use the term "Indigenous peoples," as it is the international term most commonly selected by Indigenous peoples to describe themselves. However, Indigenous peoples in Canada often use the term "Aboriginal" or "Native" to describe themselves; as a result, I have included these terms as well, particularly when focusing on the local context. Occasionally, the term "Indian" is included when popularly used by Native people (such as the term "American Indians").

by Indigenous scholars are grounded in a real sense of, and sensitivity towards, what it means to be an Indigenous person. . . . Contained within this imperative is a sense of being able to determine priorities, to bring to the centre those issues of our own choosing, and to discuss them amongst ourselves. (Smith, 1999: 38)

For Indigenous peoples, telling our histories involves recovering our own stories of the past and asserting the epistemological foundations that inform our stories of the past. It also involves documenting processes of colonization from the perspectives of those who experienced it. As a result, this chapter, as an attempt to decolonize the history of Eastern Canada, focuses on Indigenous communities' stories of land theft and dispossession, as well as the resistance that these communities manifested towards colonization. It relies primarily on the endeavours of Indigenous elders and scholars who are researching community histories to shape its parameters. Knowledge-carriers such as Donald Marshall Senior and Indigenous scholars who carry out research on behalf of Indigenous communities such as Daniel Paul, Sakej Henderson, and Georges Sioui are my primary sources. For broader overviews of the colonization process, I draw on the works of Aboriginal historians such as Olivia Dickason and Winona Stevenson. In some instances, I rely on non-Native scholars who have consulted Native elders, such as Peter Schmalz, or who have conducted research specifically *for* Indigenous communities involved in resisting colonization (where those communities retain control over ownership of the knowledge and how it is to be used), such as James Morrison. In instances where no other information is available, the detailed work of non-Native scholars such as Bruce Trigger and J. R. Miller is used to make connections between different events and to document regional processes. The issues at hand are whether the scholar in question is Indigenous and the extent to which the scholar documents the perspectives of Indigenous communities about their own pasts.

As history is currently written, from outside Indigenous perspectives, we cannot see colonization *as* colonization. We cannot grasp the overall picture of a focused, concerted process of invasion

and land theft. Winona Stevenson has summarized how the "big picture" looks to Aboriginal peoples: "Mercantilists wanted our furs, missionaries wanted our souls, colonial governments, and later, Canada, wanted our lands" (Stevenson, 1999: 49). And yet, this complex rendition of a global geopolitical process can obscure how these histories come together in the experiences of different Indigenous nations "on the ground." It also obscures the *processes* that enabled colonizers to acquire the land, and the *policies* that were put into place to control the peoples displaced from the land. As a decolonization history, the perspectives informing this work highlight Aboriginal communities' experiences of these colonial processes, while challenging a number of the myths that are crucial to Canadian nation-building, such as the notion that the colonization process was benign and through which Canada maintains its posture of being "innocent" of racism and genocide. Other myths about Native savagery and the benefits of European technologies are challenged by Native communities' accounts of their own histories and are explored below.

Mercantile Colonialism: Trade and Warfare

The French and early British trade regimes in Canada did not feature the relentless slaughter and enslavement of Indigenous peoples that marked the Spanish conquest of much of "Latin" America. Nor did they possess the implacable determination to obtain Indigenous land for settlement, by any means necessary, that marked much of the British colonial period in New England. Thus the interval of mercantile colonialism in Canada has been portrayed as relatively innocuous. And yet, northeastern North America was invaded by hundreds of trade ships of different European nations engaged in a massive competition for markets; an invasion instrumental in destabilizing existing intertribal political alliances in eastern North America. It is impossible, for example, to discount the central role that competition for markets played in the large-scale intertribal warfare that appears to have developed, relatively anomalously, throughout the sixteenth, seventeenth, and eighteenth centuries in much of eastern Canada and northeastern United States. Oral history and arche-ological evidence demonstrate that these wars were unique in the history of these Indigenous nations.

It is important to take into consideration the extent to which the new commodities offered by the Europeans gave obvious material advantages to those nations who successfully controlled different trade routes. Inevitably, however, as communities became reliant on trade to obtain many of the necessities of life, access to trade routes became not only desirable but actually necessary for survival (particular as dis-eases began to decimate populations, as the animal life was affected, and as missionaries began to make inroads on traditional practices).[2] These pressures resulted in such extreme levels of competition be-tween Indigenous nations that an escalation into continuous warfare was almost inevitable. . . .

Warfare and trade among Indigenous nations profoundly changed the ecology of the land and way of life for nations of many regions. Yet these should not be seen as evidence of Indigenous savagery or of a breakdown of Indigenous values;[3] rather, these profound changes, in part, resulted from the severe pressures caused by the intense competition of European powers during mercantile colonialism to depopulate entire regions of all fur-bearing animals.

Disease and Christianization in the Huron-Wendat Nation

Although French colonial policies focused primarily on the fur trade, under the terms of the Doctrine of Discovery, the monopolies they granted to different individuals in different regions included the man-datory presence of Christian missionaries.[4] The missionaries relied on trade wars (and the epidem-ics frequently preceding or accompanying them) to harvest converts from Indigenous populations physically devastated by mass death. Nowhere is this more obvious than among the Huron-Wendat people.

The Wendat, whom the Jesuits labelled "Huron," were the five confederated nations of the territory known as Wendake (now the Penetanguishene Peninsula jutting into Georgian Bay). It was made up of twenty-five towns, with a population that peaked at thirty thousand in the fifteenth century (Sioui, 1999: 84–5). The Wendat relied both on agriculture and fishing, and until extensive contact with French traders began in 1609, they enjoyed remarkable health and an abundance of food.

Georges Sioui suggests that Wendat commu-nities first came into contact with disease through the French, who were dealing with large groupings of Wendat living together as agricultural people. It was not until 1634, however, when the Jesuits, who had visited in 1626, returned to set up a mission that the Wendat encountered a continuous wave of epi-demics, which culminated in the virulent smallpox epidemic of 1640 that cut their population in half (Trigger, 1994: 51). So many elders and youths died in the epidemics that the Wendat began to experi-ence serious problems in maintaining their tradi-tional livelihoods and grew extremely dependent on French trade for survival. The epidemics also had a catastrophic effect on the Wendat worldview. The psychological shock of such an extreme loss of life

---

2. Losing access to the European trade appears to have been devastating for many communities. In *The Ojibwa of Southern Ontario* (Toronto: University of Toronto Press, 1991), Peter S. Schmalz recounts how Captain St Pierre arrived at Madeline Island in 1718 to find an isolated community of Ojibway who had, over the past twenty-two years, lost access to the fur trade as a result of geographic isolation, war with the Iroquois, and the deadly trading competition between the French and the English, which involved continuously cutting off each others' markets. After a century of growing dependence on European technology, the community no longer had the endurance to hunt without guns or the skills to make stone, bone, and wood tools and utensils to replace the metal ones they had become dependent on using. The women had lost many of the skills of treating skins (when they were able to obtain them) for clothing. St Pierre found a ragged and starving community, desperate to enter into trade relationships again. It is not a matter, after all, simply of individuals "roughing it" and re-adapting to Indigenous forms of technology. Indigenous communities had to be able to live off the land on a scale that would keep whole communities viable.

3. Contemporary attacks on Aboriginal harvesting, as well as the distrust that many environmentalists apparently hold for Native communities' abilities to maintain ecological relationships with the environment, have only been accelerated by the interest on the part of some historians in "debunking" notions of the viability of Aboriginal ecological relationships in the past. Calvin Martin, for example, has advanced theories that suggest Aboriginal peoples lost their respect for animals during the fur trade because of the breakdown of their spiritual framework, which was caused by illness contracted from Europeans.

4. The Doctrine of Discovery was the formal code of juridical standards in international law that had been created by papal edict to control the different interests of European powers in the different lands they were acquiring. For its primary tenets, see Ward Churchill, *Struggle for the Land: Indigenous Resistance to Genocide, Ecocide and Expropriation in Contemporary North America* (Toronto: Between the Lines, 1992), p. 36.

was experienced as sorcery, as the introduction of a malevolent power into the Wendat universe (Sioui, 1999: 86).

It was into this weakened population that the Jesuits managed to insinuate themselves, using their influence in France to have French traders withdrawn and replaced by Jesuit lay employees. The Jesuits sought to impress the Huron with their technological superiority and allowed their traders to sell certain goods, particularly guns, only to Christian converts (Trigger, 1994: 54). As the number of Christian converts grew in response to such virtual blackmail, the Jesuits gradually obtained enough power in the communities to forbid the practising of Wendat spiritual rituals. . . .

Many lost their tribal status in Kansas, but a small group of Wyandot acquired a reserve in northeastern Oklahoma where they continue to live today. A small number of Wendat remained in Ontario and maintained two reserves in the Windsor region. In the early nineteenth century, both reserves were ceded and sold by the Crown. A small acreage remained and was occupied by a group known as the Anderdon band. This band, consisting of the remaining forty-one Wendat families in Ontario, were enfranchised under the *Indian Act* in 1881, at which point they officially ceased to exist as "Indians." Their land base was divided up into individual allotments. Despite the loss of a collective land base and "Indian" status, the descendants of the forty-one families in Windsor still consider themselves Wendat (Trigger, 1994: 55–61). . . .

The catastrophic changes that the Huron-Wendat have undergone are perhaps less important than the fact that they have survived as a people, and that their worldview has changed but remains fundamentally Wendat. These myths of savagery and of a "loss of culture" form an essential part of contemporary settler ideology—a justification for the denial of restitution for colonization, the backlash against Aboriginal harvesting rights, and policies of repression against Native communities. Through exploring Huron-Wendat history informed by their own realities, a culture regarded as "dead" by the mainstream speaks to us about its contemporary world.

The Mi'kmaq: Diplomacy and Armed Resistance

Not all nations faced the Wendat experience of Christianization. The Mi'kmaq nation was perhaps unique in the way it used Christianity as a source of resistance to colonization in the earliest years of contact with Europeans.

Mi'kmaki, "the land of friendship," covers present-day Newfoundland, St-Pierre and Miquelon, Nova Scotia, New Brunswick, the Magdalen Islands, and the Gaspé Peninsula. It is the territory of the Mi'kmaq, which means "the allied people." The Mi'kmaq nation became centralized during a fourteenth-century war with the Iroquois Confederacy. Since then it has been led by the Sante Mawiomi, the Grand Council, and has been divided into seven regions, each with its Sakamaws or chiefs. It is part of the Wabanaki Confederacy, which includes the Mi'kmaq, the Abenakis in Quebec, the Maliseets in western New Brunswick, and the Passamaquoddies and Penobscots in New England (Richardson, 1989: 78). . . .

The Mi'kmaq people were the first Native people in North America to encounter Europeans, and were aware of the political implications of contact. The French entered their territory in earnest in the sixteenth century and had set up small maritime colonies by the early seventeenth century. Knowledge of the genocide of Indigenous peoples in the Caribbean and Mexico by the Spanish . . . reached the Mi'kmaq by the mid-sixteenth century. In response to this information, and to the spread of disease that increased with greater contact, the Mi'kmaq avoided the French coastal settlements and consolidated their relationships with other Eastern nations of the Wabanaki Confederacy (Henderson, 1997: 80–1). However, Messamouet, a Mi'kmaw[5] scholar and prophet who had travelled to France and learned of how the Europeans conceptualized law and sovereignty, developed another option known as the "Beautiful Trail," which would involve the Mi'kmaq nation negotiating an alliance with the Holy See in Rome. . . .

---

5. Mi'kmaq people generally wish to be referred to in the terms of their own language, rather than through the generic term "Micmac," which had been applied to them. My limited understanding of the Mi'kmaq language suggests to me that individuals and family groups are referred to as "Mi'kmaw," while the nation and its language is referred to as "Mi'kmaq." My apologies to those who are better language speakers, for whom my use of terminology may not be accurate enough.

By building an alliance with the Holy See, the Mi'kmaq nation sought recognition as a sovereign body among the European nations. In this way, Mi'kmaki could resist the authority of the French Crown. In 1610, Grand Chief Membertou initiated an alliance with the Holy See by negotiating a Concordat that recognized Mi'kmaki as an independent Catholic Republic. As a public treaty with the Holy See, the Concordat had the force of international law, canon law, and civil law. Its primary effect was to protect the Mi'kmaq from French authority "on the ground"... . Under the Concordat and alliance, the Mawiomi maintained a theocracy which synthesized Catholic and Mi'kmaq spirituality and maintained Mi'kmaq independence from the French Crown.[6]

In 1648, the Treaty of Westphalia ended the Holy See's rule over European monarchies. The treaty's settlement of territorial claims placed some lands under the control of nation-states and others under the control of the Holy See: Mi'kmaki "reverted" to Mi'kmaq control and all protections ceased to exist.

Unfortunately for the Mi'kmaq, the French were not the only colonial power to invade their world. What the British sought was not furs and missions but land where they could build colonies for their surplus populations. . . . Nineteen out of twenty Indigenous people who came into contact with the British succumbed to disease. The British initiated a number of attacks against Indigenous villages, attacks which often escalated into full-scale wars. British slavers scoured the Atlantic coast for Indigenous people who were sold in slave markets all over the world. Indeed, they began raiding Mi'kmaq territory for slaves in the mid-1600s (Stannard, 1992: 238; Churchill, 1994: 34–5; Forbes, 1988: 54–8; Dickason, 1992: 108).

As the British encroached north from New England to Nova Scotia, the Mi'kmaq responded with open resistance. From the mid-1650s until the peace treaty of 1752 (which was reaffirmed in the treaty of 1761), they waged continuous warfare against the British, fighting land battles and capturing almost one hundred British ships. As the long

war proceeded, and the Mi'kmaq were gradually weakened, the ascendant British developed policies to exterminate the Mi'kmaq. They used a variety of methods, including distributing poisoned food, trading blankets infected with diseases, and waging ongoing military assaults on civilian populations (Dickason, 1992: 159; Paul, 2000: 181–2). . . . The British introduced scalping policy as another method of extermination. For two decades, the British paid bounty for Mi'kmaq scalps and even imported a group of bounty hunters known as Goreham's Rangers from Massachusetts to depopulate the surviving Mi'kmaq nation (Paul, 2000: 207).

Those who survived this genocide were destitute, left with no food and without the necessary clothing to keep warm in a cold climate. Many were reduced to begging. Thousands died of starvation and exposure until limited poor relief was implemented on a local basis. Others eked out a bare existence selling handicrafts, cutting wood for whites, or working as prostitutes (which resulted in outbreaks of venereal disease). Those who struggled to acquire individual land plots were denied title; as a result, it was not uncommon for Mi'kmaw families to engage in the backbreaking labour of clearing and planting a patch of land, only to find that when they returned from fishing, hunting, or gathering excursions, white squatters had taken the land (Redmond, 1998: 116–17). When the British opened up the region for white settlement, they refused to set aside land for the Native peoples. . . .

By the early 1800s, the Mi'kmaq population had fallen from an estimated two hundred thousand to less than fifteen hundred people. Most whites were predicting that the Mi'kmaq would soon become extinct. During this period, Mi'kmaw leaders continuously petitioned London, finally managing to obtain a handful of small reserves. . . . The Mi'kmaq endured policies that tried to centralize and liquidate the few reserves that had been created, divide their bands, and dissolve their traditional governance. These policies aimed in every way to erase their existence.

---

6. The independence enjoyed by the Mi'kmaq under the Concordat did not sit well with the Jesuits who came to Acadia to minister to both Acadian colonists and Mi'kmaqs. The Mi'kmaq rejected the Jesuits' authoritarian ways, after which the Jesuits attended only to the Catholics of New France. Mi'kmaki continued a relatively anomalous independence from French missionaries and colonists for most of the period of French ascendancy in North America and indeed, for the most part considered themselves, and were considered as, allies with the French Crown in its escalating war with the British in North America.

Since the signing of the 1752 treaty, which brought an end to warfare, the Mi'kmaq have sought to resolve the ongoing land and resource theft, with little success. In 1973, the *Calder* case decision forced the Canadian government to recognize that it had some obligation to deal with land claims. . . .

In exploring Mi'kmaq resistance efforts—negotiating a Concordat with the Holy See, waging the longest anti-colonial war in North America, surviving policies designed to exterminate them—we see a picture of Native peoples as resourceful and capable of engaging a powerful enemy in armed conflict for a significant period of time. Perhaps even more important, we see Mi'kmaq people as actors on an international stage, engaging the European powers not only through warfare but through diplomacy, signing international treaties as a nation among nations. . . .

It is impossible to understand contemporary struggles for self-determination without this view of Native peoples as nations among other nations. Today, the spirit that enabled the Mi'kmaq to resist genocide is being manifested in the continuous struggles over the right to fish. . . . It is believed that Canada usurped lands accorded to the Mi'kmaq under the Concordat's international law. By re-establishing communication with the Holy See, the Mawiomi wish to recreate its partnership in ways that enhance the autonomy and spiritual uniqueness of the Mi'kmaq (Henderson, 1997: 104).

Geopolitical Struggles between the Colonizers and Indigenous Resistance in the Great Lakes Region

The British entered the territory now known as Canada from two fronts: the East Coast region (primarily for settlement purposes) and Hudson's Bay (under the charter of the Hudson's Bay Company for the purpose of the fur trade). . . .

The struggle between Britain and France over the Great Lakes region had profound effects on the Iroquois and Ojibway peoples who lived there. The trade struggle between Europeans forced, first, one party, and then the other, to lower the prices of trade goods relative to the furs that were traded for them. Ultimately, when warfare broke out, the effect was devastating, as colonial battles fought in Native homelands destroyed these regions and drew Native peoples into battles, primarily to ensure that a "balance of power" resulted (which would ensure that both European powers remained deadlocked and that one power would not emerge victorious over another).[7]

In 1763, the warfare between France and Britain ended when France surrendered its territorial claims in North America. . . . Because it was important for Britain to reassert its formal adherence to the Doctrine of Discovery and to ensure that its claims to eastern North America would be respected by other European regimes, the British government consolidated its imperial position by structuring formal, constitutional relations with the Native nations in these territories. The Royal Proclamation of 1763 recognized Aboriginal title to all unceded lands and acknowledged a nation-to-nation relationship with Indigenous peoples which the Indian Department was in charge of conducting. Department agents could not command; they could only use the diplomatic tools of cajolery, coercion (where possible), and bribery (Milloy, 1983). The nation-to-nation relationship was maintained until the end of the War of 1812 when the post-war relationships between Britain and the American government became more amicable and made military alliances with Native nations unnecessary.

In the meantime, Britain's ascendancy in the Great Lakes region marked a disastrous turn for Native peoples. . . . It was also obvious to Indigenous people that one unchallenged European power was far more dangerous to deal with than a group of competing Europeans. During this desperate state of affairs, a number of Indigenous nations attempted to

---

7. Many of the Indigenous nations affected by this warfare appeared to have fought strategically to ensure that a balance of power between competing Europeans was maintained. It is significant that as the French and British became locked in a death struggle, the Ojibway appear to have signed a pact of non-aggression with the Iroquois. In general, as the extent of European interference in their affairs became crucial, many of the Great Lakes nations appear to have resisted fighting each other by the mid-eighteenth century. See Schmalz, *The Ojibwa of Southern Ontario*, p. 58.

form broad-ranging alliances across many nations in an effort to eliminate the British presence from their territories, culminating in the Pontiac uprising of 1763.

Pontiac, an Odawa war chief, was inspired by the Delaware prophet Neolin. He wanted to build a broad-based multinational movement whose principles involved a return to the ways of the ancestors and a complete avoidance of Europeans and their trade goods. At least nineteen of the Indigenous nations most affected by the Europeans shared this vision. Their combined forces laid siege to Fort Detroit for five months, captured nine other British forts, and killed or captured two thousand British. Within a few months, they had taken back most of the territory in the Great Lakes region from European control.

Between 1764 and 1766, peace negotiations took place between the British and the alliance. The British had no choice in the matter; the Pontiac uprising was the most serious Native resistance they had faced in the eighteenth century (Dickason, 1992: 182–4). As a consequence, the British were forced to adopt a far more respectful approach to Native peoples within the fur trade and to maintain far more beneficial trade terms. However, the dependency of many of the Indigenous nations on British trade goods and their different strategies in dealing with this dependency weakened the alliance and it could not be maintained over the long term.[8] This, unfortunately, coincided with the British plan to devise ways of removing the military threat that Native peoples clearly represented, without the cost of open warfare. The primary means they chose were disease and alcohol.

There is now evidence to suggest that the smallpox pandemic—which ravaged the Ojibway and a number of the Eastern nations including the Mingo, Delaware, Shawnee, and other Ohio River nations, and which killed at least one hundred thousand people—was deliberately started by the British (Churchill, 1994: 35). The earliest evidence of this deliberate policy is the written request of Sir Jeffrey Amherst to Colonel Henry Bouqet at Fort Pitt. In June 1763, Amherst instructed Bouqet to distribute blankets infected with smallpox as gifts to the Indians. On June 24, Captain Ecuyer of the Royal Americans noted in his journal, "We gave them two blankets and a handkerchief out of the smallpox hospital. I hope it will have the desired effect" (Wagner and Stearn, 1915: 11–5). . . .

The "chemical warfare" of alcohol was waged against the Ojibway in a highly deliberate manner. Major Gladwin articulated this policy clearly: "The free sale of rum will destroy them more effectively than fire and sword." The effects of widespread alcohol distribution were immediate.

In the Great Lakes region, chemical and germ warfare were used by the British as the primary means to acquire land and impose control. . . . The Pontiac uprising demonstrated the power of Indigenous nations organized in armed resistance to colonization. . . . These changes to Indigenous ways of life had long-term and highly significant effects on the possibilities of maintaining sovereignty and resistance to European expansion. The centuries-long fur trade changed the course of Indigenous history in Eastern Canada, as the considerable military power of the Indigenous nations was subverted by their need for trade goods to support their changing way of life.

Ojibway Experiences of Colonization

Immigration, Deception, and Loss of Land

As the fur trade spread further west, the British government consolidated its hold over the Great Lakes area by implementing settlement policies. At the end of the American Revolution, Loyalists poured into the territory that had become known as Upper Canada, bringing new epidemics of smallpox that decimated the Ojibway around Lake Ontario. . . .

---

8. Schmalz, *The Ojibwa of Southern Ontario*, has suggested that during the Pontiac uprising, the Ojibway and other nations were too divided by their dependence on European trade goods and by the inroads that alcohol was making in the communities to successfully rout the British from the Great Lakes region, as they might have been capable of doing in earlier years. Although driving the British out of the region was undoubtedly the wish of some of the Ojibway communities, there were other communities situated far away from encroaching British settlement, but equally dependent on European technology, that were less certain of the threat the British ultimately posed.

Between 1781 and 1830, the Ojibway gradually ceded to the British most of the land north of what is now southern Ontario. The British knew that the Ojibway were aware of the warfare being committed against Native peoples in the United States, where uncontrolled, violent settlement and policies of removal were being implemented. Using this knowledge to their advantage, the British presented land treaties as statements of loyalty to the Crown and as guarantees that the lands would be protected from white settlement. Through the use of gifts and outright lies, to say nothing of improperly negotiated and conflicting boundaries, most of the land of southern Ontario was surrendered over a fifty-year period. The British used the following procedures to negotiate land treaties:

1. By the Proclamation of 1763, the rights of Indigenous peoples to the land were acknowledged.
2. The Indigenous peoples of each area were called to consider a surrender of lands, negotiated by traders or administrators that they already knew and trusted.
3. Only the chiefs or male representatives were asked to sign.[9]
4. The surrender was considered a test of loyalty.
5. The area ceded was deliberately kept vague.
6. Some compensation, in the form of gifts, was given.
7. In many cases, the land was left unsettled for a few years, until disease and alcohol had weakened potential resistance. When the settlers began to come in and the Native people complained, they were shown the documents they had signed and told there was no recourse (Schmalz, 1991: 123). . . .

Settler Violence and Loss of Land

When the first two waves of land cessions were over in what is now southern Ontario, two million acres remained in the hands of Native peoples. Over the next fifty years, the British exerted continuous pressure on the Saugeen Ojibway, whose territories of the Bruce Peninsula and its watershed were still unceded. Eager to acquire their land, the British developed a new way of obeying the letter of the law while violating its spirit—they began to use the threat of **settler violence** to force land surrenders. The constant encroachment of armed, land-hungry settlers forced the Saugeen Ojibway to continuously retreat, negotiating small land surrenders, a piece at a time. Often the treaties were negotiated with individuals who had no authority within their communities to negotiate treaties; these treaties, therefore, were illegal. . . .

A large influx of settlers, primarily refugees from the Irish potato famine and from English industrial slums, put pressure on the colony for even greater tracts of land. Once again, armed squatters were allowed to invade and seize lands. . . .

The above discussion demonstrates how the British fur trade interests in Upper Canada were gradually supplanted by settlement policies, which allowed the Crown to use whatever means were at hand to consolidate its hold over former "Indian" territories. These policies resulted in the endless misery of relocation and land loss for the Ojibway people, of what is now southern and central Ontario, and left many unresolved claims for restitution of stolen lands. These claims include the efforts of the Caldwell Ojibway to obtain a reserve[10] after being forced off their land near Lake Erie during the first wave of land grabs in the early 1800s, and the

---

9. Excluding Native women from the process was central to its success. In eastern Canada, Native women's voices were in many cases considered extremely authoritative in matters of land use. Excluding them from the signing process made land theft that much easier, by allowing those who did not control the land to sign it over. See Kim Anderson, *A Recognition of Being: Reconstructing Native Womanhood* (Toronto: Sumach Press, 2001).

10. The traditional territory of the Caldwell band is Point Pelee, which is now a national park. The Caldwell band were involved in the War of 1812 as allies to the British Crown, where they were known as the Caldwell Rangers. After the war in 1815, the British Crown acknowledged their efforts and their loyal service and awarded them their traditional territory "for ever more." But it wasn't classified as a reserve, and meanwhile, British soldiers who retired after the war were awarded most of the land. By the 1860s the few remaining members of the Caldwell band that were still living on their traditional territories were beaten out of the new park by the RCMP with bullwhips. By the 1970s, the Caldwell band members dispersed throughout southern Ontario began to take part in ritual occupation of the park to protest their land claim. A settlement process is currently in effect (Anonymous Caldwell band member, interview with author, 1999).

monumental struggles around fishing rights waged by contemporary Saugeen Ojibway communities.[11]

Moving North: Resource Plunder of Ojibway and Cree Territories

The consolidation of the land and resource base of what is now northern Ontario . . . took place within the twentieth century.

Once the land base in southern Ontario was secure, business interests in the colony looked to the rich resources in the north. Within a few years, the vast timber forests were being cut, and the growing presence of mineral prospectors and mining operations in northern Ontario caused a number of Ojibway leaders to travel to Toronto to register complaints and demand payment from the revenues of mining leases. When there was no response to these or other entreaties, the Ojibway took matters into their own hands and forcibly closed two mining operations in the Michipicoten area. Soon troops, which were not called in to protect the Saugeen Ojibway from violent white settlers, were on the scene to quell the "rebellion," and government investigators began to respond to the issues that leaders were bringing to them (Dickason, 1992: 253). The Ojibway

wanted treaties, but they demanded a new concession—that reserve territories be specified before the treaties were signed. After considerable discussion and many demands from the Ojibway leaders, the Robinson-Huron and Robinson-Superior Treaties were signed in 1850. These treaties ceded a land area twice the size of that which had already been given up in southern Ontario, yet much smaller than the Ojibway had hoped for), and provided the bands with a lump-sum payment plus annual annuities of $4 per year per person. Most important, hunting and fishing rights to the entire treaty area were to be maintained.

With these treaties, the colony gained access to all the land around Lake Huron and Lake Superior, south of the northern watershed. All land north of this was considered Rupert's Land, the "property" of the Hudson's Bay Company. . . . Inherent in the concept of "Canada," then, was the notion of continuous expansion, a Canadian version of "manifest destiny," no less genocidal than the United States in its ultimate goals of supplanting Indigenous peoples and claiming their territory.

Under section 91(4) of the Constitution Act, 1867, the Canadian federal government was given constitutional responsibility for "Indians and Lands reserved for the Indians," while section 109 gave the provinces control over lands and resources within

---

11. After a series of struggles towards resolving historic land claims, the Chippewas of Nawash, one of two remaining Saugeen Ojibway bands, were recognized in 1992 as having a historic right to fish in their traditional waters. This decision led to three years of racist assaults by local whites and organized fishing interests, including the sinking of their fishing boats, the destruction of thousands of dollars of nets and other equipment, assaults on local Native people selling fish, the stabbing of two Native men in Owen Sound and the beating of two others. No charges were laid by the Owen Sound Police or the OPP for any of this violence until the band called for a federal inquiry into the attacks ("Nawash Calls for Fed Inquiry into Attacks," *Anishinabek News*, June 1996, p. 14).

Meanwhile, the Ontario Ministry of Natural Resources, in open defiance of the ruling recognizing the band's rights, declared a fishing free-for-all for two consecutive years, allowing anglers licence-free access to the waters around the Bruce Peninsula for specific weekends throughout the summer ("Fishing Free-for-all Condemned by Natives," *Anishinabek News*, July 1995, p. 1).

In 1996, despite considerable opposition, the band took over the fishery using an *Indian Act* regulation that severed their community from the jurisdiction of the provincial government (Roberta Avery, "Chippewas Take Over Management of Fishery," *Windspeaker*, July 1996, p. 3). The other Saugeen Ojibway band on the peninsula, the Saugeen First Nation, announced the formation of the Saugeen Fishing Authority and claimed formal jurisdiction of the waters of their traditional territory. They demanded that sports fishermen and boaters would have to buy a licence from them to use their waters. The provincial government recognized the claims of neither bands, instead demanding they limit their catch and purchase licences from the provincial government in order to be able to fish at all (Roberta Avery, "Fishery in Jeopardy, Says University Researcher," *Windspeaker*, Aug. 1996, p. 16).

By 1997, a government study into fish stocks in Lake Huron revealed that certain fish stocks were severely impaired. While the report was supposed to be for the whole Lake Huron area, it in fact zeroed in on the Bruce Peninsula area a number of times, feeding the attitudes of non-Natives about Native mismanagement of the fishery (Rob McKinley, "Fight Over Fish Continues for Nawash," *Windspeaker*, Sept. 1997, p. 14). To add to the difficulties, in 1997, Atomic Energy of Canada announced their desire to bury 20,000 tonnes of nuclear waste in the Canadian Shield. This brought to the band's attention the extent to which the fishery was already affected by nuclear contamination from the Bruce Nuclear Power Development on Lake Huron, 30 km south of the reserve (Roberta Avery, "No Nuclear Waste on Indian Land," *Windspeaker*, April 1997, p. 4).

provincial boundaries, subject to an interest "other than that of the Province in the same" (Morrison, 1992: 4). . . .

In the late 1890s, the Liberal regime of Oliver Mowat, dominated by timber "barons" whose immense profits had been made through logging central Ontario and the Temagami region, was succeeded by the Conservative regime of James Whitney. Proponents of modern liberal capitalism, the Conservatives pushed aggressively ahead with northern development, focusing on railways, mining, and the pulp and paper industry (Hodgins and Benidickson, 1989: 88–9). Three northern railways were constructed to access timber, develop mineral resources, and access potential hydroelectric sites to power the resource industries. The railways opened up the territory to predators at an unprecedented rate. As a rule, if the presence of Cree or Ojibway people hindered development, the newly created Department of Indian Affairs relocated them away from the area.

It is important to understand the scale of the mineral wealth taken from the lands of the Ojibway and Cree in the past century, at great disruption to their lives and without any compensation. Since the early 1900s, the Cobalt silver mines brought in more than $184 million; Kirkland Lake gold mines produced $463 million; and Larder Lake produced $390 million (Longo, 1973: 66–107). Meanwhile, the Porcupine region, one of the greatest gold camps in the world, produced over $1 billion worth of gold and had the largest silver, lead, and zinc mines in the world (Guilbert and Park, Jr, 1986: 863).

Across northeastern Ontario, hydroelectric development was sought primarily for the new mining industry. In 1911, however, timber concessions for the pulp and paper industry were granted, mainly to friends of government ministers, on condition that

hydroelectric dams be built to power them out of the industry's money. In many cases, pulp cutting and dam construction proceeded well before permits were granted to do so.[12]

Reasserting a Silenced History

This chapter has introduced only a few examples of Indigenous writers, or non-Native historians working with Elders, who have recorded Indigenous nations' stories of their past. These stories introduce new perspectives to what is considered "Canadian" history. . . .

Writing from the perspectives of the Indigenous nations enables specific communities to give a full and honest account of their struggles with colonizers intent on their removal and elimination as peoples, and to name the racism, land theft, and policies of genocide that characterize so much of Canada's relationships with the Indigenous nations. Even more important, Indigenous peoples are not cast as faceless, unreal "stick figures" lost in a ferment of European interests, but as the living subjects of their own histories. . . .

It perhaps goes without saying that the histories of Indigenous nations will decentre the histories of New France and Upper Canada as organizing themes to the histories of this land. Canadian historians who are currently considered the experts could work in conjunction with Indigenous peoples wanting to tell their stories of the land. But the works of the experts alone, which provide powerful and detailed histories of the Canadian settler state, do not represent the full picture. It is the voices of Indigenous peoples, long silenced, but now creating a new discourse, which will tell a fuller history.

---

12. Howard Ferguson, then minister of Lands and Forests, had so consistently awarded timber and pulpwood concessions without advertisement, public tenders, or even formal agreements on price to individuals like Frank Anson who founded the powerful Abitibi Power and Paper Company, that he was found guilty in 1922 of violating the *Crown Timber Act*—one of the few whites to ever be prosecuted for disobeying federal legislation concerning Indigenous land. See Morrison, "Colonization Resource Extraction and Hydroelectric Development."

References

Churchill, Ward. *Indians Are Us? Culture and Genocide in Native North America*. Toronto: Between the Lines, 1994.

Dickason, Olive. *Canada's First Nations*. Toronto: Oxford University Press, 1992.

Forbes, Jack D. *Black Africans and Native Americans: Color, Race and Caste in the Evolution of Red-Black Peoples*. Oxford: Basil Blackwell, 1988.

Guilbert, John M., and Charles F. Park, Jr. "Porcupine-Timmins Gold Deposits," in *The Geology of Ore Deposits*. New York: W.H. Freeman and Company, 1986.

Henderson, J.S.Y. *The Mi'kmaw Concordat*. Halifax, NS: Fernwood Publishing, 1997.

Hodgins, Bruce W., and Jamie Benidickson. *The Temagami Experience: Recreation, Resources and Aboriginal Rights in the Northern Ontario Wilderness*. Toronto: University of Toronto Press, 1989.

LaRocque, Emma. "Preface—or 'Here Are Our Voices—Who Will Hear?'," in Jeanne Perrault and Sylvia Vance, eds., *Writing the Circle: Native Women of Western Canada*. Edmonton: NeWest Publishers, 1993.

Longo, Roy M. *Historical Highlights in Canadian Mining*. Toronto: Pitt Publishing, 1973.

Milloy, John S. "The Early Indian Acts: Developmental Strategy and Constitutional Change," in I.A. Getty and A.S. Lussier, eds, *As Long as the Sun Shines and the Water Flows: A Reader in Canadian Native History*. Vancouver: University of British Columbia Press, 1983.

Morrison, James. "Colonization, Resource Extraction and Hydroelectric Development in the Moose River Basin: A Preliminary History of the Implications for Aboriginal People." Report prepared for the Moose River/James Bay Coalition, for presentation to the Environmental Assessment Board Hearings, Ontario Hydro Demand/Supply Plan, November, 1992.

Paul, Daniel N. *We Were Not the Savages: A Mi'kmaq Perspective on the Collision between European and Native American Civilizations*. Halifax: Fernwood Books, 2000.

Redmond, Theresa. "'We Cannot Work Without Food': Nova Scotia Indian Policy and Mi'kmaq Agriculture, 1783–1867," in David T. McNab, ed., *Earth, Water, Air and Fire: Studies in Canadian Ethnohistory*. Waterloo, ON: Wilfrid Laurier University Press, 1998.

Richardson, Boyce, ed. *Drumbeat: Anger and Renewal in Indian Country*. Toronto: Summerhill Press and the Assembly of First Nations, 1989.

Schmalz, Peter S. *The Ojibwa of Southern Ontario*. Toronto: University of Toronto Press, 1991.

Sioui, Georges E. *Huron Wendat: The Heritage of the Circle*. Vancouver: University of British Columbia Press, 1999.

Smith, Linda Tuhiwai. *Decolonizing Methodologies: Research and Indigenous Peoples*. London: Zed Books, 1999.

Stannard, David E. *American Holocaust: The Conquest of the New World*. Toronto: Oxford University Press, 1992.

Stevenson, Winona. "Colonialism and First Nations Women in Canada," in Enakshi Dua and Angela Robertson, eds, *Scratching the Surface: Canadian Anti-Racist Feminist Thought*. Toronto: The Women's Press, 1999.

Trigger, Bruce G. "The Original Iroquoians: Huron, Petun, and Neutral," in E.S. Rogers and D.B. Smith, eds, *Aboriginal Ontario: Historical Perspectives on the First Nations*. Toronto: Dundurn Press, 1994.

Wagner, E., and E. Stearn. *The Effects of Smallpox on the Destiny of the Amerindian*. Boston: Bruce Humphries, 1945.

CHAPTER 6

Indigenous Nationhood

Chris Andersen

The "nation" form, it seems, has become a near-ubiquitous source of collective self-understanding through which we perceive and act on the social world. So ubiquitous, in fact, that Ernest Gellner (1983) once remarked that we must have a nationalist allegiance as we have a nose and ears.[13] A second doyen of the nations and nationalism literature, Eric Hobsbawm (1990), suggested similarly that, were aliens to land on this planet following a nuclear war that wiped it clean of sentient beings but left untouched our libraries and archives, the last two centuries of human history would be incomprehensible without reference to the power of the nation and its associated nationalism.[14] If either view is correct, it isn't because it speaks to national origins outside the processes of modernity central to Western Europe: by definition, these were excluded.

Without suspending the nation form's link to modernity, we must understand it as a theory (and a claim) to political legitimacy and cultural unity, always already caught on the horns of two opposing sets of social forces, one centripetal and the other centrifugal.[15] Centripetally, the elemental power of *state* cultural projects acts as pivotal claims making that labours to reproduce the apparent naturalness of settler nations as culturally unified forms of individual and collective self-identification. In contrast, centrifugal forces of cultural difference perpetually undercut and thus belie such claims, producing what Homi Bhabha (1990) has elsewhere described as its "deep ambivalence."[16] Pre-colonial Indigenous presence in particular shines a light on the conceptual and material fragility of settler nation-state claims to legitimacy in a manner unmatched by any other form of perceived difference.

Critical Indigenous studies scholars stand at the forefront of analyzing the relationship between Indigenous and settler claims to nationhood. In this context, two related uses of "nation" have gained currency: one that conceptually equates it with *tribe*

and, in doing so, seeks to explore the distinctiveness of tribal histories; and another that differentiates between the substance and goals of Indigenous and settler nationalisms. This discussion has largely taken place in the context of previous literature about *non*-**Indigenous nationhood**, which has settled into two broad camps of arguments: those who stress a fundamental *continuity* and those who argue for a basic *discontinuity* between national and pre-national forms of sociation. While those in the continuity camp often position ethnicity as a central resource utilized in and by nationalist claims, others have explained nationalism and nations as hallmarks of modernity and of the associated development and expansion of industrial capitalism and, with it, the growth of the *nation-state* as a for(u)m of political legitimacy.[17] In this sense, nations and the state that sustains them act as teleological markers of progress over previous ethnic tribalism. And though such conceits complicate envisioning nationhood outside of a context of modernity, examples of pre-modern nations exist even within a European context.[18]

Whether or not one agrees with nationalism's necessary links to modernity, nation-states have become central to a serious contemporary discussions of nation, Indigenous, or otherwise—not simply (or even) for the reasons emphasized by Hobsbawm (1990), Gellner (1983), or Anderson (2006), but rather because modern states have become such authoritative sites of power that no sustained nation building can be envisioned that does not in some way position itself for or against the modern states material and symbolic authority.[19] As I discuss later, official state agents occupy a dominant position within Canada's larger colonial field,

13.　Ernest Gellner, *Nations and nationalism* (Ithaca: Cornell University Press, 1983).

14.　Eric Hobsbawm, *Nations and nationalism since 1780: Programme, myth, reality* (Cambridge University Press, 1990).

15.　Stuart Hall, "The question of cultural identity." In *Modernity: An introduction to modern societies*, edited by Stuart Hall, David Held, Don Hubert, and Kenneth Thompson, 595–634 (Cambridge: Polity Press, 1995).

16.　Homi Bhabha, "Introduction: Narrating the nation." In *Nation and narration*, edited by Homi Bhabha, 1–7 (London: Routledge, 1990).

17.　Most notably associated with Anthony Smith, *The ethnic origins of nations* (Oxford: Blackwell Press, 1986). See also Scott Lyons, *X-marks: Native signatures of assent* (Minneapolis: University of Minnesota Press, 2010) and Benedict Anderson, *Imagined communities: Reflections on the origins and spread of nationalism*, 3rd edition (London: Verso, 2006). Also, Gellner, *Nations and nationalism*; Hobsbawm, *Nations and nationalism since 1780*.

18.　For an example of a beautiful discussion of pre-modern Czech nationalism, Derek Sayer, *The coasts of Bohemia: A Czech history* (Princeton, NJ: Princeton University Press, 1998).

19.　Industrialization and elites' invention of traditions: the growth of a centralized, educated populace producing a common "high" culture: or print capitalism enacting the same, respectively.

and any Indigenous "turning away" must continue to account for its presence, even if only to dismiss it as a political act.[20]

Of course, states have existed in one form or another for thousands of years prior to nation-states and, with varying levels of sophistication and efficiency, have coordinated a number of activities crucial to growth and maintenance of increasingly demarcated territorial spaces. While sociologist Max Weber (1978) famously defined states in terms of their ability to produce a monopoly over the legitimate use of force, over the past five centuries states have proven central to the coordination of economic and spiritual well-being as well.[21] Michel Foucault (1973) for example, has explored the (d)evolution of states from entities that reserve for themselves the "right to kill" to entities that labour to efficiently ensure a narrow range of freedoms within which subjects are asked to act responsibly ("the right to life").[22] Especially in the twentieth century, these intertwined government rationalities ("life" and "death") have manifested themselves in various public policy programs.

For our purposes, the cultural power of states thus lies not just in their claims to the monopolization of the legitimate means of physical violence but in their "symbolic violence" as well (a Bourdievian concept that bears a family resemblance to ideology). That is, states possess a singular ability to legitimize, as obvious or natural, what are in fact historical and thus ultimately arbitrary visions of the world. They possess a nearly unparalleled power to "make people see and believe, to get them to know and recognize, to impose the legitimate divisions of the social world and, thereby, to make and unmake groups."[23] For Bourdieu, if social reality is always produced

through classification struggles, powerful categories like those ordained by state actors possess the power to construct social reality even as they seek ostensibly to describe it, and thus they cannot be as easily dismissed as we might think.

It is in this sense that Stuart Hall (1995) positions nations and national identities as the end result of particular claims to a cultural unity and homogeneity.[24] States are, to borrow Bbahha's (1990) term, powerful narrators of nation, and state-sanctioned discourses of nationalism deeply influence the ways we understand the social world and ourselves more generally.[25] They attempt to (re)produce sentiments and institutions of unity, homogeneity, and commonality in a number of ways (a common language, religion, education system, currency, and so on) but among the most powerful devices they use to produce legitimacy of policy rationalities are the two sites explored earlier: the courts and the census. These two fields are indicative of how official authority operates, and their associated legitimacy helps us to make sense of the comparative inability of the Métis Nation to make claims to Métis peoplehood, in these areas and in others.

Although it is tempting to think about "nationness" only in centripetal, archetypical moments (such as the Olympics, the FIFA World Cup, or, in Canada, the World Cup of Hockey), we should remind ourselves that "the nation" is not an ahistorical or a-contextual "thing" but, rather (the result of) an ongoing struggle between unequally, "symbolically armed" protagonists. Thus, the claims to popular political legitimacy or a common cultural heritage that underlie state-sanctioned nationalistic sentiment are just that: claims. Hall (1995) explains that far from representing an underlying unit, such

---

20. Taiaiake Alfred, *Wasase: Indigenous pathways of action and freedom* (Peterborough, ON: Broadview Press, 2005); Glen Coulthard, "Subjects of empire: Indigenous peoples and the 'politics of recognition' in Canada." *Contemporary Political Theory* 6.4 (2007): 437–460.

21. For those interested in reading about these issues at an introductory level, see Richard Robbins, *Global programs amid the culture of capitalism* (Boston, MA: Pearson Education, 2011).

22. Michel Foucault, *History of sexuality. Volume 1, An introduction* (New York: Vintage Books, 1978).

23. Pierre Bourdieu, *Language and symbolic power*. Edited and introduced by John Thompson; translated by Gino Raymond and Matthew Adamson (Cambridge, MA: Harvard University Press, 1991), 221.

24. Hall, "The question of cultural identity," 614–615. See also, Anderson, *Imagined communities*; Gellner, *Nations and nationalism*; and Hobsbawm *Nation and nationalism since 1780*, for a discussion of "nation" as common culture, including the perception of common roots and territory, along with their associated symbols.

25. Bhabha, "Introduction."

claims in fact represent authoritative *attempts* to envision various differences (racial, gendered, class-based, hetero-normative, and so on) *as though* they constituted such a unity.[26] However, such claims are always scored and fissured by various internal points of strain, stress, and tension and therefore possess a discursive and material fragility otherwise un-marked by their own displays of power, spectacular or banal. Bhabha (1990) has expressed this national fragility in what he terms a "deep ambivalence," never more marked than when we catch it in the act of its composition.[27]

Indigenous nations now reside in the interiors of the territorial claims and thus amidst the cultural "pull" of our "captor nations."[28] Contemporary Indigenous articulations of nationhood thus ring a discordant note to the trumpeting of settler claims in that they offer contrasting memories of invasion, attempted conquest, and (re)settlement that belie the seemingly natural association between "nation" and "state."[29] This counter-narrative requires settler national narratives to be understood in terms of the physical and symbolic violence they enact to produce their legitimacy, and they ask us not only to think about prior claims to such territories but about the people-to-people negotiations through which territories were shared and collectivities governed.

In this spirit of discordance, Indigenous studies scholars and our progenitors have stripped the concept of nation of its teleological conceits to stake out a conceptual claim that, by definition, settler nationalism is enacted on territories owned by Indigenous nations. Many Indigenous studies practitioners have thus co-opted the term's narrower conceptions to demonstrate how thoroughly it characterizes the numerous and varied tribes in the pre-contact and pre-colonial world. If modernist discourse differentiates between tribal and national configurations by rendering the former as "other," Indigenous studies scholars have stressed in contrast that these others are and have always been nations.[30]

Indigenous studies nationhood scholarship is extensive and growing. Two broad trends offer discussions useful for my analysis. The first has turned on a straightforward substitution: "nation" for "tribe." Despite "whitestream" nationalism scholarship's attempts to situate the modern basis of nation-hood as necessarily non-tribal, Indigenous Studies scholars have positioned "tribe" as possessing equal (though different) collective historical and political consciousness, as well as a relationship to territory, one far more complex and relational than that of state-bounded Europe.[31] Along these lines, notions like self-determination and sovereignty have been wedded to a more specific focus on the nuances and complexities of individual nations, their histories, and their present configurations of power (on their own and/or in their relations with other nations, Indigenous, or otherwise).

The scholarly genealogy of "nation" is not much explored in Indigenous Studies, however—in a sense, the literature has simply adapted the former use of "tribe" to serve for "nation." In the humanities, for example, authors following on Simon Ortiz's (1981) seminal discussion have forwarded sophisticated discussions of "literary nationalism"[32] that emphasize the richness and distinctiveness of tribal/national literary traditions, both before and during colonialism.[33] These efforts have positioned national literature as an important aspect of "imagining

26. Hall, "The question of cultural identity."

27. Bhabha, "Introduction," 3.

28. Paul Chartrand, "'Terms of division': Problems of 'outside-naming' for Aboriginal people in Canada." *Journal of Indigenous studies* 2.2 (1991): 1–22.

29. Audra Simpson, "Paths toward a Mohawk Nation: Narratives of citizenship and nationhood in Kahnawake." In *Political theory and the rights of Indigenous peoples*, edited by Duncan Ivison, Paul Patton, and William Sanders, 113–136 (Cambridge, UK: Cambridge University Press. 2000), 116.

30. Lyons, *X-marks*.

31. Claude Denis, *We are not you: First Nations and Canadian Modernity* (Broadview Press, 1997).

32. Robert Warrior, *Tribal secrets: Recovering American Indian intellectual traditions* (Minneapolis: University of Minnesota Press, 1995); Jace Weaver, *That the people might live: Native American literatures and Native American community* (Minneapolis: University of Minnesota Press, 1997); Jace Weaver, Craig Womack, and Robert Warrior, *American Indian literary nationalism* (Minneapolis: University of Minnesota Press, 2006).

33. Simon Ortiz, "Towards a national Indian literature: Cultural authenticity in nationalism." *MELUS* 8.2 (1981): 7–12.

community" and thus as a central symbolic stake in the Indigenous pursuit of the sovereignty usurped by settler nation-states. Similarly, more social scientific approaches have emphasized the concept of Indigenous nationhood as a marker of autonomy: Deloria and Lytle differentiate between nationhood and self-government (the former marking autonomy while the latter evidences subjection to Western forms of power), while Alfred (1995) positions nationhood as a distinctively formed culture and collectivity at war with nation-states.[34]

A second, related Indigenous Studies trend has attempted to rescue the "use value" of "nation" from the territorial and categorical conceits of its European contexts. The basic question that seems to motivate this rescue attempt is whether or not Indigenous nationhood requires the same sort of centralization and clear territorial boundaries that buttress European rhizomatic movement from nationhood to statehood. Anticipating by a number of years the discussions that would follow, Mohawk scholar Alfred (1995) argues, with respect to European-based theories of nationalism, that "[t]heorists have created a model of nationalism based upon a narrow view of one aspect of European history and applied it as the global standard."[35] Similarly, Mohawk scholar Simpson poses a foundational challenge to the over-valorization of the European-based nation model:

> "the nation" receives its analytical particularities in the process and the place that it is articulated through. In other words, if it is industrial England that defined those processes under discussion, "the nation" will be positioned and defined in just that context. Hence, the nation will exhibit the characteristics of industrialisation, of

concomitant alienation from the means of production, and is understood as a form of social organization that is arrived at through the false consciousness of its people.[36]

Anderson's (2006) foundational logic of "nation" allows us purchase to think about the ways in which Indigenous society differed from the "pre-nation" societies of Europe.[37] For example, he argues that European nationalism emerged as a form of "deep, horizontal comradeship" in the face of the previous "divinely-ordained, hierarchical dynastic realm."[38] Of course, if we take Alfred (1995) and Simpson (2000) seriously (as we must), we might well ask: Why would we seek to impose a model of nationhood, constructed in the very specific material and symbolic circumstances of eighteenth-century, status-obsessed Europe, onto (Indigenous) societies without the "divinely-ordained, hierarchical dynastic realm" and already deeply steeped in the "horizontal comradeship" (in the case of Indigenous communities, through their complex **kinship** webs) that these new feelings of European "nation-ness" aspired to?

Along these lines, Cherokee Nation scholar Daniel Heath Justice (2006) argues that Indigenous nationhood—even pre-state forms—should not be conflated with the kinds of "whitestream" (Denis 1997) nationhood "dependent upon the erasure of kinship bonds in favour of a code of patriotism that places loyalty to the state above kinship obligations."[39] Less hierarchical in character, with power diffused across different (and different kinds) of statuses, Indigenous nations turn on their ability to recognize "other sovereignties without that recognition implying a necessary need to consume, displace or become absorbed by those nations."[40] Similarly,

---

34. See Alfred, *Heeding* and Vine Deloria and Clifford Lytle, *The nations within: The past and future of American Indian sovereignty* (New York: Pantheon Books, 1984); Deloria and Lytle emphasize Indigenous nationhood as a marker of autonomy (13).

35. Alfred, *Heeding*, 9.

36. Simpson, "Paths toward a Mohawk Nation," 118.

37. Anderson, *Imagined communities*.

38. Ibid., 7.

39. See Daniel Heath Justice, *Our fire survives the storm: A Cherokee literary history* (Minneapolis: University of Minnesota Press, 2006), 23; Denis, *We are not you*.

40. Justice, *Our fire*, 24.

Chippewa scholar Champagne refers to nations as "distinct cultural and political groups" but suggests that while Western understandings of nation and nationalism tend toward the secular, Indigenous understandings of nation and nationalism incorporate other-than-human beings.[41]

The two authors who most extensively position their constructions of Indigenous nationhood in relation to the previous genealogical frameworks of Western European thinking, however, include Mohawk scholar Audra Simpson (2000) and Ojibway/Dakota scholar Scott Lyons (2010).[42] Simpson (2000) situates her argument for Mohawk nationalism in light of both Gellner's 1983 "processes of modernity" and Anderson's 2006 "cognition and creation" as failing to account for the social and historical contexts within which Mohawk nationalism was produced. Noting a "well documented" nationhood that pre-dated contact with Western polities, Simpson (2000) offers a "bifurcated" Indigenous nationhood, forced to exist within the parameters of colonial/settler ones and, as such, one that necessarily "mix[es] parts, [drawing] from Iroquois teachings, from ancestral and immediate past, and from the neocolonial present"—not, perhaps, in pursuit of statehood (the usual horizon of modernist national thinking) but, rather, in pursuit of an "abstraction—a principle, such as sovereignty, for moral victory or simply for *respect*" (emphasis in original).[43]

In contrast, and borrowing similarly from Gellner's (1983) and Smith's (1986) discussions of the relationship between nationhood and modernity, Lyons (2010) argues that while Native tribes may have historically possessed "a shared culture requiring protection" (a primary marker of nationhood), they lacked the "territorial, educational and legal aspects" of a nation.[44] Hence, markers like kinship culture—often associated with Indigenous nationalism—are, for Lyons, precisely why Indigenous societies are manifestly *not* nations but,

rather, "ethnics" (people with a shared sense of culture but lacking a public culture and history, the *actual* bases of nationhood), Lyons (2010) argues that nationalism constitutes the political process through which ethnics become nations. In an Indigenous context, nations practise nationalism while ethnics (tribes) practice "cultural resistance." Thus, for Lyons, nationalism (Indigenous or otherwise) is always about the march to statehood: "[r]emember, it is one's aspiration for a state that produces nationalism, and it is nationalism that produces the nation."[45]

While Simpson (2000) and Lyons (2010) disagree on the origins and substance of Indigenous nationhood, their work shares in common a political rather than merely cultural orientation for Indigenous nationhood. This preference holds important consequences for understanding the relationship between modernist discourse and exclusive settler claims to nationalism and the original—and, from their standpoint, necessary—(dis)place(ment) of Indigenous collectivity within such a growing imaginary.

Recall our earlier discussion of Hall's (1995) positioning of "nation" as including both political and cultural elements. While settler nations and their associated states offer nationalism as legitimate claims to cultural unity, deep cultural fissures—the presence of "Others"—nevertheless traverse and thus destabilize such claims (just as they originally helped to stabilize these entities historically by serving as "exteriors"). The central importance of *difference* to colonial projects (institutionalized in racialized, gendered, and heteronormative hierarchies, to name but a few) was discussed earlier, but we should note here that while all political claims are cultural in the sense that they are embedded in specific meanings and social contexts, in settler nation-states, not all cultural claims are political. In fact, colonial nation-states' historical genealogies make it exceedingly clear that, especially in an Indigenous context,

41. Duane Champagne, "In search of theory and method in American Indian studies." *American Indian Quarterly* 31.3 (2007): 353.

42. Examples include Mohawk scholar Audra Simpson (2000) and Ojibway/Dakota scholar Scott Lyons (2010).

43. Simpson, "Path toward a Mohawk Nation," 118, 221.

44. Lyons, *X-marks*, 121.

45. Lyons argument is compelling only if one takes for granted Western European contexts for understanding nationhood as the only manner in which nationalism can be "located" analytically (132).

cultural claims (that is, claims to cultural difference) are often not political claims.[46] Indeed, modern nation-states and their institutions (such as the courts) often frame issues in terms of culture precisely to avoid discussions about their political basis.[47]

Hence, and given what Simpson (2000) refers to as the "enframing power" of modern states, presenting the case for Indigenous nationhood in terms of cultural difference induces a Foucauldian "enunciative poverty" (120) that never simply distinguishes it from that of settler nationhood; it also *subordinates* it.[48] Justice explains that "[c]ulture alone is voyeuristic; it gives access without accountability, and it fetishizes the surface at the expense of deeper significance."[49] Similarly, Kristina Fagan (2004) argues that Aboriginal "cultures" are positioned as quaint and vaguely non-threatening by the dominant Canadian society: "they represent a non-challenging form of difference where Aboriginal peoples become yet another culture in the mosaic."[50]

What does it mean to speak of Indigenous nationhood in political rather than cultural terms? To pose the question slightly differently, what may be gained, if anything, by articulating Indigenous nationhood in terms of political rather than cultural difference? If by political difference we mean to again demonstrate how-we-are-different-from-settlers, then little differentiates it from cultural claims, however legitimate. However, Simpson's (2000) earlier discussion of Indigenous nationhood, which presents as its end point "the desire . . . for an abstraction—a principle, such as sovereignty, for moral victory or simply for *respect*" (emphasis in original), transports us to a very different analytical space.[51] What abstraction or principle might we aspire to in our assertion of our nationhood, if not to demonstrate our cultural or political difference?

In his discussion of Indigenous nationhood and sovereignty, Womack (1999) offers a compelling alternative. Rather than conceptualizing Indigenous nationhood in terms of difference, he suggests we do so in terms of our *separateness*.[52] Womack's argument is made in the specific context of literary canon, but it resonates more broadly. Arguing similarly in a Canadian context, Denis (1997) suggests that "it is not so much difference that matters, as separateness—and indeed wanting to self-govern expresses a will to be separate, autonomous, whether or not you want to do things differently than your neighbour" (82).[53] Emphasizing cultural difference (however legitimate it may be) denies us a historiography on equal footing with that of settler histories; conversely, rooting claims in political separateness cuts to the political core of what separates Indigenous nationalism from settler nationalism: our ability to envision a consciousness as Indigenous nations prior to the presence

---

46. See Denis, *We are not you*; Kristina Fagan, "Tewatatha:wi: Aboriginal nationalism in Taiaiake Alfred's *Peace, power and righteousness: An Indigenous manifesto.*" *American Indian Quarterly* 28.1 (2004): 12–29; Daniel Heath Justice, "The necessity of nationhood: Affirming the sovereignty of Indigenous national literatures." In *Moveable margins: The shifting spaces in Canadian literature*, edited by Chelva Kanaganayakam. 143–159 (Toronto: Tsar Publications, 2005); Daniel Heath Justice, *Our fire survives the storm*.

47. See Chris Andersen, "Residual tensions of empire: Contemporary Métis communities and the Canadian judicial imagination." In *Reconfiguring Aboriginal-state relations, Canada: The state of the federation*, 2003, edited by Michael Murphy, 295–305 (Montreal and Kingston, McGill-Queen's University Press, 2005); Michael Asch, "The judicial conception of culture after *Delgamuukw and Van der Peet.*" Review of Constitutional Studies 5.2 (2000): 119–137; Glen Coulthard, "Resisting culture: Seyla Benhabib's deliberate approach to the politics of recognition in colonial contexts." In *Realizing deliberative democracy*, edited by D. Kahane, D. Leydet, D. Weinstock, and M. Williams, 138–154 (Vancouver: UBC Press, 2009); Joyce Green, "The difference debate: reducing rights to cultural flavours." *Canadian Journal of Political Science* 31 (2005): 133–144: N. Kompridis, "Normativizing hybridity/neutralizing culture." *Political Theory* 33.3 (2005): 318–343; "The unsettled and unsettling claims of culture: A reply to Seyla Benhabib." *Political Theory* 34.3 (2006): 389–396; Jeremy Patzer, "Even when we're winning, are we losing? Métis rights in Canadian courts." In *Métis in Canada: History, Identity, Law, and Politics*, edited by Christopher Adams, Gregg Dahl, and Ian Peach, 307–336 (Edmonton: University of Alberta Press, 2013).

48. Michel Foucault, *The history of sexuality. Volume 1, An introduction* (New York: Vintage Books, 1978), 120; Jacques Derrida, *Positions*. Translated and annotated by Alan Bass (Chicago: University of Chicago Press, 1981), 41.

49. Justice, *Our fire survives the storm*, 151.

50. Fagan, "Tewatatha:wi," 12.

51. Simpson, "Paths toward a Mohawk Nation," 121.

52. See Craig S. Womack, *Red on Red: Native American literary separatism* (Minneapolis: University of Minnesota Press, 1999); Warrior, *Tribal secrets*.

53. Denis, *We are not you*, 82.

of settler nations.[54] Whether or not we operate in ways that appear similar to settler self-understandings is—or at least, should be—beside the point.

Hence, Womack's (and Denis's) notion of political "separateness" is a crucial corrective to a focus on difference. It offers a form of conceptual autonomy for the creative position-taking forced upon us by our resistance to and (yes) incorporation of colonial rationalities and intervention strategies. Likewise, it requires little demonstration of our difference from whitestream normativity as a basis for collective authenticity.[55] A focus on our cultural difference, by contrast, not only inhibits a complex recounting of the *intactness* of our history and our communities/nations in the face of the massive impact of settler nation-state intervention in the lives of Aboriginal community members but also reduces the likelihood of public recognition of our modernity.[56]

At least as a matter of logic, positioning Indigenous nationhood in terms of a respect for Indigenous immediacy or complexity carries less of this kind of conceptual baggage.[57] It encourages a proliferation of the "positions," "dispositions," and tensions through which Aboriginality is produced and practised, but it doesn't demand a demonstration of how our lived experiences differed/differ from those of the non-Aboriginal communities we live/d alongside. This is not to say, however, that "anything goes" when envisioning Indigenous nationhood—as with all forms of collective self-imagining, Indigenous nations will be haunted by the tendrils of history, culture, political consciousness, and the many colonial ironies within which we find ourselves situated as contemporary (modern) Indigenous peoples. One of the most telling moments of the *Powley* case (an important 2003 Supreme Court of Canada Aboriginal rights case) comes in the form of an exchange, in the oral arguments, between two justices and an intervenor, about the extent to which Aboriginal rights can be allowed to change and how—or whether—the courts should or could protect Indigenous modernity.[58]

Whether we side with the continuity argument or the discontinuity argument, the idea of a nation/people is distinctive in international and Canadian literature as affording a right to *self-government* in a manner that does not adhere to "local" community governance. A vast literature has explored the myriad relations around the idea of Indigenous self-government: we need not reproduce it here.[59] The aspect of self-government most analytically important to this discussion of nationhood lies not in its ability to define citizenship codes or, for example, to sanction deviance—*internal* aspects, in other words. Rather, it speaks to the ability of Indigenous nations to enter into nation-to-nation relationships with other Indigenous nations and with colonial nation-states. In this context, RCAP defines an Aboriginal nation as "a sizeable body of Aboriginal people with a shared sense of national identity that constitutes the predominant population in a certain territory or collection of territories."[60] Its tautology notwithstanding, this definition is useful because it emphasizes the nation's relational character.

54. Simpson, "Paths toward a Mohawk Nation."

55. See also, Lyons, *X-marks*.

56. See also generally, Philip Deloria, *Indians in unexpected places* (Lawrence: University of Kansas Press, 2004).

57. See Sam Deloria, "Commentary on nation-building: The future of Indian nations." *Arizona State Law Journal* 34 (2002): 55–62. Deloria articulates this issue clearly "Nobody visits Liechtenstein periodically to make sure they are sufficiently poor and sufficiently culturally distinct from their neighbors to merit continued political existence. They're just around. So when we're waxing eloquent about . . . cultural sovereignty and all other kinds of sovereignty, be damned careful that we're not saying to this society, 'In exchange for a continued political existence, we promise to maintain some kind of cultural purity,' because you think it's going to be by our standards. Hell no . . . it's going to be by THEIR standards." 58–59 in Kim TallBear, "Genomic articulations of Indigeneity," *Social Studies of Science* 43.4 (2013): 515; also, Chris Andersen, "Critical Indigenous studies: From difference to density" *Cultural Studies Review* 15.2 (2009): 97–115; Brendan Hokowhitu, "Indigenous existentialism and the body." *Cultural Studies Review* 15.2 (2009): 101–118.

58. Oral arguments, 2003, *R. v. Powley*, Supreme Court of Canada (File No.: 28533), March 17th. Labrador Métis Nation Factum. 2003. *R. v. Powley*. Supreme Court of Canada File No.: 28533). Congress of Aboriginal Peoples Factum. 2002. *R. v. Powley*, Supreme Court of Canada (File No.: 28533); Métis Nation of Ontario (joint with Métis National Council) (2003) *R. v. Powley*, Supreme Court of Canada (File No.: 28533).

59. For a broad discussion of the major debates and conclusions in a Canadian context see Yale Belanger and David Newhouse, "Reconciling solitudes: A critical analysis of the self-government ideal." In *Aboriginal self-government in Canada: Current trends and issues*, edited by Yale Belanger, 1–19 (Saskatoon, SK: Purich Publishing, 2008).

60. Royal Commission on Aboriginal Peoples (RCAP), *Report of the Royal Commission on Aboriginal Peoples*. 5 volumes (Ottawa: Minister of Supply and Services. 1996, vol. 2, ii).

The Relationality of Nationhood/Peoplehood

Discussions of Indigenous nationhood often focus on its internal dimensions. This is a legitimate research strategy given that, for centuries, colonial powers have largely assumed that no such thing as Indigenous nationhood exists and that Indigenous culture and society is noteworthy only to mark its primitiveness or backwardness and, in that context, its eventual demise and disappearance. The little discussion on the *relationality* of Indigenous nationhood has thus concerned itself (again, legitimately) with denaturalizing colonial attempts to dismantle it. Though Canadian section 3 jurisprudence and legislation has, with several exceptions, been content to recognize Indigeneity in terms of "community," I will lay out in more detail what I think makes nationhood/peoplehood a specific *kind* of community and, likewise, what separates it from the community-as-settlement discourses that largely shape juridical discussion around non-treaty based Aboriginal rights.[61]

The idea of peoplehood has become a mainstay of the international Indigenous literature, particularly that which is linked to the United Nations. Little of this literature focuses on what it is exactly that makes Indigenous peoples *peoples*, however. Instead, the focus has been on what makes us Indigenous. In this context, the UN includes several elements central to their working definition of Indigeneity:

- Self-identification as indigenous peoples at the individual level and accepted by the community as their member;
- Historical continuity with pre-colonial and/or pre-settler societies;
- Strong link to territories and surrounding natural resources;
- Distinct social, economic or political systems;
- Distinct language, culture and beliefs;
- Form non-dominant groups of society;
- Resolve to maintain and reproduce their ancestral environments and systems as distinctive peoples and communities.[62]

Indigeneity is usually defined in terms of contemporary self-identification as such, attachment to a pre-colonial (if not pre-contact) Indigenous and cultural distinctiveness that normally plays out through the establishment of our *difference*.

As a rule, "peoplehood" and "nationhood" are largely employed interchangeably. In the infamous *Re: Quebec Succession* case in which the Supreme Court of Canada was asked to address the issue of whether Quebec could legally secede, the Justices note that although the right of a people to self-determination is an anchor of international law, "the precise meaning of the term 'people' remains somewhat uncertain" (1998, para. 123). Only slightly more precisely, they argued that "a people" does not necessarily mean the same thing as the entire population of a state and that it possesses a distinctive language and culture (1998, para. 124).

In a similar way, current United Nations rapporteur and noted Indigenous scholar James Anaya (1996) defines peoplehood as "comprising distinct communities with a continuity of existence and identity that links them to communities, tribes or nations of their ancestral past," creating a conflation between "community" and "people."[63] Elsewhere, he uses "peoples" interchangeably with "group" and "population." And though at one point the RCAP (1996) explains that "nation" and "people" are overlapping (thus intimating a difference between them), they use them largely interchangeably.[64]

The public documentation around peoplehood is not concerned so much with a distinction between

61. See Chris Andersen, "Settling for community? Juridical visions of historical Métis collectivity in and after *R. v. Powley*." In *Contours of Métis landscapes: Family, mobility and history in northwestern North America*, edited by Nicole St.-Onge, Carolyn Podruchny, and Brenda Macdougall, 392–421 (Norman: University of Oklahoma Press, 2012).

62. "Who are Indigenous peoples?" http://www.un.org/esa/socdev/unpfii/documents/5session_factsheetl.pdf.

63. James Anaya. *Indigenous peoples in international law* (New York: Oxford University Press, 1996), 3.

64. James Anaya, "The evolution of the concept of Indigenous peoples and its contemporary dimensions." In *Perspectives on the rights of minorities and Indigenous peoples in Africa*, edited by Solomon Dersso, 23–42 (Cape Town. South Africa: Pretoria University Law Press, 2010).

peoplehood and nationhood but, rather, with differentiating these and allied concepts from more biological-cum-racial designations of Indigeneity. As RCAP explains, "The term Aboriginal peoples refers to organic political and cultural entities that stem historically from the original peoples of North America, not to collections of individuals united by so-called 'racial' characteristics. The term includes the Indian, Inuit and Métis peoples of Canada" (1996, vol. 2, ii).[65] The distinction between "local communities" and nations or peoples is a useful one: "We use terms such as a First Nation community and a Métis community to refer to a relatively small group of Aboriginal people residing in a single locality and forming part of a larger Aboriginal nation or people" (1996, vol. 2, ii).[66] The distinction asks us to imagine broader geographical spaces and more explicit political conversations about who owns that space and what may be undertaken in, on, or beneath it.

RCAP's definition of community proceeds roughly apace with Canadian section 35 case law that conflates community with settlement. Distinguishing between community-as-settlement and community-as-nation or people, however, is important for sorting through more and less racialized claims to Indigeneity. That is, claims to peoplehood speak to a "positive core" of Indigenous peoplehood, which in turn speaks to the kinds of historical political relationships that sustained Indigenous peoples' collective consciousness and identity.[67]

What does it mean to suggest that peoples are political rather than cultural? In a colonial country such as Canada, culture is pinned to Indigeneity in the form of cultural *difference* and, as we might suspect, in such contexts it is difficult to be both "different" and "not-different." A legion of legal jurisprudence and its commentary, for example,

has grappled with the issue of which aspects of Indigeneity are protectable by a riddle the court most notoriously solved, in *R. v. Van der Peet* (1996), in terms of pre-*contact* community activities. This has subsequently been inched along to pre-colonial activities (in *Powley*) but nonetheless, the fundamental assumption lying at the heart of these discussions is that real Indigeneity *was* rather than *is*—the more modern we appear, the manifestly less Indigenous we must be. This truism, perhaps expressed most starkly in juridical logics, nonetheless lies at the heart of official Canadian discourses of Indigeneity more broadly.

One approach for situating Indigenous peoplehood politically—and perhaps offering hope for moving beyond this fixity—has been to focus on aspects of Canadian common law that emphasize historical *relationships*. Legal scholar Jeremy Webber defines Indigenous peoplehood in terms of the "intersocietal relationships" that arose during the early colonial period of North America.[68] He speaks in terms of *intersocietal norms* "that are fundamentally intercommunal, created not by the dictation of one society, but by the interaction of various societies through time."[69] Early interrelations between Indigenous peoples and settlers produced a diplomatic context that not only produced more stable and predictable conduct (or, at least, expectations of such conduct) but also provided grounds for criticizing conduct that departed from those emerging norms.[70] Tully (2008) argues that although the kinds of relationships in which intersocietal norms were produced "were surrounded by a sea of strategic relations of pressure, force and fraud. . . . Aboriginal peoples and newcomer Canadians recognize[d] each other as equal, coexisting and self-governing nations and govern[ed] their relations with each other by

65. RCAP, *Report of the Royal Commission on Aboriginal Peoples*, ii.

66. Ibid.

67. See Paul Chartrand and John Giokas, "Defining 'the Métis people': The hard case of Canadian Aboriginal law." In *Who are Canada's Aboriginal peoples? Recognition, definition, and jurisdiction*, edited by Paul Chartrand, 268–304 (Saskatoon, SK: Purich Publishing. 2002).

68. Jeremy Webber, "The jurisprudence of regret: The search for standards of justice in Mabo." *Sydney Law Review* 17 (1995a): 5–28; Jeremy Webber, "Relations at force and relations of justice: The emergence of normative community between colonists and Aboriginal peoples." *Osgoode Law Journal* 33 (1995b): 623–660.

69. Webber, "Relations of force," 626.

70. Ibid., 628–629.

negotiations, based on procedures of reciprocity and consent."[71]

Relationally based approaches offer an important corrective to colonial Aboriginal rights law that magnanimously seeks to find accommodation of Indigenous viewpoints within a colonial framework already thoroughly saturated with a colonial commonsense that incorrectly reads today's material and symbolic inequalities into historical configurations of power. Webber (1995a) cautions us to instead be attentive to the initially inchoate but increasingly stable "procedures, settled rules for the relations between colonists and indigenous peoples. They came to constitute a body of truly cross-cultural norms, born of the interaction between peoples and departing in significant ways from what either party would have required if it had been able to impose its own sense of justice."[72] While we should not use this to fashion a "Pollyanna" narrative of a history, free of conflict or turmoil, it equally requires us to give pause to the narratives like those fashioned by British Columbia Supreme Court Chief Justice Alan McEachern in delivering the decision on *Delgamuukw v. The Queen* in 1991—a narrative that, while widely admonished, displayed broad similarities to both historical and contemporaneous Aboriginal policy.[73]

Intersociality, or inter-normativity, is part of a broader discussion about how to properly characterize early interrelations between settlers and Indigenous peoples and about the fundamentally intersocietal character of Canadian common law. We may note with Slattery (2000) a major feature of the doctrine of Aboriginal rights important to a discussion of peoplehood: ancient custom. Like Webber, Slattery explains the doctrine of Aboriginal rights as, in part, formed in light of the "inter-societal" law that governed early interactions between settlers and Indigenous peoples worked out in practice along the eastern seaboard of Indigenous territories now claimed by the United States and Canada, culminating formally in the *Royal Proclamation of 1763*.[74]

Much of the Canadian discussion around Indigenous "peoples" is juridically based, at least partly the result of including Aboriginal "peoples" in section 35 of the Constitution Act, 1982. Chartrand and Giokas (2002) argue that, in a juridical context, the "Métis people" must "be defined in light of the purposes of recognizing Aboriginal rights," a principle also enshrined in Canadian Aboriginal rights law (for example, *R. v. Sparrow* 1990).[75] Analogous to Webber's and Slattery's discussion, Chartrand and Giokas (2002) define peoplehood in terms of historical political relationships with the Crown (277) because they reflect an important part of the fiduciary doctrine that governs Canada's constitutional relationships with Aboriginal peoples.[76] We might well add to this, of course, evidence of relationships with other Indigenous peoples.

Chartrand and Giokas (2002) emphasize what they term a "positive core" of peoplehood. This is important for my argument because they are suggesting that throughout the twentieth century, official Canadian recognition practices have taken place in the shadow of a deep racialization in which two kinds of Indigenous individuals and communities exist: Status and non-Status Indians. The federal government in particular has staked a financial claim in establishing hard boundaries between these categories and likely cares little how Indigenous individuals actually self-identify. Thus, Chartrand and Giokas argue, a peoplehood-based discussion must begin with historical inquiry to identify collectives with a history of formal Crown–Indigenous

---

71. James Tully, *Public philosophy in a new key: Volume I* (Cambridge: Cambridge University Press, 2008), 226.

72. Webber, "The jurisprudence of regret," 75.

73. Janna Promislow, 2010. "'Thou wilt not die of hunger or I bring thee merchandise.' Consent, intersocietal normativity, and the exchange of food at York Factory, 1682–1763." In *Between consenting peoples: Political community and the meaning of consent*, edited by Jeremy Webber and Cohn Macleod, 77–114 (Vancouver: UBC Press. 2010).

74. Brian Slattery, "Making sense of Aboriginal rights." *Canadian Bar Review* 79 (2000): 198–200.

75. Chartrand and Giokas, "Defining 'the Métis people'," 277.

76. For a broader discussion of this issue and for a discussion on "intersocietal law" more generally, see J. Borrows, 2002, *Recovering Canada: The resurgence of Indigenous law* (Toronto: University of Toronto Press, 2002) and Brian Slattery, "Understanding Aboriginal rights." *Canadian Bar Review* 66 (1987): 727–783; 'Making sense of Aboriginal rights'; and "The generative structure of Aboriginal rights." In *Moving toward justice: Legal traditions and Aboriginal justice*, edited by John Whyte, 20–48 (Saskatoon, SK: Purich Publishing, 2008).

relations and, for that matter, in formal Indigenous–Indigenous relations as well.[77]

The legal peoplehood debate has resulted in the valuable insight that peoplehood is at a fundamental level not only about internal practices of membership but about formal, externally oriented practices as well. As such, we should look for evidence of historical peoplehood in the formal interrelations *between* peoples (including but not limited to imperial powers) prior to the imposition of colonialism. This is a far cry from, for example, the kinds of recent claims that are rooted not in a pre-colonial claim to a positive core of peoplehood but, rather, in terms of a correction to the violation of the principles of natural justice that have severed descendants from their ancestors' historical Indigenous communities. It also requires us to think carefully about contemporary claims to Indigeneity based on links to historical fur trade communities, especially when these claims fail to work through the complexities of those relationships to their historical claim region's (other) Indigenous peoples.

Case Law

Alberta (Aboriginal Affairs and Northern Development) v. Cunningham. [2011] 2 SCR. 670.
Calder v. British Columbia (Attorney-General). 1973. S.C.R. 313.
Delgamuukw v. British Columbia, [1991] 3 W.W.R. 97 (BCSC).
Enge v. Mandeville et al. 2013 NWTSC 33.
Her Majesty in Right of Newfoundland and Labrador v. The Labrador Métis Nation. 2007 NLCA 75.
The Labrador Métis Nation v. Her Majesty in Right of Newfoundland and Labrador. 2006 NLTD 119.
Manitoba Métis Federation Inc., et al. v. Attorney General of Canada, et al., 2011, SCC case information, 33880.
Manitoba Métis Federation Inc. v. Canada (Attorney General), 2013 SCC 14.
R. v. Castonguay, 2006 NBCA 43 (CanLII).
R. v. Castonguay, [2003] I CNLR. (NBPCt).
R. v. Daniels, 2013 FC 6.
R. v. Goodon, 2008 MBPC 59 (CanLII).
R. v. Hirsekorn, 2013 ABCA 242.
R. v. Hopper, [2004] NBJ No. 107. (Prov. Ct.).
R. v. Howse, [2002] BCJ No. 379 (BCSC).
R. v. Laviolette, 2005 SKPC 70.
R. v. Norton, 2005 SKPC 46 (CanLII).
R. v. Nunn, 2003, unreported, Provincial Court of British Columbia. Court File No. 30689H (Penticton).
R. v. Powley, 2003 SCC 43.
R. v. Sparrow, 1990, C.N.L.R. 160 (SCC).
R. v. Van der Peet, [1996] 4 CNLR 177 (SCC).
R. v. Willison, [2006], BCJ No. 1505 (BCSC).
R. v. Willison, [2005], BCJ No. 924 (BCProvCt).
Re Secession of Quebec, [1998] 2 S.C.R. 217.
R. v. Powley Files
Trial transcripts, five volumes (transcription of original Ontario Court of Justice testimony).
Oral arguments, 2003. R. v. Powley, Supreme Court of Canada (File No.: 2853) March 17th.
Labrador Métis Nation Factum. 2003. *R. v. Powley,* Supreme Court of Canada (File No.: 28533).
Congress of Aboriginal Peoples Factum. 2002. *R. v. Powley,* Supreme Court of Canada (File No.: 28533).
Métis Nation of Ontario (joint with Métis National Council) (2003). *R. v. Powley,* Supreme Court of Canada (File No.: 28533).

PART 3

Additional Readings

Asch, Michael. *On Being Here to Stay: Treaties and Aboriginal Rights in Canada.* Toronto: University of Toronto Press, 2014.
Andersen, Chris. *Métis: Race, Recognition, and the Struggle for Indigenous Peoplehood.* Vancouver: UBC Press, 2014.

77. Chartrand and Giokas, "Defining 'the Métis people'," 272.

Dunbar-Ortiz, Roxanne. *An Indigenous Peoples' History of the United States*. Boston, MA: Beacon Press, 2014.

Goeman, Mishuana. *Mark My Words: Native Women Mapping Our Nations*. Minneapolis, MN: University of Minnesota Press, 2013.

Harris, Cole. *The Resettlement of British Columbia: Essays on Colonialism and Geographical Change*. Vancouver, BC: University of British Columbia Press, 1997.

Hill, Susan M. *The Clay We Are Made Of: Haudensaunee Land Tenure on the Grand River*. Winnipeg, MB: University of Manitoba Press, 2017.

Innes, Robert Alexander. *Elder Brother and the Law of the People: Contemporary Kinship and Cowessess First Nation*. Winnipeg, MB: University of Manitoba Press, 2013.

Leroux, Darryl. *Distorted Descent: White Claims to Indigenous Identity*. Winnipeg, MB: University of Manitoba Press, 2019.

Lyons, Scott Richard. *X-Marks: Native Signatures of Assent*. Minneapolis, MN: University of Minnesota Press, 2010.

Ramirez, Renya K. *Native Hubs: Culture, Community, and Belonging in Silicon Valley and Beyond*. Durham, NC: Duke University Press, 2007.

Relevant Websites

Canadian Geographic Indigenous Peoples Atlas of Canada
https://indigenouspeoplesatlasofcanada.ca/
An atlas created by The Royal Canadian Geographic Society, The Assembly of First Nations, Inuit Tapiriit Kanatami, The Métis Nation, The National Centre for Truth and Reconciliation, and Indspire containing maps, photography, historical items, and also information related to Truth and Reconciliation in Canada.

Map of Ontario Treaties and Reserves
https://www.ontario.ca/page/map-ontario-treaties-and-reserves
An interactive website inviting users to learn about, understand, and place themselves into relationship with more than 40 treaties and nation-to-nation political agreements in what is currently Ontario, Canada.

Native Land
https://native-land.ca/
Native Land Digital is a non-profit organization mapping Indigenous territories in ways that are intended to "change, challenge, and improve" understandings of land and territories with a focus on language, meaning, history, and relationships.

Transforming Relations: A Collaborative Collection
https://transformingrelations.wordpress.com/category/land-struggles/
This student-driven website based at Trent University provides an overview of ally engagements with lands and environmental justice movements of relevance to Indigenous nations including anti-fracking, pipeline development, and tar sands exploitation.

We Are All Treaty People
http://www.otc.ca/
The Office of the Treaty Commissioner in what is currently Saskatchewan Canada promotes respect, understanding, and information about treaties, treaty relationships, and reconciliation with archival, educational, events-based resources and a news forum on its website.

Films

Inuit Cree Reconciliation. Dir. Zacherias Kunuk and Neil Diamond. Kingulliit Productions, 2013.
Is the Crown at War with Us? Dir. Alanis Obomsawin. National Film Board of Canada, 2002.
Kanehsatake: 270 Years of Resistance. Dir. Alanis Obomsawin. National Film Board of Canada, 1993.
nîpawistamâsowin We Will Stand Up. Dir. Tasha Hubbard. National Film Board of Canada, 2019.
The Pass System. Dir. Alex Williams. Tamarack Productions, 2015.

Trick or Treaty? Dir. Alanis Obomsawin. National Film Board of Canada, 2014.
Two Worlds Colliding. Dir. Tasha Hubbard. National Film Board of Canada, 2004.
Wake Up! Dir. Jessie Short. Jessie Short, 2015.

Key Terms

- Dispossession
- Indigenous nationhood
- Kinship
- Métis
- Nation-building

- Peoplehood
- Relationality
- Settler violence
- Urbanity/Indigeneity binarism

Discussion Questions

1. What role do spatial understandings play in ongoing Settler colonialism, dispossession, and the disavowal of Indigenous identities?

2. What is meant by racialization? How did racialization impact Indigenous peoples and of what service is it to the ongoing history of Settler colonialism, lands theft, and dispossession?

3. What is the significance of Chris Andersen's peoplehood-based approach to historical inquiry? How does it address Settler–Indigenous/Indigenous–Indigenous relations, the "enframing power" of Settler States, and the contradictions inherent in European-based definitions of nationhood?

4. Bonita Lawrence writes that ". . . . in order for Canada to have a viable national identity, the histories of Indigenous nations, in all their diversity and longevity, must be erased." What does she mean by this and what are the implications of this reality for *both* Indigenous and non-Indigenous peoples?

Activities

Research the land on which your school, home, or community is built. To which Indigenous nation does it belong? What is the history of Settler colonialism or resistance against settlement on this land? Are there any historical grievances over this land? What are they? What are the central differences in these grievances?

Watch the 2002 National Film Board production *Is the Crown at War with Us?* (written and directed by Alanis Obomsawin). How might you analyze the actions of non-Indigenous fishermen with respect to race, space, and the law? Discuss the role of violence in upholding the boundaries of race and space under Settler colonialism. Where does this film and its history fit in relation to Lawrence's article on the history of Indigenous resistance in Eastern Canada?

Watch the 2006 television drama *One Dead Indian* (written by Hugh Graham and Andrew Wreggit, directed by Tim Southam). How might you analyze the actions of the provincial government and police with respect to racism, resistance, and the law? Where do their actions stand in relation to the findings and recommendations of the Ipperwash Inquiry? How did the inquiry process bring us closer to decolonizing relations between Indigenous peoples and majority Canadians? What needs to be done in both the short term and long term for these to be fully implemented?

PART 4

Indigenous Refusal, Settler Sovereignty, and Border Imperialism

Editor Introduction

In the fall of 2010, Richard Desautel made his way from his home in Inchelium, Washington across the US/Canada land border to what is currently called British Columbia. Soon after on 14 October, he shot a cow elk near Castlegar, BC and was later charged under s. 11(1) of the Province's wildlife legislation for hunting without a license. Desautel, an enrolled member of the Colville Indian Tribe in the United States, was said to be in contravention of Canadian law, which stipulates that having the right to hunt requires that one is a resident of BC and has a license to hunt. Soon after, Desautel filed defense litigation for the charge arguing that he had an Aboriginal right to hunt, protected by s. 35(1) of Canada's Constitution Act. Despite being an US citizen, he argued, he too is a Sinixt person: he shot the cow elk within his ancestral territory of the Sinixt, which exceeds the borders of British Columbia and Washington State. After 10 years in lower courts, his grievance finally made its way to the Supreme Court of Canada (SCC) in the fall of 2020 (R. v. Desautel, 2021). On 23 April 2021, the SCC said that Desautel had a right to hunt in Canada, protected under s. 35(1). The Court ruled that, in any given instance, a person claiming s.35(1) protection might in some instances be a non-Canadian citizen.

The case of Richard Desautel is but one example revealing a crack in the foundation of Settler carceral projects of exclusion and social and spatial delineation. R. v. Desautel represents a victory of sorts for Indigenous peoples in both Canada and the United States. The case recognizes that "the Aboriginal peoples of Canada" noted in s. 35(1) of the Canadian Constitution includes peoples "who were already here, who moved, or who were forced to move elsewhere when First Europeans arrived." Of course, R. v. Desautel did not address in any substantive way issues we hope this chapter might invite among readers; specifically, the ways in which people become of a place or out of place in white Settler colonial societies (Sharma, 2020). Nor did the Desautel case address the US-Canada border as a concomitant site of Indigenous genocide and antiblack violence whereby technologies of racism "premised on the social grammar of Black people as nonhumans" and enslaveable were refined (Maynard, 2019: 128). Finally, the Desautel case did not work in a way that is transformative of Settler colonialism and the racism that is necessary for the legal expropriation of Indigenous lands, sovereignty, and our legislative assimilation.

Canadian courts are not neutral arbiters of justice (Cannon, 2014; Monture, 2006). R. v. Desautel did not start by questioning the very legitimacy of the US-Canada border, or for that matter, a doctrine of discovery that would have us believe today that lands were terra nullius, empty or unoccupied, prior to the imposition of the US and Canadian border. Rather, R. v. Desautel—like other constitutional law involving "Aboriginal peoples"—sought to reconcile the prior existence of Indigenous peoples with the unilateral assertion of Crown **sovereignty** (Asch, 2014). The sovereignty of Indigenous peoples' existence before the so-called "gift" of US-Canadian **citizenship** is never questioned by settler states or in courtrooms and nations. In Settler colonial contexts, Crown sovereignty and the imposition of territorial boundaries proceeds without question. Indeed, the modern concept of citizenship and the borders drawn by nation-states are often taken for granted or regarded to be immutable (and ahistorical) facts of nature, enabling the cultivation and bolstering of nationalism(s), the justification of the inhumane treatment of migrants, and the construction of migrants and Indigenous peoples as "illegal aliens" (Sharma, 2020).

On both sides of the US-Canadian border, we have already witnessed the complex ways in which these matters of Indigeneity and Crown sovereignty play themselves out politically and legally. Some 92 years prior, in 1928, Paul K. Diabo argued similarly regarding his right to traverse the US-Canada border—not as a US or Canadian citizen, but as an Indigenous person from a nation whose existence pre-dated the origin of both nation-states. Diabo, a Mohawk from Kanawake, was deemed an "illegal alien" in the United States, where he had been employed as an ironworker. Arguing against his looming deportation, Diabo suggested he had a right to cross the international border without restriction or interference as recognized by the Jay Treaty of 1794 (see Reid, 2007). The District Court of the United States for the Eastern District of Pennsylvania ruled favorably that he had indeed the right to live and work in the USA. The court suggested the right was at once recognized and affirmed by the Jay Treaty. In other words, and as Audra Simpson (this volume) points out, the right of free passage was not created by the Jay Treaty. It existed long before the treaty itself came about in November 1794 and needed only to be recognized and affirmed.

Canadian courts are by no means as enlightened in their interpretation of the right of free passage. In Mitchell v. Minister of Natural Resources, Canadian crown attorneys were consumed with the matter of cultural continuity and the unfair advantage of acknowledging Mohawk economic jurisdiction between both nation-states (A. Simpson, this volume). Mike Mitchell, an Indigenous person from Akwesasne Mohawk Territory, crossed the international boundary line bringing goods in 1988. He was charged with violating the Canadian Customs Act after not paying duty. Like Diabo, Canadian lower courts upheld Mitchell's 1794 Jay Treaty rights. However, the Supreme Court of Canada ruled in 2001 that the determining factor establishing Mitchell's right of free passage is rooted in, and indeed sources from, his Indigenous "culture." As Audra Simpson (this volume) argues, culture is part of "an interpretive process in Canada of using especially static and culturalist methodology to mete out recognition." Culture is used to disprove our sovereignty as Indigenous nations, which pre-dates the constitution of either the US or Canada, two different countries divided by an international boundary line. In Settler states, our only existence is that of citizens firmly ensconced in the nationalism of either nation-state. Racism and Settler colonialism complicate the crossing of international borders.

Crossing the US-Canadian border is still today not without the hazards experienced by Mitchell, Diabo, and Desautel. Likewise, the original nuances of racism and Settler colonial dominance have not been sorted out in settler courtrooms or internationally. As Rickard (this volume) suggests, our crossings have been mired from the very first historic instance in the racism of border officials. Indeed, these matters have not changed despite the passage of time. Kalman (2021) documents the myriad experiences of Mohawks crossing the international border of Canada and the United States as well as the Provinces of Quebec and Ontario. His work provides a decidedly ethnomethodological exploration of Mohawk border experiences. Audra Simpson (2014: 182–185) has also documented the detainment of Iroquois Nationals seeking to play lacrosse internationally using Haudenosaunee passports. Finally, a government report from Canada found that there was still trouble utilizing these passports at the border as of 2017 (relevant websites, this volume). In Canada, the state is well aware of issues involving Indigenous peoples and the border. Recommendations have been precise and very clear about what it is that needs to take place in order to uphold the sovereignty of Indigenous peoples who traverse international borders.

The US-Canada border must be understood and further interrogated as a site of geopolitical dominance, racism, and Settler colonial regulation. Recognizing that settlement in either country did not terminate the interests of Indigenous peoples arising from prior occupation—including especially freedom of movement within and use of territories—our third edition centres the experience of Haudenosaunee where the experience of **border imperialism** is concerned. We draw upon matters involving the right of free passage as this relates to Haudenosaunee in particular because it is familiar to us as Onyota'a:ka, but it is also clear that issues involving border imperialism and the right of free passage is one that impacts Indigenous peoples across all nations, as seen in the case of Richard Desautel (also see Bellfy, 2013; Hele, 2015). Though North America is also comprised of the US-Mexico border, we wish to shift the focus and examine critically the US-Canadian border as a site of geopolitical dominance and settler colonial regulation. We trace but one dimension of the vastly understudied **refusal** by Indigenous peoples in both countries to relinquish jurisdiction and accept the limitations imposed upon them by white settler borders and the perceived "gift" of US or Canadian citizenship. In following this analytic, it will be important to address several important issues, especially the right of free passage, Indigenous governance and sovereignty, anti-blackness (Maynard, 2019), and racialized and migrant exclusion (Walia, 2021). We wish to centre and explore the possibilities, challenges, and contradictions raised by resistances to border imperialism in this section from an Indigenous-centered and decolonizing perspective. It is necessary to illuminate and realize a more critical, historicized, and decolonizing politics of place, mobility, and political consciousness.

In Chapter 7, Rickard traces his own personal activism and lobbying efforts concerning the right of free passage for Haudenosaunee along the US-Canada border. In detailing this rich and vastly under-studied matter of history and Indigenous sovereignty, the article provides an important glimpse of 1920s political-based community organizing by Haudenosaunee; the founding of the **Indian Defense League of America**; the making of early Indigenous-settler solidarity alliances, and the refusal by Ukwehuwe to recognize or even accept the re-spatialization of Turtle Island as a carceral project of international boundary-making and border imperialism that continues today. As Rickard suggests, the matter of "Canadian" or "American Indianness" is a falsehood, at once created and then perpetuated by the colonizer to have us believe as Indigenous nations that our movement is between and across nation-states instead of original homelands. Rickard reminds the reader that we are sovereign—and not racialized –nations of people with accordant rights under the Jay Treaty, established in the first historic instance of Indigenous-settler contact.

Audra Simpson, in Chapter 8, explores similarly Rickard's earlier historical analysis concerning the right of free passage, in particular the refusal by Haudenosaunee today to accept the criminalization of economic activities across international boundaries dividing territories without their consent. These activities, at times termed "smuggling" by settlers, are always tied up in the criminalization of Indigenous peoples as effectively out of place in white Settler colonialism which misrepresents, mischaracterizes, and fails to recognize Haudenosaunee as original occupants of the land. Simpson explores the matter of "**failed consent**"—indeed, a concept that is coined by the author herself to draw attention to the maintenance of Kanienkehaka ways of knowing. As Simpson suggests, it is redundant to consider a refusal to consent to colonial mappings and Settler occupations as an act of mere resistance or reaction of any sort. Rather, the act of failed consent takes place whenever we merely exist as Haudenosaunee, or assert our very presence as Haudenosaunee peoples through knowing, being, and doing. *Especially* at the US-Canada border.

CHAPTER 7

The Border Crossing

Clinton Rickard

The year 1925 began a long struggle to secure the border crossing rights for our Indian people as guaranteed by the old treaties, which were still in existence. These were specifically Article 3 of the Jay Treaty of 1794 and Article 9 of the Treaty of Ghent of 1814. The United States government had ignored these treaties in passing the new immigration legislation, and it was now up to us and our sympathizers to carry on the fight to gain justice.

I now had to take a great amount of time away from my farm to travel and to write letters to Indian and white friends and to government officials, for I was receiving mall all the time from Indians, and I was also obliged to protest to the government this prohibition of our free movement across the border. In all my work, my wife Elizabeth provided constant encouragement and assistance. . . . Our house was always open to visitors and strangers, and they came frequently, often staying long periods. Sometimes, we would not even know the person in distress who called at our door, but we took him in. As I became better known in this work, the visitors became more numerous. . . .

On September 11, 1925, Henry Hull, commissioner general of the Bureau of Immigration, United States Department of Labor, replied to a previous letter of mine by saying that North American Indians might be admitted over the border if they were coming temporarily for business or pleasure, since this was permitted by the 1924 Immigration Act. . . .

We therefore had only a partial victory. The fight was a long way from being completely won. In fact, on September 7, Chief Hoheoneane had been turned back at the border with no explanation given. . . .

I had previously written to Senator James W. Wadsworth, Jr., and Indian Commissioner Charles H. Burke on this border crossing problem. . . . I wanted the senator to ask the Secretary of Labor to notify the immigration stations along the border, especially at Buffalo, Niagara Falls, Lewiston, and Rochester, of the fact that there was no ruling excluding North American Indians from crossing the border for temporary purposes. We could see, however, that there was much more work ahead of us.

In appreciation for my work in opening the border, in the fall of 1925 the Algonquin Indians of Maniwaki presented me with a beautiful Indian costume made out of moose hide and expertly beaded.
. . .

For many years it had not been the custom to dress in Indian fashion on our reserve. . . . I began wearing my costume on all special and ceremonial occasions and also encouraged other Indians to wear Indian clothing. I received much opposition from

Fighting Tuscarora: The Autobiography of Chief Clinton Rickard, ed. Barbara Graymont (Syracuse: Syracuse University Press, 1973), 69–89. © Barbara Graymont. Reproduced with permission from the publisher.

some of my Tuscarora people on this account and was even accused of "going back to the blanket." This opposition has gradually been overcome. . . .

In December 1925 we faced a new setback at the border. On December 17, I went to Grand River to attend the condolence for departed Cayuga chiefs at the Sour Springs Longhouse. It was at this time that Alexander J. General was condoled to succeed his brother Levi General and to assume his title and chiefly name of Deskaheh. I took with me Job Henry, a Tuscarora from Grand River who had married one of our women and had lived and worked on our reserve for thirty years, with the exception of occasional visits back to Grand River. On the way back to the United States December 18, we tried to cross at Lewiston Bridge but were turned back by the immigration official whose name, as nearly as I could make out, was John McClay, and told to go to the Lower Arch Bridge in Niagara Falls, which was eight miles away. He certainly was no gentleman but talked to us as though we were dogs. I had been subjected to much embarrassment and delay by this same man on several past occasions when I tried to cross the border alone but was released when I showed him letters from Senator Wadsworth and Indian Commissioner Burke.

We followed McClay's instructions and proceeded to Niagara Falls. In the meanwhile, McClay telephoned on ahead and told the immigration office at that bridge to hold us. At the Lower Arch Bridge, we were asked why we tried to pass there when we were rejected at Lewiston. Then I was allowed to pass bat Job Henry was refused on the grounds that he was illiterate, which he was. In fact, he spoke only the Indian language and little or no English. A 1917 Immigration law barred illiterates from the United States and now for the first time this law was being used against my people. Job Henry, aged fifty-five, had a wife and two sons on our reservation. He had lived ten years straight on our reservation, from 1895 to 1905, and after that time he and his family returned occasionally to the Grand River Reserve. . . . The 1917 law acted to separate him from his family and to leave these poor people in much emotional and financial distress. This was a great wrong perpetrated against the descendants of the original inhabitants of this continent by the descendants of European immigrants. Some of these border officers were themselves recent immigrants from Europe and could not even speak good English.

Nor was this all. Our people were continually stopped when trying to cross the border, despite the fact that no order had come from Washington to bar Indians. Just the contrary, in fact, for the letter I had from Immigration Commissioner Hull indicated that Indians might be admitted on a temporary basis. This discrimination against our people was directly the result of race prejudice on the part of some immigration officers. They held the power, and they were using it to humiliate and distress us.

I took up the case of Job Henry immediately. I wrote letters to Senator Wadsworth and to the Immigration Bureau in Washington. Senator Wadsworth gave us much assistance in supporting our right to cross the border at will. I myself went to the main office of the district director of immigration in Buffalo to protest this unjust exclusion and to plead the case of our Indian people who wished to cross the border. I had told the immigration officials that Job Henry was a native American whose ancestors had been here for centuries and who had been unjustly stopped at the border and separated from his wife and children. I did not consider that there was any such thing as "Canadian Indian" or "United States Indian." All Indians are one people. We were here long before there was any border to make an artificial division of our people.

While I was in the Immigration Office in Buffalo, January 22, 1926. I was advised by Arthur Karnuth of that office that he had received word from Washington to allow Job Henry to enter this country for a temporary period of six months. This was a great victory for us, but still a limited one. . . .

I had to interpret for Job while the immigration people questioned him. They kept asking him: "Are you a Canadian Indian?" And the poor man would reply: "Yes, yes."

I stood that as long as I could and then I interrupted and said: "No, he is not a Canadian Indian in any way whatsoever. He is a true North American Indian, even as I am. Our ancestors were here long before you people and your ancestors were. We should therefore not be restricted from moving about on this continent, which is our homeland."

Congressman S. Wallace Dempsey helped us to get Job's stay extended for one year. But our struggle had to go on to open up the banter to our people in accordance with the Jay Treaty and the Treaty of Ghent. Also, it was our belief that the white man's border should never be used to separate our people. We once had complete freedom to go sad come at will before the white man took the country away from us. But this continent was still our country, too. We could not bear to have our lives restricted as though we were aliens in our own land. This was why Job's fight and the fight for all my people had to continue until righteousness prevailed.

In 1926, the Algonquins made me their wampum keeper so that the Indian agent or the Royal Canadian Mounted Police would not seize the belts, as has been done on the Six Nations Reserve at Grand River. . . .

These wampum belts had an interesting history. The ancestors of these Algonquins came originally from Lake of Two Mountains, Oka. They left that place because the French priest there was bothering them, and went to the neighborhood of Maniwaki. . . . About 1895, the Canadian Indian Act was extended to Maniwaki. Mrs. Meness' father, John Tenasen,[1] had been elected a chief . . . His brother, Peter Tenssco, said that the Indians no longer needed the wampum belts because they were going to use the Indian Act. The wampum was then put away and nearly forgotten.

In the 1920s, a man named Philip Nattoway had the wampum belts in his possession. . . .

When Frank Meness went up to visit Philip Nattoway one day, the old man told Frank that he better take the wampum belts down to Maniwaki where they would be cared for property. Frank did so and finally brought them over to me for safekeeping in 1926.

Both of these belts are very old and have the hand-made shell wampum beads strung together on rawhide strips, in the traditional manner. The larger belt is . . . known as the Grand Council Wampum Belt, and the diamonds represent the tribes.[2] The other is known as the Hudson Bay Wampum Belt. . . .

The belt tells how the Indians accepted the white man as a friend and allowed a trading post in their territory. . . .

I was also given five strands of white wampum tied together. This was used in tribal meetings. The people touched the strings to signify that they agreed to a proposal under consideration.

A couple of years later, in appreciation for my work on behalf of Indians, I was given a small belt called the Peace Belt. . . . Ever since I received it, I have used this belt to inform people, both Indian and white, about Indian history. I have also used it in adoption ceremonies, pledging the adoptees to spread peace wherever they go.

I have now kept the wampum safely all these years. Several times people have tried to get the belts away from me. . . . During these many years. I have often displayed these ancient and sacred wampum belts to instruct the people in their meaning, but always I have protected them carefully, as I have been charged.

In early 1926, I became acquainted with David Hill, a Mohawk Iron Six Nations Reserve who was living in Niagara Falls, New York. Huron Class, the Indian evangelist, appealed to Dave for help on the border question, telling him that many of the Indians crossing the border were forced to lie as to their origins, saying they were from the Cattarangus or Allegany Reservation or our Tuscarora Reservation so that they would be permitted entry into the United States. Claus thought this was a very bad situation.

Dave agreed and asked: "What can we do about it?"

Huron told him: "I was over at Chief Clinton Rickard's last week and I saw copies of the two treaties he has that say our people have the right to cross the border."

"I'd like to go over to see this Chief Rickard," Dave said. . . .

Dave received quite a shock when he first laid eyes on me. I was dressed in old, worn-out work clothes. . . . I stood, bushy-headed, with an old hat

---

1. The name was originally *Tentensee* or *Tentensi*, meaning Blue Jay. White people, who had difficulty pronouncing it, made it *Tenasco*.

2. The tribes represented may possibly be the so-called Seven Nations of Canada. This alliance was formed by the French during the French and Indian War to aid them in their imperial struggles with the British. The tribes of the Seven Nations were the three Lake of Two Mountain groups–Algonquin, Nipissing, and Mohawk—Abnaid of St. Francit, Caughnawaga Mohawk, Huron of Lorette, and Cayuga and Onondaga of Oswegatchie. The Oswegatchies later joined the émigré Caughnawagas who settled at St. Regis and were absorbed by them.

and tattered clothes, looking for all the world like a tramp. . . .

From that point on, Dave and I worked very closely together. . . .

One March day in 1926, Dave met a Mohawk friend, Leslie Martin, on the street in Niagara Falls. . . . Dave told Leslie about the border trouble and said they ought to have an organization, if only they had a place to meet and organize.

Leslie said: "You can have my house any time." He lived right in Niagara Falls, New York, and thought this would be a good central place.

They agreed on a meeting time. . . .

There we talked about the necessity of having an organization to work for our rights.

During the summer and fall, we worked on getting an organization together. On December 1, 1926, we finally formed the Six Nations Defense League. We later broadened our organization by changing the title to the Indian Defense League of America. We encouraged our friends in other areas to form branches of the league to unify themselves for our fight and to make our cause better known. Our first goal was to obtain our border-crossing rights. . . . This was an all-Indian organization. We later began adopting some of our faithful white friends who had given us much assistance, and they were thereupon made honorary, but not voting, members of our league. We also made a place as honorary members for those persons who had less than 50 percent Indian blood.

I wrote up the following brief set of regulations for our organization . . .

After our league was organized, I continued with my travels and speaking engagements to publicize our problem both to Indians and to whites. . . . It was my job, and that of other Indians, to tell these people the truth and to encourage them to become active on our behalf in fighting for justice.

Another tactic I used during the summertime to publicize our cause was to dress in my Indian costume and visit the tourist camps around Niagara Falls to speak to the many visitors who came to that city from all over the nation. I told these people of our problem and asked them to write to their congressmen when they returned home. In this way we were able to gain new friends and also put more pressure on the government to secure our rights.

We did have a number of friends in government who sympathized with our cause. Among those most active in our defense were Congressmen S. Wallace Dempsey and Clarence MacGregor of New York and Senators James W. Wadsworth, Jr., of New York and William King of Utah. Senator—later Vice-President—Charles Curtis also gave much encouragement. . . .

The border problem was very complicated, for it involved not only the simple rights of crossing but also the head tax of $8.00 on immigrants. . . . I asked him to get a writ of habeas corpus, and this he did. So the girls were out of jail in about two weeks' time. They could then be free while awaiting their court case.

Early in 1927, I took two trips to Washington to testify on Congressman Dempsey's border-crossing bill, H.R. 16864, but we were not able to get it out of committee. Attorney Codd accompanied me in February. . . .

We began having trouble with Attorney Codd about this time. He submitted to as a bill for $731.00 for his work on deportation cases on behalf of seven people we were interested in helping. The Indian Defense League paid him $371.00 on account, but not one of these cases was ever called. . . . We accordingly dismissed Codd.

This man Codd was not to be outdone, however. He began working with a factional group in the Indian Defense League at Grand River, convincing them that he was just the one to solve the border problem. My Indian people sometimes find it hard to work together, and this fact often leads to unwise decisions. Jealousy is one of the most serious factors in causing Indians to defeat themselves.

To add to our difficulties, hostility to our cause developed among my own Tuscarora people. Most unfortunate of all, the man who was the most active against the free border crossing was our head chief, J. Warren Brayley. For many months, he had been writing here and there to officials in Canada and the United States saying that the Tuscarora Nation was opposed to the entry of Indians from Canada into the United States. He wrote to Congressman S. Wallace Dempsey . . . The letter stated that these "Canadian Indians" wanted to cross the border in order to take employment away from United States Indians. "Not only that but they come over to our reservation and squat on our lands and use our firewood, and Sundays when our Tuscaroras go to church we see these Canadian Indians drunk and disorderly." His said, furthermore, that the "Tuscarora Nation of New York Indians are opposed to letting down the bars of the Immigration Act. We are favorable to more strict enforcement of said laws." Congressman Dempsey told me that we would have to overcome the effects of this letter. . . .

I immediately called a council of our Tuscarora chiefs . . .

Chief Johnson explained to the council and especially to Chief Williams that the Jay Treaty rights belonged to all our people and not just to Indians from Canada. If we asked that this right be annulled, then we would be depriving ourselves and setting a dangerous precedent. . . .

This noble speech by Philip Johnson saved the day for us. The council thereupon passed the following resolution without a dissenting vote:

Legally constituted council of the Tuscarora Indians was held at the Council House February 26, 1927.

Whereas there is what is known as Dempsey Hill No. H.R. 16864 also a Wadsworth Bill S. 4304 both regarding Immigration Act of 1924, and whereas that there is a letter written by Warren Brayley purporting that this letter was the spirit of the Tuscarora Nation as against the passing of the above said bills,

Resolved herewith the Tuscarora chiefs in council moved and seconded carried unanimously: That the said chiefs are sincerely and humbly requesting the great U.S. Congress to pass either of the said bills pending.

Vice-President, Chief Clinton Rickard
Secretary for the Council,
Chief Edgar H. Rickard

I went to Washington and placed this resolution before the Committee on Immigration and Naturalization. I also testified against a bill that had been introduced that would have allowed only Iroquois Indians to cross the border. . . . The congressmen then asked me what the Jay Treaty said,

and I told them that it referred to Indians in general but not specifically to any tribe or tribes. I added that I was working to restore the Jay Treaty as read. The congressmen saw my point and told me that they would take up the matter when Congress reconvened that fall.

Despite the resolution passed by our Chiefs' Council, sentiment against Indians coming over to our reservation from Canada was growing, and feeling was beginning to be high against me among my own Tuscarora people. I was accused of bringing "Canucks" over. Children pick up what their parents say and leant their thoughts and habits. So it was that some of the schoolchildren came to taunt my son William became of my work on securing our border-crossing rights. One day after school, four boys grabbed William and beat him unmercifully in order to get even with me. Then they threw him to the ground and jumped up and down on his chest.

When William did not come home from school for hours, I went out looking for him and finally found him at 10:00 o'clock at night, half dead. lying in a ditch. I took him to the doctor and learned that his chest had been crushed.

William only partially recovered from that beating. . . . He eventually developed emphysema and bronchiectasis and was unable to finish school or ever enjoy completely good health when he became a man. He used to remark in his later years that those four boys, then grown, never amounted to anything in their lives. . . .

I received further discouragement from a man who was one of the best-known members of our tribe. This was the Smithsonian ethnologist John Hewitt—or J. N. B. Hewitt, as he was known professionally. He came to my house in his car one day especially to talk me out of my work in securing our treaty rights.

He said: "Chief, when the government takes anything away from you, you'll never get it back."

I was very annoyed at this and told him: "We are going to centime on and on and eventually obtain justice for our people."

I was not going to be turned aside by anyone, no matter how educated he was. But it is interesting to note that John Hewitt's eider brother, Alvis Hewitt, was a member and faithful supporter of our Indian Defense League.

The reason I was so certain of the rightness of my work was because I had always appealed to the Great Spirit to bestow upon me the knowledge and wisdom to defend the rights of my people. I did not let a night go by without seeking this guidance before I lay down to sleep. I do feel that the Great Spirit answered my prayers.

On August 7, 1927, there was to be a dedication of the new Peace Bridge which linked Buffalo, New York, with Fort Erie, Ontario. This ceremony was to be attended by many outstanding dignitaries, including Prime Minister Stanley Baldwin of Great Britain and the Prince of Wales and the Duke of York.

. . . A delegation of eight Algonquins from Barriere and Maniwaki therefore made this long trip. . . .

At the border, they were absolutely refused entry. I received a message to come and help them. I dropped everything and went to the border, where I met a stone wall of refusal from the officials. After an argument of about half an hour, I did finally succeed in securing their entry. . . .

Our Defense League did have its own Peace Bridge celebration on August 6, 1927. This was a big affair, held at The Front, the large park near the Peace Bridge in Buffalo, and featured Indian dances and a speech by City Judge Patrick J. Keeler. . . . Our Six Nations Confederacy was the first League of Nations and was known as the Great Peace. This was why we wanted to perpetuate the symbol of peace in oar own day.

I kept the eight Algonquin visitors at my house until they could get money from their reserve to go home. . . .

In 1927, a famous case on the border fight was tried in Philadelphia. A Caughnawaga Mohawk Ironworker named Paul K. Diabo had been arrested in Philadelphia in 1925 for illegal entry into the United States and ordered deported on the grounds that he might become a public charge. This despite the feet that he was earning $70 a week working on the Delaware River Bridge! Diabo had traveled continually across the border from 1912 to 1925 while pursuing his profession but was finally caught up in the tangle of the Immigration Act of 1924. Diabo retained a Philadelphia law firm to defend him and determined to fight this case to the finish.

On February 20, 1926, I began corresponding with James H. Ross, a Canghnawaga Mohawk friend of Diabo's living in Philadelphia, and told him about my work on the border problem. In a later letter in March, I offered to send him or the lawyer copies of all the documents I had gathered which pertained to Indian rights in crossing the border. I learned that the law firm of William N. Nitzberg in Philadelphia was handling Diabo's case. . . .

Early in 1927, William N. Nitzberg argued the case before Judge Oliver B. Dickinson in the District Court of the United States for the Eastern District of Pennsylvania. I wrote to the judge before he rendered his decision and sent him copies of treaties and other documents relating to Indian border-crossing rights.

On March 19, 1927, Judge Dickinson rendered his decision in favor of our people as follows:

> The boundary line to establish the respective territory of the United States and of Great Britain was clearly not intended to, and just as clearly did not, affect the Indians. It made no division of their country. The Jay Treaty of 1794 recognized this fact in the provision that the Indians residing on either side of the line, which was between the United States and Great Britain and established as a boundary line, should be unaffected in their right to pass the line at will. It has been argued to us pro and con. that this treaty was abrogated by the War of 1812. We do not see that the rights of the Indians are in any way affected by the treaty, whether now existing or not. The reference to them was merely the recognition of their right, which was wholly unaffected by the treaty; except that the contracting parties agreed with each other that each would recognize it. The right of the Indian remained, whether the agreement continued or was ended. The question of the right of a relator to enter the territory of the United States does not turn upon any treaty with Great Britain, although, of course, if we have an agreement to permit him to enter, we will make good ear promise, unless it has been duly revoked.

The turning point of the question of whether the Indians are included among the members of alien nations whose admission to our country is controlled and regulated by the existing immigration laws. The answer, it seems to us, is a negative one. From the Indian view-point, he crossed no boundary line. For him this does not exist. This fact the United States has always recognized, and there is nothing in this legislation to work a change in our attitude.[3]

I quote this historic decision at length because it represented an important turning point in our fight. For the first time, our viewpoint was reinforced by a high United States judge. This decision could therefore not be ignored.

. . . On March 9, 1928, the Third Circuit Court upheld Judge Dickinson's decision, and the Solicitor General of the United States decided not to carry the appeal further.[4]

Meanwhile, in the fall of 1927 there were eleven bills introduced in Congress favoring our right to cross the border. . . .

I knew that we had a lot of support behind us and were close to winning our case. . . .

On January 21, 1928, I was invited to a meeting at the Six Nations Reserve at Grand River. The Indian Defense League delegated four of us, including David Hill and myself, to attend. We drove the ninety miles in an open car in zero weather, with gale winds at sixty-five miles an hour. When we arrived at the reservation, we had to walk the last four miles because the roads were not cleared of snow and my auto-mobile could not get through. We bad started our trip at 4:00 P.M. and arrived at 8:00 P.M.

The meeting was held in 69 Corners Hall, which was packed with people. . . . Some of the ladies were there cooking cabbage and turnips and tea and charging a small sum for this lunch in order to raise money to pay the lawyer.

I had letters with me from Washington, from senators and congressmen and others, and from

various people across the country. . . . We therefore did not need any lawyers to take our money. I had come to warn my people of this fact.

Chauncey Garlow . . . spoke to the people in Mohawk, which he knew I did not understand, but which Dave Hill translated for me, and warned the people that I was leading them to the great pit. I think he would have been more of a gentleman if he had spoken in English. . . .

I spoke to the people for an hour warning them about the attorneys and told them that all the hard work was nearly completed. . . .

It was plain to me at the time that the greatest trouble with us Indians was in looking too much to some of the white people and in being afraid of them. We were afraid of offending them. . . . This is what we in our organization, the Indian Defense League, have tried to overcome. We have provided a way for Indians to work together and to speak out on their own.

During the early months at 1928, Senator King's bill was progressing very well in Congress. It passed the Senate on March 21 and went to the House. There, Congressman Clarence MacGregor substituted this bill for his, and it passed on March 29. President Coolidge then signed the till into haw on April 2,1928.[5]

My wife heard this news over our radio and relayed it to me. I was to dated that I took file whole day off. After three long years of struggle we had finally won! . . .

Many letters of appreciation came to me after the border fight was won. One of those letters that I cherished file most was from W. W. Husband, Second Assistant Secretary of Labor, who had given support to our cause all along. It is dated April 26,1928, and says:

My dear Chief Rickard:
Mr. Horner acknowledged receipt of your letter and the picture which you so kindly sent me, but I want to tell you personally that I appreciate your kindness

3. 18 F. (2d) 282.

4. 25 F. (2d) 71.

5. Public, No. 234, April 2,1928.45 Stat. 401.

in remembering me in this way. It is certainly an excellent picture of you, and you may be sure that we were all interested in seeing you in the splendid regalia which you had with you on one of your trips to Washington.

As I have said in another letter, you certainly are to be congratulated on the successful outcome of your work in behalf of your people in connection with the modification of the Immigration Law.

I made a trip to Grand River after our bill had passed . . . There was a council on this matter at the Sour Springs Long-house, and the building was packed. . . .

When I took off my coat and stepped to the middle of the floor, they applauded for about five minutes before I was able to speak. Then I told them the whole history of our struggle. . . .

During our border fight, we had difficulties with various lawyers who had represented as briefly on different occasions. When I first began working on the border case, I consulted Attorney George P. Decker of Rochester. He told me to forget about writing letters because it would only waste postage. He would take the case himself, he said, but it would cost between $800 and $1,000. . . . R. M. Codd, Jr., was hired by a faction at Grand River, headed by Chauncey Garlow, after I had warned them not to hire him. He submitted a bill to them for $500 for the victory that we had won in Congress . . . Codd also had another money-making project to present He was going to sell identification cards to Indians for a dollar apiece. These cards were to have the person's photograph attached. In other words, this was to be a sort of passport to get Indians across

the border. I went to the district director of immigration is Buffalo and asked about this proposal. He told me it was entirely unnecessary and that Indians should save their money. Passports were only for foreigners.

After our bill had passed Congress . . . I wanted to preserve this moment in history and have a thanksgiving observance after our many years of effort. Dave agreed and we began to work on the program.

The planning took three months. There was, first of all, to be a parade which would come across the bridge from Niagara Falls, Ontario, to Niagara Falls, New York . . . We wanted to stress Indian culture particularly and also the Indian as he was two hundred years ago. Two chiefs from Maniwaki, Quebec, came in mid-June to help me. I also had the cooperation of the chamber of commerce and the mayors of the two cities.

The celebration was held on July 14, 1928, and was a great success. People said that Niagara Falls had never seen anything like it before. Indians came from all over to participate. . . . We had a band, Indian dancers, and a lacrosse game at the park grounds. . . . The entire program was very satisfactory to everybody concerned and accomplished just what we wanted it to do. It celebrated our victory and publicized our culture to white people.

Many people at the time thought that this celebration would mark the end of our struggle. We had won. Why continue our organization or our publicity? It was true that I was relieved to be out from under the burden of this long campaign to win the border-crossing right but I felt that we could not rest on our victories. . . . Since we were sure that we would have much to do in the future, we determined to continue the Defense League.

CHAPTER 8

Subjects of Sovereignty

Indigeneity, The Revenue Rule, and Juridics of Failed Consent

Audra Simpson

I. Introduction: Settler Sovereignty and the Problem of Indigeneity

This article is an anthropological examination of the way in which indigeneity and sovereignty have been conflated with savagery, lawlessness, and "smuggling" in recent history. The national "problem" of indigenous smuggling is reconstructed here as it was portrayed in the public eye, largely via the media, and then through conflict-of-laws cases concerning the interpretation and applications of the "revenue rule." Different understandings of sovereignty led to the "public problem" of smuggling. National laws outlawing smuggling implied that one view of sovereignty was more legitimate than others—that is, settler law over indigenous law. In the end, the smuggling problem was an index of the fragility of settlement itself, a fragility that was demonstrated repeatedly through the maintenance of legal boundaries and jurisdiction, the collection of taxes, and anxiety over whose law and whose jurisdictions should prevail when affronts to those boundaries had been made.

. . . The Canadian media framed smuggling as an abuse of a system of indigenous rights recognized

under Canadian law and hence a problem for any recognition by the Canadian sovereign of indigenous sovereignty. The "problem" of smuggling was then constructed through the courts as wrongdoing by tobacco companies and as a question of how the United States, as a sovereignty, could assist Canada, as a sovereignty, thereby missing the larger, critical context of Iroquois[6] trade practices and treaty interpretation across the borders of the United States and Canada, and the recognition of indigenous sovereignty.

II. Smuggling and Its Jurisdictional Implications

The Canadian Broadcasting Corporation (CBC) documentary, *The Dark Side of Native Sovereignty*,[7] broadcast in 1996, subjected Mohawk trade and traffic to an intense form of scrutiny. . . .

The role of "Big Tobacco" in illegal trade in cigarettes from Canada to the United States for eventual sale back into Canada culminated in a 2001 Racketeering Influenced and Corrupt Organizations (RICO) suit.[8] This suit was filed by the government of Canada against R. J. Reynolds and others, a conglomeration of tobacco manufacturers, for

---

---

6. "The Iroquois" is a French transliteration of a word that refers to the *Haudenosaunee*, or "People of the Longhouse," as they call themselves. This is a confederacy of six indigenous nations: Mohawk, Oneida, Onondaga, Cayuga Seneca, and Tuscarora, that extended their dominion across what is now the northeastern United States and pans of Canada. They now reside on fifteen reservations and unrecognized, traditional communities and cities spanning the borders of the United States and Canada.

7. Canadian Broadcasting Corporation's Witness television broadcast Aug. 20, 1996 (transcript on file with author).

8. Canada v. R. J. Reynolds Tobacco Holdings, Inc., 268 F.3d 103 (2d Cir. 2001).

conspiring to circumvent tax laws in Canada.[9] It is asserted in the court decision that "[a]t least some of the smuggling was conducted by selling the Canadian cigarettes to residents of the St. Regis/Akwesasne Indian Reservation . . . on the New York–Canadian border."[10] . . .

In so doing, the court reinforced settler sovereignty—in an older, territorially based model—by not believing the argument that the defendants had been acting in good faith, based on their aboriginal right to trade, guaranteed to them by the Jay Treaty of 1794. Under the treaty, the defendants, as members of a "border tribe," were legally allowed to trade across the border as long as their goods were intended for trade with another indigenous nation.[11] . . .

III. Indigenous Sovereignty

The rights and sovereignty of the Iroquois, or Haudenosaunee ("People of the Longhouse"), are ensconced in their long history as indigenous peoples in what is now North America. Their own governmental systems, political theory, and law (or *Kaienerekowa*, "Great Law of Peace"), as well as treaty- and trade practices in what is now northeastern and southeastern Canada, buttressed and continue to buttress their understandings of territory. . . .

In the CBC's documentary, *Troubled Waters*,[12] which preceded *The Dark Side of Sovereignty* . . . the narrative of the documentary . . . is dramatized by fears of Indian lawlessness:

> Dust settles on the smuggling capital of Canada. Across the river, Loran Thompson is getting ready for another busy night. . . . Just across the river from Thompson's dock is Cornwall Island, located on the Canadian half of Akwesasne. Mohawks

don't recognize the international border that cuts through the water. For them, it's all Indian territory and smuggling is a dirty word here. They call it sovereignty. They maintain a treaty signed almost 200 years ago [that] gives Mohawks the right to trade freely among themselves."[13]

With this, the director de-historicizes the historical respatialization—or reconfiguring one's understanding of a particular space—of Akwesasne through colonial boundary making. He renders this respatialization a simple matter of the refusal of Indians to recognize what is apparent, an international boundary that has been drawn through the water, which is in the minds of *Akwesasnero:non* (people of Akwesasne) *their* water. . . . Mohawks . . . refused to consent to colonial mappings and occupations of their territory. Such refusals, or failures to consent, require a legal response to contain the refusers, a move that then incites settler anxiety about the containabilty of Indian bodies and practices. That the territory and the people of Akwesasne cross four state and provincial boundaries and jurisdictions as well as an international boundary line bifurcating their territory,[14] that this territory was divided without their explicit consent, that their boundaries of this space are different than those mapped by relatively new nation-states and peoples, was not up for discussion or analysis. It is simply the Indians' perceived misrecognition of boundaries (and the inability to contain their trafficking and their economic practice) that was the issue.

. . . Mohawks and other Iroquois transporters had a much smaller role in this "problem" than was represented in these early documentaries. . . . The overemphasis on Indian activities was important in solidifying the fragile sovereignty of a settler

---

9. *Id.*

10. *Id.* at 106.

11. Treaty of Amity, Commerce, and Navigation art. 3, Nov. 19, 1794, U.S.–Gr. Brit., 8 Stat. 116, 12 Bevans 13.

12. Canadian Broadcast Corporation's Fifth Estate television broadcast, Sept, 28, 1993 (transcript on file with author).

13. *Id.*

14. Akwesasne means "where the partridge drums." Lewis Henry Morgan, League of the Iroquois 474 (1996). Akwesasne is a Mohawk reservation that is bifurcated by the international boundary line between Canada and the United States and is also surrounded by, or lies within, New York State, Ontario, and Quebec.

nation-state—a sovereignty that, it will be seen, requires, along with taxation, the vanquishing, through law, of indigenous sovereignties.

. . . Disallowing the possible role of Indian political orders (for example, the legitimacy of the trading under the Jay Treaty) or of public argument about these issues, perpetuated the notion that there are actually only *two* legitimate political regimes in play—Canada and the United States. And the "extraterritoriality," the cross-border question of the *R. J. Reynolds* case, which made the issue a choice-of-law matter, was simply a question of deciding, between the two countries, whose law would apply and which of these two unquestionably legitimate political regimes had incurred harm.

Mohawk and other Iroquois traders had their sovereignty and sovereign right to trade repeatedly criminalized and effaced by analyzing the issues as a "smuggling" problem. Their aboriginal right to commerce across borders under the Jay Treaty was ignored . . .

Indigenous "smuggling" was a sign of failed consent to recognize territorial designations by third parties, of **settler fragility**, "Sovereignty" is articulated differently by Mohawks in their traditional trade practice, a practice that necessarily involves a grounded knowledge and deep critique of settler law and that is misperceived as criminal, even when it is an explicit expression of treaty rights guaranteed to the Mohawks as a border tribe.

IV. Challenges to Sovereignty: Lost Revenues and Histories of Failed Consent

A. The Problem of Lost Revenues

. . . *R. J. Reynolds* offers an occasion for insight into the legal process of how "empire" is negotiated, where legal and political territories are acquired and new boundaries and political subjects are decided through the space of courts. In doing so, the terms—and the process—of political recognition are laid bare for analysis. This is a case in empire-building because its complicated legal reasoning both responds to and effaces, again, indigenous people's claims of their "aboriginal" right to trade, upholds and reinforces the singular forms of sovereignty (even where distributions in capital deterritorialize sovereignty *à la* Hardt and Negri[15]), and disables the very possibility of indigenous participation in a contemporary trade network. In *R. J. Reynolds*, the possibility of a third legal system at work was not admitted into the analysis, thus solidifying settler sovereignty as normal, natural, and ultimately just.

B. Histories of Failed Consent

In contrast, Mohawks interviewed in the films spoke of an alternative mapping of territory. . . . Consider the history embedded in these remarks:

> You are a cunning People without Sincerity, and not to be trusted, for after making Professions of your Regard, and saying every thing favorable to us, you . . . tell us that our Country is within the lines of the States. This surprises us, for we had thought our Lands were our own, not within your Boundaries.[16]
>
> The white Man put that there, not us, I don't know why we have to put up with this bullshit.[17]

More than two hundred years separate these utterances, yet not much seems to have changed in the Iroquois perspective concerning the border. The central point of each lament, although inflected differently, remains the same: the perception of territory that underpins Iroquois people's right to cross

---

15. *See* Michael Hardt & Antonio Negri, Empire (2000; extensively analyzing this respatialiation of authority, sovereignty, and capital globally).

16. Alan Taylor, *Divided Ground: Upper Canada, New York, and the Iroquois Six Nations*, 22 J. Early Rep. 66 (2002).

17. This quote is provided by the author from her personal experience of overhearing one Mohawk man speaking to another over dinner about border issues, at a Red Lobster in Lachine, Quebec, during the late 1990s. *See* Audra Simpson, To the Reserve and Back Again; Kahnawake Mohawk Narratives of Self, Home and Nation 200 (unpublished Ph.D. dissertation, McGill University, August 2003) (providing greater discussion of this quote).

the border dividing the United States from Canada is radically different from that of either nation. These border utterances speak from the perception of the Northeast as a territory that belongs to the Iroquois, and as a place that was divided and is administered without their consent.

. . . Why is there such a radical difference between their self-perception and the ways in which Iroquois border-crossings are administered? Why is there such incommensurability between Iroquois' perceptions of the treaty relationship and those of the regimes that now interpret it? What accounts, then, for the dissonance between Iroquois self-perception and state-perception? . . .

What then is the basis in law for Iroquois self-perception, sense of jurisdiction, and movement across the border? It is largely the nation-to-nation, or "linking arms,"[18] metaphor of equality among people, reflective of the treaty relationship, that serves as an interpretive frame for Iroquois engagements with other nations, be they indigenous or nonindigenous.[19] . . . But the most important among these treaties for cross-border articulations is the Jay Treaty of 1794.[20] . . .

In the Jay Treaty, the right to traverse the boundaries of the US-British divide freely and without levy was guaranteed for Indian people who were operating in what has been defined as their cultural traditional "nexus" of trade.[21] This is laid out explicitly in Article III of the Jay Treaty:

> It is agreed that it shall at all Times be free to His Majesty's Subjects, and to the Citizens of the United States, and also to the Indians dwelling on either side of the said Boundary Line, freely to pass and repass by Land or Inland Navigation, into

the respective Territories and Countries of the Two Parties on the Continent of America. . . .

> No Duty of Entry shall ever be levied by either Party on Peltries brought by Land, or Inland Navigation into the said Territories respectively, nor shall the Indians passing or repassing with their own proper Goods and Effects of whatever nature, pay for the same any Impost or Duty whatever.[22]

This explicit right to pass, then, implicitly leaves the legal regimes of Canada and the United States with the power to define who those Indian nations are and how that right to pass shall be rendered and respected. As well, and very critically, the regimes of the United States and Canada were bequeathed the power to choose whom they would recognize as members of these communities. It is prudent now to map out how these longstanding forms of recognition then speak to local forms of recognition, and more critically, how they speak to indigenous notions of citizenship-formation and territory. . . . Such connections may illuminate as well how these identifications and legal and interpretive acts are reformulated in practice and how they are not only "resisted," but circumvented, denied, or ignored.

V. Brushing Up Against the State: Transhistoric Narratives of Home and of Treaty

. . . The Jay Treaty got its first test of indigenous mobility and citizenship with the case of *United*

---

18. The notion of "linking arms together" is more than mere imagery or a discursive device. It is the narrative of the League and reflected in the Hiawatha bell that represents the confederation of six nations. Becker extends this notion of linking arms together to the "covenant chain" agreed to between the Iroquois and the English, a chain of friendship that recognized and then elaborated alliances between nations for the purposes of trade. These are the understandings of friendship between equals that the Iroquois would bring to the treaty-making process itself. *Id.* at 985–56; *see also* Robert Williams, Linking arms Together: American Indian Visions of Treaty and Peace (1999) (providing a book-length treatment of the interpretive space of treaty).

19. *Cf.* Becker, *supra* note 36.

20. Treaty of Amity, Commerce, and Navigation, Nov. 19, 1794, U.S.–Gr. Brit., 8 Stat. 116, 12 Bevans 13.

21. Bryan Nickels, *Native American Free Passage Rights Under the Jay Treaty: Survival Under United States Statutory Law and Canadian Common Law*, 24 Brit. Colum. Int'l & Common L. Rev. 315 (2001) ("However, to claim the free passage right in Canada, a U.S. Indian has to demonstrate a cultural or historical "nexus" to the specific area in Canada he wishes to visit.").

22. Treaty of Amity, Commerce, and Navigation art. 3, Nov. 19, 1794, U.S.–Gr. Brit., 8 Stat. 116, 12 Bevans 13.

States ex rel Diabo v. McCandless"[23] in 1927.[24] With the passage of the Indian Citizenship Act of 1924,[25] Indians in the United States were made citizens of the United States,[26] and those in Canada who travelled and worked within the United States were rendered "aliens." . . . Citizenship criteria determined by the Act omitted Canadian forms of recognition that afforded rights to Indians in Canada. Nonetheless, because Iroquois on both sides of the border had histories of crossing the border[27] and knew that this passage was a right recognized by the Jay Treaty, they believed that they had a right to pass through the Canadian–U.S. border as indigenous nationals rather than as "aliens."

Diabo was, by all legal reports, one hundred percent Iroquois, indigenous, and not, therefore, an "alien,"[28] except, of course, under the terms of the Citizenship Act. . . . Diabo petitioned for a writ of habeas corpus on the ground that, as a member of a North American Indian tribe, he was exempt from immigration laws as guaranteed under Article III of the Jay Treaty. The United States District Court for the Eastern District concurred and held that the right to cross the border was in fact an aboriginal right, a right that was inherent—one recognized and confirmed (not created) by the treaty:[29]

[T]he rights of the Indians are [not] in any way affected by the treaty, whether now

existent or not. The reference to them was merely the recognition of their right, which was wholly unaffected by the treaty, except that the contracting parties agreed with each other that each would recognize it . . . *From the Indian view point, he crosses no boundary line. For him this does not exist.*[30]

The court's decision was confirmation throughout Iroquois country that Iroquois rights were legally recognized, affirmed, and active, in spite of the major setback that the Citizenship Act posed for the particular form of recognition that they desired—that of sovereign nations.

Both the Citizenship Act and the Johnson-Reed Immigration Act of 1924, which included exclusionist measures against both Native Americans and Asians . . . These laws, as well as band-council governance[31] were resisted in Iroquois communities on both sides of the border, since any form of foreign citizenship meant the dissolution of traditional governance and membership and the growing power of the settler state *within* Iroquois communities.

These resistances to, and struggles with, state forms were not limited to a few periods and places. . . .

The Indian Defense League of America (IDLA) was formed at Tuscarora in 1926 by Clinton Rickard specifically to address the cross-border rights of Iroquois peoples.[32]

---

23. 18 F.2d 282 (E.D. Pa. 1927).

24. *See* Gerald. F. Reid, *Illegal Alien? The Immigration Case of Mohawk Ironworker Paul K. Diabo,* 151) Proc. of the Am. Phil. SOC'Y 61–78 (2007) (offering a recent historical reconstruction of this event).

25. 8 U.S.C. § 1401 (1924).

26. For a discussion of the effects of this Act on the sovereignty of Native American nations in the United States and, in particular, for his discussion of the resistances against this Act by Iroquois and other peoples, see Robert Porter, *The Demise of the Ongwehonweh and the Rise of the Native Americans: Redressing the Genocidal Act of Forcing Citizenship Upon Indigenous Peoples,* 15 Harv. Blackletter L.J. 107–183 (1999).

27. *See* Beth LaDow, *The Medicine Line: Life and Death on North American Borderland* (2001) (detailing the history of the U.S.–Canadian border from the Gros-Ventre, Blackfoot, and Settler vantage points).

28. Diabo v. McCandless, 18 F.2d 282, 283 (E.D. Pa. 1927).

29. *Id.;* Sharon O'Brien, *The Medicine Line: A Border Dividing Tribal Sovereignty, Economies and Families,* 53 Fordham L. Rev. 315 (1984).

30. *Diabo,* 18 F.2d at 283 (emphasis added).

31. Band Councils are the administrative governments authorized by the government of Canada on Indian reserves to administer The Indian Act, "[a]n Act respecting Indians." The Indian Act is an overarching piece of legislation enacted by the Parliament of Canada in 1876 that recognizes certain indigenous peoples in Canada as "status" Indians who then have rights and provisions based on this recognition as legal wards of the state. Band Councils supplant indigenous forms of governance and have been vigorously contested for this. John Tobias argues that the Act was conceived to "protect, civilize and assimilate" Indians in Canada. It also laid the foundation for all further legislation regarding the lives of Indians which were in the cases of Western Indians and others, rejected. John Tobias, *Protection, Civilizaton and Assimilation, in* Sweet Promises: A Reader in Indian-White Relations 132–133 (J. R. Miller ed., 1991).

32. Jolene Rickard, The Indian Defense League of America 48 (1995).

The IDLA was inspired by the work of the Deskaheh[33] (Levi General) at Six Nations and embodied the effort to assert Iroquois sovereignty and to affirm Iroquois treaty rights. Deskaheh worked tirelessly to get Six Nations recognized as a member nation within the League of Nations. . . . When Deskaheh's struggle to gain international recognition failed, he made a radio address explaining the Iroquois position vis-à-vis land and sovereignty, exhorting Americans to "know their history" and argued for an understanding of citizenship as a colonizing technique. Of this he argued,

> Your governments have lately resorted to new practices in their Indian policies. In the old days, they often bribed our chiefs to sign treaties to get our lands. Now they know that our remaining territory can easily be gotten from us by first taking our political rights away in forcing us into your citizenship, so they give jobs in their Indian offices to the bright young people among us who will lake them and who, to earn their pay, say that your people wish to become citizens with you and that we are ready to have our tribal life destroyed and want your governments to do it. But that is not true.[34]

He died days later in the home of Clinton Rickard on the American side of the border on the Tuscarora Indian Reservation. The circumstances of his death were symbolic of his struggle and for the struggle of Iroquois peoples at the time: he died on the Tuscarora reservation, exhausted and sick from the struggle in Geneva and with the medicine being delivered to him from Six Nations unable make it across the border because of immigration restrictions.[35] His final words were to "fight for the line," meaning fight for the border and Iroquois people's right to cross.[36] . . .

VI. Borders of Blood

With the passage in 1934 of the Indian Reorganization Act, blood became a legal marker of Indian identity in the United States at the federal level[37] and the INS determined that the amount of Indian blood that Indians from Canada had to possess was fifty percent in order to gain passage into the United States.[38] . . .

The racialization of Indian identity in the United States correlates to the differing conceptions of Indian relationships to the state and to Indian citizenship through time. These were conceptions of recognition that moved Indian tribes away from the semisovereign status of "domestic and dependent nations" and into the conceptual and legal ambit of racialized minorities. Much like the East Indians who immigrated to Canada,[39] Indians in the United States and Canada appear completely outside of the frame of U.S. citizenship, from which the U.S. Constitution excluded them by virtue of their perceived incapacity for civilization and taxability.[40] However, unlike the East Indians in Canada, indigenous peoples within the United States were not geographically distant people, or foreign people who represented reprehensible or anxiety-provoking

---

33. "Deskaheh" is a hereditary chief of the Iroquois Confederacy. Levi General was a Cayuga from Six Nations who occupied the title of Deskaheh until his death.

34. Deskaheh, Levi General, *The Last Speech of Deskaheh, in* Basic Call TO CONSCIOUSNESS 48–54 (Akwesasne Notes, ed. 2005).

35. RICKARD, *supra* note 65, at 48.

36. *Id.* at 51.

37. The Indian Reorganization Act (Wheeler-Howard Act) was enacted in Congress on June 18, 1934. Section 19 defines "Indian" in three terms, the final term being related to blood quantum: "The term 'Indian' as used in this Act shall include all persons of Indian descent who are members of any recognized Indian tribe now under Federal jurisdiction, and all person[s] who are descendants of such members who were, on June 1, 1934, residing within the present boundaries of any reservation, and shall further include all other persons of one-half or more Indian blood."

38. 48 U.S.C. § 206 (1934).

39. For a greater treatment of this subject, see generally Radhika Vyas Mongia *Race, Nationality, Mobility: A History of the Passport,* 11 Pub. Culture 527, 527–556 (1999).

40. *See* Smith, *supra* note 78, at 133.

cultural differences to the American or Canadian legal eye; they were, from their earliest moments of interaction, recognized and indigenous sovereigns, not foreigners seeking to immigrate, nor citizens.

This initial exclusion, which was based on the semisovereign status, or "independent" status of Indians and the taxable standard of citizenship, was in contrast to the deliberate exclusion of African Americans and Asian Americans in that it was not yet based on racialized criteria.[41] However this non-racialized standard of difference and recognition for Indians would soon change.[42] . . .

This diminution began with the Dawes Severalty Act of 1887, which granted U.S. citizenship to Indians who rescinded their tribal membership and their aboriginal rights to land and who accepted the apportioning of their land into fee-simple plots.[43] . . .

Citizenship is, in this rendering, a political identity rather than a racial one, and, as such, Indians were citizens only in geographic "spots."[44] More racialized forms of recognition began in part

with *Mosier v. United States*,[45] which acknowledged blood to be the proper form of identification for Indians.[46] . . .

The American recognition of blood or quantifiable notions of race (or difference) was not completely consistent with Canadian forms of recognition, but was consistent with the racialization of identity that had long been occurring in the United States through the legacy of slavery and through the courts.

The landscape in Canada was, and still is, different than that in the United States; but in some respects, it is quite similar. Unlike the racialized interpretation of crossing in the United States, Canada would take an extreme culturalist position in interpreting the Jay Treaty.[47] When Akwesasne Grand Chief Mike Mitchell tested Jay Treaty going "the other way"—from the United States to Canada—to renew trade relations with the Mohawk reserve community of Tyendinaga, his rights to trade within Mohawk territory were not respected. In his trial, archaeological evidence

---

41. *Id.* at 135.

42. *Id.* at 136.

43. The Dawes Severalty Act of 1887 is much more complicated than the above sentence indicates. Converting from communal forms of ownership (or stewardship) to individual forms of property required much more than a shift in territorial boundaries. The Dawes Severalty Act served to consolidate State power through its expropriation of massive amounts of land and the apportioning of land, based on Western notions of private property, appropriate ownership, and land tenure. The Dawes Severalty Act also instituted an astonishing twenty-five-year wait for allottees to qualify for ownership while they were required to pay rent on their land. After that time, they finally owned their land, or "qualified," according to the civility standards of the local Indian agent, for the actual ownership of their land.

44. In the United States, there is no overarching form of policy regarding membership in an Indian tribe or nation, as in Canada. The process of determining membership occurs through the implementation of the Dawes Severalty Act, which first created membership lists for the allotment of land and did so according to the subjective tests of civility and, at times, the astonishing physical anthropology administered by Indian Agents or anthropologists, who allotted Indians land based on their reading of Native peoples' bodily characteristics. These characteristics—curly hair, big feet, straight hair, et cetera—were read as indexes of racial purity and thus, cultural purity. The purer a person was in indigenous culture, the more likely he was to be deemed less competent and less able to hold land in private ownership. David L. Beaulieu, *Curly Hair and Big Feet: Physical Anthropology and the Implementation of Land Allotment on the White Earth Chippewa Reservation*, 8 Am. Indian Quart. 281, 281–314 (1984).

45. 198 F. 54 (8th Cir. 1912).

46. *Id.* at 57.

47. This extreme culturalist position was laid out in Canadian law in 2001. Mitchell v. M.N.R., 1 S.C.R. 911 (2001). The legal strategy of Akwesasne had moved from a Treaty-rights argument to an aboriginal-rights argument. The Treaty-rights approach failed with *Francis v. The Queen*, S.C.C. (1956), which denied Jay Treaty rights to the Akwesasne Mohawk Lewis Francis, who was transporting consumer goods from the United States to Canada for his own use. The court denied Francis' Treaty rights, reasoning that Britain, not Canada, was a signatory to the Jay Treaty. In a 1988 test case, Mike Mitchell brought goods from the United States' side of the border into Canada, for delivery to the Mohawk community of Tyendinaga, northwest of Akwesasne. He was charged with violating the Customs Act by not paying a duty. The appellate court upheld his Jay Treaty rights. However, by the time the case got to the Supreme Court of Canada in 2001, the arguments were no longer about the Treaty, but about aboriginal rights to trade, generally, because Mitchell's act was framed as the exercise of his traditional and cultural right to trade within the territory belonging to Mohawks. This argument accorded with the definition of aboriginal rights laid out in the Constitution Act of Canada, which affirms "existing aboriginal treaty rights of Canada." The argument also fleshed with aboriginal rights as defined in *R. v. Van der Feet*, 2 S.C.R 507 (1996). There they are considered cultural rights, which are defined as such because they are tied to cultural practices that were in play prior to settler occupancy.

was used to deny the Mohawk claim to an aboriginal right to travel and to trade with other Mohawks and trade north of the St. Lawrence River. Based on the culture test laid out in *Van der Peet*, this trade north of the St. Lawrence was deemed *not* to be a significant part of Mohawk culture and thus not a right to be upheld by the Supreme Court of Canada:

> In *Mitchell*, . . . the Supreme Court insisted on the idea that, in order to found a right, a practice does not have to be absolutely unchanging over time: it is allowed to have changed so as to remain relevant to its time, but it must demonstrate a definite continuity. . . . In *Mitchell*, however, the border marked by the Saint-Lawrence River is absolute: while changes to the way trade is carried out are permitted, the Court explicitly refuses to apply the same dynamic reasoning with regard to the territory on which such trade takes place.[48]

These different interpretations regarding boundaries and territory are part of an interpretive process in Canada of using especially static and culturalist methodology to mete out recognition. Culture *is* allowed to change, but elements within in it must maintain the same value and meaning through time. The practice must remain evident to the juridical eye and to the expert eyes of archaeologists, historians, and anthropologists, and it must be evident through time. This expert juridical frame for recognizing rights to territory has real implications, as well, for the ways in which Indians born in Canada exercise their rights to cross back to Canada and to conduct more contemporary forms of trade. It is a constant form of contention between Iroquois and all settler regimes that they encounter.

VII. The Revenue Rule and State Sovereignty

. . . The visibility of Indian governmental bodies through the form or arrests and through the nationally televised documentaries of *Troubled Waters*, in 1993, and *The Dark Side of Native Sovereignty*, in 1996, served as spectacles. . . .

Although the revenue rule stated "that one sovereign will not enforce the tax judgments or claims of another sovereign,"[49] the problem was not cast in these terms because the problem, in the early and mid-1990s in Canada, became something else through the focus on Indians as the visible smugglers. The role of Big Tobacco was yet to be revealed and remained invisible, unnoticeable in the earliest public scrutiny of tobacco smuggling. Iroquois nationals and, in particular, Mohawks—and their sovereignty—were, by contrast, very visible. . . .

Perhaps because of an unawareness of the corporate defendants' position, the "smuggling problem" in an earlier iteration was conflated with indigenousness, and indigenousness with Mohawks. Mohawks were then equated with lawlessness, and lawlessness with indigenous sovereignty.

Indigenous sovereignty carried the residue of savagery. As Aristotle and others who have relied upon his reasoning have argued, savagery is a condition of beast-like association that is defined as being without law.[50] As the discussion and analysis of public texts on smuggling illustrated, it was Mohawk invocations of sovereignty and the *practice* of sovereignty through their exercising of the Jay Treaty right to cross that made their move toward "savagery" and "lawlessness" possible in the public mind. This representational chain of equivalencies and conflations reduced sovereignty to aboriginality and in this, to racialized and temporalized bodies and locales. These bodies were reduced to entities

---

48. Claude Denis, *Indigenous Citizenship and History in Canada: Between Denial and Imposition, in* Contesting Canadian Citizenship: Historical Readings 113, 123 (Robert Adamoski et al., eds. 2002).

49. Attorney Gen. of Canada v. R. J. Reynolds Tobacco Holdings, Inc., 268 F3d 103, 106 (2002) (overruled on other grounds).

50. *See*, e.g., Aristotle, Politics 11 (Ernest Baker trans., Oxford Univ. P. 1995) ("Man, when perfected, is the best of animals; but if he is isolated from law and justice he is the worst of all.").

that were legally confounding and spectacular; the entities became newsworthy in their failure to conform to economic norms and to consent to citizenry by conforming to taxation regimes.

To be taxed is to be a citizen;[51] to evade this is to be a savage, improper, or lawless citizen. The publicizing of this "lawlessness," as with the nationally televised documentaries discussed above, incited national anxieties and fiduciary norms around taxation that then took the shape of public concern. However, to be an indigenous person in Canada is also to occupy a different space for citizenship, one that from its inception "evades" taxation because of the legally defined status of "wardship" that recognized Indians occupy. This legal status has been called "citizens plus" in liberal policy,[52] a naming that sought to capture the perceived duality of their legal category: they were citizens of a "first nation" (the aboriginal one) and also citizens of the nation-state that now frames that first nation (the settler society). This policy did not take into account the way the category of "citizens plus" also signified to Indians an executive or settler fiat: the recognition, in Hegelian terms, was a one-sided recognition, a legal event ensconced in time and in law that signaled the descent of their ability to be recognized as Indians and the strangulation of their governmental systems. Indigenous governmental systems were not recognized; what was recognized was the differentiation of those systems according to criteria defined by first Britain, and then Canada. . . .

VIII. Implications of the Indigenous Smuggling Crisis

. . . In the context of one settler society—Canada—indigenous trade practice, predicated upon indigenous historical and legal experiences in territories the Canadians claim as their own, became "smuggling," and smuggling had to be contained immediately through representational practice, such as the media, but representational practice that mirrored the law. What the media images did was remove "sovereignty" from the domain of the currently conventional sovereign, from the boundaries of the nation-state in which the practice of smuggling presumably occurred, and conflated it with aboriginally, and with indigeneity, in the public eye. Thus, sovereignty appeared not to belong to the state, but to belong instead to those who worked within and through settler-state borders through criminalized trade. The sovereignty of the nation-state under which such trading practices occurred is never discussed explicitly, for to do so would reveal its fragility. Focusing upon indigenous trade practices, however, reveals that fragility; but these trade practices must be stripped of their historical place and criminalized, so as not to reveal the temporal dimension of conquest.

. . . If the law is not upheld and maintained, then chaos will, or might, ensue. So, order requires that the modalities and practices of indigenousness "trade" or "commerce" be conflated with "smuggling" and that Indian recognition be closely regulated so that the temporality and justness of their claims are adjudicated not by Indians, but by those who now occupy their space. Law is the primary means through which that process occurs and, in law, settler colonialism maintains itself.

Events leading up to *R. J. Reynolds* were sieved through media representations that fomented this anxiety and fear of uncontainment. The images of criminal "warriors" were set side by side with *contraband* cigarettes, cigarettes that were contraband because they eluded being taxed, they were not providing revenue for Canada, and, as such, they were themselves the synecdoche for unsettling settlement, the unbounding of the place of Canada, as Canada itself—a claim of property, of seizure through law and citizenship without consent. Indigenous trade and traffic in cigarettes thus agitated the foundation of nation-state formation as a form of property, the indigenous' actions, which the Iroquois argued were

---

51. Ensin F. Isin & Bryan S. Turner, *Investigating Citizenship: An Agenda For Citizenship Studies*, 11 Citizenship Studs. 5, 5 (2007).

52. This was first coined in the Hawthorn Report in Canada in 1966. A Survey of The Contemporary Indians of Canada: A Report on the Economic, Political, Educational Needs and policies 13 (H. B. Hawthorn, ed. 1966), *available at* http://www.aincinac.gc.ca/pr/pub/srvy/sci3_e.html (last visited May 29, 2008) ("Indians should be regarded as 'citizens plus;' in addition to the normal rights and duties of citizenship, Indians possess certain additional rights as charter members of the Canadian community.").

an exercise of *their sovereign* right to trade in their territories, questioned not only the claiming of a settler state, but of citizenship itself. The exercise of their own sovereignty then revealed the fragility of the sovereign status of the settler state, which had never achieved a proper or robust form of consent from the indigenous political subjects themselves, who refused to act as subjects and be contained, or to be taxed.

IX. Conclusion

The representational history of Indian "lawlessness" does not have its beginning with cigarette "smuggling" in the 1990s. Its genealogy extends back to the earliest moments of recorded encounter, when Indians appeared to have no law, to be without order, and thus, to be, in the colonizer's most generous articulation of differentiation, in need of the trappings of civilization. . . . Designating "savagery" was required for the forceful imposition of law, as was designating brutishness. So the law in Canada—and to a less-focused and less-encompassing extent, that in the United States—has attempted to define and regulate Indian behavior, to protect, and, in different iterations, to confine and contain the indigenous in certain spaces. The 1876 Canadian Indian Act, when compared to the 2,500 pieces of legislation that comprise the rubric of federal Indian law in the United States, is a uniform body of law that has sought to do all of the above. . . . *R. J. Reynolds* and related decisions revealed the ways in which law regarding Indians was a failed episode of consent, consent to a form of sovereignty that is clear and that unambiguously accords with territories of conquest. It also fails to regulate fears of lawlessness while uncovering the role that "indigenous savagery" has had in furthering settler capitalism. Finally, it diminishes indigenous rights to trade and to act as sovereigns in their own territories.

PART 4

Additional Readings

Bhatia, Amar. "Re-peopling in a Settler-Colonial Context: The Intersection of Indigenous Laws of Adoption with Canadian Immigration Law." AlterNative 14, no. 4 (2018): 343–353.

Dunbar-Ortiz, Roxanne. Not "A Nation of Immigrants" Settler Colonialism, White Supremacy, and a History of Erasure and Exclusion. Boston, MA: Beacon Press, 2021.

Rosas, Gilberto. *Barrio Libre: Criminalizing States and Delinquent Refusals of the New Frontier*. Durham, NC: Duke University Press, 2012.

Luna-Firebaugh, Eileen M. "The Border Crossed Us: Border Crossing Issues of the Indigenous Peoples of the Americas." *Wicazo Sa Review*. 17, no. 1 (2002): 159–181.

Maynard, Robyn. "Black Life and Death Across the U.S.-Canada Border: Border Violence, Black Fugitive Belonging, and a Turtle Island View of Black Liberation." *Journal of the Critical Ethnic Studies Association*. 5, nos. 1–2 (2019): 124–151.

Nickels, Bryan. "Native American Free Passage Rights under the 1794 Jay Treaty." *Boston College International and Comparative Law Review*. 24 (2001): 313–339.

Simpson, Audra. *Mohawk Interruptus: Political Life Across the Border of Settler States*. Durham, NC: Duke University Press, 2014.

Relevant Websites

Border Crossing Issues and the Jay Treaty
https://sencanada.ca/content/sen/committee/421/APPA/Reports/APPA-JayTreatyReport_e.pdf
The Standing Senate Committee on Aboriginal Peoples produced a report documenting the challenges faced
by First Nations with respect to Canada-US border crossings and recommended further inquiry by the federal
government to explore and address these complex issues of sovereignty, citizenship, and security.

Report on First Nation Border Crossing Issues
https://www.rcaanc-cirnac.gc.ca/eng/1506622719017/1609249944512
A 2017 report produced by the Ministers of Indigenous and Northern Affairs, Public Safety, and Immigration,
Citizenship and Refugees Canada documenting Canada-US border crossing challenges, impacts, and
potential solutions in response to the Standing Senate Committee on Aboriginal Peoples recommending
consultation with First Nations.

Jay's Treaty: Primary Documents in American History
https://guides.loc.gov/jays-treaty
The Treaty of Amity Commerce and Navigation signed between His Britannic Majesty and The United States
of America (Jay's Treaty) on 19 November 1794 is a primary source document maintained by the US Library of
Congress.

No One Is Illegal
http://www.nooneisillegal.org/
No One Is Illegal is a network of international activists committed to justice for migrants and refugees including undocumented facing persecution and/or deportation within nation-state based contexts of withholding
and/or imposing citizenship.

Films

Little Caughnawaga: To Brooklyn and Back. Dir. Reghan Tarbell, National Film Board of Canada, 2008.
You're on Indian Land. Dir. Mort Ransen, National Film Board of Canada, 1969.
The Border Crossed Us. Dir. Rachael J. Nez (Diné), Native Voices at the University of Washington, 2005.
The Wall/El Muro. Dir. Ramon and Rosalva Resendiz, Cat Herder Films, 2018.
The Creator's Game: The Quest for Gold and the Fight for Nationhood. Dir. Candace Maracle, VTape, 2011.

Key Terms

- Border Imperialism
- Citizenship
- Failed Consent
- Indian Defense League of America

- Refusal
- Settler Fragility
- Sovereignty

Discussion Questions

1. How are Canadian and US citizenship considered a "gift" of both nation-states and why?

2. How does referring to Canada and the US as a "nation of immigrants" misrepresent the
    history of Indigeneity, Settler colonialism, and the violence inherent in lands dispossession,
    labor exploitation, deportation, and slavery?

3. How has Canada and the US worked to control the movement of Black and migrant bodies through border imperialism, historically and still today? How do we explain the racialized exclusion of Black and migrant bodies? What might it mean to envision both belonging and immigration from an Indigenous perspective?

4. What is meant by the "right of free passage?" What role does the Jay Treaty play in the right of free passage and why? How is the sovereignty of Indigenous nations being impacted by the Canada-US border and what sorts of decolonizing solutions exist?

Activities

Read Audra Simpson's article "Subjects of Sovereignty" (Chapter 8) and organize a class discussion about Mort Ransen's film *You're on Indian Land.* According to Simpson, what is it that makes "savagery and lawlessness" possible in "the public mind" and how is this represented in the film? What does it mean to describe Canadian law as a "failed episode of consent" and how is this embodied in the "settler anxiety" depicted in the film?

Read "Deskeheh: An Iroquois Patriot's Fight for International Recognition" and "The Last Speech of Deskeheh." What is it that Deskeheh wished to convey to his audience and to whom was he speaking? Informed by your discussion and reading, write a letter and petition to the UN General Assembly about how and why the border contravenes Indigenous (Haudenosaunee) sovereignty.

Read the 1794 Jay Treaty (see relevant websites, this section) and organize a class discussion about Candace Maracle's 2011 film *The Creator's Game: The Quest for Gold and the Fight for Nationhood*. What does the film convey about Haudenosaunee sovereignty and the right of free passage? What sections of the Jay Treaty are most applicable to the film and why?

PART 5

Racialization, Colonialism, and Gender Binaries

Editor Introduction

On 5 May 2021, Athlosa Native Family Healing Services of London, Ontario held a virtual Sharing Circle in honour of the annual National Day of Awareness for the Missing and Murdered Indigenous Women and Girls in Turtle Island. One of us, Lina, participated in this event. Throughout the afternoon, many shared stories of pain, survival, and healing that either they directly or someone close to them had experienced due to **gendered violence** against Indigenous women. A recurring theme surfaced in these stories: while in precolonial times women held much power in their nations, eventually they became marginalized and oppressed in Canadian society and vulnerable to violence. Many participants believed that we must remember that gender inequity and gendered violence are not "traditional"; it is not who we are, and we need to bring back gendered balance in our communities. Part Five of our text examines how transformations of gendered experiences and relations intersect with Settler colonialism. We stress that it is everyone's responsibility—male, female, trans, and **Two-Spirit**—to challenge the **sexism** and **heteropatriarchy** that has invaded our personal and communal relations (Sunseri, 2011). As Cannon (2019) argues, we have all indeed, been "impacted by sexism—as Indians, and as men and women" (2019: 119).

Sunseri opens the discussion by examining how the Canadian state's colonial and assimilatory policies imposed systems of governance and notions of Indigeneity upon Indigenous peoples. These colonial constructs linked legal Indigenous identity with notions of blood quantum and reserve residency. Since 1850, the point at which the category of "Indian" was established in law, **Indian status** has received increasing attention by courts of law, policy makers, and politicians in Canada. Section 12 of the 1951 Act and Section 6 of the 1985 legislation made distinctions between male and female Indians in establishing the entitlement of persons to be registered as Indians, and through "the implementation of the reserve system made invidious distinctions between men and women" (Cannon, 2019: 112). Until December 2010, following the historic case of *McIvor v. Canada*, as well as the passing of the Gender Equity in Indian Registration Act, these sections treated the children of men and women who married non-Indians differently and unequally under the law. Indian status embodied a long history of discrimination aimed at Indigenous communities, especially Indigenous women (see Cannon, 2014; see also the *Hele v. Attorney General of Canada* decision in 2020 which ruled that unmarried women could not be enfranchised under the 1951 **Indian Act**). These, and all other colonial policies, as Sunseri in Chapter 9 states, "have had a gendered impact because Indigenous women's rights from the early colonial policies have been specifically and more negatively impacted."

Like participants at the virtual event agreed, and as Sunseri in Chapter 9 points out, Indigenous women in precolonial times participated equally in the economic, political, and cultural life of their nations, and no gender was considered superior to others. Moreover, Indigenous genders were more fluid, with no expectation for anyone to embody fixed characteristics of masculinity or femininity. Instead, all genders were self-determined and free to express their own sexuality without the double standards that were more commonly found in Western heterosexual societies of that time. Settler colonialism altered such fluidity and egalitarianism by stripping women of their traditional responsibilities and roles, by denying them legal Indian status if they married nonstatus males, and by constructing damaging stereotypes that made them vulnerable to gendered violence.

Indigenous children were taught Western gendered and heteronormative values in residential schools. Indigenous sexuality was treated as sinful. As we envision a future for Indigenous peoples to live outside of racist and colonial structures, a gender analysis must be at the core of such a journey. We need to restore and reclaim traditional ways of governing and being that were once empowering for all genders. However, because Western heteropatriarchy has left an impact on Indigenous relations, those of gender and sexuality included, we need to be less essentialist, divisive, and instead more open to critical dialogues about "traditional" narratives.

Pyle (Chapter 10, this volume) engages in this critique. She asks specifically, "what does it mean for something to be traditional? How are certain practices and ideas determined to be traditional?" She reminds us that traditions have always changed over time and that colonialism altered Indigenous understanding and treatment of gender and sexuality, thus impacting Two-Spirit people. There has been an increase in misogyny, homophobia, transphobia, and gendered violence in Indigenous communities following European contact. While it might be true that originally Indigenous nations valued women, we cannot ignore the current problems associated with sexism and heteropatriarchy. Pyle warns us that reclaiming traditional gender roles could "reproduce colonial heteropatriarchy and [affirm] essentialist so-called natural differences between men and women, and naturalizing and idealizing heterosexuality."

Both Indigenous womanhood and mothering were disempowered through colonialism. It is tempting therefore to want to reclaim Indigenous notions of womanhood and motherhood. But the link between women's biological characteristics and their social roles can be disempowering to those who cannot or choose not to give birth, or to those who do not identify with womanhood at all, or not exclusively. As Pyle suggests, we must therefore recognize the diversity of experiences and identification of gender and sexuality; otherwise we could end up perpetuating other forms of exclusion and oppression.

Restoring gender balance and complementarity in our nations should mean healing all peoples. It must mean embracing diverse and fluid expressions of gender and sexuality while rejecting heteropatriarchal constructs. Fortunately, we are seeing instances of such movements. A recent example includes the coming-out story of 14-year-old Rowennakon Doxtater from Kahnawake, located near Tiotiake (Montreal, Quebec). When Doxtater started to identify as male with the support of his family and community, a prefix was added to his name in the Mohawk language. Adding words in the language to reflect our contemporary context brings a sense of pride and relief for young people and families. Rowennakon and his family share that gender diversity was not stigmatized or considered a taboo in Indigenous traditions, and that we need to at once, and again, become accepting of all human beings, and to recognize the various gifts that each of us brings to the community (CBC News, 2021c).

Reconciling and overturning sexism, heteropatriarchy, and cismisogyny is everyone's responsibility: men, women, cis, trans, and Two-Spirit individuals. As Cannon (2019) suggests, heteropatriarchy is also an issue belonging to cisgendered men. We must remember that racism, sexism, and patriarchy were all used to dispossess Indigenous peoples as part of a colonial agenda. The reason we need to dismantle heteropatriarchy is because it is a system of colonial dominance and oppression that seeks to obliterate our very existence as Indigenous peoples (Cannon, 2019: 22). The Indian Act and other colonial policies made heterosexuality compulsory by requiring that Indian status be acquired through only male and female unions, and by slowly devaluing Indigenous women's autonomy and power (ibid.). Sexism and patriarchy affects Indigenous peoples collectively. Men too must therefore look at how colonialism might have given them power, however limited, over women. They must work alongside all other genders to reinstate both balanced and equitable relations.

CHAPTER 9

Intersections of Colonialism, Indigeneity, Gender, and Nationalism

Lina Sunseri

Canada 150 Celebration: Exactly What Are We Celebrating?

2017 marked the 150th anniversary of the Canadian Confederation. Both during the preparations for this social phenomenon and throughout 2017, Canadians were invited to join in the celebration of the "founding" of the nation and in the process to promote the vision of a multicultural, diverse, just society to the rest of the world. However, many Indigenous peoples . . . did not jump onto the celebratory bandwagon, and some publicly criticized the Canadian governments

for spending so much money on the commemorative events. Undoubtedly, for many settler Canadians the country has been a welcoming place that they are proud to call home, and for some it is a refuge from previous conflict zones. Hence for them, 2017 could be a year to celebrate. However, the reality for Indigenous peoples has been very different.

As Rachael Yacaaʔal George states, for "Indigenous peoples, this year marks 150-plus years of resistance against an ongoing colonial assault. It is a reminder of our strength, our resilience, and the vitality of our nations. It is a moment to recognize our resistance and resurgence, as well as the work that still needs to be done" (2017: 49). So perhaps there was room for some celebration for Indigenous peoples, but it was not directed toward the Canadian state but toward themselves for having survived centuries of settler colonialism.

Colonialist Instruments of Assimilation

The transformation from independent, striving Indigenous nations to colonized peoples in Canada began with the establishment of pieces of lands "reserved" for "Indians" through legislations such as the 1857 Act for the Gradual Civilization of the Indian Tribe and the 1859 Civilization and Enfranchisement Act. These acts allowed for increasing dispossession of Indigenous traditional territories, settlement of Indigenous nations into small areas, and the eventual control of Indigenous peoples by colonial administrators of the Canadian state, which heightened with the passing of the 1876 Indian Act (Sunseri, 2011).

The Indian Act "provided for the appropriation of Indigenous territories and the accumulation of capital . . . imposed an elected band council system of governance upon Indigenous nations . . . [which] represented an imposition to already established traditional governance" (Cannon & Sunseri, 2017: xiv–v). A major colonial instrument of the act was the institutionalization of the legal category of Indianness through imposition of an Indian status category constructed by the stale. Indeed, the Indian Act represents "the very first instance of racialized thinking and institutionalized racism in Canada" (ibid.: xv). While before colonialism each Indigenous nation had its own specific criteria of national belonging and identity (for example, Oneida and other nations of the Haudenosaunee followed a matrilineal line of descent to one of the three clans, and anyone could be adopted into a clan as long as the clan mother welcomed them), eventually the Indian Act imposed its own construction of Indian, which was patriarchal as well as racist. Only those registered as Indians in the Indian registry can live on reserves and have a fiduciary relationship with the Canadian state. Such definitions are not traditionally Indigenous but creations of the colonial state, which linked legal Indigenous identity with notions of blood quantum and a lifestyle associated with reserve residency (Sunseri,

2011). Although a series of amendments to the act have occurred through the decades, it is still in existence and a reminder, therefore, to Indigenous peoples that we still live in a colonized world (hence, the impossibility of celebrating Canada 150 for most of us, Indigenous and non-Indigenous).

Such colonial policies involving Indigenous identity are not foreign to Indigenous peoples outside of Canada. In Hawaii currently, there are "popular notions of cultural authenticity and biological differences through the use of blood quantum, notions that have been reinforced by the law" (Kauanui, 2008: 2). This policy, similar to Canada's Indian Act, is closely linked to racist and sexist assumptions and practices. "Racialization is the process by which racial meaning is ascribed—in this case to Kanaka Maoli through ideologies of blood quantum" that gives preference to patrilineal constructions of Indigeneity (ibid.: 3). It replaces Indigenous Hawaiian criteria of national belonging that were more fluid, inclusive, and less patriarchal with colonial ones that eventually "undercut indigenous Hawaiian epistemologies that define identity on the basis of one's kinship and genealogy . . . with destructive political consequences for indigenous peoples" (ibid.: 3). The consequences include lingering divisions within Indigenous communities about who is "an authentic Indian and internalization of patriarchal practices of belonging." Reducing the legal eligibility of status Indians ultimately serves the purpose of genocide, since "histories of genocide are made possible through rigid assertions of difference between real Indians' and Others" (Cannon & Sunseri, 2017: 19). Moreover, the consequences have had a gendered impact because Indigenous women right from the early colonial policies have been specifically and more negatively targeted. And even as recently as 2017, Indigenous people, and women in particular, are still experiencing legislative concepts of Indianness in Canada.

Gender and Colonialism at a Crossroad

It is important to note that, just as is the case with colonial experiences globally, gender identities and relations have never been identical across all Indigenous peoples worldwide, either pre or after contact with settler colonials. Hence, "[w]hile we can never claim to adequately represent the extremely nuanced diversity of Indigenous maternal [and other] experience, Indigenous peoples do share some values, epistemologies, and worldviews, including a belief in the centrality of strong powerful women" (Lavell-Harvard & Anderson, 2014: 2).

Indigenous Gender Relations Prior to Settler Colonialism

In North America, Indigenous gender relations were quite egalitarian, and women were valued for their roles as life-givers, carriers of culture, and participants in the economy and other activities in their nations (Anderson & Lawrence, 2003; Cannon & Sunseri, 2017; Lavell-Harvard & Anderson, 2014; Sunseri, 2011; Valaskakis, Stout, & Guimond, 2009). "Referencing the teachings of the Dakota nation, Anderson has explained that according to our traditions Indigenous women not only literally 'birth the people' they are also given a 'lifetime responsibility to nurture the people'" (Lavell-Harvard & Anderson, 2014: 3). Haudenosaunee societies have also been reported as having a gendered power balance whereby all sexes worked together and shared responsibilities in all spheres of their nations, with no sex seen as superior to the others (Sunseri, 2011). Women held important leadership roles: they sat in separate women's councils in the confederacy, Clan Mothers appointed—and could remove—hereditary male chiefs, they held jurisdiction over adoption rules and declaration of wars, and they held the land communally by following their matrilineal and matrilocal rules (ibid.). Moreover, Indigenous nations of North America treated gender roles as complementary but not dichotomous (Tsosie. 2010: 32). "For example, in the Southwest [of the US], men and women have complementary roles in planting, growing, harvesting, and preparing corn . . . it would be inappropriate to say that one gender has primary responsibility for growing corn. It is an obligation of both genders, but it manifests in distinct duties and responsibilities" (ibid.). Indeed, for the well-being of their nation. Indigenous gender identities were fluid, and all individuals were self-determined in their own sexuality (Sunseri, 2011).

Outside of North America, we can see similar patterns. For example, Kanaka Hawaiians "had a range of models of gender and sexual diversity. . . . Both men and women were autonomous in all conjugal relations . . . bisexuality was normative and . . . polygamy and polyandry also were not uncommon. . . . High-ranking Hawaiian women and men held governing positions as paramount chiefs and lesser chiefs before the formation of the monarchy in the early nineteenth century" (Kauanui, 2017: 49). Sami women, together with men, lived off traditional economies and "made use of own expertise within the Sami landscape" (Eikjok, 2007: 108). Women had responsibility for agriculture, were producers of food and clothing, and held ownership over the reindeer industry (ibid.).

However, settler colonialism had a major negative impact on gender relations in Indigenous territories globally. Eventually, the imposition of patriarchal notions of gender and sexist discriminatory laws devalued Indigenous women, and gender equity diminished. In its place we begin to see gender inequality and an attack on Indigenous women's lives, with its legacies still felt in today's world.

Gendered Impacts of Settler Colonialism

Indigenous feminist scholars (Green, 2007; 2017; Suzack, Huhndorf, Perreault, & Barman, 2010) have recently increased awareness of the interconnections between colonialism and gender discrimination and inequality that have affected Indigenous peoples. Their analyses have highlighted how "colonialism affects both Indigenous men and women, but not identically" (Green, 2017: 5). The ongoing consequences of setter colonialism for Indigenous women have included racist and sexist laws that have robbed them of rights to their territories and entitlements to legal Indian status in Canada; inability to practise Indigenous self-determination in children and family relations; poor economic and social conditions; decrease in their leadership roles; and high risk to many forms of violence. As the following section shows, "there is no doubt that colonialism was shaped by patriarchy and racism and that Indigenous peoples were subjected to the consequent normative assumptions and structural processes" (ibid.).

Not surprisingly, settler colonial institutions such as schools and churches played a pivotal role in "producing and reproducing ideologies about what it means to be a man or a woman or a family" (St Denis, 2017: 51), and such meanings exclude Indigenous notions and practices. While prior to settler colonialism, most Indigenous societies valued women, their conditions were drastically altered (Sunseri, 2011). The changes occurred shortly after early contact with Europeans, who judged the Indigenous women they encountered against their own preconceived "cult of true womanhood" (ibid.: 89). Their ideal saw women confined within restrictive domestic spheres, subordinate to their patriarchs, and forced to accept double standards of sexuality. "This Victorian ideal of womanhood was seen as proof of civilization, whereby European women had been liberated of their burden of hard public labour and could now reserve their labour for a docile, feminine role" (ibid.; see also Olsen Harper, 2009; Stevenson, 1999; Wesley-Esquimaux, 2009).

Since Indigenous societies were structured upon gender egalitarianism and women, especially in matrilineal/matrilocal nations, were autonomous leaders, they were seen as a threat to the patriarchal order of the colonizing structures (Lavell-Harvard & Anderson, 2014). Consequently, colonizers set out to "denigrate, disempower, and dehumanize [them], thereby serving a racist and sexist colonial agenda" (ibid.: 4). A locus of such disempowerment lay in Indigenous familial and communal relations, and laws such as the Indian Act and residential schools indeed targeted these Indigenous traditional practices.

The Indian Act, although its most oppressive sections have been removed, has been the main instrument of colonialism in Canada because its main goal from its inception has been to assimilate all Indians into mainstream Canadian society, thus getting "rid of the Indian problem." A major way it has attempted to accomplish this is by establishing "a narrow definition of 'Indian' . . . the fewer Indians that Canada recognizes, the less land must be allocated as reserves, the more people who are excluded from bands, the more quickly the government-recognized Indian population shrinks. The faster bands shrink and ultimately disappear, the more quickly the land may be taken by Canada" (Eberts, 2017: 79).

The definition of Indian has historically been a patrilineal one: "an Indian was any male person of Indian blood, or any child of such a person, or any woman married to such a male person. In 1951 . . . it terminated the Indian status of Indian women who married non-Indian men and prevented these women from passing Indian status to their children" (Sunseri, 2011: 90). Patriarchal definitions of Indigeneity were also imposed in other settler colonies like Hawaii (Kauanui, 2008). Such sexist laws removed Indigenous women of their ability to equally pass on their legal Indigenous status to their offspring and to fully participate in the daily social and political activities in their communities. This was quite a change from the autonomy and leadership roles they had held in their nations, especially for Indigenous women of traditionally matrilineal societies like the Haudenosaunee. Indeed, as Eberts argues, "this places Indian women at a great legal disadvantage" (2017: 79).

In 1985, after Indigenous women fought the Canadian state both nationally and internationally through recourse to the United Nations, Canada passed Bill C-31, through which "women who had lost status when they married non-Indians were eligible to apply to acquire status under section 6(1) (c)" (ibid.). However, Bill C-31 ended the one-parent rule for determining status, requiring in its place that now "those with section 6(2) status would have to parent with a registered Indian in order to be able to confer status on their children. . . . And that is a new host of inequality among Indians brought about by the vexed provisions of the Indian Act" (ibid.: 87). More recently, the *McIvor v. Canada* legal judgment "restores federal recognition to the grandchildren of Indian women who were involuntarily enfranchised (i.e., legally assimilated) because of sexism and Indianness" (Cannon & Sunseri, 2017: 62). However, the Canadian courts did not recognize the racialization embedded in its ongoing definition of Indian status, hence they have not addressed the racialized injustice that they have continued to apply to Indigenous peoples (ibid.). As well, not all of the sexist implications have been removed from the Indian Act Aside from the issues arising from the status criteria, the Indian Act imposed new forms of governance in the established reserves, modelled after the European electoral system, and until the

Ongoing Sexist Discrimination in the Indian Act

In November 2017, the Canadian Senate passed an amendment to Bill S-3 to address a Quebec Court judge's ruling that had asked the federal government to make changes to the Indian Act to restore status to all women and their descendants who had lost it after marrying someone not registered as Indian. However, as Dr Lynn Gehl and other activists have argued, this new bill falls short of eliminating all the existing sexist discrimination. The bill restores status to those who "married-out" post-1951, but those of pre-1951 will have to wait. As it stands, the federal government is promising that it will consult with First Nations groups to address the remaining gap and will report on that process to the Parliament within three months, a year, and then three years after the passing of the bill. But as critics have pointed out, there is nothing forcing the government to actually eliminate all the sexist discrimination. As Pam Palmater, an Indigenous scholar, has pointed out, "a promise for future equality doesn't reach the Charter guarantee of equality" (*Winnipeg Free Press*, 2017).

mid-1960s, women could not participate in the elections or hold office, nor could they own property. This should lead us to question exactly what kind of progress, what kind of liberation, did modern civilization projects like settler-colonial nation-statehoods bring to Indigenous women!

Transformations in gender relations were also made possible through the residential schools in Canada and in similar educational systems in other settler colonial places like New Zealand (Lavell-Harvard & Anderson, 2014) and Hawaii (Kauanui, 2017). In these schools, Indigenous girls and boys learned new gender norms that reinforced patriarchal and heteronormative ideals. As well, they were taught to view their Indigenous sexuality as sinful and Indigenous parenting practices as uncivilized and inferior to those of European families. Together with residential schools, the child welfare system in Canada also attacked traditional family structures by removing children from what they viewed "dysfunctional" homes. Most often, children were apprehended by the state either because their families broke away from Euro-Canadian nuclear family, middle-class values, or because families could not properly meet their needs because of social inequities resulting from centuries of settler-colonialism (Cannon & Sunseri, 2017). "Breakdowns of traditional Aboriginal kinship and family structures are attributed to these experiences and they impact parenting across generations, disrupting traditional systems of social support" (Baskin & McPherson.

2014: 113). What were once sovereign families structured around gender equity were broken spiritually, psychologically, and emotionally. Sexism and patriarchy slowly penetrated Indigenous communities, and the lingering traumatic effects are still evident today, as the Truth and Reconciliation Commission of Canada reported (TRC, 2015). Current social ills affecting Indigenous women must be examined through a critical analysis of the damage settler colonialism continues to cause, and one evidence is the tragic loss of Indigenous women's lives through gendered violence.

Gendered Colonial Violence against Indigenous Women

To better grasp the height of the issue of violence against Indigenous women, we can begin with the reported numbers across different regions of the world: in Canada, an RCMP report documented more than 1000 missing or murdered Indigenous women and girls (MMIVVG) in Canada between 1980 and 2012 (Lavell-Harvard & Brant, 2016). In the US, "one in three Native American women have been raped or experienced attempted rape, and the rate of sexual assault on Native American women is more than twice the national average" (Dunbar-Ortiz, 2014: 214). In Guatemala, Mayan Ixil women "were often raped during the civil war as part of the systematic and intentional plan to destroy the social fabric and thereby ensure the destruction of the Ixil population" (Jayakumar, 2014: 132). While the violence experienced by Indigenous women is similar in some ways to that of other women because of their shared gender variable, it is quite different, since it has been shaped by its link to colonial violence.

To begin with, as Amnesty International reported in 2010, Indigenous women of Canada are at least 3.5 times more likely to experience violence than non-Indigenous women. Moreover, their homicides are disproportionally unresolved or not taken seriously by police and other justice systems (Cannon & Sunseri, 2017: 79). Indigenous scholars and activists have repeatedly argued that violence against Indigenous women is connected to colonial policies, laws, attitudes, and stereotypes of Indigenous peoples in general but particularly affect women. This colonial history has placed Indigenous women's lives at very high risk of many forms of violence, including sexual exploitation, assault, and murder (Bourgeois, 2017; Cannon & Sunseri, 2017; Eberts, 2017; Olsen Harper, 2009).

Indigenous women's lives remain at risk today. For example, a study conducted in the US revealed that "from the early mid 1960s up to 1976, between 3,400 and 70,000 Native women were coercively, forcibly, or unwittingly sterilized permanently by tubal ligation or hysterectomy" (Ralstin-Lewis, 2005: 71). These state-sponsored procedures led to a decrease in the birthrate of Indigenous women so must be considered a program to reduce the Indigenous population, a genocidal practice. Indigenous women in the United States who were coerced and/or forced into these medical procedures were often very poor and dependent on the state and health care professionals, therefore vulnerable. Moreover, they most likely lacked the medical and legal knowledge needed to make an informed decision about their reproductive rights. Lastly, "because all titles to land in the United States must, at some point, follow a path from the original inhabitants of the country to the United States government, the property can only be owned after the aboriginal title can be extinguished" (ibid.: 83). Reducing the Indigenous population through forced sterilization cleared the path to such extinguishment of Indigenous lands and natural resources, therefore indicating the genocidal implication of such medical procedures.

The violation of Indigenous women's reproductive rights has also occurred in Latin American countries like Peru, where more than 200,000 women were sterilized between 1996 and 2000 (Cavallo, 2016). Health care providers in Canada have also performed such unjust procedures, as reported by Dr Boyer and Dr Bartlett in 2017 (Hamilton & Quenneville, 2017). Using anecdotal evidence, the report stated that "women felt pressured and harassed to sign consent forms while under the trying conditions of labour" (ibid.). The report made recommendations to prevent future violations, and these included: creating an advisory council that would include Indigenous elders and community members, hiring Indigenous workers, and setting up a support group. Additionally, a United Nations committee has recently recommended that Canada criminalize any further involuntary sterilizations of Indigenous women, a move applauded by the Assembly of First Nations of Canada (Smoke, 2018).

Even the singular variable of Indigeneity has put Indigenous women at risk of violence, since racist and sexist portrayals of Indigenous women as promiscuous, easy, wild, associated with the label of "squaw," which emanated from early accounts by European traders and missionaries, still affect the minds of many in Canada. In turn, these stereotypes influence their behaviour against Indigenous women, at times leading to violence (Cannon & Sunseri, 2017: 79). As well, the Canadian state itself has been complicit in this violence (Bourgeois, 2017; Eberts, 2017). As Bourgeois argues, "the political consolidation of the Canadian State in 1867 marks the starting point of an aggressive multipronged colonial war waged by the Canadian State against Indigenous women and girls" (2017: 261). For example, colonial rules of status registration in the Indian Act discriminated against Indigenous women and their children, often pushing them outside of their communities and into urban settings. Once in the cities, racism and poor socioeconomic conditions have made them vulnerable to sexual exploitation and violence (ibid.).

This vulnerability has been compounded by the multigenerational impacts of residential schools and the child welfare systems (ibid.). We must identity "the violence and intergenerational trauma caused by the Indian residential school system as an underlying factor of the violence against MMIWG" (ibid.: 263). As a matter of fact, many of the missing and murdered Indigenous women and girls in Canada have had a history either with the residential school system or the child welfare agencies (ibid.). Hence, the state has been partly guilty in the ongoing violence inflicted upon Indigenous peoples, and women in particular. Its justice apparatus has also been complicit in this because it has failed to adequately protect Indigenous women and girls. When Amnesty International reported the alarming cases of missing and murdered Indigenous women and girls in Canada, it pointed out how the police and the courts had not taken the issue seriously. With the support of the media, often more attention was given to "the high risk lifestyle" of the victims rather than to the crime itself (Olsen Harper, 2009; Bourgeois, 2017; Cannon & Sunseri, 2017). "Canada (injustice system has long used prostitution as justification for minimizing the violence perpetrated against Indigenous women and girls and for exonerating perpetrators" (Bourgeois, 2017: 265).

It was not until 2015 that the Canadian federal government, after decades of outcry and activism by Indigenous groups and allies, initiated the Missing and Murdered Indigenous Women and Girls Inquiry to examine both the roots and consequences of violence against Indigenous women and girls and the steps needed to stop it. The inquiry needs to critically look at the role of the colonial state, the influence of racist and sexist attitudes and policies on violent behaviours, and the complicit roles of the media and the justice system in order to fully comprehend the causes of the violence. In addition, it needs to be transparent, be trauma and culturally competent, be accessible to Indigenous communities, and have good long-term support systems for both the survivors and their families as well as the staff of the inquiry, and as much as possible it should be staffed by Indigenous women and men. Ultimately, the results of the inquiry should constitute initial steps toward healing and recovery and actions toward a more equitable relationship between Indigenous peoples and settler nation-states and their residents.[1] . . .

References

Anderson, Kim, & Lawrence, Bonita (eds.). (2003). *Strong women stories: Native vision and community survival.* Toronto: Sumach Press.

Baskin, Cyndy, & McPherson, Bela. (2014). Towards the wellbeing of Aboriginal mothers and their families: You can't mandate time. In D. Memee Lavell-Harvard & Kim Anderson (eds.), *Mothers of the initions: Indigenous mothering as global resistance, reclaiming and recovery* (pp. 109–30). Bradford, ON: Demeter Press.

Bourgeois, Robyn. (2017). Perpetual state of violence: An Indigenous feminist antioppression inquiry into missing and murdered Indigenous women and girls. In Joyce Green (ed.), *Making space for Indigenous feminism* (2nd edn., pp. 253–73). Halifax, NS: Fernwood Publishing.

Cannon, Martin J., & Sunseri, Lina (eds.). (2017). *Racism, colonialism, and Indigeneity in Canada: A reader.* Don Mills, ON: Oxford University Press.

Cavallo, Shena. (2016). Peru fails to deliver for Indigenous women. *Open Democracy.* Available at https://opendemocracy.net/democraciaabierta/shena-cavallo/peru-fails-to-deliver.

Dunbar-Ortiz, Roxanne. (2014). *An Indigenous peoples history of the United States.* Boston: Beacon Press.

Eberts, Mary. (2017). Being an Indigenous woman is a "high-risk lifestyle." In Joyce Green (ed.), *Making space for Indigenous feminism* (2nd edn., pp. 69–102). Halifax, NS: Fernwood Publishing.

Eikjok, Jorunn. (2007). Gender, essentialism and feminism in Samiland. In Joyce Green (ed.), *Making space for Indigenous feminism* (pp. 108–23). Black Point, NS: Fernwood Publishing.

George, Rachael Yacaa?al. (2017). Inclusion is just the Canadian word for assimilation: Self-determination and the reconciliation paradigm in Canada. In Kiera L. Ladner & Myra J. Tait (eds.), *Surviving Canada: Indigenous peoples celebrate 150 years of betrayal* (pp. 49–62). Winnipeg, MB: ARP Books.

Green, Joyce (ed.). (2007). *Making space for Indigenous feminism.* Black Point, NS: Fernwood Publishing.

---

1. On 3 June 2019, after this chapter was written, the final report of the Missing and Murdered Indigenous Women and Girls Inquiry was released. The report included 231 Calls for Justice and characterized the violence against Indigenous women and girls as "genocide." The report can be found at www.mmiwg-ffada.ca/final-report.

Green, Joyce (ed.). (2017) *Making space for Indigenous feminism* (2nd edn.). Halifax, NS, and Winnipeg, MB: Fernwood Publishing.

Hamilton, Charles, and Quenneville, Guy. (2017). Report on coerced sterilization of Indigenous women spurs apology, but path forward unclear. *CBC News.* Available at https://www.cbc.ca/news/canada/saskatoon/report-indigenous-women-coerced-tubal-ligations-1.4224286.

Jayakumar, Kirthi. (2014). The impact of sexual violence on Indigenous motherhood in Guatemala. In D. Memee Lavell Harvard & Kim Anderson (eds.), *Mothers of the nations: Indigenous mothering as global resistance, reclaiming and recovery* (pp. 131–46). Bradford, ON: Demeter Press.

Kauanui, Kēhaulani J. (2008). *Hawaiian blood: Colonialism and the politics of sovereignty and Indigeneity.* Durham, NC: Duke University Press.

Kauanui, Kēhaulani J. (2017). Indigenous Hawaiian sexuality and the politics of nationalist decolonization. In Joanne Barker (ed.), *Critically sovereign: Indigenous gender, sexuality and feminist studies* (pp. 45–68). Durham, NC: Duke University Press.

Lavell-Harvard, Memee, D., & Anderson, Kim (eds.). (2014). *Mothers of the nations: Indigenous mothering as global resistance, reclaiming and recovery.* Bradford, ON: Demeter Press.

Lavell-Harvard, Memee, D., & Brant, Jennifer (Eds.). (2016). *Forever loved: Exposing the hidden crisis of missing and murdered Indigenous women and girls in Canada.* Bradford, ON: Demeter Press.

Olsen Harper, Anita. (2009). Sisters in spirit. In Gail Guthrie Valaskakis, Madeleine Dion Stout, & Eric Guimond (eds.), *Restoring the balance: First Nations women, community, and culture* (pp. 175–200). Winnipeg, MB: University of Manitoba Press.

Pasternak, Shiri. (2014). Occupy(ed) Canada: The political economy of Indigenous dispossession. In The Kinonda-niimi Collective (eds.), *The winter ire danced: Voices from the past, the future, and the Idle No More Movement* (pp. 40–44). Winnipeg, MB: ARP Books.

Ralstin-Lewis, Marie. (2005). The continuing struggle against Indigenous women's reproductive rights. *Wicazo Sa Review,* 20(1), 71–95.

Smoke, Penny. (2018). UN committee recommends Canada criminalize involuntary sterilization.

CBC News. Available at https://www.cbc.ca/news/uncommittee-involuntary-sterilization-1.4936879.

St Denis, Verna. (2017). Feminism is for everybody: Aboriginal women, feminism and diversity. In Joyce Green (ed.), *Making space for Indigenous feminism* (2nd edn., pp. 42–62). Halifax, NS: Fernwood Publishing.

Stevenson, Winona. (1999). Colonialism and First Nations women in Canada. In Enakshi Dua & Angela Robertson (eds.), *Scratching the surface: Canadian antiracist feminist thought* (pp. 49–80). Toronto, ON: Women's Press.

Sunseri, Lina. (2011). *Being again of one mind: Oneida women and the struggle for decolonization.* Vancouver, BC: University of British Columbia Press.

Suzack, Cheryl, Huhndorf, Shari M., Perreault, Jeanne, & Barman, Jean (eds.). (2010). *Indigenous women and feminism: Politics, activism, culture.* Vancouver: University of British Columbia Press.

Teves, Stephanie Nohelani, Smith, Andrea, & Raheja, Michelle H. (2015). *Native studies keywords.* Tucson, AZ: University of Arizona Press.

Truth and Reconciliation Commission of Canada. (2015). *Honouring the truth, reconciling for the future: Summary of the final report of the Truth and Reconciliation Commission of Canada.* Ottawa: Government of Canada.

Tsosie, Rebecca. (2010). Native women and leadership: An ethics of culture and relationship. In Cheryl Suzack, Shari M. Huhndorf, Jeanne Perreault, & Jean Barman (eds.), *Indigenous women and feminism: Politics, activism, culture* (pp. 29–12). Vancouver: University of British Columbia Press.

Valaskakis, Gail Guthrie, Stout, Madeleine Dion, & Guimond, Eric (eds.). (2009). *Restoring the balance: First Nations women, community, and culture.* Winnipeg, MB: University of Manitoba Press.

Wesley-Esquimaux, Cynthia C. (2009). Trauma to resilience: Notes on decolonization. In Gail Guthrie Valaskakis, Madeleine Dion Stout. & Eric Guimond (eds.), *Restoring the balance: First Nations women, community, and culture* (pp: 13–34). Winnipeg, MB: University of Manitoba Press.

Winnipeg Free Press. (2017). Accessed at https://www.winnipegfreepress.com/local/contentious-bill-on-indian-status-backcd-by-senate-heads-to-house-456559293.html.

CHAPTER 10

Reclaiming Traditional Gender Roles

A Two-Spirit Critique

Kai Pyle

. . . My lived experiences as a Métis/Anishinaabe Two-Spirit person, combined with my readings of scholars in Native feminism and queer Indigenous studies, cause me to question the ways that heteropatriarchy is often present even when we attempt to decolonize our attitudes toward gender and sexuality.[2] Calls for a return to traditional gender roles are deeply intertwined with concern about Indigenous authenticity: What are the truest or purest forms of Indigenous gender roles? What kinds of gender roles were present before colonization? Likewise, such calls raise questions about the nature of tradition: What does it mean for something to be traditional? How are certain practices and ideas determined to be traditional? Is being traditional reason enough for us to follow certain paths? If not, how do we determine what is the best pathway into the future? Though the demand for authenticity is a powerful spectre for Indigenous peoples, decolonization means recognizing that change has always been a part of our traditions, and that we are in control of our own cultures. . . .

Heteropatriarchy and "Traditional Gender Roles"

Indigenous feminists and other women of colour writers have amply dissected how modern gender is shaped by and used as a tool of colonization.[3] One of the goals of colonizing Indigenous peoples has always been to eliminate Indigenous understandings of gender, and in particular to subjugate Indigenous women and Two-Spirit people, whether through outright destruction or through assimilation. Nineteenth- and twentieth-century Indian boarding schools in the United States and residential schools in Canada were primary locations for indoctrinating Indigenous peoples into colonial roles. From the moment they arrived, Native children were separated into groups of boys and girls and marched off to be forcibly outfitted with clothing and hair made to fit white standards.[4] Today the assimilative project continues through institutions like schools, foster care, welfare, and health care, as well as in the form of the ever-present white-dominated media that saturates our daily lives. The results of this project

---

Kai Pyle, "Reclaiming Traditional Gender Roles: A Two-Spirit Critique." In Sarah Nickel and Amanda Fehr, eds., *In Good Relation: History, Gender, and Kinship in Indigenous Feminisms*, Winnipeg: University of Manitoba Press, © 2020.

---

2. Some of the readings that have been particularly influential in my thinking include Arvin, Tuck, and Morrill, "Decolonizing Feminism"; Driskill, "Doubleweaving Two-Spirit Critiques"; and the many contributors to Green, *Making Space for Native Feminism*, 1st ed.

3. For an overview of the Indigenous feminist project, see Arvin, Tuck, and Morrill, "Decolonizing Feminism," 9.

4. Hunt, "Embodying Self-Determination," 106.

are visible in the legacy of misogyny, homophobia, transphobia, domestic violence, sexual assault, and other forms of abuse in Indigenous communities today.

In response to this assault on Indigenous peoples and ways of life, one approach to redressing gendered violence in Indigenous communities has been a call to return to "traditional gender roles." M. Annette Jaimes and Theresa Halsey cite Native women such as Laura Waterman Wittstock, Beverly Hungry Wolf, and Clara Sue Kidwell, who argue that "recovery of traditional forms [of gender roles] is more than ever called for."[5] . . . Over time, certain tropes based in these rediscoveries have become near standard understandings in Pan-Indian circles.[6] Politically savvy Native politicians drop references to how they honour and respect "our" women, or to how their men are warriors in the fight for sovereignty. Even scholars such as Paula Gunn Allen have argued that all Indigenous peoples were originally matriarchal, which Elders from various communities I have spent time in dispute.[7] I have heard Anishinaabe people claim that our ancestors were matrilineal, for example, when Elders have repeatedly told me that we have always passed down our clans through the male line. These claims point to a climate in which Indigenous people consider it desirable to reclaim some kind of "traditional" gender roles, where "traditional" generally signifies "before European contact."

While it is admirable that people are concerned with addressing gendered colonization, we must take care to question where these tropes come from and what purposes they serve. Though many may claim that their people have always held women in high regard, Indigenous women themselves have pointed out repeatedly that misogyny and sexism are deep-rooted problems within Native communities. The logic of claiming "high regard" for women while ignoring the present reality of these problems can lead to silencing Native women. Dine scholar Jennifer Nez Denetdale writes about how Dine women have been kept out of leadership positions in tribal government on the basis that "traditional" women's roles, though "highly regarded," do not include such positions.[8] Images of male warriorhood in the American Indian Movement contributed to men keeping women off the frontlines and discounting the role they played behind the scenes in furthering the movement's achievements. . . .

The real problem with many of the gender-roles presented as traditional today, particularly in Pan-Indian circles, is that they reproduce colonial heteropatriarchy under a thin Indigenous veneer. Heteropatriarchy purports to establish a biological root of gender, claiming empirical differences between men and women that determine their aptitudes, inclinations, and abilities. At the same time, it places these qualities in a hierarchy in which men are superior to women and deserve control over women. The demands of heteropatriarchy regulate behaviour according to these gendered prescriptions. Among these prescriptions, sexuality is a very prominent concern, and heteropatriarchy mandates a particular heterosexuality (always within patriarchal frameworks, so that the man is in the leading, controlling position) that nobody is capable of living up to in practice. And while heteropatriarchy exists as an ideal enforced by individuals and infrastructures, its ideology simultaneously insists that it is a natural thing arising simply from "the way things are," and that those who do not fulfill its requirements are deviants.[9]

---

5. Jaimes and Halsey, "American Indian Women,"334.

6. I use the term "Pan-Indian" throughout this chapter to refer to the communities, both physical and ideological, that diverse Indigenous peoples have created together based in a group identity as "Indian." While urban Indigenous communities often have developed Pan-Indian identities and practices due to the diversity of people in a small area, Pan-Indian ideas are also present within most tribal communities to some extent as a result of communication and interaction between them since the late 1800s and even before. While many Pan-Indian ideas and practices have their roots in the histories of specific Indigenous groups, things like powwows, the medicine wheel, and the concept of Turtle Island (to give a few examples) have become dispersed throughout Indigenous communities in North America to the extent that their roots have sometimes been forgotten.

7. Allen, The Sacred Hoop, 2.

8. Denetdale, "Chairmen, Presidents, and Princesses."

9. Arvin, Tuck, and Morrill, "Decolonizing Feminism," 13.

Heteropatriarchy is intimately tied up in the colonial project. The settler-colonial nation-state requires compliance with heteropatriarchy in order to continue its colonizing project. Settler men become leaders of the family and the nation who subdue the "wilderness" (and the Indigenous) through force, while settler women participate by colonizing through domestication of the newly conquered spaces. Settler children, the products of "proper" heterosexual relations, are icons of the nation-state's future, and often serve as symbols whose protection demands further colonization through calls to "protect our children's futures." Additionally, a key part of the colonization of Indigenous people through assimilation has involved forcing them to conform to heteropatriarchal ideology. . . .

Because of our history of colonization and assimilation, Indigenous people have also internalized heteropatriarchal ideas, and these ideas are sometimes even invoked for a purpose similar to the settler state's invocation: to protect and strengthen the (in this case, Indigenous) nation. Same-sex marriage bans in the Cherokee and Navajo nations were passed through appeals to tribal sovereignty arguing that "homosexual activists" aimed to destabilize their nationhood.[10] In support of the ban, many invoked a "tradition" of heterosexuality. . . . Joanne Barker writes that both the Cherokee and Navajo passed their bans "in the name of Christian patriotism," yet at the same time she cautions against asserting any sort of binary between assimilated Christians and unassimilated traditionals.[11]

In fact, heteropatriarchy *can be* found in even the most non-Christian Indigenous communities. At one Anishinaabe ceremonial event I attended, for example, the teachings given by both male and female Elders to young girls instructed them that their primary duty was to be demure, pure, and supportive of their male relatives. At the same time, boys were being instructed that they should be strong leaders. . . . Emma LaRocque recalls one Elder

who declared that "man is the law, and woman is to serve the man and to nurture the family."[12] Whether these are indeed identical to pre-contact teachings is not important. What matters is that these teachings today reinforce a status quo where women are subordinate to men. . . .

Perhaps the clearest example off the way heteropatriarchy plays out in spiritual communities that consider themselves to be "traditional" (i.e., non-Christian) is the trope of Indigenous womanhood as motherhood. I have encountered the rhetoric of Native womanhood as motherhood in many groups that aim to decolonize spirituality and activism throughout the midwestern United States and western Canada. . . . Emma LaRocque notes that even the extraordinarily nuanced book *A Recognition of Being* by Cree/Métis scholar Kim Anderson, which considers Indigenous women's gender roles extensively, lends to reinscribe childrearing as the ultimate designator of womanhood.[13]

In this trope, Indigenous womanhood is linked inextricably to the duty of motherhood, or of caring for the family and home more generally. Women's power is said to come almost exclusively from the power to give birth. Although this may seem less problematic because women's status is considered to be complementary but "equal" to men's, there are unavoidable difficulties with equating womanhood entirely with motherhood. Legal scholars Emily Snyder, Val Napoleon, and John Borrows write: "This motherhood rhetoric ultimately obscures, mischaracterizes, and too narrowly frames Indigenous women's options, choices, and contributions within their societies. This is particularly problematic when women's responsibilities and contributions as citizens are only framed in relation to nurturing and caring for the nation. While 'mothering the nation is espoused as something to take pride in as a highly respected role, this discourse too often forecloses a multitude of other functions and roles that Indigenous women assume in their societies.[14]

---

10. Barker, *Native Acts*, 189.

11. Barker, 190.

12. LaRocque, "Métis and Feminist," 55.

13. LaRocque, 63.

14. Snyder, Napoleon, and Borrows, "Gender and Violence," 611.

Like colonial heteropatriarchy, the equation of womanhood with motherhood posits a biological link between women's bodies and their social roles, which ignores women who cannot give birth or do not wish to, as well as people who can give birth but do not identify with womanhood. As Snyder, Napoleon, and Borrows note, it can easily erase other roles that women currently have and historically had in Indigenous societies, such as their participation as traders, diplomats, leaders, healers, warriors, artists, and more. . . .

It is also important that we interrogate the notion of "tradition" itself and question the idea that these gender prescriptions have been in place since time immemorial. First, the strange similarity of these tropes regarding gender across Indigenous communities in North America should be noted. There are over 500 Indigenous nations in the United States alone, and each has its own body of traditional teachings. . . . Making a concerted effort to explore and excavate individual teachings of our own peoples may be one way to counteract the tendency to erase the diversity of Indigenous gender. When we perpetuate stereotyped, generalized roles as "traditional," we lose the opportunity to examine the individual teachings each Indigenous nation has about gender. . . .

In addition, I often hear people in Indigenous communities speak of the "traditional" in unspecified terms that imply there is a singular, unified understanding of what "traditional" means. . . .

Looking to the history of gender and sexuality among Indigenous peoples, it is crucial to recognize the diversity in both ideal roles and in actual practice over a great span of time and space. I end this section with an appeal to other Indigenous people who are seeking justice for colonization and gendered violence. Just as we must not disavow change that has happened in the past, we must also take care not to reject change in the present simply because it is new. . . .

Two-Spirit Critiques

Because Two-Spirit people are particularly targeted by heteropatriarchy as deviants . . . we are well placed to notice the ways that "traditional gender roles"

have been made non-inclusive. Two-Spirit people are often especially harmed by appeals to tradition, as many Indigenous people have internalized the belief that only cis-gender heterosexuality is "traditional" and view LGBTQ Indigenous people as being overly colonized and even corrupted. Many Two-Spirit people are thus denied access to their communities and cultures. Even when they are able to access these things, too frequently the roles that Two-Spirit people could take in their communities have been forgotten. In the article "My Pronouns Are Kiy/Kin," Lindsay Nixon raises difficult questions that confront Two-Spirit people who wish to take part in ceremony:

> How then do I move through these spaces and honour creation in ways that connect to the Two Spirit life that surrounds me? How can I navigate moving between these defined spaces present at water ceremony—between keeping the fire and praying for the water? Would I be respected in both spaces if I tried to move in a fluid nature through and within them, like the fluidity I feel about the space my own embodied gender takes up within community? Could I occupy the womens space, for example, if I didn't wear a skirt? Could I keep the fire with the men if I did? Would I still be welcomed and accepted into ceremonial spaces that have previously filled my spirit in ways that I cannot describe, if I were honest about the ways that felt right for me to flow through those spaces like the very water we prayed over?[15]

These questions reveal the struggle that Two-Spirit people face in balancing their desire to participate in their communities and cultures and their desire to be true to themselves.

Since the 1970s, Two-Spirit people have begun to reclaim the stories of ancestors who were "like us." Researchers such as Will Roscoe, Walter L. Williams, Beatrice Medicine, and Sabine Lang have dug up archival records and oral histories that show that in

---

15. Nixon, "My Pronouns Are Kiy/Kin."

some places and at some times, Two-Spirit people were accepted, highly regarded, and essential parts of their communities. Here too, however, tradition is sometimes weaponized against Two-Spirit people. Again and again I have heard Two-Spirit people, including myself, agonize over whether or not they are "traditional" enough to call themselves "Two-Spirit" or to call themselves by the word in their language used for a Two-Spirit person. "Two-Spirit" is often defined in terms of "traditional-ness," even by Two-Spirit people themselves. An article by Tony Enos published on 28 March 2017 in *Indian Country Today* stated that as opposed to being gay, which simply means being attracted to the same gender, "claiming the role of Two Spirit is to take up the spiritual responsibility that the role traditionally had. Walking the red road, being for the people and our children/youth, and being a guiding force in a good way with a good mind are just some of those responsibilities."[16] While these are all admirable things, requiring them of Two-Spirit people simply in order to claim the term itself forces Two-Spirit people to conform to unreasonable standards of tradition. . . .

Unfortunately, even attempts to empower Two-Spirit people can reinforce the idea that Two-Spirit people should be held to higher standards of "traditionalness" to be considered authentic. Historical studies have emphasized the "special roles" of Two-Spirit people, such as their roles as spiritual leaders, namegivers, medicine people, fortune tellers, and exceptional artisans. Native people, including Two-Spirit people themselves, repeat these roles as a way to boost the esteem of modern Two-Spirit people. Although these roles are important to know and recognize, they can sometimes obscure the fact that our Two-Spirit ancestors were also simply regular people who laughed, loved, worked, cried, and lived their lives, just as their non-Two-Spirit siblings did. Indigenous women and men today do not carry out all the same roles that they did 200 years ago, and though they may strive to reclaim some, we do not require them to do so before considering them men and women. Neither should Two-Spirit people be held to that impossible standard.

Despite these challenges, Two-Spirit people have often been successful in reclaiming and rebuilding traditions that are not steeped in heteropatriarchy. At the Great Lakes Gathering in the summer of 2016, a gathering for those concerned for the waters of the Great Lakes, the ceremonial breakout groups included a group for Two-Spirit-identified people. The tent was lined with flags printed with the message "Gender is fluid like nibi [water]." Lindsay Nixon expands on this: "Recently nîtisân Erin Marie Konsmo gifted me the first teaching I had ever received about the potentiality of genderless water. The fluidity of water taught wiya about the fluidity of wiya gender, of niya gender. While I would never devalue teachings and ceremony shared with me that associate feminine spirit to water, I also want to be honest about the ways that I experience my spiritual connection to water and other kin—human and otherwise."[17] Nixon's words reveal the possibility of Two-Spirit teachings that recognize the experiences of Two-Spirit people and connect them to their kin, as Nixon says, "human and otherwise." These teachings do not have to replace the teachings about men and women but can complement them and offer alternative ways of looking at gendered teachings.

In academia, Two-Spirit scholars are also doing fruitful work in creating new ways of looking at the place of queer Indigenous people in their communities. In a 2014 issue of the journal *Transgender Studies Quarterly*, transgender Stó:lō/Tsimshian scholar Saylish Wesley describes a community-centred approach to creating space for Two-Spirit people within Indigenous nations. Wesley was unable to find evidence of precolonial roles of Two-Spirit people among her people, which meant she had to try a different method of developing her identity and community roles. She uses a methodology drawn from another Stó:lō scholar, Jo-Ann Archibald's story-work, to recount how she was able to reconnect with her grandmother after struggling with their relationship due to Wesley's transition. After becoming her grandmother's apprentice in the art of basket weaving, they managed to reach an understanding that resulted in her

---

16. Enos, "8 Things You Should Know About Two Spirit People."

17. Nixon, "My Pronouns Are Kiy/Kin."

grandmother coining a phrase in their language to refer to Wesley's identity and role. Since then, Wesley has even offered this phrase to other Two-Spirit Stó:lō people as a possible name for their identity if they want it. Relying as it does not on rigid conformity to imagined tradition but on existing relationships between Two-Spirit people and their kin, Wesley's account of the journey that she, her grandmother, and their community took together to reincorporate Two-Spirit people as valued members of their nation serves as a powerful model for other Indigenous people wishing to do the same.[18]

I want to end with a story from my own experience. I was at an Indigenous language camp when a group of women invited me to join their drum group to perform at the camp's ending ceremony, which I eagerly agreed to. In our last practice session together before the event, the eldest woman who was our leader informed us that we should all wear long skirts for the performance. Immediately I became anxious and unsure what to do as a Two-Spirit person. Finally, I got up the courage to go talk to the leading woman. I explained to her that I was Two-Spirit and that I did not feel comfortable wearing a skirt. She did not know what to do, having never encountered this issue, so together we called her Elder, a Cree woman in her nineties. After we explained the issue, she was quiet for a minute. When she spoke, she told us she did not know anything about Two-Spirit people. However, it had always been taught to her that wearing a skirt was about respecting oneself before the Creator. If a person felt that wearing a skirt would not be respecting them, would actually be disrespecting who they felt they are, then it was clear that they should do what would be respectful of their identity. With the Elder's blessing, I wore pants as we drummed and sang before the entire camp.

The attempt to (re)build healthy Indigenous gender roles is not merely an activity of academic interest. The youth I worked with as a group leader continuously brought up problems with gendered relationships in their community: men and women alike speaking of women badly and treating them poorly, queer and trans youth being excluded from cultural events, children raised with strict gender prescriptions that did not allow them to flourish. Influences of colonization, colonial trauma, and colonial heteropatriarchy have left indelible marks on the ways we relate to one another. The harmful effects of these forces are visible in the lives of our people from the earliest of ages. We must work against the hegemony of heteropatriarchal roles in our lives collectively and create ways of relating based in Indigenous ethics. . . .

Using Indigenous feminist and queer theory, they demonstrate how we can improve health outcomes in Indigenous communities by providing decolonized and Indigenous-centred articulations of gender, sex, and sexuality that push past the gender binary and heteronormativity prevalent in health curricula and settler-colonial society. Here, I suggest that by putting Two-Spirit perspectives at the forefront, we may be better able to avoid the pitfalls of heteropatriarchy that harm not just Two-Spirit people but all Indigenous people. With gender and gendered relations so intimately tied up in the ability of Indigenous nations to survive and thrive, allowing Two-Spirit people to take the lead may open up new ways to think about sovereignty, self-determination, and nation as well.

PART 5

Additional Readings

Anderson, Kim, and Rob Innes. *Indigenous Men and Masculinities: Legacies, Identities, Regeneration*. Winnipeg: University of Manitoba Press, 2015.

18. Wesley, "Twin-Spirited Woman."

Cannon, Martin J. *Men, Masculinity, and the Indian Act*. Vancouver: University of British Columbia Press, 2019.

Chacaby, Ma-Nee A. (with Mary Plummer). *A Two Spirit Journey: The Autobiography of a Lesbian Ojibwa-Cree Elder*. Manitoba: University of Manitoba Press, 2016.

Green, Joyce, ed. *Making Space for Indigenous Feminism (2nd edition)*. Halifax & Winnipeg: Fernwood Publishing, 2017.

Nickel, Sarah and Amanda Fehr, eds. *In Good Relation: History, Gender, and Kinship in Indigenous Feminisms*. Winnipeg: University of Manitoba Press, 2020.

Sunseri, Lina. *Being Again of One Mind: Oneida Women and the Struggle for Decolonization*. Vancouver: University of British Columbia Press, 2011.

Yee, Jessica, ed. *Feminism for Real: Deconstructing the Academic Industrial Complex of Feminism*. Ottawa: Canadian Centre for Policy Alternatives, 2011.

Relevant Websites

He Inoa Mana (A Powerful Name)
https://youtu.be/A5nQZ7_ApM4
Hinaleimoana Wong-Kalu is a Kanaka Maoli cultural practitioner, educator, and transgender woman who centres her Indigenous and Chinese roots through the lens of Indigeneity, history, relationships, kinship, responsibility, and sex/gender/cultural identity.

Native Women's Association of Canada
https://nwac.ca/
The Native Women's Association of Canada (NWAC) provides media-based, archival, and community-based resources related to the health and wellness of Indigenous women and children, including events such as press releases, and historically, a voice for federally unrecognized and recognized women politically.

Native Youth Sexual Health Network
https://www.nativeyouthsexualhealth.com
The Native Youth Sexual Health Network is an organization by/for Indigenous youth that explores issues of sexual and reproductive health, rights, and justice and provides support to Indigenous youth.

Rainbow Resource Centre
https://rainbowresourcecentre.org
The Rainbow Resource Centre is a community-based organization located in Winnipeg, Manitoba that provides information, support, public awareness on issues related to sexual orientation, gender diversity, and antihomophobia education.

Films

Drunktown's Finest. Dir. Sydney Freeland. The Film Sales Company, 2014.
Fire Song. Dir. Adam Garnet Jones. IMDb, 2015
First Stories—Two Spirited. Dir. Sharon A. Desjarlais. National Film Board of Canada, 2007.
Freedom Road: Women/Ikwewag. Dir. Angelina McLeod. National Film Board of Canada, 2019.
Kuma Hina (A Place in the Middle). Dir. Dean Harmer/Joe Wilson. Dean Harmer, 2015.
Mohawk Girls. Dir. Tracey Deer. Rezolution Pictures and National Film Board of Canada, 2005.
Onkwa-nistensera: Mothers of Our Nations. Dir. Dawn Martin-Hill. Indigenous Health Research Development Program, 2006.

Key Terms

- Indian status
- Indian Act
- Gendered violence

- Two-Spirit
- Heteropatriarchy
- Sexism

Discussion Questions

1. What role do racism and Settler colonialism play in the marginalization and ongoing discrimination of Indigenous women and Two-Spirit individuals in Canada? What are some concrete examples?

2. How did the *Indian Act* redefine Indigenous belonging and identity? How do these redefinitions impact gender relations?

3. What does it mean to suggest that the *Indian Act* "normalized heterosexuality" (Cannon, 2019: 14)? What is it that links sexism, heteropatriarchy, and Settler colonialism?

4. How is reclaiming tradition both empowering and disempowering? Why is putting an end to sexism and gender inequality requisite to decolonizing?

Activities

Invite an Indigenous activist to discuss the impact of colonial policy and the *Indian Act* on their identity and/or leadership.

Watch the 2008 National Film Board production *Club Native* (written and directed by Tracey Deer). How is the status Indian collective represented in the film? How are issues of racialization being addressed? How have definitions of Indianness become central to people's own self-identification? What is the difference between the racism institutionalized through federal legislation and the racism employed to resist further colonial encroachment? How are men impacted by histories of sexism and heteropatriarchy? What needs to happen before these voices are heard?

Watch the 2007 film *Two Spirits* (written and directed by Ruth Fertig). What factors contribute to Joey Criddle's experience in terms of gendered and erotic diversity? What is it that defines his aspirations as a Two-Spirit man and activist?

PART 6

Gendered Violence

Editor Introduction

Over ten years ago, the Native Women's Association of Canada (2015) stated that

> for years, communities have pointed to the high number of missing and murdered Aboriginal women and girls in Canada. As of March 31, 2010, Native Women's Association of Canada (NWAC) has gathered information about 582 cases from across the country.... Aboriginal women face life-threatening, gender-based violence, and disproportionately experience violent crimes because of hatred and racism ... [they are] 3.5 times more likely to experience violence than non-Aboriginal women ... [and] that homicides involving Aboriginal women are more likely to go unsolved.

Being Indigenous ourselves, reading/hearing such statistics affects us at a deep personal level because the women that have been reported as missing and/or murdered are members of our communities; they are our relatives. When the Pickton's murder case captured the attention of the media and ordinary Canadians, we shared the following questions with our Indigenous relations: "How can this be? How is it possible that so many of our sisters have gone missing, or been killed? Why don't the police, the State, the media seem to care? Would they have cared if the women were middle-class white women? Why are Indigenous women the target of such tragic violence?" These questions are still asked years later. February 14 is the annual vigil to commemorate our relatives that have gone missing, and events occur throughout the country in order to gather together, share stories, and reiterate our commitment to bring needed social change. Throughout the COVID-19 pandemic it has been difficult to gather together on this important day, but virtual events have still taken place, and on 14 February 2021 one of us, Lina, attended an event organized by an Indigenous social agency in London, Ontario. It was a powerful and emotional gathering of survivors of gendered and sexual violence, their families, and community members, where teachings were shared and songs sung in order to help us heal and move forward. The objective of the readings in this part of the text is to analyze the gendered violence affecting Indigenous communities, examine some of its structural roots, and look at how Indigenous people have organized to respond to this alarming issue.

Canada is a settler colonial nation-state built upon the dispossession of Indigenous lands, and the ongoing domination of Indigenous peoples by the settler-society is symptomatic of Canada's contemporary ills. Moreover, "the effects of colonialism are gendered, and the colonial gaze has a gender-specific derogatory and essentialized frame for Indigenous women" (Bourgeois, in Chapter 11). Indeed, contemporary gendered violence against Indigenous peoples is linked to a long history of **colonial violence** directed against Indigenous nations, but distinctly felt by women. Canadian colonial policies, laws, and social inequalities have been partly responsible for pushing "many Indigenous women and girls into precarious situations—ranging from inadequate housing to sex work—where there is a heightened risk of violence" (Amnesty International, 2014: 3; see also Bourgeois, 2015).

Alongside colonial laws and policies, racist ideas about Indigenous women constructed by early Settlers have greatly contributed to the sexual violence. Specific components of the gendered element of colonialism have been the myth of the "squaw," which led to sexualization and objectification of women; sexist and patriarchal legal definitions of the "Indian" under the Indian Act, which imposed patrilineality and patriarchy on many previous matrilineal societies; and residential schools and the child welfare system wherein children were physically and sexually abused. As Acoose (1995) has argued, Indigenous women were constructed as sexually promiscuous savages, easily available to European men, eventually making them vulnerable to sexual violent acts. The perpetrators of such violence were able to escape punishment because Indigenous women were viewed as disposable, violable bodies. These sexist, demeaning, and racist stereotypes of Indigenous women have been used to justify past and persistent sexual and colonial violence, and are at the root of the epidemic of **Missing and Murdered Indigenous Women and Girls** (MMIWG) in Canada.

In addition to the aforementioned colonial ideologies and state's policies and laws that devalued Indigenous women and made them vulnerable to sexual and gendered violence, the Canadian justice system has also failed to protect Indigenous women while often criminalizing them. For example, it used prostitution as justification for minimizing the violence Indigenous women experienced, resulting in police inaction in resolving cases dealing with Indigenous women who were perceived to be involved in "risky lifestyles."

In Chapter 11, Bourgeois examines the long-fought battle by the Native Women Association of Canada and Indigenous communities to demand that the Canadian government investigate the systemic causes of the violence and take action to reduce it. This battle originated from the **Sisters in Spirit** initiative headed by Native Women's Association of Canada and funded by the Government of Canada. This initiative established supportive networks for the families of the missing and murdered women, documented the life stories of the women, and drew attention to the issue of violence against Indigenous women both nationally and internationally. The Sisters in Spirit strongly believed that in order to eliminate the sexualized and racialized violence against Indigenous women, we needed to first eradicate the negative racist attitudes that have birthed such violence, and which, as Bourgeois argues in Chapter 11, are directly linked to Canadian State's laws and policies.

A decade after the Amnesty International's report *Stolen Sisters* and the development of the Sisters in Spirit initiative, the numbers of Missing and Murdered Indigenous women had disturbingly increased, leading people and organizations across the country to repeatedly demand for the government to have an inquiry; however, it was not until the Liberal government came into power that this finally took place in 2015. Although this move was perceived as encouraging, as Bourgeois argues, the inquiry needed to take a feminist antioppression approach, drawing attention to the Canadian State's role in the violence.

In June 2019 the federal government released the Final Report of the Missing and Murdered Indigenous Women and Girls Inquiry, which included 231 Calls for Justice. The report found that Indigenous women and girls are much more likely to be targets of violence than non-Indigenous women and defined this level of violence as a genocide rooted in historical colonial discriminatory ideologies, laws, policies, and poor socioeconomic conditions. The Calls for Justice contained in the report stressed the importance of substantive equality for Indigenous peoples, and a decolonizing approach that recognizes inherent Indigenous rights. They also called for services and programs to be driven by Indigenous communities and be sufficiently funded. Finally, moving forward, all levels of government must be committed to transform the structures that have sustained the violence against Indigenous women and girls (National Inquiry into Missing and Murdered Indigenous Women and Girls, 2019).

The initial optimism that followed the launch of the inquiry and its ultimate report has increasingly deteriorated, as years have passed and little concrete action has been taken to address the identified issues and root causes. In 2021 the federal government released a national action plan that has received criticism by many Indigenous communities and organizations. Kupki 7 Chief Judy Wilson at a press conference called the action plan "a slap in the face" for not taking true accountability for the creation of the systems that contributed to the gendered and sexual violence. Although the national action plan promises to spend over 2 billion on the implementation of the Calls for Justice, Chief Wilson argues that the plan is missing concrete immediate action, timelines, and full consultation and participation from the survivors and their families (CBC News, June 2021e). Moreover, the action plan must be representative of diverse communities, cultures, organizations, and professionals with expertise in legal and justice matters, be trauma-informed, and inclusive by facilitating and supporting the participation of female survivors of violence, their families, men, youth, Elders, leaders, trans and Two-Spirit people.

Indeed, trans and Two-Spirit individuals are an important part of the conversation that cannot be left out when it comes to MMIWG, as they tend to face even higher rates of violence. In Chapter 12, Alex Wilson closely examines how Indigenous trans and Two-Spirit women are more likely to be sexually and physically assaulted than heterosexual Indigenous women. Additionally, they often don't feel supported or safe in their own communities or in the wider Canadian society. Similarly to Pyke in Chapter 10, Wilson argues that a common narrative that essentializes women and women's roles is rooted in binary constructions of gender and sexuality, and marginalizes Two-Spirit, trans, and queer Indigenous peoples, further increasing their vulnerability to violence. Through colonialism, assimilation policies have displaced traditional beliefs and practices that had been inclusive and respectful of differences of gender and sexual identities. As a result, Two-Spirit people are subject to heterosexism and homophobia, contributing to feelings of isolation and high cases of suicide, especially among the youth who are struggling to find acceptance of their forming identities.

As Wilson points outs, "there is much work to be done, then, to undo the work that has been done upon us." This requires us to reclaim sovereignty over our Indigenous bodies, just as we work toward reclaiming sovereignty over our lands, languages, ceremonies, and governance. A feminist antiracist framework to analyse and address the sexual and gendered violence must pay close attention to the ways in which Two-Spirit, trans, and queer Indigenous peoples have been particularly affected by colonial ideologies and policies. Their perspectives and needs need to be fully incorporated in any future implementation of the recommendations made in the final report of the inquiry, and by Indigenous communities and organizations.

CHAPTER 11

Perpetual State of Violence

An Indigenous Feminist Anti-Oppression Inquiry into Missing and Murdered Indigenous Women and Girls

Robyn Bourgeois

For decades, thousands of Indigenous women and girls from across Turtle Island (as many Indigenous peoples refer to the territory that constitutes North America . . .) have been stolen from our communities through a violent social phenomenon now commonly referred to as "missing and murdered Indigenous women and girls" (MMIWG). In every province and territory, in urban centres, small towns, reserves, and rural locations, Indigenous females of all ages and from all walks of life have been brutally murdered or have disappeared, fate officially unknown. In its wake, the violence has left families and communities devastated, many of whom have had to fight to have Canadian state institutions, including police forces, the judicial system, and, indeed, federal, and provincial/territorial governments, take this violence seriously.

. . . [T]he Government of Canada under the leadership of Prime Minister Justin Trudeau is conducting a national public inquiry into this violence. "Not high on our radar" (CBC News Online 2014) for the previous Conservative government of Stephen Harper, this national inquiry represents a long and hard-fought battle on the part of Indigenous women (many of whom are family and friends of the murdered and missing) and their communities for a formal government investigation of the violence of MMIWG. Mandated to occur between September 1, 2016, and December 31, 2018, the inquiry will be led by five commissioners, all but one of whom are Indigenous women, including representation from each of the three major Indigenous groups in Canada (First Nation, Inuit, and Métis). The commissioners have been tasked with investigating the "systemic causes of all violence—including sexual violence—against Indigenous women and girls in Canada," as well as the "institutional policies and practices implemented in response [to this violence], including the identification of practices that have been effective in reducing violence and increasing safety" (Government of Canada 2016). The commissioners have also been directed to make recommendations on "concrete and effective action that can be taken to remove systemic causes of violence and to increase the safety of Indigenous women and girls in Canada," as well as the "ways to honour and commemorate the missing and murdered Indigenous women and girls" (Government of Canada 2016).

In the lead up to this inquiry, which included public consultation on its creation and content, some Indigenous women began organizing and articulating the critical need for inclusion of Indigenous feminist perspectives in this national inquiry. In Vancouver, long-time Indigenous feminist activist Fay Blaney (Xwemalhkwu), in her role as co-chair of

Robyn Bourgeois, "Generations of Genocide — The historical root of missing and murdered Indigenous women and girls." In Kim Anderson, Maria Campbell, and Christi Belcourt eds. *Keetsahnak: Our Missing and Murdered Indigenous Sisters.* The University of Alberta Press, © 2018.

the February 14 Memorial March Committee, held a press conferencing demanding that, in addition to consulting families, the inquiry process needed to "make room for groups that have worked with vulnerable women for years and are uniquely well-placed to address [the] sexism, racism, and violence that shadow so many victims' lives" (Stueck 2016). Blaney was afraid that feminism would be left out of the inquiry: "it needs to proceed from a feminist perspective . . . this is an issue of Indigenous women's equality . . . I didn't hear this coming from them" (CBC News Online 2016).

If this inquiry is to achieve its goals of understanding the systemic causes of MMIWG and critically examining the institutional practices and policies in response to this violence, it is imperative that the commissioners consider Indigenous feminist perspectives. To demonstrate their importance, I offer an Indigenous feminist anti-oppression inquiry into MMIWG that draws attention to the Canadian state's roles in this violence. As a settler colonial state, Canada has an historical and ongoing investment in violence against Indigenous women and girls—and, indeed, all Indigenous peoples—in order to secure and retain unfettered access to Indigenous lands. Through its laws, policies and institutions, the Canadian state has inflicted extreme violence on Indigenous communities in explicitly gendered and sexualized ways that simultaneously secure patriarchy, white supremacy, and colonial domination. At the same time, it has colonized—attempted to silence and subvert—the efforts of Indigenous women and their allies to address this violence.

The framework I advance is what I call an Indigenous feminist *anti-oppression* framework, emphasizing its overriding commitment to ending all forms of domination and violence. It draws on Indigenous and non-Indigenous feminist, anticolonial/decolonizing, critical anti-racism, and anti-oppression theories, and is influenced by my anti-violence work with Indigenous women and their communities.

. . . [T]his framework starts from a place of honouring and respecting the knowledge and experiences of Indigenous women and girls. As "experts" in their own lives, their leadership and perspectives must be included in any discussion, decision, and action with the potential to impact their lives. As the popular political slogan states, "nothing about us without us."

This framework recognizes the simultaneous impact of colonialism, racism, and patriarchy on the lives of Indigenous women and girls and their communities, and advocates dismantling these dominant systems of oppression collectively.

> *An Indigenous feminist anti-oppression framework emphasizes its overriding commitment to ending all forms of domination and violence.*

Efforts to examine and eradicate these dominant systems of oppression, then, must pay close attention to how they operate in and through one another, and address them simultaneously. However, in doing this work, it is critical to avoid what Fellows and Razack (1998) call "the race to innocence." The danger here is that we use our oppression in one system to avoid examining our privilege in another and, thus, our complicity in the oppression of others. Because of the multiple systems of oppression involved, our lives are simultaneously shaped by oppression and privilege. Ignoring our privileges not only secures our complicity in the oppression and violence perpetrated against others, but also, ultimately, against ourselves: "attempts to change one system while leaving the others intact leaves in place the structure of domination that is made of interlocking hierarchies" (Fellows and Razack 1998: 336). Examining our privilege(s), then, is an essential part of the practices to achieve freedom for any of us. In the words of the Aboriginal Women's Action Network (AWAN), an Indigenous feminist women's group based in Vancouver, this requires "a collective definition of freedom" recognizing that "your freedom is tied to ours and ours to yours" (2011).

MMIWG: The Scope of a "National Tragedy"

In a Western society that demands statistical evidence to support claims, it has been challenging to pinpoint exact numbers of missing and murdered Indigenous women and girls across Canada. For example, at the conclusion of the Sisters in Spirit (SIS) initiative—a five-year, federally funded ($5 million) research, education, and policy initiative addressing the root causes and trends related to MMIWG—in March 2010, the Native Women's Association of Canada (NWAC) had documented 582 cases since the 1960s, identified through reports from families and consultation of public records (much of it from government documents). Around this same time, Walk4Justice, a grassroots organization led by Indigenous activists Skundaal/Bernie Williams (Haida/Nuchatlaht/Stellat'en) and Gladys Radek (Gitxsan/Wet'suwet'en), claimed to have identified more than three thousand cases of MMIWG (Williams and Radek 2010: 2). While the two organizations might have collaborated to produce an enhanced database of cases, they were never given the chance: in the second round of federal funding for their work on MMIWG, ongoing work on NWAC's database of cases was prohibited. . . .

Instead, the federal government funded a national operational overview of Royal Canadian Mounted Police (RCMP) files pertaining to MMIWG, finding 1,181 cases (1,071 homicides and 164 missing women and girls) (RCMP 2014: 3). A significant issue with these numbers (and, indeed, other police-force statistics) is the absence of established guidelines for determining how police officers collect information relating to Indigenous peoples, meaning that the Indigeneity of some victims might not be identified in case files (NWAC 2010:15). Moreover, concerns have been voiced that the deaths of some women and girls have mistakenly been deemed "accidental" instead of suspicious death or homicide in police investigations (NWAC 2009; Moore and Trojan 2016).

For families and communities, the death of one Indigenous woman or girl is too much, let alone the thousands suggested by these estimates. An "accurate" count is unnecessary: far too many Indigenous women and girls have gone missing or been murdered over the last few decades.

More than half of [NWAC's] cases involved females under age 31, and many of the women were mothers. "Knowing the number of women who were mothers," the organization contends, "speaks to the intergenerational impact of women who have gone missing or been found murdered, and the need to provide supports and services to the children left behind" (NWAC 2010: 24). This analysis also found that Indigenous women and girls were more likely to be killed by strangers (16.5 percent of cases) than non-Indigenous women (6 percent of cases). Finally, the report contends that nearly half of all cases remain unsolved (2010:17), with different clearance rates across the provinces and territories (2010: 18).

The final report of the RCMP operational overview also provides important insights into this violence. It confirmed what many have known for decades: Indigenous women have been disproportionately targeted for violence. Despite representing 4.3 percent of the female population, Indigenous women constituted 11.3 percent of missing females and 16 percent of female homicide cases in Canada between 1980 and 2010 (RCMP 2012). Moreover, statistics derived between 1996 and 2011 show that Indigenous women were, on average, five and a half times more likely to be victims of homicide than non-Indigenous women. They calculated the average age of Indigenous female homicide victims as thirty-five. Finally, Indigenous women were only slightly more likely (39 percent) than non-Indigenous women (31 percent) to be involved in criminal activity at the time of their murder (RCMP 2012).

This report also captures some interesting insights about perpetrators: in 90 percent of homicide cases, Indigenous women knew their perpetrators, a rate consistent with non-Indigenous women. However, they were more likely to be killed by acquaintances (30 percent compared to 19 percent), but less likely to murdered by a current or former spouse (29 percent compared to 41 percent) (RCMP 2014). Perpetrators were also more likely to have consumed "intoxicating substances" prior the homicide (71 percent of cases involving Indigenous women compared with 31 percent of cases involving non-Indigenous women), but "less likely to have, or be suspected of having, a developmental disorder (10 percent compared to 20 percent)" (RCMP 2014: 13).

Finally, this report contends, in contrast with NWAC, that the majority of cases have been solved. The RCMP (2014) claims a female homicide solve rate of nine out of every ten deaths, regardless of ancestry (88 percent for Indigenous women and 89 percent for non-Indigenous women). They did, however, confirm NWAC's finding of variance in clearance rates across the provinces and territories.

State of Perpetual Violence

How did we get to the point where violence against Indigenous women and girls is a "normal" part of life? As Indigenous women have been telling the Canadian state for decades through their participation in state-sponsored anti-violence initiatives, including previous investigatory commissions such as the Canadian Panel on Violence Against Women (1991–1993) and the Royal Commission on Aboriginal Peoples (1991–1996), the extreme forms of violence Indigenous women and girls experience in contemporary Canadian society are a direct consequence of settler colonial domination (Bourgeois 2014).

Understanding the connection between the two requires critical interrogation of the Canadian state. Canada is a settler colonial nation built on the historic and ongoing domination of Indigenous peoples and the occupation and exploitation of stolen Indigenous lands (Green 2014; Coulthard 2014). This colonial project succeeds through racist and sexist ideologies that portray Indigenous people as inferior, deviant, and inherently dysfunctional. The effects of colonialism are gendered, and the colonial gaze has a gender-specific derogatory and essentialized frame for Indigenous women. A powerful component of this ideology has been the myth of the "squaw": the dominantly held belief in the inherent sexual availability and, thus, violability of Indigenous women and girls (Acoose 1995; Smith 2005). This ideological dehumanization of Indigenous females justifies both settler domination over Indigenous peoples and lands and violence perpetrated against Indigenous women and girls. Indeed, within this system, violence against Indigenous women and girls is the most efficient means to securing and maintaining the colonial order of things in settler society.

Alongside physical violence, colonialism depends on structural forms of violence to marginalize and oppress Indigenous women and girls and, by extension, their communities and nations. Perpetuated through social and political institutions, these structural forms of violence further increase the vulnerability of Indigenous women and girls to physical violence. In the discussion that follows, I explore some of the ways in which the Canadian state has perpetuated and enabled violence against Indigenous women and girls.

The Violence of the Indian Act

The political consolidation of the Canadian state in 1867 marks the starting point of an aggressive multipronged colonial war waged by the Canadian state against Indigenous women and girls. With its roots in policies that predate the 1867 "confederation" of Canada, the federal Indian Act has been central to this process. Since its enactment in 1876, this racist legislation has defined almost every aspect of being an Indigenous person in Canada, including legally defining which of us "officially" count and don't count as "Indians" and, therefore, who the Canadian state is obligated to provide for under existing and future treaty obligations (Eberts 2014: 148).

However, the core legal definition of an "Indian" has largely been "any male person of Indian blood reputed to belong to a particular band, and any child of such person and any woman who is lawfully married to such a person" (Gibbins and Ponting, cited in Comack 2014: 62). Defined through men, the Indian Act imposed patrilineality and patriarchy on many previously matrilineal and matriarchal societies, therefore severely limiting the safety and social security these orderings of our communities had provided. Through sexist marriage and lineage provisions that unfairly target Indigenous women and their children only, the Indian Act has eliminated millions of "official" Indians for whom the federal government would carry responsibility through treaty obligations, with the effect of forcibly removing untold numbers of women and children from their nations and communities (an act of human trafficking, as I have argued elsewhere (Bourgeois 2015)). While Bill C-31 eliminated the controversial marry-out clause (a woman lost her status under the Indian Act if she married a man without status; however, a man who did the same not only retained his status, but status under the Act was also extended to his wife and children) in 1985, sex discriminatory lineage and membership components continue to target Indigenous women and children (Cannon 2011, 2014); and Indigenous women reinstated under Bill C-31 have experienced challenges and resistance to returning to their home communities (Dick 2006). By excluding Indigenous women from status under the Indian Act, these sex discriminatory provisions, as Mary Eberts argues, promote family fragmentation and community exile that eliminate critical sources of support and heightens the vulnerability of Indigenous women and children (2014: 152–153).

The Indian Act has contributed to the oppression of Indigenous women and girls in other ways. By imposing democratically elected band council governance on reserve communities, the Indian Act undermined and eliminated many of our traditional matriarchal forms of leadership and governance (Anderson 2000, 2009). To strengthen this blow, Indian women were prohibited from participating in these elections or serving on these band councils between 1876 and 1951. The effect was the patriarchal ordering of Indian governance and leadership across Canada, with the interests, perspectives, and needs of Indian men foregrounded in the governance of our communities (Anderson 2009). While this exclusion was repealed, its legacy continues to be felt through underrepresentation of Indian women within band and national (Assembly of First Nations) Indian governance (although their numbers are increasing) (Anderson 2009: 100). This legacy is also felt in the underfunding of Indigenous women's leadership and governance—exemplified by the four-decades-long battle of NWAC to secure equal access to funding and political fora as other national Indigenous organizations including the Assembly of First Nations (AFN) (representing the interests of status Indians in Canada) and the Congress of Aboriginal Peoples (CAP) (representing the interests of Métis and non-status Indigenous peoples) (Anderson 2009).

Human Trafficking and Extermination

Alongside the legislative assault of the Indian Act, the Canadian state has enabled and perpetuated violence against Indigenous women and girls through its institutions, most notably the Indian residential school and child welfare systems. As the Truth and Reconciliation Commission (TRC) (2015) made clear, gross neglect and all forms of physical and sexual abuse were prevalent and came to define the experiences of Indigenous girls and young women in the state and church-run Indian residential school system, which operated in Canada from the 1820s until 1996.

The intergenerational trauma created through the dehumanizing and violent residential school system continues to reverberate throughout our communities, with the consequence of increased violence within our communities. The research of NWAC through its SIS initiative identified the violence and intergenerational trauma caused by the Indian residential school system as an underlying factor of the violence experienced by MMIWG (NWAC 2010).

The Injustice System

The Canadian legal system (laws, courts, and police) has a long history of failing to protect Indigenous women and girls from violence, while simultaneously exonerating perpetrators and erasing this violence—thanks largely to the sexualized and racialized discourses of inferior and degenerate Indigenous femininity (Razack 2002; Erickson 2011; Eberts 2014). Instead of protecting them, the legal system has tended to criminalize Indigenous women who encounter it, exhibited by very high rates of incarceration (Hylton 2002; Erickson 2011; Comack 2014).

Prostitution presents a perfect example of this. The dominant colonial discourse, of the inherently sexual availability and violability of Indigenous females has, throughout Canadian history, enabled the conflation of Indigenous femaleness with prostitution (Comack 2014; Bourgeois 2014), which is reinforced, in turn, by the high numbers of Indigenous women and girls who, whether by choice, need, or force, have been involved in the sex trade. As I have argued elsewhere (Bourgeois 2014), Canadian colonial history demonstrates that the state has frequently employed prostitution as a means of legally securing control over Indigenous women and, by extension, their nations and communities. Criminalization of Indigenous ceremonies, such as the potlatch, and implementation of the pass system were justified, in part, by concerns about the immorality posed by the prostitution of Indian women. Moreover, an amendment to the Indian Act in 1892 created a distinct legal category for Indian women charged with prostitution, increasing its criminal severity from a "common nuisance" and summary offence to crime against morality and an indictable offence (Erickson 2011: 62–63). Current Canadian criminal code provisions continue to criminalize Indigenous women involved in prostitution.

At the same time, Canada's (in)justice system has long used prostitution as justification for minimizing the violence perpetrated against Indigenous women and girls and for exonerating perpetrators. Erickson's (2011) study of Prairie courts between the late 1880s and early 1900s shows that perpetrators often employed the stereotype of Indigenous sexual promiscuity, including accusations of prostitution, to their legal advantage. In her analysis of the trial surrounding the 1995 murder of Pamela George (a Saulteaux woman originally from the Sakimay First Nation) in Regina, Razack (2002) demonstrates how, one hundred years later, prostitution continues to over-define Indigenous femininity, with the effect of minimizing the violence of perpetrators through separation from the Canadian colonial project requiring violence against Indigenous women and girls. Razack uses similar analysis on the murder of 36-year-old Cindy Gladue (Cree) in Edmonton in 2011, demonstrating the central role that prostitution played in making both the murder and the courts' response to it a form of colonial terror and extraordinary violence (Razack 2016).

Prostitution is also at the root of Canadian state inaction in response to violence against Indigenous women and girls, perhaps best exemplified in the case of Vancouver's missing women. Between the late 1970s and early 2000s, at least sixty-eight women disappeared and/or were murdered from Vancouver's Downtown Eastside (DTES) community. While most commonly portrayed in mainstream media as a community of abject poverty, addiction, criminality, and prostitution (Culhane 2009; Hugill 2010), the DTES is also a caring community whose members, along with families and friends of the missing and murdered women, recognized this pattern of violence and sought police and governmental responses. However, the actual or perceived involvement of these women in prostitution resulted in police inaction. The final report of the British Columbia Missing Women Commission of Inquiry surrounding these cases points to the criminalization of prostitution under Canada's criminal code

as producing an adversarial relationship between police and women in the DTES, which contributed to the delay in catching serial killer Robert Pickton, who was preying on this community (Oppal 2012). We also know from this report that police officers and administrative staff made disparaging remarks and refused to take action because of the real or perceived involvement of the missing women in prostitution.

The result of this blatant inaction was sixty-eight missing and murdered women. Despite being formally indicted for the murders of twenty-five of these women and suspected in the deaths of many more, Pickton was only convicted of second-degree murder in six of these cases and sentenced to life in prison. While justified by the Attorney General for British Columbia as a move to curtail additional expenditures of time and energy to pursue charges that couldn't expand on Pickton's existing life sentences, the decision not to pursue those additional charges or prosecute additional cases against Pickton may be interpreted by some as representing this ongoing pattern of minimizing violence against Indigenous and non-Indigenous women associated with prostitution.

Colonizing Indigenous Women's Resistance

Another significant way that the Canadian state has perpetrated violence against Indigenous women and girls in Canada is through its repeated and sometimes aggressive attempts at colonizing (silencing and subverting) Indigenous women's anti-violence efforts. The National Inquiry into Missing and Murdered Indigenous Women and Girls has been a long time coming and must be understood as the outcome of decades of arduous and heartbreaking organizing and effort on the part of Indigenous women, their organizations, communities, and allies. For example, in Vancouver, under the leadership of Indigenous women (many of whom are family and friends of missing or murdered women), the DTES community has organized an annual memorial and march for missing and murdered women since 1991. For twenty-five years, this event has demanded the Canadian state take action to address violence against Indigenous women and girls. Since the 2000s, Indigenous women have organized solidarity events in major cities (including Edmonton, Winnipeg, Toronto, Thunder Bay, and Montréal), as well as many rural and Indigenous communities. Notably, with the arrival of the Winter Olympics in 2010, organizers attempted to displace this event from its usual date (February 14) and location to accommodate the games. Organizers and participants resisted and instead secured the highest-ever attendance for this event to that point.

. . . NWAC has played a critical role in securing Canadian state response to the issue of MMIWG. Founded in 1974, NWAC is a national organization representing the interests of Indigenous women in Canada. Birthed from the need to address sexism in the Indian Act, NWAC has expanded to address key social, economic, and political issues impacting their constituents, including all aspects of violence against Indigenous women and girls. In addition to their work on MMIWG, the organization has addressed family violence, sexual exploitation and trafficking, and Canadian state violence (such as sex discrimination in the Indian Act and matrimonial property rights).

NWAC's efforts to obtain a Canadian state response to violence against Indigenous women officially began in 2002, when it raised the issue in a report to a United Nations special rapporteur investigating human rights violations in Canada. In 2004, NWAC collaborated with Amnesty International Canada on the report *Stolen Sisters: A Human Rights Response to Discrimination and Violence Against Indigenous Women in Canada,* condemning Canada for failing to protect Indigenous women and girls from violence. Building on the attention created by that report, NWAC pursued the federal government for funding, and after more than a year and a concerted media campaign, succeeded in securing a commitment of five million dollars over five years (2005–2010) for the SIS initiative. In addition to conducting research, NWAC developed educational content and programming, including resources aimed at educating Indigenous women and girls about safety; assisting families and friends of MMIWG; and informing the state and the broader Canadian and global societies about the issue. They advised the Canadian state on how best to respond to this violence, and deployed an aggressive media campaign to raise awareness of the issue and demand further action on the part of the state.

However, the arrival of the Harper Conservative regime in 2006 contributed to the colonization of these efforts. NWAC was placed under state surveillance through increasing demands for more thorough accounting of the work of SIS: when I met with SIS director Kate Rexe in 2009, she shared with me the initiative's most recent annual report to the government, encompassing several large binders. While NWAC had pursued a second round of funding to continue its work well in advance of the conclusion of the original agreement, it wasn't secured until well after the initial funding agreement had terminated.

When I interviewed Rexe in 2012 as part of my doctoral research, she indicated that this process had been plagued by delays by the state's repeated replacement of their central contact within the Status of Women, resulting in multiple restarts to the whole negotiation process. Moreover, in a recent interview, Rexe reported, "every time NWAC submitted funding proposals to Status of Women any reference to Sisters in Spirit was scratched out or came with a clear message—that program no longer existed once the funding ran out. The name couldn't even be used" (Aboriginal Peoples Television Network 2015).

After this protracted and hostile back and forth, which led to Rexe resigning from her position, NWAC secured a second commitment of funding from the Government of Canada at the drastically reduced rate of $1.89 million over three years. The organization was prohibited from referring to its work on MMIWG as "Sisters in Spirit," referring to it instead by the title "From Evidence to Action." They were also officially prohibited from continuing their research on the database of cases of MMIWG, although it has recently been suggested this work continued in secret (Aboriginal Peoples Television Network 2015). NWAC was permitted to continue holding its annual SIS vigils (October 4), facilitate knowledge exchanges, and conduct community engagement workshops. NWAC was also permitted to continue lobbying work, which it has done vehemently to ensure that the perspectives of Indigenous women and girls are present in the debates surrounding recent significant political moments in Canada, including the B.C. Missing Women Commission of Inquiry and changes to the Canadian criminal code surrounding prostitution. During this time, NWAC also supported the RCMP when it was conducting its national operational overview.

This (his)story repeated itself in NWAC's third attempt to secure funding. Despite submitting a proposal more than six months in advance of their funding conclusion of April 2014, the organization was unable to secure a final commitment until well after that end date thanks to problematic negotiations with the Government of Canada. In 2014, the Canadian state approved a pittance of $750,000 for the organization's current three-year initiative, "Project PEACE" (Prevention, Education, Action, Change, and Evaluation).[1]

For the duration of his entire nine-year tenure as Prime Minister of Canada, Stephen Harper refused to consider holding a national public inquiry into MMIWG. As Indigenous women and girls were disappearing and dying in the hundreds across this country, Harper turned a deaf ear while he and his government calculatedly sabotaged Indigenous women's efforts to address this violence. Advancing his "tough on crime" political agenda, Harper funnelled millions into policing, including funding the RCMP operational overview and creating a national missing persons centre. As critics have pointed out, this amounts to investment in the ongoing criminalization and incarceration of Indigenous peoples. His government also refused to address much of the social, political, and economic marginalization and exclusion that makes Indigenous women and girls highly vulnerable to exploitation and violence.

Conclusion

In this new era of truth and reconciliation under Prime Minister Justin Trudeau's Liberal regime, Indigenous peoples are increasingly being invited to participate in state-sponsored efforts, such as the national inquiry into MMIWG, to address our existing relationship with Canada. As Indigenous peoples, we cannot forget that, for too long, this has been an intensely violent and exploitative relationship and, thus, we need to approach such opportunities with extreme caution. We cannot forget that this is a settler colonial nation and state with an enduring and significant investment in our oppression and elimination.

For this inquiry to make meaningful change in the lives of Indigenous women and girls, several things need to happen. First, as the experts of our own lives, the commissioners need to privilege the perspectives of Indigenous women and girls in all aspects of their work and provide adequate funding, support, and opportunities so that as many Indigenous women and girls as possible can contribute to this process. This is not intended as a statement of exclusion of the participation and perspectives of others, but instead to ensure that Indigenous women and girls play a central role in the discussions and decision-making surrounding their lives. Second, it will require the commission take a hard look at the Canadian State's role in the violence of MMIWG and make recommendations that move towards addressing state complicity, specifically through dismantling settler colonial domination in Canada. Finally, it will require a humble but courageous Canadian state that acknowledges its violence and takes immediate and meaningful steps to address and eliminate it. No doubt, this will require a radical revisioning and restricting of the Canadian nation and state that eliminates settler colonial domination (and, indeed, all forms of oppression)—however, it's the only way to end the rampant violence inflicted on Indigenous women and girls.

1. See https://nwac.ca/policy-areas/violence-prevention-and-safety/project-peace/.

References

Aboriginal Peoples Television Network. *Stephen Harper's Longest War: Missing and Murdered Indigenous Women*, 2015. aptn.ca/news/2015/09/09/stephen-harpers-longest-war-missing-and-murdered-Indigenous-women/.

Acoose, Janice. *Iskwewak—Kah'Ki Yaw Ni Wahkomakanak: NeitherIndian Princesses Nor Easy Squaws.* Toronto: Women's Press, 1995.

Amnesty International. *Stolen Sisters: A Human Rights Response to Discrimination and Violence against*

Indigenous Women in Canada, 2002. amnesty.ca/sites/amnesty/files/amr200032004enstolensisters.pdf.

Anderson, Kim. *A Recognition of Being—Reconstructing Native Womanhood*. Toronto, ON: Sumach Press, 2000.

———. "Leading by Action: Female Chiefs and the Political Landscape." In G.G. Valaskakis, M.D. Stout and E. Guimond (eds.), *Restoring the Balance: First Nations Women, Community and Culture*. Winnipeg. MB: University of Manitoba Press, 2009.

Bopp, Michael, Judie Bopp, and Phil Lane Jr. *Aboriginal Domestic Violence in Canada:* Ottawa: The Aboriginal Healing Foundation, 2003. ahf.ca/downloads/domestic-violence.pdf.

Bourgeois, Robyn. "Warrior Women: Indigenous Women's Anti-Violence Engagement with the Canadian State." Unpublished doctoral thesis. Toronto: University of Toronto, 2014.

———. "Colonial Exploitation: The Canadian State and the Trafficking of Indigenous Women and Girls in Canada." UCLA *Law Review* 62 (2015): 1426–1463.

Cannon, Martin J. "Revisiting Histories of Legal Assimilation, Racialized Injustice, and the Future of Indian Status in Canada." In M.J. Cannon and L. Sunseri (eds.), *Racism, Colonialism, and Indigeneity in Canada*. Toronto, ON: Oxford University Press, 2011.

———. "Race Matters: Sexism, Indigenous Sovereignty, and *McIvor*." *Canadian Journal of Women and Law* 26, no. 1(2014): 23–50.

CBC News. "Full text of Peter Mansbridge's interview with Stephen Harper," 2014. cbc.ca/news/politics/full-text-of-peter-mansbridge-s-interview-with-stephen-harper-1.2876934.

———. "Murdered women's inquiry must confront barriers Indigenous women face in Canadian society," 2016. cbc.ca/news/canada/british-columbia/missing-women-carolyn-bennett-inquiry-feminism-1.3407921.

Comack, Elizabeth. "Colonialism Past and Present: Indigenous Human Rights and Canadian Politics." In J. Green (ed.), *Indivisible: Indigenous Human Rights*. Halifax & Winnipeg: Fernwood Publishing, 2014.

Coulthard, Glen Sean. *Red Skin, White Masks: Rejecting the Colonial Politics of Recognition*. Minneapolis and London: University of Minnesota Press, 2014.

Culhane, Dara. "Their Spirits Live Within Us: Aboriginal Women in Downtown Eastside Vancouver Emerging into Visibility." In S. Applegate Krouse and H. A. Howard (eds.), *Keeping the Campfires Burning: Native Women's Activism in Urban Communities*. Lincoln and London: University of Nebraska Press, 2009.

Dick, Carolyn. "The Politics of Intragroup Difference: First Nations' Women and the *Sawridge* Dispute." *Canadian Journal of Political Silence* 39, 1 (2006): 97–114.

Eberts, Mary. "Victoria's Secret: How to Make a Population of Prey." In J. Green (ed.), *Indivisible: Indigenous Human Rights*. Halifax & Winnipeg: Fernwood Publishing, 2014.

Erickson, L. *Westward Bound: Sex, Violence, the Law, and the Making of a Settler Society*. Vancouver, BC: UBC Press, 2011.

Fellows, Mary Louise, and Sherene Razack. "The Race to Innocence: Confronting Hierarchical Relations among Women." *The Journal of Gender, Race & Justice*, 335 (1998).

Government of Canada. *Aboriginal Women and Family Violence*, 2008. onwa.ca/upload/documents/aboriginal-women and familyviolence p d.

———. *Terms of Reference for the National Inquiry into Missing and Murdered Indigenous Women and Girls*, 2016. aadnc-aandc.gc.ca/eng/1470141425998/147014150 7152.

Green, Joyce. "Constitutionalising the Patriarchy: Aboriginal Women and Aboriginal Government." *Constitutional Reform*, 1, 1–4 (1993):11–20.

———. "Taking Account of Aboriginal Feminism." In J. Green (ed.), *Making Space for Indigenous Feminism*. Black Point & Winnipeg: Fernwood Publishing, 2007.

———. "From Colonialism to Reconciliation Through Human Rights." In J. Green (ed.), *Indivisible: Indigenous Human Rights*. Halifax and Winnipeg: Fernwood Publishing, 2014.

Hugill, David. *Missing Women, Missing News: Covering the Crisis in Vancouver's Downtown Eastside*. Halifax and Winnipeg: Fernwood Publishing, 2010.

Hylton, J. "The Justice System and Canada's Aboriginal Peoples: The Persistance of Racial Discrimination." In W. Chan and K. Mirchandani (eds.), *Crimes of Colour: Racialization and the Criminal Justice System in Canada*. Peterborough, ON: Broadview Press, 2002.

Moore, Holly, and Martha Trojan. 2016. "'No foul play' found in deaths of dozens of Indigenous women, but questions remain." CBC *News Online*. <cbc.ca/news/canada/manitoba/unresolved-cases-of-missing-and-mnrdered-Indigenous-women-1.3651516>.

NWAC (Native Women's Association of Canada). *Voices of Our Sisters in Spirit: A Report to Families and Communities*, second edition, 2009. nwac.ca/wp-content/uploads/2015/05/NWAC_Voices-of-Our-Sisters-In-Spirit_2nd-Edition_March-2009.pdf.

———. *What Their Stories Tell Us: Research Findings from the Sisters in Spirit Initiative*. Ottawa: Native Women's Association of Canada, 2010. nwac.ca/wp-content/uploads/2015/07/2010-What-Their-Stories-Tell-Us-Research-Findings-SIS-Initiative. pdf.

———. *Sexual Exploitation and Trafficking of Aboriginal Women and Girls: Literature Review* and Key Informants—Final Report, 2014. nwac.ca/wp-content/uploads/2015/05/2014_NWAC_Human_Trafficking_and_Sexual_Exploitation_Report.pdf.

Oppal, W. *Forsaken: The Report of the Missing Women Commission of Inquiry, Volume I*. Victoria, BC: Province of British Columbia, 2012.

Perrin, Benjamin. *Invisible Chains: Canada's Underground World of Human Trafficking*. Toronto: Viking Canada.

Razack, Sherene H. *Looking White People in the Eye: Gender, Race, and Culture in Courtrooms and Classrooms.* Toronto: University of Toronto Press, 1998.

———. "Gendering Disposability" *Canadian Journal of Women and the Law*, 29, no. 2 (2016): 285–307.

Royal Canadian Mounted Police. *Missing and Murdered Aboriginal Women: A National Operational Overview.* Ottawa: Government of Canada, 2014. rcmp-grc.gc.ca/warn/media/460/original/0cbd8968a049aa0b44d343e76b4a9478.pdf.

Shenher, Lori. *That Lonely Section of Hell: The Botched Investigation of a Serial Killer Who Almost Got Away.* Vancouver: Greystone Books, 2015.

Smith, Andrea. *Conquest: Sexual Violence and American Indian Genocide.* Cambridge, MA: South End Press, 2005.

Stueck, Wendy. "Inquiry into Missing and Murdered Women Needs Funding, Advocates Say." *Globe and Mail*, 2016. theglobeandmail.com/news/british-columbia/inquiry-into-missing-and-murdered-women-needs-funding-advocates-say/artide28140337/.

Truth and Reconciliation Commission. *Honouring the Truth, Reconciling for the Future Summary of the Final Report of the Truth and Reconciliation Commission of Canada*, 2015. trc.ca/websites/trcinstitution/index.php?p=890.

Williams, Bernie, and Gladys Radek. "Walk4Justice Summary," 2010. unbc.ca/sites/defeult/files/assets/northern_fire/email_attachments/walk4justice_summary2010. pdf.

CHAPTER 12

Skirting the Issues

Indigenous Myths, Misses, and Misogyny

Alex Wilson

Introduction

Over the past few years, five of my Indigenous trans and two-spirit-identified friends have been murdered. I grieve the violent ends of the lives of my bright spirited sisters.

I grieve, just as deeply, the violence that we know is an all too present threat in the lives of two-spirit people. A recent study showed that, in comparison to the general population, two-spirit women are four times more likely to be sexually or physically assaulted, and they are 50 per cent more likely to be assaulted than Indigenous women who are heterosexual.[2] Nearly half of the trans and two-spirited participants in another study reported that they had been chased, and a similar proportion had been threatened with physical violence because of their sex/gender identity. Perhaps most troubling is the fact that many queer and trans Indigenous youth do not feel supported, welcome, or safe in

Wilson, Alex, "Skirting the Issues: Indigenous Myths, Misses and Misogyny." In Kim Anderson, Maria Campbell, and Christi Belcourt, eds., *Keetsahnak: Our Missing and Murdered Indigenous Sisters*. The University of Alberta Press, © 2018.

2. Keren Lehavot, Karina L. Walters, and Jane M. Simoni, "Abuse, Mastery, and Health among Lesbian, Bisexual, and Two-Spirit American Indian and Alaska Native Women," *Cultural Diversity and Ethnic Minority Psychology* 15, no. 3 (2009): 275–284.

their own families and communities or in ceremonial spaces. Violence, oppression, and perceived loss of culture all generate societal by-products such as suicide. And, sadly, the suicide rate amongst two-spirit people is ten times higher than that of any other group.

Our communities have witnessed, grieved, and spoken out loudly about our many missing and murdered Indigenous women, and the issue is finally gaining much-needed attention at a national level. A narrative that essentializes women and women's "roles," however, has accompanied this shift. The essentializing narrative, which is rooted in a binary construction of gender, risks further marginalization of two-spirit, trans, and other LGBTQ Indigenous people, and generates confusion about what constitutes tradition.

Skirt Shaming

A few years ago I was asked by a friend to attend a ceremony in a small community outside of the city. I had been to a quite a few sweat lodges in my life, taking part either to acknowledge significant events or rites of passage or because someone had asked for my support, and this time, without question or hesitation, I honoured my friend's request. When we arrived at the place where the ceremony would be held, I was glad to see a few familiar faces. I was introduced to the Elders and others who were standing around the fire before I was led to the lodge. I changed into my usual sweat lodge attire of a T-shirt and shorts and awaited instruction from the hosts. It was then that a (non-Native) woman whom I had met earlier came out of the change area and stood beside me. She asked my name again, stating that she had a "government name" and an "Indian name" and told me both. She asked me what my Indian name was. For the third time, I gave my name, and then, chuckling, asked where she was from. Wearing a long flannel nightgown, she suggested that I should change my clothes. "No," I replied, "this is what I have always worn to sweats." Her interrogation continued: "Who are your teachers?" She stated that I would have to go change out of the shorts and T-shirt because women must wear a dress or skirt for ceremonies. Just then, one of my friends overheard the exchange and chimed in: "Her parents are her teachers, and her grandparents." The woman stormed off, advising me that she was going to tell the Elders.

Sakihiwawin, Love in Actions

In Swampy Cree there exists a natural law, expressed by the term *sakihiwawin*. It is the natural order of the cosmos, which we, in turn, reflect as love in our actions.

Over a decade ago, a group of two-spirit people was called together by Elder Mae Louise Campbell. I am not too sure what led up to it—perhaps someone had a vision or a dream—but Elder Campbell had put word out that she was inviting two-spirit people to her land so that we could build a two-spirit drum. Word spread fast and soon we were in a convoy of three or four vehicles heading out to her land. When we arrived, she greeted us and said that she was honoured to have us. We were to build what we understood would be the first modern-day two-spirit drum in the region. As she showed us how to prepare the skin and build the drum frame, she told us stories about two-spirit people. When we had finally pieced the drum together, it was time to bless it in a sweat lodge ceremony. When that part of the ceremony was completed, we left the lodge one by one.

The experience had been so powerful that, at the feast for the drum that followed, we were all content and silent. After the building ceremony, we held weekly drum group practices and eventually decorated the drum by painting and "dressing" it. Today many two-spirit people have come and gone from the drum group, some passing on to the spirit world, but the drum continues as a reminder of our shared collective power. The drum reminds me that our relations extend beyond interpersonal to spiritual and ancestral connections. While others who present themselves as teachers had enforced "protocols" that attempted to shame and exclude me and other two-spirit or trans people from ceremony, Elder Campbell, by bringing us into ceremony to make and play our drum, had recognized and honoured us as who we are.

Connected to Body, Connected to Land[3]

I am a two-spirit member of the Opaskwayak Cree Nation. My family clan name is Wassenas, which translates as "reflecting light from within." That light is one form of the inextinguishable energy that has been passed to me from my ancestors and through my family and community. In our traditional spirituality, we find guidance in a Great Mystery; that is, that we are connected to everything by spiritual energy, joining us in a limitless circle that encompasses the past, present, and future. Following from this are the Cree principles of kakinow ni wagomakanak (we are in relationship with the land, waters, plants, animals, and other living creatures), a-kha ta neekanenni miso-an (we are all equally important), sakihiwawin (a commitment to act in ways that express love), and mino pimatisiwin (we are responsible to live in conscious connection with the land and living things in a way that creates and sustains balance—or, as my father translates from our dialect, to live beautifully). We understand that the nature of the cosmos is to be in balance and that when balance is disturbed, it must and will return.

Restoring Balance

Two-spirit identity is one way in which balance is being restored to our communities. Throughout the colonial history of the Americas, aggressive assimilation policies have been employed to displace our own understandings, practices, and teachings around sexuality, gender, and positive relationships, and replace them with those of Judeo Christianity.[4] To recognize ourselves as two-spirit

is to declare our connection to the traditions of our own people.

The term *two-spirit* first came to a Cree person who was a teacher. She shared it with a gathering of Indigenous LGBTQI people from across North America (held in southern Manitoba in 1990).[5] The term was taken up quickly as a self-identifier, and many two-spirit people understand it to mean that each of us possesses a particular balance of masculinity and femininity or male and female energy. As a self-identifier, *two-spirit* acknowledges and affirms our identity as Indigenous peoples, our connection to the land, and values in our traditional cultures that recognize and accept gender and sexual diversity.

When the term *two-spirit* first appeared, the meaning most often attached to it reflected a binary construction of gender identity. This has changed. As the two-spirit activist Cheyenne Fayant-McLeod states, "Two-spirit means being queer and Indigenous, not that you are half man half woman. Depending on which tribe you're from, who your grandparents are, and what your ancestors have experienced, there are many, many different stories about what being queer means in Indigenous communities."[6] As another observed, our current understandings of the identity of LGBTQI people is "evolving or changing, and the term *two-spirit* is a placeholder until something comes along that more accurately fits the full continuum of who we are in the contemporary context."[7]

The recognition and acceptance of gender and sexual diversity is reflected in the language, spirituality, and culture of our own people. Our Cree dialect does not include gender-distinct pronouns. Rather, our language is "gendered" on the basis of whether or not something is animate (that is, whether or not

3. "Connected to body, connected to land" is one of the many Indigenous teachings shared the Native Youth Sexual Health Network (discussed later in this chapter).

4. Martin Cannon, "The Regulation of First Nations Sexuality," *Canadian Journal of Native Studies* 18, no. 1 (1998): 1–18; Quo-Li Driskill, Chris Finley, Brian Joseph Gilley, and Scott Lauria Morgensen, eds., *Queer Indigenous Studies: Critical Interventions in Theory, Politics, and Literature* (Tucson: University of Arizona Press, 2011); Alex Wilson, "Two-Spirit Identity: Active Resistance to Multiple Oppressions," *Directions: Research and Policy on Eliminating Racism* 5, no. 1 (Spring 2009): 44–46.

5. Albert McLeod, *Two-Spirited People of Manitoba Inc.*, accessed January 24, 2018, https://twospiritmanitoba.ca/we-belong.

6. Fayant-McLeod quoted in Michele Tyndall, "Two Spirit Reclaiming Acceptance through Education," *Regina Leader-Post*, June 17, 2013.

7. Dylan Rose, personal communication, August 2011.

it has a spiritual purpose and energy). Our creation story takes us back to the stars and the central figure or character Weesageychak, represented by the constellation other people call Orion. A trickster and a teacher, Weesageychak shifts gender, form, and space to playfully teach us about our selves and our connection to the wider universe, land and waters, living things and each other.

Cultural Disruption

When European newcomers first began to explore and settle our lands, they brought with them their commitment (rooted in their own cultures, spirituality and ways of being) to **heteropatriarchy** and gender binaries. They saw the acceptance of gender and sexual diversity that prevailed in our lands as sinful and threatening. As the Spanish explorer Cabeza de Vaca stated in the early 1500s, it was "a devilish thing."[8] Historic records show that violence on the bodies of Indigenous people who did not conform to the gender and sexual norms of the European newcomers began soon after their arrival. In 1513, forty Indigenous people whom the explorer Balboa had identified as "sodomites" were executed.[9] The imposition of Christianity, Canada's Indian Act, and other laws that apply only to Indigenous peoples, and the residential and boarding school systems imposed by the Canadian and American governments continued the work of Columbus and his fellow explorers. As part of an ongoing effort to assimilate Indigenous peoples, we were forcibly separated from each other and from our traditional cultures, lands, spirituality, languages, and ways of being. Throughout, our bodies, genders, and sexualities have been regulated in a continuum of violence. Penalized and punished for our acceptance of gender and sexual variance, many of us learned that the most certain way to survive was to take these teachings underground, out of sight of the colonizers.

These experiences continue to affect our people, communities, and nations. Today, some of our

traditional Elders and spiritual teachers have adopted and introduced understandings and practices that were not part of their own cultures prior to colonization and the imposition of Christianity. This came up in a recent queer pride celebration in a small community. The celebration included a sweat lodge ceremony, and when two-spirit and other participants arrived to take part in the ceremony, the Elder leading the ceremony demanded that those in the group change their clothing to conform to what he perceived their gender to be. He added the warning that if he suspected that they had dressed in a way that did not conform to his assumptions about their gender identity, they would be required to prove that they were female or male. In the face of this direct assault on their body sovereignty and gender self-determination, some people left the ceremony.[10] Others stayed for fear that they would be disrespecting the organizers and the Elder and others, or for fear that they would be punished.

The role of Elders in our communities includes sharing with youth traditional teachings that will help them understand their own experiences, including their expressions of gender identity and sexuality. However, in most of our Indigenous cultures, where gender and sexual diversity were once accepted and valued, our traditional teachings, ways of being, spirituality, and languages were disrupted and displaced through the processes of colonization, Christianization, and assimilation. The result (as the incident described above demonstrates) is that some of our own present-day cultural teachings and practices extend the continuum of violence that two-spirit people have been subject to since colonization began.

In our home communities, two-spirit people are frequently subject to interconnected homophobia, transphobia, and misogyny, and in the larger society they are additionally subject to structural and individual racism and classism. This has had devastating impacts on the two-spirit community. The suicide rate for LGBTQ Indigenous youth is ten times

8. Alvar Núñez Cabeza de Vaca, "Naufragios de Alvar Núñez Cabeza de Vaca," in Historiadores primitives de Indias (Vol. I), ed. Enrique de Vedia, trans. Ed Strug (Madrid: M. Rivadeneyra, 1852), 538.

9. Johnathan Goldberg, Sodometri.es: Renaissance Texts and Modern Sexualities (Stanford, CA: Stanford University Press, 1992).

10. Members of this group contacted me directly to tell me of this experience.

higher than that of any other group in the United States. Thirty-nine per cent of two-spirit women and 21 per cent of two-spirit men have attempted suicide.[11] In a recent study of transgendered and gender non-conforming Indigenous people in the United States, nearly one-quarter lived in extreme poverty; elevated rates of HIV were found among participants, and more than half of respondents (56%) had attempted suicide.[12]

Coming In

There is much work to be done, then, to undo the work that has been done upon us. When we call ourselves two-spirit people, we are proclaiming sovereignty over our bodies, gender expressions, and sexualities. In my own research with Cree and Ojibwe two-spirit people, I heard many stories of "**coming in**."[13] Coming in does not centre on the declaration of independence that characterizes "coming out" in mainstream depictions of the lives of LGBTQI people. Rather, coming in is an act of returning, fully present in our selves, to resume our place as a valued part of our families, cultures, communities, and lands, in connection with all our relations.

We do not do this work alone. Idle No More is an international grassroots movement that brings Indigenous and non-Indigenous people together to honour the sovereignty of Indigenous people and Nations, and to protect the land and water. Idle No More was organized in resistance to oppressive colonial ideologies and laws, and its activities have included public education on the regulation of sexuality and gender.[14] Another organization doing liberating work is the Native Youth Sexual Health Network. This organization was created by and for Indigenous youth, and works across issues of sexual and reproductive health, rights, and justice throughout Canada and the United States, with activities that include education, advocacy, and outreach with two-spirit and LGBTQ youth.[15]

In both these movements, Indigenous sovereignty over our lands is inseparable from sovereignty over our bodies, sexualities, and gender self-expression. This connection is at the root of the very contemporary understanding of identity held by many two-spirit youth today.

Walking as Sisters

Walking With Our Sisters now includes two-spirit and trans people not legally recognized as women in their discussions of the unreported cases of missing and murdered Indigenous women.[16] The projects No More Silence and It Starts with Us have begun compiling a community-run database that documents the violent deaths of Indigenous, two-spirit, and trans women.[17] Across Canada, communities have drawn on the RED dress Project and mounted their own displays to mark the absence of their missing sisters who are missing or have been murdered, and in many communities, empty red pant suits, T-shirts, or other articles of clothing have been hung alongside red dresses to mark the absence of their two-spirit and trans loved ones and, more generally, to

11. Karen C. Fieland, Karina L. Walters, and Jane M. Simoni, "Determinants of Health Among Two-Spirit American Indians and Alaska Natives," in *The Health of Sexual Minorities: Public Health Perspectives on Lesbian, Gay, Bisexual and Transgender Populations,* ed. Ilan H. Meyer and Mary E. Northridge (Springer, 2007), 268–300, e-hook.

12. National Center for Transgender Equably, *Injustice at Every Turn: American Indian and Alaskan Native respondents in the National Transgender Discrimination Survey* (Washington, DC: National Center for Transgender Equality, 2012).

13. Alex Wilson, "N'tadmowin inna nah': Our Coming in Stories," *Canadian Woman Studies* 26, no. 3–4 (2008): 193–199; Alex Wilson, "N'tacimowin inna nah': Coming in to Two-Spirit Identities" (PHD diss., Harvard Graduate School of Education, 2007).

14. Idle No More, accessed May 10, 2016, www.idlenomore.ca; Laura Zahody, "Idle No More Organizers Reach Out to Queer Community," in *The Winter We Danced: Voices from the Past; the Future, and the Idle No More Movement,* ed. the Kino-nda-niimi Collective (Winnipeg: ARP Books, 2014), 287–289.

15. "Healthy Sexuality & Fighting Homophobia & Transphobia," Native Youth Sexual Health Network, accessed June 15, 2015, http://www.nativeyouthsexualhealth.com/youthphotoprojecLhtml.

16. "Our Sisters," Walking With Our Sisters, accessed March 21, 2016, http://walkingwithoursisters.ca/about/our-sisters/.

17. *No More Silence* (blog), accessed March 26, 2016, http://nomoresilence-nomoresilence.blogspot.ca/; It Starts with Us website, accessed March 26, 2016, http://www.itstartswithus-mmiw.com/.

recognize that not ah women are most appropriately represented by a dress.

Bringing—and keeping—our two-spirit and trans loved ones into the movement to undo the violence that removes the lives and presence of Indigenous women from our families and communities is a crucial recognition of the fact that, for Indigenous women and two-spirit and trans people, our gender identity has put us at elevated risk of violence, oppression, marginalization, and loss of our place in our culture and community. The hashtag #MMIWG2S is a good start, but we must go further and embrace all of what that means.[18] We must address the interconnections between misogyny, homophobia, transphobia, classism, ablism, and racism. We must name misogyny and homo/transphobia in our own communities. We must acknowledge and protect the bodies and people who have been most impacted by colonial violence and have the courage to stand in the truth of and celebrate our own pre-colonial understandings of gender and sexual diversity. And we must include two-spirit and trans people in every discussion of murdered and missing Indigenous women and the inquiry process.

Generations of our peoples have been forced to march along the long and brutal path of colonization—but we are still here. Stall showing up. And still very alive, speaking up for each other and for our missing and murdered loved ones, standing together in grief, anger, ceremony, and love to demand change.

Author's Note

Portions of this paper have previously been published in Alexandria Wilson, "Two-Spirited People, Body Sovereignty and Gender Self-Determination," *Red Rising Magazine,* last modified September 21, 2015, http://redrisingmagazine.ca/two-spirit-people-body-sovereignty-and-gender-self-determination, and as "Our Coming in Stories: Cree Identity, Body Sovereignty and Gender Self-Determination," *Journal of Global Indigeneity* 1, no. 1 (2015), http://ro.uow.edu.au/jgi/.

---

18. In the hashtag #MMIWG2S, 2S is understood to refer to both two-spirit and trans people.

PART 6

Additional Readings

Anderson, Kim, Maria Campbell, and Christie Belcourt, eds. *Keetsahnak: Our Missing and Murdered Indigenous Sisters.* Edmonton: The University of Alberta Press, 2018.

Dean, Amber. *Remembering Vancouver's Disappeared Women: Settler Colonialism and the Difficulty of Inheritance.* Toronto: University of Toronto Press, 2015.

Florence, Melanie. *Missing Nimama.* Richmond Hill, ON: Clockwise Press, 2015.

Hargreaves, Allison. *Violence against Indigenous Women: Literature, Activism, Resistance* Waterloo, ON: Wilfrid Laurier University Press, 2017.

Iskwé, and Erin Leslie. *Will I See?* Winnipeg: Highwater Press, 2016.

Lavell-Harvard, D. Memee, and Jennifer Brant, eds. *Forever Loved: Exposing the Hidden Crisis of Missing and Murdered Indigenous Women and Girls in Canada.* Bradford, Ontario: Demeter Press, 2016.

National Inquiry into Missing and Murdered Indigenous Women and Girls. *Reclaiming Power and Place: the Final Report of the National Inquiry into Missing and Murdered Indigenous Women and Girls.* Ottawa: Government of Canada, 2019.

Razack, S. "Gendered Racial Violence and Spatialized Justice: The Murder of Pamela George," *Canadian Journal of Law and Society* 15, 2 (2000): 91–130.

Smith, Ariel. "Indigenous Cinema and the Horrific Reality of Colonial Violence" (Decolonization Blog). Available at: https://decolonization.wordpress.com/2015/02/13/indigenous-cinema-and-the-horrific-reality-of-colonial-violence/.

Stote, Karen. *An Act of Genocide: Colonialism and the Sterilization of Aboriginal Women*. Halifax: Fernwood Publishing, 2015.

Relevant Websites

Ariel Smith
www.arielsmith.com
Ariel Smith is an artist of mixed Nēhiyaw Iskwew and Jewish ancestry whose work uses a surrealist, expressionist, and horror genre aesthetic to expose and explore the history of gendered racial and colonial violence.

Government of Canada National Inquiry into Missing and Murdered Indigenous Women and Girls
www.mmiwg-ffada.ca
This is the official Federal Government of Canada's website that contains the final report of the Inquiry, and other relevant information on the MMIWG.

I Am a Kind Man: Kizhaay Anishnaabe Niin
www.iamakindman.ca
I Am a Kind Man is an initiative by Indigenous men across Ontario to teach that violence against women is against traditional teachings and that men, together with women, have a communal responsibility to stop the abuse and violence.

Moose Hide Campaign
www.moosehidecampaign.ca
The Moose Hide Campaign is an effort by a group of Indigenous men to take a stand against violence against Indigenous women.

Native Women's Association of Canada
www.nwac.ca
This is the official website of the Native Women's Association of Canada. It contains the Sisters in Spirit Report and Fact Sheet on MMIW.

The REDress Project-Jaime Black
www.jaimeblackartist.com/exhibitions
An installation art project taking place across Canada and the United States as a visual reminder of the thousands of Indigenous women and girls that have gone missing and murdered.

Films

Everything Is Connected. Dir. Doug Cuthand. Sixties Scoop Indigenous Society of Saskatchewan and Iskwewuk-E-wichiwitochik. 2021.

Finding Dawn. Dir. Christine Welsh. National Film Board of Canada. 2006.

How Do We Stop Aboriginal Women from Disappearing? TEDx Talks by Beverly Jacobs. 2014. Available at: https://www.youtube.com/watch?v=8NtkmnJ2Q3w.

Missing: The Documentary. Dir.Young Jibwe. Animikii Films. 2014. Available at: https://www.youtube.com/watch?v =wSS6mRaMSHA.

The Red Dress. Dir. Michael Scott. National Film Board of Canada. 1978.

This River. Dir. Erika MacPherson and Katherena Vernette. National Film Board of Canada. 2016.

Key Terms

- Coming In
- Missing and Murdered Indigenous Women and Girls (MMIWG)
- Sisters in Spirit
- Colonial violence

Discussion Questions

1. Drawing from both Robyn Bourgeois and Alex Wilson's readings, discuss how violence against Indigenous women and Two-Spirit individuals is similar to and yet different from violence against non-Indigenous women. Next, propose some strategies that could be used to properly address and eliminate such forms of violence.

2. How are the experiences of gendered and sexual violence of Indigenous queer, trans, and Two-Spirit identified individuals different from those of heterosexual Indigenous and non-Indigenous women? How have those experiences been shaped by colonial constructs of gendered and sexual identities? What can the "Coming In" stories discussed by Wilson teach us about proclaiming sovereignty over Indigenous bodies?

3. Discuss some of the ways in which the Canadian State has both perpetuated and enabled gendered and sexual violence against Indigenous peoples, paying particular attention to the Indian Act and the residential schooling system.

4. In the reading, Robyn Bourgeois argues that in order to understand the systemic causes of the gendered and sexual violence experienced by Indigenous peoples, the Missing and Murdered Indigenous Women and Girls Inquiry needed to take an Indigenous Feminist Anti-Oppression framework. What does that framework entail, and how could it help us to understand the systemic causes of the violence, and to eradicate it?

Activities

Browse through the Missing and Murdered Indigenous Women and Girls National Inquiry website available online (see above) and read the Final Report. How do its findings and recommendations fit with Bourgeois's argument that it is imperative that the MMIWG Inquiry commissioners "consider Indigenous feminist perspectives"?

Visit the I Am a Kind Man and the Moose Hide Campaign websites listed above. Why and how are Indigenous men taking initiatives to respond to and eliminate gendered violence? Through their engagement, how do you think they might be reconceptualizing Indigenous masculinities?

PART 7

Family, Belonging, and Displacement

Editor Introduction

On 11 June 2008, Prime Minister Harper officially apologized on behalf of the Canadian State and ordinary Canadians to the survivors of the **residential schooling** system, and Indigenous peoples in general, for the many forms of abuse that happened in the schools and for other negative impacts inflicted on individuals, their families, and communities. This apology recognizes that the impacts of colonial policies, like residential schooling, are still ongoing in Indigenous communities. Contrary to what some might wish to believe, colonialism is not a thing of the past and a new path of reconciliation and healing must be taken. The year 2021 marked a time of pain, anger, sadness, and shock for many Canadians, as thousands of unmarked gravesites at former residential schools have been located across the land. For most Indigenous peoples this triggered painful memories of traumatic stories we have been told by our relatives, but for many Canadians the discovery of the gravesites was a shock, an awakening of the racist and colonial history upon which their country had been built on, an often hidden story of the abuse and violence that occurred in those schools. This section of the book examines the impact of racism, Settler colonialism, and displacement on familial relations and nationhood, in particular the impact of these legacies on traditional ways of knowing, loving, caring, and nurturing.

As Ing (2006) has argued, through the separation of children from their families and communities, the State had hoped that the traditional cultures of Indigenous peoples would be forgotten, and assimilation to mainstream society would take place. In 2008, the House of Commons reported that this policy was racist because it deemed Indigenous cultures to be inferior to that of Euro-Canadians. It reported the many violent forms of abuse that happened inside the walls of the schools, as well as the long-term impact on the bodies, minds, spirits, and hearts of the survivors and their families that is still being felt today.

Indigenous children were expected to suppress their sexuality, were punished for speaking their language and for maintaining bonds with their siblings, and suffered abuse from their teachers and schoolmates in residential schools. Children were left with feelings of shame about their Indigenous identity; they did not learn positive parenting skills, confusing love with violence and self-hate. When returning to their communities, they no longer possessed the love, confidence, self-esteem, cultural knowledge, and oftentimes, the language, to form positive relationships with their families. Many turned to negative coping behaviours to escape the internal turmoil, sometimes involving alcoholism and other addictions, as well as violence.

The residential schooling system was part of an overall attack on Indigenous family structures by the Canadian State and the Euro-Christian systems that made up Settler colonialism. As Lavell-Harvard and Anderson point out in their article, **Indigenous mothering** was directly targeted by the racist, sexist, and patriarchal colonial structures. Prior to colonialism, in Indigenous societies, women and mothers held much power and were regarded as the carriers of water of life. As such, they held responsibility to nurture not just their families, but also the whole people, and had authority and decision-making powers at least equal to those of men in their nations. Given that Indigenous mothering practices were "seen as a threat to the patriarchal order of the colonized" (Lavell-Harvard and Anderson, in Chapter 13) because they did not entail Indigenous women being submissive to the males of their families and communities, Indigenous families had to be disrupted and restructured. Some of the ways this was done was by constructing negative stereotypes of Indigenous women, disciplining them into monogamous patriarchal nuclear units, and eventually through the apprehension of Indigenous children from their families to residential schools, to foster care, or to be adopted to non-Indigenous families.

While the impact of such attacks on Indigenous families has undoubtedly been traumatic and damaging, Indigenous women and their communities have always fought to maintain and/or revitalize the "more empowering cultural beliefs, traditions, and practices of our ancestors", and to maintain a "definition of womanhood and mothering premised upon strength and capability." Their resilience has made it possible to teach the next generations of the richness of Indigenous mothering practices and heal from the traumatic experiences brought by colonial policies.

In December 2015, the Truth and Reconciliation Commission Report was released, detailing the history and legacy of the residential schooling system on both the children that attended those schools and their families (TRC, 2015). The report included 94 calls to action, some of which are specifically tied to child welfare: to reduce the number of Indigenous children in care; to develop culturally appropriate parenting programs for Indigenous families; to provide resources to Indigenous communities and organizations so that Indigenous families can stay together whenever possible; and to require that child welfare decision makers be trained on the impacts of residential schools system on children and caregivers (TRC, 2015).

Indigenous communities and organizations took the federal government to court in order to seek compensation for the discriminatory child welfare policies in Indigenous communities, and for the removal of children from their families during the well-known Sixties Scoop. After long years of court battles, survivors of the Sixties Scoop have achieved over $700 million in settlement, and an Agreement in Principle has also finally been reached to compensate First Nations communities for the government's failure to fairly and adequately fund children and family services in reserves, and to implement the Jordan's Principle as previously mandated by the courts. These two historic settlements, if fully and promptly acted upon, are positive steps towards the reconciliation path recommended by the TRC, and will assist in keeping Indigenous families together.

Lynn Gehl's reading examines another policy that has also discriminated against many Indigenous people and children: the Aboriginal Affairs and Northern Development Canada's (now renamed Indigenous and Northern Affairs Canada) unstated paternity policy that denied Indian status registration to children whose father's signature did not appear on their birth certificate, as it assumed unknown and/or unstated paternity to mean a non-Indian man. While the sexist discriminatory practice of this policy has already been covered in Part Five of this volume, Gehl's chapter highlights how this policy particularly impacted women's children by denying them their Indian status, and in doing so, diminished their ability to be full members of their Indigenous nations. As Gehl argues, this policy denied many children the ability to be legal Indians, members of their bands, and to have treaty rights. Furthermore, she points out, the policy "relies on a discourse . . . and practice that blames and targets mothers and their babies . . . sometimes . . . due to an abuse of power and sexual violence such as incest and rape, mothers may not obtain the father's signature on the child's birth registration form because they do not want the father to know about the child or have access to the child." Indeed, there might exist a myriad of complex and private reasons for not being able/willing to state a child's paternity. However, the policy strove to regulate Indigenous women's choices and intimate lives, and in many cases, it further victimized them and influenced Indigenous familial arrangements and relations. In the end, this "legislative silence presently coded in the *Indian Act* was manipulatively crafted by sexist and racist patriarchs as a mechanism to then create discriminatory policy at the departmental level" (Gehl, Chapter 14 in this volume).

After decades of legal challenges to the sexist discriminatory policy in the *Indian Act*, in 2017 the Canadian Senate passed an amendment to Bill S-3 to eliminate all existing sexist discriminations. Initially, the federal government paused the implementation of the Senate's mandate, stating that it needed to first consult with First Nations communities, but finally in August 2019 promised that it would proceed to remove any remaining sexist inequalities in the Act, and to extend Indian Status to those prevented from it because of the 1951 cut-off rule (CBC News, August 2019a).

Despite the genocidal nature of residential schooling, the child welfare system, and other State policies, both authors speak of their own resilience and the courage of Indigenous people to survive the racist colonial attacks on Indigeneity. This is evident through efforts to recover both traditional gender and familiar relations, and to pass on these traditions to the younger generations. They have done so by both by educating oneself in the history of residential schools, as well as through their family members who have experienced this history, so that we can make sense of the lingering effects existing in our families and nations, and to find again our inner strength to heal and move forward.

CHAPTER 13

Indigenous Mothering Perspectives

D. Memee Lavell-Harvard and Kim Anderson

After centuries of persecution and oppression, the simple fact that we are still here, as proud Indigenous mothers, at the heart of our families, communities, and nations, signifies the strength of our resistance. Whether this resistance has been overt, as our sisters engage in constitutional challenges or human rights demonstrations, or covert, as we silently reconnect with the land and

Lavell-Harvard, D. Memee and Kim Anderson. "Introduction: Indigenous Mothering Perspectives." In *Mothers of the Nations: Indigenous Mothering as Global Resistance, Reclaiming and Recovery*, Demeter Press: Bradford ON Canada, Copyright © 2014.

teach our children the ways of our ancestors, our efforts have ensured the continued survival of our people.

Our traditions remind us of the power of motherhood. In the Indigenous nations that we (Lavell-Harvard and Anderson) come from, we are taught that the women are the water carriers; they carry the waters of life and, therefore, water represents the female element. It is this belief in one's own ability that like the water we can adapt to and eventually overcome any obstacle—that inspires resilience and persistence in the face of adversity. Sylvia Maracle (Mohawk) explains:

> The other thing to remember about the water is that it is the strongest force on the earth . . . Even the wind can't do what the water can do . . . that is our role in terms of tradition; we have the capacity as women to take those shapes, but also to make those shapes. We recognize that we don't have the kind of power where you bang your fist on the table, but that we have the power of the water—that sort of every day going against something that ultimately changes the shape of the thing. (quoted in Anderson, *A Recognition of Being* 185)

Indeed, like the waves that eventually wear away the rocks on our shores, the strength of our women is subtle but relentless. Such characteristics are unquestionably powerful tools in both the everyday struggles for survival as Indigenous mothers, as well as the larger struggles to challenge, subvert, deconstruct, and eventually break free from the oppressive structures of the racist, sexist, patriarchal society in which we find ourselves.

Although we set out to achieve the impossible, since "writing about an 'Indigenous ideology of motherhood' is, of course, an exercise in making generalizations about peoples who are extremely diverse" (Anderson, "Giving Life to the People" 761), we have . . . found some common themes within the experiences of Indigenous mothering across the globe. While we can never claim to

adequately represent the extremely nuanced diversity of Indigenous maternal experience, Indigenous peoples do share many values, epistemologies, and worldviews, including a belief in the centrality of strong powerful women. Unfortunately, as a graduate student recently reminded Lavell-Harvard when she glibly called out "the White Man" when asked to identify our greatest enemy, the one thing that we all have in common is a history of resistance; the experiences of colonization, oppression, and marginalization have been all too similar the world over. While this shared experience may determine the field upon which we must choose our battles, it does not define who we are at heart as Indigenous mothers since Indigenous mothering is, in essence, about something much larger, and much older, and much more empowering.

Interestingly, it is our shared experience of exclusion from society that provides a fertile ground for the revitalization and maintenance of empowering mothering practices. In the Canadian context, many of our mothers, grandmothers, and great-grandmothers before us found that an "Indian" or "half-breed" woman could never be assimilated enough to be accepted by colonial society (Van Kirk). As a result, the large scale inability (or more likely the conscious refusal) of Indigenous women to adapt to the western institution of motherhood instigated the apprehension of generations of Indigenous children and subsequent placement into residential schools or foster care where they could be isolated from the influence of their "backward" mothers. Despite the concerted and often brutal efforts of both church and state to erase Indigeneity, it became apparent that our cultures, the very essence of who we are, could neither be overcome, nor beaten out.

Traditionally, our women were respected and valued within our communities. Arising out of our role as mothers, as the givers of life, the role of Indigenous women is to care for and nurture life once it is brought into the world and, by extension, to care for and nurture our nations (Anderson, *A Recognition of Being*). Referencing the teachings of the Dakota nation, Anderson has explained that according to our traditions Indigenous women not only literally "birth the people" they are also given a "lifetime responsibility to nurture the people:"

> It's not just women's responsibility to the children—we have a responsibility to all of the people. We have to. We are the life givers. We are the life force of the nation. Our responsibility is to everyone; male and female, young or old, because we are that place from which life emanates. And there is nothing greater than that. (Ivy Chaske, quoted in Anderson, *A Recognition of Being* 169)

Bringing forth and nurturing new life is understood to be the basis of the creation of our nation. Thus, unlike western ideologies that denied women decision-making power in the family and positioned them in a role equivalent to a family servant, Indigenous mothers historically had responsibility for the life they created and, by extension, for the whole family and the entire community. With such responsibility came authority and the "right to make decisions on behalf of the children, the community and the nation" (Anderson, "Giving Life to the People" 171).

Unfortunately for our people, a fundamental belief in the equality and interdependence of all people, and the resulting egalitarian social structures found in many Indigenous societies, as well as the empowered women therein, were seen as a threat to the patriarchal order of the colonizers. In the North American context, Indigenous women not only birthed each new generation, they were simultaneously "bearers of a counter-imperial order," and so their subjugation was "critical to the success of the economic, cultural and political colonization" of the "new world" (Smith 15). The very existence of women who were subject to the authority of neither fathers nor husbands had the potential to throw into question the supposed natural order of patriarchal hierarchies and could therefore not be tolerated. As Andrea Smith has argued, the subsequent and continued "demonization of Native women can be seen as a strategy of white men to maintain control over white women" (21) thereby reinforcing **patriarchy**, and simultaneously destroying the social structures of Indigenous nations. In Canada and the United States, Eurowestern "matrons" were sent to Indigenous communities to train the women, in a largely unsuccessful attempt to encourage acceptance of a more acceptable role as docile and subservient housewives and mothers in patriarchal nuclear families (Rutherdale, Jacobs).

Dua, Stevenson, Smith, and Monture-Angus have all described the many ways in which the colonial imagination constructed the "myth" of the Indigenous woman in North America in order to denigrate, disempower, and dehumanize her, thereby serving a racist and sexist colonial agenda. According to Dua, departures from the traditional patriarchal nuclear family model were seen as a danger to the social order and fears of miscegenation were intimately mixed with fear of "degeneration" into so-called "primitive patterns of social and family practices" in North America (254). Through their missions, the early French colonizers actively worked to replace the functional gender, sexual, and familial relations in Indigenous communities with patriarchal relationships based on monogamy, discipline, and dependency for women. While such attempts were generally resisted (as the dismayed accounts of missionaries attest), they were not without effect, as familial relationships that had served the Indigenous people well since time Immemorial were disrupted.

Indeed, even when Indigenous ceremonies, dances, or gatherings were outlawed, and our very survival was dependent upon compliance with the dictates of colonial society, our grandmothers learned how to effectively hide any indicators of adherence to our traditions by actively cultivating the outward appearance of conformity. We have been persecuted for as long as we can remember, not only because we were different in a society with very little tolerance for diversity, but because society deemed our differences, our heathen legacies, as a threat to the maintenance of social order. It is therefore not surprising that many of us learned at a very young age the importance of deception. Thus began a long tradition of "keeping up appearances" as a strategic form of resistance, and as a result many of us find ourselves living double life as we construct and work to maintain a facade of normalcy in order to evade the always vigilant gaze of the larger society.

In retrospect, it was a blessing in disguise that Indigenous women were never completely or effectively assimilated enough to become the kind of wife and mother idealized in western patriarchal society. While non-Indigenous women are struggling to break free from the constraints of the patriarchal family and the oppression of motherhood, many of our women have resisted (or been excluded) and, as a result, have always existed outside these particular paradigms. Andrea O'Reilly explains that feminist mothering functions as a counter narrative or "oppositional discourse: its meaning is constructed as a negation of patriarchal motherhood" (797). In this context, as it is defined in oppositional ways, feminist mothering is still responding to, and therefore structurally and conceptually influenced by, the parameters and definitions of patriarchal mothering. In this manner, the revolutionary power of feminist mothering is hobbled as the terms of the debate and the field of battle are already set by the traditions of patriarchal society. However, generations of resistance and resilience means those Indigenous women do not necessarily face the same dilemma as we work instead to reclaim and revitalize the more empowering cultural beliefs, traditions, and practices of our ancestors.

Indigenous women have had to become practiced at resistance in order to survive in a system that functions globally to subjugate and oppress both Indigenous peoples and women generally, and, therefore, Indigenous women particularly. Generations of strong women have provided the foundation for such resistance, for, as Anderson explains, the "guidance that women receive from their mothers, aunts and grandmothers, shapes the way they learn to understand themselves and their positions in the world" ("Giving Life to the People" 123). Having had to learn how to resist subjugation and how to survive under the weight of oppression, previous generations of Indigenous mothers have maintained a definition of womanhood and mothering premised upon strength and capability that was distinctly different from the negative images and subservient female role offered by mainstream society. Indeed, according to the definition of womanhood cultivated by Western society, the so-called "true woman is self-contained within her nuclear family, with specific and separate roles for men and women and with an economic dependence on men, in such a way that motherhood is one's true occupation" (Snorton 57). In contrast, for Indigenous women, the role of wife and mother did not historically preclude working outside the home and was certainly not defined by dependency.

In land-based communities, given that the men were often away from the community for long periods, women were not only encouraged, but expected to be independent and self-reliant. Women were therefore neither prevented, nor discouraged from learning tasks that were traditionally seen to be men's work and, moreover, engaging in such work was not seen *so* take sway from one's femininity (Anderson, Berkin, Brown, Landes). The provision of foodstuffs and resources for the family often relied heavily upon tasks traditionally performed by women, thereby negating any possibility of women being dependent upon their husbands and creating, instead, relationships characterized by interdependence and equality (Anderson. "Giving Life to the People"). For centuries, strength, independence, and self-reliance have defined our mothers, and interdependent supportive networks of kin have shaped Indigenous motherhood; the legacy of which continues to influence our collective experience today.

. . . Indigenous mothering practices challenge patriarchal norms and even notions like gender complementarity . . . Indigenous approaches to healthy beginnings, which include food intake during pregnancy encourages us to see how healthy beginnings involve re-connecting to mother earth.

"Healthy beginnings" for Indigenous peoples ultimately leads to reclaiming pre-natal, birth and postnatal care . . . [R]eclaiming Indigenous centered care and the resurgence of Indigenous midwifery . . . is a heartening example of how the circle comes around, for here we have Indigenous women reclaiming an Indigenous vision of healthy beginnings in a modern urban context.

. . . Indigenous mothers envision themselves through the oppressive colonial practices that have led to poverty, poor health, child welfare intervention and sexual violence . . . these women must navigate through experiences of "being up, feeling down and stress up" as they steadfastly work to raise their children without adequate support . . . navigating the child welfare system while simultaneously working to address alcohol and drug substance misuse . . . more time is needed to allow the mothers to heal, build partnerships with and between service providers, implement holistic approaches and learn from each other.

[O]ne might incorporate traditional Indigenous mothering practices in a modern context . . . through a series of principles that she has applied as an Indigenous single mother living in mostly urban contexts, including spiritual based living, integrating interconnectedness, environment centered thinking, self-sufficiency and self-discovery, recognizing and nurturing gifts, apprenticeship training, self-determination, working with communal food and water, nurturing relationships, employing free trade and gifting, working with restorative justice, restoring public rites of passage, employing circle talk, working with consensus, and leadership from below.

. . . we are not alone in our communities, territories and nations—that there is a global context of resistance, reclaiming and recovery among Indigenous mothers and their allies.

Works Cited

Anderson, Kim. "Giving Life to the People: An Indigenous Ideology of Motherhood." In pp. 761–781 in Andrea O'Reilly, ed. *Maternal Theory: Essential Readings.* Toronto, ON: Demeter Press, 2007.

——. *A Recognition of Being.* Toronto, ON: Sumach/Canadian Scholars' Press, 2000.

Berkin, Carol. *First Generations: Women in Colonial America.* New York: Farrar, Straus, and Giroux, 1996.

Brown, Judith. "Economic Organization and the Position of Women Among the Iroquois," pp. 151–187 in Wm. G. Spittal, ed. *Iroquois Women: An Anthology.* Oshweken, ON: Iroquois Printing and Craft Supplies, 1990.

Dua, Enakshi. "Beyond Diversity: Exploring the Ways in which the Discourse of Race has Shaped the Institution of the Nuclear Family," pp. 237–260 in Enakshi Dua and Angela Robertson, eds. *Scratching the Surface: Canadian Anti-Racist Feminist Thought.* Toronto, ON: Women's Press, 1999.

Jacobs, Margaret. *White Mother to a Dark Race: Settler Colonialism, Maternalism, and the Removal of Indigenous Children in the American West and Australia, 1880–1940.* Lincoln: University of Nebraska Press, 2009.

——. "Working on the Domestic Frontier: American Indian Domestic Servants in White Women's Households in the San Francisco Bay Area, 1920–1940." *Frontiers: A Journal of Women's Studies* 1 and 2 (2006): 127–161.

Landes, Ruth. *The Ojibwa Woman. 1971.* New York: Norton and Company, 1974.

Monture-Angus, Patricia, and Mary Ellen Turpel. *Thunder in my Souk A Mohawk Woman Speaks.* Halifax: Fernwood Publishing. 1995.

O'Reilly, Andrea. "Feminist Mothering," pp. 792–821 in Andrea O'Reilly, ed. *Maternal Theory: Essential Readings.* Toronto, ON: Demeter Press, 2008. Print.

Rich, Adrienne. *Of Woman Born: Motherhood as Experience and Institution.* New York: Norton, 1976.

Rutherdale, Myra. "Mothers of the Empire: Maternal Metaphors in the Northern Canadian Mission Field," in Alvyn Austin and Jamie S. Scott, ed. *Canadian Missionaries, Indigenous Peoples: Representing Religion at Home and Abroad.* Toronto: University of Toronto Press, 2005.

Smith, Andrea. *Conquest: Sexual Violence and American Indian Genocide.* Cambridge, MA: South End Press, 2005.

Snorton, Teresa E. "The Legacy of the African-American Matriarch: New Perspectives for Pastoral Care," pp. 50–65, in Jeanne Stevenson Moessner, ed. *Through the Eyes of Women.* Minneapolis: Fortress Press, 1996.

Stevenson, Winona. "Colonialism and First Nations Women in Canada," pp. 49–80, in Enakshi Dua and Angela Robertson, ed. *Scratching the Surface: Canadian Anti-Racist Feminist Thought.* Toronto, ON: Women's Press, 1999.

Van Kirk, Sylvia. "Colonized Lives: The Native Wives and Daughters of Five Founding Families of Victoria," pp. 170–199, in Mary Ellen Kelm and Lorna Townsend, ed. *In the Days of our Grandmothers: A Reader in Aboriginal Women's History in Canada.* Toronto, ON: University of Toronto Press, 2006.

CHAPTER 14

Protecting Indian Rights for Indian Babies

Canada's "Unstated Paternity" Policy

Lynn Gehl, Gii-Zhigaate-Mnidoo-Kwe, and Algonquin Anishinaabe

Through Aboriginal Affairs and Northern Development Canada's (AANDC)[1] unstated paternity policy many Indigenous people and children are denied Indian status registration due to the lack of a father's signature on their birth certificates. I write this article for Indigenous community members, Indigenous women's organizations, and people caring for Indigenous women and their children to learn and draw from.

History of the Sex Discrimination in the *Indian Act*

Eventually, through the imposition of colonial policy and laws, it was through the process of Indian status registration whereby Indigenous people became, and continue to be, entitled to their treaty rights. It is because of this relationship between Indian status registration and treaty rights that many people conflate "treaty" and "status" as in a "treaty status" Indian. Initially the legislative process of defining who was an Indian followed an Indigenous model, meaning being an Indian was more about community relationships and affiliation and thus broad and inclusive. Despite this inclusive beginning, through the

application of an increasingly narrow definition of Indian status, the government of Canada began limiting the number of people entitled to Indian status, and through this process began eliminating the federal government's treaty responsibilities established in 1764 during the *Treaty at Niagara* (Miller, 2004; Gehl, 2014). This process of narrowly defining and controlling who an Indian was, and is, is commonly referred to as eliminating the "Indian problem" (Scott qtd. in Troniak, 2011).

When it was determined that the process of enfranchising Indians and eliminating Indigenous treaty rights was proceeding at a snail's pace, Indian women and their children became the target of patriarchal and racist regime. Through a series of legislative acts dating back to the 1857 *Gradual Civilization Act*, Indian women and their children were enfranchised when their husband or father was enfranchised. It was through the 1869 *Gradual Enfranchisement Act* where Indian women, along with their children, who married non-Indian men (a.k.a. marrying out) were enfranchised, denied Indian status registration and thus their treaty rights (Miller, 2004). At this time, as per the European model of the world, women were considered chattel or appendages of their husbands and therefore if, and when, they married a non-Indian man they

1. Note that as of publication the department is no longer referred to as the AANDC but has instead been renamed as Indigenous and Northern Affairs Canada. This change was implemented in the days after Justin Trudeau's election as prime minister in 2015.

too became a non-Indian person (Gehl, 2006, 2013). Eventually, the process of eliminating status Indians through sex discrimination was codified in section 12(1)(b) of the 1951 *Indian Act* (Gilbert, 1996). Significant to this discussion is another form of sex discrimination first codified in the 1951 *Indian Act*: the double-mother clause. Essentially, through the double-mother clause a person was enfranchised at the age of 21 years if both their mother and paternal grandmother (two generations of non-Indigenous mothers) were non-Indians prior to their marriage (Eberts, 2010).

With this loss of status, Indian women also lost their treaty rights, their right to live in their communities, their right to inherit property, and their right to be buried in the community cemetery. Further, through this sex discrimination "Aboriginal women have been denied opportunities to hold leadership positions within their communities and organizations and have been excluded from high-level negotiations among Aboriginal and Canadian political leaders" (McIvor, 2004: 108).

Ogitchidaa Kwewag

As most know, many Indigenous women have worked tirelessly to eliminate section 12(1)(b) of the *Indian Act* and its intergenerational effects. I think it is appropriate to refer to these Indigenous women as Ogitchidaa Kwewag, an Indigenous term that best translates to a brave woman who is dedicated to the safety, security, and service of her family, community, and nation. On the national and international scale it is Mary Two-Axe Early, a Mohawk woman from Kahnawake, Quebec, who in 1966 began to speak publicly about the matter, where eventually she approached the Royal Commission on the Status of Women (Jamieson, 1978). It was in 1971 when now icon of Indigenous women's rights Jeannette Corbiere-Lavell, an Anishinaabe woman from Manitoulin Island, Ontario, took the matter of section 12(1)(b) to court arguing it violated the *Canadian Bill of Rights*. Yvonne Bedard, from Six Nations, Ontario, was also addressing the sex

discrimination, and it was in 1973 when both their cases were heard together at the Supreme Court of Canada (scc) level. Unfortunately, relying on a patriarchal line of reasoning, the scc ruled that because Indian women who married non-Indian men "had equality of status with all other Canadian married females," there was no sex discrimination to resolve (McIvor, 2004: 113).[2]

Although this 1973 scc decision was a setback, in 1981 Sandra Lovelace, a Maliseet woman from Tobique First Nation, New Brunswick, appealed to the United Nations Human Rights Committee (UNHRC) regarding section 12(1)(b). Because her marriage and loss of status registration occurred prior to the *International Covenant on Civil and Political Rights* the UNHRC declined to rule on the matter of sex discrimination. Nonetheless, the UNHRC did rule that the *Indian Act* violated section 27 of the International Covenant, which protected culture, religion, and language. Through this ruling it became evident that Indigenous women did have rights that international fora were willing to stand behind and protect (McIvor, 2004).[3]

Largely due to the actions of these Ogitchidaa Kwewag, combined with the patriation of Canada's *Constitution* in 1982 intact with the *Charter of Rights and Freedoms*, in particular section 15—the sex equality section—in 1985 the *Indian Act* was amended.[4] Through this amendment to the *Indian Act* many Indigenous women, involuntarily enfranchised for marrying non-Indian men, were re-instated as status Indians, and many of their children were *newly registered* as status Indians for the first time. Statistics Canada reports that by the end of 2002, more than 114,000 individuals gained Indian status registration through the 1985 amendment (O'Donnell and Wallace, 2012). Through this process, many re-instated women re-gained, whereas their newly registered children gained for the first time, First Nation band membership and entitlement to their treaty rights that were protected through the 1764 *Treaty at Niagara*. Indian status registration entitlement for the grandchildren of these reinstated Indian women, however, is another matter.

---

2. See also Monture Angus, 1999; S. Day, 2011.

3. See also Monture-Angus, 1999; Silman, 1987; Stevenson, 1999.

4. 17 April 2012 marked the thirtieth anniversary of the Charter of Rights and Freedoms. Possibly needless to say, I did not celebrate.

Although many think the 1985 amendment to the *Indian Act* was for the purpose of establishing equality between men and women, and foremost to achieve compliance with the equality provisions of the *Charter of Rights and Freedoms*, it in fact failed. Through the creation of the second-generation cut-off rule, the grandchildren of women once enfranchised for marrying out continued to be denied Indian status registration and consequently all that went with it such as band membership and their treaty rights. Succinctly, the second-generation cut-off rule is a process whereby after two successive generations of parenting with a non-Indian parent, either mother or father, the loss of status registration occurs.[5] While the second-generation cut-off rule applies to all births after 1985—the descendants of Indian men included—it was applied immediately in a retroactive way to the descendants of the re-instated Indian women one generation sooner. Through this discriminatory process, Corbiere-Lavell has stated, "Three of my five grandchildren do not have legal rights to be members of my community" (as cited in Keung, 2009: np).

To understand this legislative complexity is not a simple task. First, it is important to understand that because of the 1985 amendment, Indian status registration is now stratified into two main subsections: 6(1) and 6(2). While subsection 6(1) status, and its many paragraphs (sub-subsections)—(a) (b) (c) (d) (e) and (f)[6]—allows a parent to pass on Indian status to his or her children in his or her own right, subsection 6(2) status does not. This means a 6(2) parent must parent with another status Indian in order to pass on Indian status registration to his or her children. For this very reason many people refer to 6(1) as a stronger form of status, and 6(2) as a weaker form. Certainly, this distinction is useful at conveying some of the legal complexity created in 1985.

Within the stronger form of Indian status registration, paragraph 6(1)(a) is the best form of status.

When the *Indian Act* was amended, Indian men and all their descendants born prior to April 1985, the date of amendment, were all registered under paragraph 6(1)(a), whereas the Indian women who married out were only registered under paragraph 6(1)(c) and their children were only registered under the weaker form of status registration subsection 6(2). As a result of this difference in Indian status registration, and as suggested above, the grandchildren of Indian women became immediate targets of the second-generation cut-off rule. This of course means that the sex discrimination was not eliminated. Rather, through **Bill C-31** the sex discrimination was passed on to the children and grandchildren of Indian women once enfranchised for marrying out (Eberts, 2010).[7] It is precisely in this way that the 1985 amendment to the *Indian Act* through Bill C-31 was "failed remedial legislation" (Eberts, 2010: 28).

As most know by now Sharon McIvor and her son Jacob Grismer's situation is illustrative of the government of Canada's continued reluctance to resolve the sex discrimination. Through the 1985 amendment McIvor was designated as a 6(2) Indian, the weaker form of status registration which thus prevented her from passing on status to her children in her own right because the Indian status granted descends from her Indian women forbearers versus her Indian men forbearers (McIvor, 2004).[8] For 25 years, McIvor continued the important work of eliminating the sex discrimination that the children and grandchildren of Indian women once enfranchised continue to face (S. Day, 2011).[9]

An ally to Indigenous women, Mary Eberts, relying on her critical legal perspective, offers her comments and analysis on the McIvor decision. Eberts explains that Madam Justice Ross of the British Columbia Supreme Court agreed with McIvor's legal team that the comparator group for McIvor and her son Grismer was the Indian men who married non-Indian women and their children who on

---

5. While many may argue that it was in 1985 when the enfranchisement process was removed from the Indian Act, I disagree. It is my contention that enfranchisement has a new form: the second-generation cut-off rule.

6. Outside of my discussion of 6(1)(a) and 6(1)(c) and how AANDC applies them to Indigenous women and men in an unequal manner, I do not discuss the other paragraphs (sub-subsections) of 6(1). This discussion is beyond the scope of this paper.

7. See also Gehl, 2006, 2013; Gilbert, 1996; McIvor, 2004.

8. See also Eberts, 2010.

9. See also Day and Green, 2010; Eberts, 2010; Haesler, 2010.

17 April 1985, were registered as status Indians under 6(1)(a) of the *Indian Act*. Through applying this comparator group Ross J. ruled that the "preference for descent of status through the male line is discrimination on the basis of sex and marital status" (Eberts, 2010: 32). Ross J. ruled that 6(1)(a) must be equally applied to Indian men and their descendants and the Indian women once enfranchised and their descendants (Eberts, 2010). Alternatively stated, the children and grandchildren of both Indian men and the Indian women who married out should all be registered under 6(1)(a) of the *Indian Act*. This ruling was cause for celebration.

Unfortunately, through yet another questionable line reasoning the Court of Appeal narrowed the scope of Justice Ross' legal remedy by using a comparator group for Grismer thereby completely ignoring McIvor's situation of her inability to pass on status registration to her grandchildren. Yet it was McIvor, not her son, who brought the matter of sex discrimination to court. The new comparator group which Justice Harvey Groberman relied on was the grandchildren once enfranchised through the double-mother clause codified in section 12(1)(a)(iv) that came into effect on 4 September 1951. As discussed above, through the double-mother clause a person was enfranchised at the age of 21 years when both their mother and paternal grandmother were non-Indians prior to their marriage. This change means that McIvor's son is only entitled to 6(1)(c) and his children 6(2) status.[i]

In relying on this comparator group Groberman J.A. narrowed the scope, where as a result, and in line with Bill C-31, the legal remedy found in **Bill C-3** fails to resolve all the sex discrimination. It is precisely for this reason that Eberts (2010) has argued the "Court of Appeal decision is a deep disappointment" and further "is, in fact, almost a case-book example of judicial activism producing bad law" (ibid., 39–40).

One can determine, through Justice Groberman's reasoning many caveats remain in the *Indian Act*'s current form. First, the grandchildren of Indian women once enfranchised, and born prior to 4 September 4, 1951—when the double-mother clause

was first enacted—will continue to be denied Indian status registration, yet the grandchildren of Indian men in this same situation are registered. Second, grandchildren of Indian women born through common law relationships rather than the institution of marriage will continue to be denied status registration. Third, the female children (and their descendants) of Indian men who co-parented with non-status women in common law union will continue to be excluded, yet the male children (and their descendants) of Indian men who co-parented with non-status women in common law union have status. Fourth, the grandchildren of Indian women once enfranchised and now re-instated are only entitled to 6(2) status and therefore will not be able to pass on status to their children born prior to April 17, 1985, yet the grandchildren of Indian men are registered under 6(1)(a). Clearly, it is in these ways that matrilineal descendants remain targets of sex discrimination (McIvor and Brodsky, 2010).

Unfortunately, on 5 November 2009, the SCC refused to hear the appeal in the case of *McIvor v. Registrar, Indian and Northern Affairs Canada*. Although Brodsky and McIvor argued Bill C-3 as inadequate remedial legislation, in January 2011 it passed into law. Thus, despite the *Charter of Rights and Freedoms*, in particular section 15 which states women have the right to live free from racial and sex discrimination, like Lovelace before her, McIvor has been forced to pursue the elimination of the sex discrimination beyond the domestic arena. Shortly after Bill C-3 became law McIvor filed a complaint against Canada with the UNHRC (S. Day, 2011). In taking on this process McIvor herself has argued, "Canada needs to be held to account for its intransigence in refusing to completely eliminate sex discrimination from the *Indian Act* and for decades of delay" (as cited in Haesler, 2010: np). Similarly, the Director of the Women's Legal Education and Action Fund (LEAF), Joanna Birenbaum (2010), has argued that forcing Indigenous women such as McIvor "to endure the emotional and financial hardship of years and years of additional protracted litigation to remove the remaining areas of sex discrimination in the status provisions is unconscionable" (ibid., np).

---

i In the original publication of this article and a subsequent re-publication, [it was] stated that Sharon's son, Charles Jacob Grismer, was registered as 6(1)c when in fact he was registered as 6(1)c.1. The goal was 6(1)a.

Notwithstanding these issues and arguments, it is estimated that as many as 45,000 grandchildren of Indian women once enfranchised for marrying out will gain the right to status registration through this more recent amendment (Day and Green, 2010; O'Donnell and Wallace, 2012). They will now also be more likely to be entitled to First Nation band membership and their treaty rights.

In sum, despite the efforts of Ogitchidaa Kwewag—Two-Axe Early, Corbiere-Lavell, Bedard, Lovelace, and more recently McIvor—the 156 year (as of 2013) history of the sex discrimination in the *Indian Act* continues. This is the case, regardless of the fact that Indigenous women have dedicated over fifty years to its elimination (Eberts, 2010: 42). Although living in a post-*Charter* era, for me and possibly many others, the equality outlined in section 15 of the *Canadian Charter of Rights and Freedoms* has no real practical value beyond that of a pitiful and meaningless fictional story. Through living, observing, and thinking about the process of remedial legislation—both in 1985 and 2011—I have come to realize that Canada manipulates legislative change as an opportunity to create new forms of sex discrimination rather than eliminate it. The next section of this article discusses yet another form of sex discrimination that has not received much attention: **unknown and unstated paternity** and the *Indian Act*.

Unknown and Unstated Paternity and the *Indian Act*

Traditional Knowledge

After assessing the needs of the Indians of Lower Canada, the 1845 Bagot Commission reported on child rearing practices stating, "an event of this nature [child of unknown or unstated paternity] does not cast a stigma upon the mother, nor upon the child, which is usually adopted into the tribe" (App. EEE, section 1, Indians of Canada East). Similarly, in his work on the Algonquin Nation of the Ottawa River, F.G. Speck observed it was the Chief's responsibility to take care of orphaned children (1915: 21). Further to this, Gordon Day has stated, "the basic unit of Algonquin society was the family: the father and mother, grandparents, children and adopted children" (1979: 3).

In my process of understanding the Indigenous family model, parenting, and community membership, I also turn to Anishinaabe governance laws, in particular the Clan System of Governance. Through clan teachings such as the need to keep our blood clean, men and women were encouraged to seek new genetic material from outsiders as the diversity assured the health and wellness of the people. In addition to this, it was common practice for Indigenous nations to adopt, kidnap, and assimilate young children when membership loss due to disease and war was great. In this way, parenting and community membership was not always reducible to the biological parents. Pamela D. Palmater (2011) arrives at a similar realization of the limitations of blood as the criteria in determining identity and nationhood when she argues, "blood is not only unnecessary as an indicator of our identities; it is completely irrelevant" (ibid., 218). Rather, it is the social cultural aspect that determines who we are such as the deeply rooted connections to our nations that include family, larger community relations, and traditional territories, as well as the collective history, values, and beliefs that we share in common with one another (Palmater, 2011). Cannon (2008) concurs with this broader understanding of identity and belonging, offering there exists in Indigenous culture an "ancient context" that informs us of the importance of respecting women and the responsibilities they carry (ibid., 6).

Legislative History

As the historical record, my family oral history, traditional governance practices, and sacred teachings inform, eventually the *Indian Act* began to impose European definitions and practices on who was and who was not an Indian child, even though the inclusion of all children regardless of paternity disclosure was once traditional Indigenous practice. In 1927, section 12 of the *Indian Act*, which remained in place until 4 September 1951, stated that "Any illegitimate child may, unless he has, with the consent of the band whereof the father or mother of such child is a member, shared in the distribution moneys of such band for a period exceeding two years, be, at any time, excluded from the membership thereof by the Superintendent General" (as cited in Gilbert, 1996: 34). This criterion was broad and inclusive in that all that was required was the sharing of band funds. From 4 September 1951 through 13 August 1956 the criteria of who was an Indian shifted slightly where the test was "the Registrar had to be *satisfied* that the father was not an Indian in order to omit adding a name to the register" (as paraphrased in Gilbert, 1996: 33, emphasis mine). The criteria shifted once again from 14 August 1956, through 16 April 1985, where section 12(2) stated that illegitimate children were automatically added to the Indian register whereby the band had twelve months to protest. This provision protected Indigenous mothers and their children. That said, if and when a protest was made and the Registrar determined that the father of the child was a non-Indian person then the child's name was removed from the official Indian register (Gilbert, 1996: 33). In summary, although regulated by legislation, and although the inclusive process was once narrowed, it was eventually re-expanded to include all children regardless of non-paternity disclosure unless a successful protest was made. This process of inclusion remained in place until 1985.

Aboriginal Affairs' Unstated Paternity Policy Explained

Along with the issues that McIvor continues to pursue, today there is an additional form of sex discrimination of which few are aware. This sex discrimination is particularly disconcerting as it places many Indigenous children at risk of being denied their entitlement to Indian status registration and consequently First Nation band membership and treaty rights. This sex discrimination pertains to the Indigenous children whose father's signature is not on their birth certificate. Today, when a child is born and for some reason the father is unable to or does not sign the birth certificate AANDC assumes the father is a non-Indian person as defined by the *Indian Act*. This AANDC unstated paternity policy which I prefer to call "unknown and unstated paternity" is best thought of as the application of a negative presumption of paternity, and it occurs whether the parents are married or not. Succinctly, a father's signature must appear on a child's long form birth certificate as it is the long form birth certificate, and both parental signatures, that are relied upon in determining if a child is entitled to Indian status registration.

Interestingly, as with the sex discrimination that McIvor continues to challenge, this sex discrimination was created through the remedial action of the 1985 amendment to the *Indian Act*. What is really important here is that in actuality today the *Indian Act* is silent on this very matter of missing fathers' signatures. Regardless of this legislative silence, through AANDC's unstated paternity policy these children are placed at risk for the denial of Indian status registration. More particularly, when administrating applications for status registration, this policy instructs the assumption of a non-Indian father to all applicants where a father's signature is lacking. Through this unfair negative assumption of paternity, when a mother is registered under section 6(1), the stronger form of Indian status, and a status Indian father does not sign the birth certificate the child is only registered under 6(2). While this child is entitled to Indian status registration, when a mother is registered under 6(2), the weaker form of Indian status, and a status Indian father does not sign the birth certificate the child is deemed a non-status person (Gehl, 2006, 2013).

What is really dubious about this policy assumption is that AANDC relies on a discourse—unstated paternity—and practice that blames and targets mothers and their babies. Clearly there is the need to understand the situation from the perspective of mothers.[10] My own reasoning informs me that sometimes, due to an abuse of power and sexual violence such as incest and rape, mothers may not obtain the father's signature on the child's birth registration form because they do not want the father to know about the child or have access to the child. Such situations may be best referred to as unreported and unnamed paternity. Again relying on my own reasoning sometimes a mother may record the father's name on the child's birth registration form, yet he refuses to sign the form because

---

10. I need to qualify that many women conceived through the sexual violence that occurred during their Residential School and Day School experience. In these situations it is highly unlikely that the father's signature would be recorded on the birth registration form.

he needs to protect his standing in the community, and/or a marriage to another woman, and/or to avoid having to make child support payments, and/or the loss of his driver's license should he not make his child support payments. Such situations may be best referred to as unacknowledged and unestablished paternity.

Further, I have been told that in some situations mothers do record the father's name on the birth registration form, but because the father's signature is not obtained, an official of the government of Canada blanks-out his name. Alternately stated, an official removes the father's name from the birth form. Still further, I have also been told that in many situations the father may not be present during the birth of the child, such as when the mother is flown outside of her community to give birth as many communities are not equipped to fulfill this necessary area of health care. Moreover, once again my own reasoning informs me that sometimes the father dies prior to the birth of his child. Such situations may be best referred to as unrecognized paternity. What is more, a child may be conceived through the sexual violence of rape, gang rape, sexual slavery, or through prostitution where, as a result, the mother does not know who the father is and, possibly needless to say, could care less who he is as she has other matters to address. These latter situations may best be named unknown paternity.[11]

Statistics and Figures

According to Stewart Clatworthy (2003) between 1985 and 1999 as many as 37,300 children of so-called unstated paternity were born to status Indian mothers registered under 6(1). During this same time period as many as 13,000 children of so-called unstated paternity were born to status Indian mothers registered under 6(2). Through AANDC's policy, these latter 13,000 children were immediately denied Indian status registration and, therefore, potentially band membership and treaty

rights. Mann (2009) provides the percentage rates of so-called unstated paternity respective to age for section 6(1) mothers which, unsurprisingly, is higher for younger mothers. For example, mothers under the age of 15 years had a rate of 45 per cent. Mothers aged 15 to 19 had a rate of 30 per cent. Further, mothers aged 20 to 24 had a rate of 19 per cent, mothers aged 25 to 29 had a rate of 14 per cent, whereas mothers aged 30 to 34 had a rate of 11 per cent. Although these statistics represent rates for mothers registered under 6(1), it is not unreasonable to assume that similar rates also apply to mothers registered under 6(2).

Administrative Remedies Offered and My Thoughts

According to Clatworthy (2003) 53 per cent of so-called unstated paternity cases are unintentional, while the remainder, 47 per cent are intentional. Unintentional situations emerge due to compliance issues such as the father's signature not being achieved because of his absence during the birth, the dissolution of the relationship, and the inability to pay administrative charges for changes requested after amendment deadlines have passed. Intentional situations emerge because of unstable relationships, a father's denial of paternity, confidentiality concerns of the mother, child custody concerns, mothers afraid of losing Indian status registration or First Nation band membership, and an unwillingness to pay administrative fees for birth registration changes (Clatworthy, 2003: 16–18). Moving from this limiting framework Clatworthy offers a number of administrative remedies. These remedies include the development of a national policy; First Nation leadership development; the production of new resource materials for parents; education initiatives for parents; and the development of birth and status registration kits for parents (ibid., 19–22). For the most part these remedies emerge from an androcentric position.

11. While thinking through all these situations we also need to keep in mind that while a mother, grandmother, or great-grandmother may know the father, this does not mean a child, a grandchild, or great-grandchild knows. Further, these categories—unstated, unreported, unnamed, unacknowledged, unestablished, unrecognized, and unknown paternity—also apply to the paternity of one's grandfather and/or great-grandfather.

Fiske and George (2006) critique Clatworthy for failing to explore in greater detail why Indigenous mothers might not disclose who the father is. They argue, paternity disclosure can at times place women in "jeopardy, perhaps endanger them, and at the very least cause social conflicts where a man either denies paternity or refuses to acknowledge it to state authorities" (Fiske and George, 2006: 4). Similarly, the Native Women's Association of Canada (NWAC) (2007) has noted, "Issues related to personal safety, violence, or abuse may provide a reason for a woman deciding to disassociate herself with a former partner or spouse" (ibid., 1). Adding, "mothers may wish to avoid custody or access claims on the part of the father: leaving the paternity unstated forms a partial protection against such actions by a biological father who may be unstable, abusive or engaged in unhealthy behaviours" (NWAC, 2007: 1). Mann (2009) adds intentional situations also emerge when a mother knows who a father is yet is unwilling to identify and name the father when the pregnancy is the result of abuse, incest, or rape (ibid., 33). Certainly Fiske and George, NWAC, and Mann are getting closer to the issues and reality that many Indigenous women are forced to endure in a sexist and racist patriarchal society.

Mann (2005) offers her own discussion of administrative remedies. In some ways they do pick up where Clatworthy left off. Mann suggests: access to travel funding for fathers when mothers have to leave the community to give birth, birth forms signed in the community prior to the mother leaving to give birth, increased administrative support in communities, and alternatives to notarization when there is the need to amend birth registration forms (ibid., 21). In offering this discussion of remedies, Mann admits that they will serve little in situations where a mother for some very legitimate reason cannot or will not disclose the name the father. Mann then proceeds to offer several recommendations: the use of affidavits or declarations as proof of paternity by either the mother or father, or at the very least allow for affidavits or declarations to identify who the father is when the child is the result of sexual violence such as incest or rape; provide necessary resources when affidavits or declarations are required; the need for

educational initiatives for both men and women; conduct research to determine additional administrative remedies; and conduct research where key stakeholders such as First Nation women and First Nation representatives are included throughout the development of policy or legislative change (ibid., 26). In this way, Mann's analysis moves in the right direction extending Clatworthy's limitations. But there is more thinking and research required.

Certainly, administrative remedies are within AANDC's jurisdiction, and while these remedies offered by Clatworthy and Mann are on the right track—again, Mann more so—my own thinking informs me that they do not begin to consider and thus address situations where a father, for whatever reason, while accepting paternity refuses to officially acknowledge paternity and sign their child's birth certificate. For example, it is common knowledge that sometimes fathers go through a period of insecurity and jealously when their partner becomes pregnant. When I think about this state of being I view it as analogous to the postpartum depression–psychosis continuum that some mothers experience after childbirth. While this state of pathology has yet to be identified, named, and defined in the Diagnostic and Statistical Manual of Mental Disorders, and thus effectively addressed in our societal structures, many people know that it is during a woman's pregnancy when a father is more likely to become neglectful, abusive, and consequently likely to refuse to acknowledge paternity and sign a child's birth certificate.

Nor for that matter, and again drawing from my thinking, do these administrative remedies offered by Clatworthy and Mann address situations where a mother does not know who the father is due to situations of rape or gang rape by unknown perpetrators. While in some situations of sexualized violence a mother may know who the perpetrator is, in other situations she may not. Moreover, there may be more than one perpetrator. In addition, and this time drawing from my own experience of being denied Indian status, these administrative remedies offered do not address situations where an individual such as myself does not know who her grandfather was or is, and has no way of determining his identity. Like the Ogitchidaa Kwewag before me, I am forced to take the matter of an unknown paternity in my lineage, and consequently the denial of Indian status registration, through Canada's legal system.

That said, I think it is also important to understand that these remedies and recommendations offered by Clatworthy and Mann do not address situations where a non-Indigenous woman has a child with an Indian man yet for some reason is unable to attain the father's signature on their child's birth certificate. Certainly administrative remedies, whether at the policy level or legislative level, need to incorporate the realities of non-Indigenous mothers who have parented with Indian men. Further research is required, research that includes non-Indigenous mothers of Indigenous children as a stakeholder group.

As a measure of fairness, objectivity, and to assure this article is comprehensive, readers will find it interesting to know that AANDC (2012) offers three administrative remedies on this topic. First, AANDC recommends that applicants for Indian status have their birth certificate amended. Second, a statutory declaration signed by the applicant's mother and biological father should be provided. Third, in the event that a biological father is uncooperative, unavailable, or deceased, it is suggested that the applicant provide a statutory declaration from the biological father's family members that affirms what they believe. These remedies fail to address many of the issues discussed by Clatworthy, Mann, and myself and as such fail to crest the horizon of the issues.

Summary and Conclusion

Despite decades of advocacy and litigation work by Indigenous women that eventually led to amendments to the *Indian Act*, under AANDC's current regime of determining Indian status registration, and as of 1985, a father must sign his baby's birth certificate for his Indian status registration to be factored into the child's eligibility. Otherwise, through an unstated paternity policy the Registrar of AANDC applies a negative assumption of paternity whereby the child may not be entitled to Indian status and consequently band membership, and their treaty

rights. This assumption of non-Indian paternity is sex discrimination.

What is particularly disturbing about AANDC's unstated paternity policy is the way it targets Indigenous mothers and children. As I have discussed in this article, women sometimes conceive through an abuse of power such as in situations of incest, rape, gang rape, sexual slavery, and prostitution where as such the terms un reported, unnamed, unacknowledged, un-established, unrecognized, and unknown paternity are more appropriate descriptors than the inadequate "unstated."

Through the creation of the 1985 AANDC unstated paternity policy it is now clear to me that the remedial legislation intended to eliminate the sex discrimination was little more than an opportunity for Canada to manipulate the legislative change process into an opportunity to create new and worse forms of sex discrimination. While many people may correctly argue additional research is required in remedying AANDC's unstated paternity policy, it is my contention that a well-defined research methodology alone will not resolve the issues faced by Indigenous women. It is my view that the legislative silence presently coded in the *Indian Act* was manipulatively crafted by sexist and racist patriarchs as a mechanism to then create discriminatory policy at the departmental level. AANDC's unstated paternity policy is a new low for the Canadian state that is "morally reprehensible" (McIvor, 2004: 133).

It is precisely this AANDC unstated paternity policy that is preventing me from Indian status registration and consequently First Nation band membership in my kokomis' (grandmother's) community, citizenship in the broader Anishinaabek citizenship endeavour, as well as access to my treaty rights such as health care. When AANDC denies me Indian status registration they deny me important aspects of my identity as an Indigenous person, and as a result my right to live mino-pimadiziwin (the good life) as an Algonquin Anishinaabekwe. It is precisely for this reason, as well as for young mothers and their babies, that I continue my effort.

References

Aboriginal Affairs and Northern Development Canada. *Unstated Paternity on Birth Certificate: Quick Facts on Documentation Required*. 12 April 2012. Retrieved from http://www.aadncaandc.gc.ca/eng/1334234251919.

Bagot Commission Report. "Report on the Affairs of The Indians in Canada," *Journals of the Legislative Assembly of the Province of Canada*, 1844–1845. App. EEE.

Bagot Commission Report. "Report on the Affairs of The Indians in Canada," *Journals of the Legislative Assembly of the Province of Canada*, 1847. App. T.

Birenbaum, J. *Women's Legal Education and Action Fund (LEAF) calls on the Conservative Government to withdraw its opposition to Amended Bill C-3* [News Release]. 5 May, 2010. Retrieved from http://www.leaf.ca/media/releases/Press_Release_May_5_2010_Bill_C-3.pdf.

Cannon, M. J. *Revisiting Histories of Gender-Based Exclusion and the New Politics of Indian Identity*. 2008. Retrieved from http://fngovernance.org/ncfng_research/martin_cannon.pdf.

Clatworthy, S. *Factors Contributing to Unstated Paternity*. 20 January 2003. Retrieved from http://dsp-psd.pwgsc.gc.ca/Collection/R2-255-2003E.pdf.

Day, G. M. "The Indians of the Ottawa Valley," *Oracle* 30 (1979): 1–4.

Day, S. "153 Years of Sex Discrimination Is Enough," *The Star*. 6 January 2011. Retrieved from http://www.thestar.com/opinion/editorialopinion/article/916682—153-years-of-sexdiscrimination-is-enough.

Day, S., and J. Green. "Sharon McIvor's Fight for Equality," *Herizons* 24, no. 1 (2010): 6–7.

Eberts, M. "McIvor: Justice Delayed—Again," *Indigenous Law Journal* 9, no. 1 (2010): 15–46.

Fiske, J., and E. George. *Seeking Alternatives to Bill C-31: From cultural Trauma to Cultural Revitalization through Customary Law*. Ottawa, ON: Status of Women Canada, 2006.

Gehl, L. *The Truth that Wampum Tells: My Debwewin on the Algonquin Land Claims Process*. Halifax and Winnipeg: Fernwood Publishing, 2014.

Gehl, L. "'The Queen and I': Discrimination against Women in the Indian Act Continues," pp. 162–171 in A. Medovarski and B. Cranney, eds, *Canadian woman studies: An introductory reader*, 2nd edn. Toronto, ON: Inanna Publications and Education Inc, 2006.

Gehl, L., with H. Ross. "Disenfranchised Spirit: A Theory and a Model," *Pimatiziwin: A Journal of Aboriginal and Indigenous Community Health* 11, no. 1 (2013): 31–42.

Gilbert, L. *Entitlement to Indian Status and Membership Codes in Canada*. Scarborough, ON: Carswell Thomson Canada Ltd., 1996.

Haesler, N. "B.C. Aboriginal Woman Taking Status Battle to the UN: Sharon McIvor Says Canada Continues to Discriminate under Indian Act," *Vancouver Sun*. 12 November 2010. Retrieved from http://www.vancouversun.com/life/Aboriginal+woman+taking+status+battle/3817575/story.html.

Jamieson, K. *Indian Women and the Law in Canada: Citizens Minus*. Ottawa, ON: Minister of Supply and Services, Canada, 1978.

Keung, N. "'Status Indians' Face Threat of Extinction: In Some Communities, Last Children with Historic Rights Will Be Born as Early as 2012," *The Toronto Star*. 10 May 2009. Retrieved from http://www.thestar.com/news/canada/article/631974.

Mann, M. M. "Disproportionate & Unjustifiable: Teen First Nations Mothers and Unstated Paternity Policy," *Canadian Issues* (Winter 2009): 31–36.

Mann, M. M. *Indian Registration: Unrecognized and Unstated Paternity*. June. Ottawa, ON: Status of Women Canada, 2005. Retrieved from http://www.michellemann.ca/articles/Indian%20Registration%20-%20Unrecognized%20and%20Unstated%20Paternity.pdf.

McIvor, S. D. "Aboriginal Women Unmasked: Using Equality Litigation to Advance Women's Rights," *Canadian Journal of Women and the Law* 16, no. 1 (2004): 106–136.

McIvor, S., and G. Brodsky. *Equal registration status for Aboriginal women and their descendants: Sharon McIvor's comments on Bill C-3, An Act to promote gender equity in Indian registration by responding to the Court of Appeal for British Columbia decision in McIvor v. Canada (Registrar of Indian and Northern Affairs)*. 13 April 2010. Submission to the House of Commons Standing Committee on Aboriginal Affairs and Northern Development.

Miller, J. R. *Lethal legacy: Current Native Controversies in Canada*. Toronto: McClelland & Stewart, 2004.

Monture-Angus, P. *Thunder in my Soul: A Mohawk Woman Speaks*. Halifax, NS: Fernwood Publishing Company Ltd., 1999.

Native Women's Association of Canada. *Aboriginal women and unstated paternity: An issue paper*. 20–22 June 2007. Retrieved from http://www.laa.gov.nl.ca/laa/naws/pdf/nwac-paternity.pdf.

O'Donnell, V., and S. Wallace. *First Nations, Métis and Inuit women*. 24 February 2012. Retrieved from http://www.statcan.gc.ca/pub/89-503-x/2010001/article/11442-eng.htm.

Palmater, P. D. *Beyond Blood: Rethinking Indigenous Identity*. Saskatoon, SK: Purich Publishing Limiting, 2011.

Silman, J. *Enough Is Enough: Aboriginal Women Speak Out*. Toronto, ON: The Women's Press, 1987.

Speck, F. G. *Family Hunting Territories and Social Life of Various Algonkian Bands of the Ottawa Valley*. Canada: Department of Mines, Geological Survey Memoir 70. Anthropological Series no. 8 (1915): 1–30.

Stevenson, W. "Colonialism and First Nations Women in Canada," pp. 49–80 in E. Dua and A. Robertson, eds. *Scratching the Surface: Canadian Anti-Racist Feminist Thought*. Toronto, ON: Women's Press, 1999.

Troniak, S. *Addressing the Legacy of Residential Schools*. 2011. Retrieved from http://www.parl.gc.ca/Content/LOP/ResearchPublications/2011-76-e.pdf.

PART 7

Additional Readings

Anderson, Kim. *A Recognition of Being: Reconstructing Native Womanhood*, 2nd edn. Toronto: Women's Press, 2016.

Castellano, Marlene Brant, Linda Archibald, and Mike De-Gagné. *From Truth to Reconciliation: Transforming the Legacy of Residential Schools*. Ottawa: Aboriginal Healing Foundation, 2008.

Gehl, Lynn. *Gehl v. Canada: Challenging Sex Discrimination in the Indian Act*. Regina: University of Regina Press, 2021.

Ing, Rosalyn. "Canada's Indian Residential Schools and Their Impacts on Mothering," pp. 157–172 in Lavell-Harvard, Dawn Memee, and Jeanette Coribiere Lavell, eds, *"Until Our Hearts Are on the Ground": Aboriginal Mothering, Oppression, Resistance, and Rebirth*. Bradford, ON: Demeter Press, 2006.

Lavell-Harvard, D. Memee, and Kim Anderson, eds. *Mothers of the Nations: Indigenous Mothering as Global Resistance, Reclaiming, and Recovery*. Bradford, ON: Demeter Press. 2014.

Makokis, Leona, Ralph Bodor, Avery Calhoun, and Stephanie Tyler. *Ohpikinâwasowin/Growing a Child: Implementing Indigenous Ways of Knowing with Indigenous Families*. Black Point, NS: Fernwood Publishing, 2020.

Palmater, Pamela D. *Beyond Blood: Rethinking Indigenous Identity*. Saskatoon: Purich Publishing Limited, 2011.

Truth and Reconciliation Commission of Canada. *What We Have Learned: Principles of Truth and Reconciliation*. Ottawa: Government of Canada, 2015.

Relevant Websites

First Nations Child and Family Caring Society of Canada
http://fncaringsociety.com
This is the official website of the First Nations Child and Family Caring Society of Canada, and it contains information, resources, and networks to assist Indigenous families.

Indigenous and Northern Affairs Canada, "Statement of Apology to Former Students of Indian Residential Schools,"
http://www.aadnc-aandc.gc.ca/eng/1100100015644/1100100015649.
This website contains the official apology given by the Canadian federal government to the survivors of the residential schooling system.

Films

A Place Between: The Story of an Adoption. Dir. Curtis Kaltenbaugh. National Film Board of Canada, 2007.
Birth of a Family. Dir. Tasha Hubbard. National Film Board of Canada, 2016.
Club Native. Dir. Tracey Deer. National Film Board of Canada with Rezolution Pictures, 2008.
Jordan River, the Messenger. Dir. Alanis Obomsawin. National Film Board of Canada. 2019.
We Can't Make the Same Mistake Twice. Dir. Alanis Obomsawin. National Film Board of Canada, 2016.
We Were Children. Dir. Tim Wolochatiuk. National Film Board of Canada, 2012.

Key Terms

- Bill C-3
- Bill C-31
- Indigenous mothering
- Patriarchy
- Residential schooling
- Unknown and unstated paternity

Discussion Questions

1. There is much evidence that residential schooling has had lasting intergenerational impacts on Indigenous communities. What are some of these impacts and how have communities enacted healing processes for survivors and their families?

2. How do Lavell-Harvard and Anderson define "Indigenous Mothering"? Why and how was traditional Indigenous mothering seen as a threat to "the patriarchal order of the colonizers"? How, despite centuries of colonialism, have Indigenous mothering practices persisted, albeit in altered forms?

3. Discuss how the sex discrimination codified in section 12(1)(b) of the *Indian Act* denied many Indigenous women their legal Indian status, and consequently created barriers for their familial and communal rights and responsibilities.

4. How did the Unstated Paternity Policy under the *Indian Act* contravene the *Charter of Rights and Freedoms*? Why does Gehl argue that recent remedial legislative process still failed to justly address systemic discrimination?

Activities

Watch the documentary *Unrepentant: Kevin Annett and Canada's Genocide* (available online). Discuss the ongoing implications of residential schools on both Indigenous and non-Indigenous identities.

On 11 June 2008 the Government of Canada officially apologized for the residential school system. Watch the apology online and discuss your thoughts about it. Should Canada have apologized for residential schooling? Is saying "sorry" enough? What other concrete actions are needed for reconciliation and healing to begin, and to move forward? To prepare for this activity, read one or both of the following: (a) Sara Ahmed, "The Politics of Bad Feeling," *Australian Critical Race and Whiteness Studies Association Journal* 1 (2005): 72–85; (b) Megan Boler, "The Risk of Empathy: Interrogating Multiculturalism's Gaze," *Cultural Studies* 11, 2 (1997): 251–71.

Indigenous Rights, Citizenship, and Nationalisms

Editor Introduction

On 13 September 2007 the United Nations adopted the Declaration on the Rights of Indigenous Peoples. The Declaration itself provided an overview of Indigenous peoples, including a framework for realizing a future of more just relations. States were urged to implement a series of steps to safeguard the rights of Indigenous nations. Moreover, and with great significance to the themes raised in this section of the anthology, the document acknowledged that "Indigenous peoples have suffered from historic injustices as a result of, inter alia, their colonization and dispossession of their lands, territories and resources." It recognized "the urgent need to respect and promote the inherent rights of Indigenous peoples which derive from their political, economic, and social structures and from their cultures, spiritual traditions, histories and philosophies, especially their rights to their lands, territories, and resources."

The Declaration was not legally binding on member States and does not signify a threat to their sovereignty. Nevertheless, Canada rejected this landmark document in September 2014 at the UN General Assembly. In choosing to reject the Declaration, the Conservative government at that time failed to acknowledge the distinct nature of equity claims and the historicity of Indigenous rights. On 12 November 2015, the newly appointed Indigenous and Northern Affairs Minister Carolyn Bennett announced that the Liberal government would implement the UN Declaration on the Rights of Indigenous Peoples. The move, she said, was to reflect the commitment that Prime Minister Justin Trudeau made when elected to build a better and healthier nation-to-nation relationships with Indigenous peoples, one whereby the State will fully consult and obtain consent from Indigenous peoples on any matters that directly affect them and their lands. This new direction is one full of promise and hope for Indigenous peoples, and many of our Indigenous relatives and friends have been saying that in fact, they are more "cautiously optimistic" that a future more positive relationship with the Canadian State can be built, and that respect for our inherent Indigenous rights might finally happen.

As both authors in this section point out, Indigenous rights are as unique as the peoples themselves. They are rooted in the inherent and never-before-extinguished rights of nations as well as a colonial experience wherein people were dispossessed—and continue to be dispossessed—of lands. Indigenous peoples do not wish to integrate into mainstream structures, but rather wish to have their rights and nation-to-nation relationships affirmed. These demands derive from, and indeed shape, what it means to be Indigenous in the contemporary world.

Alfred and Corntassel (2005) suggest that contemporary Indigenous struggles are an affirmation of identity. The demand to have Indigenous rights affirmed is inherently decolonizing in nature. Remembering our ceremonies, traditions, laws, and autonomous nations is a journey of what they refer to as "self-conscious traditionalism." This type of traditionalism is a "reconstruction of traditional communities based on the original teachings and orienting values." Indigenous peoples are in a unique position relative to the Canadian political make-up. As Henderson (2002) writes, Indigenous peoples have a unique constitutional heritage enabling sui generis rights. Canada is "based on the foundation of shared sovereignty" (ibid., 419), since our ancestors agreed to a treaty relationship: he writes, "a relationship between nations . . . a belief in autonomous zones of power, freedom, and liberties" (ibid., 422). Although Canada has not respected our treaty rights, they are nonetheless real and binding to the parties originally promising to uphold them.

Bonita Lawrence's article brings attention to the fact that despite Indigenous peoples' inherent right to self-government and title to land, contemporary self-government and **comprehensive claims policy** negotiations are still constraining Indigenous peoples. Canada still unilaterally decides what constitutes Aboriginal culture and what can be discussed in a self-government negotiation process, and it continues to not address questions of compensation of loss of lands and resources. What has transpired throughout modern treaties is that self-government is implied to merely apply to internal matters, and it is limited to "pre-contact" cultures, therefore it definitely does not translate into a right of sovereignty in the international sense, hence further legitimizing the Canadian State's control over Indigenous peoples.

Given the power imbalances between the Canadian State and Indigenous nations, First Nations often feel pressured into accepting terms within a settlement claim that do not fairly address historical wrongs, and might even further damage them. As Lawrence points out, one of the most crucial concerns is that claims negotiations demand either a full extinguishment of title or modified rights. In either case, Crown sovereignty is maintained and what most often occurs is further loss of lands and resources. Lawrence's critiques are quite timely because the Algonquins of Ontario have been in the process of voting on a Proposed Agreement-in-Principle. Many Algonquin members have been critical of the agreement and have encouraged all Algonquins to reject it. They highlight a few important components of the Agreement that would negatively impact their peoples: extinguishment of Algonquin Aboriginal title with no compensation for loss of lands and resources; only 1.3 per cent of their traditional lands will be transferred to the Algonquins; and the end of tax exemption by becoming a municipal type of government (Kebaowek First Nations, 2016). More recently, the voting on this important land claim settlement has become a contentious matter, as the legitimacy of at least over 4000 Algonquin members eligible to vote has been questioned (see Gehl, 2022 for further discussion). Lawrence's cautions are indeed evident in current self-government negotiations, and the latter do not come near to the promised nation-to-nation relationship that this country was to embark upon under the leadership of Prime Minister Justin Trudeau.

Indigenous rights of self-determination are ultimately tied to the ability to freely decide on matters of membership to each specific Indigenous nation. As Audra Simpson's article reveals, this is a very complicated task, and Indigenous nations, as they have always done, continue to imagine and construct alternative discourses of citizenship. In it, she addresses the complexities embedded in matters of citizenship, in particular the current challenges present in her community, the Kahnawake Mohawk nation. As with other nations, Canada imposed a definition of membership at Kahnawake through the *Indian Act*. Traditional ways of defining **nationhood** and national membership have been disrupted through the *Indian Act*, especially patrilineal definitions of citizenship which robbed Mohawk women who "married out" of a right to be defined as Mohawk (Indian for that matter) and granted such rights to white women who "married in." In 1985 the State, in its attempt to redress gendered injustice granted "reserves" the right to define their own membership.

Out of this history, Kahnawake passed a code of 50 per cent **blood quantum** as a criterion for membership to protect a small land base against those who are perceived to not have sufficient Mohawk blood.

Alongside band membership, other lived experiences of citizenship do exist in the community, such as those of Status Indians (who might or not have band membership) and "feeling" citizenship. All of these varied narratives and lived experiences of citizenship, Simpson reminds us, are collective experiences connecting all the people, (re)acting against the State's imposition, as well as against each other in the process. And they are living legacy of colonialism; as the Mohawk nation moves forward to a decolonizing future, "the challenge to the community is to harden these pieces of knowledge, these critiques and these possibilities into a membership policy that may accommodate the simultaneity of these experiences, these different trans-historic discourses (and people) so that these '**feeling citizenships**' may then become *lived* citizenships for *all*."

After centuries of colonial transformations, it is difficult to remember Indigenous traditional systems of governance, and given the high levels of despair most Indigenous nations live under, it might be hard to resist the Canadian State's pressures in self-government and land claims negotiations. However, true warriors have always resisted colonial impositions and have insisted on the inherent rights to follow our own traditional ways of governing and be *equal* participants in a nation-to-nation relationship.

CHAPTER 15

Aboriginal Title and the Comprehensive Claims Process

Bonita Lawrence

. . .

Policy Framework

The inherent right to **self-government policy** and the comprehensive claims policy were both created by Ottawa in response to constitutional changes and Supreme Court decisions that addressed Aboriginal rights and title. Both documents suggest that, within the implementation of these policies, everything is negotiable. Unfortunately, the reality is that the colonialist assumptions informing the Supreme Court decisions that constrain Aboriginal rights and title have moulded these policies as well. Both policies clearly articulate that Aboriginal laws and traditional jurisdictions cannot be part of negotiations relating to self-government or comprehensive claims, that Canada can unilaterally decide what constitutes an "integral" aspect of Aboriginal culture, that discussions on self-government will remain separate from those regarding territory (as if governance is not associated with territory), and above all, that questions of compensation will not be addressed. This last stipulation sidesteps any recognition that Canada's wealth has come (and continues to come) from appropriating Native peoples' lands and resources, and that Native poverty is therefore a direct result of Canada's wealth. Moreover, the Supreme Court decisions . . . limit what is possible to achieve by litigation, leaving Native people no other option but to negotiate with Ottawa, inevitably from a position of weakness.

When Aboriginal rights were first entrenched in the Constitution, many Native people believed that at least some aspects of their control over their own affairs would be "on the table" as part of asserting a right to self-government or making a claim based on Aboriginal title. But in 2002, when talks on a number of comprehensive claims were proceeding under this assumption, Ottawa walked away from several negotiating tables across the country, labelling them "unproductive." These tables—30 of approximately 170—dealt with various matters ranging from specific claims, to self-government negotiations, to comprehensive claims within the British Columbia treaty process. When interviewed by the CBC, then-Indian Affairs minister Robert Nault stated that he had discontinued negotiation with certain tables because Native leaders had made excessive demands. These included issues relating to Aboriginal jurisdiction and the right to enact certain laws and to resist having Ottawa delegate authority over all matters relating to self-government (Nahwegahbow, 2002: 2).

In an environment where the Supreme Court decisions regarding Aboriginal rights and title have essentially predetermined what is open to negotiation, it is perhaps not surprising that Aboriginal leaders who attempt to infuse Indigenous frameworks of understanding into Canadian processes are characterized as unreasonable and acting in bad faith. Nevertheless, it is important to explore the self-government and comprehensive claims policies in some detail, to understand these processes more clearly.

The Inherent Right to Self-Government Policy

In 1995, the federal government released its Approach to Implementation of the Inherent Right and the Negotiation of Aboriginal Self-Government Policy. The document clearly states that recognition of inherent right is based on the view that the Aboriginal peoples of Canada have the right to govern themselves in relation to matters that are internal to their communities, integral to their unique cultures, identities, traditions, languages, and institutions, and with respect to their special relationship to their land and their resources (Canada, 1995). The language here is virtually identical to that of *Van der Peet, Pamajewon,* and *Delgamuukw* in that it limits self-government to purely internal matters and "culturalizes" Aboriginal rights, so that what is to be protected are not the existence, needs, and livelihoods of Aboriginal peoples, but their pre-contact cultures. The policy explicitly states that the inherent right of self-government does not include a right of sovereignty in the international sense and will not result in sovereign independent Aboriginal nations. Instead, the participation of Aboriginal peoples in the Canadian federation will be enhanced, and they and their governments will not exist in isolation, separate and apart from the rest of Canadian society. By suggesting that Aboriginal perspectives lead only to total independence from Canada, the policy ignores any notion that these perspectives should be part of the dialogue about *how* Indigenous people are to participate within Canada.

Negotiations relating to self-government are tripartite, involving the First Nation, Ottawa, and the relevant province or territory. The policy indicates that Aboriginal jurisdictions and authorities should work in harmony with those of other governments, which suggests that some "give" is expected from the provinces in the matter of jurisdiction. However, should an Aboriginal government's law conflict with any of the laws of the province or territory, it will be overridden by provincial or territorial law. Moreover, only matters considered internal to the group, integral to its distinct Aboriginal culture, and essential to its operation as a government can be part of self-government.

Although these limitations are extremely troubling, Aboriginal people are even more concerned about the financial aspects of the negotiations. The fact that no separate funds have been provided for implementation means that the considerable costs of transitioning to self-government must come from existing federal expenditures, which will depend on available resources. Second, although the policy suggests that self-government will ensure a stable source of funding for Aboriginal governments, there are no provisions to constitutionally protect transfer payments from Ottawa to First Nations in the manner in which provinces are constitutionally protected (McNeil, 2002: 32). This leaves First Nations in a very vulnerable position, particularly given Canada's history of significantly underfunding Aboriginal infrastructure and services relating to basic needs such as housing, clean water, sanitation, and accessible health care. . . .

As of September 2011, two BC bands (Sechelt and Westbank First Nations) had negotiated self-government agreements, and nine Yukon First Nations had negotiated a self-government agreement as part of their comprehensive claim (AAND, 2011). An examination of these agreements reveals that all generally adhere to a template, suggesting that the policy framework and process determined what was to be discussed. Notably, divisions between **status and non-status Indians** are maintained: Canada will continue to fund services for status Indians who come under self-government agreements but will not do the same for non-status or Metis groups, who must seek funding agreements with their relevant provinces in order to obtain self-government. . . .

. . . The most problematic issue, . . . and one that applies equally to self-government and the comprehensive claims process, is identifying who has the right to self-government. The Royal Commission on Aboriginal Peoples carefully distinguished between Indigenous nations and local communities. It identified an Indigenous nation as a sizeable body of Indigenous people who share a sense of national identity and who constitute the predominant population in a territory or collection of territories. Local communities, on the other hand, are the smaller groupings of Indigenous people that are not themselves nations but are part of nations. The royal

commission estimated that there are probably between fifty and eighty Indigenous nations in Canada and approximately a thousand local communities (RCAP, 1996b: 178–81).

McNeil (2002: 28) points out that due to the fragmenting effect of the Indian Act's band system, many Aboriginal communities are most comfortable dealing at the band level, or at most the tribal council level, and have little skill or experience in working at the nation level. Added to this actuality is the fact that treaties and provincial boundaries bisect Indigenous nations, dividing them into different jurisdictions, with the result that envisioning a reunited nation is difficult. McNeil suggests that this fundamental area needs significant research to address ways of overcoming these divisions.

The Comprehensive Claims Policy

Federal policy assigns Aboriginal land claims to one of two broad categories. Comprehensive claims are based on the assertion of continuing Aboriginal rights and title that are not covered by a treaty or other legal vehicle. Specific claims arise from non-fulfillment of treaties or other legal obligations, or from the improper administration of lands or assets under the Indian Act or other formal agreement (Hurley, 2009: 1). Despite the stipulations of its own policy, Ottawa has agreed to negotiate a few comprehensive claims in areas governed by treaties. . . .

. . . All modern treaties, otherwise known as land claim agreements, are negotiated through the comprehensive claims policy, which came into existence in 1973 as a result of the *Calder* decision. Between 1973 and 2009, twenty-three comprehensive claims have been settled (Hurley, 2009: 1–2). However, to truly understand the comprehensive claims process, we must examine how a claim is negotiated.

Negotiating a Comprehensive Claim
Before the negotiation process can begin, a First Nation is required to submit a statement of claim, which must include "a statement that the claimant group has not previously adhered to a treaty; a documented statement from the claimant group that it has traditionally used and occupied the territory in

question and that this use and occupation continues; a description of the extent and location of such land use and occupancy, together with a map outlining the approximate boundaries; and, identification of the claimant group including the names of the bands, tribes or communities on whose behalf the claim is being made, the claimant's linguistic and cultural affiliation, and approximate population figures of the claimant group" (Canada, 1987).

The federal government funds the research stage of the process, and if the land claim is accepted, First Nations must annually secure loans or grants from Ottawa to finance their participation in the negotiations. Claims are accepted only if the Indian Affairs minister deems that they have a high probability of success. Once a claim is accepted, the minister appoints a senior federal negotiator, who receives his or her mandate from Ottawa.

The parties then enter into preliminary negotiations, outlining areas to be discussed. It is important to understand that the "Scope of Negotiations" in the comprehensive claims policy establishes very strict parameters concerning what can be put on the table, in terms of land rights, waters, fisheries, subsurface royalties, and sacred sites. It rejects concepts such as co-management or sharing environmental management with First Nations. It also establishes fiscal caps and sets limits on royalties and revenue sharing—indeed, on most areas under discussion. Perhaps most importantly, it maintains the existing constitutional division of power between Ottawa and the provinces (ibid.). Clearly, control of the process is firmly in the hands of the federal government.

The first crucial issue to consider here is the power imbalance relating to funding. Because they are borrowing money from Ottawa, Native people who launch a claim are aware that during every day of the negotiations, their debt is mounting and that it will ultimately be deducted from the final settlement. Nor are these amounts trivial. According to an Indian Affairs estimate, the cost of negotiating a land claim can range from $15 to $50 million (INAC, 2003: 22). Once this amount has been deducted from the cash settlement, the actual monies received will be significantly reduced. Although Ottawa has forgiven some of these loans, the general rule is that they must be paid, and so the first "gun" held to the head of Indigenous people is the pressure to negotiate fast

before the debt piles up. And since Ottawa controls funding, the possibility that funding may be withdrawn if agreements are not forthcoming represents an additional set of pressures.

Of course, the irony of these pressure tactics is that the poverty of Native communities, which makes them dependent on government loans for land claim negotiations exists precisely because their wealth has been expropriated via the colonial process. In seeking title to the land, they are forced to borrow money from the very government that appropriated their land and resources in the first place. The funding issue highlights the fact that modern treaty negotiations are built upon a negation of the living reality of colonial history and the power it has granted Canada. For example, Canada continually denies that it should pay compensation for centuries of occupying people's land and usurping their resources. Its negotiators repeatedly insist that "history has been dealt with" via the apology to victims of residential schooling and the $350 million healing fund, and that the cash component of treaty settlements is an exchange of "value for value" (de Costa, 2002: 8). . . .

However, the biggest government pressure tactic is that untrammeled resource development continues while the treaty is being negotiated. For many Native people, the fact that clear cutting continues to devastate their homeland or that mines are being created on their territories while they sit in negotiations are powerful incentives to keep negotiations brief and accept whatever terms are offered.

The extinguishment of title is perhaps the most crucial concern for many Aboriginal people. Critics of the comprehensive claims process have suggested that the government should not seek to extinguish Aboriginal title: instead, it should specify which rights it is seeking from Native people to develop and use land and resources (Conseil Attikamek Montagnais et al., 1986). However, given the power imbalance that permeates the comprehensive claims policy, negotiations are grounded in either the full extinguishment of title or a specification of exactly what rights Aboriginal people will retain in the land.

The 1973 comprehensive claims policy contained what were referred to as "blanket extinguishment" provisions in that Indigenous people were to "cede, release and surrender" all Aboriginal rights and interests in and to the settlement area in exchange for the benefits provided by the settlement agreement. When Indigenous people's dissatisfaction regarding this requirement was obviously impeding the progress of claims, Canada adopted a new approach in 1986. This consisted of two alternatives—modified rights and non-asserted rights. In the former, which was first employed during the Nisga'a negotiations, Aboriginal rights are modified rather than extinguished, becoming solely the rights enshrined in the treaty. Under the latter, Aboriginal rights remain unextinguished, but Indigenous groups agree not to exercise them, confining themselves solely to the rights articulated and defined in the treaty. The 1986 policy allowed for the retention of Aboriginal rights on land that Indigenous people will hold once their claim is settled, but only insofar as such rights are not inconsistent with the treaty. . . .

If comprehensive claims are really modern treaties, it is clear that at the heart of treaty making, past and present, lies the assumption of Crown sovereignty. Indeed, as Kent McNeil (2002) demonstrates, jurisprudence in this area is instructive. McNeil compares four Supreme Court cases—*Simon, Sioui, Sparrow,* and *Delgamuukw*—to reveal the inconsistencies in the establishment of sovereignty. The *Simon* case of 1985 considered the rights accrued under the 1752 Treaty of Peace and Friendship between the Mi'kmaq and Britain; *Sioui,* which dates from 1990, involved a 1760 treaty between the Hurons of Lorette and Britain. The court viewed the Mi'kmaq and the Hurons as "quasi-sovereign nations" who were treaty signatories with Britain, and it recognized a range of rights under the two treaties. By comparison, in *Sparrow* and *Delgamuukw,* the court saw the Musqueam, the Gitksan, and the Wet'suwet'en as having been subjugated simply because Britain had asserted sovereignty over British Columbia in 1846. McNeil highlights the contradictions here: According to the court, British sovereignty at the time of the two eighteenth-century treaties was not yet established in Eastern Canada, even though the British had been in the area for over a century. But in 1846, when a treaty between Britain and the United States established the forty-ninth parallel as the boundary between their respective western possessions, it conclusively proclaimed British sovereignty over the whole of British Columbia, even though the

British had barely entered the west coast at this time. McNeil emphasizes the necessity of conducting research into how British sovereignty can supersede Indigenous jurisdiction—how it is that European settlement automatically confers Crown sovereignty, and indeed, how sovereignty can be asserted when no treaties are established with Indigenous people.

Although Crown sovereignty lies at the heart of the treaty relationship between Aboriginal people and the Crown, sacredness has been central to treaties between Aboriginal peoples themselves. According to the report of the Royal Commission on Aboriginal Peoples (RCAP, 1996a: 68–9), treaties were of the highest order of diplomatic relations across the continent and were maintained through the use of ceremony, replete with rituals, oratory, and specific protocols such as the exchange of wampum belts and smoking the sacred pipe, all of which were conscientiously observed by treaty partners. Indigenous terminology relating to treaties reveals an extraordinary attention to detail and to the various types of treaties. In the Ojibwa language, for example, there is a difference between *Chi-debahk-(in)-Nee-Gay-Win,* an open agreement with matters to be added to it, such as the Lake Huron Treaty of 1850, and *Bug-in-Ee-Gay,* which relates to "letting it go"—treaties requiring no further terms. However, treaties were always regarded as living entities to be renewed in ceremonies, which in turn renewed relationships. Nations cemented treaties with each other for purposes of trade, peace, neutrality, alliance, the use of territories and resources, and protection, resulting in far-reaching geopolitical alliances ranging from the Wendat Confederacy, which united four nations of similar dialects, to the Wabanaki Confederacy, the Iroquois Confederacy, and the Blackfoot Confederacy, each of which united diverse nations with many languages. Once formed, these confederacies were strengthened by the demands of the fur trade and became mechanisms for dealing with European colonists.

During the fur trade, Europeans entered into treaties according to Indigenous protocols, but this dynamic changed once Native people began to lose control of their territories. Particularly in Eastern Canada, the waning of the fur trade and its replacement with settlement policies, the drastic decline in Indigenous populations due to epidemics and warfare, and the growth of internecine divisions brought about by religious conversion and other destabilizing factors all contributed to this loss of power for Indigenous nations in their dealings with Europeans (Lawrence, 2002: 41). In this situation, it was all too easy for Europeans to negotiate treaties that were ostensibly about peace and trade but were subsequently revealed to focus on land cession (ibid.). As a result, between 1781 and 1830, most of southern Ontario was surrendered to Europeans. Between 1814 until the census of 1851, the white population of what is now southern Ontario multiplied by a factor of ten, from 95,000 to 952,000 (Miller, 2009: 94). Given the attenuated power that Native peoples now commanded, the old alliances between themselves and Europeans were abandoned.

With Confederation and the increasing power of the Canadian state came an accelerated process of land acquisition treaties in Western Canada and the North, so that in less than fifty years, eleven numbered treaties had been signed, claiming all the land stretching from Lake Superior to the Rockies and north to the Arctic Ocean.

Lynn Gehl (2009: 5) has compared these **historic treaties** with the **modern treaties** of the comprehensive claims policy. She has discovered that, with the exception of the Nunavut settlement, the modern treaties involved First Nations obtaining self-government powers only at the level of a municipality.[1] In examining the numbered treaties, she also found that Treaties 1, 2, and 5 allocated 32 acres per person, whereas the other numbered treaties apportioned 120 acres per person. Under the terms of the Nisga'a Agreement, each individual received 80 acres.

And yet, this does not compare with the situation of the Lheidli T'enneh, a band near Prince George. With a traditional territory of 10,000 square kilometres, the band was offered 29 square kilometres, 7 of which were reserve lands that it already held. This band, whose land borders Treaty 8 territory, would have been entitled to 140 square kilometres had it signed that treaty a hundred years ago (de Costa, 2002: 4). In April 2007, it voted to reject the treaty that it had spent thirteen years and $1 billion

negotiating with the federal and provincial governments. Only 47 percent of its 234 members voted in favour of the treaty. In general, it appears that modern treaties, at least those south of the sixtieth parallel, seek to leave Native people with less land than the historic treaties ever did.

In fact, more than any other aspect of Canadian policy, treaties grounded in European terms, both historically and in the modern era via the comprehensive claims policy, reveal the ongoing colonialism at the heart of Canadian society. It is not merely that Canada assumed sovereignty over the land with no clear basis under its own laws, it is also the hostile and mean-spirited attitude that Canada displays regarding any notion that it should now share the land in the traditional Aboriginal manner of negotiating treaties. Indeed, Canada appears determined to keep the door slammed shut on any possibility of real Native participation in activities on traditional lands. Ultimately, there is little difference between, on the one hand, historical treaty making and policies based on assimilation, and on the other, modern treaty making and policies based on containment and the notion that Native peoples will be domesticated through subordination to Canadian authority and therefore finally neutralized as sovereign entities.

Perhaps not surprisingly, the comprehensive claims policy has been challenged on a number of levels. For example, John Olthuis and Roger Townshend (1996), who voice many criticisms of the policy, assert that equity and compensation must be assessed according to the value of the assets on the date they are restored, not on the date in which they were improperly taken....

Rejecting the Politics of Recognition

A number of Aboriginal scholars have questioned the entire process of seeking recognition from settler governments. Glen Coulthard (2008: 188) notes that for the past thirty years, the self-determination efforts of Indigenous people in Canada have

---

1. The Nunavut Agreement involved an entire territory where the Inuit were a majority population and therefore received some jurisdictions similar to provinces. For the terms of the agreement, see Government of Nunavut (1993).

increasingly been cast in the language of "recognition." Coulthard applies the term "**politics of recognition**" to various recognition-based models of liberal pluralism that seek to reconcile Indigenous claims to nationhood with Crown sovereignty via the accommodation of Indigenous identities in some form of renewed relationship with the Canadian state. This may involve the delegation of land, capital, and political power from the state to Indigenous communities, generally through land claim agreements, economic development initiatives, and self-government packages. Coulthard argues that instead of establishing co-existence grounded on the ideal of mutuality, the politics of recognition in its contemporary form is reproducing the configurations of colonial power that Indigenous struggles for recognition sought to transcend in the first place.

In noting that our identities—as individuals and as groups—do not exist in isolation, Coulthard (ibid., 196) suggests that if our identities are shaped by recognition, they can also be distorted by misrecognition, so that distorting representations of Indigeneity serve to damage Aboriginal people and prevent them from flourishing. In an analysis based on the work of Frantz Fanon, Coulthard observes that the long-term stability of a colonial structure of dominance depends as much on the "internalization" of racist forms of asymmetrical and non-mutual modes of recognition as it does on brute force. According to Fanon, a colonial configuration of power must be attacked at two levels if one hopes to transform it; these are the objective level, where power is maintained through the appropriation of land and resources, and the subjective level, where ideological structures of dominance are ensconced in racist "recognition."

From this perspective, the politics of recognition can address colonial injustice only in reformist terms. The promotion of state redistribution schemes that grant certain "cultural rights" and economic concessions to Indigenous communities through land claims and self-government agreements fails to address the objective level of power that colonialist states have accrued via land and resource theft. The liberal recognition paradigm enables colonialist states to maintain power by "managing" land claims to their own benefit.

The second problem with the recognition paradigm relates to the subjective realm of power relations. Most recognition-based proposals rest on the problematic assumption that the flourishing of Indigenous peoples as distinct and self-determining is dependent on being recognized by the settler state. For Fanon, only resistance struggles—Coulthard calls them "transformative practices," such as struggles for cultural regeneration—are capable of enabling subjugated people to deconstruct the racist misrecognition that is so harmful.

When recognition is not accompanied by the transformative practice of cultural resistance, the fundamental self-transformation that comes with decolonization cannot occur. Under the politics of recognition, the colonized may receive constitutionally protected rights but cannot challenge the subjugation of their sovereign rights that is inherent in the process of delegating power. Indeed, those who engage in the politics of recognition must accept the infantilization and belittling of Indigenous societies that ensues when colonizers define the "integral" aspects of their "special cultures," delegating self-government that does not entail real Indigenous control and structuring land claims so as to permit no self-determination. In addition, Coulthard suggests that Indigenous people who work within the politics of recognition are in grave danger of adopting the limited and structurally contained terms of recognition as their own, so that in effect they identify with what he calls "white liberty" and "white justice."

As Coulthard (ibid., 195) points out,

Anybody familiar with the power dynamics that currently structure the Aboriginal rights movement in Canada should immediately see the applicability of Fanon's insights here. Indeed, one need not expend much effort at all to elicit the countless ways in which the liberal discourse of recognition has been limited and constrained by the state, politicians, corporations and the courts in ways that pose no fundamental challenge to the colonial relationship. With respect to the law, for example, over the last thirty years the Supreme Court of Canada has consistently refused to recognize Indigenous peoples' equal and self-determining status, based on the Court's adherence to legal precedent founded on the white supremacist myth that Indigenous societies were too primitive to bear fundamental political rights when they first encountered European powers. Thus, even though the Court has secured an unprecedented degree of recognition for certain "cultural" practices within the colonial state, it has nonetheless failed to challenge the racist origin of Canada's assumed authority over Indigenous peoples and their territories.

Coulthard's arguments reveal that, far from being liberatory, the politics of recognition is increasingly what Canada *needs* in order to absorb an Indigenous presence into its liberal democratic framework and to convince the world that it is *not* a colonial state. It seeks to demonstrate that "its" Indigenous peoples—tamed and domesticated—have become reconciled with the state and are happily co-existing within it, now that Canada protects its "special" cultures. For Indigenous people to step back from the politics of recognition—to refuse to be "reconciled" to Canada under such terms, and instead, to seek strength in their own traditions and their own land-based practices—may not challenge the brute force of colonial power, but it does delegitimize it.

Coulthard's reasoning is supported by Taiaiake Alfred (2005), who asserts that the large-scale "statist" solutions offered by Canada, such as land claim negotiations and self government, merely provide a good living for those who represent their people in such contexts. At the same time, however, the great majority of Native people do not benefit from such practices, and indeed, are bearing the brunt of a racist society that denigrates their identities as Indigenous people and has done its best to erode and destroy Indigenous peoples' traditional frameworks of identity as ensconced in language and relationship to the land. The result is weakened and isolated people, too often consumed by addictions and tremendously unhealthy. Alfred suggests that a strategic focus on self-help for many Native people who are struggling with addiction and poor health is fundamentally necessary for decolonization, whereas those who are stronger and able to engage in critical resistance should concentrate on delegitimizing Canada's liberal democratic facade and reclaiming traditional practices on the land. . . .

References

AAND. "Self Government." Aboriginal Affairs and Northern Development, 2011. http://www.aadnc-aandc.gc.ca/.

Alfred, Taiaiake. *Wasáse: Indigenous Pathways of Action and Freedom.* Toronto: Broadview Press, 2005.

Canada. *Comprehensive Claims Policy.* Ottawa: Minister of Supply and Services Canada, 1987.

———. "The Government of Canada's Approach to Implementation of the Inherent Right and the Negotiation of Aboriginal Self-Government Policy." Aboriginal Affairs and Northern Development Canada, 1995. http://www.aadnc-aandc.gc.ca/eng/.

Conseil Attikamek Montagnais, Council for Yukon Indians, Dene Nation, Métis Association of the N.W.T., Kaska-Dena, Labrador Inuit Association, Nishga Tribal Council, Taku River Tlingit, and Tungavik Federation of Nunavut. "Key Components of a New Federal Policy for Comprehensive Land Claims." 30 October 1986. http://www.carc.org/.

Coulthard, Glen. "Beyond. Recognition: Indigenous Self-Determination as Prefigurative Practice," in L. Simpson, ed., pp. 187–204, *Lighting the Eighth Fire: The Liberation, Resurgence, and Protection of Indigenous Nations.* Winnipeg: Arbeiter Ring, 2008.

De Costa, Ravi. "Agreements and Referenda: Recent Developments in the British Columbia Treaty Process." Paper presented at "Negotiating Settlements: Indigenous Peoples, Settler States and the Significance of Treaties and Agreements," Institute for Postcolonial Studies, Melbourne, 29 August 2002. http://www.atns.net.au/.

Gehl, Lynn. "Land Settlements Not Improving," *Anishinabek News,* July–August 2009, 5.

Government of Nunavut. *Agreement between the Inuit of the Nunavut Settlement Area and Her Majesty the Queen in Right of Canada,* 1993. http://www.gov.nu.ca/hr/site/doc/nlca.pdf.

Hurley, Mary C. "Settling Comprehensive Land Claims," Parliamentary Information and Research Service, Library of Parliament, 21 September 2009. http://www2.parl.gc.ca/Content/LOP/ResearchPublications/prh0916-e.pdf.

inac (Indian and Northern Affairs Canada). *Resolving Aboriginal Claims: A Practical Guide to Canadian Experiences.* Ottawa: inac, 2003.

Lawrence, Bonita. "Rewriting Histories of the Land, Colonization and Resistance in Eastern Canada," in Sherene Razack, ed., pp. 23–46, *Race, Space and the Law: Unmapping a White Settler Society.* Toronto: Between the Lines Press, 2002.

McNeil, Kent. "The Inherent Right of Self-Government: Emerging Directions for Legal Research." A Research Report prepared for the First Nations Governance Centre, Chilliwack, BC. November 2002.

Miller, J.R. *Compact, Contract and Covenant: Aboriginal Treaty-Making in Canada.* Toronto: University of Toronto Press, 2009.

Olthuis, John, and H.W. Roger Townshend. "Is Canada's Thumb on the Scales? An Analysis of Canada's Comprehensive and Specific Claims Policies and Suggested Alternatives," in *Canada, for Seven Generations: An Information Legacy of the Royal Commission on Aboriginal Peoples*, 63 174–63877. Ottawa: Libraxus, 1996.

rcap (Royal Commission on Aboriginal Peoples). Report of the Royal Commission on Aboriginal Peoples. Vol. 1, *Looking Forward, Looking Back.* Ottawa: Ministry of Supply and Services, 1996a.

———. Report of the Royal Commission on Aboriginal Peoples. Vol. 2, *Restructuring the Relationship.* Ottawa: Ministry of Supply and Services, 1996b.

CHAPTER 16

The Gender of the Flint

Mohawk Nationhood and Citizenship in the Face of Empire

Audra Simpson

. . .

Narrating Territory and Rights

Even a dog could be buried in Kahnawà:ke, and we [the women who lost their Indian status upon out-marriage] could not! (Mary Two-Axe Early, ca. 1983)

The transition from property holder and status giver to a rank that is, upon death, beneath that of a dog

requires a sudden and swift shift in power. . . . The utterance of Mary Two-Axe Early cited above tell us that notions of status and rights, and the complex of both that constitutes "political membership," must be tied up with something more than the power of the state. Why? Canada does not bury members in Kahnawà:ke; families do, and they do so in accordance with Mohawk Council of Kahnawà:ke (or traditional Longhouse) rules on membership and jurisdiction. Thus, the decision that allows dogs to be buried in the community and not women (who had lost their status) and *then* to cite this as a matter of injustice, references something deeper than the state. There is another story, another working even of *value* at play. There is evidence here of a local and Indigenous notion of "the utilitarian good" that is historically driven and striving to be consensus based, attempting to recover and manage the vicissitudes of lawful and unlawful forms of dispossession that are borne by women today in various forms: dispossession of their rights as Indians, of their land, and of their lives. The agency exercised within the community, then, is an agency and instrumentality that work upon these notions "on the ground," notions that work in some relation to notions of territory.

. . . A traditional woman whom I interviewed from another Mohawk community answered my questions on Mohawk identity, nationhood, and territory in this way:[2]

Q: *Please give me some words to describe Mohawk people; how would you describe Mohawks to someone that does not know us?*

A: *Strong, peace loving, funny . . .*

Q: *Are these qualities the same for women as they are for men?*

A: *These qualities are more pronounced in women.*

Q: *Please tell me what nationhood is to you?*

A: *This is the disappearance of the boundaries between our reserves. In the ideal world, we would move through our traditional territory with no impediments, we would restore our relationship with the land as women. We would be free to do these things and not stay on the "ghettos" that they call reserves.*

Territory is a large issue in her discourse on identity and nationhood and was throughout the course of the interview. She wanted to see the traditional territory of Mohawk people, which extends down from Kanehsatà:ke into the Ohio Valley, restored. In relation to this territory, she said, women are "the caregivers and own the territory, and the caregivers of the children and keep the communities going while the men are away." This is a neotraditional argument that takes the "traditional," precontact role of women and transposes it onto the contemporary. . . .

Here we are not yet finished with blood quantum or ideas about purity, as women still seem to carry the burden of this shift. Thus local membership options—such as matriliny, blood, and (in the case of one interlocutor in my data set) formal Canadian citizenship[3]—should also be viewed as adaptations, and somewhat sensible ones, to a colonial scene. Iroquois membership prior to the ascent of the settler state on the Canadian side of the international boundary line was about clan membership, and clan membership was transmitted through the woman's line. Particularly in light of the importance of women as clan bearers and as landowners in traditional Iroquois communities, blood quantum and the disregard for these *traditional* lines of descent—along with hooking ideas about nationhood to colonial forms of membership—seem especially problematic and self-defeating. If Iroquois women were the "mothers of the nation," then how could the nation continue without them in authoritative, structural positions of power?

. . . So how indeed could this "sudden and swift" shift in power occur? Land diminished rapidly; resources dwindled; being Indian mattered differently, and became hinged, perhaps, to a notion of decision making and loyalty to the community land base.

---

2. A "traditional woman" would be defined as someone who self-consciously practices "tradition," and rejects the authority of the settler nation-state to define her or accord her rights. She does not vote in federal or provincial elections, she does not pay taxes, she uses a "red card" (with her clan, not her band number) to cross the US–Canadian border, she may refuse to use a provincially issued Medicare card to obtain health care. "Traditional" would entail a very adamant stance in terms of sovereignty, which is why much of the Iroquoianist literature on "culture" can exasperate contemporary ethnographers and ethnographic understandings of sovereignty. In 1997, way before I started formal fieldwork, I witnessed a "traditional" man refuse medical attention in a hospital in Chateauguay (the municipal suburb next the reserve) because he did not recognize the Province of Quebec or Canada.

3. One man told me that his vision of community membership in Kahnawà:ke was predicated on recognition within the Longhouse; however, he had no problem personally with identifying as a Canadian, nor with concealing that he was Indian (as his mother had instructed) from kids that he played with in the Maritimes because they might beat him up if they knew. His willingness to "pass" as white in his youth was tied to fears surrounding the presence of the Ku Klux Klan and their violent attacks against visible minorities.

Thus being Indian and having status became tied to notions of personal and individual responsibility. Women were told, "If you marry out, then you have to leave."[4] Interlocutors told me, "I always knew what would happen if I married out" (mind you, one woman in my data set purported to *not* know this) .... These adaptations were tied as well to notions of territory that moved along with labour and travel beyond the confines of Kahnawà:ke. It is to this new "diasporic" space that disenfranchised women and their children, along with the shifting community of travellers and workers, would have to relocate. In this way, policy and cultural practice forced a new, gendered territorial imperative; this is especially the case if the women remain committed to the community and to their identities as Mohawks, transmitting this identity to their children. They may have had to leave the community proper, the bounded space of the reserve, but their activities in Chateauguay, Brooklyn, Ottawa, or elsewhere may have oriented them toward home or a re-created "home" away.

How does this predicament manifest itself in the present? This excerpt is from a woman who awaits recognition:

> And so when we come out and we are [talking] about the things [that] are going on with the community, I am sure that the band council is not . . . going to Ottawa and telling the minister everything that he's doing to the people over there. You see, and yet he is saying "We are providing the services, we're doing everything that we're supposed to," but only to the few that they select. Now what about the rest of the population?
>
> Now you've got people living off-reserve, because the community has rejected them—those people are not necessarily familiar with the daily activities that are going on in the community, so what they have done is basically removed themselves from having to deal with those situations on a daily basis. . . .

I mean life is hell there! I mean, it is not the best, I'll be the first to say it, living there; you gotta be damn tough to live there. And in order to survive there, you have to be really tough. Now some people might have gotten tired by it, and decided, "I'm gonna go live off the reserve where I won't have to deal and face those things on a daily basis, where somebody's telling me, 'Leave, you don't belong here,' facing the discrimination on a daily basis." Which is what we encounter.

I encounter it daily there; you never know what's going to happen from one moment to the next. I mean water and sewage is one thing, landfill is another, getting slapped in the face [when I got] my letter from the Education Centre . . . saying that they are not accepting me so that I can go ask and beg and plead to the Department to get it.... I never got rid of it—certificates of possession, with letters of rejection....

I mean at every turn we are getting slapped in the face—every single turn—which should be normal things that we should be entitled to for the past seventeen years. And the federal government has been: "Well, sorry."

Now if anybody is going to . . . want us to trust them, they have to jump over a lot of loops to do that now, and hurdles, because there is no more trust. There is no trust in the councils, and there is no trust in the federal government because both have reneged on their responsibilities.

So, now we are sitting back, and this is why we are taking the position that we are taking, and this is why we are *angry*. I mean, I lived hell for *x* years, my whole entire life getting slapped in the face at every turn. I grew up in the city, them telling me "Go back to where you come from." I go to the town,[5] they tell me, "Go back to the city you don't belong here."

---

4. I have been told this, and women I interviewed told me that they also were told this.

5. People in Kahnawà:ke refer to the reserve community as "town."

Where the hell do you go? And then when you do decide to make your decision—your stance on where you are going—you still get slapped in the face daily. So life is not a bed of roses over there, but I choose to live there because it is my *right*.

I didn't get the land that I am living on by *buying* it; it was passed down from generation to generation within my family, and I am being told I am third generation, I am white, and I have no right. That is what I am being told, and yet I inherited that land; I never bought it; it has been passed down from generation to generation.

This narrative moves us through the historical spaces that one must simultaneously occupy to manage the question of rights and justice as a historically excluded woman of unambiguous Kahnawà:ke Mohawk descent. We can cull from her narrative that she is first constructed as a claimant upon the community as a non-status Indian (or in the eyes of some community members, as a non-Indian). As such, she is also being constructed as a claimant upon the resources of the community. Within her narrative, we can see that she experiences aggression from others in Kahnawà:ke, where she is told "to go back to the city." And the city, she makes clear, is also not a welcoming place for her. She wants to stay on the reserve in spite of this because it is her *right*. Now this notion of "right" that she is working with is an interesting one. It includes what she is owed by her Bill C-31 reinstatement of status and, as she makes clear toward the end of her narrative, to her position as a landowner. Her status as a landowner is owing to her descent from people who were property owners within the community. She is not directly invoking the notion of an Iroquois woman's role in pre-settler society as a caretaker of the land, but her argument is tied to the commonsense transparency embedded in the parentage of her right as a person descended from people who lived and owned land in the community. Thus it is her right to remain there. This for her is obvious; it is commonsense; and it is what she leaves us with, along with the dissent that greets her claim to this right within the community: "I am third generation, I am white, and I have no right."

. . . The following utterances will touch upon, in different ways, alternative conceptions of political membership in Kahnawà:ke and the larger body of the Mohawk nation (spread out across six different reserves in Ontario, Quebec, upstate New York, and urban areas). Consider now these propositions and how they shift and change as we move through different locales, from the reserve to the city.

Clearing 1

When interviewed in *now* magazine, an alternative weekly in Toronto Ontario, Ida Goodleaf, a Kahnawà:ke Mohawk, offered her thoughts on the blood-quantum debate on the reserve. At the time of her interview in 1994, the debate over membership requirements in the community was in "full swing." The blood-quantum requirement of 50 percent was on the books, but was not ratified by the federal government. Consternation and conflict abounded within the community. The local and outside media sought to document and discuss the "racial" requirements for membership in the community and its implications. In response to her interviewer's questions, Ida Goodleaf said, perhaps defensively, "People have got to understand that this little postage stamp [the reserve]—I've got to fight for it. . . . I only want to keep my rights and what rightfully belongs to us, and anybody that is 50-percent Indian. If we had let that go [the land, the membership requirement], we would have already lost our rights" (quoted in Sero, 1994: 15).

This discourse is from the reserve. It clearly pronounces the reserve to be in a diminished state—"this little postage stamp"—and a site of protection, of a place that must, in her mind (and the minds of others), be protected against encroachment by those who do not have sufficient blood quantum. . . . The conditions of not belonging are determined by a degree of blood that is to approximate lineage and can be discerned by people in Kahnawà:ke. Blood quantum has always been a way of talking about lineage—descent from people who themselves were imagined to have 100 percent Mohawk blood, who were on the band list, and could be reckoned by others as Indians who were from and of that place. The rights that this woman speaks of would perhaps approximate collective rights, rights that belong to a group larger than herself, contrary to the model mapped out by the geographic and rights-based flux of the previous interlocutor who does not seem to belong anywhere, and yet has individual rights to property.

Perception of Women's Roles

In 2002 I interviewed the Kahnawà:ke Mohawk who helped to draft the first blood-quantum requirement rules for the community. We were in Montreal, and when our meal had wound down I asked him, "What do you think of blood quantum? What is the legacy of C-31 in Kahnawà:ke? What about the role of our women in deciding membership?" He told me, "Look, I am 'hardline' on this issue, I believe that blood is part of identity. But I also believe that women are part of that too, they should be the decision makers; that is the way it was before white people got here, and that is the way it should be. Women should be in charge—they know what is going on in the community; the men have no idea—they are away all the time."

One sees how gendered even the exclusionary discourse can be, how tied it can be to ideas about "traditional" and actionable theories on gender (women simply are in charge) and the contemporary experience of that role of women in lives lived in the Longhouse structure of the past and transposed onto the life of the reserve today. "Men are away all the time" is a reference to the labour of ironwork, done almost exclusively by men, for the past century. It takes them down to New York City, almost always across the border to the United States. The conundrum, then, of gendered exclusion based on blood quantum is not addressed; there is no recognition that the descendants of women, and those women themselves who the Indian Act made white in the eyes of the state, are afflicted by exclusion. This man maintains a commitment to blood as the basis of recognition and rights, with shades of the more collectivist and territorially protectionist model of rights instanced by Ida Goodleaf in her *NOW* interview.

The Forest

Eventually my research took me "away" from the reserve, the surrounding cities, and the suburbs, down to the "forest," to the place of men (it seems), to New York City. I found myself leaning against a bar in Greenwich Village, talking to the ironworkers who had just finished up a day of bolting and welding on the new student services building at New York University on West Fourth and La Guardia. I was interviewing a Mohawk man from Ahkwesáhsne.

"Hey, L, tell me, what is the ideal form of membership for us? What do you think makes someone a member of the community?"

He looks at me squarely in the eye, and doesn't answer. Instead he says, "Well, can I ask *you* something?"

"Sure . . ."

"When you look in the mirror, what do you see?"

"When I look in the mirror, what do I see?"

I repeat this out loud. The question hangs awkwardly and stubbornly between us. The silence between us is louder than the song by Kate Bush and Peter Gabriel that fills the bar. He pushes me,

"I asked you, Audra, when you look in the mirror, what do you see?"

My stupefied silence is audible, and somewhat embarrassing even now, when I replay it on my mini-disc recorder. I finally answer him, I say,

"I see a nice person, L."

"Well, that is who we are, then—that is the answer to the question."

These utterances and narratives gathered and produced during fieldwork testify to the shifting content and positioning on the question of membership and citizenship *within* the political membership. Here we have different notions of rights, and what rights *should* be like, as well as the gendered valences of their form, their role, and the implications of this to contemporary territory.

The particular history of Indian women and territory in Canada factors into this analysis of territory and citizenship as the central subject of historical and legal exclusion, a subject whose (dangerous) Indigeneity was legally eliminated upon marriage to a non-Indian man. When she left her moral and "racial" community, she joined "civilization" through heterosexual practice. "Civilization" and citizenship (and geographic banishment from her family) was then achieved through the legal union with a non-Indian man. This completely counters

Iroquois perceptions of gender roles (and thus a woman's access to institutional power) within communities where women are the carriers of the names, the owners of the land, the ones who appoint chiefs. These narratives pivot through the different ways in which these roles and responsibilities punctuate territory and how they mark it, but also how "rights" are subject to ongoing deliberation and debate.

The final narrative, a conversation I had with an ironworker in a bar, flips it all back into my face—gender roles, legal status, informal status—as he pushes me to define myself. I am struck now at how completely indifferent I was to gender and to responsibility, and defined myself in completely attributional terms that are not part of official discourse. "I see a smart person," "I see a funny person," "I see a person who is ethically challenged by these policies that are unfair." These transcendent qualities such as "nice" and "funny," when intertwined with a just genealogical configuration and authority to act on that configuration, may be the things that matter the most to the project of moving away from the choking grip that settler colonialism has on Indigenous governance and, consequently, membership and citizenship.

Yet there is no place in the formal political discussion for qualities; roles, history, and tradition are the terms of appeal. And it is no wonder; those were the very things that the Indian Act and its gendered imposition upon communities sought to change. During the course of my research, I attended as many community meetings on membership as I could. During one of these meetings, I witnessed a Kahnawà:ke woman stand up and read a prepared statement to the councillors, who are sometimes known as "elected chiefs." Here I paraphrase her letter: "Why is it that we as Mohawk women were important, that we owned the land, gave children their clans, and now we cannot even own land or build a house in this community?" This woman's mother is Mohawk and is from the community, and her father is non-Indian. Because she is not married to her Mohawk partner, she remains a "C-31" and off the band list, in spite of having grown up in the community, having a partner in the community, and having children with that Mohawk partner. What she reminds the community of in these moments and within a Mohawk Council of Kahnawà:ke meeting—what some traditional people would say is an authoritative space of Canada and of colonialism—is that "as women we had power; why do we not still have power? Why do we, as a Mohawk community, uphold non-Mohawk ways of recognizing descent?" And, further, "Why are women such as myself, who carry the clan with them, not recognized by this official, land-granting body of this community?"[6]

. . . Membership is a social, historical, and, in the case of this study, *narrated* process that references personal and collective pasts while making itself over, parameters and boundaries and all, in a lived present. As a social, historical, and narrated process, gender is necessarily bound up in and speaks of and from the power that accrues to the settlement of space. Although membership is made over, the stories and practices in that remaking may reinterpret and subvert the metahistories (and fictions) of the state(s) in which one finds oneself; the narratives of membership may work to build a sense of nationhood not from the signs and symbols of the state, but rather from the words and interactions of the people—words and actions that are issued in the everyday moments of exchange. . . .

Feeling Citizenship

There is a difference between what is prescribed and what actually should be, and that is being worked out in the day-to-day life of the community. This difference between "membership" and "citizenship" was made clear to me through the course of an interview with a man in his early twenties, "C". . . . He is a lifelong resident of the community, yet the situation regarding his own membership is difficult.

Q: *Are you a citizen of Canada?*

A: *I live and work, for the most part, within the territorial boundaries that Canada has*

6. A good part of this meeting was devoted to land requests from community members who have to go before the community and Council to request land. They have to put themselves on the agenda, attend three meetings, and answer questions from people in attendance, if asked.

unilaterally set. For the sake of ease, when crossing the border, or in discussion or signing any forms, for the sake of simplicity, and, as I said, ease, and to get things done with rather quickly, I will say I live in Canada. I will say I live in Canada, [that] I am a Canadian citizen, for simplicity's sake,

That is not how I feel, and when it could be avoided I never say that. But of course when I am crossing the border and they ask where I live, or if they say "what country" I will say "Canada" just to avoid any problems. Of course anywhere else I never say that—that is not how I feel. I am a Mohawk of Kahnawà:ke, not a Canadian citizen.

Q: *What does that mean, to be a Mohawk from Kahnawà:ke, 'cause you said, "I will do this for the sake of ease." It is more like this citizenship of convenience.*

A: *Yes, "convenience."*

Q: *You know, it is like, "OK, don't give me a hard time, I was born . . ." Well, actually they were born in our territory, but now it looks like we were born in their territory.*

A: *We will say it was theirs, to avoid problems . . .*

Q: *So there is this citizenship of convenience, and then you also said, "This is not how I feel, but this is what I have to do, just in this situation," so what then is this other thing, the "feeling citizenship," is that a feeling citizenship?*

A: *Within Kahnawà:ke?*

Q: *Yeah, the idea, "I am a Mohawk from Kahnawà:ke?" is that your* other *citizenship? Is that your* other *. . .*

A: *That is my* primary *citizenship; that is my main citizenship. Canadian citizenship*

is sort of an ancillary citizenship, which I invoke to avoid hassle. I don't consider myself "Canadian." As I said, I am a Mohawk of Kahnawà:ke, and I feel that that is where my citizenship lies. If one would like to go even further, I could say, "I am a Mohawk of Kahnawà:ke of the Confederacy," although I see myself more limited to Kahnawà:ke. . . .

Q: *Why is that?*

A: *I see no working, legitimate Confederacy to be a part of. It [would] be different if there was a true, governing, recognized body, but there is none that I am aware of, so I limit my citizenship to "Mohawk of Kahnawà:ke," perhaps a bit further the "Mohawk nation," but no Confederacy. In my eyes it's nonexistent.*

Q: *Would you be interested in that form of citizenship if it were possible, for us?*

A: *If it were possible, yes!*

Q: *If there were those operational—you are probably thinking about institutions? If we had our clans back up? If they were . . .*

A: *Not really, but a system of nations associated together for the betterment of all Aboriginals in that group. . . .*

Q: *Iroquois?*

A: *Iroquois. That I would agree to—I feel that in a way is what we should be; it isn't agreeing to anything new and extraordinary; it is just the way it should be. . . .*

Q: *There is this "citizenship of convenience," [but] your "primary citizenship," that "feeling citizenship"—what is the content of that citizenship for you? When you say you are a Mohawk of Kahnawà:ke, what does that mean to you?*

A: *That is where I associate with most, because that is where I've grown up; that's where my feeling and loyalty lie. I have . . . what is the word I can use? I have a* bond *with the community; that's the life that I know; that's the society, the setup, the whole setup to the society, the way life evolves and revolves around certain institutions in the community, is what I am used to, and that's how I feel that my citizenship lies there; that is the life that I know. . . .*

. . . In spite of the rules of the state, in spite of the governance structure that attempts to implement them (or not implement them, or find an alternative to them), there are other workings of citizenship. . . . C's is in active and attached disaffiliation from the state—"for the sake of convenience, I am a Canadian"—yet he was unrecognized by his primary space of self-articulation—the Mohawk Nation as instantiated by a tribal or band council governance system. Even so, he maintains a sense of himself as *still* belonging, and indeed he does belong to the community, in spite of the fact that they do not *legally* recognize him. He is distanced from the settler state as well. Here he elaborates further on the bite of that exclusion, the ways in which it cuts through, in some ways, his "feeling citizenship":

Q: *Tell me what you think our ideal form of . . . Are citizenship and membership the same thing?*

A: *From my understanding, and whomever I ask, I get these gray, cloudy answers in return, so I am not quite sure. I am a* citizen *of Kahnawà:ke, but I am not a* member *of Kahnawà:ke. I am not on this mysterious list that no one seems to have any information about.[7] So although I dearly love Kahnawà:ke, there are many positions I will never be able to hold until this membership issue is cleared up, so I don't know much about it, other than, I don't think it to be fair. There are those who leave the community, as I said—we all come*

back to Kahnawà:ke, but there are those who leave for twenty-five years and they come back and they're a member, and they will have all these opportunities that I won't, even though I've never left. I don't think that's fair. But I think there's a distinction—one could be a citizen without being a member.

Q: *Interesting, and that citizenship is based on. . . . Let me push you on that then—how is that different; explain it to me?*

A: *Citizenship is—as I said—you live there; you grew up there; that is the life that you know. That is who you are. Membership is more of a legislative enactment designed to keep people from obtaining the various benefits that Aboriginals can receive. So I am a citizen; I live there; that is who I am; yet, I cannot be a member because of these laws, which I feel is unfair. If I had been there my whole life, I should have the same opportunity to run for Council that anyone else can. Yet I cannot.*

Q: *Do you think that's because of public sentiment, the Indian Act, is that because of . . .*

A: *I don't know what you know, or what others know—this is an area that I can't get straight answers from; no one seems to know.*

"No one seems to know" was laced through much of his discourse on C-31 and on his own predicament. However, people do seem to *know* the different forms of recognition that are at play in the exercising of rights, and that knowledge translates in the "feeling side" of recognition. I want to return us now to the community meeting that I discussed prior to this interview in order to compare the difference between my interlocutor's critical point on the difference between "citizenship" and "membership."

At the same meeting at which the woman read her letter to the community and to Council—a

---

7. He is referring to the locally controlled "band list."

community member with an especially complicated membership, but with an official membership no less—stood up and made an impassioned speech about the perils of blood quantum and its similarity, in his mind, to Nazi policies on race purity. During his narrative, a woman sitting near him said loudly to the woman sitting next to her, "He shouldn't even be here" and then repeated herself, louder. When he reached the point in the trajectory of his argument about how Mohawk identity was about clan and language, not blood, she said even louder to no one in particular, "Then speak in Indian." This discursive challenge to his authority to speak on matters of culture was testament to the unfairness of the situation presented by these different cases. What I wish to suggest is that these *living, primary, feeling citizenships* may not be institutionally recognized, but are socially and politically recognized in the everyday life of the community, and people get called out on them—there is little room or toleration for an inconsistency in one's own situation and what is considered just—hailing at that moment, that which makes it unjust: the Indian Act, for example. One who has rights that another does not because of gender inequality and then pronounces on the "best way" in spite of his or her privilege will get pushed, discursively—will get reminded. The challenge to the community is to harden these pieces of knowledge, these critiques and these possibilities into a membership policy that may accommodate the simultaneity of these experiences, these different trans-historic discourses (and people), so that these "feeling citizenships" may then become *lived* citizenships for *all.*

These feeling citizenships are narratively constructed, hinge upon sociality, and are tied in ways to the simultaneous topography of colonialism *and* Iroquoia—where certain women reside outside the boundaries of the community because they have to, and others remain in; where the forces of social, primary, "feeling" citizenships may work to enfold all into a narrative frame of collective experience. The narratives that connect these people deal heavily in the currency of "who we are, of who they are, of what rights we should have, of what we shall be in the future." They are a relentless process and practice, as Mohawks come up against the state and against each other, as they enfold each other into ambits of critique, refusal, care, and ambivalence in spite of forces that would have them completely banished.

I wish to argue here that the case of political membership is one that narrates "who we are" while archiving the living legacy of colonialism through recitation and reminder. These narratives are more, however, than colonial recitations of exclusion; they embed *desire* in ways that speak between the gulfs of the past and the present, whether this might be, as we have seen, for traditional modes of governance within the nation-state of Canada or the Mohawk nation (itself a member nation in the Iroquois Confederacy), for a limited form of self-government within the boundaries of the community, or for an abstraction such as justice. No matter what the final object of that desire may be, the narratives of citizenship in this study are laden with desires that want in some ways to affect the differentials of power that underwrite notions of nationhood and citizenship away from the politics of recognition and into other unfolding, undetermined possibilities. This desire is made from the intimacy, the knowledge, and the messiness of everyday life, and from the bonds of affection and disaffection that tie people into communities and communities into nations, even if they are unrecognizable or unrecognized.

Reference

Sero, Peter. "Bloodlines Cross Mohawk Country," *Now* (6–12 October): 14–20.

PART 8

Additional Readings

Alfred, Taiaiake and Jeff Corntassel. "Being Indigenous: Resurgences Against Contemporary Colonialism," *Government and Opposition* 40, no. 4 (2005): 597–614.

Cobb, Daniel M. *Say We Are Nations: Documents of Politics and Protest in Indigenous America since 1887*. Chapel Hill, NC: University of North Carolina Press, 2015.

Dhillon, Jaskiran. *Prairie Rising: Indigenous Youth, Decolonization, and the Politics of Intervention*. Toronto: University of Toronto Press, 2017.

Hill, Susan M. *The Clay We Are Made Of: Haudenosaunee Land Tenure on the Grand River*. Winnipeg: University of Manitoba Press, 2017.

Gehl, Lynn. *The Truth That Wampum Tells: My Debwewin on the Algonquin Land Claims Process*. Halifax & Winnipeg: Fernwood Publishing, 2014.

Lawrence, Bonita. *Fractured Homeland: Federal Recognition and Algonquin Identity in Ontario*. Vancouver: University of British Columbia Press, 2012.

Palmater, Pamela D. *Indigenous Nationhood: Empowering Grassroots Citizens*. Halifax & Winnipeg: Fernwood Publishing, 2015.

———. *Beyond Blood: Rethinking Indigenous Identity*. Saskatoon: Purich Publishing, 2011.

Simpson, Audra. *Mohawk Interruptus: Political Life across the Borders of Settler States*. Durham: Duke University Press, 2014.

Sunseri, Lina. *Being Again of One Mind: Oneida Women and the Struggle for Decolonization*. Vancouver: University of British Columbia Press, 2011.

Relevant Websites

Defenders of the Land
http://www.defendersoftheland.org/
The Defenders of the Land describe themselves as "a network of Indigenous communities and activists in land struggle across Canada, including Elders and youth, women and men." According to their website, the organization "was founded at a historic meeting in Winnipeg from November 12–14, 2008. Defenders is the only organization of its kind in the territory known as Canada—Indigenous-led, free of government or corporate funding, and dedicated to building a fundamental movement for Indigenous rights."

IGOV Indigenous Speaker Series. Dr. Audra Simpson talks on Mohawk Interruptus
https://www.youtube.com/watch?v=FWzXHqGfH3U
Dr. Audra Simpson delivers a lecture at the IGOV on alternative discourses of Mohawk citizenship.

Yellowhead Institute
https://yellowheadinstitute.org/
The Yellowhead Institute is an Indigenous-led research centre producing policy perspectives intended to (re-) shape Indigenous governance, facilitate Indigenous-Settler alliances, research opportunities, government accountability and public education.

Films

Fractured Land. Dir. Fiona Rayher and Damien Gillis. Crown-source funding, 2015.
Kanehsatake: 270 Years of Resistance. Dir. Alanis Obomsawin. National Film Board of Canada, 1993.
Haida Gwaii: On the Edge of the World. Dir. Charles Wilkinson. Shore Films Inc., 2015.
The Road Forward. Dir. Marie Clements. National Film Board of Canada, 2017.
Trick or Treaty. Dir. Alanis Obomsawin. National Film Board of Canada, 2014.

Key Terms

- Self-government policy
- Comprehensive claims policy
- Status and non-status Indians
- Historic/modern treaties

- Politics of recognition
- Nationhood/citizenship/membership
- Feeling citizenship
- Blood quantum

Discussion Questions

1. What are the differences between nationhood, citizenship, and membership? What does Simpson mean by "feeling citizenship"? And how does this "feeling citizenship" relate to the other three terms?

2. How has a blood-quantum criterion on membership to an Indigenous nation resulted in a gendered exclusion? How does such exclusion contrast to matrilineal/matrilocal traditional Indigenous governances?

3. Discuss how negotiations relating to the inherent right to self-government have not served the interests and goals of Indigenous Nations in Canada very well. What would be a better strategy for Indigenous peoples to undertake?

4. By referring to Glen Coulthard, what does Lawrence mean by the term "politics of recognition"? Why are both Coulthard and Lawrence critical of a politics of recognition? What do they propose as a better alternative?

Activities

Watch the film *Sewatokwa'tsher'at: The Dish with One Spoon* (2008), directed by Dawn Martin-Hill. Discuss the notions of nation and nationalism as presented in the film: what do many white residents in Caledonia imagine Canadian nationalism to be? What kinds of Canadian national narratives inform these white residents' actions? How do you account for the discrepancy between representations of Six Nations' actions on the one hand as peaceful resistance against colonialism, and on the other hand, as terrorist? What role does race play in this discrepancy? How does the film show the connections between colonial concepts of race, entitlement, and land?

Watch the film *Trick or Treaty* (2014), directed by Alanis Obomsawin. Discuss how the development of modern treaties shown in the film highlight some of the arguments presented by Lawrence's reading.

Decolonizing Indigenous Education

Editor Introduction

On 11 June 2008, Stephen Harper, Canada's Prime Minister of that time, and three other political leaders stood in the House of Commons and offered a public apology to former students of Indian residential schools. The nation watched and listened as the leaders spoke of religious orders that ran these institutions, the brutality that defined them, and, indeed, Canada itself who funded them. Forgiveness should never be assumed. Surrounded by media and religious officials, Indigenous political leaders took turns responding to the apology, each of them recounting its impact on our families and nations. The event itself marked a turning point in Canadian history. However, and to follow from our second edition of *RCIC*, we share grief and shock over recent findings about the now thousands of unmarked graves and the refusal by governments to take seriously the matter of **colonial reparations** and the history of racism, Settler colonialism, and Settler laws in Canada.

We believe that Indigenous and non-Indigenous education in Canada must focus on the very concept of Canadian nation-building and citizenship, and how these are rooted in histories of racism and settler colonialism. In Canada, the history of education is rooted in missionary schooling. Early schools were aimed at making all Canadians productive members of an emerging capitalist economy. For Indigenous peoples, this was a particularly violent and disruptive process, involving at times their forcible removal from homes and communities. Pedagogically, our ancestors were subjected to instruction premised on colonial superiority, in turn marking them as inferior along with their knowledge and cultures. The histories of racism and of Canadian education are unmistakably linked and inseparable for Indigenous peoples. Ideologies of racism continue, furthermore, to shape modern educational contexts and structure a devastating series of outcomes. The actual inner workings of these sorts of dynamics that still continue today with child appropriations enacted at the hands of the Canadian Child Welfare system (Obomsawin, 2016) and also IRS Grievances (Thielen-Wilson, 2014) must come to be understood by all Canadians, and something must be done to repair the history of Settler colonial violence. Colonial reparations must become a focus of public education in Settler colonial Canada to follow.

Public apologies and mournful settler populations do not in themselves remedy years of colonial displacement. They cannot undo a century of cognitive, pedagogical, and linguistic supremacy that continues to shape the experience of schooling for us as nations. Upon recent developments concerning the discovery of unmarked graves, we have become increasingly disappointed and dismayed. The modern face of racism is with us today as Indigenous peoples as it always has been: through disrespect, misunderstanding, and most especially white Settler supremacy. Racism no longer rests at the hands of Euro-Christian orders charged with the responsibility of "civilizing" Indian children. Instead, racism exists each time an Indigenous child is taught a history that neither describes nor reflects her experience as an Indigenous person; or conversely, is denied a vocabulary with which to describe and challenge histories of colonization that continue to shape his everyday life. It is precisely these kinds of practices that contribute to Indigenous peoples being pushed out of institutions of formal learning.

Despite ameliorative efforts, the systemic barriers facing Indigenous peoples in educational contexts appear endemic to Canadian society. The failure to acknowledge and understand these matters, structurally speaking, including the complexity of challenges that limit improvements to education and pedagogical change, needs to be taken seriously. A stage was set in June 2015 for educational reform in Canada following recommendations made by the Truth and **Reconciliation** Commission in its final report. The Commission issued 94 items in what it referred to as a "call to action," including recommendations to revitalize education by "building student capacity for intercultural understanding, empathy, and mutual respect" (2015: 331). We feel especially passionate as scholars in providing for –and continuing to develop—an educational and pedagogical model that is concerned with the history of lands dispossession, partnership and co-existence, historical foci, racism, and the history of white Settler colonialism in Canada (see Cannon, Chapter Sixteen).

Calls to invigorate education with a focus on Settler–Indigenous relationship-building and rejuvenation cannot be underestimated. Indeed, the idea echoes prior calls by the Association of Canadian Deans of Education who called for attention to "Non-Indigenous Learners and Indigeneity" (2010: 7) where educational reform is concerned, granting it precisely the same and equivalent status as "Culturally Responsive Pedagogies" (ibid., 6) and "Affirming and Revitalizing Indigenous Languages" (ibid., 7). The message to educators was clear in both 2010 and 2015: public education about the history of residential schools in Canada is necessarily based on pedagogical and programmatic efforts aimed at Settler decolonization and colonial reparations.

Given calls by both TRC and the ACDE that all Canadians take responsibility for colonial reparations, we continue, as in prior volumes of this textbook, to explore in Part Nine the role of public education in reconciling, and more importantly, disrupting colonial relations of power. In light of prior developments concerning racism, Indian Residential Schools, and the findings concerning unmarked graves of children, we do not ask how non-Indigenous peoples—including educators— might work to acquire cultural competence or come to better understand Indigenous peoples' customs, cultures, or languages. Rather, we are concerned with educational change and reform and indeed with critical and anticolonial perspectives that forgo a culturalist line. We ask in particular how non-Indigenous peoples might work to expose the violence engendered in privileged ways of knowing, including the advantages that accrue to individuals by virtue of race, Settler colonialism, cis-heternormativity, and social/economic capital.

As Cree/Métis scholar Verna St Denis outlines in Chapter Fifteeen, culturally relevant education is only a partial solution to educational disparities and dropout rates, inadequate on its own for explaining or redressing the status quo of racism and structural inequality. She questions how the concept of culture itself—especially in educational anthropology—has come to both define and provide a solution to educational problems. The effect has been to ignore the impact of colonization in favour of celebrating—and working to revitalize—as much culture as possible. But there is reason to be skeptical of culture lending itself to any real or transformative change. Indeed, St Denis (2004: 36) suggests that "cultural revitalization and restoration" has achieved the status of **cultural fundamentalism** in having become "the primary goal of those involved in promoting Aboriginal education." As she suggests, a decolonizing education must be centered on **cultural revitalization** as well as antiracist and anticolonial pedagogy.

Martin Cannon in Chapter Sixteen is concerned with reform-based educational and programmatic initiatives centred on exposing and apprehending the violence of Settler colonialism and law. He asks how schools might be invigorated so that all people teaching and learning within them are better able to consider, know about, name, and challenge their investments in colonial dominance and complicity. He asks how schools might seek to ensure that all Canadians know about, interrogate, and restore respectful Settler-Indigenous and nation-to-nation based relationships. As Cannon suggests, reconciliation must move beyond a mere acknowledgment of privilege and instead, place words into real, tangible action and change.

CHAPTER 17

Rethinking Culture Theory in Aboriginal Education

Verna St Denis

Will teaching Native culture remedy the many wounds of oppression? (Hermes, 2005: 23)

Introduction

. . . When racialized conflict between Aboriginal and white Canadians erupts in a way that makes it clear that collective action is required, more often than not, what is recommended is not anti-racism education but cross-cultural awareness or race-relations training for the primarily "white" service providers, including police officers, social workers, and teachers. Usually the recommended cross-cultural awareness or race-relations training does not include a critical race theory analysis that might explore "how a regime of white supremacy and its subordination of people of color have been created and maintained" (Ladson-Billings, 1999: 14). Rather than acknowledging the need for a critical examination of how and why race matters in our society, it is often suggested that it is Aboriginal people and their culture that must be explained to and understood by those in position of racial dominance. A recent example is the Stonechild Inquiry that recommends race-relations training that will include "information about Aboriginal culture, history, societal and family structures" (Wright, 2004: 213).

This chapter explores how the culture concept and the discipline of anthropology came to occupy such an important role in the conceptualizing and theorizing in the lives of Aboriginal people and especially in Aboriginal education. This knowledge is important because of the effects that the culture concept and discipline has had on the capacity for defining and suggesting solutions to Aboriginal educational problems. For example, in both explaining and seeking solutions to low achievement and high dropout rates for Aboriginal students, the call is usually made for "culturally relevant" education rather than the need for a critical race and class analysis. This chapter will suggest that a cultural framework of analysis is partial and inadequate on its own for explaining Aboriginal educational failures and that culturally based solutions can inadvertently contribute to further problems.

Current concepts of Aboriginal education and the sub-discipline of educational anthropology evolved during the same time period and are as related as are anthropologists and Indians in North America. As has been observed, the discipline of anthropology was "invented across the 'red/white' color line" (Michaelson, 1999: xvi). Both Aboriginal and American-Indian educators have acknowledged the predominance of the culture concept and anthropology in Aboriginal and American-Indian education. In a review of literature on American-Indian education, Deyhle and Swisher (1997: 117) observed that, "over the past 30 years, we found that the largest body of research was grounded in educational anthropology and sociology." Furthermore they state that this research "used the concept of culture as a framework for the analysis of schooling and the behaviour of Indian students, parents and their communities" (ibid.).

In the 1960s much of the educational anthropology literature suggested that racialized minority children failed in school because their cultural beliefs and practices predisposed them to failure, and they were, therefore, described as being "culturally deprived" or even "deviant" (McDermott, 1997). In the 1970s some adjustments were made to the cultural framework for analyzing educational failure, suggesting that it was not so much that some children were culturally deprived or culturally disadvantaged but that their way of life was merely "culturally different"— not better or worse than that valued by schools, but definitely different (McDermott, 1997). The subsequent educational interventions suggested that cultural differences needed to be celebrated rather than eradicated. This shift in emphasis was meant to advantage Aboriginal and American-Indian children whose culture would now be celebrated and observed through research that would focus on learning styles and **acculturation** processes.

This shift towards prescribing the celebration of cultural difference as a means to bring about educational equality provided a foundation for the growing focus on the importance and necessity of cultural and language revitalization for Aboriginal students. American-Indian educators and researchers Tippeconnic and Swisher note that, "beginning in the 1960s and into the 70s a revival of 'Indianness' in the classroom was now encouraged" (1992: 75). In a Canadian review of policy on Aboriginal education, Abele, Dittburner, and Graham also explain that between 1967 and 1982 Aboriginal education was increasingly regarded as a "means for the revitalization of Indian cultures and economies" (2000: 8).

As part of this cultural revitalization, the provision of culturally relevant education assumed great importance for improving the educational success of Aboriginal students, and the health and well-being of Aboriginal communities in general. This shift to regarding education as the means to revitalize Aboriginal culture and language is often attributed to processes of decolonization and, in Canada, to the policy outlined in "Indian Control of Indian Education" (National Indian Brotherhood, 1972). The idea that culture and language could be revitalized, and that Aboriginal people needed a "positive" cultural identity as a prerequisite to success in education and in life more generally, can also be understood to be derivative of anthropological concepts and theorizing.

In writing this chapter, I have been informed by my own experiences and professional knowledge as an Aboriginal teacher and educator. By the time I arrived on campus as a university student in the late 1970s, the move towards decolonizing education by Aboriginal people in Canada was already moving forward with the adoption of the policy position outlined in "Indian Control of Indian Education" (National Indian Brotherhood, 1972). With the recognition of this policy came the establishment of Indian cultural centres, Indian Teacher Education programs, cultural survival schools, and Indian and Native Studies departments across the country (Posluns, 2007). It was a very exciting time for us Aboriginal students since we could now pursue specialized studies in Aboriginal education and Native Studies.

In 1978 I enrolled in the Indian Teacher Education Program at the University of Saskatchewan. I was going to become an "Indian" teacher. I was younger than most students in the program at that time, and, although both my parents had spoken Cree, I myself was not fluent in Cree. Indian Teacher Education programs were at the forefront in calling for the cultural and language revitalization of Indian cultures, and Indian teachers were to play a significant role in this revitalization. In this educational context I sensed I was in trouble—I was well aware that my lack of fluency in my indigenous language placed me at a disadvantage. The analysis offered here in this chapter is one attempt to make sense of this "trouble."

I didn't realize back then the role that anthropological concepts and theory had in the formulations of Aboriginal education through notions like "cultural discontinuity," "cultural relevance," "cultural difference," and "acculturation/enculturation." As a student and teacher of Aboriginal education and Native Studies, I never imagined that studying anthropology and its concepts would be useful in unravelling some of the ways in which we interpret the problems and solutions we have named and pursued in Aboriginal education.

Although I have now been involved in Aboriginal education for almost three decades, it is only in the past decade that I realized I needed to know more about anthropology. I had avoided learning about anthropology partly because anthropology and history were two mainstream disciplines that Native Studies and Aboriginal education had rallied against in the 1970s and 1980s. I regarded the discipline of anthropology, as some in the late 1960s referred to it, as the "child of colonialism" (Cough, in Caulfield 1969: 182) and therefore not worthy of attention. It was Rosaldo's *Culture and Truth: The Remaking of Social Analysis* (1989) that introduced me to a critique of classic notions in anthropology. Reading this book marked the beginning of my efforts to develop an understanding of how anthropologically informed social analysis has impacted the development of Aboriginal education. This chapter offers an analysis of how those of us in Aboriginal education have been historically and discursively constituted within and by anthropological theory and research.

I began to understand that the social and cultural analysis prevalent when I first enrolled in the Indian Teacher Education Program was informed not only by "Indian philosophy and worldview" but also by the social and cultural analysis practised by American anthropologists who combined psychology and anthropology through their focus on culture and personality and acculturation studies. The culture and personality movement and acculturation studies inspired psychologists and anthropologists who were interested in cross-cultural education, and who contributed to the development of educational anthropology. In turn, the social and cultural analysis offered by scholars of educational anthropology influenced the conceptualizing of Aboriginal/Indian education. As someone who has been involved in Aboriginal/Indian education for almost 30 years, I find there is still much to learn about this legacy of anthropological ideas, concepts, problems, and solutions that helped to shape Indian education.

European Philosophical and Intellectual Legacies

Culture is . . . itself the illness to which it proposes a cure. (Eagleton, 2000: 31)

. . . Efforts to develop a history of the culture concept invariably requires attempts to make sense of the relationships between the varied usages of the concepts of "culture" and "civilization," and "Romanticism" and "Primitivism" within European thought and social practice. . . .

Both Romanticism and Primitivism have influenced our understanding of "culture" and "civilization" through articulations of self and Other. Scholarly writing about the history of the development of modern notions of culture is often situated within histories of Romanticism, if not Primitivism. Although Romanticism and Primitivism are two different social and intellectual developments, there is some overlap and similarities between these two schools of thought. And although neither Romanticism nor Primitivism has been consistently or constantly invoked in European imagination and fantasies of the Other, one of their recurring and enduring emphases is a valorization of the Other, as a way to critique and register dissatisfaction with European society (Stocking, 1986). . . .

Herder conceptualized "culture" as the "uniquely distinct" way of life, values, and beliefs of a people; culture was what distinguished one people from another (1774: 44f.). . . .

Herder's conceptualization of "culture" has lent itself to a belief in "cultural essentialism" and "cultural determinism" that is elaborated upon in Boasian anthropology. . . . It suggests an essential culture that is able to exist in the realm of the spiritual.

Herder also signalled language as important to the delineation of a nation, because within language dwells a people's "entire world of tradition, history, religion, principles of existence; its whole heart and soul" (Herder, in Malik, 1996: 78–9). This idea that the culture of a people is invoked through its language and stories is further developed in the efforts made in Aboriginal education to participate in cultural and language revitalization, as it was also an idea brewing within anthropological studies of culture and personality and acculturation.

Another of Herder's beliefs was in the "incommensurability of the values of different cultures and societies" (Malik, 1996: 78). . . .

This idea of the incommensurability of different cultures would eventually propel and motivate anthropology's interest in what makes people different. The idea would lend itself not only to an exaggeration of human difference but also a negative evaluation of these differences, making possible notions like folks who suffer, not from colonial oppression but, from "cultural incongruence," and "cultural discontinuity," both of which were seen as tangible threats to cultural self-preservation despite whatever cultural exchanges and accommodations have been made by cultural Others (Biolsi, 1997).

The idea of the "incommensurability" of cultures led anthropologists in search of "an Indian culture incommensurably alien from [their own]" (Biolsi, 1997: 140)—in other words, the search for the "real" Indian (Biolsi, 1997; Waldram, 2004). The belief in twentieth-century social analysis about the incommensurability of different cultures encourages a trivializing of the impact of colonial oppression by attributing the effects and the conditions of oppression to this very factor of incommensurability. In the example of Aboriginal people, effects of oppression are cast as "value conflicts" between white and Indian cultures, suggesting that inequality is inevitable, and merely an effect of different orientations to work, education, and family. When the affects of oppression are attributed to a "conflict of values" it is easy to see how the remedy then becomes cross-cultural awareness training or a "race"-relations program that does not disrupt the status quo of structural inequality while seemingly responding.

Understanding American Anthropological Legacies

. . . Through concepts like "enculturation," this idea of a culture as a conditioning process became a central concept in educational anthropology, and suggested research into the "enculturation processes" of culturally different students, families, and communities. In addition, this idea that culture is a conditioning process implied that it is not people who create culture through the conditions of their everyday lives, but rather "culture" that creates people. It is as if culture is an object with its own agency divorced from people. This objectification of culture also suggests that culture is something to be "lost" and "found." It is as if people are no longer agents; culture happens to them. A notion like "cultural determinism" then becomes possible. Cultural determinism has been used to justify racism; hence the notion of "cultural racism" (Hall, 1982; Gilroy, 1990) that becomes another way to justify discrimination. . . .

This idea of culture as an entity outside of people provides a foundation for the belief in the potential for "cultural revitalization" and the very idea that culture can be retrieved. While the idea that culture resides deep inside one's "core" may be reassuring in the early stages of an engagement with cultural revitalization, when that "traditional" culture fails to appear or reveal itself, it can be very troubling. This failure of culture to appear becomes a very different kind of problem. It is a problem long familiar to those anthropologists who have been keenly interested in "authentic" and "real" Indians or the "primitive," and for whom evidence of "cultural change" would suggest otherwise, namely that culture is mutable.

Many have critiqued anthropologists' interest and fetishization of the most exotic and primitive

Other (e.g., Biolsi, 1997; Caulfield, 1969; Deloria, 1969; Rosaldo, 1989). The implications for regarding cultural change as a threat and as a negative process continue to have repercussions for "Others" such as Aboriginal people....

Not only was cultural change regarded as dangerous for the "primitive" Other, but "rapid" cultural change was regarded as even more detrimental. Culture was something primitive people "had," and it was understood that "primitive" people needed culture more than "civilized" people did....

Educational anthropology would embrace the above ideas and to a large degree so would Aboriginal education. This conceptualization has resulted in that claim that it is "cultural discontinuity" between the school and the Aboriginal family and community and the inability of Aboriginal students to make adequate cultural adjustments that causes high levels of school failure for Aboriginal students despite evidence that racism and classism are equally, if not more compelling reasons for these levels of school failure (Ledlow, 1992). Culturally relevant education, rather than anti-oppressive education, has become a common-sense solution. As well, the idea that "primitives" learn less by instruction than by imitation led to research focusing on understanding different "learning styles" and with the effect of creating a new set of stereotypes about the nature of Aboriginal learning styles....

This method of anthropological social analysis, exemplified by Benedict and Mead, compared and contrasted cultures as a whole and paved the way for cross-cultural comparisons that continue to remain popular in educational research. In particular, this method has been used as a way of explaining the low academic achievement of Aboriginal students....

Acculturation studies ... promoted ideas that the retention of "indigenous belief systems" was essential for Indians to adequately adjust to rapid social change (Waldram, 2004). Anthropologists were often not interested in documenting the creative and successful ways in which Indians were making cultural adaptations to their continually changing environments (Deloria, 1969). This was especially the case if anthropologists were particularly interested in finding the most "incommensurable" and exotic Indian (Biolsi, 1997). Further advancing the belief that culture was a "cure," studies of acculturation,

such as those conducted among the Hopi, claimed that "Personality disorders and social breakdown characterize Hopi communities that have lost their values and their ceremonies" (Thompson, 1946: 210, in Waldram, 2004: 37). This idea that Indian culture is "lost" and that Indians have lost their culture is a deceptively benign but very common way to refer to the effects of colonial and racial oppression on Aboriginal people. In acculturation studies, suggesting that "maintaining essential, internal cultural integrity" (Thompson, 1950, in Waldram, 2004: 35) is necessary for exploited and colonized people, has become a popular and common way to blame the victim of oppression.

The problem of inequality is now attributed to the Indian who does not have "cultural integrity" rather than the social, economic, and political context that does not recognize the human rights of Aboriginal people. Acculturation, and Culture and Personality studies, contributed to reducing the effects of colonial and racial oppression to a problem of an identity crisis. Restoring the Indian has become the imperative rather than ensuring social and political justice. The anthropological interest in a timeless and unchanging cultural Indian demeans Aboriginal and American-Indian Peoples who have had to constantly adjust to and live with the context of ongoing and normalized racism.... The idea that cultural adaptation is regarded as "broken" relegates Indians as interesting to the degree that they can serve as windows to the past, ignoring the effects of colonization by aiming to celebrate and recoup as much "traditional" culture as possible.

As many have stated, Boas and his many students "never showed any real interest in studying the situation of conquest and exploitation" (Caulfield, 1969: 184, italics in original). This failure by the anthropology of that time to explore the consequences and situation of exploitation continued to have repercussions for at least the early years in the development of Aboriginal education by and for Aboriginal people rather than examining the situation of conquest and exploitation, anthropologists like Benedict were more interested in bringing attention to "the desperate urgency of doing anthropological field work before the last precious and irretrievable memories of traditional American Indian cultures were carried to the grave"

(Mead, 197: 3). . . . Here we have an anthropology that cared more about "Indian culture" than the people of that culture, yet another example of the belief in a culture as something outside and existing independently of its people.

This background knowledge of anthropology provides a basis to better understand the published conference proceedings of the first conference of educational anthropology. That conference helped initiate the field of Educational Anthropology, which has had its own set of implications for Aboriginal education.

The Legacy of Educational Anthropology

. . . In 1954, the anthropologist George Spindler hosted a conference that brought together several educators and anthropologists; among them were anthropologists Margaret Mead, Alfred Kroeber, and Cora DuBois. Several papers were presented, along with remarks by formal discussants; conference proceedings were published in the book *Education and Anthropology* (Spindler, 1955a) and later republished in the edited collection, *Education and Culture: Anthropological Approaches* (Spindler, 1963). . . .

Some of the many concepts utilized in the papers and the discussions that followed included ones familiar to those who work in the area of Aboriginal education, including: cultural transmission; enculturation; acculturation; cultural awareness; bicultural, monocultural, and intercultural learners; cultural gap; and cultural discontinuity.

Conference participants acknowledged that the discipline of psychology made it possible to combine educational and anthropological interests (Frank, 1955). Participants agreed that exploring cultural processes of socialization was one way in which anthropology could contribute to education. Socialization processes were understood to vary from culture to culture, and it was those "differences" that could form the basis of investigation in developing educational anthropology. Building on acculturation and personality studies in anthropology, educational anthropology would also explore processes of cultural change, cultural adaptation, and cultural continuity. Knowledge of socialization

practices and processes could, in turn, help educators and schools assist culturally different students adjust to change. . . .

This idea that schools and education are the site for cultural continuity and cultural transmission has become accepted wisdom in Aboriginal education (see, e.g., Royal Commission on Aboriginal Peoples, 1996). Through the conceptual framework of educational anthropology, schools are increasingly instructed to become a place where "culturally relevant" education should occur so as to ensure cultural continuity and cultural transmission for the Aboriginal child. But in light of massive cultural change in regards to how Aboriginal people live, the task of providing culturally relevant education can prove to be perplexing and challenging for the well-intentioned Aboriginal teacher who asks, "what is it exactly that you want to be taught in the classroom, the parents say let's teach culture in a classroom, but they don't come out and say what they mean by culture" (Friesen and Orr, 1995: 22). In the context of ongoing cultural change, this line of questioning remains relevant, but it is also the legacy of an anthropology that was once intent on "reconstructing traditional culture" (Asad, in Stocking, 1991: 318).

By combining psychology and anthropology, the field of educational anthropology would pursue investigations that would seek to explain the impact of differences between the cultural values and beliefs of the culturally different child and the teacher. . . . It was proposed that this cultural knowledge could help teachers understand how "imitation, participation, communication, and informal methods" socialize members into one's culture, as well as how "cultural motivation incentives, values and school learning" are related (Quillen, 1955: 3).

Four decades later, this theorizing about difference has, more often than not, resulted in the production of stereotypes and classist and racist constructions of the culturally different child (Laroque, 1991; Razack, 1998). This anthropological orientation to understanding "difference" is now used to endorse the current demand that human service providers be "culturally competent" in their delivery of services. Without examining the impact of racism and classism, this requirement for cultural competency has the potential to repeat stereotypes of Aboriginal people rather than focusing on how racial dominance and poverty continue to detrimentally impact Aboriginal people (Razack, 1998; Schick and St Denis, 2005). . . .

There is no single straightforward trajectory to understanding how, when, and why the concept of culture, as opposed to the need for social and political justice, has come to occupy such a large role in articulating Aboriginal education. . . .

The politics of this articulation of culture as a concept associated with the Other, and the nation as a concept associated with the civilized person, has a long history, not only in anthropology but, in Western and European thinking, in general. It is not common for those in a position of racial dominance to risk relativizing their own way of life by describing it as a "culture": as Eagleton puts it, "One's own way of life is simply human; it is other people who are ethnic, idiosyncratic, culturally peculiar" (2000: 27). . . .

A review of literature reveals that teachers often have low expectations of Aboriginal and American-Indian students (Ambler, 1997; Delpit, 1995; Flail, 1993; Strong, 1998; Tirado, 2001; Wilson, 1991). Low expectations justify the lack of instruction and attention to Aboriginal students. Tirado (2001) found that teachers have a tendency to size up American-Indian students as underachievers; they don't expect the kids to do anything, so they don't teach them. Wilson found that "even before teachers knew the [Aboriginal] students, they prejudged them. They could not have imagined that these students would ever be successful. Students were classified as unable to cope with a heavy academic load" (1991: 379). As a result, Aboriginal students are often placed disproportionately in vocational or special needs classes (Wilson, 1991). Rather than encouraging an examination of the ways in which class and racial bias impact educational processes, the legacy of the 1954 conference of anthropologists and educators has resulted in a large body of educational research primarily interested in "culture" as the explanatory concept for understanding how the culturally Other would or would not adjust to school. . . .

The idea that the cultural Other is not able to make cultural adjustments without a great deal of trauma is an idea that continues to have a negative effect on discussions of how to improve educational achievement for Aboriginal students. To a large extent these discussions tend to promote a stereo-typed idea of the Aboriginal student as vulnerable and non-resilient and enables the avoidance of addressing the far more difficult questions of racism and classism in education. . . .

This idea of the Aboriginal cultural Other as unwilling and unable to adapt to changing social, economic, and political contexts is a long entrenched assumption that justifies oppression and inequality. For example, Sarah Carter (1986, 1996), a prairie Canadian historian, challenges the taken-for-granted assumption that Aboriginal people were unwilling and unable to adapt to a farming-based economy. Carter uncovers the extent to which white settlers and the Canadian government colluded to ensure that Aboriginal farmers failed at farming. The introduction of the pass and permit system prevented Aboriginal farmers from succeeding by limiting their ability to purchase farm machinery, limiting what produce they could grow, and limiting when and where they could sell their produce.

The All Hallows School in British Columbia, a boarding school attended by both Aboriginal and white girls between 1884 and 1920, described in the work of Barman (1986), provides another historical and educational example of unwarranted assumptions about Aboriginal people unwilling and unable to adapt to change. The establishment of the All Hallows School was a case in which Aboriginal parents welcomed change and the opportunity to adjust to a changing world by requesting that a school be established for their girls.

Because of inadequate financial resources, the All Hallows School could only function if white girls were allowed to attend alongside Indian girls. In the first years of the school, the Indian and white girls seemed content with their integrated schooling situation. Then a white parent protested about this integrated situation, so the effort was made to separate the white and Indian girls. But in his annual report, the bishop in charge of the school commented that the Indian girls were as intellectually capable as the white girls, claiming that at times the Indian girls had "the answers all respects being equal, and sometimes superior, to anything that could be expected from white children of the same age" (Barman, 1986: 117). Not only did the Indian girls achieve academically, but they also could from time to time serve as junior teachers, and their ability to learn the practices of another culture was demonstrated in two Indian girls, who alongside eight white girls passed the Royal Academy of Music exam.

These Indian girls did not seem to suffer any crisis due to the culture difference between the school and their home and community. When the Indian girls returned home for holidays and summer vacation, they often freely maintained contact with the teachers through letters. At least for one Indian girl, the only source of cultural conflict involved the dilemma of attending a potlatch even though it was "forbidden by law" (Barman, 1986: 118). In a letter to the sisters at the school, this student tried to persuade them that the potlatch is not something they should be afraid of because it is just "our way of praying" (Barman, 1986: 119).

Eventually the Indian and white girls were physically separated, although still offered equally challenging academic programs. But then the curriculum for the Indian girls shifted from a full academic program to one that included teaching them how to weave baskets. Finally, a shift in government policy led to closing the school, a policy change justified by a larger concern that it was unwise to offer Indians an education that would allow them "to compete industrially with our people" (Minister of Indian Affairs, 1897, in Barman, 1986: 120). Throughout the proceeding decades, Aboriginal people continued to be denied the high-quality education for which First Nations treaty negotiators assumed they had signed on. The inability of an anthropology and, in turn, an educational anthropology to acknowledge the effects of "conquest and exploitation" of the cultural Other continues to reverberate.

As Biolsi (1997) explains, anthropologists such as those present at the time of that 1954 conference were typically not interested in Indians who accepted that change was inevitable. As a result, these examples of Indian farmers and the All Hallows School would not have drawn their attention. Not only were anthropologists not interested in Indians wanting to figure out how to adapt to the changing world around them, but anthropologists also typically maligned these Indians for not being "real" Indians (Biolsi, 1997; Waldram, 2004).

Conclusion

> More powerful than their knowledge of cultural difference is their knowledge of the big picture—the context of socioeconomic and cultural oppression of Native Americans. (Hermes, 2005: 21)

We started out a few decades ago in Aboriginal education believing that we could address the effects of racialization and colonization by affirming and validating the cultural traditions and heritage of Aboriginal peoples. There is increasing evidence that those efforts have limitations. As I have argued elsewhere, cultural revitalization encourages misdiagnoses of the problem (St Denis, 2004). It places far too much responsibility on the marginalized and oppressed to change yet again, and once again lets those in positions of dominance off the hook for being accountable for ongoing discrimination. It is to the advantage of the status quo to have Aboriginal people preoccupied with matters of authenticity. If cultural authenticity is the problem then we don't have to look at what is the immensely more difficult task of challenging the conscious and unconscious ways in which the ideology of white identity as superior is normalized and naturalized in our schools and nation, both in the past and in the present (Francis, 1997; Willinsky, 1998).

Instead of doing anti-racism education that explores why and how race matters, we can end up doing cross-cultural awareness training that often has the effect of encouraging the belief that the cultural difference of the Aboriginal "Other" is the problem. Offering cultural awareness workshops can also provide another opportunity for non-Aboriginals to resent and resist Aboriginal people. Offering cultural awareness education has become the mainstream thinking about proper solutions to educational and social inequality. In her research exploring the qualities of effective teachers of American Indians, Hermes, an American-Indian educator, found that "more powerful than [teachers'] knowledge of cultural difference is their knowledge of the big picture—the context of socioeconomic and cultural oppression of Native Americans" (2005: 21). We often hear that addressing racism or doing anti-racism education is too negative and that we need to focus on a more positive approach. However, that often means tinkering with the status quo. As Kaomea suggests, when schools offer benign lessons in Hawaiian arts, crafts, and values, this approach tends to erase Hawaiian suffering, hardship, and oppression. "It is time to tell more uncomfortable stories" (Kaomea, 2003: 23).

References

Abele, F., C. Dittburner, and K.A. Graham. "Towards a Shared Understanding in the Policy Discussion about Aboriginal Education," pp. 3–24 in M.B. Castellano, L. Davis, and L. Lahache, eds, *Aboriginal Education: Fulfilling the Promise*. Vancouver and Toronto: University of British Columbia Press, 2000.

Ambler, M. "Without Racism: Indian Students Could Be Both Indian and Students," *Tribal College Journal* 8, no. 4 (1997): 8–11. Available at http://www.tribalcollegejournal.org/themag/backissues/spring97/spring97ee.html; accessed 8 October 2002.

Barman, J. "Separate and Unequal: Indian and White Girls at All Hallows School, 1884–1920," pp. 110–131 in J. Barman, Y. Hebert, and D. McCaskill, eds., *Indian Education in Canada*, Volume 1: The Legacy. Vancouver: University of British Columbia Press, 1986.

Biolsi, T. "The Anthropological Construction of 'Indians': Haviland Scudder Mekeel and the Search for the Primitive in Lakota Country," pp. 133–159 in Thomas Biolsi and L.J. Zimmerman, eds, *Indians and Anthropologists: Vine Deloria Jr. and the Critique of Anthropology*. Tucson: University of Arizona Press, 1997.

Carter, S. "'We Must Farm to Enable Us to Live': The Plains Cree and Agriculture to 1900," pp. 444–470 in R.B. Morrison and C.R. Wilson, eds., *Native Peoples: The Canadian Experience*. Toronto: McClelland and Stewart, 1986.

Carter, S. "First Nations Women in Prairie Canada in the Early Reserve Years, the 1870s to the 1920s: A Preliminary Inquiry," pp. 51–75 in C. Miller and P. Chuchryk, eds., *Women of the First Nations: Power, Wisdom, and Strength*. Winnipeg: University of Manitoba Press, 1996.

Caulfield, M. D. "Culture and Imperialism: Proposing a New Dialectic," pp. 182–212 in D. Hymes, ed., *Reinventing Anthropology*. New York: Pantheon Books, 1969.

Deloria, V., Jr. *Custer Died for Your Sins: An Indian Manifesto*. Norman, OK: University of Oklahoma Press, 1969/1988.

Delpit, L. *Educating Other People's Children: Cultural Conflict in the Classroom*. New York: New Press, 1995.

Deyhle, D. "Constructing Failure and Maintaining Cultural Identity: Navajo and Ute School Leavers," *Journal of American Indian Education* 31 (1992): 24–47.

Deyhle, D., and K. Swisher. "Research in American Indian and Alaska Native Education: From Assimilation to Self-determination," *Educational Review* 22 (1997): 113–194.

Eagleton, T. *The Idea of Culture*. Oxford: Blackwell Manifestos, 2000.

Francis, D. *National Dreams: Myth, Memory and Canadian History*. Vancouver: Arsenal Pulp Press, 1997.

Frank, L.K. "Preface," pp. vii–xi in G. Spindler, *Education and Anthropology*. Stanford: Stanford University Press, 1955.

Friesen, D.W., and J. Orr. "Northern Aboriginal Teachers' Voices." Unpublished manuscript, University of Regina, Saskatchewan, 1995.

Hall, J. L. "What Can We Expect from Minority Students?" *Contemporary Education* 64, no. 3 (1993): 180–182.

Herder, J.G. *Another Philosophy of History Concerning the Development of Mankind. Translation of Auch eine Philosophie der Geschichte zur Bildung der Menschheit.* Frankfurt am Main: Suhrkamp, 1774/1967.

Hermes, M. "Complicating Discontinuity: What about Poverty?" *Curriculum Inquiry* 35, no. 1 (2005): 9–26.

Kaomea, J. "Reading Erasures and Making the Familiar Strange: Defamiliarizing Methods for Research in Formerly Colonized and Historically Oppressed Communities," *Educational Researcher* 32, no. 2 (2003): 14–25.

Ladson-Billings, G. "Just What Is Critical Race Theory, and What's It Doing in a Nice Field Like Education?" pp. 7–30 in L. Parker, D. Deyhle, and S. Villenas, eds., *Race Is . . . Race Isn't: Critical Race Theory and Qualitative Studies in Education*. Boulder, CO: Westview Press, 1999.

Larocque, E. "Racism Runs through Canadian Society," pp. 73–76 in O. McKague, ed., *Racism in Canada*. Saskatoon: Fifth House, 1991.

Ledlow, S. "Is Cultural Discontinuity an Adequate Explanation for Dropping Out?" *Journal of American Indian Education* 31 (1992): 21–36.

McDermott, R. P. "Achieving School Failure, 1972–1997," pp. 110–135 in G. Spindler, ed., *Education and Cultural Process: Anthropological Approaches*, 3rd edn. Prospect Heights, IL: Waveland Press, 1997.

Malik, K. *The Meaning of Race: Race, History and Culture in Western Society*. New York: New York University Press, 1996.

Mead, M. Ruth Benedict: *A Humanist in Anthropology*. New York: Columbia University Press, 1974.

Michaelson, S. *The Limits of Multiculturalism: Interrogating the Origins of American Anthropology*. Minneapolis: University of Minnesota Press, 1999.

National Indian Brotherhood. "Indian Control of Indian Education." Ottawa: National Indian Brotherhood, 1972.

Posluns, M. *Speaking with Authority: The Emergence of the Vocabulary of First Nations' Self-Government*. New York: Routledge, 2007.

Quillen, J. I. "An Introduction to Anthropology and Education," pp. 1–4 in G. Spindler, *Education and Anthropology*. Stanford: Stanford University Press, 1955.

Razack, S. *Looking White People in the Eye: Race, Class and Gender in the Courtrooms and the Classrooms*. Toronto: University of Toronto Press, 1998.

Rosaldo, R. *Culture and Truth: The Remaking of Social Analysis*. Boston: Beacon Press, 1989.

Royal Commission on Aboriginal Peoples. *Report on the Royal Commission on Aboriginal Peoples*. 5 vols. Ottawa: Canada Communications Group, 1996.

Schick, C., and V. St Denis. "Troubling National Discourses in Anti-racist Curricular Planning," *Canadian Journal of Education* 28, no. 3 (2005): 295–317.

Spindler, G. *Education and Anthropology*. Stanford: Stanford University Press, 1955a.

———. "Anthropology and Education: An Overview," pp. 5–22 in G. Spindler, *Education and Anthropology*. Stanford: Stanford University Press, 1955b.

———. *Education and Culture: Anthropological Approaches*. New York: Holt, Rinehart and Winston, 1963.

St Denis, V. "Real Indians: Cultural Revitalization and Fundamentalism in Aboriginal Education," pp.

35–47 in C. Schick, J. Jaffe, and A. Watkinson, eds. *Contesting Fundamentalisms*. Halifax, NS: Fernwood, 2004.

Stocking, G. W., Jr. "Essays on Culture and Personality," pp. 3–12 in Stocking, ed., History of Anthropology Vol. 4. *Malinowski, Rivers, Benedict and Others: Essays on Culture and Personality*. Madison: University of Wisconsin Press, 1986.

Strong, W. C. "Low Expectations by Teachers within an Academic Content," Paper presented at the Annual Meeting of the American Educational Research Association San Diego, CA, 1998 (ERIC Document Research Service No. ED 420 62).

Tippeconnic, J. W., III, and K. Swisher. "American Indian Education," pp. 75–78 in M.C. Alkin, ed., *Encyclopedia of Education Research*. New York: MacMillan, 1992.

Tirado, M. "Left Behind: Are Public Schools Failing Indian Kids?" *American Indian Report* 17 (2001): 12–15. Available at Wilson Web. Accessed 9 October 2002.

Troulliet, M. R. "Anthropology and the Savage Slot: The Poetics and Politics of Otherness," pp. 17–44 in R. G. Fox, ed., *Recapturing Anthropology: Working in the Present*. Santa Fe, NM: School of American Press, 1991.

Waldram, J. *Revenge of the Windigo: The Construction of the Mind and Mental Health of North American Aboriginal Peoples*. Toronto: University of Toronto Press, 2004.

Willinsky, John. *Learning to Divide the World: Education at Empire's End*. Minneapolis: University of Minnesota Press, 1998.

Wilson, P. "Trauma of Sioux Indian High School Students," *Anthropology and Education Quarterly* 22 (1991): 367–383.

Wright, D. H. *Report of the Commission of Inquiry into Matters relating to the Death of Neil Stonechild*, 2004. Available at http://www.stonechildinquiry.ca/.

Zenter, H. *The Indian Identity Crisis: Inquires into the Problems and Prospects of Societal Development among Native Peoples*. Calgary: Strayer Publications, 1973.

CHAPTER 18

Teaching and Learning Reparative Education in Settler Colonial and Post-TRC Canada

Martin J. Cannon

This paper is focused on the implementation of a critical and decolonizing approach to social justice education and pedagogy. I envision an anti-colonial approach to thinking critically and differently about culture, citizenship, colonial settlement, and settler colonial reconciliation. I suggest that schools in settler colonial Canada work to realize original nation-to-nation political relationships and reform-based educational and programmatic initiatives concerned with exposing and apprehending the violence of settler colonialism and law. I outline an approach to education concerned with colonial reparations, restitution, and what it might mean to realize and articulate a program of settler decolonizing in Canadian schools.

I envision my audience to be teachers and learners who wish to implement an anti-colonial and decolonizing approach to social justice education and pedagogy. I do not suggest non-Indigenous peoples—including educators—might work to acquire "cultural competence" or come to better understand Indigenous peoples' customs, cultures, or languages. Rather, I wish to name and consider the role of non-Indigenous peoples—including educators—in transforming pedagogical and reform-based programmatic initiatives centered on **Indigenous-Settler** relationships rejuvenation and nation-to-nation relationships building. I ask in particular: how might schools be invigorated so that all people teaching and learning within them are better able to consider, know about, name, and challenge investments in colonial dominance and complicity?

The answer to that question starts with land, specifically the lands dispossession that has taken place under settler colonialism. Schools must provide a way of thinking differently about matters of land, the history of colonial settlement, and the ways we relate to each other as peoples and as nations. Schools must also work to illuminate, interrupt, and then eliminate the harm experienced by Indigenous nations under ongoing settler colonialism.

Canada's Truth and Reconciliation Commission (TRC) has asked that we think about reconciliation. For me, that means: how might we restore right relations? I have come to reflect on this matter from a perspective that centres Indigenous-Settler relationships building and rejuvenation. In what follows, I propose that relationships building in the Canadian context take place in a way that centres a few crucial items. A priority among them is land, specifically lands dispossession, the role of law, lands reclamation, colonial reparations, and Indigenous-Settler relationships building as a starting point in education. The paper points to the limits of multiculturalism, and relatedly, problematic formulations concerning culturalism when it comes to centring land and Indigenous peoples.

. . . I provide an overview and reflexive commentary on two graduate postsecondary courses

I developed and teach that explore directly the role of education in creating a new and productive dialogue between Indigenous and non-Indigenous peoples.

The Question of Land and Multiculturalism

Multiculturalism has not done a particularly good job at inviting questions about lands dispossession, Indigenous sovereignty, and self-determination. . . . Multiculturalism does nothing to invite a critical conversation about "competing moral visions" of democracy and sovereignty; nor does it invite Settlers to think about where it is that they stand in relation to the land and what it might mean to relinquish control or leave.

Conversations about decolonization and decolonizing education are rarely concerned with relinquishing settler sovereignty and lands appropriation. Instead, they have become too tightly scripted in ways that are often concerned only with how teachers might best integrate Indigenous culture in Canadian schools (St. Denis & Schick, 2003). This not only raises obvious questions about cultural appropriation (Battell Lowman & Barker, 2015, p. 40), but also enacts a reprehensible relation of power in locating the origin of colonial grievances in cultural incommensurability when they really involve lands theft. As Razack (2015) writes:

> The pernicious idea that it has all been simply a cultural misunderstanding persists in education. We have yet to develop anti-colonial pedagogies that would invite students to examine their complicity in ongoing colonialism, one in which Indigenous peoples are disproportionately incarcerated and overrepresented in deaths in custody. While universities are happy to promote courses on Indigenous knowledge . . . there is less willingness to consider issues of Indigenous sovereignty and colonial violence. (p. 207–208)

Canadian schools should do more than acquire facts and information about Indigenous culture and then distribute them in what amounts to a cultural competence approach. The invitation to cultural competence and/or sensitivity training has already been shown in services provision literature to place dominant individuals into inevitable positions of power and superiority (Allan, 2006; Jeffery & Nelson, 2009; Pon, 2009). Within these frameworks, Indigenous peoples are positioned as those to be helped and tolerated, or at the very least as those without sovereignty or historic colonial grievances concerning land and colonial injustice.

Under the current culturalist regime in education, non-Indigenous peoples normally are not asked to remedy systemic inequities or processes of identity making that are rooted in Indigenous inferiority and settler superiority. They are not required to know their own culture, institutions, or law, or to recognize and nuance their own complicity and responsibility. Rather, the objective is only to learn as much as possible about Indigenous peoples, which re-enacts a historical process of land entitlement and settler futurity and is complicit in the removal of Indigenous peoples—violently if necessary—from settler spaces of belonging (Razack, 2002; 2015).

If reconciliation is to be truly meaningful, Canadians need to learn about, identify, and then relinquish structural advantages acquired through settler colonialism and privilege (Macoun, 2016). It will require moving beyond a sole focus on Indigenous peoples to what I once called a "changing of the subject in education," the idea that non-Indigenous people must come to know, understand, and challenge their own investment and implication in colonial dominance and self-identification (Cannon, 2012).

Land, Relationships, and Settler Decolonizing

The TRC called repeatedly on all Canadians to think about and improve relationships with Indigenous peoples. In fact, this need for settler decolonizing was made abundantly and consistently clear throughout the commission's public events and hearings, where Justice Murray Sinclair stated numerous times: "Indian Residential Schools is not an Aboriginal problem. It is a problem that all people in Canada need to think about and address" (Government of Canada, 2010, pp. 7–8). I want to think seriously about what it might mean to take Senator Sinclair's assertion literally and to heart. I think we need to ask three central questions in response to this call, notably: How is scholarly literature concerning critical pedagogy and educational reform bringing us closer to, or facilitating, conversations about whose problem the history of settler colonialism actually is? What are we doing in Canadian classrooms and how much of that work addresses histories of racism and settler colonialism? How are schools seeking to ensure that Canadians know about, interrogate, and restore respectful relations with Indigenous peoples as nations?

It is incumbent upon schools to take these questions seriously. If the history of colonization is a problem facing all Canadians, then it is each and every Canadian who needs to acknowledge and understand how this is so. We need to think of frameworks that start not only with Indigenous peoples, or even with Indigenous culture and worldviews, but with the identity-making processes—many of them racialized—that are specific to settler colonialism and non-Indigenous peoples.

I am not suggesting the focus of educational discourse should shift solely to settler populations; rather, I suggest that non-Indigenous peoples shoulder equally, if not principally, the responsibility of teaching themselves and others about the history of settler colonialism.

. . . In seeking to reconcile colonial pasts, specifically histories of racism, settler colonialism, and residential schools, Canadians should seek to learn about, identify, and then relinquish structural advantages acquired through settler colonialism and privilege.

Restoring right relations in the way I am describing was fundamentally a part of a report produced for Canadians some 27 years ago by the *Royal Commission on Aboriginal Peoples*. The RCAP report (1996) identified four principal stages of native/ newcomer relationships throughout history: the Separate Worlds, Contact and Cooperation, Displacement and **Assimilation**, and Negotiation and Renewal stages.

Signs of a failed relationship are as evident today as they were in 1996, especially in the violence of settler colonialism. Consider the nature in which men still learn to view Indigenous women's bodies as disposable and that crimes can be committed against

them with impunity (Deer, 2015; Razack, 2002). There is also physical and often state-sanctioned violence, including the threats, stones-throwing, and gunshots experienced by our communities in retaliation for land grievances, acts of reclamation, and unbroken assertions of sovereignty (Alfred, 2005; Mackey, 2016; McCarthy, 2016; Monture, 2015). . . . What are schools doing to teach of these matters of life and death? How are Canadian schools obliged to identify, combat, and correct for a culture of entitlement and ignorance that contributes to— if not creates—the conditions of ongoing colonial violence?

The truth is that a decolonizing education in settler colonial and post-TRC Canada is necessarily a matter of life and death. It endeavours to place genocide, theft of lands, Indigenous nationhood, colonial reparations, gendered racial violence, and border imperialism (Walia, 2013) at the forefront of curricula. It invites Settlers to become conscious about and apprehend their own complicity in settler colonialism. . . .

Land itself is key to thinking about "a revolutionary critical pedagogy that can inform Indigenous struggles for self-determination" (Grande, 2004, p. 25). . . .

There is an opportunity to disrupt the history of settlement when we start with land in both classrooms and in pedagogy. Histories of slavery and migration are indeed part of these conversations in important ways, all of which are complicated by versions of democratic citizenship being offered up in schools based on settler futurity and Indigenous erasure. Clearly, not all migrants are settlers. . . . How are non-Indigenous peoples being invited into conversations about a relationality to land—especially its corporatization and appropriation—at home, globally, and transnationally?

Schools are challenged to invigorate conversations about settler colonialism and citizenship education. . . .

We need to think about land, each other, and our agency as citizens in relational terms. Current models of education often preclude these sorts of understandings. Sovereignty is (mis-) interpreted as involving property alone (Grande, 2004, p. 54). This preclusion does nothing to facilitate a conversation about settler-Indigenous relationships building, border imperialism, and relationships building and/or rejuvenation across multiple subject positions. It offers instead a propertied, exclusivist, and indeed colonial model of citizenship under which there is little reason or room to imagine or engage with a more respectful, reciprocal, and "peaceful coexistence" with Indigenous nations (Grande, 2004, p. 61).

Land, Relationships, and Indigenous Sovereignty

. . .

It is necessary to critically analyze sovereignty and the way we have come to think about the world around us in propertied terms, and to think more expansively about the idea in relational ways. The word "relational" is important here because sovereignty *is* relational: it depends on our mutual entanglements, our affective transactions, and our interdependence as *Ukwehuwe* and Settlers. As Taiaiake Alfred (2009) writes, "irredentism has never been in the vision of our peoples" (p. 182). Borrows (2010) states similarly: "secession is largely a colonizer's activity. It is rare for Indigenous peoples in Canada to talk about severing their relations with others" (p. 167). How then will schools address this call for Indigenous-Settler relationships rejuvenation, recuperation, and the rebuilding of nation-to-nation political relationships?

. . .

Schools have not worked effectively enough to combat ignorance related to the theft of Indigenous land, or to inform or educate people about ongoing encroachment as sanctioned by settler colonial violence and law. Before reconciliation is possible in a post-TRC and highly apologetic Canada, it is necessary for Settlers to accept that ignorance is not the sole cause of conflict. McCarthy (2016) argues that education will be unable to play any role in assuaging a conflict stemming from Indigenous land grievances and reclamation so long as "non-Native people . . . want what native people have" (p. 179). . . .

McCarthy concludes: "There will be no decolonization in Canada simply because non-Native people learn more about Indigenous history and culture. Better knowledge must be accompanied by the

return of land to alter settler colonialism's structural foundation" (p. 280).

Notwithstanding McCarthy's important criticism, I would suggest that taking a materialist, anticolonial, and decolonizing approach to Indigenous education in settler colonial and post-TRC Canada is an important step toward transforming relationships. Such an approach would reject a possessive individualism which has always functioned as ideological justification—and an explanation—for occupying stolen land (Thielen Wilson, 2012, p. 54). . . .

A decolonizing education could make a difference across barricades, especially if we consider the violence and disavowal experienced by some communities in retaliation for land grievances, reclamation, and affirmations of Indigenous sovereignty (Mackey 2016; McCarthy, 2016; Monture, 2015). Canadians do not usually think in critical ways about lands, or about the direct action that is used at times to occupy and protect them. Furthermore, they do not even have to think about land itself, or what it might mean to stand in a reciprocal relationship with land as the Mother beneath our feet. Indeed, Sheelah McLean reflects on a much more common oppositional way of thinking that is evident when extralegal and direct action is taken by Indigenous peoples to occupy land, one in which "the Canadian public are socialized to believe that barricades are violent" (as cited in Lilley & Schantz, 2013, p. 121). As McLean writes:

> The mainstream media, along with our schools, churches, and government work very hard to create and maintain that perception, which inhibits people from seeing the violence inherent to colonial society and from understanding barricading as an act of protection (as cited in Lilley & Schantz, 2013, p. 121).

Classroom-based, pedagogical, and programmatic initiatives must necessarily transform this way of thinking. Schools should also be challenged to think instead about how to foster a collective responsibility to reject settler capital and lands exploitation, and the ecological devastation brought on by both. . . .

Teaching Law, Land, and Settler Colonial Dispossession

Each and every Canadian ought to receive mandatory education about law, land, and the history of settler colonialism. Settlers cannot possibly hope to restore a peaceful coexistence across the Indigenous-Settler divide until such time that Canadian law—not to mention education—recognizes and affirms a nation-to-nation political relationship (Turner, 2013). . . .

The "Doctrine of Discovery" is an exemplary ideological formulation administered today by settler courts to lay ongoing claim to stolen land. Lindberg (2010) suggests the Doctrine of Discovery is used as "a rationale to take Indigenous lands on the basis of constructed . . . deficiencies and inhumanity" (p. 94). It is "a dogmatic body of shared theories predicated on a notion of 'first' and 'discovery,'" which enables ideological assertions about the "rightful and righteous settlement of Indigenous peoples' lands" (Lindberg, 2010, p. 94; also see Fitzpatrick, 2003). The Doctrine of Discovery is firmly ensconced in settler colonial law. The settler nation perpetuates these racialized ideas of discovery, especially through its Constitutional Law. The settler nation never questions its own right to legitimately possess land or to interfere with Indigenous sovereignty in Canada, let alone define and then legislate over those it calls 'Indians' and 'Aboriginals.'

Canadian law is based on the supremacy of settler sovereignty. It is based on racialized notions of conquest, discovery, and a unilateral entitlement to land. As Razack (2015) rightfully observes, "*even when the settler state is at its most expansive in acknowledging Aboriginal rights*, the premise remains that history begins with the sovereignty of the settler state" (p. 12, emphasis mine). Even at their most expansive, courts in general remain steadfast in refusing to acknowledge Indigenous peoples as nations, or for that matter, anything beyond "Aboriginal title," understood in Canadian law to mean "a legal right to . . . ancestral lands where their title has been neither surrendered nor validly extinguished" (McNeil, 1997, p. 135). Aboriginal rights have always to be "reconciled with Crown sovereignty" despite them being inherent rights bestowed by the Creator (Borrows, 2002, p. 8; Mackey, 2016, p. 10; see also Tully, 2000, p. 45). This tautological and deeply re-colonizing move protects settler sovereignty, as does foreclosing examinations of the category 'Aboriginal' in general (Alfred, 2005, pp. 126–130).

Canada has not addressed but has instead reinforced its colonial existence through the language of law and rights discourse. As Monture (2006) wrote, constitutional law is by no means an arbiter of colonial reparations or even social justice (see also Cannon, 2019). Maracle (2003) writes of the *Constitution* in particular:

> Section 35 has created the biggest and saddest sham in our history of having to endure plenty of shams perpetuated by colonial authority. Prior to the entrenchment of Aboriginal Rights in the constitution, we were fighting for the recognition of a nation-to-nation relationship, not fighting to cement the colonizer's magic foot print. (p. 314)

These matters of *re-colonization*—that is, the process whereby Indigenous peoples are subsumed by a legal apparatus serving settler interests and sovereignty—need to be understood, taught thoroughly, and addressed by Canadian schools. Schools need to teach how the sovereign right of Indigenous nations to exercise jurisdiction over our lands and territories has been reduced to a pattern of rights and rights infringement.

. . .

Schools must start to teach that the law in Canada is a system intended to divest our nations of sovereignty and land (Turpel, 1989/90, 1991). This system demands that our grievances always be reconciled, foremost with Crown sovereignty and then in the interests of settler futurity. Moreover, settler courts put into place criteria intended to freeze our 'Aboriginal rights' into a context pre-dating *Ha dih nyoh* (the word in my language for white settler). . . . In courtrooms—as in classrooms and settler culture—Indigenous peoples are expected to live in a world of long ago. If as Indigenous peoples we have in any way consumed modernity, our grievances are rendered suspect (Cannon & Sunseri, 2018, pp. 19–21).

The "integral to the distinctive culture" bias in Canadian constitutional law is as repugnant as it is insidious. . . .

An anti-colonial and decolonizing education seeks to explore these matters of Crown sovereignty and supremacy in settler colonial contexts. Specifically, it provides an understanding of the law in Canada, and interrogates whose authority it is to decide on what is "integral to the distinctive culture." . . . Before any reconciliation can take place in Canada, schools must challenge themselves and others to correct for a system of settler law and culture that contributes to, if not creates the conditions for ongoing lands dispossession and violence.

An understanding of settler law was missing from my own formal K-12 education as an Indigenous person growing up in Canada. . . . I suggest that education must centre matters involving law and racialization (i.e., Indianness), including how blood quantum ways of thinking are intended to denigrate Indigenous peoples' genealogical connection to territory and place in ways that further lands dispossession (Cannon, 2019; also see Kauanui, 2008, pp. 11, 34–35).

Schools ought also to provide a more thorough critique of settler colonial history and law, especially the ecological violence that is still invariably a part of empire building. . . . In relation to the world around us, it is more necessary than ever to call on Settlers to participate in matters concerning environmental sustainability, and in ways that rejuvenate our interdependence as sovereign nations. Formal education should work to more effectively challenge a system that exploits us all.

Envisioning Anticolonial and Reparative Education in the Canadian University

. . . In terms of my own teaching, I am invested in transformative anti-colonial pedagogies, and in fostering collaborations in both research and practice. . . .

Ten years ago, I created a course intended to explore issues of *Race, Indigeneity, and the Colonial Politics of Recognition*. This course . . . sets a scholarly context and framework for contemplating complex matters of citizenship, colonialism, and multiculturalism. In the interest of moving forward with colonial reparations in Canada, it is imperative that non-Indigenous peoples give thought to Canadian citizenship in scholarly and educational contexts, including the complex matters of difference, diversity, and colonial entanglements that comprise them. As Thobani (2007) writes of this matter: "Canadian citizenship remains predicated upon the erasure of Aboriginal sovereignty, and *unless this institution can be transformed in relation to the realization of Aboriginal sovereignty, it will remain an instrument of colonial dispossession*" (p. 250; emphasis mine).

. . .

In an effort to assist students to better understand (and remember) the history of Indigenous-Settler relations in Canada, I designed and developed another course in 2011 entitled *Centering Settler-Indigenous Solidarity in Theory and Research*. . . . I encourage graduate students to contribute to an ever-increasing body of peer reviewed scholarly literature concerned with Indigenous-non-Indigenous relationships. My motivation stems in part from realizing that I work and teach in one of the most diverse graduate programs in the country, and that before reconciliation can take place, Canada will require precisely these sorts of education-related initiatives in schools, along with a diverse population of graduates who are learned in both imagining and defining them.

The history of Indigenous-Settler relations extends well beyond the informal and official exchanges Indigenous peoples have had historically, and still have today, with the state and with white settlers. . . .

The story of Indigenous and racialized peoples' relationships is being told in a growing body of scholarly literature. I believe all students in Canada should read this literature and make a contribution of their own to its development. We should be challenged collectively in settler colonial and post-TRC Canada to engage with matters of difference, racialization, citizenship, and relationships rejuvenation, including nuances across multiple subject positions. The relevance of this engagement extends well beyond Canada, the classroom, and the academy.

Conclusion

Part of the work I envision going forward in Canada, indeed informed by this paper, involves working with teachers and graduate students in particular to contemplate pedagogical and/or programmatic initiatives aimed at settler decolonizing and relationships building in schools and the classroom. Teacher education must become a central part of envisioning a process of relationships rejuvenation and nation-to-nation building. I believe that reconciliation can only take place when Settlers start to move beyond a simple acknowledgement of privilege to place words into real, anticolonial, transformative, and pedagogical action. I hope this is something that all Canadians will come to think more about, including the ways in which Settlers might begin to and further engage with the 94 *Calls to Action* offered by the TRC (2015) and the ideas and conversations that ought to be happening in Canadian schools about law, land, and settler decolonizing. More importantly, I hope the emphasis being placed on relationships building and learning will truly transform Canadian education.

Nyawen Skannoh.

References

Alfred, T. (2009). Restitution is the real pathway to justice for Indigenous peoples. In *Aboriginal healing foundation research series. Response, responsibility, and renewal: Canada's truth and reconciliation journey* (pp. 178–187). Ottawa, ON: Aboriginal Healing Foundation.

Alfred, T. (2005). *Wasàse: Indigenous pathways of action and freedom*. Peterborough, ON: Broadview Press Ltd.

Allan, B. (2006). Remembering, resisting: Casting an anti-colonial gaze upon the education of diverse students in social work education. In G. J. S. Dei and A. Kempf (Eds.) *Anti-colonialism and education: The politics of resistance* (pp. 257–270). Rotterdam, NL: Sense Publishers.

Borrows, J. (2010). *Canada's Indigenous constitution*. Toronto, ON: University of Toronto Press.

Borrows, J. (2002). *Recovering Canada: The resurgence of Indigenous law*. Toronto, ON: University of Toronto Press.

Cannon, M. J. (2019). *Men, Masculinity, and the Indian Act*. Vancouver, BC: University of British Columbia Press.

Cannon, M. J. (2012). Changing the subject in teacher education: Centering Indigenous, diasporic, and settler colonial relations. *Cultural and pedagogical inquiry*, 4(2), 21–37.

Cannon, M. J., & Sunseri, L. (2018). (Eds.) *Racism, colonialism, and Indigeneity in Canada: A reader*, 2nd edition. Toronto, ON: Oxford University Press.

Deer, S. (2015). *The beginning and end of rape: Confronting sexual violence in Native America*. Minneapolis, MN: University of Minnesota Press.

Fitzpatrick, P. (2003). Doctrine of Discovery. In D. Theo Goldberg and J. Solomos (Eds.) *A companion to racial and ethnic studies* (pp. 25–30). Malden, MA: Blackwell Publishers.

Grande, S. (2004). *Red pedagogy: Native American social and political thought*. New York, NY: Rowman and Littlefield Publishers, Inc.

Jeffery, D., & Nelson, J. J. (2009). The more things change . . . the endurance of "culturalism" in social work and healthcare. In C. Schick and J. McNinch (Eds.), *"I thought Pochahontas was a movie." Perspectives on race/culture binaries in education and service professions* (pp. 91–110). Regina, SK: Canadian Plains Research Center Press.

Kauanui, J. K. (2008). *Hawaiian blood: Colonialism and the politics of sovereignty and Indigeneity*. Durham, NC: Duke University Press.

Lilley, P. J., & Shantz, J. (2013). From idle no more to Indigenous nationhood: Growing roots, upholding sovereignty, and defending the land. *Upping the anti: A journal of theory and action*, 15, 113–127.

Lindberg, T. (2010). The Doctrine of Discovery in Canada. In R. J. Miller, J. Ruru, L. Behrendt, & T. Lindberg (Eds.) *Discovering Indigenous lands: The Doctrine of Discovery in the English colonies* (pp. 89–125). Oxford University Press.

Lowman, E. B., & Barker, A. J. (2015). *Settler: Identity and colonialism in 21st century Canada*. Halifax, NS: Fernwood Publishing.

Mackey, E. (2016). *Unsettled expectations: Uncertainty, land and settler decolonization*. Winnipeg, MB: Fernwood Publishing.

Macoun, A. (2016). Colonising white innocence: Complicity and critical encounters. In S. Maddison, T. Clark, & R. de Costa (Eds.) *The limits of Settler colonial reconciliation: Non-Indigenous people and the responsibility to engage* (pp. 85–102). Singapore: Springer Nature Singapore Pte Ltd.

Maracle, L. (2003). The operation was successful, but the patient died. In A. Walkmen & H. Bruce (Eds.) *Box of treasures of empty box?: Twenty years of section 35* (pp. 308–314). Penticton, BC: Theytus Books Ltd.

McCarthy, T. (2016). *In divided unity: Haudenosaunee reclamation at Grand River*. Tucson, AZ: The University of Arizona Press.

McNeil, K. (1997). The meaning of Aboriginal title. In M. Asch (Ed.) *Aboriginal and treaty rights in Canada: Essays on law, equality, and respect for difference* (pp. 135–154). Vancouver, BC: University of British Columbia Press.

Monture, P. (2006). Standing against Canadian law: Naming omissions of race, culture, and gender. In E. Comack & K. Busby (Eds.) *Locating law: race/class/gender/sexuality connections*, 2nd edition (pp. 73–93). Halifax, NS: Fernwood Publishing.

Monture, R. (2014). *We share our matters: Two centuries of writing and resistance at Six Nations of the Grand River*. Winnipeg, MB: University of Manitoba Press.

Pon, G. (2009). Cultural competency as new racism: An ontology of forgetting. *Journal of progressive human services*, 20(1), 59–71.

Razack, S. H. (2015). *Dying from improvement: Inquests and inquiries into Indigenous deaths in custody*. Toronto, ON: University of Toronto Press.

Razack, S. (2002). Gendered racial violence and spatialized justice: The murder of Pamela George. *Canadian journal of law and society*, 15(2), 91–130.

Royal Commission on Aboriginal Peoples (RCAP). (1996). *The Report of the Royal Commission on Aboriginal peoples. Gathering Strength* (Vol 3). Ottawa, ON: Minister of Supply and Services.

St. Denis, V. & C. Schick. (2003). What makes anti-racist pedagogy in teacher education difficult? Three popular ideological assumptions. *The Alberta journal of educational research*, 49(1), 55–69.

Thobani, S. (2007). *Exalted subjects: Studies in the making of race and nation in Canada*. Toronto, ON: University of Toronto Press.

Thielen-Wilson, L. (2012). White terror, Canada's Indian Residential Schools, and the colonial present: From law towards a pedagogy of recognition (Unpublished doctoral dissertation). University of Toronto, Toronto, Canada.

Tully, J. (2000). The struggles of Indigenous peoples for and of freedom. In D. Ivison, P. Patton & W. Sanders (Eds.) *Political Theory and the rights of Indigenous peoples* (pp. 36–59). Cambridge, UK: Cambridge University Press.

Turner, D. (2013). On the idea of reconciliation in contemporary Aboriginal politics. In J. Henderson & P. Wakeham (Eds.) *Reconciling Canada: Critical perspectives on the culture of redress* (pp. 100–114). Toronto, ON: University of Toronto Press.

Turpel, M. E. (Aki-Kwe). (1991). Aboriginal peoples and the Canadian Charter of Rights and Freedoms: Contradictions and challenges. In E. Comack & S. Brickey (Eds.), *The social basis of law: Critical readings in the sociology of law*, 2nd Edition (pp. 223–237). Halifax, NS: Garamond Press.

Turpel, M. E. (1989/90). Aboriginal peoples and the Canadian Charter: Interpretive monopolies, cultural differences. *Canadian human rights yearbook*, 6, 3–45.

Truth and Reconciliation Commission of Canada. (2015). Honouring the Truth, Reconciling for the Future. Ottawa, ON: Truth and Reconciliation Commission of Canada.

Walia, H. (2013). *Undoing border imperialism*. Oakland, CA: AK Press.

PART 9

Additional Readings

Sheila Cote-Meek *Colonized Classrooms: Racism, Trauma and Resistance in Post-Secondary Education*. Fernwood Publishing, 2014.

Cote-Meek, Sheila and Taima Moeke-Pickering (eds.) *Decolonizing and Indigenizing Education in Canada*. Toronto: Canadian Scholars Press, 2020.

Dion, Susan D. *Braiding Histories: Learning from Aboriginal Peoples' Experiences and Perspectives*. Vancouver: UBC Press, 2009.

Florence, Melanie. *Residential Schools: The Devestating Impact on Canada's Indigenous Peoples and the Truth and Reconciliation Commission's Findings and Calls for Action, 2nd Edition*. Toronto: James Lorimer & Company Ltd., Publishers, 2021.

Grande, Sandy, ed. *Red Pedagogy: Native American Social and Political Thought, 10th Anniversary Edition*. New York: Rowman and Littlefield, 2015.

Jacobs, Beverley. "Response to Canada's Apology to Residential School Survivors," *Canadian Woman Studies* 26, 3–4 (2008): 223–225.

Simon, Roger I. "Towards a Hopeful Practice of Worrying: The Problematics of Listening and the Educative Responsibilities of Canada's Truth and Reconciliation Commission," pp. 129–142 in Jennifer Henderson and Pauline Wakeham, eds., *Reconciling Canada: Critical Perspectives on the Culture of Redress*. Toronto: University of Toronto Press, 2013.

Thielen-Wilson, Leslie. "Troubling the Path to Decolonization: Indian Residential School Case Law, Genocide, and Settler Illegitimacy." *Canadian Journal of Law and Society* 29, 2 (2014): 181–197.

Truth and Reconciliation Commission of Canada. *Honouring the Truth, Reconciling for the Future: Summary of the Final Report of the Truth and Reconciliation Commission of Canada*. Truth and Reconciliation Commission of Canada, 2015.

Relevant Websites

Orange Shirt Society
https://www.orangeshirtday.org/
This website contains important information regarding the annual September 30th Orange Shirt Day and resources, including teacher resources, concerning IRS in Canada and calls on all Canadians to remember the history of Indian Residential Schools by listening to the stories of IRS survivors and their families.

Colours of Resistance Archive
http://www.coloursofresistance.org
This website was developed by the Colours of Resistance Network, a grassroots organization concerned with opposing global capitalism, and contains a number of useful articles and resources concerning antiracist and anticolonial engagements with Indigenous solidarity.

Leanne Simpson and Glen Coulthard on Dechinta Bush University, Indigenous land-based education and embodied resurgence
https://decolonization.wordpress.com/2014/11/26/leanne-simpson-and-glen-coulthard-on-dechinta-bush-university-indigenous-land-based-education-and-embodied-resurgence/
Leanne Simpson and Glen Coulthard discuss Dechinta Bush University in this audio interview, providing a scholarly and participatory land-based pedagogy and practice that (re-)connects and (re-)embeds students in an anticolonial and land-centred way of knowing.

Transforming Relations: A Collaborative Collection
https://transformingrelations.wordpress.com/?s=education
This student-driven website, based at Trent University, provides an overview of ally engagements with Settler-colonialism and the numerous initiatives and resources available to and surrounding them.

Truth and Reconciliation Commission of Canada
http://www.trc.ca/websites/trcinstitution/index.php?p=3
This website provides information about the history of residential schools, the Truth and Reconciliation Commission of Canada, the programs available to individuals and communities affected by the legacy of residential schools, and final reports issued in summer 2015.

Films

Cold Journey. Dir. Martin Defalco. National Film Board of Canada, 1975.

The Fallen Feather: Indian Industrial Residential Schools and Canadian Confederation. Dir. Randy Bezeau. Kinetic Video, 2007.

Hi-Ho Mastahey! Dir. Alanis Obomsawin. National Film Board of Canada, 2013.

Indian Horse. Dir. Stephen Campanelli. Elevation Pictures, 2017.

Pelq'ilc (Coming Home). Dir. Helen Haig-Brown and Celia Haig-Brown. V Tape, 2009.

Understanding and Finding Our Way: Decoloninzing Canadian Education. Dir. Alison Duke. Oya Media Group, 2021.

We Were Children. Dir. Tim Wolochatiuk. National Film Board, 2012.

We Can't Make the Same Mistake Twice. Dir. Alanis Obomsawin. National Film Board, 2016.

Key Terms

- Acculturation
- Assimilation
- Colonial reparations
- Cultural revitalization

- Cultural fundamentalism
- Indigenous–Settler relations
- Reconciliation

Discussion Questions

1. How did residential schools encourage the genocide of Indigenous peoples and with what set of consequences? How do these strategies manifest themselves in contemporary contexts?

2. How does a focus on cultural education erase the systemic violence of Settler colonialism? What are the implications of turning dehumanization, disparities in educational attainment, and educational reform into a problem of culture, cultural incommensurability, or cultural misunderstanding?

3. What does Cannon mean by a "truly transformative education" and what needs to become the focus of educational discourse in Settler colonial and post-TRC Canada? Why?

4. How do anthropological notions of cultural difference manifest themselves in services delivery and educational contexts today? How does this tendency detract from conversations about racism and Settler colonialism?

Activities

Rosemary Henze and Lauren Vanett (1993) suggest in their article "To Walk in Two Worlds—Or More?: Challenging a Common Metaphor of Native Education" that a two-world metaphor leaves the matter of culture both pre-determined and yet grossly under-defined. How does the film *Cold Journey* (NFB, 1975) produce a two-world metaphor, with what series of consequences, and as Henze and Vanett ask explicitly: "how do students who learn to walk in two worlds know when they have accomplished their task?" (ibid., 123) Are non-Indigenous students impacted by a two-world metaphor? How?

Read the 94 "Calls to Action" offered by Canada's Truth and Reconciliation Commission in their Final Report from 2015. Which of these action items most resonates with you and why? As a class, discuss individual and collective strategies for placing one of these items into action.

Read Roger Simon's "Toward a Hopeful Practice of Worrying" and Sara Ahmed's "The Politics of Bad Feeling" and organize a class discussion about the recommendations provided by the Truth and Reconciliation Commission of Canada in their report *Honouring the Truth, Reconciling for the Future*. What does the Commission say overall and with respect to public education about the history of residential schools? What recommendations would your class make for educational reform in Canada based on the TRC report? How might schools elicit empathy among Canadians that makes possible a restorative project, a claiming of responsibility for the colonial past, and a more just and equitable future?

PART 10

Indigenous Research and Methodologies

Editor Introduction

While reviewing relevant literature and editing the two articles for this part of the text, memories of our graduate studies started to come to us: the limited choices we had of published Indigenous scholarship, how we wanted to ensure our research methodologies were respectful of our communities, the challenges we encountered in our university when the institution's expectations and demands of what constituted "knowledge" and "ethical protocols" clashed with those of our own community and our selves. What helped us through it was reading the works of Indigenous scholars like Linda Tuhiwai Smith, Margaret Kovach, Marie Battiste, and others whose words resonated with our experiences and commitment. Influenced by Linda Tuhiwai Smith, Sunseri has argued, "for the most part, Western research has been part of an imperialist and colonialist agenda towards Indigenous peoples. Historically, social researchers, while achieving the status of authoritative voices of research about Indigenous peoples, have often disrespectfully represented our Indigenous cultural knowledge and disregarded our own established ethical protocols" (2007, 94). Western social research about Indigenous peoples was used to represent them as the "Other," proliferating negative and damaging stereotypes and classifying them as a "problem" whose solutions were proposed by Western "experts."

As Absolon points out in her article, Indigenous peoples had always possessed rich traditions of knowledge and research methodologies, yet these eventually waned somewhat. As she further argues, "the waning of traditional science among Indigenous peoples was not voluntary or spontaneous. It was caused by the historical denial, degradation, and even destruction [of it] . . . traditional science was replaced with belief systems based on western scientific thought." Western science, and Western research methodologies became normalized as the only valid form of knowing, marginalizing if not completely silencing Indigenous knowledge and research methodologies. Despite this, Indigenous knowledge survived due to the resistance and resilience of our ancestors, and pioneer Indigenous academics, as named above, became influential in reclaiming our spaces in the sciences and academia, in our own terms and by decolonizing research. Due to their efforts, it is now not as difficult for Indigenous graduate students to review and use Indigenous scholarship for their own work and have Indigenous research methodologies accepted by their own institutions. What is Indigenous research, then? What distinguishes it from others?

Indigenous research recognizes knowledge to be dynamic, earth-centred, and to "exist in relationships with Creations . . . , inseparable from the lived experiences of Indigenous people and so is relevant to our day-to-day lives, knowledge is personal" (Johnston et al., in Chapter 19). One of its main purposes is to contribute to the overall struggle for Indigenous sovereignty; hence it needs to be as much as possible for and by Indigenous researchers working within healthy relationships. As Johnston, McGregor, and Restoule in Chapter 19 and Absolon in Chapter 20 point out, Indigenous research is a relationship: the researcher has a relationship with their own self, with their families, with knowledge keepers, with research participants, with their ancestors, with the future generations, the land, and the Creator. To help to establish good relationships, it is good practice for the researcher to share their own personal story and social location; this allows to better assess their credibility, accountability, and the validity of their research and knowledge, as well forming a reciprocal relationship. We, the editors of this text, shared our personal stories and identified our familial and community connections in the introductory chapter, as we agree that this a responsible and ethical way to conduct any Indigenous research.

Johnston et al. (Chapter 19) outline four specific principles that ought to guide Indigenous research: respect, responsibility, relevance, and reciprocity. The first, respect, means that the researcher must behave with respect in all relationships they engage in while doing research, be humble, acknowledge the sources of the acquired knowledge, and ensure to provide honest representation of that knowledge. The researcher must act responsibly and be accountable for their own actions throughout the research process, as well as take necessary steps to ensure the knowledge that has been shared will not be used to harm the participants or the community. Indigenous research ought to be relevant to the community, and be part of the broader goal of empowering and decolonizing Indigenous communities and society. Lastly, research should be reciprocal, meaning that any findings, results, benefits should be shared with the community so to maintain a well-balanced relationship.

In Chapter 20, Absolon discusses her overall research journey, and describes one specific research project. She points out how important it is for her to connect with the medicines, the plants, the animals, the land, and the Creator when doing research. For her, this is what Indigenous research is about: to honour our oral cultural traditions, and pass them on to the future generations. "Indigenous knowledge is as old as life. Indigenous re-search can now be guided by a re-emergence and assertion of Indigenous knowledge." This knowledge comes from our ancestors, and above all is sacred, and ought to be carried out by establishing holistic healthy relationships, following the 4 Rs outlined above.

Absolon proceeds to describe a research project she undertook and how she ensured to follow Indigenous research methods. First, she identified what Indigenous research methodologies graduate Indigenous researchers were using, what specific methods they were employing. She reviewed graduate theses, connected with Indigenous researchers, got together with them, and in group learning circles, they all shared their experiences in a reciprocal, respectful way. They employed culturally centred methods, and collectively, gathered knowledge, made meaning, supported each other, and decided on whole research process. Hence, the research was respectful, responsible, relevant, and reciprocal.

It has been inspirational and exciting to read many books and articles on Indigenous knowledge and research methodologies for this part of the text. Indigenous scholarship in general, and particularly that dealing with Indigenous research methodologies, has truly bloomed from the time two of us were graduate students. As Johnston et al. state in Chapter 19, "Indigenous research is as diverse as the peoples who engage in the process, yet the varied approaches . . . share the common feature of being different from other, non-Indigenous, approaches to research." Indigenous research is one that prioritizes Indigenous scholarship, Indigenous traditional knowledge and protocols, Indigenous needs, and Indigenous sovereignty.

Relationships, Respect, Relevance, Reciprocity, and Responsibility

Taking Up Indigenous Research Approaches

Rochelle Johnston, Deborah McGregor, and Jean-Paul Restoule

Can we speak of a single Indigenous research paradigm? Indigenous research is as diverse as the peoples who engage in the process, yet the varied approaches we collectively refer to as "Indigenous research" share the common feature of being different from other, non-Indigenous, approaches to research (Chilisa, 2012; Mertens, Cram, & Chilisa, 2013; Rigney, 2006; Wilson, 2008). Indigenous research scholarship has been pivotal in clarifying this difference, putting it in context, and providing a theoretical lens through which we can better understand and promote research that prioritizes the aspirations, needs, and values of Indigenous peoples and knowledges (Kovach, 2009; Lambert, 2014).

... What is it about this methodology that makes research Indigenous? Like the concept of Indigeneity itself, the answers are multiple, complex, and contested (Chilisa, 2012; Paradies, 2016), and better approached in context than with fixed definitions. There are some key elements that stand out, however. For example, Indigenous research offers a clear commitment to recognize and support diversity and nationhood – intellectual self-determination, if you will. Indigenous research explicitly recognizes traditional and contemporary Indigenous knowledge traditions, the value of community leadership and support, and the community's ownership of knowledge. Indigenous research holds the potential to regenerate and revitalize the life of Indigenous peoples and communities along with the "knowing" that sustains their ongoing vitality.

In a similar vein, "Indigenist" research, as described by Lester Rigney (2006), is an emancipator, seeking to help "chart our own political and social agendas for liberation from the colonial domination of research and society" (p. 39). According to Rigney, Indigenist research focuses on three principles: "the involvement in resistance as the emancipatory imperative in Indigenous research; the maintenance of political integrity in Indigenous research; and the privileging of Indigenous voices in Indigenous research" (2006, p. 39). Rigney also makes clear that while Indigenist research must benefit Indigenous communities, it is by no means "anti-intellectual" or "atheoretical," nor is it meant only for Indigenous peoples. What it does offer is a clear opportunity for Indigenous voices and perspectives, and thus is a critical starting point for addressing vitally important issues affecting Indigenous and non-Indigenous peoples alike.

The Transformation of Indigenous Research

Indigenous research methodologies arise from Indigenous worldviews (Geniusz, 2009; Kovach, 2009; Lambert, 2014), but they are also shaped by centuries of struggle to survive and overcome colonialism. Indigenous research seeks to expose epistemic violence and domination (Walton, 2013) and poses a counter-narrative to Western research approaches. We are indebted to the work of Maori scholar Linda Tuhiwai Smith (1999), which explains how research has been used by Europeans to colonize Indigenous peoples around the world. We build on this foundation and focus on the opportunities and challenges of using research as a tool to achieve sovereignty or self-determination. However, Indigenous research methodologies are not simply a response to colonialism; they have existed for thousands of years (Wilson, 2008). Indigenous research methodologies reflect how knowledge is understood and sought in the context of the worldviews, ontologies, and epistemologies of diverse Indigenous nations.

Decolonizing Research

Decolonization has become a critical aspect of moving away from the colonizing research that has consistently dehumanized Indigenous peoples over time, and of resisting Euro-Western theories and research (Brown & Strega, 2015). Despite its vital importance, decolonizing research is difficult, uncomfortable, and risky. We must go into the belly of the beast to critique colonialism (Absolon, 2011). This includes taking an honest look at the wrongdoings perpetrated by non-Indigenous people, as well as the ways in which Indigenous people have sometimes participated in our own oppression (Wilson, 2008).

The paradox of decolonizing research arises from having to resist continued attempts to eradicate Indigenous ways of being and knowing, while recognizing the fact that beneficial research can indeed entail cross-cultural encounters, particularly if said research is firmly grounded in an Indigenous paradigm, as Maori education researcher Graham Smith (cited in Kovach, 2009) believes:

My view was that we needed to put some Indigenous theory tools or, in a New Zealand sense, Maori tools on the wall of the university alongside of all the other theoretical tools and all the other research methodologies, so that we would have a more effective and wider choice of options. . . . We also now have our own ways of doing things. It is not an either/or situation, and I think this is a really important point to emphasize. (pp. 88–89)

Cross-cultural relationships can cultivate ethical possibilities that foster collaborative research in support of the aspirations of Indigenous communities. These research relationships can create ethical space for research negotiations (Johnson & Larsen, 2013), and, as Deborah McGregor (2013) points out, may respectfully "create space for difference among nations, peoples, knowledges, traditions and values" (p. 162). Collaborative research can also be rooted in Indigenous research traditions that are embodied in treaty relationships (Latulippe, 2015; Luby et al., this volume).

Decolonizing research means designing and carrying out research in ways that honour Indigenous knowledges and communities rather than privilege colonizing institutions, such as the academy. As Anishinaabe scholar Kathy Absolon (2011) explains, "our search for knowledge constitutes a search for power" (p. 55). In an Indigenous research paradigm, Indigenous communities, researchers, and research participants, rather than academic "experts," become the final arbiters of the value of the research. As Kovach (2009) explains, centring power in Indigenous communities could mean following community research protocols, convening community advisory committees, and ensuring research participants have control in their relationship with the researcher.

Knowledge and Knowing

As Cree scholar Shawn Wilson (2008) points out, "all knowledge is cultural" (p. 91). Indigenous knowledge is rooted in, congruent with, and respectful of the "beliefs, values, principle's, processes and contexts" of the worldview of a particular Indigenous nation

(Absolon, 2011, p. 22). Kovach (2009) writes that, according to Indigenous worldviews, there is a responsibility to transmit Indigenous knowledge from one generation to another. Further, "[l]anguage [in this case, Indigenous languages] matters because it holds within it a people's worldview" (Kovach, 2009, p. 59).

Writing from an Anishinaabe worldview, Absolon (2011) describes knowledge as alive and dynamic because it is "earth-centered and harmoniously exists in relationships with Creation" (p. 49). Similarly, Wilson (2008) speaks of ideas as entities, with Spirit, with whom we can form relationships. Indigenous methodologies are also drawn from the land, as Tuck and McKenzie (2015) point out: "Indigenous knowledges emerge and exist within a universe that is relational and responsive" (p. 95). They add, "Reciprocity in Indigenous methodologies takes a different tenor because of its cosmological connotations, concerned with maintaining balance not just between humans, but with energies that connect and thread through all entities in the Universe" (p. 95). Indigenous knowledge is inseparable from the lived experiences of Indigenous people and so is relevant to our day-to-day lives (Wilson, 2008, pp. 100–101). Knowledge is personal.

Knowledge is also political, because knowledge is power. Further, given Indigenous people's "struggle to live and be well in a society that is opposed to bur survival as Indigenous people" (Wilson & Restoule, 2010, p. 33), Indigenous research is a tool of resistance (Brown & Strega, 2015).

Knowledge is bigger than we are, something we can uncover only a part of. It was here before we were: "Knowledge is received or gifted from all living things and from the spirit world" (Wilson & Restoule, 2010, p. 33). According to Absolon (2011), coming to knowledge is an open-ended process; it is difficult to predict where we might end up, what we might come to know. Knowledge is also organic, because it "is cyclical and circular and follows the natural laws of Creation" (Absolon, 2011, p. 31). Indigenous knowledges are derived from land and place (Lambert, 2014; Johnson & Larsen, 2013; Tuck & McKenzie, 2015). Indigenous place-based research methods enable interactions, engagement, and reciprocity in knowledge exchange with the natural world. As Vanessa Watts (2013) points out, "Place-Thought is based upon the premise that land is alive and thinking and that humans and non-humans derive agency through the extensions of these thoughts" (p. 21). In this sense, research is not solely the domain of humans; the land, place, and non-humans also generate knowledge.

Why Seek Knowledge?

Knowledge is not sought purely for the sake of it – it always serves a purpose, not least because for Indigenous people the struggle for sovereignty is ongoing. Given the brutality and scope of colonization, having an Indigenous person seek knowledge of their own nation is, in and of itself, a powerful rationale for conducting research: "Resistance is a subtext to the journey [in search of knowledge]; resistance to being silenced and rendered invisible, insignificant, uncivilized, inhuman, non-existent and inconsequential" (Kovach, 2009, p. 91).

Indigenous knowledges must be reclaimed from the past, privileged in the present, and transmitted to the next generation (Absolon, 2011). However, reclamation is not just about resisting the extermination of Indigenous knowledges; it is about "stop[ping] it from being misused and misunderstood" (Wilson & Restoule, 2010, p. 35). Part of achieving sovereignty is ensuring that research done *about* Indigenous people is done *by* Indigenous people (Absolon, 2011). Knowledge sovereignty means Indigenous people decide why, what, and when knowledge is being sought and the methods being used to seek it. It also means that Indigenous people are valued as the experts, and Indigenous standards are used to judge whether what is learned is really "true" (Wilson, 2008).

Research as Relationship

Indigenous research methodologies can be understood as processes for establishing, strengthening, and coming into closer relationship with knowledge. However, other relationships – between the researcher and their research participants, between the land the research is taking place on and all its inhabitants, among the people who learn or read about the research once it is completed, between the ancestors and future generations – must also be honoured. Wilson (2008) believes that these two sets of relationships, researcher to knowledge and researcher to the rest of the cosmos, are interdependent. This is consistent with trail blazing Blackfoot academic Leroy Little Bear's assertion that "[t]he function of Aboriginal values is to maintain the relationships that hold Creation together" (cited in Absolon, 2011, p. 49). The researcher is nested in concentric circles of relationships. The researcher must consider their relationship with self, with family, with those that provide guidance in carrying out the research, with the research participants, with the broader community, with the ancestors and future generations, with the environment and land, and with the Creator (Suchet-Pearson, Wright, Lloyd, Burarrwanga, & Hodge, 2013). Because researchers are constituted by their relationships, and their research is the relationship between themselves and the knowledge they are seeking, a researcher must begin by exploring their own location and subjectivities. Learning something of the researcher's personal story may help research participants decide what to share of their own stories, and how to share them (Kovach, 2009, p. 98). As discussed above, knowing the researcher's location allows others to assess the researcher's credibility, and thus the validity of the research. It also makes the researcher conscious of their biases (Kovach, 2009). In this sense, the researcher becomes "knowable" to research participants, thus disrupting the power dynamics inherent in conventional Western research relationships. Locating oneself may involve identifying one's own nation, culture, clan, land, and historical and personal experiences (Absolon, 2011). What usually emerges from locating oneself is an understanding of one's reasons for undertaking the research (Absolon, 2011). Further, self-location is not a one-time act. The process of doing research changes us, as well as the world around us (Wilson, 2008).

Once we understand ourselves in relation, it is possible to carry out research that is true to ourselves. Wilson (2008) talks about the importance of having your own voice in the research, and Absolon (2011) concurs, writing that "I want my words to reflect my way of thinking, being and doing" (p. 15). An extension of this congruency is ensuring the same values inform one's research as inform one's day-to-day life (Kovach, 2009).

From self, one moves to the next level of the concentric circle, which is family. In his book, Wilson (2008) devotes significant attention to the generations that came before (his parents) and after him (his children), and traces how his identity as a Cree man and a Cree researcher is constituted by those relationships. Family relations can also serve as a network through which the researcher connects to those people in the community with whom they need to speak in order to carry out the research (Weber-Pillwax, in Wilson, 2008). Wilson (2008) also mentions that connecting to potential research participants through family members and other intermediaries gives research participants the opportunity to decline participating without having to directly turn down a request. As with self, families have also been colonized. In the process of carrying out her research, Kovach, who was adopted into a white family as a child, furthered her journey to reclaim her Cree-Saulteaux relations. Kovach's (2009) research journey led her back to her traditional territory.

Moving outwards from family, there is community, and within that community there are Elders and traditional knowledge keepers who have expertise in cultural knowledge and ways to access spiritual knowledge. While some researchers, like Wilson and Restoule (2010) engage with Elders as research participants, learning from Elders can be viewed as a critical component of an Indigenous; research methodology no matter what the topic (Simpson, 2000).

Research also brings one into relationships through time and space and between material and spiritual worlds. As Nuu-chah-nulth scholar Richard Atleo (2004) describes, the petition that must be made between material and spiritual worlds is embodied in the term *oosumich*. Across time, we have a responsibility to the ancestors and future generations (Absolon, 2011). Tobacco can be used to communicate intentions to the ancestors about the research (Wilson & Restoule, 2010), As Anishinaabeg scholars Deborah McGregor and Sylvia Plain (2014) observe:

> Our teachers in the Anishinaabe tradition include non-human forms such as animals, trees, waters, rocks, etc. They are our relatives and we continue to learn and seek guidance from them as we always have. Recognizing our relatives as a source of knowledge forms an integral aspect of our theoretical foundation. This means our

knowledge is rooted in the Earth and the place we come from: where our ancestors are. (p. III)

As the above quote connotes, relationships in Indigenous research extend beyond human agents to include all beings, what Western science would call "living" and "non-living." **Relational accountability** includes literally all relations. Sandra Suchet-Pearson and colleagues (2013) observe that "these relations include not only human relations but limitless 'nonhuman' entities, what are usually described in Western contexts as the elements, animals, trees, landscapes and so on" (p. 33). Haudenosaunee/Anishinaabe scholar Vanessa Watts (2013) adds, "When thinking about agency with reference to Place-Thought, where can it be located? I find it in animals, in humans, in plants, in rocks, etc. How did I come to think that these different entities and beings had agency in the first place? From stories/histories" (p. 25). Research, then, is not strictly a human endeavour. Just as a researcher is accountable to their research participants and community, so they have responsibilities toward the land and all our relations (Wilson, 2008).

The Other Rs of Indigenous Research: Respect, Responsibility, Relevance, Reciprocity, and Refusal

We enact relational accountability with all these entities, human and non-human, physical and metaphysical, through research. So then how must we behave in these relationships in order to carry out research in a good way? Restoule (2008), following Kirkness and Barnhardt (1991), takes the four Rs of education – respect, responsibility, relevance, and reciprocity – and applies them to doing research, noting that these actions are inscribed within relationships, a fifth "R," just discussed.

Most fundamentally, the researcher must behave with respect in relationships. Respect is one of the Seven Grandfather Teachings of the Anishinaabek and forms a cornerstone principle in ethical research conduct. While the idea of respect exists in many different cultures and contexts, ways of showing respect

seem to differ greatly. Showing respect in the context of carrying out research using an Indigenous approach is similar in many ways to showing respect in our day-to-day lives. While a research relationship is different, it is not that different – the normal courtesies of relating to one another still apply. The researcher must not only strive for egalitarian relationships between themselves and their research participants, but also among the research participants (Wilson, 2008). There is also a burden on the researcher to adapt to the research participants' ways of thinking about and doing things, not the other way around (Wilson & Restoule, 2010). This may require extraordinary patience and flexibility on the part of the researcher.

In showing respect, the researcher must express humility. They must ask permission before doing things and ensure everyone participating in the research is doing so voluntarily. The researcher must also show respect to the individuals and communities they work with by acknowledging the source of the information that is shared, and by ensuring an honest representation of *the individuals' and communities'* knowledge. Unless there is a compelling reason not to, acknowledging the people who participated in the research by name is a way of showing respect and gratitude (Wilson, 2008). However, it is not just people whom researchers must respect. Natural laws that govern the way we relate with all of Creation also need to be honoured (Absolon, 2011).

Responsibility in the context of Indigenous research methodologies is about more than taking responsibility as a researcher; it is about taking responsibility as a human being embedded in a network of relationships. Wilson (2008) calls this being accountable to your relations. Relational accountability is not just about the researcher being responsible to a research participant; it holds the family and community of those two people, and all their other relations, accountable for the research being done in a good way. A researcher must take personal responsibility for the knowledge shared through the research, to ensure it is not misused, as well as for the new knowledge that arises through the research, to ensure that it does not lead to any harm: "The new relationship [that comes with bringing a new idea into being] has to respect all of the other relationships around it" (Wilson, 2008, p. 79). Indigenous research is about relationships and responsibilities. As such, research participants also hold responsibilities.

Research must serve a purpose. Relevance to the community is also a critical concern. Ideally, the research is initiated by an Indigenous community who has requested or expressed a need or desire for research. In some cases, concerns that impact Indigenous communities more broadly are the catalyst for including a particular community or members of that community in the research work. Accountability to the broader community as well as to the particular relationship formed in the course of the research project mean that the work, the questions raised, the outcomes, and the process to undertake the research all have to be relevant to the community. Each of these aspects of the research has to be understood by the community members involved as at least indirectly, or ideally directly having bearing on their lives.

Reciprocity actualizes the principle of serving the community. The researcher feeding back the results of the research to those who contributed, sharing their own story with the research participants (Kovach, 2009, p. 98), or offering tobacco to an Elder (Wilson & Restoule, 2010) are all forms of reciprocity (Absolon, 2011). However, many Indigenous researchers also aim to have their research improve conditions in Indigenous communities (Kovach, 2009). Reciprocity also makes its way into other aspects of the research process. For example, Kovach (2009) reminds us that when we work through relationships, participants choose the researcher as much as the other way around.

Reciprocity is also a way of maintaining balance in research relationships (Kovach, 2009). As Wilson and Restoule (2010) explain, in the context of tobacco offerings, reciprocity is about establishing a mutual relationship. Further, disrespecting the relationship or acting unethically in the context of research invites the reciprocal process of natural justice: "If a person deliberately mistreats other creatures, that action will invoke natural justice: So they will receive similar treatment either to themselves or their descendants . . . even to seven generations" (Wilson, 2008, p. 107).

Mohawk scholar Audra Simpson's (2007) seminal work on ethnographic refusal points to questions about what communities and participants in research may *refuse* to disclose or share. Refusal represents sovereignty in research: some matters are "more our business than others" (p. 68). Refusal is a principle of Indigenous research that explicitly recognizes that "the goals and aspirations of those we talk to inform the methods and the shape of our theorizing and analysis" (Simpson, 2007, p. 68). Simpson's insights are critical: they directly challenge the image of the "uncooperative" or "uninformed" research participant. Tuck and McKenzie (2015) add that "[r]efusal is a powerful characteristic of Indigenous methods of inquiry, pushing back against the presumed goals of knowledge production, the reach of academe, and ethical practices that protect the institutions instead of individuals and communities" (p. 148). Indigenous methods and practices are original, varied, and seemingly contradictory, yet they fundamentally base their efforts on Indigenous self-determination in research.

Closing Thoughts, and Questions on the Ways Forward

. . . The values and principles of the six Rs we have outlined should guide any research undertaking with(in) Indigenous communities, no matter the researcher's social location and position relative to the community(ies) participating in research. That being said, each of us will follow a different research path depending upon these locations; we will form different relationships with the Indigenous research approaches and with the Indigenous communities with which we connect.

Entering into research is entering into relationship. It is a relationship with others, human and non-human, micro to macro. Through it all, how the researcher conducts themselves in those relationships is critically important; their approach must consider and embody feelings, values, context, process, and outcome. We should strive to *be* good in our relations and to *do* good in our relations. If research is conducted in the same good way, with the same spirit and intent, then we will have done research that meets a high standard of accountability to all our relations.

References

Absolon, K. (2010). Indigenous wholistic theory: A knowledge set for practice. *First Peoples Child and Family Review, 5*(2), 74–87.

Absolon, K. E. (2011). *Kaandossiwin: How we come to know.* Halifax, NS: Fernwood Publishing.

Atleo, R. (2004). *Tsawalk: A Nuu-chah-nulth worldview.* Vancouver, BC: UBC Press.

Brown, L., & Strega, S. (2015). *Research as resistance: Revisiting critical, Indigenous, and anti-oppressive approaches. Toronto, ON: Canadian Scholars Press.*

Chilisa, B. (2012). Indigenous research methodologies. Thousand Oaks, CA: Sage.

Geniusz, W. (2009). Our knowledge is not primitive: Decolonizing botanical Anishinaabe teaching. Syracuse, NY: Syracuse University Press.

Johnson, J., & Larsen, S. (Eds.). (2013). *A deeper sense of place: Stories and journeys of Indigenous-academic collaboration.* Corvallis, OR: Oregon State University Press.

Kirkness, V., & Barnhardt, R. (1991). First Nations and higher education: The four R's – respect, relevance, reciprocity, responsibility. *Journal of American Indian Education, 30*(3), 1–10.

Kovach, M. (2009). *Indigenous methodologies: Characteristics, conversations and contexts.* Toronto, ON: University of Toronto Press.

Lambert, L. (2014). Research for Indigenous survival: Indigenous research methodologies in the behavioral sciences. Pablo, MT: Salish Kootenai College Press.

Latulippe, N. (2015). Bridging parallel rows: Epistemic difference and relational accountability in cross-cultural research. *The International Indigenous Policy Journal, 6*(2). Retrieved from http://ir.lib.uwo.ca/iipj/vol6/iss2/7. DOI: 10.18584/iipj.2015.6.2.7.

McGregor, D. (2013). Towards a paradigm of Indigenous-non-Indigenous collaboration in geographic research. In J. Johnston & S. Larsen (Eds), *A deeper sense of place: Stories and journeys of Indigenous-academic collaboration* (pp. 157–178). Corvallis, OR; Oregon State University Press.

McGregor, D., & Plain, S. (2014). Anishinabe research theory and practice; Place based research. In A. Corbiere, M. A. Corbiere, D. McGregor, & C. Migwans (Eds.), *Anishinaabe-win niiwin: Four rising winds* (pp. 93–114). M'Chigeeng, ON; Ojibwe Cultural Foundation.

Mertens, D., Cram, F., & Chilisa, D. (Eds.). (2013). *Indigenous pathways into social research.* Walnut Creek, CA: Left Coast Press Inc.

Paradies, Y. (2016). Beyond black and white: Essentialism, hybridity and Indigeneity. In C. M Lennox & D. Short (Eds.), *Handbook of Indigenous peoples' rights* (pp. 24–34). London, UK; Routledge.

Restoule, J.-P. (2008). *The five R's of Indigenous research: Relationship, respect, relevance, responsibility, and reciprocity.* Lecture presented at Wise Practices II: Canadian Aboriginal AIDS Network Research and Capacity Building Conference, Toronto, ON.

Rigney, L. (2006). Indigenous Australian views on knowledge production and Indigenist research. In N. I. Goduka & J. E. Kunnie (Eds.), *Indigenous peoples' wisdom and power: Affirming our knowledge through narratives* (pp. 32–50). London, UK: Ashgate Publishing.

Simpson, A. (2007). Ethnographic refusal: Indigeneity, "voice," and colonial citizenship. *Junctures, 9,* 67–80.

Simpson, L. (2000). Anishinaabe ways of knowing. In J. Oakes, R. Riew, S. Koolage, L. Simpson, & N. Schuster (Eds.), *Aboriginal health, identity and resources* (pp. 165–185). Winnipeg, MB: Native Studies Press.

Smith, L. T. (1999). Decolonizing methodologies: Research and Indigenous peoples. New York, NY: Zed Books.

Suchet-Pearson, S., Wright, S., Lloyd, K., Burarrwanga, L., & Hodge, P. (2013). Footprints across the beach: Beyond researcher-centered methodologies. In J. Johnson & S. Larsen (Eds.), *A deeper sense of place: Stories and journeys of Indigenous-academic collaboration* (pp. 21–40). Corvallis, OR: Oregon State University Press.

Tuck, E., & McKenzie, M. (2015). *Place in research: Theory, methodology, and methods.* New York, NY: Routledge.

Walker, P. (2013). Relationship with humans, the spirit world, and the natural world. In D. Mertens, F. Cram, & B. Chilisa (Eds.), *Indigenous pathways into social research* (pp. 299–316). Walnut Creek, CA: Left Coast Press Inc.

Watts, V. (2013). Indigenous Place-Thought and agency amongst humans and non-humans (First Woman and Sky Woman go on a European world tour!). *Decolonization: Indigeneity, Education & Society, , 2*(1), 20–34.

Wilson, D. D., & Restoule, J.-P. (2010). Tobacco ties: The relationship of the sacred to research. *Canadian Journal of Native Education, 33*(1), 29–45.

Wilson, S. (2008). *Research is ceremony: Indigenous research methods.* Halifax, NS: Fernwood Publishing.

CHAPTER 20

Indigenous Re-Search

Kathleen E. Absolon

...Miigwech Cocomish, miinwa Shaumish...
Miigwech nsitam miinwa kaandaassiwin
Miigwech minobaamaadsiwin
Niin bemoose miinwa niin ndanewaad
kaandossiwin
Miigwech wedookwishin G'chi Manidoo...
(Minogiizhigokwe)

Indigenous Peoples' Cultural History and Research

Knowledge quests and knowledge searchers are all around us. Indigenous peoples have always had means of seeking and accessing knowledge Yet Indigenous searchers are usually caught in the context of colonial theories and methodologies. We tend to spend a lot of time there while compromising the development of our own knowledge.... Far too often, as Indigenous people, we are negotiating the sensitive area of research as both researched and researcher.

... Traditionally, research has been conducted to seek, counsel and consult; to learn about medicines, plants and animals; to scout and scan the land; to educate and pass on knowledge; and to inquire into cosmology. The seeking of knowledge has been usually solution-focused and often has had an underlying purpose of survival. Searching for knowledge was congruent with the principles, philosophies, customs, traditions, worldview and knowledge of a particular nation (Absolon and Willett 2004; Battiste 2000b; Battiste and Henderson 2000a; Deloria 1996). Today, Indigenous re-searchers are committed to rediscovering that congruency between worldview and methodology (Absolon and Willett 2004; Alfred 2005; Archibald 1997; Sinclair 2003; Wilson 2001).

Oral Traditions and Narrative

In keeping with my Anishinaabe culture, I begin by paying respect to the oral traditions and knowledge that I was raised with and that guide Aboriginal methodologies of searching. Vine Deloria (1996: 36) explains that oral tradition is the "non-western, tribal equivalent of science," where Indigenous experiences and knowledge are passed from generation to generation and where that knowledge explains the nature of the physical, emotional, mental and spiritual worlds of the people.

I return to the bush because that is where my first teachings about searching began. The animals, the earth and Creation are the original teachers of the Anishinaabek. As an Anishinaabe *kwe*, my search for knowledge and life began at home in the bush, where I was taught to fish, hunt, trap and go

Kathleen E. Absolon, "Indigenous Re-Search." In *Kaandossiwin: How We Come to Know*, Black Point, Nova Scotia: Fernwood Publishing © 2011.

berry picking. Searching is so intrinsic to living in the bush that we can connect this tradition to our contemporary search for knowledge. The ethics of our search are instilled in the land, and I agree with Peter Cole (2000, 2006) on Indigenous ethics when he states that we learned to give thanks and express our intentions, actions and feelings for what we needed and took from the earth. Indigenous ethics are implied in life itself and exercised through the teachings. If we needed the bark from a tree, expressing thanks, intentions and actions would precede the taking. Thus, the origins of any feast, basket, lodge or canoe would have been honoured and a consciousness of its Spirit respected.

When going on a search, negotiating the bush requires an understanding of the laws of nature. These laws are non-negotiable, meaning we must be prepared. Also, when going on a spiritual search for guidance and knowledge, we need to follow a process. Searching the land, in sacred spaces or human spaces, is guided by the nature of how we exist. In retrospect, I realize certain principles and philosophies guided my searches for life, berries, fiddle-heads, mushrooms or fish. *Preparation* is essential to any search: bring *semaa* (tobacco), be of a good heart and mind, think about your route, wear the proper clothing, gather your tools, bring food and water and plan for the unexpected. Announce yourself and your intentions; share this with others. In our search for berries we *started with our own knowledge.* Know where to begin looking and know how to find your path. Thus, in my search for principles of Indigenous methodologies, I begin with my own knowledge of searching in the bush. I was taught to *attune* to the land and what the animals were doing. *Announcing my intentions* to the land or warning the creatures of my presence was a central philosophy that *respected* the animals and our *relationship* to Creation. I learned to offer a prayer with *semaa* to acknowledge the Spirits of the land. I learned to *watch* the animals and birds, particularly the bears. Bears love blueberries too. Walking the land and negotiating the elements of the bush called for another principle: *do not get lost.* As a young child, I learned to *identify landmarks* from which I could locate my position and from where I would retrace my steps. Sometimes I used markers along the way in the form of rocks, broken twigs

or flag tape to identify the path I had taken and to guide me safely home. Trees, rivers, creeks and landscapes also were important in finding my way. Markers were essential because after a while the bush begins to all look the same. You might think you know where you came from—and some very knowledgeable people do, such as my mother and grandparents—but I am not as skilled and require physical markers to guide my path home. *Listening and walking carefully* were other principles central to my search. My eyes *watched* for animals and obstacles and helped me to retain balance in my steps. I listened for animals to ensure that I wouldn't startle a bear. I used a stick to shake the lower juniper bushes or bang on the rocks to warn snakes or other small creatures of my presence. In practising these principles I learnt about *demonstrating respect* for the land and its inhabitants. In my search I might not find what I sought, but that did not mean giving up; it just meant I would need to try another day. Thus I learned about *persevering.* I learned to walk through the bush *patiently,* knowing that my search would take time. Sometimes I would find an abundance of berries and would pick for hours, reaping the gifts of Creation. For that, I was always grateful: *gratitude* is another principle. On other occasions, I would find other medicines and foods. Sometimes, I would just find myself and would spend the day in the bush with Creation. Always, searching in the bush was guided by principles, and it felt good to come home with baskets full of berries and a *sense of connection, understanding and knowing.*

Indigenous cultural histories are rich and have been passed from one generation to the next since time immemorial. Our lived experiences are records of these histories. Cultural histories speak about the cosmology of the universe and our location in it. Such histories have been carried on from generation to generation via oral traditions of storytelling, ceremony, songs, teachings, ritual and sharing. Each nation retained, recorded and recounted its own cultural histories. These histories were/are relevant and meaningful to the lives, culture and survival of each Indigenous nation. Intertwined in histories were methodologies from which purpose and meaning were actualized. The "hows" to life's questions and quests were pivotal to seeking answers. These "hows" are central to Aboriginal methodologies as

Indigenous re-searchers claim and articulate what is Aboriginal in our research practices and processes.

... As Indigenous scholars, we are challenged to take back control and change the way research is conducted within our communities, peoples and cultures. We are being given the task to re-write and re-right our own realities and truths (see also Hart 2009). An acknowledgement of Indigenous re-search methods in communities and research contexts is pivotal to this task. If we intend to theorize and re-search as Indigenous scholars, then we must identify what that means and how that happens.

Indigenous Science and Knowledge

> Indigenous knowledge Is the property of those individuals, their communities and their Nations. It is inappropriate for outside researchers to document such knowledge for the sole purpose of thesis, dissertations and academic advancement. (Leanne[1])

Undeniably, the waning of traditional science among Indigenous peoples was not voluntary or spontaneous. It was caused by the historical denial, degradation and even destruction of "traditional Elders, keepers of knowledge [who] were deliberately murdered" (Colorado 1988: 51). Sacred birch bark scrolls, knowledge bundles and ceremonial objects were confiscated, destroyed and outlawed. Traditional science was replaced with belief systems based on western scientific thought, which "created the illusion that western science is THE Universal Truth with THE true methods. As a result, since the invasion of the Americas, the science that has studied Native life has been Western science" (50–51, uppercase in original). Truth was then explained within European paradigms. Pam Colorado led Indigenous critiques of western science colonialism as "**intellectual imperialism**" and called for the strengthening of "traditional Native science and to block further penetration of traditional Native science by Western science" (50). In the 1960s, the first generation of

Indigenous scholars and activists in the academy applied sociocultural models of social science research using history as a methodological tool and addressing historical, economic and political issues. The voices of Indigenous peoples and Indigenous re-searchers began to re-emerge and call into question western theoretical models. Whisperings in the wind carried forward notions that Indigenous peoples might have a science of their own (Colorado and Collins 1987). And so, along with feminist and critical scholars, Indigenous scholars criticized the limitations of western science and actively advanced methodologies which embraced our own historical, social, political, economic, spiritual and cultural realities (Absolon and Willett 2004; Archibald 2008; Bishop 1998b; Cole 2006; Colorado 1988; Deloria 1996; Duran and Duran 2000; Fitznor 2002; Graveline 1998, 2000; Kenny 2000; Kovach 2005, 2009; Little Bear 2000; McPherson and Rabb 2001, 2003; Martin-Hill 2008; Thomas 2005; Wilson 2008).

Shawn Wilson (2003, 2008) identifies the development of Indigenous research paradigms on a continuum of four stages. The first finds Indigenous re-searchers working solely from a western paradigm, with few Indigenous people present in academia. The second and third stages move toward integration of western and Indigenous paradigms, with the third illustrating a stronger thrust toward decolonization. The fourth, and most recent stage has Indigenous re-searchers illuminating their own worldview using Indigenous paradigms. As an Indigenous searcher, my focus is on these recent developments. Indigenous paradigms are increasingly receiving recognition and respect as Indigenous scholars re-search and teach from their own distinct stance. Indigenous paradigms enable Indigenous re-searchers to talk back and assume control of our own search for knowledge (Calliou 2001; Hart 2009; Talbot 2002). When we indigenize or Aboriginalize (Fitznor 2002) research, Indigenous worldviews and perspectives are affirmed (Cardinal 2001; Simpson 2001; Sinclair 2003; Steinhauser 2002). Indigenous critiques are vital to create space for Indigenous paradigms and methodologies in Indigenous searches to emerge.

---

1. Voices from the conversations are cited with the first name only.

The concept "we are all related" informs the wholistic and relational nature of Indigenous methodologies. Indigenous thought and knowledge guides how we search for knowledge — a search that considers reciprocity and interdependence.

Indigenous knowledge is as old as life. Indigenous re-search can now be guided by a re-emergence and assertion of Indigenous knowledge. You will see the depth and breadth of such knowledge reflected by Indigenous searchers throughout this book in our stories and narratives. Here, I pause to stress the significance and extent of Indigenous knowledge within Indigenous re-searchers' consciousness. Indigenous knowledge is knowledge that is wholistically derived from Spirit, heart, mind and body. Indigenous forms of knowledge production accept intuitive knowledge and metaphysical and unconscious realms as possible channels to knowing (Colorado 1988; Deloria 2002; Little Bear 2000).

Many Indigenous searchers from diverse nations share common principles regarding Indigenous worldviews.[2] It is a given, for instance, that Indigenous worldviews are wholistic and relational. "Most Aboriginal worldviews and languages are formulated by experiencing an ecosystem" (Henderson 2000a: 259). Indigenous worldviews teach people to see themselves humbly within a larger web or circle of life. This web contains our relationships to one another and to all of Creation. Indigenous knowledge lives in the animals, birds, land, plants, trees and Creation. Relationships among family and kinship systems exist within human, spiritual, plant and animal realms. Indigenous knowledge systems consider all directions of life: east, south, west, north and beneath, above and ground levels. Life is considered sacred and all life forms are considered to have a Spirit. We manifest this knowledge in our humility in offering thanks for life and in seeking life's direction.

Knowledge for Indigenous peoples exists in the heart and Spirit too. Indigenous knowledge comes from ancestral teachings that are spiritual and sacred in origin (Ermine 1995). It exists in our visions, dreams, ceremonies, songs, dances and prayers. It is not knowledge that comes solely from books but is lived, experiential and enacted knowledge. It is cyclical and circular and follows the natural laws of Creation. Indigenous knowledge is earth-centered, with ecology-based philosophies derived out of respect for the harmony and balance within all living beings of Creation. Indigenous knowledge occupies itself with the past, present and future. The past guides our present, and in our present we must consider the generations to come. Our ancestors have used their knowledge to respect the laws of Creation, while subsisting on the land, since our earthwalk began. Thus, research that is derived from Indigenous knowledge certainly entails methodologies that demonstrate respect and reverence within these understandings. Indigenous re-search is about being human and calls all human beings to wake from the colonial trance and rejoin the web of life.

My Own Search: A Journey of Making Meaning

> G-chi' manidoo, what is it that you ask of me?
> Chi-Miigwech for helping me on my search
> Help me to listen with an open mind
> And to see with an open heart
> Help me to recognize the leadership and wisdom of those before me
> And to honour the knowledge of those today and those of the past
> Give me the landmarks so that I can remember my own path for those to come.
> Help me to not get lost on this search
> And to gather with humility and integrity
> Zhiway miishnaun G-chi' Manidoo . . .
> Chi'miigwech G'chi'Manido for your guidance
> (Minogiizhigokwe)

My own search involved a process of preparing, searching and making meaning.

---

2. Absolon 1993; Allen 1986; Battiste and Henderson 2000b; Benton-Banai 1988; Brant Castellano 2000; Cajete 2000; Colorado 1988; Fitznor 2002; Graveline 2000; Gunn Allen 1991; Hart 2002 Henderson 2000a; Holmes 2000; Kovach 2005; Martin 2002; Nabigon 2006; Thomas 2005.

Preparing: The Purpose of My Search

I have always known that there are Indigenous ways of searching for knowledge; I just didn't have a path to communicate this. I do now! The purpose of my search was to make what we know visible by identifying what Indigenous methodologies graduate Indigenous re-searchers are using and how they are employing those methodologies within the academy. I want to provide other Indigenous re-searchers with methodological options based in Indigenous worldviews. I chose graduate research theses because they would articulate their methodologies and demonstrate the varied ways that Indigenous researchers are searching in the academy. Like searching for berries, I searched in fields that I was familiar with, which was primarily the social sciences. Searching for these would enable me to reveal and empower Indigenous methodologies and worldviews within re-search contexts.

Searching: How I Searched and What I Did

My gathering process was eclectic, flexible and organic. A multi-method approach best suited the wholism of Indigenous culture (Denzin and Lincoln 2003; Sinclair 2003) and provided rich berries in my search. My search combined the following:

1. a review of selected Indigenous graduate theses;
2. individual conversations with Indigenous searchers; and
3. a group learning circle with Indigenous searchers.

I choose theses by and conversations with Indigenous peoples who were conscious of their own locations: culturally, colonially and politically. I choose theses whose methodologies explicitly revealed an Indigenous consciousness and worldview. I brought to this task my own experiences as an Indigenous re-searcher and much prior reading and study. The first element of my search involved identifying Indigenous graduate re-search projects and re-searchers within the academy m Canada. Before selecting the theses and researchers, I had done a lot of work and reading on Indigenous knowledge and worldview m my life, teaching, research and course work. I came to the. search with my own Indigenous knowledge and understandings. My existing relationships and knowledge of the circle of Indigenous searchers within the Canadian academy allowed me access to people I already had a relationship with and whose research I was aware of. This harvest presents a synthesis of my experiences, the literature and all the berries I gathered during my search.

I cite the written and spoken words of the graduate re-searchers differently than the literature citations. I use only the first names of participants for their written and spoken words. In the written thesis work of participants I cite the year to distinguish the thesis from their spoken voice. In this manner I create space for all the re-searchers to have a central place and voice herein.

Making Meaning: Reading the Landscape of Indigenous Searches

Making meaning implies the process of interpreting and finding meaning in all the berries I gathered. It is also known in its western form as data analysis. Surprisingly, reading other Indigenous theses was delightful. First of all, I thought they would be dry and boring, filled with academic jargon, I wasn't looking forward to reading them at all. Yet, I was searching to see what the landscape looked like. Some theses I couldn't put down because they were so articulate, meaningful and relevant. Some theses were narratives filled with personal stories of the research journey. They helped me demystify my own doctoral search. It was as if I was being mentored and shown how to proceed with my search through the thesis projects. One of my fears of writing was that my writing wouldn't be academic enough, in the western sense. That fear evaporated while reading other Indigenous theses. The most amazing and captivating dissertations were written in very accessible and personal styles. The searchers wove themselves into their projects. Each dissertation was unique and taught me about Indigenous methodology. Reading them excited me and gave me hope that we are making legitimate space for Indigenous methodologies in academic re-search. I encourage others to read projects by Indigenous searchers for they will nurture and nourish you on your search.

Having Conversations

Having conversations meant travelling over the land to meet people in spaces that we both agreed upon. Searching for Indigenous scholars to converse with led to the bluest of blue blueberry patches. While travelling and having conversations about how we search for knowledge I met with leading Indigenous scholars and we shared and wove our stories together. My baskets of knowledge were full and I felt content with this harvest. After gathering berries I now had to make meaning of it all. Making meaning of the conversations refers to analyzing them and turning berries into jam or pie or sauce (Marsden 2005). After all the searching, gathering and making meaning I present this book as my giveaway. To see the details of how I made meaning, go to the Theses Canada web portal to view my full dissertation.

Prayer and dreaming were sources of support, guidance and direction during the phase of analysis and making meaning of the conversations. During this phase I was preoccupied with how I would sort, and more importantly, represent all the information I had gathered. I dreamt of a petal flower, which I use later, where I present the bounty of my harvest.

I felt a strong need to embody the process of working with all the knowledge and information I gathered. Making pies after all is very hands on and creative. So one day, I stopped typing at my computer, got up and started working with textiles and tapestry. Eber Hampton (1995b), in his thesis process, identified his need to set his research aside and return to it to redo the analytic process. Stepping back for a while provided time and space to mentally, emotionally, spiritually and physically breathe, contemplate and reflect on the process. I needed to embody the knowledge that I was working with and do something physical and manual. I chose textiles because I can sew and bead and enjoy creating. From my dream I fashioned a tapestry representation. I pulled out ribbons and assorted materials. After experimenting with a variety of designs I chose black cloth as a background to represent space. A bright red circle surrounds the sunflowers, creating a wholistic framework.

In the centre sits a red circle with a deer hide medicine wheel, representing self and central tendencies. Outside the red circle, sunflowers situated in e our directions represent and reinforce the wholistic nature of Indigenous methodologies All the sunflower appliqués are accompanied with words identifying Indigenous methodological tendencies in search for knowledge. Making meaning involved prayer, dreaming, visual arts and tapestry. Creating this tapestry took me on a journey from my head to my heart and Spirit. It removed me from cerebral analysis and brought me to another level, where I was able to wholistically conceptualize what I had gathered. In creating the tapestry I thought about what I had learnt and what I needed to represent. I thought about my dreams and honoured them. I thought about the people I talked to and whose work I read. As I sewed and embroidered, I embodied my search in the tapestry. I didn't plan on it then, but the tapestry became the local point of sharing in the learning circle.

The Learning Circle as Giving Back

The learning circle is a small group format where the process benefits those who participate m the exchange and sharing of ideas and experiences. The intention of the learning circle was to provide an opportunity for Aboriginal re-searchers/participants to dialogue and share their re-search methodologies and the ways they bring their worldviews into their re-search within the academy. I prayed for direction, somehow trusted the universe, and along came an opportunity. I responded to a call for proposals for the Shawane Uagosiwm Indigenous re-search conference in Winnipeg, Manitoba.[3] The committee welcomed my proposal. At the conference, my session (the learning circle) was open to Indigenous re-searchers wanting to share about Indigenous methodologies.

At the time of the learning circle, I knew that my basket was full and that I did not need to gather anymore. Sharing what I was learning from my search, as a way of giving back and reciprocating other searchers' generosity became my goal. I invited

---

3. Shawane Dagosiwin translates to mean being respectful, caring and passionate about Aboriginal research. This conference was held from 31 May to 2 June 2006.

people to share their ideas, comments and thoughts on Indigenous methodologies m search for knowledge. Mainly, the sharing within the circle validated the information I had already gathered.

Many circle attendees expressed that talking about Indigenous methodologies validated possibilities and gave them hope for how they search for knowledge. The learning circle was a small example of a need for Indigenous searchers to gather and share their experiences, challenges and accomplish-merits. I offered strawberries as a token of my gratitude to the universe and to each person for listening, sharing and attending this learning circle.

These theses, conversations and gatherings are processes within a larger continuum of conversations and work being done among Indigenous researchers. Those I had the privilege of learning from and speaking with are searchers in the academy who are actively engaged in decolonization and liberation of Indigenous peoples. While in the academy, we all struggle to learn, grow, read, search and write from our own cultural, political, spiritual and personal locations. Contributing to the collective good of Indigenous well-being and humanity seems to be a shared goal of Indigenous searchers. The next part is my giveaway of what I found on my search for knowledge.

PART 10

Additional Readings

Absolon, Kathleen E. *Kaandossiwin: How We Come to Know*. Halifax & Winnipeg: Fernwood Publishing, 2011.

Archibald, Jo-Ann Q'um Q'um Xiiem, Jenny Bol Jun Lee-Morgan, and Jason De Santolo. *Decolonizing Research: Indigenous Storywork as Methodology*. London: Zed Books Ltd., 2019.

Kovach, Margaret. *Indigenous Methodologies: Characteristics, Conversations, and Contexts*. Toronto: University of Toronto Press, 2009.

McGregor, Deborah, Jean-Paul Restoule, and Rochelle Johnston. *Indigenous Research: Theories, Practices, and Relationships*. Toronto: Canadian Scholars, 2018.

Moreton-Robinson, Aileen, ed. *Critical Indigenous Studies: Engagement in First World Locations*. Tucson: University of Arizona Press. 2016.

Smith, Linda Tuhiwai. *Decolonizing Methodologies: Research and Indigenous Peoples* 3rd edition. London: Zed Books Ltd. 2021.

Sunseri, Lina. "Indigenous Voice Matters: Claiming our Spaces through Decolonizing Research." *Junctures: The Journal for Thematic Dialogue*. 9, (2007): 93–106.

Wilson, Shawn. *Research is Ceremony: Indigenous Research Methods*. Halifax & Winnipeg: Fernwood Publishing, 2009.

Wilson, Shawn, Andrea V. Breen, and Lindsay Dupré. *Research & Reconciliation: Unsettling Ways of Knowing through Indigenous Relationships*. Toronto: Canadian Scholars, 2019.

Relevant Websites

Indigenous Mentorship Network of Ontario
https://imnp.uwo.ca
The Indigenous Mentorship Network of Ontario provides mentorship to Indigenous scholars to support their community-based health research projects.

Native American and Indigenous Studies Association
https://naisa.org
This is the official website of NAISA, an "international scholarly organization that engages Indigenous issues and communities." NAISA holds an annual meeting, normally in May.

Urban Aboriginal Knowledge Network
https://uakn.org
UAKN is a "research network of urban Aboriginal communities, policy makers and academics, engages in community driven research with the goal of contributing to a better quality of life for urban Aboriginal people."

Films

Onkwanisten'hsera- Mothers of our Nations. Dir. Dawn Martin-Hill. Ontario Federation of Indian Friendship Centres. 2006.
Our People Will Be Healed. Dir. Alanis Obomsawin. National Film Board of Canada. 2017.
The Gift. Dir. Gary Farmer. National Film Board of Canada. 1998.
The Sacred Sundance: The Transfer of a Ceremony. Dir. Brian J. Francis. National Film Board of Canada. 2008.

Key Terms

- Decolonizing research
- Indigenous knowledge
- Indigenous research
- Intellectual imperialism
- Relational accountability

Discussion Questions

1. What is meant by "intellectual imperialism?" What have some of its consequences to traditional Indigenous knowledge been?

2. What is decolonizing research? What is its potential for honouring and reclaiming Indigenous knowledge and methodologies? What are some possible challenges in carrying out decolonizing research in current contexts, both inside and outside of academia?

3. In Chapter 19 it is stated that "Indigenous research methodologies can be understood as processes for establishing, strengthening, and coming into closer relationship with knowledge." In defining research as relationship, what are the 4 specific components of Indigenous research as outlined in the readings? As a researcher, how would one ensure to follow the 4 Rs of Indigenous research?

4. In Chapter 20, Kathleen Absolon describes the research practices and journey undertaken during her research project. Linking this to chapter 19, how were the 4 Rs of Indigenous Research followed?

Activities

Invite a local Indigenous researcher to share their own community-based research with the class, the types of methodologies they used in their research, and how from their perspective, their research could benefit the Indigenous community they worked with.

Browse through the Urban Aboriginal Knowledge Network at https://uakn.org, click their Research tool and browse through some of their listed Research Projects. Select and review one of the research projects, and discuss if/how the researcher(s) practiced the 4 Rs of Indigenous Research discussed by Johnston, McGregor, and Restoule in Chapter 19.

PART 11

Violence and the Construction of Criminality

Editor Introduction

"Cindy Gladue was reduced to a body part" –Globe and Mail, 2015

"Gerald Stanley trial: Jury delivers not guilty verdict in death of Colten Boushie" –The Star Phoenix, 2019

"Tina Fontaine murder case never had a chance" –Winnipeg Sun, 2018

"Report urges more re-investigations into deaths of Indigenous people in Thunder Bay, Ont." –CTV News, 2022

"Overrepresentation of Indigenous women in jails hits record levels in BC: most convictions come from what one expert refers to as survival crimes" –The Tyee, 2022

"Remembering Neil Stonechild and exposing systemic racism in policing" –The Conversation, 2019

The news headlines noted above share something in common. As Starblanket and Hunt (this volume) suggest, the incidents to which they are referring "illustrate . . . the asymmetrical treatment Indigenous peoples receive and are subjected to within the Canadian judicial system, relative to that of non-Indigenous people."

In a democratic society like Canada, supposedly the law and the justice system are to treat all who live within its borders respectfully and equally. In fact, the assumption most people have of the law is that it is fair and objective. But this presumes that the "subject of law is a universal, abstract person. . . . Indeed, law's claim to impartiality is derived from its commitment to the view that it does not deal with different types of people" (Comack and Balfour, 2004: 23). Yet, there are *different* groups with particular race, gender, class, sexuality, abilities, and ethnicities that make distinct subjects of law. Additionally, despite the myth that Canadian law and the justice system have been/are just, fair, and respectful, the reality is that racism is quite present within the legal institutions and practices. A number of studies have shown that racial minorities and Indigenous peoples have experienced racist treatment from the justice system in various ways: by the police, the courts, the enactment of discriminatory laws, and policies (Henry and Tator, 2006: 130).

One only needs to remember that it was the *Indian Act*—a law made by non-Indigenous peoples without the consent or participation of those to whom it was directed—that allowed the establishment of reserves, dispossession of lands, removal of children from their families and their placement in residential schools, and the termination of "Indian status" to those women who married unregistered males. Evidently, Canadian law has not been an instrument of justice for Indigenous peoples; instead, it has been a tool of oppression and colonialism. In this section of the book, the authors provide a critical examination of the relationship Indigenous peoples have had with the Canadian justice system, one rippled with racism, colonialism, and poor socioeconomic conditions.

We begin Part Eleven with an analysis of the **risk factors** associated with Indigenous peoples' overrepresentation in the criminal justice system. Lisa Monchalin in her chapter asserts that high residential mobility, poor living and housing conditions, poor health, low education, poor employment and low income, and unstable family environment are all linked with the cycle of crime and violence that impact Indigenous peoples in Canadian society. The symptoms of this link are visible in the high rates of suicide, addiction, and overrepresentation in the justice system. We must not view these risk factors as individual or cultural deficiencies, but rather, root them in a long history of colonialism and racism, which has resulted in Indigenous people's subjugation and discrimination in various social institutions.

The frequent residential mobility and poor living and housing conditions that many Indigenous peoples experience throughout their lives place them under a lot of stress and anxiety, leading to a higher likelihood of poverty. As Monchalin points out, "poverty is a risk factor linked to crime . . . temptation to escape from these conditions perhaps by breaking rules or through taking drugs and alcohol use." Low education is another risk factor that contributes to the overrepresentation of Indigenous peoples in the criminal justice system. Due to the legacy of residential schooling, limited opportunities for proper academic achievements in Indigenous communities, racism, and culturally irrelevant curricula in schools, many Indigenous youth do not complete high school. Ultimately this decreases their future employment and income opportunities, consequently increasing their risk of a cycle of poverty and crime. Unstable family environments, often leading to trauma, abuse, removal of children from their homes and communities, and negative experiences within the foster care system are other factors to consider when analyzing youth's vulnerability to violence and crime. The case of Tina Fontaine, mentioned above, illustrates the fatal consequence of such unstable family environments and the failure of the child welfare system to properly protect her, as she became a victim of crime. To this day, justice has yet to be served to her and her family/community.

Monchalin highlights the need for Indigenous-focused interventions, social programs, and support systems that acknowledge the root causes of overrepresentation of Indigenous peoples in the criminal justice system. She is concerned with reducing the risk factors to break the cycle of crime. Importantly, this would mean disrupting the racism and colonialism that still exist in social institutions, including the legal one, which continues to place Indigenous peoples in oppressive social conditions that limit their chances to live a life free of violence and crime. Many non-Indigenous either overtly deny the existence of racism and colonialism, or these are invisible to them, while Indigenous peoples continuously experience both in their lives, impacting their opportunities and shaping their social interacions with non-Indigenous people and Canadian social institutions. In their chapter, Starblanket and Hunt show how such denial and invisibility of racism and colonialism is part of a larger settler narrative that has been a mechanism of injustice and oppression against Indigenous peoples, especially in the Prairies. They analyze the case of Gerald Stanley, the man who shot to death Colten Boushie, an Indigenous youth, for trespassing on his farm property.

As Starblanket and Hunt point out, race/racism/colonialism were left out as possible mitigating factors to consider throughout the trial, "despite the rampant proliferation of settler stereotypes and assumptions about Indigenous peoples in the area." Such dismissal of racism in the criminal justice system is not an anomaly. In the early 2000s, when an inquiry report on the death of Neil Stonechild, an Indigenous male who was left to freeze to death by the Saskatoon police, came out, racism was also not explicitly named as the main cause of his unjust treatment by the police. As Green (2006) maintains, the report failed to recognize the structural and systemic element of racism and only treated it as a consequence of a "chasm" between the different communities.

Starblanket and Hunt maintain that the denial of race and colonialism on the part of non-Indigenous people, particularly those in the legal systems, are part of the overall settler narrative that has tried to eradicate Indigenous peoples from their lands, often by producing **treaty mythologies** and racist stereotypes of Indigenous peoples, both resulting in the criminalization of Indigenous peoples. Over time, they argue, the Canadian legal system, particularly in the Prairies, has favoured the rights of white settlers over those of Indigenous peoples. They write: "state institutions . . . operate to mask the frequent and extreme forms of violence that Indigenous people face when interacting with them." There is a continued refusal to know and name racism and colonialism in both the Stonechild report and the Gerald Stanley case. Starblanket and Hunt ask: how can we believe that the persistent racial tensions between Indigenous and non-Indigenous people, and racial stereotypes of Indigenous peoples that penetrate their interactions, did not affect at all what occurred between Stanley and Boushie at Stanley's farm? In order to truly transform the Canadian criminal justice system, we need to stop this discourse of denial. We also need to address the overall risk factors rooted in racism and colonialism that continue to disproportionally affect Indigenous peoples' interactions within it.

CHAPTER 21

Crimes Affecting Indigenous Peoples

Over-Representation, Explanations, and Risk Factors

Lisa Monchalin

INDIGENOUS PEOPLES ARE NOTABLY over-represented in the criminal justice system, both as victims and as those incarcerated.[1] This development is not new. It has been well documented for decades. What has been termed "over-representation," however, is clear evidence

---

Lisa Monchalin, "Crime Affecting Indigenous Peoples: Over-Representation, Explanations, and Risk Factors." In *The Colonial Problem: An Indigenous Perspective on Crime and Injustice in Canada*, Toronto: University of Toronto Press, © 2016.

1. Samuel Perreault, "Violent Victimization of Aboriginal People in the Canadian Provinces, 2009," *Juristat* 30, no. 44 (2011): 1–35; Samuel Perreault, "Admissions to Adult Correctional Services in Canada, 2011/2012," *Juristat* 34, no. 1 (2014).

of a major injustice, one resulting from the centuries of subjugation and mistreatment Indigenous peoples have experienced in this country, from the devastating consequences of having been, and of continuing to be, targets of colonization. We must acknowledge, consequently, that a large portion of the over-representation of Indigenous peoples in the criminal justice system is due to systemic issues of racism and discrimination and not because actual crimes have been committed.

The Victimization of Indigenous Peoples

The reality is that crime hurts—and it has always hurt. It hurt when it was committed against Indigenous peoples in the residential schools, and it hurts now because ongoing colonialism and oppression and the legacies from these experiences compound and make Indigenous peoples even more susceptible to victimization. This susceptibility is well documented. As compared to non-Indigenous groups, Indigenous peoples were,

- twice as likely to report being the victim of violent assault (i.e., physical or sexual assault or robbery) in 2009;[2]
- about six times more likely to be the victims of homicide in 2014; and[3]
- at a higher risk of being victimized multiple time.[4]

The General Social Survey undertaken in 2009 by Statistics Canada shows that 37 per cent of Indigenous peoples (aged 15 years or older) reported being a victim of a crime compared to 26 per cent of non-Indigenous peoples.[5] This is equivalent to almost 322,000 Indigenous peoples aged 15 years or older being victimized annually, an average of about 882 victimizations every day.

Indigenous women experience violence at a higher rate than any other group of women in Canada. Monture Angus explains that, for many Indigenous women, violence began in childhood and is a result of generationally layered violence. As she states, "Violence is not just a mere incident in the lives of Aboriginal women. Violence does not just span a given number of years. It is our lives. And it is in our histories. For most Aboriginal women, violence has not been escapable."[6] . . .

Resilience and Risk Factors
High Residential Mobility and Poor Living Conditions

Research shows that residential mobility—meaning moving from dwelling to dwelling on a frequent basis—is linked to higher rates of crime.[7] Many times, people and families move because of their poor socioeconomic status and limited access to proper housing, so poverty and low income are risk factors related to residential mobility. Physical environments, such as poor living conditions and crowded housing, can put stress on people and families, who are forced to live in close quarters and who struggle to make ends meet with seemingly no hope for a better future.[8] Some might turn to substance

2. Samuel Perreault, Violent Victimization of Aboriginal People in the Canadian Provinces, 2009 (Ottawa: Canadian Centre for Justice Statistics, 2011).

3. Leah Mulligan and Zoran Miladinovic, Homicide in Canada 2014 (Ottawa: Canadian Centre for Justice Statistics, 2015), 16.

4. Perreault, Violent Victimization of Aboriginal People, 7.

5. Ibid.

6. This paragraph, including the quote, draws on Monture-Angus, Thunder in My Soul, 170.

7. Robert J. Sampson and W. Byron Groves, "Community Structure and Crime: Testing Social Disorganization Theory," American Journal of Sociology 94, no. 4 (1989): 774–802.

8. Robin T. Fitzgerald and Peter J. Carrington, "The Neighbourhood Context of Urban Aboriginal Crime," The Canadian Journal of Criminology and Criminal Justice 50, no. 5 (2008): 523–557; Cathleen Knotsch and Dianne Kinnon, If Not Now . . . When: Addressing the Ongoing Inuit Housing Crisis in Canada (Ottawa: National Aboriginal Health Organization, 2011), 28; La Prairie, Dimensions of Aboriginal Over-Representation; La Prairie, "Aboriginal Over-Representation in the Criminal Justice System"; Charlotte Loppie Reading and Fred Wien, Health Inequalities and Social Determinants of Aboriginal Peoples' Health (Prince George, BC: National Collaborating Centre for Aboriginal Health, 2009), 3; J. Reading, The Crisis of Chronic Disease Among Aboriginal Peoples: A Challenge for Public Health, Population Health, and Social Policy (Victoria, BC: Centre for Aboriginal Health Research, 2009), 13.

abuse to alleviate the stress that accompanies this lack of resources or hope, or just the discomfort of sharing poor conditions and cramped living quarters. Regardless, living in a state of perpetual stress affects even an individual's body chemistry.

Indigenous peoples are more likely to be poor, to live in inadequate housing, and to have high rates of residential mobility as compared to non-Indigenous peoples. According to the 2001 census, over a 12-month period, one in five Indigenous peoples moved compared to one in seven for the general Canadian population.[9] Throughout the 1990s and 2000s, Indigenous peoples moved to cities from First Nation communities in increasing numbers, and now the majority live in urban areas (54 per cent in 2006).[10] When relocating from First Nation communities or remote communities to the city, many Indigenous people move to inner cities, as is the case in Winnipeg or Toronto, typically attracted there by lower housing prices and the presence of members of their family and community.[11] Unfortunately, moving to the inner city is usually a move from one marginalized community into another.[12] In Winnipeg for example, Indigenous peoples are disproportionately located in the inner-city area, with approximately 44 per cent of Winnipeg's Indigenous peoples residing there. The Winnipeg inner city has approximately 120,000 people in total, and Indigenous peoples constitute 20 per cent of this total, compared to a concentration of only 6 per cent in the remainder of the city.[13]

Furthermore, although the size of the disparity is declining,[14] Indigenous peoples are more likely than non-Indigenous peoples to live in crowded living conditions. In 2006, Indigenous peoples were almost four times as likely compared to non-Indigenous peoples to live in a crowded dwelling. They were also three times more likely than non-Indigenous peoples to live in a dwelling requiring major repairs, a rate unchanged since 1996.[15]

Some northern or remote Indigenous communities, and some Indigenous accommodations in inner cities, offer what can be described as third-world living conditions.[16] On October 28, 2011, the First Nation community of Attawapiskat declared a state of emergency because of a housing crisis. At the time, this community had just over 1,500 residents. After declaring a state of emergency, Attawapiskat received support from the Canadian Red Cross Society, which flew in various emergency supplies. Aid workers found community members living in makeshift tents, sheds, or shacks with plywood walls, or in condemned houses with fire and water damage.[17] Many of these places had black mould and no running water, electricity, insulation, or proper heating. Many families living in these poor conditions had children. In at least one case, a single mother with multiple children was living in a shed with no heat. With winter fast approaching in October of 2011, the community needed to get people into adequate accommodations quickly, so they could survive the cold season. In Attawapiskat, average lows reach below freezing from October through April.

In December of 2011, the government announced that it would finally send Attawapiskat

9. *Statistics Canada, 2001 Census: Analysis Series Aboriginal Peoples of Canada—A Demographic Profile (Ottawa: Minister of Industry, 2003)*, 11.

10. Statistics Canada, *Aboriginal Peoples in Canada in 2006: Inuit, Métis, and First Nations 2006 Census Findings* (Ottawa: Minister of Industry, 2008), http://wwwl2.statcan.ca/census-recensement/2006/as-sa/97–558/pdf/97-558-XIE2006001.pdf (accessed February 19, 2013); Statistics Canada, *2001 Census: Analysis Series Aboriginal Peoples of Canada*.

11. Jim Silver, with Joan Hay, Parvin Ghorayshi, Darlene Klyne, Peter Gorzen, Cyril Keeper, Michael Mackenzie, and Freeman Simard, *In Their Own Voices: Building Urban Aboriginal Communities* (Halifax: Fernwood Publishing, 2006), 16–17.

12. Ibid., 17.

13. These numbers and percentages are derived from a Statistics Canada custom tabulation based on 2001 census data, cited by Tom Carter, *Planning for Newcomers in Winnipeg's Inner City* (Winnipeg: Metropolis, 2009), 1.

14. In 2006, 11 per cent of Indigenous people were living in homes with more than one person per room, which is down from 17 per cent in 1996, according to Statistics Canada.

15. Statistics Canada, *Aboriginal Peoples in Canada in 2006*, 16.

16. See the following documentary films for examples, *Third World Canada*, DVD, directed by Andrée Cazabon (Ottawa: Productions Cazabon, 2010); *The Invisible Nation*, DVD, directed by Richard Dejardins and Robert Monderie (Ottawa: The National Film Board of Canada, 2007); *The People of the Kattawapiskak River*, DVD, directed by Alanis Obomsawin (Ottawa: The National Film Board of Canada, 2012).

17. For the details of the situation discussed here, see *The People of the Kattawapiskak River*.

22 modular homes, as well as some toilets and wood stoves. After waiting for the ice roads to freeze and become useable, the community finally received their homes in February 2012. Today, people have moved into these homes and some conditions have improved. Unfortunately, some in the community still live in mould-filled, condemned homes and sleep on cots in the healing lodge. As well, many people live in a dangerously overcrowded construction trailer (acquired from the nearby diamond mine after the company no longer had use for it). No long-term plan is in place to address the housing problem in Attawapiskat.

Attawapiskat is only one example. There are numerous communities in Canada facing similar issues. For instance, in December of 2012, just one year after Attawapiskat declared a housing crisis, Kashechewan, a neighbouring First Nation community, also declared a state of emergency. This community had 21 houses that were unfit for people to live in and survive a winter. Kashechewan was also running out of fuel, so it could no longer provide heat to homes and other buildings. In November 2011, the community had to shut down two schools, the power-generation station, the fire hall, and a health clinic because they could no longer be heated and safely operated. Fortunately, just in time, the government released funds for emergency supplies to fix the 21 houses and for fuel. Yet this First Nation community, like Attawapiskat and many others across the country, has no long-term, sustainable plan to address the linked crises of inadequate housing and poverty. In December 2012, NDP MP Charlie Angus stated that First Nation communities in his riding alone declared 13 emergencies in just 7 years, the majority of which were associated with poor

infrastructure. He went on to state, "We're always putting Band-Aids on septic wounds."[18]

What relationship do these often appalling conditions have to crime? Aside from the fact that poverty is a risk factor related to crime, imagine the difficulty, when living in these conditions, of deferring to the "way things are" and the structures and authorities that seem to keep them from changing. Imagine how hard it might be to keep even one's self-respect strong. Then imagine the temptation of escape, perhaps by breaking rules or through drug and alcohol use. As we have already seen, the consequences of yielding to these temptations, even a few times, can be more serious for Indigenous peoples than for others in terms of their relation to the criminal justice system.

Poor Health, Suicide, and Addictions

. . . Living in and trying to survive conditions of such poverty and despair has sadly led some Indigenous peoples down the road of suicide, heavy drinking, or addictions. Some of the remote First Nation communities described previously have the highest rates of suicide in Canada. In fact, the community of Pikangikum was described by sociologist Colin Samson as having one of the highest rates of suicide in the world, when its 2000 rate soared to 470 deaths per 100,000 people.[19] Suicide rates in First Nations communities have been recorded at twice the general Canadian rates. Among Inuit, the rate is even higher, being 6 to 11 times greater than that of the general population.[20]

Research has also shown heavy drinking to be linked with suicidal behaviour and to suicide and deaths from unintentional injury.[21] As Kirmayer

18. *For this crisis in Kashechewan, see Heather Scoffield, "Neighbouring Reserve to Attawapiskat Narrowly Avoids Fuel, Housing Crisis," Globe and Mail, December 2 2012, http://www.theglobeandmail.com/news/national/neighbouring-reserve-to-attawapiskat-narrowly-avoids-fuel-housing-crisis/article5899087/ (accessed February 17, 2013); the quotation is also from this article.*

19. Louise Elliott, "Ontario Native Suicide Rate One of the Highest in World, Expert Says," *Canadian Press,* November 27, 2000, http://www.hartford-hwp.com/archives/41/353.html.

20. Laurence J. Kirmayer, Gregory M. Brass, Tara Holton, Ken Paul, Cori Simpson, and Caroline Tait, *Suicide Among Aboriginal People in Canada* (Ottawa: The Aboriginal Healing Foundation, 2007), 1; see also, Laurence Kirmayer, Cori Simpson, and Margaret Cargo, "Healing Traditions: Culture, Community and Mental Health Promotion with Canadian Aboriginal Peoples," *Australasian Psychiatry* 11 (2003): S15–S23.

21. Iris Wagman Borowsky, Michael D. Resnick, Marjorie Ireland, and Robert W. Blum, "Suicide Attempts Among American Indian and Alaska Native Youth: Risk and Protective Factors," *Archives of Pediatrics and Adolescent Medicine* 153, no. 6 (1999): 573–580; Paul Kettl and Edward O. Bixler, "Alcohol and Suicide in Alaska Natives," *American Indian and Alaska Native Mental Health Research* 5, no. 2 (1993): 34–45; J. Paul Seale, Sylvia Shellenberger, and John Spence, "Alcohol Problems in Alaska Natives: Lessons from the Inuit," *American Indian & Alaskan Native Mental Health Research: The Journal of the National Center* 13, no. 1 (2006): 1–30, 2.

and his colleagues note, "Alcohol or drug intoxication may disinhibit the behaviour of individuals, contributing to the risk of suicide."[22] Yet, contrary to the horrible "drunken Indian" stereotype, many Indigenous peoples refrain from drinking alcohol. In fact, research has shown that abstinence was actually almost two times more frequent among Indigenous peoples than among non-Indigenous peoples in 1991.[23] . . .

. . . Some Indigenous peoples have indeed turned to alcohol or other substances as a way to cope with current situations of poverty and despair. According to a 2007 study, alcohol and drug abuse are cited as the most dominant types of addictive behaviours faced by Indigenous peoples in Canada.[24] For example, in some northern Innu communities, addiction to huffing solvents has been a major worry for decades. Left with no hope and living in despair, some Innu youth sniff gas or turn to suicide to escape their realities. In 2012, estimates from the RCMP suggest that about 40 to 50 per cent of Innu *children* living in the community of Natuashish are addicted to sniffing gas.[25] . . .

According to psychology professor Bruce. Alexander, people who are chronically and severely dislocated are vulnerable to addictions. As he says, "the historical correlation between severe dislocation and addiction is strong.[26] He further points out that no anthropological research shows Indigenous peoples to have had addictions before the arrival of Europeans in Canada. He contends that the dislocation of Indigenous peoples by Europeans is the ultimate precursor of addiction for Indigenous peoples. Research has shown that addictive behaviours

and substance abuse have taken a terrible toll on Indigenous peoples and contribute significantly to instances of accidents, death, disease, and illness, as well as to violence.[27]

Education and Academic Advancement

Research shows that those who advance educationally and occupationally are much less likely to be engaged in crime and much less likely to be arrested as compared to those who do not.[28] But not all people have or are able to take advantage of opportunities for advancement, and unequal access affects people early in life. When children and youth have limited opportunities for academic advancement (such as when they live in poverty or despair), their academic ambitions can decrease. When opportunities for educational advancement are available and are supported, students are opened up to more options for a viable future.

Even though Indigenous peoples have had rapidly increasing levels of educational attainment, they still lag behind the general Canadian population. In 2006, 32 per cent of Indigenous peoples in Canada were without a secondary school diploma while non-Indigenous peoples without a diploma made up only 15 per cent of the population.[29] According to a 2007–10 survey, the high-school dropout rate among Indigenous peoples aged 20 to 24, who were not living in their First Nation community, was 22.6 per cent, compared to 8.5 per cent for non-Indigenous peoples.[30] In June 2011, the Assembly

22. *Kirmayer, Fraser, Fauras, and Whitley, Current Approaches, 15.*

23. See Royal Commission on Aboriginal Peoples, *Bridging the Cultural Divide: A Report on Aboriginal People and Criminal Justice in Canada* (Ottawa: Supply and Services Canada, 1996). This report came to this conclusion after examining several studies.

24. Chansonneuve, *Addictive Behaviours.*

25. CBC, "Politicians Weight in on Gas Sniffing in Natuashish," *CBC News,* September 21, 2012, http://www.cbc.ca/news/canada/newfoundland-labrador/politicians-weigh-in-on-gas-sniffing-in-natuashish-1.1146972 (accessed February 18, 2013).

26. Bruce K. Alexander, *The Roots of Addiction in Free Market Society* (Vancouver: Canadian Centre for Policy Alternatives, 2001), 13, 14. I draw on this source for the next two sentences.

27. Chansonneuve, *Addictive Behaviours,* 28.

28. Robert J. Sampson and John H, Laub, *Crime in the Making: Pathways and Turning Points Through Life* (Cambridge, MA: Harvard University Press, 1993), 147.

29. Daniel Wilson and David MacDonald, *The Income Gap Between Aboriginal Peoples and the Rest of Canada* (Ottawa: Canadian Centre for Policy Alternatives, 2010), 15.

30. Jason Gilmore, *Trends in Dropout Rates and the Labour Market Outcomes of Young Dropouts* (Ottawa: Labour Statistics Division, Statistics Canada, 2010).

of First Nations reported that Indigenous students living in First Nation communities have a kindergarten to grade 12 completion rate of 49 per cent. In fact, the group declared, it is statistically more likely that students from First Nation communities will go to jail than graduate from high school.[31]

Many First Nation schools in Canada today are in a deplorable condition, and their students continue to be plagued by serious health concerns. For example, a 2011 report written by Gitxsan activist and academic Cindy Blackstock describes a First Nation school in Manitoba that had to be closed and replaced with portable trailers because it was "infested with snakes." The water system at this particular school had become overrun with the snakes, so "when children turned on the taps, baby snakes would come out."[32] This situation sounds like a nightmare come to life. This same report tells of another First Nations school in Manitoba that began its 2009 school year in tents because no building was available in the community.

Even when school buildings exist, they are sometimes so overcrowded that children have to go to school in shifts. It is also routine for many children living in First Nation communities to be sent away from their families and homes to attend school. This circumstance echoes the traumas of residential schools. In 2011, the Assembly of First Nations reported that 40 First Nation communities had no schools and that, in some First Nation communities, children had not been to school in more than two years.[33]

Clearly, Indigenous children living in their First Nation communities face major educational challenges, but the situation for Indigenous peoples living outside their First Nation communities is also a struggle. For example, Winnipeg, which has the highest percentage of urban Indigenous peoples in Canada as well as the largest total number of Indigenous peoples of any major city in Canada, has educational attainment rates that are much lower for Indigenous peoples as compared to non-Indigenous peoples.[34] In 2006, about 30 per cent of Indigenous peoples in Winnipeg between the ages of 25 and 64 did not have a certificate, diploma, or degree, compared to only 13 per cent of the non-Indigenous population in the same age group. Also in 2006 Indigenous youth aged 15 to 24 living in Winnipeg were found to have lower school attendance rates compared to non-Indigenous peoples, with a 58 per cent attendance rate for Indigenous youth compared to 66 per cent for non-Indigenous youth.

In 2002, a study investigating the educational circumstances of Indigenous students in Winnipeg's inner-city high schools provided a clear explanation of why the Winnipeg school system seemed to be failing Indigenous peoples. Interviews were conducted with 47 Indigenous students in the inner-city high schools, 50 Indigenous school leavers, 25 adult members of the Indigenous community, and 10 teachers, 7 of whom were Indigenous. The study concluded that the school system marginalizes Winnipeg's Indigenous students, as it does not adequately reflect their cultural values or their daily realities and feels alien to many Indigenous peoples.[35] Furthermore, the prevalence of institutional forms of racism as well as evident, direct racist actions and attitudes, including name-calling and stereotyping, was very high. The school system was described as non-Indigenous, overly Eurocentric, and colonial. For example, there were very few Indigenous teachers and very little Indigenous content in the curriculum. Some text-books still explained history in terms of the West being settled by persons of non-Indigenous ancestry, referred to as "we," thus placing Indigenous students in the less desirable "other" category.

31. *This information comes directly from the Assembly of First Nations, "Fact Sheet—Quality of Life of First Nations, June 2011," http://www. afn.ca/uploads/files/factsheets/quality_of_life_final_fe.pdf (accessed February 18, 2013).*

32. This and the following paragraph's details, including the quote, are found in Blackstock, *Jordan & Shannen*, 7.

33. Assembly of First Nations, "Fact Sheet—Quality of Life of First Nations, June 2011," http://www.afn.ca/uploads/files/factsheets/quality_of_life_final_fe.pdf.

34. Statistics for Winnipeg are from Statistics Canada, *2006 Aboriginal Population Profile for Winnipeg* (Ottawa: Minister of Industry, 2008), https://www12.statcan.gc.ca/census-recensement/2006/as-sa/97-558/p3-eng.cfm#01 (accessed February 19, 2013).

35. Jim Silver and Kathy Mallett with Janice Greene and Freeman Simard, *Aboriginal Education in Winnipeg Inner City High Schools* (Winnipeg: Canadian Centre for Policy Alternatives–Manitoba, 2002); for the following material on textbooks, see 26.

... First Nation communities, Indigenous educators, and their allies have been working to address the clear gaps in curriculum across the country, for example, by developing improved curriculum, promoting the certification of more Indigenous teachers, increasing cross-cultural awareness among students and teachers, and sharing resources and supports to improve educational outcomes for Indigenous students.[36] New Indigenous-focused schools have opened in urban areas, such as the one in Vancouver's Sir William Macdonald Elementary School. In 2011, this school opened to both Indigenous and non-Indigenous students from kindergarten to grade three. The curriculum is explained as being "respectful of local First Nations and the shared values, experiences and histories of all Aboriginal peoples. It is respectful of the shared history between Aboriginal peoples and Canada and about a shared world view between Aboriginal people and environmentalists."[37] In December 2015, the Winnipeg School Division announced that they would be establishing Cree and Ojibway bilingual language programs at their Isaac Brock School in Winnipeg, set to begin in September 2016.[38]

However, too few schools in Canada have been proactive in finding ways to improve curriculum, to prioritize Indigenous education, or to implement new polices and guidelines.[39] Both Indigenous and non-Indigenous students are still largely experiencing "the same limited and narrow curriculum." Seeds of racism are sown very early when the school curriculum is not reflective of the realities and cultures of all students, and this stereotyping in education "contributes to the lack of Canadian understanding of Aboriginal rights, culture, and traditions." More related to the point of this chapter is that Indigenous children who experience this racism and are made to feel inferior or like outsiders are more likely to become disengaged and to drop out of school, which puts them at more risk when it comes to poverty and crime.

Employment and Income

Research shows that unemployment is associated with physical and mental health problems such as stress, anxiety, depression, and increased suicide rates.[40] And it just makes sense that an employed person with an income sufficient to sustain self and family has less stress. Being employed also correlates to having a good education and to being less likely to engage in criminal activity. Studies show that people with access to quality education in their elementary and high school years and who graduate are less likely to commit crimes, as they are more likely to have stable families and to achieve employment.[41] According to the 2012 Aboriginal Peoples Survey, Indigenous adults (aged 18 to 44) who graduated from high school were more likely to be employed than those who did not.[42] Obviously, the education gap between Indigenous people and non-Indigenous people has long-term implications for earning sufficient income. Indeed, Indigenous peoples in Canada have high rates of unemployment as compared to non-Indigenous peoples. In 2006, the census showed that the unemployment rate for Indigenous people (aged 25 to 64) remained almost three times the rate for non-Indigenous people, with unemployment for Indigenous peoples at 13 per cent compared to 5 per cent for non-Indigenous peoples.[43]

36. *Coalition for the Advancement of Aboriginal Studies, Learning About Walking in Beauty*, 15.

37. Vancouver School Board, *Aboriginal Focus School*, http://www.vsb.bc.ca/aboriginal-school (accessed March 13, 2014).

38. John Woods, "Winnipeg School Division Adds Ojibway, Cree, Spanish, French Programs," *Winnipeg Free Press*, December 8, 2015, http://www.winnipegfreepress.com/local/Winnipeg-School-Division-adds-Ojibway Cree-Spanish-French-programs-360911701.html (accessed December 8, 2015).

39. The details of this paragraph, including the quote, can be found in Coalition for the Advancement of Aboriginal Studies, *Learning About Walking in Beauty*, 15, 16.

40. Juha Mikkonen and Dennis Raphael, *Social Determinants of Health: The Canadian Facts* (Toronto: York University School of Health Policy and Management, 2010), www.thecanadianfacts.org/The_Canadian_Facts.pdf (accessed February 18, 2013).

41. Dana Mitra, *Pennsylvania's Best Invesment: The Social and Economic Benefits of Public Education* (Philadelphia: Education Law Centre, 2011).

42. Evelyn Bougie, Karen Kelly-Scott, and Paula Arriagada, *The Education and Employment Experiences of First Nations People Living Off Reserve, Inuit, and Métis.* (Ottawa: Statistics Canada, 2013).

43. Aboriginal Affairs and Northern Development Canada, "Fact Sheet: 2006 Census Aboriginal Demographics," http://www.aadnc-aandc.gc.ca/eng/1100100016377/1100100016378 (accessed March 23, 2014).

Ultimately, as mentioned, the criminological research proves that lack of employment and income are risk factors for crime. And Indigenous peoples are placed at a disadvantage when it comes to getting and keeping work and receiving equitable wages. In part, this disadvantage stems from the educational gap between them and non-Indigenous peoples, but racism is also a significant factor. At an even deeper level, Indigenous people may feel that the whole system of employment and education—indeed, the complete structure of Euro-Canadian society—is culturally foreign, or even criminal, based as it is upon competitive production and consumption that discounts their ancestral teachings.

Family Environment and Child Welfare

Indigenous children are also less likely than non-Indigenous children to live with both parents. In 2001, twice as many Indigenous children lived with a lone parent compared to non-Indigenous children.[44] We know from countless research studies that the presence of two nurturing parents in the home serves as a protective factor against crime.[45] Thus, the chances of becoming involved with crime, as either victim or offender, are lower if one grows up with two nurturing parents in the home as opposed to one. . . .

. . . a stable family environment serves as a protective factor against crime . . . a supportive environment can reduce their children's risk of suffering early childhood trauma, which could increase susceptibility to crime . . . residential schools disrupted Indigenous people's families, taking children away from parents during critical times in their development. In 1951, around the time these schools started to close, a new section was added to the Indian Act entitled "General provincial laws applicable to Indians." That section (s. 88) states that "all laws of general application from time to time in force in any province are applicable to and in respect of Indians in the province, except to the extent that those laws are inconsistent with this Act" or with other similar legislation.[46] This new section cleared the way for provincial laws to apply to Indigenous peoples living in First Nation communities.

Following this change, provinces began to take Indigenous children from their homes in abominable numbers—by applying provincial child welfare laws in First Nation communities.[47] According to Lynda Gray (member of the Tsimshian Nation), these laws were not in line with Indigenous values but rather with Eurocentric beliefs and customs. When there were real safety issues in the home, she states, Indigenous families were given no support to help them deal with the intergenerational impacts of neglect and abuse resultant from residential schools.

From the 1960s through to the mid-1980s, thousands of Indigenous children were taken from their families and put into the child welfare system.[48] Many were either put into foster care or put up for adoption during what has come to be known as the "sixties scoop."[49] Patrick Johnston first coined this term in a 1983 report he wrote for the Canadian Council on Social Development.[50] Johnston recalled that he got the term from a British Columbian social worker, who told him ". . . with tears in her eyes—that it was common practice in BC in the mid-sixties to 'scoop' from their mothers on reserves almost all newly born children."[51] Many times,

44. *Statistics Canada, 2001 Census*, 9.

45. Rolf Loeber and David P.Farrington, "Young Children Who Commit Crime: Epidemiology, Developmental Origins, Risk Factors, Early Interventions, and Policy Implications," *Development and Psychopathology* 12, no.4 (2000): 737–752.

46. Indian Act, RSC 1985, c I-5. at s. 88.

47. For this paragraph, I have drawn on Lynda Gray, *First Nations 101: Tons of Stuff You Need to Know about First Nations People* (Vancouver: Adaawx Publishing, 2011), 65–66.

48. Raven Sinclair, "Identity Lost and Found: Lessons from the Sixties Scoop," *First Peoples Child & Family Review* 3, no. 1 (2007): 65–82, 65–66.

49. Marlyn Bennett, Cindy Blackstock, and Richard De La Ronde, *A Literature Review and Annotated Bibliography on Aspects of Aboriginal Child Welfare in Canada*, 2nd edition (Ottawa: First Nations Child and Family Caring Society, 2005), 22.

50. Patrick Johnston, *Aboriginal Children and the Child Welfare System* (Toronto: Canadian Council on Social Development, 1983).

51. For the quote and subsequent details, see Sinclair, "Identity Lost and Found," 66.

children were fostered or adopted out to other provinces. In some cases, children were adopted out to the United States or overseas. Approximately 70 per cent of the adopted children were placed with non-Indigenous families. Furthermore, there was often inadequate to no screening of families to ensure their suitability, and, although money was exchanged during adoption, especially when cases involved private American adoption agencies, no record exists of any money reaching the children's families.[52]

Many Indigenous children are still under the authority of the child welfare system. Indeed, Cree scholar Lauri Gilchrist of Lakehead University has described a recent "scoop" of Indigenous children as the "millennium scoop."[53] It is a scoop driven by systemic discrimination coupled with the federal government's severe underfunding of First Nations child welfare agencies.[54] . . . About 27,000 Indigenous children were in state care as of 2006; the Assembly of First Nations estimates that the number had not changed substantially as of 2010.[55] In 2008, Canada's auditor general estimated that First Nations children were six to eight times more likely to be put into foster care than other children, citing neglect as the key reason for these children's over-representation in care. Often, this neglect is driven by substance abuse or by influences typically beyond parents' control, such as poor housing and poverty.[56]

Though this problem is well known, the current government has done little to make essential changes to the existing child welfare system. Data from fiscal year 2009–10 show that First Nations Child and Family Service agencies receive approximately 22 per cent less funding than provincial agencies.[57] Also, an evaluation of the antiquated formula used to fund First Nations child and family services (Directive 20–1) shows that it currently steers agencies toward the most disruptive and expensive care options—foster care, group homes, and institutional care—because only these agency costs are fully reimbursed.[58] A result is that most Indigenous children are placed in non-Indigenous settings, where it is difficult to be exposed to and learn about Indigenous teachings and to develop a cultural identity.[59] Recent longitudinal research from the United States has proven that those who grow up in the foster care system are highly likely to become involved in crime later in life given their lack of a strong and stable nurturing family environment.[60] Given the instability in their lives, many also struggle to find jobs and adequate housing and find it hard to complete their education.

Indigenous Peoples: Young and Growing

As a result of the disruptions of colonialism, not to mention the attempts to eradicate "Indians," the numbers of Indigenous peoples diminished for a time. But now, Indigenous peoples are gaining in

52. *For abuses see, Bennett, Blackstock, De La Ronde, A Literature Review and Annotated Bibliography on Aspects of Aboriginal Child Welfare in Canada, 19–20.*

53. Sinclair, "Identity Lost and Found," 67.

54. Cindy Blackstock, John Loxlely, Tara Prakash, and Fred Wien, *Wen:de: We Are Coming to the Light of Day* (Ottawa: First Nations Child and Family Caring Society of Canada, 2005).

55. Assembly of First Nations, *Leadership Action Plan on First Nations Child Welfare* (Ottawa: Assembly of First Nations, 2006), 1, http://www. turtleisland.org/healing/afncf.pdf (accessed December 19, 2012); Assembly of First Nations, "Fact Sheet–Child Welfare, October 2013," http://www.afh.ca/uploads/files/13-02-23_fact_sheet_-_child_welfare_updated_fe.pdf.

56. Blackstock, *Jordan & Shannen*, 4.

57. Native Women's Association of Canada, *Special Submission to the Expert Mechanism on the Rights of Indigenous Peoples (EMRIP) on Access to Justice for Aboriginal Women in Canada,* March 10 (Ottawa: NWAC, 2014), 5.

58. Indian and Northern Affairs Canada, *Evaluation of the First Nations Child and Family Service Program* (Gatineau, QC: Indian and Northern Affairs Canada, Department of Audit and Evaluation Branch, 2007), 35, http://www.aadnc-aandc.gc.ca/DAM/DAM-INTER-HQ/STAGING/texte-text/aev_pubs_ev_06-07_1332356163901_eng.pdf (accessed January 16, 2013).

59. Mark Totten, "Preventing Aboriginal Youth Gang Involvement in Canada: A Gendered Approach," paper prepared for the Aboriginal Policy Research Conference, Ottawa, March 2009, 8, http://www.turtleisland.org/resources/gangsnwac09.pdf (accessed January 16).

60. This and the following sentence are informed by Mark E. Courtney, Amy Dworsky, Adam Brown, Colleen Cary, Kara Love, and Vanessa Vorhies, *Midwest Evaluation of the Adult Functioning of Former Foster Youth: Outcomes at Age 26* (Chicago: Chaplin Hall at the University of Chicago, 2011).

numbers and momentum. The Indigenous population, however, is not only growing but also young.
As mentioned, the median age of Indigenous peoples was 27.7 years in 2011, compared to 40.6 years
for non-Indigenous peoples.[61] Consider the relative
youth of the Indigenous population in light of the
fact that the age range for the highest rate of offending is from about 16 to 21.[62] The median age of federal
incarcerated persons is 32.[63] Overall, police-reported
offending rates tend to be higher among youth and
young adults, with rates increasing incrementally
for youths aged 12 to 17, peaking at age 18, and de-
creasing with age after that.[64] Based on these statistics alone, Indigenous peoples are more likely to be
incarcerated at higher rates than non-Indigenous
people.

Research in the field of juvenile justice has
shown that youth involvement in crime is due to the
interaction of various risk factors related to crime
that then have a "multiplicative effect."[65] One of
those factors is engaging in risk-taking behaviours.
Laurence Steinberg, a professor of psychology and
a leading expert on adolescent behaviour, argues
that risk-taking increases between childhood and
adolescence due to changes in the brain's socio-
emotional system that take place during puberty.[66]
These changes lead to amplified reward-seeking behaviour, which is heightened when youths are in the
company of their peers and which is driven largely by
a notable remodelling of the brain's neural pathways.

He notes that risk-taking declines between adolescence and adulthood because the brain's cognitive
control system changes. These changes increase people's ability to self-regulate their behaviours.

As Indigenous peoples experienced a 20.1 per
cent increase in population between 2006 and 2011,
and an Indigenous woman, from 1996 to 2001, was
estimated to have an average of 2.6 births throughout her life course, as opposed to 1.5 for a non-
Indigenous woman, we can expect the percentage of
youths in the Indigenous population to grow, especially in comparison to the overall demographic trend
of aging within the general population of Canada.[67]
Indeed, Indigenous children and youth under the
age of 24 made up almost one-half (48 per cent) of
all Indigenous peoples in 2006. Compare this to the
non-Indigenous population under 24, which was 31 per
cent of the overall population.[68] Population projections
show that, by 2017, Indigenous peoples between the ages
of 20 to 29 could comprise 24 per cent of Indigenous
peoples in Manitoba, 30 per cent in Saskatchewan, and
58 per cent in the North-west Territories.[69]

Canada's North has been termed "the territory
of the young" because of these statistics.[70] Indigenous
peoples between the ages of 20 to 29 comprise more
than 80 per cent of Nunavut's population, and this
proportion is projected to increase.[71] Of the 2,000 or
so residents of Attawapiskat, more than a third are
under 19 years of age, and those under the age of 35
make up three-quarters of the community.[72]

61. *Statistics Canada, Aboriginal Peoples in Canada: First Nations People, Métis, and Inuit—National Household Survey, 2011 (Ottawa: Statistics Canada, 2013),* 14.

62. Shannon Brennan, *Police-Reported Crime Statistics in Canada, 2011* (Ottawa: Ministry of Industry, 2012), 20.

63. Public Safety Canada, *Corrections and Conditional Release Statistical Overview: Annual Report 2012* (Ottawa: Public Safety Canada, 2012), 43.

64. Brennan, *Police-Reported Crime,* 20.

65. Michael Shader, *Risk Factors for Delinquency: An Overview* (Rockville, MD: US Department of Justice, 2004).

66. Laurence Steinberg, "A Social Neuroscience Perspective on Adolescent Risk-Taking," *Developmental Review* 28, no. 1 (2008): 78–106.

67. Employment and Social Development Canada, *Canadians in Context—Aboriginal Population,* http://well-being.esdc.gc.ca/misme-iowb/.3ndic.1t.4r@-eng.jsp?iid=36 (accessed August 2, 2015); Vivian O'Donnell and Susan Wallace, *Women in Canada: A Gender-Based Statistical Report: First Nations, Métis and Inuit Women* (Ottawa: Statistics Canada, Ministry of Industry, 2011), 20.

68. Statistics Canada, *Aboriginal Peoples in Canada in 2006,* 14.

69. Ibid.

70. Linda Goyette, "Still Waiting in Attawapiskat," *Canadian Geographic,* December 2010. http://www.canadiangeographic.ca/magazine/dec10/attawapiskat.asp (accessed February 18, 2013).

71. Statistics Canada, *Aboriginal Peoples in Canada in 2006,* 14.

72. Goyette, "Still Waiting in Attawapiskat."

Based on these demographics alone, Indigenous peoples have a higher chance of having contact with the criminal justice system. Given the Indigenous birth rate and the number of Indigenous people who will soon be in their child-bearing years, many more, in years to come, will enter the age ranges associated with a higher risk of offending and incarceration.[73] Furthermore, according to criminologists Julian Roberts and Ronald Melchers, Indigenous peoples experienced their "baby boom" 10 years after the rest of Canada, so its effects are also abating more slowly.[74] Over time, these various demographic factors could cause the number of Indigenous peoples incarcerated to rise even higher.[75]

The Cycle of Crime Affecting Indigenous Peoples

The Pauktuutit Inuit Women of Canada outline a cycle of abuse—in other words, a cycle of crime against children—and explain that, in the Inuit context, the cycle can be traced back to two root causes.[76] The first is a loss of culture and tradition, and the second is loss of control over individual and collective destiny. These lead to psychological trauma, the breakdown of families, alcohol and drug addiction, and increased feelings of powerlessness. Then fear, mistrust, abuse, and denial become involved, creating a cycle of abuse in which individuals can be both victim and abuser. As an Inuk elder and healer explains, "It is all about your upbringing. If a child was abused at a very early age, sexually or physically, then that's all they know, and they will continue to abuse. And it's up to the community to stop that abuse with education and awareness. The root causes come from shame, guilt and what you've learned from a young age."[77] Other crimes are also related to an experience of or a proximity to this cycle of abuse.

Through life history interviews of Indigenous males imprisoned at federal and provincial facilities in Manitoba and Saskatchewan, James Waldram found that many of the men had experienced long-term trauma and considerable violence, including physical and sexual abuse and alcoholism.[78] A survey of 249 of these men showed that 66 per cent had physical violence in their families when they were growing up; 80 per cent said that at least one parent (or foster or adoptive parent) had a problem with alcohol or drugs. Familial disruption was also a significant finding, as 35 per cent of the men interviewed had spent time in foster homes, 30 per cent had attended residential schools, and 5 per cent were adopted.

In a study on violence and street gangs in Winnipeg, researchers met with six Indigenous gang members living in the city's north end; the researchers adopted an approach intended to "... learn from the wisdom of street gangsters."[79] Ultimately, the gang members demonstrated that street gangs

73. Ron Melchers, "Aboriginal Peoples Experiences with Crime and Criminal Justice," Presentation to CRIM 3322 Aboriginal Peoples and Justice, University of Ottawa, February 4, 2011.

74. Julian Roberts and Ronald Melchers, "The Incarceration of Aboriginal Offenders: Trends from 1978 to 2001," Canadian Journal of Criminology and Criminal Justice 45, no. 2 (2003): 211–243.

75. Office of the Correctional Investigator, Spirit Matters: Aboriginal People and the Corrections and Conditional Release Act (Ottawa: Office of the Correctional Investigator, 2012), 11.

76. Pauktuutit Inuit Women of Canada, National Strategy to Prevent Abuse in Inuit Communities and Sharing Knowledge, Sharing Wisdom: A Guide to the National Strategy (Ottawa: Pauktuutit Inuit Women of Canada, 2006), 3.

77. Ibid.

78. This study used a variety of research techniques, including participant observation; survey instruments; and open-ended, ethnographic-style interviews. Initial data collection began in 1990 at the Regional Psychiatric Centre in Saskatoon, where researchers conducted participant observation and ethnographic interviews with 30 people who were incarcerated. Research continued through to 1994, when an additional phase was implemented that involved interviewing 249 Indigenous incarcerated persons at the Saskatchewan Penitentiary and Riverbend institutions in Prince Albert and the Stony Mountain Penitentiary and Rockwood Institution in Winnipeg; for these details and more, see James B. Waldram, The Way of the Pipe: Aboriginal Spirituality and Symbolic Healing in Canadian Prisons (Peterborough, ON: Broadview Press, 1997), xi, 45–46.

79. Elizabeth Comack, Lawrence Deane, Larry Morrissette, and Jim Silver, If You Want to Change Violence in the "Hood," You Have to Change the "Hood": Violence and Street Gangs in Winnipeg's Inner City (Winnipeg: Canadian Centre for Policy Alternatives, 2009), 14, http://www.policyalternatives.ca/sites/default/files/uploads/publications/Manitoba_Pubs/2009/Violence_and_Street_Gangs_091009.pdf (accessed January 17, 2013).

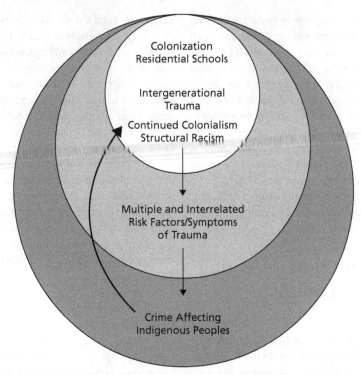

Colonization
Residential Schools

Intergenerational
Trauma

Continued Colonialism
Structural Racism

Multiple and Interrelated
Risk Factors/Symptoms
of Trauma

Crime Affecting
Indigenous Peoples

Figure 8.2 The Cycle of Crime Affecting Indigenous Peoples

and gun violence are products of poverty, **systemic racism**, and the associated consequences and conditions of these two afflictions, that is, addictions, violence, family disintegration, neglect, drugs, and abuse. All were conditions that these men experienced while they were young. The men indicated that, to them, such conditions were normal "everyday events."[80]

Research has shown that exposure to traumatic factors such as violence and abuse will carry on within families and communities, causing the next generation to suffer the same or similar effects or to resort to dangerous coping mechanisms, such as substance abuse, to "bury the pain." It is not an absolute that these traumas, in one form or another, will be passed down; nor is crime the only response to experiencing trauma. However, the chances of being involved in crime increase dramatically if a person is exposed to violence or abuse or to the other traumatic events or circumstances outlined previously. This cycle of crime is sketched out in Figure 8.2.

Only by addressing all that fuels the cycle of crime affecting Indigenous peoples—past and current trauma, racism, continuing colonialism, inequality, and Eurocentric ideologies that commodify the land and its inhabitants—can we hope to break this cycle.

80. *Ibid.,* 5.

CHAPTER 22

The Case That's "Not About Race"

Gina Starblanket and Dallas Hunt

Canada—past and present—is a settler colonial political formation. This truth is increasingly recognized by well-informed individuals. Unfortunately, not all who make their home in Canada are informed.

And, even among those who are informed, even fewer people recognize the ways in which they are implicated by, and in many cases, benefit from, contemporary structures of colonialism in everyday and innumerable ways.

Many people—informed and uninformed—see their everyday actions as divorced from colonial governing systems and institutions; many see themselves as independently self-made individuals unburdened by the violence of the colonial histories that have produced the present. But colonialism forms a scaffolding that is largely invisible to those who do not experience its harmful consequences firsthand or who deny its connection to the disproportionate levels of suffering faced by Indigenous peoples.

Thus non-Indigenous people can claim to see colonialism without ever feeling compelled to transform it. They can perceive the story, the narrative of colonization, without ever having to, or even feeling the need to, work to change its regenerative structures or foundations.

The Particulars of Settler Colonial Logics in the Prairies

Within Canada too, **settler colonialism** takes shape in distinct contexts and historical moments. Some foundational aspects are shared, such as the fact that colonialism is structurally embedded and ongoing, that it operates through an eliminatory logic, that it is heavily racialized and sexualized, and that its driving motivation is land[1]. And while the removal and containment of Indigenous peoples was and continues to be motivated by the settler drive to claim the lands, waters, and the rest of creation as their own, the particular way in which land dispossession is carried out is not identical within settler states; that is, settler states use a variety of tactics and strategies to achieve these goals. These inform the creation of regional political cultures that can contextualize the differences between settler political ideas and values across Canada, and that also shed light on the differences that exist in settler-Indigenous political relations across regions.

At least some of the distinctions in how colonialism plays out can be identified by looking at

1. *For some foundational theorizations of this, see Coulthard, 2014; Moreton-Robinson, 2015; A. Simpson, 2014; L. Simpson, 2017; Wolfe 2006.*

the particular relationships between colonial states and the types of commodities they seek to access and exploit. In contexts of settler colonialism, this commodity is the land, but also access to the land as a precondition to access and exploit other materials, including 'natural resources' and labour, among other things.

Treaty Mythologies

. . . Importantly, one of the primary mechanisms that the Canadian government and people have employed to conceal or 'soften' land theft in the prairies has been through the proliferation of one-sided, Eurocentric interpretations of the numbered treaties. The Red Pheasant First Nation and the Stanley farm are both located in Treaty 6 territory, and so any discussion of the relationship between Indigenous and non-Indigenous people in these spaces must be grounded in Treaty 6 as a living, breathing agreement that governs the relationship.

The numbered treaties were negotiated from 1871–1921, as Indigenous people in the prairies were faced with an influx of settlers and rapidly declining population of buffalo and other wild animals that were crucial to our traditional lifeways. Where the numbered treaties have been signed, Indigenous peoples agreed to share the land with newcomers but only up to the depth of a plow and in exchange for commitments from the Crown. While many Indigenous leaders were hesitant to enter into treaty relationships during the negotiation of Treaty 6, they were also mindful of the impacts that their choices would have on generations to come and sought to craft relationships with newcomers that would allow Indigenous and non-Indigenous people to live alongside and learn from one another without either being subordinate to the other (Taylor, 1985, Cardinal and Hildrebrandt, 2000).

For the most part, treaties have not been implemented in accordance with the way in which they were understood by Indigenous people, but have been confined to one-sided, Eurocentric mythologies surrounding their nature and intent. Popular assumptions surrounding the numbered treaties operate to bolster settler perceptions that both the land and Indigenous political authority have been surrendered long ago, and that treaties were one-time

transactions with little bearing upon contemporary settlers who reside in the prairies. Of course, the presumption that land could be converted into private property and exchanged for a fixed set of terms is one that flows from Canadian laws and worldviews, and is inconsistent with Indigenous laws and worldviews. It is important to understand this imposition of Canadian law on top of Indigenous law as a technique of elimination, but also as the grounds for the ongoing political mobilization of Indigenous peoples in the prairies who have always resisted a transactional understanding of treaties.

Settler treaty mythologies, then, can be understood as the selective construction and misrepresentation of treaties that originate from, but are also continually reproduced through, Canadian institutions and society (Starblanket, 2019; Green, 1995). Such mythologies are wide-ranging and configure dominant representations in multiple ways. Some situate treaties as one-time events through which Indigenous peoples consensually agreed to relinquish our rights to the land and to legal and political jurisdiction in exchange for a fixed set of terms. Interpreted in this way, treaties represent mechanisms of extinguishment of Indigenous claims against Canada's assertion of sovereignty across much of the prairie west.

A Quasi-Military Police Force

Following treaty-making, Canada sought to bolster its own legitimacy and authority by gradually placing bounds on Indigenous sovereignty and political authority through the criminalization and domestication of Indigenous people (Stark 2016). Indeed, after the Northwest Rebellion in the area of Fort Battleford in 1885, and the subsequent hangings of those who took part, Prime Minister John A. Macdonald remarked in a letter to Edgar Dewdney that "the executions . . . ought to convince the Red Man that the White Man governs" (Stonechild and Waiser 1997, 221). Until the 1951 amendments to the Indian Act, it was illegal for Indigenous peoples to even protest the conditions of our own oppression, as raising money to fund court cases in the interest of protecting our basic human rights rendered us as criminals in our own homelands. In other words, when we attempted to address colonial intrusions, our efforts were criminalized. As was our very presence outside of reserve lands.

In the prairie west, the North West Mounted Police (NWMP) were charged with bringing Indigenous people, including the Métis, within the reach of Canadian law (Harring 1998, 242). Prior to the founding of the NWMP (which was later succeeded by the RCMP), the Hudson's Bay Company (HBC) exercised certain powers of law and governance yet infrequently interfered with Indigenous peoples' existing legal and political institutions (Harring 1998, 242). Early on in Indigenous-settler interactions, the NWMP are often described as maintaining relatively favorable relations with Indigenous peoples (particularly with certain groups such as the Blackfoot), taking an active role in restricting the presence of whisky traders and unwanted visitors within Indigenous communities. However, the 1885 Northwest Rebellion, among other events, resulted in the NWMP taking on a stronger role in the enforcement of policies geared towards Indigenous repression and assimilation (Stonechild and Waiser 1997).

The exercise of law and order in the prairies, as Lesley Erickson notes, was a way for dominant groups to impose their vision of society, law, and morality on subordinate groups. Indeed, the settler construct "depended on the application of a system of law that was both discretionary and discriminatory" (2011, 19). The legal system placed primacy in the liberal individual citizen, protecting "his right to self-preservation and the pursuit of property [. . .] liberals envisaged the rights-bearing individual as the rational male, in opposition, they constructed women, indigenous peoples and the unpropertied as deficient individuals" (Erickson 2011, 22).

The contemporary experiences of both settlers and Indigenous peoples in the prairies should be contextualized by these histories. And it should come as no surprise that multiple contemporary inquiries into the interactions between Indigenous peoples

and the criminal justice system have indicated that they continue to be marked by deeply rooted forms of Eurocentrism, racism, and sexism[2]. State institutions not only deprive Indigenous people of justice but operate to mask the frequent and extreme forms of violence that Indigenous people face when interacting with them. As the attitudes and operations engendered by these structures have been rendered normative over time, they are deemed completely "lawful" even when operating at a clear and continuous disadvantage to Indigenous peoples.

Far from transcending the violence of colonialism past, Canadian institutions still function to discipline and suppress Indigenous peoples and continue to provide protections for those who commit violence against them so long as it is rationalized by what we term "settler reason."

Designed by and for European newcomers who sought to institute their own legal orders in these lands, Canadian institutions of law and policing have since functioned as an integral part of the structure of settler colonialism in what is currently called Canada. The police, in particular, have been used to carry out much of the overt violence and forms of direct oppression committed against Indigenous people in the service of the national interest. As the institutional relationship between Indigenous, federal, and provincial governments has never been reconfigured in a way that deviates from these colonial origins, it should come as no surprise that the criminal justice system continues to operate in a way that reflects its earliest mandate.

Similar to the way in which the provision of "justice" unfolded surrounding the killing of Colten Boushie, examples of racial violence and discrimination within the Saskatchewan and broader Canadian criminal justice system abound. For example, in January 1991, Leo Lachance, a Cree trapper from Big River First Nation, went to the Prince Albert Northern Pawn and Gun Shop to potentially sell a few items. The pawn shop was a popular meeting space

---

2. See, for instance, Royal Commission on Aboriginal Peoples, Bridging the Cultural Divide: A Report on Aboriginal People and Criminal Justice in Canada (Minister of Supply and Services Canada Ottawa, Canada, 1996); Aboriginal Justice Implementation Commission, Report of the Aboriginal Justice Inquiry of Manitoba (Public Inquiry into the Administration of Justice and Aboriginal People, 1991); Frank Iacobucci, First Nations Representation on Ontario Juries: Report of the Independent Review Conducted by the Honourable Frank Iacobucci (Ontario Ministry of the Attorney General, 2013); Patricia A Monture-Angus, "Lessons in Decolonization: Aboriginal Overrepresentation in Canadian Criminal Justice," in David Long & Olive Dickason, eds., Visions of the Heart: Canadian Aboriginal Issues (Oxford: Oxford University Press, 1996).

for prison guards and off-duty police officers and was owned and operated by Carney Milton Nerland, a known white supremacist and leader of the Jesus Christ Church of Aryan Nations in Saskatchewan. Soon after entering the shop LaChance was fatally shot by Nerland, his bullet propelled forward not only by his rifle, but also by centuries of settler colonial white supremacist hatred. Nerland was ultimately charged with manslaughter and given a 4 year sentence, of which he would only serve 2 years before being released on parole and placed in a witness protection program by the RCMP. What these incidents illustrate, and the plethora of cases like them (see: Pamela George, Tina Fontaine, among *many* others), is the asymmetrical treatment Indigenous peoples receive and are subjected to within the Canadian judicial system, relative to that of non-Indigenous peoples[3].

Rather than regarding the Canadian legal system as something that has, from time to time, malfunctioned, we understand the legal system to be a mechanism that was designed for, and actively continues to carry out, the elimination of Indigenous people.

The System Isn't Broken, It Was Built This Way

In our interactions with non-Indigenous institutions and populations, Indigenous peoples often find that matters of race and colonialism are deliberately left out of the picture, despite the undeniable existence of racial tensions and ongoing colonial dynamics on the prairies. Such was the case in the Stanley trial, where race relations were not mentioned once in the main trial proceedings, despite the rampant proliferation of settler stereotypes and assumptions about Indigenous peoples in the area. In the preliminary trial inquiry, witnesses were chided by the defense when they suggested that they had been subject to racist treatment by the RCMP, to the point where Judge Martel Popescul intervened in the defense's

treatment of one of the Indigenous youth to say: "I'm concerned that [. . .] you've told her a number of times that—why you think that she shouldn't think that they're racist, that she continues to think that they are, and I'm not sure that we're going to get anywhere by continuing down this road" (R. v. Stanley 2017, 334).

Outside of the courts, Scott Spencer, Gerald Stanley's lawyer, took great pains to downplay the ways that racialized logics figured into Colten's death, suggesting that he did not want the trial to "become a referendum on race," and that he saw "no evidence that race played any part in the tragic circumstances that escalated on the Stanley Farm" (quoted in CBC News 2017).

Yet, the extreme racial tensions surrounding Boushie's death have been readily apparent throughout and following this case. Indeed, many commentators and reporters reproduced stereotypes and prejudices about Indigenous peoples, some of which are explicitly grounded on ideas of racial inferiority and deficiency, and others which use more coded language, such as associations between race and criminality, vagrancy, idleness, and alcohol/drug use. The irony here is that many were employing these explicitly or implicitly racialized ideas at the exact same moment that they were dismissing race as a relevant factor in Colten's death. It seemed that race was allowed to figure into the narrative when situating Indigenous people as perpetrators of crime, but when Indigenous people have been victims of crime, we are told that we shouldn't be playing the "race card."

The **rhetoric of "the race card"** refers to the assumption that individuals who are trying to name or identify prejudice and discrimination are attempting to use their identity as a strategy to gain an advantage, or at the very least, that they are trying to bring the issue of race into contexts where it does not belong. Yet, the very notion of a 'race card' functions as a strategy to contain and discredit efforts to account for the implications of past and present experiences of racism (Edgar et al. 2019, 131).

---

3. Many Indigenous writers and educators, as well as sex workers and sex worker advocates, have spoken or written about the murder of Pamela George. That said, the most well-known and widely-read piece on the murder of Pamela George is most likely Sherene Razack's "Gendered Racial Violence and Spatialized Justice: The Murder of Pamela George," in the edited collection Race, Space, and the Law: Unmapping a White Settler Society (Razack, 2002).

In the prairies, negative perceptions of Indigenous people do not just emerge during the course of overtly racist interactions, but rather they form an unnamed and taken for granted social norm. Even as settler individuals in these spaces reproduce negative assumptions and representations of Indigenous people, they will often vehemently deny their own racism. When confronted about their race-based ideas, they can frequently be heard either refusing to admit that those views are racist, or conversely, explaining why they are *entitled* to hold and express these views. Regarding the latter, the explanations vary, but often they cite the fact that they live in a region with a high Indigenous population or work in a profession where they have to interact with many Indigenous people who have caused challenges for them. In other words, Indigenous people are to blame for the racism inflicted upon us and, in some cases, for the violence that it gives rise to.

The historical and present structures of racism and colonialism mark all interactions in the prairies; they do not only exist in select contexts. Racial tensions did not merely surface after Colten's death, but date back to the earliest interactions between Indigenous and non-Indigenous peoples in these spaces. We ask, then: how could the interactions between Gerald Stanley and the car of Indigenous youth on that farm be immune from these racialized associations? How could the Stanley family possibly be isolated from the dominant social, cultural, and political norms that mark prairie life? How could this incident be inoculated from the colonial story of the settlement of the prairie west?

Here there is a common dissociative tendency in contexts of colonialism, where there exists undeniable racialized hierarchies and patterns of discrimination that inform social interactions, yet law and politics are said to be immune from these influences[4]. Such was the case in Stanley's trial where the language of race rarely surfaced. Instead, the defense relied upon racialized associations between Indigeneity and deviance, troublemaking, and terror, and corresponding narratives of settler independence, industry, and lawfulness—without ever having to speak about race. It is precisely because these narratives are so deeply normalized in the prairies that they were able to make sense to the jury and, ultimately, help configure the outcome of the case.

The ongoing denial of settler colonialism and its racialized logics shapes popular representations of colonial histories as well as dominant understandings of Indigenous and non-Indigenous life in the prairies today. At a systemic level, narratives of colonial violence are often dismissed by settlers as a fabrication of historical revisionism while peaceful histories of colonial settlement and development are regarded as the "correct," "unbiased," or "true" version of the past and present. Even when colonial violence is acknowledged (and it is rarely acknowledged in the prairies), it is situated as a historical phenomenon that is disconnected from contemporary contexts, which obscures the many ongoing operations of settler colonialism.

At an interpersonal level, the denial of racialized hierarchies blocks the potential for Indigenous suffering to be recognized and addressed, as Indigenous people are continually told that our lived experiences of oppression are a product of our own making, markings of a broken culture, an unwillingness to join Canadian society, or a product of gratuitous self-victimization and entitlement. At the same time, preconceived assumptions and stereotypes that many non-Indigenous people hold about Indigenous people and communities are rendered invisible. They are unremarkable because they have become the fabric of everyday life in the settler colonial context of Canada; indeed, these assumptions and stereotypes are informed by narratives of savagery, of deficiency, of deviancy that have been reproduced and reified for centuries, in the process becoming sedimented and normalized. To settlers in the prairies, then, Indigenous peoples have been and always will be this way, as this is the 'natural,' normative order of things, as told to them via the logics, imaginaries, and stories that settler colonialism and its proprietors cultivate.

Yet, despite what many Canadians would like to believe, the contemporary crises of relationship between Indigenous and non-Indigenous peoples

---

4. *For more on the processes of "settler memory," see Kevin Bruyneel, 2017.*

in Canada do not exist in a vacuum. They cannot be divorced from the structures of colonialism and notions of racial hierarchy that both helped to produce, and are required to sustain, the Canadian state.

. . . The narratives that we elaborate lay bare the discrepancies between settler colonial history and the tales Canada tells about itself. In many ways, these lies—of (white) civility and neutrality, of the inability to see race or the processes of colonization—are crucial to combat as they become the fodder for narratives that naturalize the deaths of Indigenous youth on the prairies. These narratives mark Indigenous deaths as personal, subjective problems, ones unmoored from history and politics and their effects. Yet, these are not individualized issues relevant only to the actors involved, but rather are a part of a longer history and structure of settler colonial violence, the scaffolding of which attempts to frame Stanley as an exceptional, yet justified agent of violence, instead of positioning him as only one agent of violence in the longer history of force, coercion, and bodily harm enacted on Indigenous communities and their territories.

Bibliography

Cardinal, Harold, and Walter Hildebrand. 2000. *Treaty Elders of Saskatchewan: Our Dream is that Our Peoples Will One Day be Clearly Recognized as Nations.* Calgary: University of Calgary Press.

CBC News. 2017 "'I've seen no evidence that race played any part': Gerald Stanley's lawyer comments on the Colten Boushie case". *CBC News' Out in the Open,* January 6, 2017. https://www.cbc.ca/radio/outintheopen/what-does-colten-boushie-say-about-us-1.4039219/i-ve-seen-no-evidence-that-race-played-any-part-gerald-stanley-s-lawyer-comments-on-the-colten-bo-ushie-case-1.3923957.

Edgar, Alistair, Rupinder Mangat, and Bessma Momani, eds. 2020. *Strengthening the Canadian Armed Forces through Diversity and Inclusion.* Toronto: University of Toronto Press.

Erickson, Lesley. 2011. *Westward Bound: Sex, Violence, the Law, and the Making of a Settler Society.* Vancouver: UBC Press.

Green, Joyce. 1995. Towards a Détente With History: Confronting Canada's Colonial Legacy. *International Journal of Canadian Studies* 12, Fall.

Harring, Sidney L. 1998. *White Man's Law: Native People in Nineteenth-Century Canadian Jurisprudence.* Toronto: University of Toronto Press.

Starblanket, Gina. 2019. "The Numbered Treaties and the Politics of Incoherency" *Canadian Journal of Political Science* 52(3): 443–459.

Starblanket, Gina. 2019. "Constitutionalizing (In) justice: Treaty Interpretation and the Containment of Indigenous Governance." *Constitutional Forum* 28(13).

Stark, Heidi. 2016. "Criminal Empire: The Making of the Savage in a Lawless Land". *Theory & Event* 19(4).

Stonechild, Blair and Bill Waiser. 1997. *Loyal Till Death: Indians and the North-West Rebellion.* Calgary: Fifth House.

Taylor, John Leonard. 1985. *Treaty research report: Treaty six (1876).* Treaties and Historical Research Centre, Indian and Northern Affairs Canada.

Wolfe, Patrick. 2016. *Traces of History: Elementary Structures of Race.* New York: Verso Books.

Legal Cases

R. v. Stanley, 2017, E-File 2017-04-030CPStanleyG (Preliminary Inquiry)

R. v. Stanley, 2018, E-File 2018-01-290CQStanleyGf

PART 11

Additional Readings

Amnesty International Report. *Stolen Sisters: A Human Rights Response to Discrimination and Violence against Indigenous Women in Canada*. Ottawa: Amnesty International, 2004.

Comack, Elizabeth. *Coming Back to Jail: Women, Trauma, and Criminalization*. Halifax: Fernwood Publishing. 2018.

Johnson, Harold J. *Peace and Good Order: the Case for Indigenous Justice in Canada*. Toronto: McClelland & Stewart Limited. 2019.

Maynard, Robyn. *Policing Black Lives: State Violence in Canada from Slavery to the Present*. Halifax & Winnipeg: Fernwood Publishing. 2017.

Monchalin, Lisa. *The Colonial Problem: An Indigenous Perspective on Crime and Injustice in Canada*. Toronto: University of Toronto Press, 2016.

Murdocca, Carmela. *To Right Historical Wrongs: Race, Gender, and Sentencing in Canada*. Vancouver: University of British Columbia Press, 2014.

Reber, Susanne. *Starlight Tour: The Last, Lonely Night of Neil Stonechild*. Toronto: Random House Canada, 2005.

Roach, Kent. *Canadian Justice, Indigenous Injustice: the Gerald Stanley and Colten Boushie Case*. Montreal & Kingston: McGill-Queen's Univesity Press. 2019.

Starblanket, Gina and Dallas Hunt. *Storying Violence: Unravellling Colonial Narratives in the Stanley Trial*. Winnipeg: ARP Books. 2020.

Talaga, Tanya. *Seven Fallen Feathers: Racism, Death, And Hard Truths In A Northern City*. Toronto: House of Anansi Press. 2017.

Relevant Websites

Report of the Aboriginal Justice Inquiry of Manitoba
http://www.ajic.mb.ca/volume.html
The Manitoba Government created the Public Inquiry into the Administration of Justice and Aboriginal People, commonly known as the Aboriginal Justice Inquiry. The Inquiry was created in response to the trial in November 1987 of two men for the 1971 murder of Helen Betty Osborne in The Pas. The Report can be found online on the Aboriginal Justice Inquiry's website.

Cindy Gladue Murder Case
https://www.cbc.ca/news/canada/edmonton/bradley-barton-sentencing-1.6118846
This newspaper article documents the tragic death of Cindy Gladue in a hotel room, and the reaction of her family after the sentencing of her murderer.

Gerald Stanley Case
https://www.thecanadianencyclopedia.ca/en/article/gerald-stanley-and-colten-boushie-case
The Canadian Encyclopedia provides background and context about the Gerald Stanely case.

Overrepresentation of Indigenous Women in Prison
https://thetyee.ca/News/2022/05/31/Overrepresentation-Indigenous-Women-In-Jail/
This newspaper article reports on the high overrepresentation of incarcerated Indigenous women in Canada, and the socio-economic factors that contribute to it.

Films

Home Fire. Dir. Greg Miller. National Film Board of Canada. 2014.
Life on Victor Street. Dir. Kirby Hammond. National Film Board of Canada. 2012.
Nipawistamâsowin: We Will Stand Up. Dir. Tasha Hubbard. National Film Board of Canada. 2019.
Spirit to Soar: Mashkawi-Manidoo Bimaadiziwin. Dir. Tanya Talaga. Antica Production Ltd. 2021.
Two Worlds Colliding. Dir. Tasha Hubbard. National Film Board of Canada, 2004.

Key Terms

- Cycle of crime
- Race card rhetoric
- Risk factors of crime
- Settler colonialism
- Systemic racism
- Treaty mythologies

Discussion Questions

1. How has the Canadian criminal justice system in reality resulted in systemic injustice towards Indigenous peoples? What steps need to be taken for justice to take place?

2. What are the risk factors that contribute to the overrepresentation of Indigenous peoples in the cycle of crime? In particular, how does the Sixties Scoop relate to this cycle of crime?

3. Discuss the implications of "race card" rhetoric. Why is racism a conversation many non-Indigenous people wish to avoid? Why is it important to have this conversation in order to address the systemic barriers Indigenous peoples encounter with the Canadian criminal justice system?

4. Starblanket and Hunt explain how the legal system favourably protects the rights of the "rational white male" over that of Indigenous peoples. In particular, how have Indigenous women been particularly mistreated?

Activities

Review The Cycle of Crime Affecting Indigenous Peoples on Figure 8.2 in Chapter 21. In groups, draw the diagram and add the mentioned risk factors into the appropriate level(s) of the cycle. Research existing social programs and supports in your area for Indigenous peoples that work against the risk factors. Does each risk factor have an existing social program? Do you notice any significant gaps?

Research the Tina Fontaine case, and compare and contrast it with the Colten Boushie case. What were the risk factors associated with each case? Did gender play a factor in each case? If so, how?

Invite a local anticolonial activist to discuss issues of hatred and violence against Indigenous peoples in your area, and strategies to organize and bring public awareness and social change.

PART 12

Environmental Racism

Editor Introduction

Part Twelve of *Racism, Colonialism, and Indigeneity in Canada* 3rd edition is a new section exploring **environmental racism** with two edited selections by Deborah McGregor (Anishinaabe Kwe) and Anne Spice (Tlingit). We suggest up front and without hesitation that no other topic is more pressing to us as human beings in the twenty-first century than our environment and finding ways to live more responsibly and nonexploitatively with our relatives, living and nonliving, to restore balance with Yethi-nihstenha Onhwentsya [she-to-us, our mother, the earth] (Hill, 2017), to eliminate harmful extractions, and to reduce carbon emissions. We also acknowledge that defining environmental racism is itself a challenging task. As Gilio-Whitaker (2019: 21–22), a scholar of the Colville Confederated Tribes writes: "environmental racism is a narrow term that doesn't account for ways in which poor communities are affected by polluting industries, or the ways it can ignore the historic and systemic nature of racism." Any definition of environmental racism must therefore address the combined and interlocking systems of race and class discrimination (ibid.) but also those of antiblackness, as Ingrid R. G. Waldron's work linking environmental racism and its impacts on health in both Black and Indigenous communities suggests (2018).

Environmental racism requires us to think seriously about "human presence in and use of the environment" (Gilio-Whitaker, 2019: 22). We call to mind several natural resources extraction initiatives, some involving the oil and gas industry as Spice outlines in this volume, that are already doing or hold the potential to do even further terrible harm to the earth and atmosphere. In each case, these initiatives have been driven by a relentless pursuit of wealth accumulation leading to profits being channelled to the one per cent, and as the late Arthur Manuel (2017: 235) once wrote of the dirty energy market, the refusal by Canada and industry to honour, respect, or even so much as acknowledge Indigenous peoples' constitutionally protected rights and their responsibility to speak for and protect the land.

In drawing attention to the relentless pursuit of wealth accumulation and its ability to effect ecological harm, we suggest that it is both a Hobbesian mindset of mastery over nature, the blatant disrespect held by industry, settler governments, and even policing/surveillance over Indigenous peoples and their allies that defines environmental racism. It is a system of profit at any cost, the recurrent tendency to initiate and further natural resources extraction without Indigenous peoples' consent, the brutality directed toward defenders of the land through court injunctions (Manuel, Chapter 30), and a readiness to accept damage and ecological destruction on our nations, communities, and indeed working class and poor humans that are at the core of defining environmental racism. These practices each lend further service to ecological destruction, and they foreclose any further thought be given toward what it might mean to live in better relationship with the natural world, our surroundings, and the environment.

The injustices committed in the name of wealth accumulation and Settler sovereignty do not only—we wish to reiterate—impact Indigenous peoples alone. Instead, we believe they impact all humans, as Gilio-Whitaker reminds us, especially the poor. Furthermore, we cannot at times avoid being implicated in ecological destruction ourselves as the failure to respect the world around us is something all humans are implicated in. As the late Arthur Manuel, who features in Chapter 15 of this book, once wrote of his own involvement in the oil and gas industry: "I am not pretending to be some environmental angel. The fact is, I have myself earned a living off oil and gas" (2017: 235). He went on to write of Indigenous peoples, however, and in particular: "we believe that the oil and gas industry has had its day and the pipelines—far from being expanded—should be gradually turned off" (ibid.). As Manuel suggests, the demand for environmental justice should not ultimately be read solely as an expression of Indigenous resistance.

Manuel provides a context for realizing a shared responsibility to defend the land from damage and/or destruction. In fact, we hope this section of the book will invite a more critical and collective conversation about why all peoples—not just Indigenous, Black, or poor—need to care about environmental racism. Indeed, we hope the readings show that we cannot hope to be free of ecological devastation unless the racism directed at Indigenous land defenders is seen as an issue belonging to us all as humans—Indigenous and non-Indigenous—and as working contrary to our survival as humans with water to drink, food to eat, air to breathe, and temperatures to not burn up in. Like Manuel, we wish to move away from a way of thinking about environmental racism as if it's an issue that doesn't impact non-Indigenous peoples, when, in fact, it is environmental racism that is used to wreak havoc on the earth and destroy the balance and respect between humans and environment. It is our responsibility to care about environmental racism because we all need a planet to live in.

Like Manuel, as well as Spice (Chapter 23) suggest, the demand for environmental injustice is therefore about the refusal to advance any further ecological devastation that parts with or even negates our responsibility to care for and defend the land and environment. Environmental justice demands that all human beings look inward and introspectively at how we live alongside nature—however much we are implicated—to not just haphazardly invest in alternative energy solutions, and to think seriously about the things that will cause real harm to living and non-living things. Beyond resistance, the demand for environmental justice is instead, and as Audra Simpson (2014) has written, a refusal to be eliminated or to accept the terms and conditions offered up by Settler colonial wealth accumulation to further ecological devastation and its potential to destroy. It is a demand to act more responsibly, a tenet centrally upheld by Indigenous women who, alongside other Indigenous peoples, have recognized that environmental injustice has negatively impacted their ability to maintain sustainable economies, as well as disrupting their traditional sacred relationship with Mother Earth.

Despite heavy surveillance and policing towards them, Indigenous peoples have continued to be stewards of the land, waters, and all beings as their ancestors before them. Though, as previously stated, environmental justice is a matter that affects us all, Indigenous women have led the way as defenders of land, including the late Grandmother Josephine Mandamin who co-founded the Mother Earth Water Walk to bring awareness of damage done to the waters; Autumn Peltier who continued this water protector role at a very young age and spoke to the United Nations about environmental issues; Courtney Skye of the 1492 Land Back Lane movement who are protecting lands of/near the Six Nations of the Grand River Territory against further subdivision developments; and Kanahus Manuel, a member of the Tiny House Warriors in British Columbia who is fighting against the Trans Mountain pipeline project. These brave women view their activism as an extension of mothering in their nations.

Josephine Mandamin stated in an interview: "As women we are carriers of the water. We carry life for the people. So when we carry that water, we are telling people that we will go to any lengths for the water. We'll probably even give our lives for the water if we have to" (CBC News, 26 Feburary 2016e). Mandamin's words reflect traditional Indigenous mothering practices that place women at the forefront of strength in their nations (Lavell-Harvard and Anderson, Chapter 13). In many communities, women have historically held decision-making authorities and responsibilities that derive from a culturally specific Indigenous concept of motherhood. As Lavell-Harvard and Anderson (Chapter 13) point out, Indigenous mothering means "to care for and nurture life once it is brought into the world and, by extension, to care for and nurture our nations." This extends beyond the responsibility towards our human relatives. It includes all our relations: other animals, waters, Mother Earth, and all of her creations.

Mothering itself embodies the notion of interconnectedness, an idea explored by Anne Spice in Chapter 23. She presents an Indigenous conception of **critical infrastructure** as an interconnected network of **relationality** between humans and other-than-human beings, including animals, rivers, and mountains. It is through these relationships that Indigenous people acquire a sovereign right to protect the land and its ecosystems, including protesting the development of **fossil-fuel infrastructures**. Blockades and spaces of protests, Spice argues, are not only events of resistance but also events of possibility for alternative worldviews regarding infrastructure. It stands in stark contrast to an invasive fossil-fuel version of infrastructure that threatens living and nonliving things. Indigenous peoples must use their worldview, and Indigenous feminist methodologies, to counter dominant, settler attempts to impose their own views onto Indigenous lands. The Indigenous perspective of infrastructure has sustained Indigenous peoples for thousands of years and must continue to thrive in order to prevent further colonial invasion. Indigenous women are key to unmasking the colonial violence against them and the lands that they defend.

In Chapter 24, Deborah McGregor focuses again on women to show us how the mothering role is practiced transnationally. Indigenous women throughout the globe have brought an awareness of how some nation-states and corporate actions have harmed the environment, and in the process, hurt Indigenous women in particular: by increasing their poverty, dispossessing them of their lands, and disrupting their traditional ways of governing. However, McGregor outlines some legislative Declarations that continue to call upon global leaders and citizens for environmental action, to demand that any future environmental policies include a gendered analysis, and to integrate traditional Indigenous knowledges and practices. Ultimately, Indigenous women's full participation in any policy-making at a global level is necessary in order to reverse the negative impacts that have taken place against our nations, peoples, and the environment.

CHAPTER 23

Fighting Invasive Infrastructures

Indigenous Relations against Pipelines

Anne Spice

Critical infrastructure refers to processes, systems, facilities, technologies, networks, assets and services essential to the health, safety, security or economic well-being of Canadians and the effective functioning of government. . . . Disruptions of critical infrastructure could result in catastrophic loss of life, adverse economic effects and significant harm to public confidence. (PSC 2018)

In Unist'ot'en territory in northern British Columbia, Canada, clan members of the Wet'suwet'en people have built a permanent encampment in the pathway of numerous potential and proposed pipelines. In response to the characterization of these pipeline projects as "critical infrastructure," the camp's spokesperson, Freda Huson, notes that the pipelines were proposed to run through the clan's best berry patches. By resisting pipeline construction, she explains, "what we're doing here is protecting *our* critical infrastructure." When I asked Freda to describe the difference between industry conceptions of critical infrastructure, and the infrastructures that sustain Indigenous life on Unist'ot'en *yintah* (territory), she told me this:

> So industry and government always talk about critical infrastructure, and *their critical infrastructure is making money, and using destructive projects to make that money,* and they go by any means necessary to make that happen. . . . So for us, our critical infrastructure is the clean drinking

water, and the very water that the salmon spawn in, and they go back downstream and four years, come back. That salmon is our food source; it's our main staple food. That's one of our critical infrastructures. And there's berries that are our critical infrastructure, because the berries not only feed us, they also feed the bears, and the salmon also don't just feed us, they feed the bears. And each and every one of those are all connected, and without each other, we wouldn't survive on this planet. . . . For example, the bears will eat the berries and they'll drop it, and the waste that comes out of the bear, it's got seeds in it, so that germinates and we get more berries. We need the bears in order to keep producing our berries, and same with the salmon. The bears eat the salmon as well, because once the salmon spawn, they end up dying anyways, and that becomes food for the bears, so it's not being wasted. All of that is part of the system that our people depend on, and *that whole cycle and system is our*

Courtesy of Anne Spice.

critical infrastructure, and that's what we're trying to protect, an infrastructure that we depend on. And industry and government are pushing these projects that would destroy that critical infrastructure, most important to our people. (emphasis added)

Here, Freda appropriates the term "critical infrastructure" to index the interconnected networks of human and other-than-human beings that sustain Indigenous life in mutual relation. This network stands in stark contrast to the critical infrastructures of government and industry—infrastructures that are meant to destroy Indigenous life to make way for capitalist expansion. By contrasting these two meanings under one term, she brings attention to the underlying driving force of industrial infrastructure, exposing the lie that these projects are creative/productive and instead insisting that they are regressive/destructive and embedded in a capitalist system that is fundamentally at odds with the cycles and systems that make Indigenous survival possible.

Infrastructure vis-à-vis Settler Colonialism

How, then, can an anthropology of infrastructure address the radical vision of Indigenous resistance to settler infrastructures? Larkin advocates for a systems analysis of infrastructures, and stresses that infrastructures are networks that cannot always be reduced to the technologies or materials that make them up: "infrastructures are matter that enable the movement of other matter . . . they are things and also the relation between things" (329). Larkin argues, allows us to attend to how the definition of an assemblage as infrastructure works to categorize the world. This act of definition "comprises a cultural analytic that highlights the epistemological and political commitments involved in selecting what one sees as infrastructural (and thus causal) and what one leaves out" (230). As the Canadian government's definition of "critical infrastructure"

above makes clear, these political commitments may come into conflict, as infrastructures are proposed across territories that Indigenous peoples have never surrendered to the Canadian state. This article links literature in the anthropology of infrastructure, settler colonial studies, and critical Indigenous studies to understand the emergence of "critical infrastructure" as a settler colonial technology of governance and expropriation in lands now claimed by Canada.

The government mobilizes the language of "critical infrastructure" to transform oil and gas infrastructures from industry projects into crucial matters of national interest. That authority is buoyed further by the genealogy of the concept of infrastructure itself, which Larkin shows is the genealogical descendant of Enlightenment ideas about modernity and progress. While the categorization of oil and gas technologies as "critical infrastructure" is a relatively recent move, the discursive positioning of infrastructure as a gateway to a modern future has been used in state-building projects around the world for some time now. The conflict over oil and gas infrastructures, however, is more than a disagreement about what "counts" as infrastructure and what does not. Embedded in Larkin's definition of infrastructure is a tacit assumption that infrastructures, as "things and also the relation between things," are inanimate, are not alive. Freda Huson calls attention to the salmon, the berries, and the bears that form "our critical infrastructure." This living network is not an assemblage of "things and relation between things," but rather a set of relations and things between relations. These are relations that require caretaking, which Indigenous peoples are accountable to. And they are relations that are built through the agency of not only humans but also other-than human kin. The bears and salmon create and maintain the assemblage as much as (or more than) humans do. Infrastructure, then, attempts but fails to capture the agentive and social network through which Indigenous life is produced.[1] These assemblages exist whether or not they are framed or captured by anthropological theory.

---

1. These productive networks are better described by Ruth Wilson Gilmore's (2017) concept "infrastructures of feeling." Asking how structures of feeling are produced and relations rearranged, she suggests that the Black radical tradition and other revolutionary knowledges are formed and maintained through connections that arc toward freedom and challenge the structures of racial capitalism.

The characterization of oil and gas pipelines as "critical infrastructures" constitutes a form of settler colonial invasion. Indigenous resistance to oil and gas infrastructures, through suspension, disruption, and blockages, protect our relations against the violence of settler colonial invasion, and open alternatives for living in good relation to our territories. I address each assertion by turning to a set of field insights followed by an engagement with relevant literatures in settler colonial studies and the anthropology of infrastructure.

Field Insights: Critical Infrastructure

I visited Unist'ot'en Camp for the first time in the summer of 2015. I responded to the people's call for support on the ground after increased industry pressure and police presence threatened to breach the borders of their territory and begin construction of pipelines on their land, they could not afford to trust a stranger. In May of that year, the Canadian legislature had passed Bill C-51 (House of Commons of Canada 2015), which redefined "activity that undermines the security of Canada" as "any activity . . . if it undermines the sovereignty, security, or territorial integrity of Canada or the lives or the security of the people of Canada." Activities explicitly listed include "interference with the capacity of The Government of Canada in relation to intelligence, defense, border operations, public safety, the administration of justice, diplomatic or consular relations, or the economic or financial stability of Canada," "terrorism," and "interference with critical infrastructure." An emergent category for the governance of crisis, critical infrastructure is defined by the Canadian government as the "processes, systems, facilities, technologies, networks, assets and services essential to the health, safely, security or economic well-being of Canadians and the effective functioning of the government" (PSC 2009: 2). Threats to pipeline projects, then, can be cast as threats to national (economic) security, and these definitions of critical infrastructure make it possible to place resistance to fossil fuels in the same category as domestic terrorism. Even though the reoccupation of traditional territory at Unist'ot'en Camp has always been peaceful,

in 2015 supporters worried that they could be cast as terrorists simply by helping the Unist'ot'en people to reestablish a home on the territory for which they have cared for thousands of years.

This concern was amplified by the apparent coordination between oil and gas industry personnel and police. Supporters on their way to Unist'ot'en Camp were surveilled; police checkpoints stopped cars on the logging road and issued tickets for broken taillights and cracked windshields. In between police visits meant to intimidate supporters, industry executives attempted to "negotiate" entry onto Unist'ot'en territory. These tactics mirrored the industry police collaboration that was made clear in a leaked report from the Royal Canadian Mounted Police (RCMP) Critical Infrastructure Intelligence Assessment Team entitled *Criminal Threats to the Canadian Petroleum Industry*. An unmarked binary operates throughout the report: privatized oil and gas technologies and pipelines are "critical infrastructures" in need of increased securitization and protection, while protection of Indigenous lands and ecologies is extremist ideology.

In the lands now occupied by Canada, the state's approach to Indigenous protest has shifted under Prime Minister Justin Trudeau's government, which has fully embraced the politics of recognition with its accompanying reconciliation pageantry. On National Aboriginal Day in 2016, the Trudeau administration released a statement on the government's approach to Indigenous peoples, saying: "No relationship is more important to our government and to Canada than the one with Indigenous peoples. Today, we reaffirm our government's commitment to a renewed nation-to-nation relationship between Canada and Indigenous peoples, one based on the recognition of rights, respect, trust, co-operation, and partnership" (PMO 2016). Despite these statements of "recognition," Indigenous peoples remain in a deeply subordinated relationship to Canada, and political claims to land and self-governance are repeatedly squashed in favor of cultural exchange (Coulthard 2014, A. Simpson 2014). The prime minister's statement of recognition itself embodies this by reciting the language of a nation-to-nation relationship as the route to reconciliation but ending with the facile suggestion that reconciliation can be practiced by Canadians reading more books by Indigenous authors: "I invite you to join the #IndigenousReads campaign to help raise awareness and understanding through shared culture and stories and encourage steps toward reconciliation with Indigenous peoples" (PMO 2016).

While the government shifts the focus to "shared culture and stories" and away from Indigenous claims to land and sovereignty, oil and gas infrastructures have continued to operate as emblems of national progress and resource wealth. Trudeau gave the keynote speech to a meeting of oil and gas executives in Houston, Texas, noting, "No country would find 173 billion barrels of oil in the ground and just leave them there" (Berke 2017). His speech was met with a standing ovation. The naturalization of oil and gas extraction and the securitization of pipelines as "critical infrastructures" serve to link industry profits to national security, criminalizing Indigenous dissent and recasting destructive infrastructure projects as natural outgrowths of the settler state, the intersections between official state definitions of "infrastructure" and the tactics and technologies of settler colonialism merit further explanation.

Invasive Infrastructures

This article takes up Patrick Wolfe's (2006: 388) assertion that settler colonial "invasion is a structure not an event" and turns to one of invasion's contemporary material forms: oil and gas infrastructure. Pipelines, like other modern infrastructures, are not events, but they are eventful: rooted in a settler future, they enable a material transit of empire (Byrd 2011), and this movement is hailed as an inevitable and necessary pathway to progress settler state discourse imagines "critical infrastructures" as assemblages that serve the Canadian public, need protection, and reimagine the social good in terms of the aggregate economy (Mitchell 2011; Murphy 2017). Yet as Unist'ot'en spokesperson Freda Huson makes clear, Indigenous resistance to "critical infrastructures" contests the very category of infrastructure itself, asserting alternative ontological and epistemological modes of relating to assemblages that move matter and sustain life.

Infrastructures that transport people have been identified as formations of settler colonization. The railroads that facilitated westward expansion onto Indigenous territories in Canada and the United States were deeply colonial projects that required the labor of Chinese immigrants and the displacement of Indigenous peoples in order to build capital and deliver settlers to the West (Day 2016). Manu Vimalassery describes how the land grants underwriting the Central Pacific Railroad link the assertion of settler sovereignty to underlying Indigenous claims to land; the practice of "counter-sovereignty" in this case uses railroad infrastructure to both build on and replace preexisting Indigenous sovereignties to shape and expand colonial geographies (2014: 88). Other transportation infrastructures operate this way as well. Roxanne Dunbar-Ortiz notes, the extensive roadways used by North American Native peoples as trade routes before colonization have been paved over, forming the major highways of the United States and obscuring the mobility and presence of Native peoples, both historically and presently (2014: 28–30). In crucial ways, the concept of modern infrastructure elides the supposedly "nonmodern" assemblages of Indigenous peoples that were transformed into settler property and infrastructure. Settlers acquired their "modernity" as infrastructures facilitated dispossession while disavowing their roots in Indigenous organizations of space. If settler colonialism is a structure that "destroys to replace" (Wolfe 2006), then transportation infrastructures are themselves settler colonial technologies of invasion.

Since the very beginning of the settler colonial project in North America, infrastructures have been sites of contact, violence, tension, and competing jurisdiction. The infrastructures that support oil and gas development form a network of completed and proposed projects that are embedded in the national imaginaries of settler colonies while also reaching beyond international borders. They enable the material transit of energy, as well as the ideological claims of settler sovereignty over Indigenous territory.[2] Proposed pipelines assume and assert settler jurisdiction over the unceded Wet'suwet'en territories

2. For an excellent report on the political context of pipeline infrastructures and their claims to Indigenous territories, see Mazer (2017).

in British Columbia in order to usher in prosperity for the Canadian public, and they do so in concert with transportation infrastructures. When police approached the border of Unist'ot'en territory in 2015, they told us that our actions were not allowed because we were blocking a "public highway" (a logging road). Hence, the language of infrastructure is used to delegitimize Indigenous claims to territory by replacing them with allusions to the legality of "public" access. The extraction of oil and gas is normalized, and the petro-economy invades Native lands in the name of the settler public, extending the net of economic relations reliant on oil and gas and making it harder and harder to imagine and live into relations outside of capitalism.

These are also infrastructures of white supremacy. For the Unist'ot'en clan of the Wet'suwet'en nation, resistance to the construction of pipelines in their territory is resistance to the invasion of the Canadian state onto territories that they have never ceded or surrendered to the province or the crown. Unist'ot'en people regularly remind visitors to their land that it is not Canada, it is not British Columbia: it is unceded Wet'suwet'en territory. While oil and gas companies strive to present their projects as just another national infrastructure—TransCanada's (2017) Coastal Gaslink pipeline is even pitched as a boon to other infrastructures: "Annual properly tax revenues generated from the project can also help build important infrastructure that we rely on every day like roads, schools and hospitals"—white possession continues to naturalize projects that cut through Indigenous territories in service of the national interest.

Oil and gas extraction, in particular, creates spaces of unchecked white masculinity in which incidents of violent abduction, abuse, and rape of Indigenous women and girls have skyrocketed (Gibson et al. 2017; Jensen 2017; WEA and NYSHN 2016). Attention to alternatives would recognize the work done by generations of women and Two-Spirit people to protect and maintain the assemblages that sustain Indigenous life in the face of settler colonial invasion[3]—work that the Dakota scholar Kim TallBear (2016) calls caretaking relations. In spaces of land defense and Indigenous resistance across Canada and the United States, women have led movements to protect the land and water and to reinvigorate alternatives to infrastructures threatening destruction of land and Indigenous ways of life (Kino-nda-niimi Collective 2014).

Anthropology of Infrastructure

Infrastructure is by definition future oriented; it is assembled in the service of worlds to come. Infrastructure demands a focus on what underpins and enables formations of power and the material organization of everyday life in time and space. Cowen (2017) offers an expansive definition of infrastructures as "the collectively constructed systems that also build and sustain human life," and terms the alternatives to state systems "fugitive infrastructures." Fugitivity calls our attention to the ways in which time, space, and the material world are organized by power yet constantly disrupted and remade. An analysis that dwells in "fugitivity" attends to that which can be gleaned from spaces of power (Moten and Harney 2013).

The concept of "fugitivity," however, has temporal and theoretical limitations in relation to Indigenous movements. While Indigenous movements may disrupt settler infrastructures and the capitalist relations they sustain, these movements are not transitory, fleeting, or temporary (Spice 2016). Furthermore, Indigenous peoples are not fugitives "on the run" from settler governance. Instead, resistance to invasive infrastructures requires standing in place, in our territories, and insisting on our prior and continuing relationships to the lands, kin, and other-than-human relations that those infrastructures threaten.

Indigenous blockades of "critical infrastructures" disrupt the reproduction of settler futures through assertion of Indigenous jurisdiction, placing the settler future in suspension, Shiri Pasternak and Tia Dafnos describe how blockades trigger state securitization: "Simply put, Indigenous peoples

---

3. *Gunalchéesh* (thank you) to a reviewer for pointing out that this is also true of the word "sovereignty." For a discussion of Indigenous appropriations of sovereignty, see Barker (2006, 2017).

interrupt commodity flows by asserting jurisdiction and sovereignly over their lands and resources in places that form choke points to the circulation of capital. Thus, the securitization of 'critical infrastructure'—essentially supply chains of capital, such as private pipelines and public transport routes—has become a priority in mitigating the potential threat of Indigenous jurisdiction" (2017: 3).

Movements to block critical infrastructures, such as those enacted across the country during the Idle No More movement (the "Native winter" of 2012–2013), highlight the ability of dispersed Native nations to significantly alter the circulation of capital by shutting down highways, bridges, and railroads. By participating in the politics of blockades, Indigenous activists are correctly identifying the reliance of the petro-state on energy infrastructure and forcing open the contradiction between proposed and presumed energy infrastructure on stolen land.

The naturalization of resource extraction projects alongside the suspension of Indigenous life through settler infrastructure projects combine to mask the ways in which the language of infrastructure itself can work to legitimize "modern" assemblages like pipelines while rendering invisible the living assemblages that would strengthen Indigenous sovereignty and lifeways. If, following Larkin, we turn to "what one sees as infrastructural (and thus causal) and what one leaves out" as a window into state aspirations and intentions, the Canadian context of oil and gas extraction returns the following conclusion: in the eyes of the Canadian state, oil and gas pipelines count as infrastructural, while the relations of rivers, glaciers, lakes, mountains, plants and animals and Indigenous nations are the natural resources to be modernized as commodities or subjects.

Many scholars have connected infrastructures to state promises of modernity, progress, and nationhood (Bear 2007; Coronil 1997; Ferry and Limbert 2008; Gledhill 2008; Mrazek 2002). The promise of oil, Fernando Coronil (1997) explains, allows the state to perform all kinds of "magic"; Andrew Apter (2005) explores this magic through the dramaturgy and spectacle underlying oil and the mirage of progress in Nigeria. But what of infrastructures that do not yet exist? How might spaces of anticipation,

spaces slated as "energy corridors," work as transit to capitalist petro-futures? And how might these futures be disrupted?

While anthropological definitions of infrastructure carry the political weight of state and industry projects, they have also made space to investigate the affective, social, and temporal aspects of infrastructure. Akhil Gupta (2015) explains that infrastructure can illuminate social futures, since state infrastructure projects are often long-term investments. Infrastructures "tell us a great deal about aspirations, anticipations, and imaginations of the future . . . what people think their society should be like, what they might wish it to be, and what kind of statement the government wants to make about that vision."

Pipelines, then, become an inevitable harbinger of social progress, and they are proposed across territories as if they are already bringing the benefits of their completion. The temporality of infrastructure construction further brings with it reorganizations of experience. The new socialities and relations formed through infrastructures are themselves worthy of study.

Governments intending to extend settler colonial control over Indigenous lands through pipeline construction face the continued resistance of Indigenous peoples, forcing oil and gas projects to linger for years between proposal and completion. ". . . The temporality of suspension is not between past and future, between beginning and end, but constitutes its own ontic condition just as surely as does completion." For many Indigenous peoples, the completion of pipelines includes the inevitable spill, the environmental catastrophe, the destruction of ways of life. Holding projects in suspension, then, is a key tactic of Indigenous resistance.

Indigenous feminist perspectives, however, point to how suspension also characterizes Indigenous life under settler occupation. Here we can also look to Traci Voyles's (2015) Indigenous feminist-informed *Wastelanding*; Voyles shows how the discourses about land in the Southwestern United States shape settler colonial violence: the land is cast as already wasted, allowing the continued settler appropriation of resources and reckless contamination of land and water. The settler accumulation of energy, capital, and territory is reliant on the parallel distribution of toxicity and violence to Indigenous nations, and forms of immediate state violence (like the militarized response to Standing Rock Indian Reservation water protectors) are tied to the slow environmental destruction of Indigenous homelands (Montoya 2016).

The uneven distribution of infrastructures also draws attention to who is seen as part of a society worth reproducing and who is not. Recall Harper and Trudeau advertising the future of Canada through pipelines and energy infrastructures while minimizing the threats to Indigenous sovereignty and the environment required to complete these state-building projects. The effects are dramatic abandonments and exclusions from the social benefits promised by modernity's infrastructures in order to secure resource extraction. Houses provided for Aboriginal families may look like houses, but they are not. Their pipes lead to nowhere and are constructed with cheap and crumbling materials. These "not-houses" draw attention to the way in which infrastructure can, through its pull to the literal, mask the material conditions lurking just underneath the surface.

Like many infrastructures that are subject to state investment, oil and gas infrastructures are aspirational. They anticipate the circulation of certain materials, the proliferation of certain worlds, the reproduction of certain subjects. But, sometimes, their bluster hides their tenuous nature, and their future focus creates an opening in which other possibilities can assert themselves. While Trudeau has heralded his government's approval of two major pipeline projects, another was canceled after many years of Indigenous resistance and a lack of proper consultation with Indigenous peoples (Tasker 2016). If Indigenous resistance forces pipeline projects into suspension, futures might grow in the space between proposal and completion (a space that, if Indigenous land defenders have their way, leads to the reversal of settler colonialism).

Field Insights: Relations against Pipelines

Before heading out to Unist'ot'en Camp for the second time (in 2016), I drove a rusting Toyota truck up to the Yukon territory, following my parents along the Alaska Highway and stopping to camp along the way. We were also going to meet and remeet my family.

I was nervous. Having grown up on Treaty 7 territories in southern Alberta, I felt like an interloper and outsider. The day after we arrived in Whitehorse, my auntie had a barbecue for family. Put the word out, expected a handful of people. Suddenly, the house was full. Dozens of people, all related to me. All my relations. I sat outside with a moose burger in hand, talking to a maybe cousin of mine. He convinces me to make a kinship chart. I find a piece of paper and sit down on the deck. People gather around, and I map out our relations. All of us are descendants of my great-grandmother Jenny LeBarge, though we can now trace the tree back further, back a few more generations to ancestors whose names are all Tlingit or Southern Tutchone, not the names of the places the colonizers found them. Our family name—LeBarge—is a misspelled tribute to Lake Laberge, which was named for a French-Canadian explorer. And my people weren't even really from there; we migrated in from the coast of Alaska. While explorers were lazy historians.

During the final week of the camp, after a trip out berry picking with all the youth, we get a moose. That moose is my relation; this land is my responsibility. This is when I realize I have wholly committed myself to a "next time," and the pull back to the land is so strong that when I arrive in NYC I am ill for weeks, heartsick as my connection to both territory and people wears under the strain of distance, the fast-paced crunch of capitalist time, the pressing need for me to make my "summer research" legible and theoretical and fundable.

It has become clear to me that spaces like Unist'ot'en Camp are doing more than blocking pipelines. The work of undoing settler colonial invasion requires blocking, resisting, and suspending the infrastructures of oil and gas and the systemic dominance of capitalism. It also requires attending to and caring for the networks of relations that make Indigenous survival possible. These are the relations that linked my nation to the Wet'suwet'en people before our territories felt the first footsteps of while settlers. These are the relations that bring Indigenous youth back onto the land and into material relation with the other-than-human beings that share their territories. These are the relations that connect me to other Indigenous peoples as we struggle to regain ancestral skills that we have lost. These are the Indigenous assemblages that recognize our dependence on other-than-humans for our survival as peoples. These are the relations threatened by invasive infrastructures and their toxic consequences. If the moose, the berry patches, the salmon, and the bears are destroyed, then so are we.

When Indigenous land defenders point to "our critical infrastructures," they are pointing to another set of relations that sustains the collective life of Indigenous peoples: the human and non-human networks that have supported Indigenous polities on this continent for tens of thousands of years. Indigenous peoples reject the idea that the way of life supported by pipeline infrastructure should be accelerated or intensified, and instead step into the vulnerable and volatile space between the proposal and potential completion of pipelines to protect the land, water, air, plant, and animal relations instead. By doing so, they attend to the "vital systems" that form alternatives to capitalist exploitation, alternatives to oil-soaked futures, alternatives to the unquestioned occupation of the settler state.

By performatively "seeing like an oil company" (Ferguson 2005), land defenders appropriate the language of infrastructure to question the terms of industrial invasion onto their territories. And by building alternatives based on Indigenous relations of ethics and care in the aspirational space of proposed pipeline routes, encampments like Unist'ot'en Camp challenge the destructive teleology of settler petro-futures. At Unist'ot'en Camp, the hosts remind visitors, "this is not Canada, this is not British Columbia: this is unceded Wet'suwet'en territory." We must critically analyze the tactics and strategies of colonial domination while strengthening our relations. We can do this by supporting spaces of resistance like Unist'ot'en Camp, by holding each other accountable for the relationship-building work that underlies everything we do. We can challenge the inevitability of settler colonial invasion by returning to the networks that have sustained us for tens of thousands of years on our territories and by living into better relations with each other and our other-than-human kin. We pick the berries, skin the moose, protect the water. We feed *our* critical infrastructures, in hopes that they will flourish again.

References

Apter, Andrew. 2005. *The Pan-African Nation: Oil and the Spectacle of Culture in Nigeria.* Chicago: University of Chicago Press.

Barker, Joanne. 2006. *Sovereignty Matters: Locations of Contestation and Possibility in Indigenous Struggles for Self-Determination.* Lincoln: University of Nebraska Press.

Barker, Joanne. 2017. "Introduction." in *Critically Sovereign*, ed. Joanne Barker, 1–44. Durham, NC: Duke University Press.

Bear, Laura. 2007. *Lines of the Nation: Indian Railway Workers, Bureaucracy, and the Intimate Historical Self.* New York: Columbia University Press.

Berke, Jeremy. 2017. "'No Country Would Find 173 billion Barrels of Oil in the Ground and Just Leave Them': Justin Trudeau Gets a Standing Ovation at an Energy Conference in Texas." *Business Insider*, 10 March. http://www.businessinsider.com./trudeau-gets-a-standing-ovation-at-energy-industry-conference-oil-gas-2017-3.

Coronil, Fernando. 1997. *The Magical State: Nature, Money and Modernity in Venezuela.* Chicago: Chicago University Press.

Coulthard, Glen. 2014. *Red Skin White Masks: Rejecting the Colonial Politics of Recognition.* Minneapolis: University of Minnesota Press.

Cowen, Deborah. 2017. "Infrastructures of Empire and Resistance." Verso blog, 25 January. https://www.versobooks.com/blogs/3067-infrastructures-of-empire-and-resistance.

Day, Iyko. 2016. *Alien Capital: Asian Racialization and the Logic of Settler Colonial Capitalism.* Durham, NC: Duke University Press.

Dunbar-Ortiz, Roxanne. 2014. *An Indigenous Peoples' History of the United States.* Boston: Beacon Hill Press.

Ferguson James. 2005. "Seeing Like an Oil Company: Space, Security, and Global Capital in Neoliberal Africa." *American Anthropologist* 107 (3): 377–382.

Ferry, Elizabeth, and Mandana Limbert. 2008. "Introduction." In *Timely Assets: The Politics of Resources and Their Temporalities*, ed. Elizabeth Ferry and Mandana Limbert, 3–24. Santa Fe, NM: School for Advanced Research Press.

Gibson, Ginger, Kathleen Yung, Libby Chisholm, and Hannah Quinn, with Lake Babine Nation and Nak'azdli

Whut'en. 2017. *Indigenous Communities and Industrial Camps: Promoting Healthy Communities in Settings of Industrial Change.* Victoria, BC: Firelight Group.

Gilmore, Ruth Wilson. 2017. "Abolition Geography and the Problem of Innocence." In *Futures of Black Radicalism*, ed. Gaye Theresa Johnson and Alex Lubin, digital edition. London: Verso.

Gledhill, John. 2008. "'The People's Oil'": Nationalism, Globalization, and the Possibility of Another Country in Brazil, Mexico, and Venezuela." *Focaal—Journal of Global and Historical Anthropology* 52: 57–74.

Gupta, Akhil. 2015. "The Infrastructure Toolbox: Suspension." *Cultural Anthropology,* 24 September. https://culanth.org/fieldsights/722-suspension.

House of Commons of Canada. 2015. Bill C-51, Anti-Terrorism Act, 2nd sess., 41st Parliament. http://www.parl.gc.ca/HousePublications/Publication. aspx?Language=E&Mode=I&DocId=7965854.

Jensen, Toni. 2017. "Women in the Fracklands: On Water, Land, Bodies, and Standing Rock." *Catapult*, 3 January. https://catapult.co/stories/women-in-the-fracklands-on-water-land-bodies-and-standing-rock.

Kino-nda-niimi Collective. 2014. *The Winter We Danced: Voices from the Past, the Future, and the Idle No More Movement.* Winnipeg: ARP Books.

Larkin, Brian. 2013. "The Politics and Poetics of Infrastructure." *Annual Review of Anthropology* 42: 327–343. https://doi.org/10.1146/annurev-anthro-092412-155522.

Mazer, Katie. 2017. *Mapping a Many Headed Hydra: The Struggle Over the Dakota Access Pipeline.* Infrastructure Otherwise Report no. 001. http://infrastructureotherwise.org/DAPL_Report_20170921_FINAL.pdf.

Mitchell, Timothy. 2011. *Carbon Democracy: Political Power in the Age of Oil.* New York: Verso.

Montoya, Teresa. 2016. "Violence on the Ground, Violence below the Ground." *Cultural Anthropology*, 22 December. https://culanth.org/fieldsights/1018-violence-on-the-ground-violence-below-the-ground.

Moten, Fred, and Stefano Harney. 2013. *The Undercommons: Fugitive Planning and Black Study.* New York: Minor Compositions.

Mrazek, Rudolf. 2002. *Engineers of Happy Land: Technology and Nationalism in a Colony.* Princeton, NJ: Princeton University Press.

Murphy, Michelle. 2017. *The Economization of Life.* Durham, NC: Duke University Press.

Pasternak, Shiri, and Tia Dafnos. 2017. "How Does the Settler State Secure the Circuitry of Capital?" *Environment and Planning D: Society and Space.* First published 7 June. https://doi.org/10.1177/0263775817713209.

PMO (Office of the Prime Minister). 2016. "Statement by the Prime Minister of Canada on National Aboriginal Day." 21 June. https://pm.gc.ca/eng/news/2016/06/21/statement-prime-minister-canada-national-aboriginal-day.

PSC (Public Safety Canada). 2018. "Critical Infrastructure." Modified 22 May. https://www.publicsafety.gc.ca/cnt/ntnl-scrt/crtcl-nfrstrctr/index-en.aspx.

RCMP (Royal Canadian Mounted Police). 2014. *Criminal Threats to the Canadian Petroleum Industry.* Critical Infrastructure Intelligence Assessment. Ottawa: RCMP.

Simmons, Kristen. 2017. "Settler Atmospherics." *Cultural Anthropology*, 20 November. https://culanth.org/fieldsights/1221-settler-atmospherics.

Simpson, Audra. 2014. *Mohawk Interruptus: Political Life across the Borders of Settler States.* Durham, NC: Duke University Press.

Spice, Anne. 2016. "Interrupting Industrial and Academic Extraction on Native Land." *Cultural Anthropology*, 22 December 22, 2016. https://culanth.org/fieldsights/1021-interrupting-industrial-and-academic-extraction-on-native-land.

TallBear, Kim. 2016. "Badass (Indigenous) Women Caretake Relations: #NoDAPL, IdleNoMore, #BlackLivesMatter." *Cultural Anthropology,* 22 December. https://culanth.org/fieldsights/1019-badass-indigenous-women-caretake-relations- nodapl-idlenomore-blacklivesmatter.

Tasker, John Paul. 2016. "Trudeau Cabinet Approves Trans Mountain, Line 3 Pipelines, Rejects Northern Gateway." CBC News, 29 November. http://www.cbc.ca/news/politics/federal-cabinet-trudeau-pipeline-decisions- 1.3872828.

TransCanada Corporation. 2018. "Economic Benefits." Coastal GasLink Pipeline Project, accessed 18 June. http://www.coastalgaslink.com/benefits/economic-benefits.

Vimalassery, Manu. 2014. "The Prose of Counter-Sovereignty." In *Formations of United States Colonialism,* ed. Alyosha Goldstein, 87–109. Durham, NC: Duke University Press.

Voyles, Traci. 2015. *Wastelanding: Legacies of Uranium Mining in Navajo Country.* Minneapolis: University of Minnesota Press.

Wolfe, Patrick. 2006. "Settler Colonialism and the Elimination of the Native." *Journal of Genocide Research* 8 (4): 387–409. https://doi.org/10.1080/14623520601056240.

WEA (Women's Earth Alliance) and NYSHN (Native Youth Sexual Health Network). 2016. *Violence on the Land, Violence on Our Bodies: Building an Indigenous Response to Environmental Violence.* http://landbodydefense.org/uploads/files/VLVBReportToolkit2016.pdf.

CHAPTER 24

Indigenous Feminism Perspectives on Environmental Justice

Deborah McGregor

Introduction

In this chapter, you will learn about the emergence of a distinct theoretical, methodological, and practical approach for accounting for gender in relation to environmental justice called Indigenous feminism . . .

Indigenous knowledge systems emerged as a field of study to address the hegemony of Western knowledge. Western knowledges have contributed to the colonization and continued marginalization of Indigenous peoples, women in particular (Kermoal & Altamirano-Jiménez, 2016). The importance of Indigenous knowledges is well recognized internationally and has been for decades in the environmental realm (Kermoal & Altamirano-Jiménez, 2016). Much attention has been paid to the potential benefits of IKS in addressing local, regional, and global environmental challenges. Less attention has been paid to how knowledge is specific to "gender, age, sexuality, livelihoods, and experiences of colonization" (Kermoal & Altamirano-Jiménez, 2016, p. 9). Gender differentiation and specialization means that men and women hold different knowledges of the environment/waters and furthermore have different priorities. "Indigenous women's knowledge extends beyond the activities done by women and involves a system of inquiry that reveals Indigenous processes of observing and understanding and the

protocols for being and participating in the world" (Kermoal & Altamirano-Jiménez, 2016, p. 11).

In this chapter, the concept of Indigenous feminism will be applied to environmental and water justice. This is achieved by analyzing international Indigenous environmental/water declarations generated by Indigenous women. What characteristics define a unique approach to environmental and water justice? What actions have Indigenous women taken to address their distinct experiences and concerns? What do Indigenous women envision as their future? These are some of the questions that will be addressed.

Indigenous/Aboriginal Feminism

Until recently, very little had been written specifically about Indigenous feminism (Huhndorf & Suzack, 2010). The relevance of Indigenous feminism in Indigenous societies has been questioned in some circles as it is argued that women enjoyed far more power, respect, and autonomy than their European counterparts (Green, 2007). The reality is that colonization has "involved their removal from positions of power, the replacement of gender roles with Western patriarchal practices and exertion of colonial control

McGregor, Deborah, In Gül Çalişkan, ed., *Gendering Globalization, Globalizing Gender: Postcolonial Perspectives*, Don Mills: Oxford University Press, © 2020.

over Indigenous communities through the management of women's bodies and sexual violence" (Huhndorf & Suzack, 2010, p. l). Further, the contemporary lived reality of Indigenous women is primarily that of racist, colonial, and patriarchal forms of oppression evidenced in both settler society and Indigenous societies. This is in part due to the forced imposition of colonial patriarchy in Indigenous societies and the subsequent internalization of such ideologies. Indigenous women are doubly subjugated because they experience oppression in dominant society and often in their own. This was evident in the public inquiry on Missing and Murdered Indigenous Women and Girls, which recognized that Indigenous women experience far more violence historically and currently than other women (Ambler, 2014).

Indigenous feminism, applying a gendered analysis, reveals violence of all kinds, at various levels and scales, in processes of historical and contemporary colonialism. If gender was an organizing principle to colonize societies of Indigenous peoples, to undermine Indigenous women, their political, economic, social, cultural, and spiritual role, then decolonization must also include a gendered aspect (Kermoal & Altamirano-Jiménez, 2016). Indigenous feminist analysis and activism "must aim to understand the changing circumstances, the commonalities, and the specifics of Indigenous women across time and space; it must seek ultimately to attain social justice not only along gender lines but also along those of race, class and sexuality" (Huhndorf & Suzack, 2010, p. 3).

Anti-colonial Analysis and Indigenous Feminism

Anti-colonial analysis and Indigenous feminism have their own theorists, practices, and spheres of engagement and generate space for addressing environmental/water (in)justice from a gendered lens (in this chapter, that of women). These frames of analysis are evident and asserted by Indigenous women around the world, as seen in the stated declarations of Indigenous women at various fora. Indigenous women have distinct contributions to make to the international dialogue on the global environmental crisis, in particular environmental/water justice

issues including climate change. The next section examines three international declarations prepared by Indigenous women over the past two decades: the Beijing Declaration of Indigenous Women (1995); the Mandaluyong Declaration (2010); and the Lima Declaration (2013). These declarations exemplify anti-colonial and feminist articulations of how women and the people (and non-humans) they care for are affected by a continuing colonial agenda, manifested in capitalism, globalization, and trade liberalization.

Case Studies in Applying Anti-colonial and Indigenous Feminism

Indigenous women in the Global South and North are linked through coming together at various international environmental and sustainable development gatherings to collectively assert their own voices and perspectives. Indigenous women, often in opposition to the dominant environmental/sustainable development paradigm, not only offer invaluable and necessary critiques but also provide a plan of action for a more just future. Three case studies form the basis of the next section: the Beijing Declaration of Indigenous Women; the Mandaluyong Declaration of the Global Conference on Indigenous Women, Climate Change and REDD Plus; and the Lima Declaration: World Conference of Indigenous Women: Progress and Challenges Regarding the Future We Want.

The Beijing Declaration of Indigenous Women (1995)

Indigenous women involved in the development of the Beijing Declaration of Indigenous Women, convened as part of the fourth World Conference on Women, provided a powerful anti-colonial critique of what is referred to as "**recolonization.**"

> "The 'New World Order' which is engineered by those who have abused and raped Mother Earth, colonized, marginalized, and discriminated against us, is being imposed on us viciously. This is recolonization coming under the name

of globalization and trade liberalization" (Beijing Declaration of Indigenous Women, 1995, 1, article 6).

We, the women of the original peoples of the world have struggled actively to defend our rights to self-determination and to our territories which have been invaded and colonized by powerful nations and interests. We have been and are continuing to suffer from multiple oppressions; as indigenous peoples, as citizens of colonized and neo-colonial countries, as women, and as members of the poorer classes of society. In spite of this, we have been and continue to protect, transmit, and develop our indigenous cosmovision, our science and technologies, our arts and culture, and our Indigenous socio-political economic systems, *which are in harmony with the natural laws of Mother Earth*. We still retain the *ethical and esthetic values, the knowledge and philosophy, the spirituality, which conserves and nurtures Mother Earth*. We are persisting in our struggles for self-determination and for our rights to our territories. This has been shown in our tenacity and capacity to withstand and survive the colonization happening in our lands in the last 500 years (b, 1, article 5; italics mine).

The women pointed out that the broader international environmental meetings failed to critique the "new world order," stating:

This poverty is caused by the same powerful nations and interests who have colonized us and are continuing to recolonize, homogenize, and impose their economic growth development model and monocultures on us. It does not present a coherent analysis of why is it that the goals of "equality, development, and peace" becomes more elusive to women each day in spite of three UN conferences on women since 1975 (Beijing Declaration of Indigenous Women, 1995, 2, article 11).

The non-economic activities of Indigenous women have been ignored and rendered invisible, although these sustain the existence of Indigenous peoples. Our dispossession from our territorial land and water base, upon which our existence and identity depends, must be addressed as a key problem (Beijing Declaration of Indigenous Women, 1995, 2, article 7).

The Beijing Declaration offers 30 proposals and demands that signify a rejection of the new world economic order and the move to a world based on responsibility and caring for the earth to sustain all life. Indigenous feminism sentiments (although not termed in that way by the Indigenous women at the gathering) in the Beijing Declaration as distinct impacts on women are outlined throughout. Asserting Indigenous feminism as a form of critique of how women are treated in the international environmental realm also includes an assertion of Indigenous world view, legal orders, philosophies, and knowledges as part of a sustainable path forward. For example, in relation to environment/water, article 22 states that Indigenous peoples will decide what "to do with our lands and territories and to develop it an integrated, sustainable way, according to our cosmovision" (Beijing Declaration of Indigenous Women, 1995, p. 3). The first article in the declaration outlines the responsibility to care for the earth and points to the knowledge, philosophy, spirituality, and natural laws that nurture the earth. However, Indigenous lifeways are not uncritically accepted, and it is clear that those aspects that are discriminatory and disadvantage women in any way should be abolished. This is similar to the critique that Indigenous feminists make of Indigenous societies, particularly the way that colonialism has been internalized in many communities. For example, article 36 advocates that Indigenous customary laws and justice systems that are supportive of women be recognized and reinforced and those that are not be eradicated (Beijing Declaration of Indigenous Women, 1995, p. 4). The Beijing Declaration centres the concerns and calls to action of Indigenous women, pointing to human rights violations and violence against Indigenous women. It outlines a set of proposals including the right to self-determination (in all aspects: health, education, intellectual and cultural heritage, and, of critical importance here, elevating the participation of Indigenous women at every level and scale in a dialogue that affects the lives, livelihood, and sovereignty of Indigenous peoples).

The Mandaluyong Declaration (2010)

The Mandaluyong Declaration of the Global Conference on Indigenous Women, Climate Change and REDD Plus, held in Legend Villas, Philippines, in 2010, conveys similar sentiments to the Beijing Declaration of 15 years earlier. Eighty women, from 60 Indigenous Nations and 29 countries, gathered to tell their own stories of how they are differently affected by the impacts of climate change on the basis of gender. The anti-colonial critique is evident in the declaration, the women clearly critical of the world economic order.

> While we have least contributed to the problem of climate change, we have to carry the burdens of adapting to its adverse impacts. This is because of the unwillingness of rich, industrialized countries to change their unsustainable production and consumption patterns and pay their environmental debt for causing this ecological disaster. Modernity and capitalist development which is based on the use of fossil fuels and which promotes unsustainable and excessive production and consumption of unnecessary goods and services, individualism, patriarchy, and incessant profit-seeking have caused climate change (Mandaluyong Declaration, 2010, para. 1).

The delegates all point to the lived experience of Indigenous peoples and in particular how women are affected by climate change. They point to the underlying causes of climate change (modernity and capitalist development that is extractive and destructive). Climate change has contributed to the undermining of traditional livelihoods, identity, and the well-being of the people, unprecedented disasters, loss of land and communities, and food and **water insecurity**, all resulting in "hunger, disease and misery" (Mandaluyong Declaration, 2010, para. 3). The combined impacts of climate change point to a loss of land and lives, which has

political and legal implications for the exercise of sovereignty.

Women are particularly compromised because of their caregiving role in families and communities: as "main water providers, we have to search and fight for access to the few remaining water resources" (Mandaluyong Declaration, 2010, para. 5). The declaration adds:

> Complicating these are the situations of multiple discrimination based on gender and ethnic identity. These are manifested in the lack of gender and culturally sensitive basic social services such as education and health and our lack of access to basic utility services such as water and energy. The systematic discrimination and non-recognition of our sustainable resource management and customary governance systems and their access, control and ownership over their lands, territories and resources persists (Mandaluyong Declaration, 2010).

In terms of Indigenous knowledge systems, the declaration points out that the norms, laws, knowledge, and values that guide sustainable resource governance are weakened by climate change. Yet, the women point out:

> We shared how we are addressing the issues of food, water and energy insecurity. How we are sustaining and transmitting our traditional knowledge to the younger generations. How we are continuing our traditional land, water and forest resources management systems. How we are exerting our best to ensure the overall health and well being of our families and communities. Our efforts to recover, strengthen, use, and adapt our traditional knowledge and our ecosystems to climate change and to transmit these to our youth are bearing some good results. . . . We shared our Indigenous ways of predicting and coping with climate change–related disasters and we hope to further strengthen these knowledge and practices (Mandaluyong Declaration, 2010, p. 3).

And point out that "we continue to use and adapt our traditional knowledge and land, water, forest and natural resource management systems to climate change" (Mandaluyong Declaration, 2010, p. v3) and stress the importance of Indigenous knowledge systems as key to the future: "Our spirituality which links humans and nature, the seen and the unseen, the past, present, and future, and the living and non-living has been and remains as the foundation of our sustainable resources management and use. We believe if we continue to live by our values and still use our sustainable systems and practices for meeting our basic needs, we can adapt better to climate change" (Mandaluyong Declaration, 2010, p. 4).

The delegates who generated the Mandaluyong Declaration advocate for the recognition and implementation of the United Nations Declaration on the Rights of Indigenous Peoples (UNDRIP) as a way to help protect peoples from the risks associated with REDD Plus. Similar to the Beijing Declaration, the Mandaluyong Declaration outlines priority work areas and actions, including:

- Awareness raising, skills training workshops, information dissemination.
- Gender analysis of policies and approaches for mitigation and adaptation.
- Skills training workshops that are gender-sensitive, including the sharing of knowledge with grassroots women's organizations.

Indigenous women call for research on climate change impacts on Indigenous women and on climate change adaptation and mitigation. Ideally, such research would be conducted by Indigenous women themselves in the following areas:

- Food security and climate impacts and roles of women.
- Traditional knowledge and community forest management and the roles of Indigenous women.
- Traditional livelihoods of Indigenous women and climate change.
- Gender dimensions of adaptation and mitigation policies and measures.

Indigenous women call for enhancement of traditional practices and systems and more specifically to "reinforce Indigenous women's traditional knowledge on mitigation and adaptation and facilitate the transfer of this knowledge to the younger generations" (Mandaluyong Declaration, 2010, article 3.4).

Indigenous women call for increased political participation and policy advocacy: "Indigenous women in political and decision making bodies and processes and in the formation of the climate agenda" at all levels and scales (global, national, regional and local), essentially enabling women to speak and advocate for themselves (Mandaluyong Declaration, 2010, article 5.2).

Indigenous women advocate for a human rights–based approach to dealing with climate change, arguing in favour of "a holistic framework for a gender-sensitive, ecosystem, human rights-based and knowledge-based approach to climate adaptation and mitigation efforts (Mandaluyong Declaration, 2010, p. 7). Although the Mandaluyong Declaration was generated by Indigenous women, the space is open for going beyond non-binary gender expressions by the inclusion of "gender-based analysis" and "sensitivity."

The Lima Declaration (2013)

The Lima Declaration: World Conference of Indigenous women: Progress and Challenges Regarding the Future We Want advocates for the principle "Nothing about us, without us" and further declares, "Everything about us, with us." The women call for "the direct, full and effective participation of Indigenous Peoples; including the vital role of Indigenous women in all matters related to our human rights, political status, and wellbeing" (Lima Declaration, 2013, para. 1). In relation to the environment:

> We, Indigenous women, affirm our responsibility to protect the Earth, our Mother. Indigenous women experience the same pain and impacts from the physical abuse and excessive exploitation of the natural world, of which we are an integral part. We will defend our lands, waters, territories and resources, which are the source of our survival, with our lives.
>
> Protection of Mother Earth is a historic, sacred and continuing responsibility

of the world's Indigenous Peoples, as the ancestral guardians of the Earth's lands, waters, oceans, ice, mountains and forests. These have sustained our distinct cultures, spirituality, traditional economies, social structures, institutions, and political relations from immemorial times. Indigenous women play a primary role in safeguarding and sustaining Mother Earth and her cycles (Lima Declaration, 2013, paras. 4 & 5).

As in the Beijing and Mandaluyong declarations, the women advocate for self-determination through the UNDRIP and human rights instruments. They point out that it is Indigenous peoples who bear the burden of social and environmental harms. Women and girls bear particularly insidious harms, including environmental violence and human rights violations.

The anti-colonial critique is evident when the women point out that the environmental crisis faced by all is due to the rise of the "exploitive model of economic growth and development" (Lima Declaration, 2013, para. 9) and the nations' failure to uphold Indigenous and human rights. They state that nations must: "recognize and respect our rights to land, territories and resources as enshrined in Indigenous customary law, the UNDRIP, and other international human rights instruments" (Lima Declaration, 2013, para. 10).

> Finally, we affirm that Indigenous women have knowledge, wisdom, and practical experience, which has sustained human societies over generations. We, as mothers, life givers, culture bearers, and economic providers, nurture the linkages across generations and are the active sources of continuity and positive change (Lima Declaration, 2013, para. 15).

The Indigenous feminist and indigenous knowledge perspectives are evident in that the declaration affirms that women have knowledge and expertise that can contribute to the well-being of the earth and peoples. The women bring forward the distinct concerns, issues, and experience of Indigenous women, in addition to the unique contributions women

make to addressing challenges at every scale. As in the other declarations, Indigenous sovereignty is asserted and understood as central to a sustainable future.

Conclusion

Indigenous women can offer distinct contributions to combatting the current environmental crisis based on their responsibilities and knowledge systems that have supported Indigenous societies for millennia. For decades, Indigenous women from across the globe have gathered to share their experiences, concerns, and knowledges and to advocate for a sustainable future. The Beijing, Mandaluyong, and Lima declarations by Indigenous women are anti-colonial in their character as they uncover the underlying reasons for ongoing environmental recolonization, dispossession, and violence. However, each declaration also lays out future priorities and plans.

It should be noted that there is a significant gap in recognizing gender beyond the man/woman binary, and work needs to be done to ensure that Indigenous non-binary gender expressions are accounted for.

Tying It Together

This chapter's main purpose was to point out that Indigenous women face unique challenges that are tied to the fate to the earth. The distinct concerns of women can be addressed by Indigenous feminism. This chapter also informs you that gender must be considered more broadly and include non-binary persons. While gender analysis has been and continues to be discussed in detail in many settings, there remain many international, national, and local fora where this is unfortunately not the case. This is especially true in regard to both Indigenous feminism and climate change policy development.

An anti-colonial analysis reveals the underlying ideologies that have resulted in the global environmental crisis. An Indigenous feminist analysis reveals that there are considerations unique to Indigenous women that UNDRIP and other human rights instruments hold as key to addressing.

Call to Action

Support the goals and aspirations of Indigenous women outlined in the declarations noted in the chapter. There are many ways in which this can be done in everyday practice; just some are mentioned here. Recognize that whatever happens to women happens to the earth and whatever happens to the earth happens to women. Support Indigenous women in their efforts to protect the environment whenever you can. Educate yourself: attend and participate in presentations, workshops, lectures given by Indigenous women in your community or school. Also, educate others: for example, explain to friends, family, and colleagues the importance of self-determination of Indigenous peoples through the United Nations Declaration on the Rights of Indigenous Peoples. Support non-binary people and facilitate their voices and experiences whenever possible. Support land/water-based education to reconnect with Mother Earth. If your school or community does not provide it, then demand it. You can also listen to the voices of women online. There are many resources that can be found on the Internet (videos, presentations) of women offering their own voice. When they arise, support women during times of disaster or emergencies by fundraising. Finally, follow the Lima Declaration principle: "Nothing about us, without us." This means, no decision, discussion, dialogue, or conversation about Indigenous women should occur unless Indigenous women are equal participants with a strong voice. If you do not see Indigenous women in a meeting/workshop/conference yet people are talking about issues related to and affecting Indigenous women, then call participants out and demand for the participation of Indigenous women in the discussion.

Indigenous women have not been silent; they have voiced their concerns and outlined calls to action and plans of action, such as those put forward in the Mandaluyong Declaration, that have not been heeded. The challenge for all of us is to listen and to act on the knowledge Indigenous women share.

REFERENCES

Ambler, S. (2014). *Invisible women: A call to action. A report on missing and murdered Indigenous women in Canada.* Ottawa, ON: Speaker of the House of Commons. Retrieved from: http://ywcacanada.ca/data/research_docs/00000359.pdf.

Beijing Declaration of Indigenous Women. (1995). Beijing Declaration of Indigenous Women. Fourth World Conference on Women. Retrieved from http://www.ipcb.org/resolutions/htmls/dec_beijing.html.

Green, J. (Ed.). (2007). *Making space for Indigenous feminism.* Winnipeg. MB: Fernwood Publishing.

Huhndorf, S.M., & Suzack, C. (2010). Indigenous feminism: Theorizing the issues. In Cheryl Suzack, Shari Huhndorf, Jeanne Perreault, and Jean Barman (Eds), *Indigenous women and feminism: Politics, activism, culture* (pp. 1–17), Vancouver, BC: University of British Columbia Press.

Hunt, S. (2015). The embodiment of self-determination. Beyond the gender binary. In M. Greenwood, C. Reading, & S. de Leeuw (Eds), *Determinants of Indigenous peoples' health in Canada* (pp. 104–119). Toronto, ON: Canadian Scholars' Press.

Johnson, J.T., Cant, G., Howitt, R., & Peters, E. (2007). Creating anti-colonial geographies: Embracing Indigenous peoples' knowledges and rights. *Geographical Research,* 45(2), 117–120. doi: 10.1111/j.1745-5871.2007.00441.x.

Kermoal, N., & Altamirano-Jiménez, I. (Eds). (2016). *Living on the land: Indigenous women's understanding of place.* Edmonton, AB: Athabasca University Press.

Lima Declaration. (2013). The Lima Declaration: World Conference of Indigenous Women: Progress and Challenges Regarding the Future We Want. World Conference of Indigenous Women. Retrieved from: http://www.un.org/en/ga/president/68/pdf/6132014Lima-Declaration_web.pdf.

Louis, R.P. (2007). Can you hear us now? Voices from the margin: Using Indigenous methodologies in geographic research. *Geographical Research*, 45(2), 130–139. https://doi.org/10.1111/j.1745-5871.2007.00443.x.

Mandaluyoug Declaration. (2010). Mandaluyong Declaration of the Global Conference on Indigenous Women, Climate Change and REDD Plus. Manila, Philippines. Retrieved from: http://www.tebtebba.org/index.php/all-resources/file/144-indigenous-womens-declaration-on-cc-and-redd.

Native Youth Sexual Health Network. (2014). Violence on the land, violence on our bodies: Building an Indigenous response to environmental violence. Retrieved from: http://landbodydefense.org/uploads/files/VLVBReportToolkit2016.pdf.

Williams, L., Fletcher, A., Hanson, C., Neapole, J., & Pollack, M. (2018). *Women and climate change impacts and action in Canada—Feminist, Indigenous, and intersectional perspectives*. Canadian Research Institute for the Advancement of Women and the Alliance for Intergenerational Resilience. Retrieved from: http://www.criaw-icref.ca/images/userfiles/files/Women%20and%20Climate%20Change_FINAL.pdf.

PART 12

Additional Readings

Crosby, Andrew and Jeffrey Monaghan. *Policing Indigenous Movements: Dissent and the Security State*. Halifax: Fernwood Publishing, 2018.

Estes, Nick. *Our History Is the Future: Standing Rock versus the Dakota Access Pipeline, and the Long Tradition of Indigenous Resistance*. Brooklyn, NY: Verso. 2019.

Gilio-Whitaker, Dina. *As Long as Grass Grows: the Indigenous Fight for Environmental Justice, from Colonization to Standing Rock*. Boston: Beacon Press, 2020.

Howe, Miles. *Debriefing Elsipogtog: the Anatomy of a Struggle*. Halifax: Fernwood Publishing, 2015.

Liboiron, Max. *Pollution is Colonialism*. Durham: Duke University Press, 2021.

Luby, Brittany. *Dammed: The Politics of Loss and Survival in Anishinaabe Territory*. Winnipeg: University of Manitoba Press, 2020.

McGregor, Deborah. 2018. "Indigenous Environmental Justice, Knowledge, and Law" *Kalfou*. 5, 2 (2018): 279–296.

Waldron, Ingrid R.G. *There is Something in the Water: Environmental Racism in Indigenous and Black Communities*. Halifax: Fernwood Publishing, 2018.

Relevant Websites

Honor Earth
https://www.honorearth.net/
Honor Earth is a website originating in an initiative by Winona LaDuke and musicians Indigo Girls, intending to raise public awareness and financial and political resources to support grassroots Native environmental groups.

Idle No More
https://idlenomore.ca/
This is the official website of the Idle No More movement.

Lakota Peoples Law Project Action Center
https://action.lakotalaw.org/nodapl/
The website provides history, background, resources, and discussions of how to take action in securing justice for Indigenous and Lakota peoples in campaigns of child well-being, health and safety, voting rights, and defending the environment from harmful extraction projects.

Unist'ot'en/No Pipelines
https://unistoten.camp/no-pipelines/
The Unist'ot'en No Pipelines weblink provides background, a timeline, testimonials, and resources linked to a number of campaigns to protect and defend the land where pipeline projects have the potential to threaten, disrupt, or destroy them.

Water Song: Indigenous Women and Water
https://www.kosmosjournal.org/news/water-song-indigenous-women-and-water-in-canada/
This weblink provides an article describing the relationship between Indigenous women, communities, and water with an emphasis on the participation of Indigenous women in local, regional, and national water dialogues, and on key principles for supporting women as "keepers of the water."

Films

Inuit Knowledge & Climate Change, Dir. Z. Kunuk, Isuma.TV, 2010.
The Lake Winnipeg Project: Camp Morningstar. Dir. Kevin Settee. National Film Board of Canada. 2021.
Six Miles Deep. Dir. Sara Roque. NFB. 2009.
Stand. Dir. Antony Bonello and Nicolas Teichroch. Dendrite Studio. 2013.
There is Something in the Water. Dir. Elliott Page and Ian Daniel. Netflix. 2019
The Water Walker. Dir James Burns. Seeing Red 6 Nations, Contour Films Inc. 2019.
Water Warriors. Dir. Michael Premo. New Day Films. 2017.
The Whale and the Raven. Dir. Mirjam Leuze. National Film Board of Canada. 2019.

Key Terms

- Critical infrastructure
- Environmental racism
- Environmental/water security
- Fossil-fuel infrastructure
- Indigenous relationality
- Mandaluyong Declaration
- Recolonization

Discussion Questions

What are Indigenous peoples refusing in their resistance to oil and gas pipelines, according to Spice? Why has their resistance been labeled as "domestic terrorism" by the federal and provincial governments, and the oil and gas corporations? What are some possible consequences for treating their resistance as a form of extremism that needs to be contained and policed?

Why was the Keystone XI pipeline a controversial proposal, according to Spice? What can be learned from its revocation following the resistance of Indigenous peoples to its terms and construction?

What roles have Indigenous women played in environmental justice and Indigenous governance? How would you describe these roles and where do they originate from? How can we see their activism as a resistance to both racism and sexism?

Consider the statements in The Lima Declaration: "Nothing about us without us," and "Everything about us, with us." What do these statements mean? How do they relate to the calls made in the Mandaluyong Declaration?

Activities

Review Freda Huson's explanation of Indigenous infrastructure in Spice's chapter. In groups of two or more, create a visual map of the various connections outlined in Huson's description. How is every element connected? Can more elements be added to display further interconnectedness? What is the impact of oil and gas infrastructure on these elements, and how might this be illustrated on the map?

Visit a body of water (a river, a lake, or beach) and participate in a garbage cleanup. Consider how your participation in maintaining this body of water has a positive impact on humans and other-than-humans. Draw a map to visualize this relationship.

Write a persuasive letter to the Prime Minister of Canada advocating that the Federal Government consider and heed one or more of the declarations made by Indigenous women. Outline how the knowledge systems of Indigenous women and their bond to nature are key to understanding climate impacts and establishing climate action plans.

Poverty, Economic Marginality, and Community Development

Editor Introduction

On 22 January 2016 in La Loche, a small Dene community in northern Saskatchewan, a 17-year-old male shot and killed four people and injured seven other community members. Aside from directly impacting the small community, this event shocked all of Canada; however, we need to contextualize this tragedy, to better understand its complex roots, and ultimately find proactive preventive strategies for the future.

La Loche is a community that has struggled for many years with poverty, unemployment, addictions, and alarmingly high numbers of youth suicides. As a member of La Loche told a CBC news reporter, "there is lack of everything . . . we don't have nothing" (CBC News 2016b). Agreeing with this community member, the Métis Nation president Clément Chartier added that such poor social conditions are linked to the loss of traditional economic systems since the 1960s, and the consequent long history of high unemployment rates, lack of social programs, and lack of other resources. This harsh reality has been felt particularly hard by the youth, who, feeling helpless about their future and having lost a strong cultural identity, have resorted to violence, either towards others or towards themselves. To grasp the severity of the existing conditions in remote northern Indigenous communities like La Loche, one only needs to learn that the average for suicide in La Loche was 61.1 per 100,000 according to a 2010 report. The event that took place in La Loche on 22 January 2016 must not be looked at in isolation from the social conditions that have surrounded the community for many decades. What happened on that day is strongly connected to a history of neglect and other colonial injustices that La Loche and many other Indigenous nations have endured.

The links between Indigenous peoples, poverty, and development policy have, in recent years, received attention by social researchers and analysts who have reported that "development itself has failed to provide answers to human suffering and disadvantage" (Eversole, McNeish, and Cimadamore, 2005: 1). Moreover, it has finally been internationally recognized that "[I]ndigenous peoples are nearly always disadvantaged relative to their non-[I]ndigenous counterparts. Their material standard of living is lower; their risk of disease and early death higher . . . there is a 'cost' to being Indigenous" (ibid.: 2). Their socioeconomic conditions have been described to belong to that of "Fourth World" communities, minority populations in their own lands who suffer from a lack of political power, economic subjugation, and social and cultural stigmatization (Dick, 1985).

Rather than treating these conditions as outcomes of individual faults or bad personal choices, we must recognize that poverty and economic marginalization are also linked to past and ongoing policy injustices, racist colonial attitudes, and discrimination. Legal and educational barriers routinely impact on the ability of Indigenous peoples to prosper. Indeed, as Cora Voyageur and Brian Calliou (2003: 121) explain, economic underdevelopment is not a "Native problem." They write: "the Canadian state's institutionalized and oppressive, economic and legal structures have played a key role in Aboriginal community underdevelopment, which has resulted in the increasing dependency of some Indigenous peoples on the state" (ibid.). They also observe that "the Canadian state, through its federal and provincial jurisdictions, often legislates access to land and resources that benefits corporate interests and is detrimental to Aboriginal peoples" (ibid.: 125). A "blame-the-victim" ideology is therefore inadequate in analyzing current Indigenous economic conditions as it fails to recognize how racism and colonial attitudes and policies have significantly contributed to both the creation and the maintenance of those conditions. Such ideology treats economic marginalization as a consequence of Indigenous peoples' outmoded value system and their unwillingness to let go of their "Indianness." These racist ideologies disallow close examination of any systemic barriers that have created and maintained Indigenous underdevelopment.

The points made above were reiterated in December 2009 at the Oneida of the Thames Longhouse, at their mid-winter ceremonies to honour Mother Earth and all her natural gifts. During the ceremonies, new members of the nation were welcomed and given traditional Oneida names. At the end of the first day of the ceremonies our spiritual Elder gave us teachings about the ceremonies and also remarked that as the original peoples of the land we should resist assimilation and reawaken our traditions and ways of governing. He reminded us of our responsibility to protect our lands and natural resources from some "development" projects that in actuality are threatening the climate, the waters, the trees, and the overall well-being of our nations. We are not against all modern technological developments, or participation in the Canadian economy, but we do want sustainable economies that do not destroy the environment and Mother Earth; we must ensure that our present economies safeguard "all our relations" for the next seven generations. This sentiment resembles what other Indigenous scholars have said about ecology and our responsibilities to ensure its sustainability (see Manuel, 2017).

Indigenous peoples all over Turtle Island have not forgotten the responsibilities that our Elder reminded us of. They have always been keenly aware of the negative impacts that both the Canadian State's laws and private corporations' activities have had on Indigenous territories and ways of life. They have always resisted any threats against Mother Earth and all of its creations.

In the winter of 2012–2013 all of Canada saw evidence of such resistance when the **Idle No More Movement** "swept the country over the holidays, took most Canadians, including then Prime Minister Stephen Harper and his Conservative government, by surprise" (Palmater, Chapter 25, in this volume). This movement was initiated by four women who wanted to bring to Canadians' attention the inevitable negative impacts that the then proposed **Bill C-45** (which eventually came into effect) would have on the environment, and on Indigenous territories and rights. More on the Idle No More movement's role in both bringing awareness of Indigenous people's issues and resisting colonialism will be examined in Part 15.

The participants of the Idle No More movement effectively, with the use of social media and grassroots activism, brought to light the broader issues that have affected Indigenous peoples, such as dispossession of lands, disrespect of treaty rights, violence against Indigenous women, and the very poor socio-economic conditions under which most Indigenous communities live. When, during the period of the movement, Attawapiskat **Chief Theresa Spence** went on a hunger strike until the representatives of the Crown, including the Prime Minister, agreed to meet with First Nations leaders to discuss both Bill C-45 and the broader social issues that the Idle No More spoke about, Canada and the rest of the world could no longer be in denial or silent about the broken relationship between the Canadian State and Indigenous nations. As Palmater states, in Chapter 25, "her strike is symbolic of what is happening to First Nations in Canada. For every day that Spence does not eat, she is slowly dying, and that is exactly what is happening to First Nations, who have lifespans up to 20 years shorter than average Canadians."

Other activists of Idle No More reminded those who were curious of the demands made by Indigenous peoples that "the political economy of Canada rests on claims of ownership to all lands and resources within our national borders . . . [and that] Indigenous labour and lands have shaped the political economy of Canada, right from the railroad development to current resources exploration and extractions" (Pasternak, 2014: 40–2). Acknowledging this would dispel the myth that "it is hard-earned tax dollars of Canadians that pays for housing, schools, and health services in First Nations" (Jay, 2014: 109). In reality, it is Indigenous peoples who have been subsidizing the rest of Canada, given that the Canadian economy has heavily relied on the natural and other resources drawn from Indigenous lands, most of which are unceded territories. The Idle No More movement has intended to make everyone aware of this reality, and has demanded, as Palmater states, "for Canada to negotiate the sharing of our lands and resources, but the government must display good faith by withdrawing the legislation and restoring the funding to our communities. Something must be done to address the immediate crisis faced by the grassroots in this movement." It is time to end the continuing colonial relationship; none of us can remain idle, Indigenous peoples and allies alike.

In Chapter 26, Calliou and Wesley-Esquimaux consider which approach to Indigenous community development would be most effective in improving the poor socioeconomic conditions that Indigenous communities are currently experiencing. What is needed is a blended approach that revitalizes Indigenous traditional cultural principles and values, they argue, while building internal capacity to take advantage of economic opportunities. This approach would have to differ from past assimilationist ones that blamed Indigenous peoples for their own economic conditions, and followed a Western liberal philosophy that promoted values such as individualism and competition that do not fit well with most Indigenous collectivist values. A Western approach of community development often adopts a "best practices" measure of success and leadership that, as Calliou and Wesley-Esquimaux suggest, are not universally applicable to all communities, especially Indigenous ones. This is because they do not take into account the unique cultures, knowledges, experiences, and assets that Indigenous communities possess.

As an alternative to the best practices model, Calliou and Wesley-Esquimaux propose "wise practices," defined as "locally-appropriate actions, tools, principles, or decisions that contribute significantly to the development of sustainable and equitable conditions." These practices require effective leaders with intelligence, wisdom, ethical judgment, adaptability to constant and rapid changes, and commitment to work for the welfare of others. The **wise practices model** uses a specific set of elements to define success: identity and culture, leadership, strategic vision and planning, good governance and management, accountability and stewardship, performance evaluation, collaborations, partnerships, and external relationships. Success is not measured by wealth accumulation, but rather a goal towards a public good aimed at "protect[ing] and enhanc[ing] Indigenous community's identity and culture" so that they can share the resources of this land and enjoy equitable economic opportunities into the future.

CHAPTER 25

Why Are We Idle No More?

Pamela Palmater

The Idle No More movement, which has swept the country over the holidays, took most Canadians, including Prime Minister Stephen Harper and his Conservative government, by surprise. That is not to say that Canadians have never seen a native protest before, as most of us recall Oka, Burnt Church, and Ipperwash. But most Canadians are not used to the kind of sustained, coordinated, national effort that we have seen in the last few weeks—at least not since 1969. 1969 was the last time the federal government put forward an assimilation plan for First Nations. It was defeated then by fierce native opposition, and it looks like Harper's aggressive legislative assimilation plan will be met with even fiercer resistance.

In order to understand what this movement is about, it is necessary to understand how our history is connected to the present-day situation of First Nations. While a great many injustices were inflicted upon the indigenous peoples in the name of colonization, indigenous peoples were never "conquered." The creation of Canada was only possible through the negotiation of treaties between the Crown and indigenous nations. While the wording of the treaties varies from the peace and friendship treaties in the east to the numbered treaties in the west, most are based on the core treaty promise that we would all

live together peacefully and share the wealth of this land. The problem is that only one treaty partner has seen any prosperity.

The failure of Canada to share the lands and resources as promised in the treaties has placed First Nations at the bottom of all socio-economic indicators—health, lifespan, education levels and employment opportunities. While indigenous lands and resources are used to subsidize the wealth and prosperity of Canada as a state and the high-quality programs and services enjoyed by Canadians, First Nations have been subjected to purposeful, chronic underfunding of all their basic human services like water, sanitation, housing, and education. This has led to the many First Nations being subjected to multiple, overlapping crises like the housing crisis in Attawapiskat, the water crisis in Kashechewan, and the suicide crisis in Pikangikum.

Part of the problem is that federal "Indian" policy still has, as its main objective, to get rid of the "Indian problem." Instead of working toward the stated mandate of Indian Affairs "to improve the social well-being and economic prosperity of First Nations," Harper is trying, through an aggressive legislative agenda, to do what the White Paper failed to do—get rid of the Indian problem once and for all. The Conservatives don't even deny it—in fact

Courtesy of Dr. Pamela Palmater.

In Kino-nda-niimi Collective, eds., The Winter We Danced (Winnipeg: ARP Books, 2014), 37–40. Used by permission. Originally appeared in The Ottawa Citizen, 28 December 2012.

Harper's speech last January at the Crown–First Nation Gathering focused on the unlocking of First Nations lands and the integration of First Nations into Canadian society for the "maximized benefit" of all Canadians. This suite of approximately 14 pieces of legislation was drafted, introduced, and debated without First Nation consent.

Idle No More is a coordinated, strategic movement, not led by any elected politician, national chief or paid executive director. It is a movement originally led by indigenous women and has been joined by grassroots First Nations leaders, Canadians, and now the world. It originally started as a way to oppose Bill C-45, the omnibus legislation impacting water rights and land rights under the Indian Act; it grew to include all the legislation and the corresponding funding cuts to First Nations political organizations meant to silence our advocacy voice.

Our activities include a slow escalation from letters to MPs and ministers, to teach-ins, marches and flash mobs, to rallies, protests, and blockades. The concept was to give Canada every opportunity to come to the table in a meaningful way and address these long-outstanding issues, and escalation would only occur if Canada continued to ignore our voices. Sadly, Prime Minister Harper has decided to ignore the call for dialogue just as he has ignored the hunger-striking Attawapiskat Chief Theresa Spence.

Although Idle No More began before Chief Spence's hunger strike, and will continue after, her strike is symbolic of what is happening to First Nations in Canada. For every day that Spence does not eat, she is slowly dying, and that is exactly what is happening to First Nations, who have lifespans up to 20 years shorter than average Canadians.

Idle No More has a similar demand in that there is a need for Canada to negotiate the sharing of our lands and resources, but the government must display good faith first by withdrawing the legislation and restoring the funding to our communities. Something must be done to address the immediate crisis faced by the grassroots in this movement.

I am optimistic about the power of our peoples and know that in the end, we will be successful in getting this treaty relationship back on track. However, I am less confident about the Conservative government's willingness to sit down and work this out peacefully any time soon. Thus, I fully expect that this movement will continue to expand and increase in intensity. Canada has not yet seen everything this movement has to offer. It will continue to grow as we educate Canadians about the facts of our lived reality and the many ways in which we can all live here peacefully and share the wealth.

After all, First Nations, with our constitutionally protected aboriginal and treaty rights, are Canadians' last best hope to protect the lands, waters, plants, and animals from complete destruction—which doesn't just benefit our children, but the children of all Canadians.

CHAPTER 26

Wise Practices Approach to Indigenous Community Development in Canada

Brian Calliou and Cynthia Wesley-Esquimaux

Introduction

Indigenous peoples in Canada face many challenges because of the impact of globalization, rapid technological change, and a neo-liberal market economy with its shrinking governmental support. Many Indigenous peoples continue to live in substandard conditions and poverty. However, they also face many opportunities, since much of the industrial development of natural resources occurs on their traditional territories. Recent Supreme Court of Canada case law states that they need to be consulted and accommodated in any development projects that might impact their Aboriginal rights. Thus, there is an urgent need for effective leadership for Indigenous communities to adapt to this external change and to build the internal capacity to take advantage of economic opportunities. Developing effective Indigenous leaders requires a blended approach of revitalizing traditional cultural principles and values while teaching them the core competencies required for success in the modern business world. The wisdom of Indigenous knowledge systems must also be developed, along with Western knowledge and skills to run the governments, organizations, and businesses of today's Indigenous communities.

In this chapter, we describe a wise practices approach to successful community economic development. This wise practices approach is informed by a review of literature on best practices in Indigenous business, economic development, and community development. From this literature review, we identified seven elements that are essential for **modern Indigenous leaders** to cultivate in order to lead their communities through the rapid changes that are occurring. In addition, the modern Indigenous leader must meet the community's needs and aspirations, while preserving his or her community's culture and traditions.

Approaches to Indigenous Economic Development

There have been many approaches to Indigenous economic development, most often imposed upon First Nations communities by governments or non-governmental organizations. Such approaches have often been assimilationist in nature. They argued that adhering to cultural values, traditions, and knowledge actually placed Indigenous peoples at a disadvantage. Within the assimilationist stream is modernization theory, which views industrialization and technological advances as part of an inevitable progress (Calliou and Voyageur 2007). Thus, modernists argue that economic underdevelopment among most Indigenous peoples is due to outmoded economic organization and ideas. Modernists further state that if Indigenous peoples do not undergo industrialization and are unable to change with the times, then their disadvantaged position vis-à-vis the Canadian economy is really of their own doing. This "blaming the victim" stance does not recognize the societal, institutional, and structural barriers that restrict Indigenous participation in the market economy. The modernization theory is reflected in the neo-liberal view of a capitalist, market-driven economic system that supports Western liberal democratic values such as individualism, consumerism, individual property ownership, and wealth accumulation. Such notions often set up a clash of cultural values with Indigenous peoples, who generally have a strong belief in collectivism, a spiritual connection to the land and its resources, and a history of sharing the land rather than exclusive ownership of it.

Other theories have challenged modernization theory by highlighting the overt and systemic structures that marginalize Indigenous peoples from the economy. The metropolis-hinterland theory argues that at the root of legal and political barriers are the metropolitan centres run by elites who exploit the raw materials of the hinterland regions, where Indigenous peoples generally live, and then sell the finished products back to the outlying areas (Davis 1971). Colonialist theory argues that Indigenous communities are essentially internal colonies that are exploited for economic gain by the dominant society, which uses them as a source for cheap resources and unskilled labour (Frideres 1988; Abele 1997, 129). Dependency theory argues that underdevelopment can only be understood by analyzing the economic and power relationships between developed and underdeveloped economies (Dos Santos 1971; Frank 1966). Indigenous peoples have become dependent upon the productive relationships established by the capitalist metropolises of developed countries. Thus, world systems related to a global capitalist economy benefit some regions and lead to the underdevelopment of others (Wallerstein 2004). Robert Anderson (1999) set out a "contingency" theory wherein he argues that while there are world systems at play, Indigenous peoples' participation in the global economy is contingent upon a number of factors, many of which can be controlled by Indigenous peoples themselves. This contingency approach takes agency and social relations seriously, and emphasizes a community-driven approach to economic development where the community is an active agent in development and controls its pace and nature. Indigenous peoples in Canada have been advocating for greater self-government, respect for their rights to their traditional lands and resources, and an active role in economic development on their traditional lands. Government policy has been established through history to play a role in Indigenous economic development.

Federal Government Policy on Indigenous Economic Development

Historically, Indigenous peoples in Canada adapted well to the presence of the new settler populations, especially during the fur trade, where they played prominent roles (Ray 1974). Indigenous peoples also began to adapt somewhat successfully to the new agricultural economy, and it was government policy that began to impede Indigenous communities' agricultural success by restricting their ability to sell their products (Carter 1990). Indigenous peoples in Canada also adopted seasonal labour as a way to earn an income and continue their traditional livelihood of hunting, fishing, and trapping (High 1996; Elias 1990). It is only relatively recently that Indigenous peoples have been marginalized from the economy—from the early 1920s onward (Tough 1992).

Federal government policy had an assimilationist agenda early on, and residential school policy had a significant impact on Indigenous identity and cultural capital (Tobias 1976; Milloy 1999). State-sponsored welfare programs also led many Indigenous citizens to become dependent (Helin 2006). Furthermore, policy and laws such as the Indian Act imposed further barriers to Indigenous involvement in the national economy and limited the possibilities of success (Calliou and Voyageur 2007, 140). As one commentator stated, in all liberal democracies such as Canada, Indigenous peoples are transformed into "politically weak, economically marginal and culturally stigmatized members of national societies" (Dyck 1985, 1).

More recently, the Canadian federal government has attempted to deal with Indigenous involvement in the economy through a variety of policies. The federal government instituted a policy in 1989 entitled the Canadian Aboriginal Economic Development Strategy (CAEDS), which was a partnership between three federal government departments. The Department of Indian and Northern Development funded programs in community economic and resource development; the Department of Employment and Immigration funded training and skills development; and the Department of Industry, Science and Technology funded programs in business development.

More recently, in 2009, the Conservative federal government instituted a new policy entitled the Federal Framework for Aboriginal Economic Development (FFAED), which strongly reflects the Conservative government's neo-liberal approach to the "good society." Their policy efforts are focused on opening up Canada's natural resources for the world to exploit. Of course, the natural resources are on traditional Indigenous lands. This market-driven approach to Indigenous participation in the national economy sees the policy focus on partnerships with private industry, a strong emphasis on northern development, especially of its natural resources, a results-based approach to any funding investments, and enabling legislation (Oppenheimer and Weir 2010).

Much government policy and many non-governmental organizational approaches to Indigenous economic development focused on capacity development and training, particularly in business, management, and leadership development. Some Indigenous institutions were established to carry out such training, including the Council for the Advancement of Native Development Officers, the Indigenous Leadership Institute, the Aboriginal Financial Officers Association, and the National Centre for First Nations Governance. Many post-secondary institutions also established training programs to meet this need (O'Connell, Oppenheimer, and Weir 2010). Each of these institutions uses a variety of methods to deliver the training. One method to learning in the areas of leadership, management, and business is the best practices approach.

Best Practices in Business and Management

Leadership development programs use a variety of methods and approaches to teach leadership and management (McGonagill and Pruyn 2010). Besides formal lectures in post-secondary institutions, many organizational or community leaders also rely on the best practices case study approach to develop leaders and look for ways to improve (Leskiw and Singh 2007).

So what are best practices? One definition states that best practices are the "methodologies, strategies, procedures, practices and/or processes that consistently produce successful results" (Foy, Krehbiel, and Plate 2009, i). A best practice is "a proven method, technique, or process for achieving a specific outcome under a specific circumstance and in an effective way" (Calliou and Wesley-Esquimaux 2010, 5).

Best practices are essentially documented case histories of innovation and performance success in a specific practice area. They provide guidelines for others to learn from because of the detailed analysis of the practice under study.

Critique of the "Best Practices" Concept

There is an assumption that calling practices "best practices" means they can inspire others and encourage leaders to improve their own practices. The assumption is that these documented stories can make a difference to those who study them, and that the knowledge can be transferred into action using the best practice case study as a guide. Best practices case studies are also used as a benchmark against which to compare one's own community or organization. Although there is some truth to each of these assumptions, there is a growing skepticism about the universality of best practices.

There is much utility in learning from best practices case studies. However, as one education scholar put it, best practices can unrealistically elevate expectations, best practices' "too confident hope ordinarily smashes against the rocks of reality," and the attempt to implement best practices "ordinarily diverts attention away from the practical to the theoretic" (Davis 1997, 1). Some commentators caution that we cannot assume that what is successful in one situation, context, or culture will necessarily work in a completely different one (Krajewski and Silver, n.d.). Others have raised the issue of universality, asking the following: How could this supposed objective, universal standard of best practice "take into account context and values, subjectivity and plurality? How could it accommodate multiple perspectives, with different groups in different places having different views of what quality was or different interpretations of criteria?" (Dahlberg, Moss, and Pence 1999, 4). Thus, the term "best practices" is often decontextualized and cannot always be generalized into another context or culture.

Furthermore, another question arises: What criteria determine what is "best"? It is often a Western corporate standard. It reflects a certain ideological lens—that of the neo-liberal market. Certainly, the criteria of what successful or best practice is can differ between Western liberal democracies and Indigenous peoples. Cornell (1987) argues that the middle-class dream of success in the United States is not necessarily the same definition of success that most Native Americans have. Thus, best practices tend to reflect hierarchical evaluative criteria that also tend to exclude local and Indigenous knowledge and ways of doing. For case studies to resonate and be relevant, they need to allow for other perspectives, knowledge, and experiences. There has been a similar assumption that Western-based knowledge and experience with respect to leadership, management, and business practices have an objective quality that can be universally applied to other cultures. Hofstede (1980, 1983) has argued that the failure of many international development initiatives during the 1960s and 1970s was partly due to the lack of cultural sensitivity in the transfer of management ideas. In fact, culture matters. Many Indigenous scholars are arguing that modern management and business practices and knowledge are important for Indigenous peoples, but that they must be reconciled with and built upon traditional cultural values and knowledge (Wuttunee 2004; Smith 2000; Neilsen and Redpath 1997; Newhouse 2000; Calliou 2005).

Finally, some commentators have argued that best practices in adult education are running the risk of eroding the traditional grounding in an ethic of the common good and of social justice (Bartlette 2008). Indigenous communities that involve themselves in successful business enterprises do so for the collective good, for social purposes, and to maintain their cultural identity (Anderson 2001; Champagne 2004).

More Indigenous people have argued that there is something missing in how Indigenous community and leadership development is approached (Snowball and Wesley-Esquimaux 2010; Thoms 2007). They argue that an approach other than best practices must be developed, one that makes a space for Indigenous knowledge, experiences, and stories "learned on the frontlines through socio-cultural insight, ingenuity, intuition, long experience, and trial and error" (Thoms 2007, 8).

The Wise Practices Approach to Economic and Leadership Development

Taking the foregoing critique into account, and in order to resonate with Indigenous leaders, we adopt the notion of "wise practices" as an alternative term to "best practices." Wise practices are best defined as "locally-appropriate actions, tools, principles or decisions that contribute significantly to the development of sustainable and equitable conditions" (Calliou and Wesley-Esquimaux 2010, 19). Rather than aspiring to be universal, as best practices try to be, wise practices are "idiosyncratic, contextual, textured, and not standardized" (Davis 1997). Thus, wise practices recognize the wisdom in each Indigenous community and in the community's own stories of achieving success. The concept of wise practices recognizes that culture matters.

Wise practices are thus based on what so many Indigenous scholars have argued: the importance of an Indigenous identity and strong cultural ties (King 2008; Calliou 2005; Grint and Warner 2006; Cowan 2008; Ottmann 2005b). Indigenous perceptions of leaders' characteristics also inform the wise practices approach, as is illustrated by the words of

Taiaiake Alfred (1999, 10) citing Leroy Little Bear, a Blackfoot philosopher and scholar:

> A culture attempts to mold its members into ideal personalities. The ideal personality in Native American cultures is a person who shows kindness to all, who puts the group ahead of individual wants and desires, who is a generalist, who is steeped in spiritual and ritual knowledge—a person who goes about daily life and approaches "all his or her relations" in a sea of friendship, easy-going-ness, humour, and good feelings ... She or he is a person expected to display bravery, hardiness, and strength against enemies and outsiders. She or he is a person who is adaptable and takes the world as it comes without complaint.

These characteristics of ideal persons reflect the principles of wisdom: fluid intelligence; ethical judgement; actions undertaken for noble and worthwhile purposes; working for the welfare of others; and having a metaphysical or spiritual quality (Kok 2009). Theorists and practitioners in organizational studies and leadership development are increasingly becoming interested in wisdom. They see a need for wisdom to be practised by leaders, managers, and business persons who must make complex decisions in this period of rapid change, uncertainty, and paradox, all the while considering the welfare of others and the planet (Cooperrider and Srivastva 1998; Korac-Kakabadse, Korac-Kakabadse, and Kouzmin 2001; Weick 2004; Kageler et al. 2005; Sternberg 2005; Knudtson and Suzuki 1992). In order for leaders to practise wisely, they need to have well-developed intuitive powers to move beyond existing ideas or rules. In fact, wisdom "requires one to respect tradition and experience," and issues a leader faces "can be considered reflexively from a cultural-historical perspective" (Kok 2009, 54). Collective knowledge impacts learning, and many theorists now see knowledge as a socially shared resource. Knowledge "can only be exploited to its maximum degree when complemented by wisdom" (Kok 2009, 55). Indigenous traditional knowledge offers traditional teachings in order to prepare people to live as good human beings who can coexist respectfully and who have a respectful relationship with their environment.

Ottmann (2005b) argues that Indigenous leadership development began with childhood encouragement and direction from the elders, and with inspiration and support from other leaders. Thus, the shared values and beliefs of the community shaped a future leader. Indeed, Little Bear (2011, 77) has stated that individuals are going to have their own "personal interpretation of the collective cultural code; however, the individual's worldview has its roots in the culture—that is, in the society's shared philosophy, values, and customs."

A wise practices approach to developing Indigenous leadership examines the "wisdom of practice" and documents case studies that are "thickly textured, robust, subject matter specific, and richly contextualized" (Davis 1997, 3). The expansion of these detailed, descriptive, and interpretive case studies will illuminate the wisdom of successful practices, especially the construction of the meaning of culturally appropriate leadership practices in the service of the common wealth.

There is a growing body of Indigenous scholarship exploring the use of wise practices and wisdom in a variety of disciplines, such as business (Erakovic et al. 2011), mental health and addiction (Snowball and Wesley-Esquimaux 2010), and social work (Nabigon and Wenger-Nabigon 2012).

A wise practices model also reflects a strengths-based approach to community economic development. It recognizes that there are many gifts and strengths in a community that strategies for growth can build upon. This assets-based planning method provides for an inventory of assets, including cultural assets (Cunningham and Mathie 2002). This is also referred to as an appreciative inquiry approach, where strengths are identified as a starting point rather than problems or shortcomings (Cooperrider and Whitney 2005; Bushe 1998). Certainly, one of the strengths of an Indigenous community is its local knowledge and experience, that is, the oral histories and traditional teachings held by elders and other wisdom keepers.

The methodology for researching and documenting wise practices is multidisciplinary, using arts-based research methods to visually capture the wise practice case study story (Brearley, Calliou, and Tanton 2009; Brearley and Darso 2008). The wise practices approach uses a qualitative research method to carry out a naturalistic inquiry that allows for a community to find its voice and narrate its own story of achievement, highlighting its strengths and local knowledge and experience. It also uses a participatory action research method that embraces principles of community participation and reflection, empowerment, and emancipation of the people seeking to improve their social situation (Walter 2006).

The wise practices approach involves a journey that goes backwards in order to move forwards. Interviews of community or organizational leaders elicit the story from when the idea for the venture began, documenting all its characters and its journey, including the assorted trials and tribulations that led to ultimate success. The resulting case studies use the storytelling method to inform and inspire other leaders to undertake their own community initiatives in a wise way. This is merely a wise practice in itself, since traditionally Indigenous leaders learned from past stories before making a decision about future action.

Wise Practices Seven Elements of Success Model

Drawing on the conclusions from the best practices literature review that we explained earlier, we have identified seven key factors of success for Indigenous community economic development. Our selection of the success factors was also informed by competency map research we undertook through focus groups at The Banff Centre. The findings supported the importance of culture and identity for Indigenous leaders (Calliou 2005). We call this our wise practices model, which sets out the following seven elements of success:

1. Identity and culture
2. Leadership
3. Strategic vision and planning
4. Good governance and management
5. Accountability and stewardship
6. Performance evaluation
7. Collaborations, partnerships, and external relationships

We will discuss each of these seven key success factors in turn.

Identity and Culture

The first key factor is *identity and culture,* which is to say that leaders of Indigenous communities have stated clearly that for any Indigenous leader to be competent in advocating and representing their community's interests, they must have a strong understanding of, and grounding in, their culture, traditional knowledge, and historical connection to their traditional territories (King 2008; Grint and Warner 2006; Cowan 2008). This became very clear in our competency map research (Calliou 2005). Other Indigenous scholars have also found this to be the case (Ottmann, 2005b). This key success factor supports current claims about the importance of identity at work and authentic leadership (Gini 1998; Jaros 2012; Cooper, Scandura, and Schriesheim 2005; Gooty and Michie 2005).

Leadership

The second factor is *leadership.* Effective leadership is key to successful community economic development. The term "leadership" is a verb, that is, it refers to action taken by someone to turn ideas into actions and thus into results. It does not need to be related to someone in authority; leadership can be practised by essentially anyone at any level. Warren Bennis and Burt Nanus (1985) defined leadership as that which "gives an organization its vision and its ability to translate the vision into reality." Leaders must be action oriented in order to transform ideas into action, lead change, and achieve results. They must practise courageous leadership in order to change the status quo and improve the conditions of the community. Also, Sonia Ospina and others argue that values-based leadership towards social justice, what they term "social change leadership," is about leadership that is collective or shared, and that both beliefs and behaviours are important (Foldy and Ospina 2005).

Strategic Vision and Planning

Third is the key factor *strategic vision and planning.* Leaders must set out long-term visions for the community that inspire and motivate community members to support strategic plans that bring positive change. Such strategic plans provide a basis for decision making and help to focus scarce resources on their collective strategic goals. They allow the community or organization to be proactive rather than reactive (Cornell 1998; Anderson and Smith 1998; Guyette 1996).

Good Governance and Management

The fourth factor is *good governance and management*. Leaders must set up good governance and management structures and systems to effectively carry out the goals and program needs for their communities (Cornell and Kalt 1990; Cornell 2007; Cornell and Jorgensen 2007; Calliou 2008). Building effective institutions and processes allows leaders and managers to come and go while the government or organization continues to operate. Stable governance and management sends a strong message to potential external partners that they can rest assured that the Indigenous community or organization operates professionally.

Accountability and Stewardship

The fifth factor relates to *accountability and stewardship*. Good leaders and managers act as stewards of the community resources and are accountable for their decisions and actions (Block 1993; Davis, Donaldson, and Schoorman 1997; Hernandez 2008; Leithwood 2001; Fox 1992). Being open and transparent about their decision making and spending builds community trust in them. Leaders or managers can show how they are accountable by openly reporting how decisions were made, scarce resources allocated, and results achieved.

Performance Evaluation

Next is the sixth factor, *performance evaluation*. This refers to being accountable and practising stewardship of community resources by measuring for results of decisions made and dollars invested in the various strategies undertaken. Evaluating the performance of the initiatives undertaken by leaders ensures that they are achieving the most value for each dollar invested in their projects (Martz 2013; Meier 2003). Evaluation of human resources is another important measurement that ensures that staff

performance is tied to strategic objectives and that results are being achieved. Thus, one is essentially carrying out performance management (Bacal 1999). However, there is a growing literature critiquing evaluation approaches and calling for an Indigenous evaluation framework that makes room for culturally competent evaluations (Chouinard and Cousins 2007; LaFrance and Nichols 2010; Aton et al. 2007).

Collaborations, Partnerships, and External Relationships

Finally, the seventh factor is *collaborations, partnerships, and external relationships*. External partnerships are often necessary for an Indigenous community's success. Indigenous communities often need external financial support, as well as external support in other areas. Thus, good working relationships with external funders, bankers, investors, suppliers, and trading partners are key to success. Being self-governing means being interdependent, that is, having networks and external trading partners. Many Indigenous communities enter into partnerships, co-operatives, or joint ventures (Wuttunee 2002; Fraser 2002; Hammond Ketilson and MacPherson 2002).

Conclusion

Through a literature review of best practices in Indigenous community and economic development, we were able to provide an empirical basis for our wise practices model for successful community economic development, with its seven elements that increase the likelihood of success. The concept of wise practices, in contrast to the concept of best practices, provides a space for Indigenous knowledge and local experience in order to lay a foundation for a strengths-based approach to community economic development. It recognizes that culture matters, and that wise practices case studies can inspire and provide wisdom that can teach us ways to build our communities and our local economies. It also recognizes that each community has its own wisdom, experiences, and strengths to build upon.

The wise practices model sets out various elements for Indigenous leaders to become familiar with and learn aspects of, so that they have the competencies to lead change, inspire hope, and take advantage of economic opportunities for their communities. The economic success that can be achieved through such a model is not merely for wealth accumulation, but rather is for the public good. It is for what one commentator described as "tribal capitalism," and another called "capitalism with a red face" (Champagne 2004; Newhouse 2000). This represents capitalism as a means to an end—a triple bottom-line approach to economic development that seeks to protect and enhance an Indigenous community's identity and culture.

As Indigenous communities face rapid changes coming from external sources, they are in need of competent leadership to adapt to this change. Developing leaders' knowledge, skills, and virtues can be accomplished in part by learning from and being inspired to action by wise practices case studies. Leadership for change is necessary, but a wise practices approach also supports the continuance of traditional knowledge as a foundation for the change, so that identity and culture are preserved.

References

Abele, Frances. 1997. "Understanding What Happened Here: The Political Economy of Indigenous Peoples." In *Understanding Canada: Building on the New Canadian Political Economy*, edited by Wallace Clement, 118–140. Montreal: McGill-Queen's University Press.

Alfred, Taiaiake. 1999. *Peace, Power, Righteousness: An Indigenous Manifesto*. Toronto: Oxford University Press.

Anderson, Robert B. 1999. *Economic Development Among the Aboriginal Peoples in Canada: The Hope for the Future*. North York: Captus Press.

———. 2001. "Aboriginal People, Economic Development and Entrepreneurship." *Journal of Aboriginal Economic Development* 2 (1): 33–42.

Anderson, Joseph S., and Dean Howard Smith. 1998. "Managing Tribal Assets: Developing Long-Term Strategic Plans." *American Indian Culture and Research Journal* 22 (3): 139–149.

Aton, Kanani, Fiona Cram, Alice J. Kawakami, Morris K. Lai, and Laurie Porima. 2007. "Improving the Practice of Evaluation Through Indigenous Values and Methods: Decolonizing Evaluation Practice – Returning the Gaze From Hawai'i and Aotearoa." *Hulili: Multidisciplinary Research on Hawaiian Well-Being* 4 (1): 319–348.

Bacal, Robert. 1999. *Performance Management*. New York: McGraw-Hill.

Bartlette, Deborah. 2008. "Are 'Best Practices' Hurting Adult Ed: McIntyre and the Globalisation of Practice." Unpublished paper presented at Thinking Beyond Borders: Global Ideas, Global Values 27th National Conference, online proceedings of the Canadian Association for the Study of Adult Education, University of British Columbia, Vancouver.

Bennis, Warren, and Burt Nanus. 1985. *Leaders: Strategies for Taking Charge*. New York: Harper & Row.

Block, Peter. 1993. *Stewardship: Choosing Service Over Self-Interest*. San Francisco: Berrett-Koehler.

Brearley, Laura, and Lotte Darso. 2008. "Vivifying Data and Experience Through Artful Approaches." In *Handbook of the Arts in Qualitative Research: Perspectives, Methodologies, Examples and Issues*, edited by Ardra L. Cole and Gary J. Knowles, 639–652. Thousand Oaks: Sage Publications.

Brearley, Laura, Brian Calliou, and Janice Tanton. 2009. "An Aesthetic Approach to Leadership and Organizational Development: The Deep Listening Model for Research and Cultural Renewal." Unpublished paper presented at the Asia-Pacific Researchers in Organization Studies 13 Conference, Monterrey, Mexico, December 7–9.

Bushe, Gervase R. 1998. "Appreciative Inquiry with Teams." *Organization Development Journal* 16 (3): 41–50.

Calliou, Brian. 2005. "The Culture of Leadership: North American Indigenous Leadership in a Changing Economy." In *Indigenous Peoples and the Modern State*, edited by Duane Champagne, Karen Jo Torjesen, and Susan Steiner, 47–68. Walnut Creek: AltaMira Press.

———. 2008. "The Significance of Building Leadership and Community Capacity to Implement Self-Government." In *Aboriginal Self-Government in Canada: Current Trends and Issues*, edited by Yale Belanger, 332–347. 3rd ed. Saskatoon: Purich Publishing.

Calliou, Brian, and Cora J. Voyageur. 2007. "Aboriginal Economic Development and the Struggle for Self-Government." In *Power and Resistance: Critical Thinking About Canadian Social Issues*, edited by Wayne Antony and Les Samuelson. 4th ed. Halifax: Fernwood Publishing.

Calliou, Brian, and Cynthia Wesley-Esquimaux. 2010. "Best Practices in Aboriginal Community Development: A Wise Practices Approach." Unpublished report, the Banff Centre, Indigenous Leadership and Management. http://www.banffcentre.ca/indigenous-leadership/library/pdf/best_practices_in_aboriginal_community_development.pdf.

Carter, Sarah. 1990. *Lost Harvests: Prairie Indian Reserve Farmers and Government Policy*. Montreal: McGill-Queen's University Press.

Champagne, Duane. 2004. "Tribal Capitalism and Native Capitalists: Multiple Pathways of Native Economy." In *Native Pathways: American Indian Culture and Economic Development in the Twentieth Century*, edited by Brian Hosmer and Colleen O'Neill, 308–329. Boulder: University Press of Colorado.

Chouinard, Jill A., and J. Bradley Cousins. 2007. "Culturally Competent Evaluation for Aboriginal Communities: A Review of the Empirical Literature." *Journal of Multidisciplinary Evaluation* 4 (8): 40–57.

Cooper, Cecily D., Terry A. Scandura, and Chester A. Schriesheim. 2005. "Looking Forward But Learning From Our Past: Potential Challenges to Developing Authentic Leadership Theory and Authentic Leaders." *The Leadership Quarterly* 16 (3): 475–493.

Cooperrider, David L., and Suresh Srivastva, eds. 1998. *Organizational Wisdom and Executive Courage*. San Francisco: New Lexington Press.

Cooperrider, David L., and Diana Whitney, 2005 *Appreciative Inquiry: A Positive Revolution in Change*. San Francisco: Berrett-Koehler.

Cornell, Stephen. 1987. "American Indians, American Dreams, and the Meaning of Success." *American Indian Culture and Research Journal* 11 (2): 59–70.

——. 1998. "Strategic Analysis: A Practical Tool for Building Indian Nations." Harvard Project Report No. 98–10. Cambridge: John F. Kennedy School of Government, Harvard University.

——. 2007. "Remaking the Tools of Governance: Colonial Legacies, Indigenous Solutions." In *Rebuilding Native Nations: Strategies for Governance and Development*, edited by Miriam Jorgensen, 57–77. Tucson: University of Arizona Press.

Cornell, Stephen, and Miriam Jorgensen. 2007. "Getting Things Done for the Nation: The Challenge of Tribal Administration." In *Rebuilding Native Nations: Strategies for Governance and Development*, edited by Miriam Jorgensen, 146–172. Tucson: University of Arizona Press.

Cornell, Stephen, and Joseph P. Kalt. 1988. "Sovereignty and Nation-Building: The Development Challenge in Indian County Today." *American Indian Culture and Research Journal* 22 (3): 187–214.

——. 1990. "Pathways from Poverty: Economic Development and Institution-Building on American Indian Reservations." *American Indian Culture and Research Journal* 14 (1): 89–125.

——. 2000. "Where's the Glue? Institutional Bases of American Indian Economic Development." *Journal of Socio-Economics* 29 (3): 443–470.

Cowan, David A. 2008. "Profound Simplicity of Leadership Wisdom: Exemplary Insight From Miami Nation Chief Floyd Leonard." *International Journal of Leadership Studies* 4 (1): 51–81.

Cunningham, Gord, and Alison Mathie. 2002. "From Client to Citizens: Asset-Based Community Development as a Strategy for Community Driven Development." The Coady International Institute, St. Francis Xavier University, Nova Scotia. http://dspace.cigilibrary. org/jspui/bitstream/123456789/10369/1/From%20 Clients%20to%20Citizens%20Asset%20Based%20 Community%20Development%20as%20a%20

Strategy%20For%20Community%20Driven%20 Development.pdf?1.

Dahlberg, Gunilla, Peter Moss, and Alan Pence. 1999. *Beyond Quality in Early Childhood Education and Care: Postmodern Perspectives*. London: Routledge.

Davis, Arthur K. 1971. "Canadian Society and History as Hinterland Versus Metropolis." In *Canadian Society: Pluralism, Change and Conflict*, edited by Richard J. Ossenberg, 6–32. Scarborough: Prentice-Hall.

Davis, O. L., Jr. 1997. "Beyond 'Best Practices' Toward Wise Practices." *Journal of Curriculum and Supervision* 13 (1): 1–5.

Davis, James H., Lex Donaldson, and F. David Schoorman. 1997. "Toward a Stewardship Theory of Management." *Academy of Management Review* 22 (1): 20–47.

Dos Santos, Theotonio. 1971. "The Structure of Dependence." In *Readings in the U.S. Imperialism*, edited by K. T. Fann and Donald C. Hodges, 225–236. Boston: Extending Horizons.

Dyck, Noel, ed. 1985. *Indigenous People and the Nation-State: Fourth World Politics in Canada, Australia and Norway*. St. John's: Memorial University of Newfoundland.

Elias, Peter Douglas. 1990. "Wage Labour, Aboriginal Relations, and the Cree of the Churchill River Basin, Saskatchewan." *Native Studies Review* 6 (2): 43–64.

Erakovic, Lijijana, Manula Henare, Edwina Pio, and Chellie Spiller. 2011. "Wise Up: Creating Organizational Wisdom Through an Ethic of *Kaitiakitanga*." *Journal of Business Ethics* 104 (2): 223–235.

Foldy, Erica, and Sonia Ospina. 2005. "Toward a Framework of Social Change Leadership." Research paper no. 2010-05, NYU Wagner. http://ssrn.com/abstract=1532332.

Fox, Jonathan. 1992. "Democratic Rural Development: Leadership Accountability in Regional Peasant Organizations." *Development and Change* 23 (2): 1–36.

Foy, Malcom, Rick Krehbiel, and Elmar Plate. 2009. "Best Practices for First Nations Involvement in Environmental Assessment Review of Development Projects in British Columbia." Unpublished report, New Relationship Trust, Vancouver. http://www. newrelationshiptrust.ca/downloads/environmental-assessments-report.pdf.

Frank, Andre Gunder. 1966. "The Development of Underdevelopment." *Monthly Review* XVII (2): 17–31.

Fraser, Sarah Jane. 2002. "An Exploration of Joint Ventures as a Sustainable Development Tool for First Nations." *Journal of Aboriginal Economic Development* 3(1): 40–44.

Frideres, James. 1988. "The Political Economy of Natives in Canada." In *Native Peoples in Canada: Contemporary Conflicts*, edited by James Frideres, 366. 3rd ed. Scarborough: Prentice-Hall.

Gini, Al. 1998. "Work, Identity and Self: How We Are Formed by the Work We Do." *Journal of Business Ethics* 17 (7): 707–714.

Gooty, J., and S. Michie. 2005. "Values, Emotions, and Authenticity: Will the Real Leader Please Stand Up?" *Leadership Quarterly* 16 (3): 441–457.

Grint, Keith, and Linda Sue Warner. 2006. "American Indian Ways of Leading and Knowing." *Leadership* 2 (2): 225–244. doi:10.1177/1742715006062936.

Guyette, Susan. 1996. *Planning for Balanced Development: A Guide for Native American and Rural Communities.* Santa Fe: Clear Light Publishers.

Hammond Ketilson, L., and I. MacPherson. 2002. "Aboriginal Co-operatives in Canada: A Sustainable Development Strategy Whose Time Has Come." *Journal of Aboriginal Economic Development* 3 (1): 45–57.

Helin, Calvin. 2006. *Dances with Dependency: Indigenous Success Through Self-Reliance.* Vancouver: Orca Spirit Publishing.

Hernandez, Morela. 2008. "Promoting Stewardship Behavior in Organizations: A Leadership Model." *Journal of Business Ethics* 80 (2008): 121–128. doi:10.1007/s10551-007-9440-2.

High, Steven. 1996. "Native Wage Labour and Independent Production During the Era of Irrelevance." *Labour/Le Travail* 37 (Spring): 243–264.

Hofstede, Geert. 1980. *Culture's Consequences: International Differences in Work Related Values.* Beverley Hills: Sage.

———. 1983. "The Cultural Relativity of Organizational Practices and Theories." *Journal of International Business* 14 (2): 75–89.

Jaros, Stephen. 2012. "Identity and the Workplace: An Assessment of Contextualist and Discursive Approaches." *Tamara: Journal for Critical Organization Inquiry* 10 (4): 45–59.

Kageler, W., V. L. Goodwin, T. M. Pitts, and J. L. Whittington. 2005. "Legacy Leadership: The Leadership Wisdom of the Apostle Paul." *Leadership Quarterly* 16 (5): 749–770.

King, Tracey. 2008. "Fostering Aboriginal Leadership: Increasing Enrollment and Completion Rates in Canadian Post-Secondary Institutions." *College Quarterly* 11 (1). http://www.collegequarterly.ca/2008-vol11-num01-winter/king.html.

Knudtson, Peter, and David Suzuki. 1992. *Wisdom of the Elders.* Toronto: Stoddart Publishing.

Kok, Ayse. 2009. "Realizing Wisdom Theory in Complex Learning Networks." *Electronic Journal of e-Learning* 7 (1): 53–60. http://www.ejel.org/volume7/issue1.

Korac-Kakabadse, A., N. Korac-Kakabadse, and A. Kouzmin. 2001. "Leadership Renewal: Towards the Philosophy of Wisdom." *International Review of Administrative Sciences* 67 (2): 207–227.

Krajewski, Henryk, and Yvonne Silver. n.d. "Announcing the Death of 'Best Practices': Resurrecting 'Best Principles' to Retain and Engage High Potentials." Unpublished article, Human Resources Association of Calgary. Accessed February 6, 2014. www.right.com/documents/newsroom/20080620141835_420216525.pdf

LaFrance, Joan, and Richard Nichols. 2010. "Reframing Evaluation: Defining an Indigenous Evaluation Framework." *Canadian Journal of Program Evaluation* 23 (2): 13–31.

Leithwood, Kenneth. 2001. "School Leadership in the Context of Accountability Policies." *International Journal of Leadership in Education: Theory and Practice* 4 (3): 217–235. doi:10.1080/13603120110057082.

Leskiw, Sheri-Lynne, and Parbudyal Singh. 2007. "Leadership Development: Learning From Best Practices." *Leadership and Organization Development Journal* 28 (5): 444–464.

Little Bear, Leroy. 2011. "Jagged Worldview Colliding." In *Reclaiming Indigenous Voice and Vision,* edited by Marie Battiste 77–85. Vancouver: University of British Columbia Press.

Martz, Wes. 2013. "Evaluating Organizational Performance: Rational, Natural, and Open System Models." *American Journal of Evaluation* 34 (3): 385–401. doi:10.1177/1098214013479151.

McGonagill, Grady, and Peter W. Pruyn. 2010. "Leadership Development in the U.S.: Principles and Patterns of Best Practice." Unpublished report, Bertelsmann Stiftung, Gütersloh, Germany. http://www.bertels-mann-stiftung.de/cps/rde/xbcr/SID-57313EB7-4601475F/bst_engI/Leadership-Development-in-the-US.pdf.

Meier, Werner. 2003. "Results-Based Management: Towards a Common Understanding Among Development Cooperation Agencies." Discussion paper ver. 5.0, Canadian International Development Agency, Performance Review Branch, Ottawa.

Milloy, John. 1999. *A National Crime: The Canadian Government and the Residential School System.* Winnipeg: University of Manitoba Press.

Nabigon, Herbert C., and Annie Wenger-Nabigon. 2012. "'Wise Practices': Integrating Traditional Teachings With Mainstream Treatment Approaches." *Native Social Work Journal* 8 (2012): 43–55.

Newhouse, David. 1999. "The Development of the Aboriginal Economy Over the Next 20 Years." *Journal of Aboriginal Economic Development* 1(1): 68–77.

———. 2000. "Modern Aboriginal Economies: Capitalism with a Red Face." *Journal of Aboriginal Economic Development* 1 (2): 55–61.

Nielsen, Marianne O., and Lindsay Redpath. 1997. "A Comparison of Native Culture, Non-Native Culture and New Management." *Canadian Journal of Administrative Sciences* 14 (3): 327–339.

O'Connell, Tom, Robert J. Oppenheimer, and Warren Weir. 2010. "Training Opportunities in Aboriginal Business, Community and Economic Development: Being Offered Through Aboriginal Organizations." *Journal of Aboriginal Economic Development* 7 (1): 19–28.

Oppenheimer, Robert, and Warren Weir. 2010. "The New Federal Framework for Aboriginal Economic Development: The Base Upon Which Future Canadian Government Policies and Programs Are Being Built." *Journal of Aboriginal Economic Development* 7 (1): 86–94.

Ottmann, Jacqueline. 2005a. "First Nations Leadership Development." Report for the Banff Centre, Indigenous Leadership and Management. www.banffcentre.ca/departments/leadership/aboriginal/library/First_Nations_Leadership_Ottmann.pdf.

———. 2005b. "First Nations Leadership Development within a Saskatchewan Context." EdD diss., Department of Educational Administration, University of Saskatchewan.

Ray, Arthur J. 1974. *Indians in the Fur Trade: Their Role as Trappers, Hunters, and Middlemen in the Lands Southwest of the Hudson Bay, 1660–1870*. Toronto: University of Toronto Press.

Smith, Dean Howard. 2000. *Modern Tribal Development: Paths to Self-Sufficiency and Cultural Integrity in Indian Country*. Walnut Creek: AltaMira Press.

Snowball, Andrew, and Cynthia Wesley-Esquimaux. 2010. "Viewing Violence, Mental Illness and Addictions Through a Wise Practice Lens." *International Journal of Mental Health and Addictions* 8 (2): 390–407.

Sternberg, Robert J. 2005. "A Model of Educational Leadership: Wisdom, Intelligence, and Creativity Synthesized." *International Journal of Leadership in Education* 8 (4): 347–364.

Thoms, Michael J. 2007. "Leading an Extraordinary Life: Wise Practices for an HIV Prevention Campaign With Two-Spirited Men." Unpublished paper, 2-Spirited People of the First Nations, Toronto.

Tobias, John. 1976. "Protection, Civilization, Assimilation: An Outline of Canada's Indian Policy" *Western Canadian Journal of Anthropology* 6 (2): 39–53.

Tough, Frank. 1992. "Regional Analysis of Indian Aggregate Income, Northern Manitoba." *Native Studies Review* 12 (1): 95–146.

Wallerstein, Immanuel. 2004. *World-Systems Analysis*. Durham: Duke University Press.

Walter, Maggie. 2006. "Participatory Action Research." In *Social Research Methods*, edited by Maggie Walter, chapter 21. Online excerpt, accessed June 9, 2014. http://lib.oup.com.au/he/study_skills/walter2e/walter_ch21.pdf.

Weick, K. E. 2004. "Mundane Poetics: Searching for Wisdom in Organization Studies." *Organization Studies* 25 (3): 653–668.

Wuttunee, Wanda. 2002. "Partnering Among Aboriginal Communities: Tribal Council Investment Group (TCIG)." *Journal of Aboriginal Economic Developments* 3 (1): 9–17.

———. 2004. *Living Rhythms: Lessons in Aboriginal Economic Resilience*. Montreal: McGill-Queen's University Press.

PART 13

Additional Readings

Andrew, Paul, Tim Aubry, and Yale Belanger, eds. *Indigenous Homelessness: Perspectives from Canada, Australia, and New Zealand*. Winnipeg: University of Manitoba Press, 2016.

Beaton, Ryan and John Borrows, eds. *Wise Practices: Exploring Indigenous Economic Justice and Self-determination*. Nanaimo: Strong Nations Publishing. 2021.

Christensen, Julia. *No Home in a Homeland*. Vancouver: University of British Columbia Press. 2017.

Kenny, Carolyn, ed. *Living Indigenous Leadership: Native Narratives on Building Strong Communities*. Vancouver: University of British Columbia Press, 2012.

Jobin, Shalene Wuttenee. *Upholding Indigenous Economic Relationships: Nehiyawak Narratives*. Vancouver: University of British Columbia Press. 2022.

Neu, Dean and Richard Therrien. *Accounting for Genocide: Canada's Bureaucratic Assault on Aboriginal People*. Halifax: Fernwood Publishing. 2020.

Sinclair, Sara, ed. *How We Go Home: Voices from Indigenous North America*. Chicago: Haymarket Press. 2020.

The Kino-nda-niimi Collective. *The Winter We Danced: Voices from the Past, the Future, and the Idle No More Movement*. Winnipeg: Arbeiter Ring Publishing, 2014.

Voyageur, Cora, Laura Brearley, and Brian Calliou, eds. *Restorying Indigenous Leadership: Wise Practices in Community Development*. Banff: Banff Centre Press. 2015.

Relevant Websites

Cooperative and community-based economy research—"Wise Practices"
https://www.uvic.ca/ncied/research/coop-community/index.php

A webpage from The National Consortium for Indigenous Economic Development that discusses a research project that utilized the wise practices lens.

National Indigenous strategy includes the 107 Calls to Economic Prosperity
https://windspeaker.com/news/windspeaker-news/national-indigenous-strategy-includes-107-calls-economic-prosperity

An article about the June 6th 2022 National Indigenous Economic Strategy (NIES) created by Indigenous leaders and organizations to guide governments and institutions towards restoring Indigenous economic prosperity.

Films

Beating the Streets. Dir. Lorna Thomas. National Film Board of Canada, 1998.
Economic Reconciliation. Dir. Andrée Cazabon. Productions Cazabon. 2019.
Kimmapiiyipitssini: The Meaning of Empathy. Dir. Elle-Máijá Tailfeathers. National Film Board of Canada. 2021.
Life on Victor Street. Dir. Kirby Hammond. National Film Board of Canada. 2012.
The People of the Kattawapiskak River. Dir. Alanis Obomsawin. National Film Board of Canada, 2012.
Our People Will Be Healed. Dir. Alanis Obomsawin. National Film Board of Canada. 2017.

Key Terms

- Modern Indigenous leader
- Wise practices model
- Idle No More Movement
- Bill C-45
- Chief Theresa Spence

Discussion Questions

1. Why does the universality of a model of best practices need to be critiqued, according to Calliou and Wesley-Esquimaux? How is this model not culturally responsive to Indigenous community development?

2. Discuss what Calliou and Wesley-Esquimaux mean in saying: "the wise practices approach involves a journey that goes backward in order to move forward." How does this approach challenge a Western view of community development?

3. Discuss the significance of the Idle No More movement both in terms of bringing awareness to the historic injustices committed against Indigenous nations in Canada, and in mobilizing a strong resistance to Settler colonialism.

4. What was the symbolic significance of Chief Theresa Spence's hunger strike? How was her individual act linked to the poor socioeconomic conditions experienced by Indigenous peoples across Canada? How did it influence the Idle No More movement?

Activities

Invite a local community worker in a social services sector to speak about issues of poverty faced by Indigenous people in the area and how the community agency is working to address these. Are any of the wise practices discussed by Calliou and Wesley-Esquimaux being employed by the agency?

Locate a recent news item that highlights the economic and social conditions of Indigenous peoples in cities. What are the main issues? Does the article link these conditions with colonialism? What solutions, if any, are offered, and how do these reflect those compare to those offered by Palmater and Calliou and Wesley-Esquimaux?

PART 14

Health

Editor Introduction

On 19 September 2008, Brian Lloyd Sinclair wheeled himself into an emergency room at Winnipeg's Health Sciences Centre. After waiting 34 hours for medical attention, he later died. Requiring only routine care to remove a blocked catheter, an inquiry later revealed that no one seemed to know what to do with Mr Sinclair, or even what he was doing there (Provincial Court of Manitoba, 2014). Among the possibilities: he was sleeping (ibid.: 70–1); waiting for another assessment (ibid.: 71–2); and possibly another bed (ibid.: 72–3). The inquiry also concluded that he was believed intoxicated—a drunk seeking shelter and warmth (ibid.: 74–8). Brian Sinclair was not intoxicated. Much to the horror and protest of selected onlookers—at times even vomiting on himself—he died alone in a wheelchair. He escaped the attention of medical personnel.

The violence directed toward Brian Sinclair and his family marks an egregious act of racism in Canada's health care system. Logan McCallum and Perry (2018) provide extensive documentation and analysis in their recent book *Structures of Indifference*. They outline the many factors contributing to Sinclair's death, the resultant dehumanization that contributes to and condones the deaths of Indigenous peoples more broadly, as well as details about the inquiry that followed. The inquiry into Sinclair's death put forward 63 recommendations to make sure it never happened again (CBC News, 2017). However, and inexcusably, these recommendations have remained ineffective because Sinclair's death is not an isolated occurrence in our institutions of Canadian health care. As recently as 28 September 2020, Joyce Echaquan, a 37-year-old Atikamekw woman, arrived at Centre hospitalier de Lanaudière in Saint-Charles-Borromée, Quebec, showing early signs of pulmonary edema (CBC News, 2021a). In a video recording posted to social media, health care professionals are heard audibly hurling demeaning and racist insults toward her. She later died of an entirely preventable death in hospital (ibid.).

The story of Brian Sinclair and Joyce Echaquan would seem atypical by health care professionals were it not for the suspicion of alcoholism and drug addiction, a pattern that is common in Settler–Indigenous encounters today. In fact, the stories of both Brian Sinclair and Joyce Echaquan are entirely consistent with a scholarly literature already suggesting that intoxication—or even suspected drunkenness and addiction—recurrently precedes Indigenous deaths in custody (Razack, 2015). It is furthermore consistent with an interview-based literature documenting the experience of Indigenous peoples in search of health care services (Browne and Fiske, 2001; Fiske and Browne,

2006). Alcohol and drugs, it is argued, works to discredit Indigenous peoples in health care contexts (ibid., Razack, 2015: 116). It fuels a deadly and racist perception that people struggling (or perceived to be struggling) with addictions are unworthy of care—a phenomenon that left an Anishinabe man dying in a wheelchair for 34 hours, and an Atikamekw woman dying from fluid in the lungs in September 2020.

Indigenous peoples do not always die due to negligence rooted in suspected alcoholism and addictions. Jordan River Anderson—a Cree boy with a complex medical condition requiring special services—died as an outcome of governments trying to decide on who would pay the bills (Blackstock, 2008). Anderson required an immediate determination, later dying in hospital because provincial governments have viewed health care for Indians as a federal responsibility. Some of us die in Canada because governments cannot decide on jurisdiction, while others die due to racial profiling. In either case, the deaths are preventable and are but two sides of the same coin. They both involve a societal and legislative history that places Settlers into positions of power and privilege over Indigenous health and well-being. These matters of life and death are not new.

The marking of Indigenous peoples as diseased, addicted, and unworthy of care—along with their deaths—are deeply historical. Kelm (1998) wrote of the discursive construction of Indigenous peoples as sick and vulnerable, arguing that it has worked under Settler colonialism to construct a population of peoples believed incapable of governing themselves. Razack (2015: 45) argues, furthermore, that the presence and/or mere suspicion of addictions and alcohol use—along with the inquiries that follow and indeed document them—is constitutive of a material and symbolic violence required for an ongoing project of Settler colonialism to ensue. "Marked as surplus, . . ." she writes, "Indigenous people [sic] are considered by settler society as the waste or excess that must be expelled" (ibid., 24).

Sick, damaged, and addicted populations are incapable of governing themselves, a conceptual if not ideological formulation that must be shown repeatedly if Settler colonialism is to lay ongoing claim to stolen lands (Kelm, 1998; Razack, 2015). Thus, when people like Brian Sinclair and Joyce Echaquan die in hospital, and in the case of Sinclair, when a subsequent order of inquiry never moves beyond sorting out whether or not he was drunk or an alcoholic, the privilege of never having to know, name, or mark Settler investments in white normalcy and difference-making persists. Unfortunately, there is a dearth of inquiry focusing on difference-making in health care services delivery. Typically, we are instead invited into a conversation about **historical trauma**, how to better procedures, offer a more compassionate or humanitarian response—especially to alcohol use (Razack, 2015: 103)—if not engage in **cultural sensitivity** training.

The invitation to **cultural competence** and/or sensitivity training places individuals—including health service providers—into positions of power and superiority (Jeffery and Nelson, 2009). Indigenous peoples are there to be helped, tolerated, if not better understood and culturally managed as different and deficit. Under this formulation, Settlers are never asked to name, transform, and/or remedy systemic inequities, or a process of identity-making that is rooted in Indigenous inferiority. They do not need to know their own culture and institutions, or to realize and nuance Settler complicity and responsibility. Rather, and in re-enacting a historical process of Settler entitlement, the objective is to steer Indigenous peoples away from an inherent ill health and poverty and toward civility, or to remove them—violently if necessary—from Settler spaces of belonging (Razack, 2002, 2015).

Cultural competence and sensitivity training ought to be looked upon with a great deal of skepticism if we consider that much of education and even literacy today—including that which is offered up pedagogically and institutionally—is based on coming to better understand a (different) culture. Polaschek (1998) wrote of New Zealand—now some 25 years ago—that health practitioners would be better off actively focusing on access to education and affordable housing versus cultural difference. Culturally safe services are not only informed and delivered through cultural sensitivity training. They require the participation of non-Indigenous peoples in terms of demarcating racism, colonialism, and a Settler entitlement to lands. **Cultural safety** requires a changing of the subject in education (Cannon, 2014; Dion, 2009; St Denis and Schick, 2003).

The COVID-19 pandemic that has unfolded since the second edition of *Racism, Colonialism, and Indigenity in Canada* has made the matter of health care services and their modes of delivery even more urgent, especially in light of the devastating impacts on Indigenous communities and how they have been disproportionately affected (CBC News, 2021b). We wish to acknowledge the many deaths in communities, some of which have impacted us personally. Poverty and overcrowding—both clear **social determinants of health** and outcomes tied to colonization directly as discussed in scholarly literature—adversely affected too many communities to mention (UBC Faculty of Arts, 2022). The deadly impacts also strained, changed, and transformed the structure of health care delivery in general, and in some cases, galvanized a noteworthy response of community-based vaccination campaigns—a matter of governance, innovation, and self-determination that must be acknowledged as a great achievement in some of our nations (ibid.). The impact of COVID-19 on Indigenous peoples and the health care system is ongoing and will require greater understanding and research in its own right (ibid.).

The authors we have selected are concerned with interrogating, intercepting, and changing the more immediate and deadly outcomes in health care situations. In particular, the readings are concerned with and critical of **culturalist** solutions to problems involving racism and colonialism in the context of health care services delivery. It is important to draw a distinction between culturalist and anticolonial approaches to health care services delivery. Janet Smylie and Billy Allan argue, for example, that cultural sensitivity training actively prevents health care practitioners from dealing effectively with issues of racism, and from producing scholarly epidemiological research illuminating the social determinants of health. They argue that Indigenous peoples are impacted by poverty, poor water quality, stress, and identity-related issues, and that this impacts health and health outcomes. The focus of research, they suggest, ought to be on health outcomes, and on remedying disparate and negative health indicators.

Brascoupé and Waters interrogate the expectations held by health care professionals today using cultural safety as a yardstick. The authors borrow the concept of cultural safety in part from New Zealand–based scholarship, pointing toward the limitations of the literature in Canada. They suggest that the responsibility of Settler populations beyond a concept of self-reflexivity and **healing** has not yet been determined. They also note that the concept of cultural safety is intended to prompt Settlers to ask critical questions about their own entitlement to lands, belonging, and a further dismantling of a Settler colonial project. Combined, the articles call for decolonizing solidarities, reform, and Settler–Indigenous relationship-building and rejuvenation as this relates to combating racism, colonialism, and disparities in health care practice and policy.

CHAPTER 27

Cultural Safety

Exploring the Applicability of the Concept of Cultural Safety to Aboriginal Health and Community Wellness

Simon Brascoupé and Catherine Waters

Introduction

1. Introduction and Definition

This paper describes and analyzes the concept of cultural safety as it pertains to Aboriginal policy and assesses its usefulness as a means of designing and developing government policy and service delivery. It seeks to draw together a range of literature sources to assess the applicability of cultural safety in a Canadian context.

The concept of cultural safety evolved as Aboriginal people and organizations adopted the term to define new approaches to healthcare and community healing ... the concept is used to express an approach to healthcare that recognizes the contemporary conditions of Aboriginal people which result from their post-contact history. . . .

To be able to introduce cultural safety into policy and delivery, policy-makers must understand what cultural safety fundamentally means, the difference it makes to policy development and delivery, and where cultural safety lies conceptually and in practice in relation to previous considerations of cultural difference.

This paper seeks to clarify and deepen the definition of cultural safety, and explore practical strategies, approaches and lessons learned that address the key drivers of risk and crisis in First Nation communities. . . .

Finally, this paper addresses the relevance of programs and services to the values, traditions, beliefs, and practices of Aboriginal people. The issue of culture and the degree to which it can and should be part of policy design and implementation are complex, but increasingly it is recognized and accepted that policy cannot be effective if it does not acknowledge and take some account of the cultural context in which it is applied. . . .

2. Literature Search

The literature search includes academic literature, focused both on health and indigenous cultures, grey literature and the Internet. . . . An Internet search included national and international literature available on the Internet (the Google search identified 6,860,000 citations for "cultural safety;" 455,000 citations for "cultural safety in health care," and 273,000 citations for "cultural safety Canada") presented a comprehensive review of relevant academic and professional research.

Simon Brascoupé and Catherine Waters. "Cultural Safety: Exploring the Applicability of the Concept of Cultural Safety to Aboriginal Health and Community Wellness." *International Journal of Indigenous Health* 5.2 (© 2009).

3. Cultural Competence and Cultural Safety Evidence Base

The evidence base for cultural competence and cultural safety is being examined from the perspective of quantitative, qualitative and traditional research methods. . . .

In a major study of the cultural competence evidence-base in health care, the National Center for Cultural Competence found some promising studies supporting health outcomes and patient satisfaction (Goode et al., 2006). . . .

The challenge is to extend the understanding of the role of *cultural competence* in health-care delivery to the concept of *cultural safety*, by distinguishing between these concepts and understanding what difference cultural safety brings to policy outcomes. . . . Cultural safety and cultural competence are key concepts that have practical meaning for Indigenous people. They form the basis for effective patient-centred care and the professional advocacy role of the general practitioner (Nguyen, 2008). . . . In Canada, there are a few studies by scholars (Smye and Browne, 2002) that explore how Aboriginal peoples experience cultural safety, to deepen the understanding of the effectiveness of cultural safety tools and interventions in nursing practice. Other researchers, like Jessica Ball (2007a), ask "How safe did the service recipient experience a service encounter in terms of being respected and assisted in having their cultural location, values, and preferences taken into account in the service encounter?" (Ball, 2007a: 1), explicitly linking service delivery to cultural respect and awareness. . . .

Finally, no cultural competency and safety research was found that focused explicitly on communities at risk or in crisis. . . .

This paper begins to map out the link between cultural safety and communities at risk or in crisis. Further research and work is needed to demonstrate how cultural safety theory contributes to community development strategies in supporting communities at risk and in crisis. . . .

Cultural Safety and Power

Throughout the literature, there is considerable reference to the concept and practice of *cultural competence*. This appears to represent a high-water mark of cultural understanding demonstrated by health-care professionals and, as the literature reveals, is taught and measured as a function of knowledge and understanding of Aboriginal culture by practitioners. . . .

Elsewhere, the literature reveals a different understanding of cultural safety. . . . This conceptualization of cultural safety represents a more radical, politicized understanding of cultural consideration, effectively rejecting the more limited culturally competent approach for one based not on knowledge but rather on power. . . .

1. The Culture Continuum or Paradigm Shift?

. . . Cultural safety is not just a process of improving program delivery; it is also part of the outcome.

Scholar Jessica Ball (2007a) supports this view of cultural safety as an outcome, but views cultural safety as a departure from cultural competence, rather than an extension of it. In essence, she sees a link between cultural sensitivity and cultural competence, but not between these concepts and cultural safety. She stresses that, while the responsibility for cultural competence lies with the service provider, cultural safety turns this on its head, transferring the responsibility (and the power) of determining how successful the experience was to the service recipient. . . .

Ball goes on to describe five principles necessary for cultural safety:

- **Protocols**—respect for cultural forms of engagement.
- **Personal knowledge**—understanding one's own cultural identity and sharing information about oneself to create a sense of equity and trust.
- **Process**—engaging in mutual learning, checking on cultural safety of the service recipient.
- **Positive purpose**—ensuring the process yields the right outcome for the service recipient according to that recipient's values, preferences and lifestyle.
- **Partnerships**—promoting collaborative practice. (adapted from Ball, 2007b: 1)

2. Multiculturalism and Cultural Blindness

. . . **Multiculturalism** can be seen, not as a "celebration of diversity," but a means of making culture and race invisible, by blurring and ultimately ignoring important differences between people into a meaningless notion of diversity. Verma St Denis, a Canadian scholar examining race and education, particularly as it pertains to Aboriginal students, argues that the danger of the "multi-culturalism myth" is that it creates an ideology of "racelessness," making race invisible when it should be acknowledged and understood, and reinforcing Whiteness as the standard of what is normal. With colleague, Carol Schick, St Denis examines racial attitudes in education in the Canadian prairie provinces, observing that the invisibility of White privilege which is accepted sub-consciously as the norm has the effect of marginalizing Aboriginal people and other racial minorities, and causing the "inferiorization" of Aboriginal people for their apparent failure to meet White measures of success and achievement (Schick and St Denis, 2005; St Denis, 2007).

York University scholar Susan Dion takes the same view of race relations in education as St Denis, underlining the need for carefully designed curricula to trace the history of the "colonial encounter" between Aboriginal and non-aboriginal people and understand 20th century issues in the light of this history. . . .

Dion, St Denis and McIntosh all relate their studies of interracial relations primarily to the field of education and curriculum-design. . . . Most interestingly, in contrast to the cultural competence model of transcultural relationships, these scholars all point to the need for White people, and White professionals in particular, to understand themselves and their own race and culture, rather than learning about their clients' races and cultures. This element of self-knowledge is integral to cultural safety and any possible redefinition of power relations.

3. Transculturalism and Cultural Safety

. . . Transcultural nursing, expounded in the writing of Leininger (1991, 1998) is, according to Ramsden, based on the traditional western approach to health care, represented by the non-Aboriginal nurse. Transcultural nursing focuses on the knowledge and understanding of Aboriginal culture of the Canadian nurse; it therefore uses as its starting point the norms of the nurse and, in this sense, represents an approach based on cultural competence, rather than cultural safety. Transcultural nursing appears to fit the model of race relations criticized by St Denis and McIntosh, where the White professional establishes the context in which the service encounter will take place. In transcultural nursing, the power to define the norm and the onus for action to understand and know about another culture fall to the nurse (Ramsden, 2002: 112–14). . . .

Ultimately, the deficiency of cultural competence is that it is, as both a concept and as a practice, too one-sided and focuses on the knowledge and training of the service provider. This focus reinforces inherent power positions and reduces the role of Aboriginal patients to one of passive receivers of culturally competent behaviours. This is not to say that cultural competence does not play a crucial part in a successful interaction, but it cannot on its own create an equal relationship.

The transformation of the relationship cannot be effected through more culture training and greater knowledge by the service provider. . . . Both parties require the capacity to play their part in successful engagements; this capacity depends on the knowledge, understanding and confidence of both, as well as their self-knowledge and cultural self-awareness. . . .

At the individual, institutional and government levels, the parties need to view cultural safety as neither an extension to cultural competence on the cultural continuum, nor as a paradigm shift, but as a navigation model to transform cross-cultural relationships.

4. Social Determinants of Health

. . . The environment in which people live has a profound effect on their health difficulties. These are known as the social determinants of health (SDOH), including poverty, unemployment, poor education, bad nutrition, poor housing, and unclean water. . . .

The focus of the literature that explicitly explores cultural safety is limited to a narrow area of healthcare delivery, specifically nursing. But to limit the discussion to nursing and health care delivery ignores the many issues, such as education, economic opportunity, and lifestyle issues (such as nutrition, smoking, and alcohol and drug consumption) that are integral to the area of health care delivery.

Although the academic and professional literature concentrates almost exclusively on a narrow range of health care delivery, it is clear that cultural safety must extend beyond health if its full implications are to be realized. . . .

In order to explore the full meaning of cultural safety and its possible application to different areas of social policy, we now analyze a number of specific policy areas which make up the context and environment for Aboriginal health and wellness.

Application to Policy Areas

. . . In this section, we examine some areas of public policy where the literature on cultural safety examines the relevance of the concept to produce . . . practical outcomes: health and the social determinants of health, education, and self-determination. In addition, in a subsequent section, the relevance of cultural safety is considered in the context of the criminal justice system. . . .

1. Health

To understand health as a policy area, it is necessary to consider the wider definition employed by the World Health Organization (WHO) and further supported by the WHO's Commission on Social Determinants of Health (SDOH). WHO reports that the most common definition of health for the last fifty years is "a complete state of physical, mental and social well-being and not merely the absence of disease or infirmity" (Ustun and Jakob, 2005, quoted in Stout, 2008: 3[sic]). . . .

Health policy regarding Aboriginal people which reflects the prescription of cultural safety could provide the policies to improve health outcomes, the institutional structures for on-going partnership and shared responsibility, and the symbolism of enlightened governance. . . .

2. Education

. . . Possibly the single most important social issue for inclusion within the cultural safety model is education, particularly at the secondary and post-secondary levels. . . .

Culturally safe teaching practices have also been the subject of considerable study, though the actual term "cultural safety" has not been transferred from the health literature. Scholar Pamela Toulouse draws on growing research when she argues that Aboriginal students' self-esteem is a key factor in success in school. She lists a number of factors that contribute to the academic success of Aboriginal students:

- Educators who have high expectations and truly care for Aboriginal students.
- Classroom environments that honour who they are and where they come from.
- Teaching practices that reflect Aboriginal learning styles (differentiated instruction and evaluation).
- Schools with strong partnerships with Aboriginal communities. (Toulouse, 2008: 1–2)

As in the health arena, the success of the bicultural educational encounter between teacher and student must be a two-way exchange, based on an equal partnership. The teacher's skills and knowledge must allow for the student to feel respected and understood. The student must feel safe in order to enter into their part of the encounter.

3. Self-Determination

. . . Used in the context of health care, the term "self-determination" . . . encompasses a variety of forms which allow Aboriginal people to regain control at some level. At the same time, it may be a matter of practicality for Aboriginal people to take advantage of those forms of self-determination which can be negotiated and agreed quickly. . . .

These could include: a strong political voice through Aboriginal organizations; inspirational community leadership and role models; the reinterpretation of historical events; use of Aboriginal languages; the formation of intertribal and international networks; recognition and respect for traditional knowledge; the establishment of Aboriginal schools, colleges, community centres, clinics, treatment centres, and cultural and spiritual institutions; the use of cultural symbols and ceremony in the community and in wider Canadian society; a greater role for Elders; the use of consensual decision-making; the use of traditional healing and justice; and negotiated treaties and agreements granting greater governance powers to First Nations. Finally, the literature on cultural safety in health care implies that self-determination exists also in the form of individual confidence and self-esteem, personal choices about treatment, an equal exchange of information with health care professionals, and a feeling of trust. . . .

The aspects of this form of self-determination, focusing on spirituality, tradition, respect, and community are in keeping with the concept of cultural safety. The cultural safety model of Aboriginal power does not advocate separateness of the Aboriginal community. . . . This is consistent with Ramsden's conception of cultural safety as, by definition, bicultural (Ramsden, 2004 [sic]; Coup, 1996) . . .; it was a way of defining a two-way relationship.

Personal and Community Healing

. . . First Nations are developing institutions and curricula to build the capacity in their youth. However, one of the legacies of colonialism is social and economic conditions that often preclude full participation in their community and . . . put communities at risk and potentially in crisis unless healing can take place. In this section we look at the subject of healing from three perspectives: the concept of healing in general, community healing, and indigenous knowledge and law.

1. Healing

The Aboriginal healing movement is based on a traditional community-based shared counselling process which includes physical, emotional, mental, and spiritual healing. It traditionally involves Elders bringing together the people involved in a dispute or harmful incident to talk, listen and learn from each other and to agree on a solution. . . .

While there are variations in the way First Nations depict the medicine wheel, generally the healing path of the medicine wheel includes a:

- Talking Lodge.
- Listening and Teaching Lodge.
- Healing Path Lodge.
- Healing Lodge . . .

Healing is . . . a society-wide exercise, whereby Aboriginal and non-Aboriginal peoples come to terms with the past and redefine the future. In this way, the healing relationship is depicted in the same way as the cultural safety model and is consistent with the writings of St Denis and McIntosh regarding the need for mutual understanding and also self-knowledge and understanding . . .

2. Community Healing

The literature on cultural safety is curiously silent on the issue of communities in crisis. The cultural safety of nurses' interaction with Aboriginal patients is defined in individual terms, with the feelings of the individual patient determining the success of the interaction. But the application of cultural safety to the wellness of a community is not considered . . .

Aboriginal communities face different challenges depending on their history and resources. It is possible to imagine other questions that could be asked in different circumstances, such as questions about the state of housing, the existence of employment opportunities, and the condition of the family. In the literature on Aboriginal communities and economic development are descriptions of communities who have healed from crisis to create a vibrant healthy life for their residents . . .

3. Indigenous knowledge and law

Indigenous knowledge is "a complete knowledge system with its own epistemology, philosophy and scientific and logical validity . . . which can only be understood by means of pedagogy traditionally employed by the people themselves" (Battiste and Henderson, 2000: 41[sic]). . . .

Indigenous knowledge allows Aboriginal people to express themselves in languages and terms which reinforce their social, spiritual, political, and cultural identity. While indigenous knowledge can be of practical use to individuals and families, in the context of cultural safety, its significance is in the recognition of and respect shown by service providers for traditional ways of doing things. . . .

Indigenous knowledge and laws strengthen Aboriginal people in claiming the respect and equality in relation to figures of authority in Canadian society, including nurses, teachers, social workers, judges, and others. . . .

It is evident that Aboriginal people can draw on the strength of their indigenous knowledge and cultures. However . . . there is the opportunity for enrichment for non-Aboriginal society as well in terms of mutual respect and understanding. In the Truth and Reconciliation Report, Anne Salmond comments: ". . . the process of opening Western knowledge to traditional rationalities has hardly yet begun" (Bielawski, 2004: 1[sic]).

Conclusion

The concept of cultural safety . . . remains confined largely to academic studies and government reports, and little hard evidence appears to have been applied to professional practice. It seems that the practicalities of cultural safety as an *outcome* rather than a *concept* have yet to be realized. . . .

[A]s several writers have discussed, the concept of cultural safety carries an explicit political component. This derives from the express transfer of power in a culturally safe exchange from the professional to the Aboriginal client, where the success of the exchange is judged by the Aboriginal person, and not the professional. Expressing cultural safety in terms of power explicitly challenges the existing power structures within institutions and wider society and can appear threatening. . . .

The differences between the concept of cultural safety versus cultural competence and transcultural practice are profound. . . .

Cultural competence (and the linked concepts of cultural sensitivity and transcultural practice) is based on the *process* of building an effective service delivery interaction with Aboriginal clients, rather than the *outcome* of the success of the interaction. However knowledgeable or sensitive the professional is, this does not in itself ensure the effectiveness of the interaction. . . .

While it is desirable that professionals be knowledgeable of Aboriginal cultures, this criterion is inadequate to ensure that the *outcome* of the interaction with Aboriginal clients is culturally safe. . . .

[F]or cultural safety to become entrenched in professional practice in health and other policy areas, including education at all levels, justice, and social work, cultural safety has to be practiced not just by individuals but also by institutions. . . .

Since the literature on cultural safety focuses strongly on the individual level of Aboriginal people interacting with health care professionals, it is largely silent on the issues of community wellness and communities at risk and in crisis. . . . However, moving from the issue of power to culture, it is possible to see links that could be explored in literature in the future.

References

Ball, J. 2007a. *Creating Cultural Safety in Speech-language and Audiology Services.* PowerPoint Presentation: Presented at the Annual Conference of the BC Association of Speech-Language Pathologists and Audiologists, Whistler, BC, 25 October 2007.

Ball, J. 2007b. "Supporting Aboriginal Children's Development," *Early Childhood Development Intercultural Partnerships*, University of Victoria, retrieved Nov. 2008, www.ecdip.org/capacity/.

Coup, A. 1996. "Cultural Safety and Culturally Congruent Care," *Nursing Praxis in New Zealand* 11 (1); 4–11.

Dion, S. 2007. "Disrupting Molded Images: Identities, Responsibilities and Relationships—Teachers and Indigenous Subject Material," *Teaching Education* 18 (4): 329–342.

Goode, T. D., M.C. Dunne, and S.M. Bronheim. 2006. "The Evidence Base for Cultural and Linguistic Competency in Health Care," *The Commonwealth Fund* 37, http://www.commonwealthfund.org/publications/publications_show.htm?doc_id=413821.

Leininger, M. 1991. "Transcultural Nursing: The Study and Practice Field," *Imprint*.

Leininger, M. 1998. "Leininger's Theory of Nursing: Cultural Care Diversity and Universality," *Nursing and Health Care 1*: 152–160.

McIntosh, P. 1988. *White Privilege: Unpacking the Invisible Knapsack*. Wellesley College Center for Research on Women.

McIntosh P. 1998. "White Privilege, Color and Crime: A Personal Account," in C. R. Mann and M. S. Zatz, eds,

Images of Color, Images of Crime: Readings. Los Angeles: Roxbury Publishing Company.

Nguyen H.T. 2008. "Patient Centred Care—Cultural Safety in Indigenous Health," *Australian Family Physician* 37 (12): 990–994.

Ramsden, I. 2002. *Cultural Safety and Nursing Education in Aotearoa and Te Waipounamu.* Wellington: Victoria University, http://culturalsafety.massey.ac.nz/RAMSDEN%20THESIS.pdf.

St Denis, V. 2007. "Aboriginal Education and Anti-Racist Education: Building Alliance across Cultural and Racial Identity," *Canadian Journal of Education* 30 (4): 1068–1092.

St Denis, V., and C. Schick. 2005. "Troubling National Discourses in Anti-Racist Curricular Planning," *Canadian Journal of Education* 28 (3): 295–317.

Smye, V. and A.J. Brown. 2002. "Cultural Safety and the Analysis of Health Policy Affecting Aboriginal People," *Nurse Researcher* 9 (3): 42–56.

Stout, M. D., and B. Downey. 2006. "Nursing, Indigenous Peoples and Cultural Safety: So what? Now what?" *Contemporary Nursing*, International Council of Nurses, http://www.contemporarynurse.com/archives/vol/22/issue/2/article/749/nursing-indigenouspeoples-and-cultural-safety.

Toulouse, P.R. 2008. *Integrating Aboriginal Teaching and Values into the Classroom.* Government of Ontario, Literacy and Numeracy Secretariat, www.edu.gov.on.ca/eng/literacynumeracy/inspire/research/Toulouse.pdf.

World Health Organization. (2008). Final Report—Closing the Gap in a Generation: Health Equity through Action on the Social Determinants of Health. Commission on Social Determinants of Health.

CHAPTER 28

The Role of Racism in the Health and Well-being of Indigenous Peoples in Canada

Billie Allan and Janet Smylie

. . . Scope and Purpose of the Review

. . . This paper explores the role of racism in the health and well-being of Indigenous peoples in Canada. It provides an overview of the historical and contemporary contexts of racism which have and continue to negatively shape the life choices and chances of Indigenous peoples in this country, and then examines the ways in which racism fundamentally contributes to the alarming disparities in health between Indigenous and non-Indigenous peoples. Indigenous peoples experience the worst health outcomes of any population group in Canada (Royal College of Physicians and Surgeons of Canada, 2013), underscoring the urgency and importance of understanding and addressing racism as a determinant of Indigenous health. . . .

[T]his paper is composed of three key sections. First, we examine racism and colonization as root determinants of Indigenous/non-Indigenous health inequities. We draw on Indigenous approaches to the social determinants of health and focus on describing specific colonial policies and how these policies have historically shaped and continue to shape Indigenous health determinants, outcomes and access to care. Second, we review the literature documenting and describing Indigenous peoples' experiences of racism in Canada and the links to health, well-being, and access to health care. Third, we review responses and interventions aimed at addressing the impacts of racism at the individual, community, health services, and policy levels. We conclude with emerging ideas and recommendations for moving forward that we hope will contribute to broader discussions and collaborative action. . . .

Methods

Telling Our Own Stories

. . . The rippling effects of the trauma and rupture caused by colonial policies have served to reinforce or seemingly legitimize racist stereotypes about Indigenous peoples.

Stereotypes of the "drunken Indian" or the hyper-sexualized "squaw,"[1] the casting of Indigenous parents as perpetual "bad mothers" (Kline, 1993) or "deadbeat dads" (Ball, 2010; Bell and George, 2006), or media portrayals of Indigenous leadership as corrupt and/or inept, all serve to justify acts of belittlement, exclusion, maltreatment, or violence at the interpersonal, societal and systemic levels. . . . Stereotypes are examples of the ways in which the dominant stories in Canadian society of who we as Indigenous peoples are and how we are, are told about us and not by us.

. . . [I]n preparing this paper, we attempted as much as possible avoid the perpetuation of deficit-based stereotyping of Indigenous peoples. Rather, we set out to support the telling of our own stories as Indigenous people about our experiences of racism and the impact of racism on our health and well-being. To accomplish this we have used a mixed methods approach. First, we have included narratives shared by our Counsel of Indigenous Grandparents with the aim of grounding our paper in their knowledge and experience and to prevent our discussion of the reality of racism in the lives of Indigenous peoples from being reduced to an intellectual exercise. . . . Second, in contextualizing our discussion of the role of racism in Indigenous health in Canada, we utilize a critical Indigenous lens to examine colonial policies and practices and their impacts on Indigenous health and well-being (Smylie, Kaplan-Myrth, and McShane, 2009). . . .

Finally, keeping in mind that the indexed published literature systematically prioritizes non-Indigenous voices and perspectives (Smylie, 2014), we draw on the results of a systematic search of multiple databases of published literature using search terms designed to identify publications regarding Indigenous populations in Canada that addressed the interface of racism/discrimination and health/health care. . . .

Racism, Colonization, and The Roots of Indigenous Health Inequities

. . . Despite the fact that race is a socially constructed category with no biological basis, it has been used for hundreds of years to argue for and promote hierarchies of supposed superiority and civility among "races" of people (Reading, 2013). . . .

Telling Another Story: Indigenous Understandings of Social Determinants of Health

Social determinants of health approaches seek to understand not only the causes of health inequities, but the causes of the causes (Rose, as cited in Marmot, 2005), such as access to income security, employment, education, food, and shelter (Smylie, 2009). The social determinants of health mark an

---

1. The stereotype of the "squaw" portrays Indigenous women as dirty, uncivilized, savage, lazy, and hypersexual; this stereotype has been linked to efforts to undermine the roles and responsibilities of Indigenous women during the early stages of colonization and to justifying the historical and ongoing physical and sexual violence experienced by Indigenous women Anderson, 2004; Gilchrist, 2010; Larocque, 1994).

important departure from strictly biomedical and health behaviour paradigms (Raphael, 2009), which can further stereotype and pathologize marginalized people by inferring that the health inequities they face are a matter of personal choice or poor genetics. . . .

The authors identify a range of proximal determinants including physical environments (including housing and infrastructure), health behaviours, education, employment, income, and food security. . . .

The authors emphasize the importance of accounting for the historic and ongoing impacts of colonization in public health strategies and communications with Aboriginal peoples, as well as the need for more detailed explanations for why particular groups are identified as at-risk. Moreover, they recommend increased specificity in identifying priority groups by attributes that increase risk (e.g., lower socioeconomic status, overcrowded housing) as opposed to ethnicity to decrease experiences stigmatization and discrimination.

Indigenous approaches to the social determinants of health also offer a significant contribution to health knowledge in centering holistic perspectives of health which may include consideration of the four aspects of self (body, heart, mind, spirit); the lifecycle; the importance of understanding our past, in the present for our future (Greenwood and de Leeuw, 2012; Loppie, Reading, and Wien, 2009; Smylie, 2009); and the understanding of ourselves in relationship to the land and our natural environment (Blakney, 2009 [sic]). . . .

Canadian Policies and The Institutionalization of Racism Against Indigenous Peoples

. . . Racist beliefs about Indigenous peoples underlie the historical and ongoing overrepresentation of Indigenous children in the care of child welfare agencies. Indigenous children were historically removed from the care of their families and communities to residential schools, a system of institutionalized education and care that lasted well over 100 years[2] and aimed to assimilate Indigenous children into European and Christian cultural norms, beliefs and practices. . . .

As concerns about poor conditions and widespread abuses surfaced, support for residential schools began to wane in the late 1940s and into the 1950s. This gave way to a new wave of assimilationist practice taken up by child welfare agencies and the social workers they employed. Beginning in the 1950s and peaking in the 1960s, there was an enormous influx of Indigenous children taken into the care of child welfare agencies which is now known as the Sixties Scoop (Sinclair, 2004). . . . The removal of children from their homes and the impact of cross-cultural adoption not only had damaging effects on the identity and well-being of adoptees, but on the families from whom they were taken (Carriere, 2005; Sinclair, 2007; Alston-O'Connor, 2010).

Overrepresentation of Indigenous children in child welfare is not a vestige of the past, but in fact remains an urgent and ongoing challenge facing Indigenous communities across Canada. . . .

The Gendered Impact of Colonial Racism: Indigenous Women's Health and Well-Being

Indigenous women in Canada carry a disproportionate burden of ill-health and disease, including higher rates of hypertension, heart disease, diabetes, cervical and gallbladder cancer, HIV/AIDS, substance abuse, mental illness, and suicide (Bourassa, McKay-McNabb, and Hampton, 2005; Dion Stout et al., 2001; Gatali and Archibald, 2003; Ghosh and Gomes, 2012; Grace, 2003; Kirmayer et al., 2007). . . .

The epidemic of violence against Indigenous women profoundly threatens our health and

2. The last residential school in Canada closed in 1996 on Gordon's First Nation in Saskatchewan. It was also the longest running residential school in Canada operating for 107 years (George Gordon First Nation, 2014).

subsequently that of our families. Aboriginal women experience higher rates than non-Aboriginal women of both spousal and non-spousal violence, and report more severe forms of violence including being sexually assaulted, choked, beaten, or threatened with a knife or gun (Mathyssen, 2011; Statistics Canada, 2013)....

Indeed . . . the Society of Obstetricians and Gynaecologists of Canada recently released a newly revised set of clinical practice guidelines for health professionals working with First Nations, Inuit, and Métis highlights which notes [sic] in its clinical tips that some women may choose to terminate their pregnancy in fear that if carried to term their child would be apprehended by the child welfare system (ibid., S31; Wilson et al., 2013). Addressing the alarming health disparities and barriers to health care experienced by Indigenous women and supporting our right to reproductive justice foundationally requires understanding the historical and contemporary racist policies and practices that shape our lives, health care access, health, and well-being.

What We Know about the Magnitude of Racism Experienced by Indigenous Peoples in Canada and Its Impacts on Health, Well-Being and Access to Health Services

In Canada, there is a range of survey data documenting the experiences of racial discrimination of Indigenous people (e.g., Regional Health Survey (RHS), Aboriginal Peoples Survey (APS), Urban Aboriginal Peoples Study (UAPS), Toronto Aboriginal Research Project (TARP), and the Our Health Counts (OHC) study) and a small but growing body of research focused on delineating the relationship between racism and Indigenous health and health care access. In this section, we provide a brief overview of existing information documenting the burden of racism experienced by Indigenous peoples followed by a synopsis of what is known about the impacts of racism on Indigenous health and well-being....

A Snapshot of Available Information Regarding Indigenous Peoples' Experiences of Racism in Canada

The Urban Aboriginal Peoples Study (UAPS) drew on an income stratified convenience sample of Aboriginal people across 11 Canadian cities. Non-Aboriginal participants from these cities were also interviewed regarding their attitudes and knowledge about Indigenous people in Canada. Of the Aboriginal participants, 43 per cent reported poor treatment as a result of racism and discrimination, and 18 per cent reported negative experiences of racism and discrimination resulting in shame, lower self-esteem or self-confidence, or the hiding of one's Aboriginal identity (Environics, 2010)....

At the provincial level in Ontario, the Urban Aboriginal Task Force (UATF) used a mixed-methods approach involving a convenience sample survey, key informant interviews, life histories, focus groups, and plenary discussions to engage Aboriginal peoples across five Ontario cities. In this study 78 per cent of participants identified racism as a problem for urban Aboriginal peoples (McCaskill and FitzMaurice, 2007). The UATF Final Report describes the racism faced by Aboriginal peoples in urban areas as widespread and systemic, impacting access to housing and employment, interactions with police and school systems, and treatment in public spaces like restaurants, shopping malls and buses (McCaskill and FitzMaurice, 2007)....

The First Nations Regional Longitudinal Health Survey (RHS) is a national health survey developed by and for on-reserve First Nations and uses a population based sampling method. In the 2002–2003 RHS 39 per cent of participants reported experiencing racism, with experiences of racism more likely to be reported by those with a completed high school education, those employed for 15 hours or more a week, and those with a disability (First Nations Centre, 2005). Findings in the 2008–2009 study indicated a slight reduction in reported racism (33 per cent); reported racism data was not stratified by education, employment, or disability in the RHS 2008–2009 National Report (FNIGC, 2012)....

Racism has undeniably had a negative impact on Indigenous identity (McCaskill and FitzMaurice,

2007), with one of the most painful outcomes reflected in the racism experienced among Indigenous peoples which is sometimes referred to as intra-group racism, internal racism, or lateral violence.

Understanding the Impacts of Racism and Discrimination on Indigenous Health and Well-Being

At present, the data addressing racial discrimination against Indigenous peoples in Canada and its effects on health is limited and piecemeal, utilizing cross-sectional samples that cannot address issues such as exposure and lag time (e.g., examining exposure to discrimination and the development of chronic diseases that develop over time) (Williams and Mohammed, 2009). . . .

In addition to the cchs based on the 2006 census sample, there have been multiple studies examining the experiences of urban Indigenous people (Currie et al., 2012b; Environics, 2010; McCaskill and FitzMaurice, 2007; McCaskill, FitzMaurice, and Cidro, 2011; Smylie et al., 2011). . . .

Despite the limitations described above, the body of research knowledge addressing the relationship between racism and Indigenous health and health care access in Canada is slowly but steadily growing. . . .

The studies of Currie et al. (2012a, 2012b) and Bombay et al. (2010) highlight the need for research that addresses the complex relationship between racism, trauma, Indigenous identity, and Indigenous health. . . . Understanding the impact of historic, collective, and intergenerational trauma in the lives of Indigenous peoples is a necessary precondition to improving health care access and service delivery. Moreover, it is foundational to informing anti-racist efforts addressing the pathologizing and dehumanizing stereotypes that have fueled the marginalization and poor treatment of Indigenous peoples in Canadian society, and to advancing awareness of how these stereotypes are reinforced by the ongoing social exclusion and inequities faced by Indigenous communities subsequent to these traumas, including poverty, unemployment, homelessness, and poor health. . . .

Race-Based Policies, Racism, and Access to Health Care

In the preceding sections of the paper we have described the historical policy context and the current state of knowledge regarding the burden of racism in the lives of Indigenous peoples in Canada. In the following sections, we turn our attention to the ways in which racism appears in Indigenous-specific health policies and within the interactions between Indigenous peoples and the Canadian health care system.

State-Imposed Indigenous Identity and Access to Health Care

. . . In the context of contemporary Indigenous health, Canada's race-based legislation has normalized the uneven distribution of health funding, resources and services according to state-constructed Indigenous identities, such that only status First Nations and Inuit peoples are entitled to the nihb program and to the Indigenous health services and support provided through the federal government via the First Nations and Inuit Health Branch. Métis and non-status First Nations lack access to these services and resources while facing the same determinants of health that have created egregious disparities in health in comparison to non-Indigenous people, such as lack of access to secure, affordable, or adequate housing, increased rates of unemployment and underemployment, food insecurity, poverty, and disproportionate rates of incarceration and child welfare apprehension (Greenwood and de Leeuw, 2012; Loppie and Wien, 2009; Smylie, 2009; Smylie and Adomako, 2009; Statistics Canada, 2008).

The nihb program provides coverage for status Indians and Inuit people registered with a recognized Inuit Land Claim organization to access a range of medical goods and services. This includes dental and vision care, prescription medications, specified medical supplies, equipment and transportation, short-term crisis intervention, and mental health programming (Health Canada, n.d.). However, simply being eligible for nihb does not necessarily ensure access since some services

require on-reserve residency in order to receive
funding for or access the service or program, and
the roster of approved services and medications is
constantly changing (Haworth-Brockman et al.,
2009; Mother of Red Nations, 2006). Moreover, the
delivery of NIHB also poses challenges to equitable
access to health services in comparison to non-
Indigenous people, particularly in northern and
remote communities. . . .

Racism in the Health Care Experience

In addition to the uneven access to health services
and resources created through the NIHB and other
race-based policies, experiences, and anticipation
of racist treatment by health care providers also
acts as a barrier to accessing needed health services for Indigenous peoples (Kurtz et al., 2008;
Tang and Browne, 2008; Browne et al, 2011).
Qualitative studies documenting the health care
experiences of Aboriginal peoples highlight an-
ticipated and actual poor treatment. For example,
in examining the experiences of Aboriginal and
non-Aboriginal persons accessing an inner-city
emergency department, Browne et al. (2011) found
that Aboriginal participants described anticipating that being identified as Aboriginal and poor
might result in a lack of credibility and/or negatively influence their chances of receiving help.
This was such a common experience that participants actively strategized on how to manage
negative responses from health care providers
in advance of accessing care in the emergency
department. . . .

Fatal Racism: The Death of Brian Lloyd Sinclair

Grandmother Madeleine Keteskwew Dion Stout of
the Well Living House Grandparents Counsel asked
that our paper include the story Brian Sinclair's
tragic and unnecessary death at the Winnipeg
Health Sciences Centre. . . .

Brian Sinclair was a 45-year-old Indigenous
man who died after a 34 hour wait in the emergency room of the Winnipeg Health Sciences
Centre in 2008. He was referred to the ER by a
community physician for a bladder infection,

which the Chief Medical Examiner of Manitoba
has suggested would have required approximately
a half hour of care to clear his blocked catheter
and to prescribe antibiotic treatment (Puxley,
2014a). Instead, Mr Sinclair died slowly and un-
necessarily of bladder infection in the waiting
room of the ER without ever receiving treatment,
despite vomiting several times on himself, and despite pleas from other ER visitors for nurses and
security guards to attend to him (Puxley, 2013a,
2013b). Mr Sinclair's body was already cold and
stiff, demonstrating the onset of rigour mortis by
the time staff responded and attempted to resus-
citate him (Puxley, 2014 [sic]).

Mr Sinclair was a double amputee, having lost
his legs to frostbite after being found frozen to the
steps of a church in 2007. He suffered a cognitive
impairment from previous substance use and had
endured homelessness, although he had housing
at the time of his death. The Sinclair family, their
legal counsel, and local Indigenous leaders asked
the provincial inquest into the matter to strongly
consider the ways in which Mr Sinclair's race, disability, and class resulted in his lack of treatment
and subsequently his death (Puxley, 2014a). In
fact, several staff testified they had assumed Mr
Sinclair was in the ER simply to warm up, watch
TV, or sleep off intoxication, while others have reported that they never saw Mr Sinclair despite the
fact that his wheelchair partially blocked the same
part of an aisle of the ER for more than 24 hours
(Puxley, 2013a, 2014a, 2014b). During inquest testimony, hospital staff and the Chief Medical Officer
of Manitoba, Dr Thambirajah Balachandra, vehemently denied the role of racism in Mr Sinclair's
death, with Dr Balachandra blithely suggesting that
even Snow White would have received the same
treatment as Mr Sinclair under the circumstances
("Brian Sinclair dead for hours," 2013). Racism, the
refusal of care and poor treatment of Indigenous
peoples in the Canadian health care system are well
documented in health research. For Mr Sinclair, the
impact of racism proved fatal. On 18 February 2014,
the family of Mr Sinclair withdrew from the provincial inquest because its failure to examine and address the role of systemic racism in his death and in
the treatment of Indigenous peoples in health care
settings more broadly (Sinclair, 2014). . . .

Racism versus Culture: Implications for Access to Health Care

We argue here for consideration of how Indigenous peoples' experiences of racism in health care systems are mischaracterized as and/or reduced to matters of "cultural difference" that are best addressed through cultural sensitivity or cultural competence approaches as opposed to anti-racism. The critique of a reliance on culture as a way to diffuse or avoid addressing racism in Canada is not new (Browne and Varcoe, 2006; Fiske and Browne, 2006; Henry, Tator, Mattis and Rees, 2000 [sic]). However, it is central to advancing understanding of and responses to Indigenous peoples' experiences of racism since Indigenous peoples have become synonymous with "culture" in the Canadian consciousness (personal communication, Grandmother Madeleine Dion Stout, 2014).

Browne and Varcoe (2006) assert that culture-focused approaches to working with Indigenous peoples (i.e., cultural sensitivity, cultural competence) require a critical analysis of how we understand culture in the first place, in order to account for the impact and influence of racism, colonialism, and our historical and contemporary contexts. This is necessary to understand and respond to the ways in which Indigenous peoples endure a disproportionate burden of ill-health and experience poorer access to social and economic determinants of health and health care that have been structurally created and maintained through historical and ongoing racism (Browne and Varcoe, 2006). Moreover, it is important to draw attention to how models such as cultural sensitivity or cultural competence maintain a focus on interactions between service users and health care providers, downloading matters of racism (under the guise of "cultural difference") to the individual and interpersonal levels and failing to address the role of systemic, institutional, and organizational racism in shaping the encounters between service users and health care providers. Cultural safety, a more recent and Indigenous model of health care, directly addresses the role and impact of racism in Indigenous inequities in health care access and health outcomes and attends to power dynamics in the interactions between health care provider and service user. . . .

Racism, Health and Health Care: Responses and Interventions

The published Indigenous-specific literature on interventions aimed at addressing racism within the context of Indigenous health and health care is very scant. . . .

Our systematic literature search for articles, which focused on racism and discrimination against Indigenous people and health or health care in Canada (but did not include "disparities" more generally) identified only descriptive literature, with not a single indexed article describing or evaluating an intervention specifically focused on addressing racism within the context of Indigenous health or health care. We did, however, locate published literature describing initiatives designed to train health care professionals to improve their "cultural competence" or their ability to provide "culturally secure" care (Saylor, 2012). . . .

What Do We Know about the Impacts of Racism on Health Services and Interventions to Address These Impacts with Respect to Indigenous Peoples in Canada?

In this section, we provide an overview of multiple examples of responses and interventions (including policy recommendations) aimed at addressing racism (including colonial policy and practice) and the impacts of racism on the health and health care of Aboriginal peoples in Canada. . . . We first acknowledge the strong individual, family and community strategies and resiliencies that are employed by Indigenous people. We then examine health care service and deliver responses; health professional and training responses (including cultural safety training); national, provincial/territorial level interventions both specific to Aboriginal health and/or health care and impacting Aboriginal health. . . .

Health Care Service and Delivery Responses

Community-Directed Indigenous Services and Programs Specific to Health

At the level of health care service and delivery, there has been a variety of developments aimed at increasing access to health care for Indigenous peoples and mitigating the impact of racism they experience in attempting to manage their health and well-being in the Canadian health care system. The emergence in recent decades of health services and programs directed by the Indigenous communities that they are designed to serve is of fundamental importance to improving the health inequities faced by Indigenous peoples in Canada.... For example, the Community Health Representatives (known as CHRs) and the National Native Alcohol and Drugs Addictions Program (NNADAP) have been managed by First Nations since inception (ibid.), and presently, a large majority of First Nations communities are administering and managing their own health services according to one of several federal contribution agreement funding models (Health Canada, 2012a).... Transfer of program and service plans that adequately ensure for escalating future costs have been notoriously difficult for First Nations to negotiate with the federal government. Below, we describe four key examples of community-directed health systems, organizations and services.

First Nations Health Authority (FNHA)

The establishment and implementation of the First Nations Health Authority (FNHA) in British Columbia has broken new ground in the efforts of First Nations communities to control their health services.... Guided by principles of respect, discipline, transparency, and culture, the overarching goal of the FNHA is to achieve better health outcomes for all First Nations in BC....

Indigenous Midwifery: Inuulitsivik Health Centre

The initiation of the maternity program at the Inuulitsivik Health Centre in Puvirnituq, Quebec also represents an important landmark example of Indigenous community controlled health services....

Urban Indigenous Health Centres: Anishnawbe Health Toronto

In the urban context, the establishment of multiple urban Indigenous health centres represents Indigenous community-controlled health services, the large majority of which are run by Indigenous boards of directors and offer both traditional healing and medical services (Association of Ontario Health Centres, n.d.)....

Indigenous Youth Leadership in Health and Well-being: Native Youth Sexual Health Network

The Native Youth Sexual Health Network (NYSHN) is an Indigenous for youth, by youth organization serving Indigenous youth across Canada and the US, emphasizing empowerment, cultural safety, reproductive justice, sex positivity, and healthy sexuality (NYSHN, n.d.)....

Community-directed Indigenous Services and Programs that Generally Impact Health

There are thousands of community-directed Indigenous services and programs across the domains of housing, education, employment, language, and culture that impact health more generally....

In Vancouver, British Columbia, the Aboriginal Mother Centre Society (AMCS) provides a transformational housing program for Aboriginal women and their children who are at risk of homelessness or child welfare intervention (AMCS, 2012).... Given the devastating impact of invasive child welfare intervention in Indigenous communities described in this paper, the AMCS represents an innovative model of service aimed at preventing or mitigating the involvement of child welfare authorities in the lives of Aboriginal women and their families and supporting their overall well-being and success....

Community Level Health and Health Impacting Services and Programs (Not Indigenous-Specific or Indigenous-Directed)

There are many important non-Indigenous specific community level health and health impacting services and programs that are making important inroads with respect to Indigenous access to health care.... Some of these mainstream centres, such as the Queen West Community Health Centre[3] in Toronto, also offer Indigenous-specific programming to meet the needs of Indigenous community members living in their catchment. . . .

Mainstream Health Institution Level Efforts to Improve Access to Health Care

Within some mainstream institutions, efforts to improve access and service for Indigenous clients has included the development of Indigenous-specific programs or services (e.g., the Aboriginal Services of Centre for Addictions and Mental Health (CAMH) based in Toronto, Ontario; the First Nations Health Programs based in the Whitehorse Hospital), or the employment of Indigenous staff in specialized roles such as Aboriginal patient navigator (APN) or Aboriginal patient liaison (APL) intended to improve access to and outcomes of health care by serving as a bridge between Indigenous patients and the health care system. . . .

Health Professional Education and Training Responses

Since 2000, there has been a steady emergence of policy statements and guidelines for medical professional and medical training organizations in Canada towards identifying and developing the competencies needed by health professionals in order to optimize the care that they provide to Indigenous individuals and communities, followed by the development of educational guidelines, curricula and training programs for medical and nursing professionals and trainees. . . .

National, Provincial, or Territorial Level Policy Responses Specific to Health and Impacting Health

In addition to federal policies regarding transferring the control of First Nations health services to

First Nations communities and the First Nations Health Authority, there are several other sets of policies and policy recommendations aimed at increasing Indigenous governance and management of Indigenous health services. . . . At the national level both the Royal Commission on Aboriginal Peoples (1996) and the Kelowna Accord (2005 [sic]) deliberations advocated for fundamental shifts in the governance and management of Indigenous health services from the federal government to Indigenous communities (First Ministers and National Aboriginal Leaders, 2005; RCAP, 1996). . . . There has been some tracking of impacts of the implementation of policy recommendations although in most cases, the track record is not encouraging. For example, in 2006 the Assembly of First Nations published a ten-year report card examining the implementation of the recommendations of the 1996 Royal Commission on Aboriginal Peoples, giving the federal government a failing grade on 37 of the 62 recommendations included in their report card. . . .

What Do We Know about the Impacts of Racism on Health Services and Interventions to Address These Impacts More Generally?

. . . Implicit bias refers to attitudes and stereotypes that occur unconsciously and inform our thinking, beliefs and behaviours (Staats, 2014 [sic]). . . .

There is an emerging body of research examining the role of health care provider implicit bias in racialized health disparities; this literature is overwhelmingly based in the US context and most heavily focused on contrasting service providers' perceptions and treatment of Black vs. white patients as Black people experience some of the most egregious and persistent health disparities among all marginalized people in the US. . . .

---

3. Queen West Community Health Centre, part of the Central Toronto Community Health Centres, offers an Aboriginal diabetes program.

Looking and Moving Forward

Count Us In: Transforming the Conversation about Racism and Health in Canada

. . . Given that much of the existing research on racism and health has been led by scholars in countries with colonial histories similar to Canada (i.e., the US, Australia and New Zealand) in which Indigenous health disparities are strikingly similar to those of Indigenous peoples in Canada, there is much that can be learned in drawing from this work to adapt existing or establish new research instruments, approaches to policymaking, programming, service provision, and anti-racism interventions. . . .

Moving the conversation of race and health forward in Canada requires engaging in a decolonizing approach to anti-racism that centres colonization in discussions and knowledge production about race and racism, fundamentally acknowledging the historic and ongoing colonization of Indigenous peoples (Lawrence and Dua, 2005). This is necessary to ensure that Indigenous peoples are no longer left out of or sidestepped in conversations of racism and health. . . .

Count Us In: Improving Indigenous Health Data Collection in Order to Address Racism as a Driver of Indigenous Health Disparities

. . . The need for meaningful data is critical to understanding and addressing the role of racism in creating and sustaining the health disparities experienced by Indigenous people in Canada. This echoes the work of scholars from Australia and New Zealand who are at the forefront of advancing knowledge addressing the impact of racism on Indigenous health (Paradies et al., 2008) and their call for research in four key areas: 1) the prevalence and experience of racism experienced by Indigenous peoples across the life course; 2) the impact of racism on Indigenous health across the life course; 3) the development of measures to assess systemic racism against Indigenous peoples; and 4) identifying best practices in addressing systemic racism against Indigenous peoples (ibid., 16). We especially argue for concerted effort to develop or adapt effective interventions addressing attitudinal/interpersonal and systemic racism towards Indigenous peoples, and to undertake bold and brave evaluation of existing anti-racism strategies and interventions.

Telling Another Story

We end where we began: we as Indigenous peoples must be the authors of our own stories. It is necessary to interrupting the racism that reduces our humanity, erases our histories, discounts our health knowledge and practices, and attributes our health disparities and social ills to individual and collective deficits instead of hundreds of years of violence, marginalization, and exclusion. The stories shared here describe the ways in which racism has shaped the lives of generations of Indigenous peoples and contributed towards our contemporary health disparities. It is time for stories of change: change in how we imagine, develop, implement, and evaluate health policies, services and education, change in how we talk about racism and history in this country. This is fundamental to shifting what is imagined and understood about our histories, our ways of knowing and being, our present and our future, and to ensuring the health and well-being of our peoples for this generation and generations to come. . . .

References

Aboriginal Mother Centre Society (AMCS). 2012. *About the Aboriginal Mother Centre Society*, http://www.aboriginalmothercentre.ca.

Alston-O'Connor, E. 2010. "The sixties scoop: Implications for social workers and social work education," *Critical Social Work* 11 (1): 53–61.

Association of Ontario Health Centres. n.d. *Aboriginal health access centres*, http://aohc.org/aboriginal-health-access-centres.

Ball, J. 2010. "Indigenous fathers' involvement in reconstituting 'circles of care'," *American Journal of Community Psychology* 45 (1–2): 124–138.

Bell, J., and R. George. 2006. "Policies and practices affecting Aboriginal fathers' involvement with their children," pp. 123–144 in J. White, S. Wingert, D. Beavon, and P. Maxim, eds, *Aboriginal Policy Research: Moving Forward, Making a Difference*, Vol. 111. Toronto, ON: Thompson Educational Publishing, Inc.

Blakney, S.L. 2010. Connections to the Land: The Politics of Health and Well-being in Arviat Nunavut. (Doctoral dissertation). University of Manitoba, Winnipeg, Manitoba.

Bourassa, C., K. McKay-McNabb, and M. Hampton. 2005. "Racism, sexism and colonialism: The impact on the health of Aboriginal women in Canada," *Canadian Woman Studies* 24 (1): 55–58.

Browne, A.J., and C. Varcoe. 2006. "Critical cultural perspectives and health care involving Aboriginal peoples," *Contemporary Nurse* 22 (2): 155–167.

Browne, A., V. Smye, P. Rodney, S. Tang, B. Mussell, and J. O'Neil. 2011. "Access to primary care from the perspective of Aboriginal patients at an urban emergency department," *Qualitative Health Research* 21 (3): 333–348.

Carriere, J. 2005. "Connectedness and health for First Nation adoptees," *Paediatrics and Child Health* 10 (9): 545–548.

Currie, C.L., T.C. Wild, D.P. Schopflocher, L. Laing, and P. Veugelers. 2012a. "Racial discrimination experienced by Aboriginal university students in Canada," *Canadian Journal of Psychiatry* 57 (10): 617–625.

Currie, C.L., T.C. Wild, D.P. Schopflocher, L. Laing, P. Veugelers, and B. Parlee. 2012b. "Racial discrimination, post-traumatic stress, and gambling problems among urban Aboriginal adults in Canada," *Journal of Gambling Studies* 29: 393–415.

Dion Stout, M., G.D. Kipling, and R. Stout. 2001. *Aboriginal women's health research synthesis project: Final report.* Ottawa, ON: Canadian Women's Health Network.

Environics Institute. 2010. *Urban Aboriginal Peoples Study: Main Report.* Toronto, ON: Author.

First Ministers and National Aboriginal Leaders. 2005. *First ministers and national Aboriginal leaders strengthening relationships and closing the gap.* [Press release]. http://www.health.gov.sk.ca/aboriginal-first-ministers-meeting.

First Nations Centre. 2005. *First Nations Regional Longitudinal Health Survey (RHS) 2002/03: Results for adults, youth and children living in First Nations Communities.* Ottawa, ON: Author.

First Nations Information Governance Centre (FNIGC). 2012. *First Nations Regional Health Survey (RHS) 2008/10: National report on adults, youth and children living in First Nations communities.* Ottawa, ON: FNIGC.

Fiske, J., and A.J. Browne. 2006. "Aboriginal citizen, discredited medical subject: Paradoxical constructions of Aboriginal women's subjectivity in Canadian health care policies," *Policy Sciences* 39 (1): 91–111.

Gatali, M., and C. Archibald. 2003. "Women and HIV," in M. DesMeules and D. Stewart, eds, *Women's Health Surveillance Report: A Multidimensional Look at the Health of Canadian Women.* Ottawa: Canadian Institute for Health Information. http://secure.cihi.ca/cihiweb/products/WHSR_Chap_26_e.pdf.

George Gordon First Nation. 2014. *History of George Gordon.* Retrieved from: http://www.georgegordonfirstnation.com/history.html

Ghosh, H., and J. Gomes. 2012. "Type 2 Diabetes among Aboriginal Peoples in Canada: A focus on direct and associated risk factors," *Pimatisiwin* 9 (2): 245–275.

Gilchrist, K. 2010. "'Newsworthy' victims?: Exploring differences in Canadian local press coverage of missing/murdered Aboriginal and white women," *Feminist Media Studies* 10 (4): 373–390.

Grace, S.L. 2003. "A review of Aboriginal women's physical and mental health status in Ontario (Commentary)," *Canadian Journal of Public Health* 94 (3): 173–175.

Greenwood, M., and S. de Leeuw. 2012. "Social determinants of health and the future well-being of Aboriginal children in Canada," *Paediatrics and Child Health* 17 (7): 381–384.

Haworth-Brockman, M., K. Bent, and J. Havelock. 2009. "Health research, entitlements and health services for First Nations and Métis women in Manitoba and Saskatchewan," *Journal of Aboriginal Health* 4 (2): 17–23.

Health Canada. 2012a. *First Nations & Inuit Health: Contribution Agreements.* http://www.hc-sc.gc.ca/fniah-spnia/finance/agree-accord/index-eng.php.

Health Canada. n.d. *First Nations Inuit and Aboriginal Health: Non-Insured Health Benefits for First Nations and Inuit.* http://www.hc-sc.gc.ca/fniah-spnia/nihb-ssna/index-eng.php.

Kirmayer, L.J., G.M. Brass, T. Holton, K. Paul, C. Simpson, and C. Tait. 2007. *Suicide among Aboriginal people in Canada.* Ottawa, ON: Aboriginal Healing Foundation.

Kline, M. 1993. "Complicating the ideology of motherhood: Child welfare law and First Nations women," *Queen's Law Journal* 18 (2): 306–342.

Kurtz, D.L.M., J.C. Nyberg, S. Van Den Tillaart, B. Mills, and Okanagan Urban Aboriginal Health Research Collective (OUAHRC). 2008. "Silencing of voice: An act of structural violence: Urban Aboriginal women speak out about their experiences with health care," *Journal of Aboriginal Health* 4 (1): 53–63.

LaRocque, E. 1994. Violence in Aboriginal communities. Ottawa, ON: Health Canada. Retrieved from: http://dsp-psd.pwgsc.gc.ca/Collection/H72-21-100-1994E.pdf

Lawrence, B., and E. Dua. 2005. "Decolonizing anti-racism," *Social Justice: A Journal of Crime, Conflict and World Order* 32 (4): 120–143.

Loppie Reading, C., and F. Wien. 2009. *Health inequalities and social determinants of Aboriginal peoples' health.*

Prince George, BC: National Collaborating Centre for Aboriginal Health.

Marmot, M. 2005. "Social determinants of health inequities," *The Lancet* 365: 1099–1104.

Mathyssen, I. 2011. *Ending violence against Aboriginal women and girls: Empowerment—A new beginning: Report of the Standing Committee on the Status of Women.* Ottawa: Standing Committee on the Status of Women.

McCaskill, D., K. Fitzmaurice. 2007. *Urban Aboriginal Task Force, Final Report.* Commissioned by the Ontario Federation of Indian Friendship Centres, Ontario Metis and Aboriginal Association and Ontario Native Women's Association. http://ofifc.agiledudes.com/sites/default/files/docs/UATFOntarioFinalReport.pdf.

McCaskill, D., K. Fitzmaurice, and J. Cidro. 2011. *Toronto Aboriginal Research Project, Final Report.* Toronto, ON: Toronto Aboriginal Support Services Council.

Mother of Red Nations: Women's Council of Manitoba. 2006. *Twenty years and ticking: Aboriginal women, human rights and Bill C-31.* Winnipeg, MB: Author. http://morn.cimnet.ca/cim/dbf/morn_billc31_complete.pdf?im_id=5088&si_id=92.

Native Youth Sexual Health Network. n.d. Areas of work. Retrieved from: http://www.nativeyouthsexualhealth.com/areasofwork.html.

Paradies, Y., R. Harris, and I. Anderson. 2008. *The impact of racism on Indigenous health in Australia and Aotearoa: Towards a research agenda (Discussion Paper No. 4).* Darwin, Australia: Cooperative Research Centre for Aboriginal Health.

Puxley, C. 2013a. "Woman tells inquest she tried to get nurses to check on man in Winnipeg ER," *Maclean's*, 24 October. http://www.macleans.ca/general/woman-tells-inquest-she-tried-to-get-nurses-to-check-on-man-in-winnipeg-er/.

Puxley, C. 2013b. "Woman in ER where man died after lengthy wait says it was obvious he needed help," *Maclean's*, 30 October. http://www.macleans.ca/general/woman-in-er-where-man-died-after-lengthy-wait-says-it-was-obvious-he-needed-help/.

Puxley, C. 2014a. "Brian Sinclair inquest to look at hospital backlogs; man died after 34-hour ER wait," CTV *News*, 5 January. http://www.ctvnews.ca/canada/brian-sinclair-inquest-to-look-at-hospital-backlogs-man-died-after-34-hour-er-wait-1.1618464

Puxley, C. 2014b. "Nurse tells inquest it didn't seem urgent to check on man in Winnipeg ER," *Maclean's*, 6 January. http://www.macleans.ca/general/nurse-tells-inquiry-it-didnt-seem-urgent-to-check-on-man-in-winnipeg-er/.

Raphael, D. 2009. "Social determinants of health: An overview of key issues and themes," pp. 2–19, in D. Raphael, ed., *Social determinants of health: Canadian perspectives*, 2nd edn. Toronto, ON: Canadian Scholars' Press Inc.

Reading, C. 2013. *Understanding Racism.* Prince George, BC: National Collaborating Centre for Aboriginal Health.

Reading, J., and E. Nowgesic. 2002. "Improving the health of future generations: The Canadian institutes of health research institute of Aboriginal peoples' health," *American Journal of Public Health* 92 (9): 1396–1400.

Royal College of Physicians and Surgeons of Canada. 2013. *Indigenous health values and principles statement.* http://www.royalcollege.ca/portal/page/portal/rc/common/documents/policy/indigenous_health_values_principles_report_e.pdf.

Royal Commission on Aboriginal Peoples (RCAP). 1996. *Report of the Royal Commission on Aboriginal Peoples. Ottawa, ON: Indian and Northern Affairs Canada.* http://www.collectionscanada.gc.ca/webarchives/20071124130216/http://www.ainc-inac.gc.ca/ch/rcap/sg/sgm10_e.html.

Saylor, K. 2012. "Development of a curriculum on the health of Aboriginal children in Canada," *Paediatric Child Health* 17 (7): 365–367.

Sinclair, R. 2004. "Aboriginal social work education in Canada: Decolonizing pedagogy for the seventh generation," *First Peoples Child & Family Review* 1 (1): 49–61.

Sinclair, R. 2007. "Identity lost and found: Lessons from the sixties scoop," *First Peoples Child and Family Review* 3 (1): 65–82.

Sinclair, Robert. 18 February 2014. *Statement of Robert Sinclair re: withdrawal of Sinclair Family from Phase 2 of the Brian Sinclair inquest.* https://dl.dropboxusercontent.com/u/8827767/Withdrawal/2014–02-18%20Statement% 20of%20 Robert%20Sinclair%20FINAL.pdf.

Smylie J., M. Firestone, L. Cochran, C. Prince, S. Maracle, M. Morley, S. Mayo, T. Spiller, and B. McPherson. 2011. *Our Health Counts Urban Aboriginal Health Database Research Project—Community Report First Nations Adults and Children, City of Hamilton.* Hamilton, ON: De Dwa Da Dehs Nye's Aboriginal Health Centre.

Smylie, J. 2009. "Chapter 19: The health of Aboriginal peoples," pp. 280–304 in D. Raphael, ed., *Social determinants of health: Canadian perspectives*, 2nd edn. Toronto, ON: Canadian Scholars' Press Inc.

Smylie, J. 2014. "Indigenous Child Well-being in Canada," pp. i–j in A. C. Michalos, ed., *Encyclopedia of Quality of Life and Well-being Research*. Dordrecht, Netherlands: Springer.

Smylie, J., N. Kaplan-Myrth, and K. McShane. 2009. "Indigenous knowledge translation: Baseline findings in a qualitative study of the pathways of health knowledge in three indigenous communities in Canada," *Health Promotion Practice* 10 (3): 436–446.

Smylie, J., and P. Adomako. 2009. *Indigenous Children's Health Report: Health Assessment in Action.* Toronto: St. Michael's Hospital.

Smylie, J., M. Firestone, L. Cochran, C. Prince, S. Maracle, M. Morley, S. Mayo, T. Spiller, and B. McPherson. 2011. *Our Health Counts Urban Aboriginal Health Database*

Research Project—Community Report First Nations Adults and Children, City of Hamilton. Hamilton: De Dwa Da Dehs Ney's Aboriginal Health Centre.

Staats, C. 2013. State of the Science: Implicit Bias Review 2014. Columbus, OH: The Kirwan Institute for the Study of Race and Ethnicity. http://kirwaninstitute.osu.edu/docs/SOTS-Implicit_Bias.pdf.

Statistics Canada. 2008. Aboriginal Peoples in Canada in 2006: Inuit, Métis, and First Nations, 2006 Census. Ottawa: Ministry of Industry, Catalogue number 7-558-XIE. http://www12.statcan.ca/census-recensement/2006/as-sa/97-559/p.../97-559-XIE2006001.pdf.

Statistics Canada. 2013. Measuring violence against women. Ottawa, ON: Author. http://www.statcan.gc.ca/pub/85-002-x/2013001/article/11766-eng.pdf.

Tang, S., and A.J. Browne. 2008. "'Race' matter: Racialization and egalitarian discourses involving Aboriginal people in the Canadian health care context," Ethnicity & Health 13 (2): 109–127.

Wilson, D., S. de la Ronde, S. Brascoupé, A.N. Apale, L. Barney, B. Guthrie, O. Horn, R. Johnson, D. Rattray, and N. Robinson. 2013. "Health Professionals Working With First Nations, Inuit, and Métis Consensus Guideline," Journal of Obstetrics & Gynaecology Canada 35 (6) Suppl 2: S1–S52.

PART 14

Additional Readings

British Columbia, Ministry of Health. Rural, Remote, First Nations, and Indigenous Covid-19 Responses Framework. Vancouver: British Columbia Ministry of Health, 2020.

Greenwood, Margo, Sarah de Leeuw and Nicole Marie Lindsay, eds. Determinants of Indigenous Peoples' Health in Canada: Beyond the Social, 2nd edition. Toronto: Canadian Scholars' Press Inc., 2018.

Jeffery, Donna, and Jennifer J. Nelson. "The More Things Change . . . : The Endurance of 'Culturalism' in Social Work and Healthcare," pp. 91–110 in Carol Schick and James McNinch, eds, "I Thought Pocahontas Was a Movie": Perspectives on Race/Culture Binaries in Education and Service Professions. Regina: Canadian Plains Research Center Press, 2009.

Kelm, Mary-Ellen. Colonizing Bodies: Aboriginal Health and Healing in British Columbia, 1900–50. Vancouver: University of British Columbia Press, 1998.

Logan McCallum, Mary Jane, and Adele Perry. Structures of Indifference: An Indigenous Life and Death in a Canadian City. Winnipeg: University of Manitoba Press, 2018.

Razack, Sherene H. Dying From Improvement: Inquests and Inquiries into Indigenous Deaths in Custody. Toronto: University of Toronto Press, 2015.

Styvendale, Nancy, J.D. McDougall, Robert Henry, and Alexander Innes, eds. The Arts of Indigenous Health and Well-Being. Winnipeg: University of Manitoba Press, 2021.

Talaga, Tanya. All Our Relations: Finding the Path Forward. Nanaimo: Strong Nations Publishing, 2018.

Relevant Websites

Aboriginal Healing Foundation
http://www.ahf.ca
An archived website providing information about funded research related to residential schools, AHF publications, press releases, and speeches about Indigenous peoples' health, healing, and wellness.

National Aboriginal Health Organization
http://www.naho.ca
This website contains a vast and comprehensive number of resources, spanning from fact sheets to multimedia items to career-based resources and numerous health related publications, including a link to the Journal of Aboriginal Health.

National Collaborating Centre for Aboriginal Health
http://www.nccah-ccnsa.ca/en/
This website was established in 2005 to support health equity through knowledge translation and exchange, and contains a newsletter, events calendar, video resources, and publications related to social determinants literature and child and family health.

Native Youth Sexual Health Network
http://www.nativeyouthsexualhealth.com
This website provides information about safer sex, sexuality, harm reduction, and reproductive health, and contains numerous outreach resources, press releases, memes, and publications including a Two-Spirit Resource Directory.

Films

A Healing Journey: Aboriginal Children's Environmental Health. NAHO, 2003.
Jidwá:doh, Let's Become Again. Dir. Dawn Martin-Hill, 2005.
My Legacy. Dir. Helen Haig Brown. Vtape, 2014.
Young Lakota. Dir. Marion Lipschutz and Rose Rosenblatt. Incite Pictures/Cine Qua Non, 2013.
The Unforgotten. Dir. Ewan Affleck et al. Build Film + Network Health. 2021

Key Terms

- Cultural competence
- Cultural sensitivity
- Culturalism
- Cultural safety
- Healing and wellness
- Historical trauma
- Multiculturalism
- Social determinants of health

Discussion Questions

1. What is meant by the terms "cultural safety" and "culturalism"? What similarities exist between them, and how are they different? What exists as an alternative to these approaches? How are the alternatives generative of (and informed by) anticolonial thinking? How would you define an anticolonial approach to health care services delivery?

2. What has it meant to belong in Canada? Who is in charge of defining how we belong in Canada, and what sorts of alternatives exist? What would it mean to position oneself differently in relation to belonging, the land, and Indigenous sovereignty? How might the alternatives ensure a restorative approach to health care and well-being in Canadian society?

3. How is it possible to die in health care contexts or custody if you are suspected of drug or alcohol use? What would it mean to challenge one's own, and others' complicity in the structural relations of colonial power and racism that are fuelled by stereotypical depictions of diseased, damaged or "drunken Indians"? How does one interrupt a structural relation of power that effects Indigenous dispossession and that is constitutive of white Settler identity and belonging?

4. What is meant by the term "health"? How does the term differ from "well-being"? What would it mean to re-define health care from a perspective that ensures the inter-relational and sovereign well-being of Indigenous peoples and Settler populations? How might this re-articulation look toward original principles involving treaty and nation-to-nation agreements and understandings?

Activities

Your class has been asked to prepare a list of recommendations related to non-Indigenous peoples who work in health care services delivery with Indigenous populations. What do you recommend and why? What is unique about your approach? How is it critical of other approaches to health care services delivery?

Helen Haig Brown depicts a portrayal of love, renewal, and intergenerational healing in her film *My Legacy*. Why is her message important, and what series of questions involving resiliency, health, and well-being are being raised?

PART 15

Resistance

Editor Introduction

Our third edition of *Racism, Colonialism, and Indigeneity in Canada* is marked by ongoing Indigenous resistance to racism and colonial dominance. From the time of the second edition's publication in 2018, we have witnessed many examples of resistance, including the resurgent and historic Land Back initiative aimed at maintaining Indigenous sovereignty and economic control across Turtle Island (landback.org); the Wet'suwet'en defending their land from the Coastal GasLink pipeline project (unistoten.camp); the insistence by Mi'kmaq lobster fishers of their sovereign right to fish without interferences by non-Indigenous peoples and Fisheries and Oceans Canada (CBC News, 12 July 2022a); Red Dress Day (lilreddressproject.ca), and the Every Child Matters movements marked by the now yearly *Orange Shirt Day* and other initiatives aimed at creating and rejuvenating "meaningful reconciliation in Canada" (National Centre for Truth and Reconciliation). Indigenous resistance, and more accurately, refusal of Settler colonial injustice (Simpson, 2014), has been steadfast from 2018. The resistances we note above are concerned with asserting Indigenous sovereignty, and they follow on the heels of Idle No More (INM) discussed in Part Thirteen of this textbook.

The Idle No More initiative grew out of flash mob dances, rallies, blockades, teach-ins, and interviews of Indigenous people all over Turtle Island in late fall of 2012 and winter 2013 (The Kino-nda-niimi Collective, 2014). It was galvanized by the efforts of Theresa Spence, the chief of Attawapiskat, who in 2012 began a fast to bring attention to the conditions of her community and demanded that then Prime Minister Stephen Harper and the Governor General (as the representative of the Crown) meet with her and other Chiefs to discuss the many issues faced by Indigenous communities, such as poverty, gendered violence, cultural loss, and environmental degradation. INM was initiated by four women (three Indigenous and one non-Indigenous) who were concerned about the impacts of the proposed federal government's Bill C-45 on the environment and on Indigenous communities. Through the use of Facebook and other social media these women initiated a dialogue about the threats to the environments, and the lack of meaningful consultation with Indigenous communities whose rights were to be mostly affected by the changes proposed in the Bill. These brave women inspired people all over the country and worldwide to "not be idle" about such political events. They encouraged all to become more informed about the historical relationship between Indigenous peoples and mainstream society, and about how the newly proposed laws would threaten our environment.

The INM was a significant moment in our Canadian history; however, we must remember that Indigenous peoples—just as the recent examples provided above suggest—have never been idle

05 b

against the ongoing colonialism and have always resisted the dispossession, discrimination, and threat to our inherent Indigenous self-determination. Hence, INM should

> be remembered—alongside the maelstrom of treaty-making, political waves like the Red Power Movement and the 1969–1970 mobilization against the White Paper, and resistance movements at Oka, Gustefson's Lake, Ipperwash, Burnt Church, Goose Bay, Kanostaton, and so on . . . most Indigenous peoples have never been idle in their efforts to protect what is meaningful to our communities—nor will we ever be." (The Kino-nda-niimi Collective, 2014: 21)

This long history of resistance represents a true commitment to the principles embedded in the original treaty/nation-to-nation relationship that our ancestors entered with the first Settlers and later the State, such as the Two-Row Wampum that has been discussed throughout this book. Indigenous nations have been faithful to this sacred relationship, and when the other party has strayed from its original intent, our people have acted to protect and nurture it, reminding others that we are meant to share the resources of this land and to act in a just and equitable way with each other. Hence, when such a relationship has been disrespected, Indigenous people have been ready to even risk their own lives in order to reawaken the true intent of the wampums. Indigenous peoples have always been vocal about following the just principles of a nation-to-nation relationship and have asked that every human being act responsibly and follow those principles in their daily lives.

INM has to be seen as a continuation of that commitment to a nation-to-nation relationship and a call to act responsibly towards *all our relations*, including our lands, waters, and all animals. The movement differed a bit from other acts of resistance: it was a bottom-up informal one, initiated and led by women, and it used social media, arts, round dances, and other culturally specific means to address important issues. It also was effective in drawing support from many non-Indigenous peoples, including environmentalists, youth, labour activists, and some politicians. It spread all over the globe, reaching Indigenous communities as far as New Zealand and Australia, who in having their own history of decolonizing movements prior to INM could identify similar experiences of historical grievances against Settler States as their Canadian counterparts. INM awakened all, Indigenous and non-Indigenous, to act responsibly and remember that treaties and original wampums are living documents from which our daily actions must flourish. The solidarity shown by many individuals gave us some hope for the future: that a just equitable relationship wherein Indigenous inherent self-determination is respected might be possible.

We do not suggest the focus of Indigenous resistance shift focus to Settler populations. Instead, we believe it is important to pay attention to the nuances and particularities of solidarity activism expressed by Black, racialized, and other non-Indigenous peoples, as well as migrant Indigenous in shouldering equally, if not principally, the responsibility of decolonization (Cannon, 2018: 167). These forms of allyship reveal the ways in which non-Indigenous people also have to play a role in challenging the structural foundations of Settler colonialism (ibid.). Likewise, it is important to pay attention to cracks in the foundations of Settler colonialism. These ruptures take place when Indigenous peoples and Settler activists call for Canada Day to be cancelled (CBC News, 2 July 2022b; idlenomore.ca); when a Prime Minister (albeit without the presence of the Governor General) must recognize the issues facing the chief of Attawapiskat and other First Nations; when a court rules favourably and affirms "existing Aboriginal and Treaty Rights" and must deal (or not) with the the Doctrine of Discovery (Financial Post, 2 January 2020); when non-Indigenous peoples join in marking Orange Shirt Day and know the importance of why, and when the Senate presents a more favourable plan for peaceful fisheries in Canada and Nova Scotia (CBC News, 12 July 2022a). These developments reveal how the ultimate goal of Indigenous erasure and disspossession has never been achieved, and that the claim to Settler existence always remains tentative, never able to rest easy, having to shift time and again in adjusting colonial modalities of power such as Settler colonial law (Landertinger, 2017). It is these failures of racism and Settler colonialism that will also require further documentation and research.

The authors of this section give illustrations of everyday acts of self-determination and resistance to colonialism as well as the great lengths to which Canada and courts must go to adjust legal modalities of power in order to maintain Settler colonial dispossession. In doing so, the authors are highlighting the ways in which Indigenous peoples are acting on their responsibility to life and lands, their people, and all creation, demanding a structural change to the current systemic inequities, and a shift towards a true shared power, a lived nation-to-nation relationship.

Corntassel and Bryce's chapter shows us that environmental destruction has made it difficult for Indigenous nations to practice sustainable self-determination. However, Indigenous peoples have not been sitting idly. For example, the Lekwungen communities are trying to revitalize and protect their traditional kwetlal food system from the effects of colonial developments, and the "Water Walkers" movement in Wikiwemikong Unceded First Nation in Ontario, Canada is resisting against the environmental pollution to our lakes and traditional waters. In both these cases, one can see that Indigenous peoples are asserting their inherent rights to sustainable self-determination, and fulfilling their responsibility to maintain a sacred traditional holistic relationship with their territories and all relations. Such assertive acts move us away from a politics of recognition that limits Indigenous peoples' self-determination.

A politics of recognition is a rights-based strategy that largely depends on the State's recognition and accommodation of Indigenous self-determination. But, as Coulthard (2014) argues, "the politics of recognition in its contemporary liberal form promotes to reproduce the very configurations of colonialist, racist, patriarchal state power that Indigenous peoples' demands for recognition have historically sought to transcend" (ibid., 3). This is because, in the current structurally unequal relationship, the colonial Canadian State still controls the definition of "Indigenous self-determination" and "Indigenous rights" and frames both the discourse of politics of recognition and any practical consequence of it. Ultimately, such a strategy has not significantly transformed the relationship between the State and Indigenous nations, especially when any Indigenous claims are viewed as a threat to Canadian "interest" or "sovereignty." Rather than wishing for such recognition by the State, Indigenous peoples, Coulthard maintains, ought to assert cultural practices of critical individual and collective self-recognition, empower themselves, and "practice decolonial, gender-emancipatory, and economically nonexploitative alternative structures of law and sovereign authority grounded on a critical refashioning of the best of Indigenous legal and political traditions" (ibid., 179). Acts taken by the Water Walkers and Lekwungen communities are examples of such types of decolonial self-recognition.

The late Arthur Manuel provides a further interrogation of the Canadian colonial state, not simply in terms of the politics of recognition, but the modes of power enforced legally by its courts to control and contain Indigenous resistance and to skirt its obligations to Indigenous peoples. He centers his own personal experience of the Sun Peaks dispute where an injuction (what he more loosely terms "**the legal billy club**") was used to contain and also criminalize the Neskonlith, leading eventually to their arrest and imprisonment. Manuel rejects the current trend toward criminalizing Indigenous resistance. He suggests that Canada begin to recognize the Aboriginal title and rights that are already enshrined in s. 35 in the 1982 Constitution, the absolute right to self-determination, and the title that has been acknowledged by courts as underlying and superseding all other layers of property rights in what is currently called Canada. He is focused on fighting the assimilationist tendencies of government policy, dependency programs, and negotiations based on extinguishment and Canada's terms of "surrender and grant back." As such, he denounces a racist doctrine of discovery, calling on Canada to implement the path to self-determination (not simply "self-government") and to sort out matters of access to lands and the sharing of benefits, jurisdiction, and the matter of domestic (and also international) legal orders that affirm the rights of Indigenous peoples.

CHAPTER 29

Practicing Sustainable Self-Determination

Indigenous Approaches to Cultural Restoration and Revitalization

Jeff Corntassel and Cheryl Bryce

Today there are approximately 370 million indigenous people living in over 70 states throughout the world, constituting five per cent of the global population. Eighty per cent of all biodiversity on the planet thrives in the twenty-two per cent of global territories home to indigenous peoples.[1] Increasingly, researchers recognize that the same forces that threaten biodiversity also threaten indigenous peoples' longstanding relationships with their homelands and the health and well-being of native communities. Ongoing environmental destruction jeopardizes the sustainable relationships indigenous nations have practiced for thousands of years, including **land-based and water-based cultural practices** such as gathering medicines, hunting, fishing, and farming. . . .

As a result of colonial encroachment onto their homelands, being indigenous today means engaging in a struggle to reclaim and regenerate one's relational, place-based existence by challenging the ongoing, destructive forces of colonization.[2] According to Mohawk scholar Taiaiake Alfred, "colonialism is best conceptualized as an irresistible outcome of a multigenerational and multifaceted process of forced dispossession and attempted acculturation—a disconnection from land, culture, and community—that has resulted in political chaos and social discord within First Nations communities and the collective

---

---

1. United Nations Development Programme, Human Development Report 2011 (New York: Palgrave Macmillan, 2011), 54.

2. The United Nations has not adopted an official definition of indigenous peoples, but working definitions, such as the one developed by the United Nations Working Group on Indigenous Populations in 1986, offer some generally accepted guidelines for self-identifying Indigenous peoples and nations:

    - Self-identification as indigenous peoples at the individual level and accepted by the community as their member;

    - Historical continuity with pre-colonial and/or pre-settler societies;

    - Strong link to territories and surrounding natural resources;

    - Distinct social, economic, or political systems;

    - Distinct language, culture, and beliefs;

    - Form non-dominant groups of society; and,

    - Resolve to maintain and reproduce their ancestral environments and systems as distinctive peoples and communities.

    For more on the complexities of defining 370 million indigenous peoples around the world, see: Jeff Corntassel, "Who is Indigenous? 'Peoplehood' and Ethnonationalist Approaches to Rearticulating Indigenous Identity," Nationalism & Ethnic Politics 9, no. 1 (2003): 75–100.

dependency of First Nations upon the state."[3] These forces of disconnection further distance indigenous peoples from their spiritual, cultural, and physical relationships with the natural world and serve to destroy the confidence and well-being of indigenous peoples.

When addressing contemporary colonialism and cultural harm, it is important to understand that the indigenous rights discourse has limits and can only take struggles for land reclamation and justice so far. Indigenous mobilization around rights-based strategies premised on state recognition of indigenous self-determination—which entails unconditional freedom to live one's relational, place-based existence, and practice healthy relationships—has serious shortcomings in terms of redressing cultural harms and loss. According to Dene political theorist Glen Coulthard, "the politics of recognition [for indigenous peoples] in its contemporary form promises to reproduce the very configurations of colonial power that Indigenous peoples' demands for recognition have historically sought to transcend."[4] It follows that indigenous self-determination is something that is asserted and acted upon, not negotiated or offered freely by the state. Based on Coulthard's description of the politics of recognition, it is clear that the rights discourse has certain limitations in relation to indigenous struggles for self-determination. Rights are state constructions that do not necessarily reflect inherent indigenous responsibilities to their homelands. Rather, rights are conditional in that the state can withdraw them at any time or selectively enforce them. Additionally, the rights discourse compartmentalizes indigenous self-determination by separating questions of governance and community well-being from homelands and relationships to the natural world. Consequently, a right to indigenous self-determination is often reduced to self-governance, when this is only one of several layers of indigenous self-determining authority. Finally, by embedding themselves within the state-centric rights discourse, indigenous peoples risk mimicking state functions rather than honoring their own sustainable, spiritual relationships with their homelands. In this context, indigenous self-determination can be rearticulated as part of a sustainable, community-based process rather than solely as narrowly constructed political or legal entitlements.

As the above discussion indicates, when approaches to indigenous cultural revitalization and self-determination are discussed solely in terms of strategies, rights, and theories, they overlook the everyday practices of resurgence and decolonization. Indigenous resurgence is about reconnecting with homelands, cultural practices, and communities, and is centred on reclaiming, restoring, and regenerating homeland relationships. Another dimension centres upon decolonization, which transforms indigenous struggles for freedom from performance to everyday local practice.[5] This entails moving away from the performativity of a rights discourse geared toward state affirmation and approval toward a daily existence conditioned by place-based cultural practices. What, then, does a process of sustainable self-determination look like in practice as indigenous peoples move from rights to practicing their everyday responsibilities? This article examines indigenous communities in Lekwungen (Songhees First Nation in Victoria, British Columbia, Canada) as they work to overcome cultural loss by reclaiming their homelands and distinct cultural practices.[6] First, however, concepts of culture and sustainability are further developed in terms of their applicability to international law.

3. Taiaiake Alfred, "Colonialism and State Dependency," Journal of Aboriginal Health 5 (2009): 52.

4. Glen S. Coulthard, "Subjects of Empire: Indigenous Peoples and the 'Politics of Recognition' in Canada," Contemporary Political Theory 3 (2007): 1–29.

5. Kahikina de Silva, "Pathways to Decolonization" class session, Indigenous Governance Program course igov 595: Reclaiming Ćelenen: Land, Water, Governance (University of Victoria: July 19, 2011). This quote is used with Kahikina's written permission.

6. For the purposes of this article, cultural practices comprise the everyday activities of indigenous peoples in relation to their homelands. Additionally, it is understood that indigenous peoples who live outside their territories continue to practice their cultures, though they express their deep relationships and connections to place in different ways on a daily basis. For example, while over 50 per cent of indigenous peoples in Canada live in urban areas, there is a multidirectional flow between urban and rural communities.

Cultural Harm and Community Resurgence

Indigenous peoples in urban areas often find ways to maintain their links to families, communities, and homelands by going "home" for ceremonies and/or practicing their ceremonial life in the cities. . . . Whether on their homelands or maintaining homeland connections through regular visits and other land-based/water-based cultural practices, indigenous peoples defy the standard reservation/off-reservation dichotomies.

One example of **community resurgence** in action is the "Water Walkers" movement in Wikiwemikong Unceded First Nation in Ontario, Canada. The movement began in the winter of 2002 in response to mounting threats of environmental pollution to community lakes and traditional waters. According to one of the leaders of this movement, Josephine Mandamin, they asked themselves, "What can we do to bring out, to tell people of our responsibilities as women, as keepers of life and the water, to respect our bodies as Nishnaabe-kwewag, as women?"[7] They decided as a group to undertake a spiritual walk around the entire perimeter of Lake Superior with buckets of water to raise awareness of the need to protect water. According to Josephine, "This journey with the pail of water that we carry is our way of Walking the Talk. [. . .] Our great grandchildren and the next generation will be able to say, yes, our grandmothers and grandfathers kept this water for us!"[8] When examining indigenous community resurgence, questions of sustainability and subsistence become key starting points for assessing cultural harm, and, ultimately, for the restoration of cultural practices. In a comprehensive United

Nations study examining indigenous peoples and their natural resource rights, Special Rapporteur Erica-Irene Daes found that "few if any limitations on indigenous resource rights are appropriate, because the indigenous ownership of the resources is associated with the most important and fundamental of human rights: the rights to life, food, shelter, the right to self-determination, and the right to exist as a people."[9]

Given that their future survival depends on it, indigenous communities adamantly assert an inherent right to subsistence living. For indigenous peoples, subsistence living involves everyday cultural, spiritual, and social interactions grounded in reciprocal relationships that sustain communities for generations. Cree activist Ted Moses discusses how self-determination and a right to subsistence are interrelated in this regard: "We may not be denied our own means of subsistence. [. . .] We may not be denied the wherewithal for life itself—food, shelter, clothing, land, water and the freedom to pursue a way of life. There are no exceptions to this rule."[10]

How does the most comprehensive indigenous rights instrument in effect today—the 2007 UN Declaration on the Rights of Indigenous Peoples—protect indigenous rights to subsistence and sustainable self-determination within Canada? While it initially voted against adoption of the Declaration (along with Australia, New Zealand, and the United States), Canada has since reversed course due to political pressure from First Nations and formally endorsed the Declaration in 2010.[11] When providing the details of its endorsement, the Canadian government emphasized that the Declaration is a "non-legally binding document that does not reflect customary international law nor change Canadian laws."[12] Notwithstanding this interpretation, some

---

7. Renée Elizabeth Mzinegiizhigo-kwe Bédard, "Keepers of the Water: Nishnaabe-kwewag Speaking for the Water," in Lighting the Eighth Fire, Leanne Simpson, ed. (Winnipeg: Arbeiter Ring Publishing, 2008), 103.

8. Ibid., 104.

9. Erica-Irene A. Daes, Final Report on Indigenous Peoples' Permanent Sovereignty Over Natural Resources, July 13, 2004, un Doc. E/CN.4/Sub.2/2004/30.

10. Ted Moses, "The Right of Self-Determination and its Significance to the Survival of Indigenous Peoples," in Operationalizing the Right of Indigenous Peoples to Self-Determination, ed. Pekka Aikio and Martin Scheinin (Tuku/Abo: Institute for Human Rights, Abo Akademi University, 2000), 161.

11. Australia, New Zealand, and the United States have also reversed their 2007 positions on the Declaration and formally endorsed UNDRIP.

12. S. James Anaya, "The Right of Indigenous Peoples to Self-Determination in the Post Declaration Era," in Indian and Northern Affairs Canada, "Canada's Statement of Support on the United Nations Declaration on the Rights of Indigenous Peoples," November 12, 2010.

international legal scholars contend that the Declaration has political and legal force because it is grounded in universally upheld principles of self-determination....

Drafted by Indigenous activists, scholars, and state delegates over the past three decades, the Declaration is comprised of 46 articles that mirror several international customary norms already in place.[13] The main articles of interest here are those which outline the rights of indigenous peoples to restorative justice, including redress for any action which has the aim or effect of depriving them of their ability to live as indigenous peoples, such as their means of subsistence (Article 20); access to health and traditional medicines (Article 24); or the right to maintain and strengthen their distinctive spiritual relationship with their traditionally owned or otherwise-used and occupied lands, territories, waters, coastal seas, and other resources (Article 25).[14]

Despite the potential for existing international legal institutions and standards to hold signatories accountable, as of this writing no global forum has yet held Canada accountable for its denial of indigenous cultural practices and everyday subsistence. In this regard, Article 46, Part 1 of the UN Declaration on the Rights of Indigenous Peoples is revealing: "Nothing in this Declaration may be interpreted as implying for any State, people, group or person any right to engage in any activity or to perform any act contrary to the Charter of the United Nations or construed as authorizing or encouraging any action which would dismember or impair, totally or in part, the territorial integrity or political unity of sovereign and independent States." While indigenous peoples do not tend to seek secession from the state, the restoration of their cultural practices is often portrayed as a threat to the territorial integrity of the countries in which they reside, and thus, a threat to state sovereignty. The politics of

recognition highlight the shortcomings of pursuing rights-based strategies for indigenous peoples desiring decolonization and restoration of their relationships to the natural world....

... How, then, do subsistence and sustainability fit into a discussion of cultural practice and continuity in indigenous communities? For indigenous peoples, sustainability is upheld by honoring longstanding, reciprocal relationships with the natural world, as well as by transmitting knowledge and everyday cultural practices to future generations.... An indigenous notion of sustainability involves upholding one's responsibilities to the land and natural world and giving back more than one takes, rather than simply residing on the land. It follows that **indigenous** sustainable self-determination is both an individual and community-driven process where "evolving indigenous livelihoods, food security, community governance, relationships to homelands and the natural world, and ceremonial life can be practiced today locally and regionally, thus enabling the transmission of these traditions and practices to future generations."[15]

Whether living in rural or urban areas, indigenous peoples are finding new pathways to resurgence and cultural continuity in order to strengthen their nations amidst ongoing colonialism and legacies of cultural harm. Rights have limits when addressing issues of cultural harm, and new indigenous movements, such as the Water Walkers, are emerging to protect indigenous lands, cultures, and communities. Terms such as *subsistence* and *sustainability* are being redefined by indigenous peoples to express their complex relationships with their homelands. Resurgence ultimately entails community reclamation, restoration, and regeneration of local cultural practices, and the Lekwungen people have begun a movement to fight for their unique way of life.

13. The Universal Periodic Review (UPR) process, which is a new inter-state mechanism of the Human Rights Council, may also be an important mechanism for mainstreaming the provisions of the Declaration into existing human rights law and establishing human rights obligations for states under review. See: Luis Rodriguez-Pinero, "'Where Appropriate:' Monitoring/Implementing of Indigenous Peoples' Rights Under the Declaration," in Making the Declaration Work: The United Nations Declaration on the Rights of Indigenous Peoples, ed. Claire Charters and Rodolfo Stavenhagen (Copenhagen: International Working Group on Indigenous Affairs, 2009), 321–322.

14. Other relevant articles in undrip include Article 8, 11, 21, 28, 29, 31, 32, and 40.

15. World Commission on Environment and Development, Report of the World Commission on Environment and Development, A/RES/42/187; posted by UN Department of Economic and Social Affairs (DESA), December 11, 1987, http://www.un-documents.net/a42r187.htm; United Nations Development Programme, Human Development Report 2011 (New York: Palgrave Macmillan, 2011), 119.

Kwetlal and Community Resurgence

... One example of everyday practices of resurgence in action comes from British Columbia, Canada. The Lekwungen ancestral homelands are also known as Victoria (Metulia) and Greater Victoria in British Columbia, Canada. Diverse ecosystems, such as the Garry Oak Ecosystem (GOE), which is known for the *kwetlal* (*camas*, a starchy bulb that has been a staple food and trade item for indigenous peoples in the region for generations), have thrived on Lekwungen territories for centuries. The GOE remains vital to the kwetlal food and trade system, and Lekwungen communities were known worldwide as the place to trade for kwetlal. ... Additionally, the University of Victoria is located in the one area where kwetlal was celebrated, harvested, pit cooked, and traded with people up and down the coast.

Lekwungen women have been the backbone of the kwetlal food system by managing it for centuries and, through their connections to kwetlal and management of their traditional homelands, have sustained their communities. This important role was passed down from mothers to daughters. Cheryl Bryce and her family have been managing their traditional Lekwungen territories for several generations, and Bryce continues to harvest kwetlal on parklands and private property despite threats to her and her family's well-being from settlers attempting to deny her access to Lekwungen homelands.[16] The struggles of Bryce and her family highlight how these foods systems have been greatly impacted by settler colonial encroachment that continues today.

In 1844, James Douglas decided to settle the new Hudson Bay Fort in Metulia (downtown Victoria) because of the beautiful kwetlal food system, and Fort Victoria became the first "box store," so to speak, in the Lekwungen ancestral homelands. Initially, the Lekwungen people maintained relations with the alien settler economy as a secondary form of trade. However, Fort Victoria was developed in the centre of the Lekwungen ancestral lands and its impacts were directly aimed at destroying the combined strength of the culture, people, and land. As a result, this trading system deteriorated over time, and led to the decline of the kwetlal food systems. Today, the kwetlal food system comprises less than five per cent of its original yield over 150 years ago.

Given that 95 per cent of the ancestors' land base for this food system is not available today, the current state of the indigenous food system is evidence of colonial development, pollution, and cultural suppression and oppression, which has led to cultural loss and the destruction of roles and responsibilities within the Lekwungen community. For example, the Lekwungen people have seven major families each with food resources, roles, and an area of land. However, as a result of colonial encroachment, gender roles relating to traditional land management and harvesting have been disrupted and fishing and planting areas governed by particular families have been encroached upon by settler populations. Additionally, local environmental conservation efforts have focused on the revitalization of the GOE, rather than on addressing the reality of indigenous food systems and community sustainability in the region.

Today, the work continues among the women with inherent family rights to the kwetlal food system. It will take generations of Lekwungen peoples acting in solidarity to reinstate cultural food systems such as kwetlal. Cultural revitalization starts with protecting the land, reinstating traditional roles, and practicing everyday acts of resurgence. Harvesting, pit cooking, and trading continue today despite the colonial disruption. However, Lekwungen homelands, roles, and nationhood remain threatened as they have been since the first contact with settlers. After all, Lekwungen homelands remain at the centre of ongoing colonial expansion. Cheryl Bryce is a Lekwungen woman visibly reinstating her role among both Lekwungen and settlers. It was around 1999 when Bryce realized she needed to educate and develop a working network toward reinstating kwetlal food systems. As a child, Bryce remembers going to parks in Lekwungen ancestral lands early in the morning with her grandmother Edna George née Norris and, upon encountering settlers, being told that they did not have the right to harvest in "Victoria parks." Within

---

16. Briony Penn, "Restoring Camas and Culture to Lekwungen and Victoria: An interview with Lekwungen Cheryl Bryce," Focus Magazine, June 2006, http://www.firstnations.de/media/06-1-1-camas.pdf.

Victoria and throughout Canada, acts of community resurgence are criminalized when it comes to regenerating one's cultural practices on original indigenous homelands, which are often considered private properties or public parklands. As an adult Bryce continues to encounter this type of ignorance coupled with threats of physical force. These experiences and her concern with the decline of the food system led Bryce to raise awareness and build networks of like-minded indigenous and settler peoples.

Bryce took the struggle for cultural restoration beyond her family and invited indigenous peoples and settlers to partake in public events such as kwetlal pit cooks and invasive plant species removal and to engage in creative awareness-building campaigns. The goals of the "Community Tool Shed" founded by Bryce focus on education and the reinstatement of indigenous food systems such as kwetlal. There is a strong educational component to this work, because Bryce has developed maps of Victoria with traditional place names and has also spoken to several school groups and residents about the history of the region, as well as their obligations to the kwetlal food systems in Lekwungen territories.[17] In order to protect the remaining five per cent of kwetlal yields and reinstate kwetlal food systems, it will take generations working at removing invasive plant species (such as Scotch Broom), pollution concerns, and colonial development.... Bryce's efforts to revitalize kwetlal food systems, as well as to regenerate community roles and responsibilities, are critical to the future survival and resurgence of Lekwungen peoples. As the Lekwungen example points out, communities must assert sustainable self-determination rather than negotiate for it. Ultimately, a community's cultural continuity is premised on direct actions to protect these sacred relationships.

Conclusion

When discussing questions of indigenous community sustainability, the previous research and an in-depth look at community resurgence on Lekwungen homelands make it clear that the revitalization of land-based and water-based cultural practices is premised on enacting indigenous community responsibilities, which "entails sparking a spiritual revolution rather than seeking state-based solutions that are disconnected from indigenous community relationships."[18] Processes of reclamation, restoration, and regeneration take on a renewed urgency given the high stakes of dispossession and disconnection from indigenous territories.

The pursuit of self-determination should be reconceived as a responsibility-based movement centred on a sustainable self-determination process, not as a narrowly constructed, state-driven rights discourse. Overall, one sees that grassroots efforts like those referenced above do not rely heavily on rights as much as they do on community responsibilities to protect traditional homelands and food systems. By resisting colonial authority and demarcating their homelands via place-naming and traditional management practices, these everyday acts of resurgence have promoted the regeneration of sustainable food systems in communities and are transmitting these teachings and values to future generations.

We also have to remember that change happens in small increments—*one warrior at a time*. As Cheryl Bryce's actions in Lekwungen demonstrate, "Measurable change on levels beyond the individual will emanate from the start made by physical and psychological transformations in people generated through direct, guided experiences in small, personal groups and, one-on-one mentoring."[19] In her role as a mentor, Bryce brings indigenous children to pull invasive species and learn more about native plants. Passing on this experiential knowledge to younger generations is crucial to the survival of indigenous communities. Additionally, the Community Tool Shed is a place where both indigenous and non-Indigenous people can come together under a common goal of protecting the land from invasive species so that native plants will flourish once again. All of these grassroots efforts begin to create awareness of these local struggles and the urgency to protect indigenous homelands.

---

17. For example, see: Cheryl Bryce and Brenda Sam, "Lekwungen People: The Traditional Territory of the Songhees and Esquimalt People" (pamphlet), 1997, http://bcheritage.ca/salish/ph2/map/lekwungen.htm.

18. Jeff Corntassel, "Toward Sustainable Self-Determination," 124.

19. Alfred, "Colonialism and State Dependency," 56.

There is also an educational component to this struggle. Bryce creates teachable moments in order to convey the history and contemporary struggles of the indigenous peoples in the region. For example, she makes bouquets out of cut-outs of kwetlal (camas) flowers, along with cedar and other native plants, and brings them to Parliament in order to remind people of the local battles being waged over the land. Bryce uses symbolism to urge people to practice healthier relationships, noting that the land itself can also heal.

By understanding the overlapping and simultaneous processes of reclamation, restoration, and regeneration, one begins to better understand how to implement meaningful and substantive community decolonization practices. Future generations will map their own pathways to community regeneration, ideally on their own terms. By moving from performance to everyday cultural practices, indigenous peoples will be recognized by future generations for how they defended and protected their homelands.

CHAPTER 30

The Legal Billy Club

Arthur Manuel

At the end of our acts of defiance, we are often met with the business end of the police truncheon. But the process of attacking us usually begins weeks and even months earlier, when the state takes in hand its legal billy club: the court injunction.

The weight of this club is provided by the racist colonial doctrines of discovery claiming that we have been fully and irreversibly dispossessed of our territories. That is the underpinning behind the Canadian state's vision of Crown land, and it is the force behind the injunctions that industry and governments use to get enforcement orders that allows them to use the police, paramilitaries and even the army to crush our efforts to inhabit the lands given to us by our Creator.

As soon as we leave our reserves to return to our land, government and industry take collateral colonial legal action in the form of the court injunction. By that means they instantly transform the Royal Canadian Mounted Police, the Ontario Provincial

Police, the Sûreté du Quebec or whatever security force is on the scene into an attack force against us. If we continue to resist, they escalate to the Canadian military, and it is notable that regarding potential opposition to pipelines the Trudeau government has already specifically warned that it will use the Canadian military against any of its citizens who try to stand in the way of the full exploitation of the country's petroleum resources.

The injunction, enforcement orders, and prosecution for contempt of court are the means by which our assertion of our rights on the ground is instantly criminalized by the Canadian state, even when it is clear that we have a very good legal case to the land in question. Colonial courts do not take into account our legal rights when issuing injunctions—they operate purely on the status quo and such unlofty principles as the "balance of convenience." Injunctions are therefore the aces up the sleeve of the government

Arthur Manuel, "The Legal Billy Club." In Arthur Manuel and Grand Chief Ronald Derrickson, *The Reconciliation Manifesto: Recovering the Land, Rebuilding the Economy*, Toronto: James Lorimer and Company Ltd Publishers, © 2017.

and industry when land is being contested. They are generally quickly granted to government and industry but rarely to Indigenous peoples. Even when we have a clear-cut case for proprietorship over our land, injunctions are granted "on the balance of convenience" to government and industry and our further activity on the land is instantly criminalized.

Injunctions are an ideal tool of oppression because they allow government and industry to skirt the substantive legal issues behind Indigenous rights to follow only the status quo concept that our lands are, at present, in possession of the settler state and until we overturn this fact, we do not have the right to exercise our own jurisdiction there.

We saw the devastating effect of injunctions as a tool to criminalize our activities in my own community, Neskonlith. When I was chief, a group of our youth and Elders moved up the mountain and set up a camp at the foot of the new Sun Peaks ski resort development on our Aboriginal title lands.

At first, the federal government avoided getting involved in this dispute and let the province deal with it. The province and Sun Peaks, which was owned by Nippon Cable, a Japanese multinational, took collateral legal action to avoid negotiating a mutually agreeable solution to this dispute. They resorted to injunctions and enforcement orders against our people, who were peacefully camping at the entrance to the construction site.

The end product of this process is often our men, women and Elders thrown face down onto the ground with handcuffs locked on their wrists. But it all begins in a surprisingly genteel manner. Polite and well-dressed and well-groomed corporate lawyers appear before a court to state that a group of Indigenous people—in our case at Sun Peaks it was a small group of youth and Elders—have moved onto and are inhabiting or blocking a section of their Aboriginal title land. They point out that the Crown does not acknowledge the Aboriginal title and even if the issue is before the courts, argues the balance of convenience for an injunction while cases are being decided elsewhere. In such cases, colonial courts generally side with the corporations and the injunctions are granted. Then the courtly manners are dispensed with. The Crown is free to show its teeth. They send in the police to move in and break heads and make arrests if we do not disperse on their command.

In our Sun Peaks dispute, over fifty arrests were made over several years and Indigenous people, including my own daughters, spent months in jail. This is unacceptable in our country. It is unacceptable anywhere in the world to have Indigenous people jailed simply for refusing to leave their own land. It is when we stand our ground we see that ultimately the power is based only on the violence they can bring to bear against us. We will fight violence with resistance and calls for justice within Canada and internationally.

As my friend Dr. Shiri Pasternak has written, "blockades are the meeting of settler and Indigenous legal orders—and not just as some tactic of civil disobedience." We must continue to assert our legal rights over our land, no matter what the consequences. And we will meet settler law at the blockade with our own Indigenous law and Aboriginal title and rights to the land.

What is most frustrating when the government uses the courts against us is the fact that, when the tables are turned and the courts actually support us, the government thinks nothing of ignoring them to the point of openly breaching court orders.

I have pointed to it before and it is one of the most worrying aspects of Canada's treatment toward Indigenous peoples: when our rights are at stake, the Canadian government consistently ignores rulings of its own courts. This should worry Canadians as well. When the judicial branch is no longer a check on executive power, democracy itself is at stake. But this is the situation in Canada with regards to Indigenous law.

For example, the federal government has maintained its comprehensive claims policy that employs a "modification" and "non-assertion" approach resulting in the de facto extinguishment of Aboriginal title, despite the fact that the federal government is required to act as a fiduciary to Indigenous peoples and to protect and implement Aboriginal title and rights, which are recognized and affirmed by Section 35 of the Canadian Constitution. As such, there is an affirmative obligation on the federal government to bring its laws and policies in line with the highest law in the country, the Canadian *Constitution Act*, and the highest court in the country, the Supreme Court of Canada.

The federal government has implemented Supreme Court of Canada decisions regarding other issues, such as same sex marriage and safe injection sites, but not regarding Aboriginal title and rights, although they have an even more stringent obligation in that regard as the fiduciary. The result is a constitutional breach, where the executive branch (the government) does not implement the binding rulings of the judiciary branch and the Constitution, the highest expression of the legislative branch. In turn, Indigenous peoples who assert and exercise their Aboriginal title and rights rather than negotiating under policies that violate the Constitution and international human rights standards are subject to executive action and criminalization.

The federal government continues to fail to live up to its constitutional obligations as a fiduciary, opposing judgements in favour of Indigenous rights instead of taking the side of Indigenous peoples. At the same time, the provincial governments do not hesitate to resort to violence against our people if we try to stand up for our rights.

PART 15

Additional Readings

Belanger, Yale D., and P. Whitney Lackenbauer. *Blockades or Breakthroughs? Aboriginal Peoples Confront the Canadian State*. Montreal & Kingston: McGill-Queen's University Press, 2015.

Bowles, Paul, and Henry Veltmeyer, eds. *The Answer Is Still No: Voices of Pipeline Resistance*. Halifax: Fernwood Publishing, 2014.

Coulthard, Glen Sean. *Red Skin White Masks: Rejecting the Colonial Politics of Recognition*. Minneapolis & London: University of Minnesota Press, 2014.

Gehl, Lynn. *Gehl v. Canada: Challenging Sex Discrimination in the Indian Act*. Regina: University of Regina Press, 2021.

The Kin-nda-niimi Collective. *The Winter We Danced: Voices from the Past, the Future, and the Idle No More Movement*. Winnipeg: ARP Books, 2014.

Lyons, Scott Richard. *X-Marks: Native Signatures of Assent*. Minneapolis: University of Minnesota Press, 2010.

Manuel, Arthur. *Unsettling Canada: A National Wake-up Call*. Toronto: Between the Lines, 2015.

McGregor, D. "Anishnaabe-Kwe, Traditional Knowledge, and Water Protection," in *Canadian Woman Studies* 26 (3/4), 2008.

Pasternak, Shiri. Grounded Authority: The Algonquins of Barriere Lake Against the State. Minneapolis: University of Minnesota Press, 2017.

Simpson, Audra. *Mohawk Interruptus: Political Life across the Borders of Settler States*. Durham, NC: Duke University Press, 2014.

Simpson, Leanne, ed. *Lighting the Eighth Fire: The Liberation, Resurgence, and Protection of Indigenous Nations*. Winnipeg: Arbeiter Ring Publishing, 2008.

Relevant Websites

Behind the Thin Blue Line: Meet a secretive arm of the RCMP in B.C.
https://www.aptnnews.ca/ourstories/cirg/%3c/
APTN investigates the origin and actions of the Community-Industry Response Group (C-IRG), a secretive industry defence arm of the B.C. RCMP, meant to dismantle blockades at pipeline protests and the federal government's "counter-terror squad."

Indigenous Action Media/Indigenous Action.
https://www.indigenousaction.org/%3c/

An archived website intended to provide communications about and direct action support for Indigenous sacred lands defense including poscasts, essays, and a print-friendly zine outlining steps to abolish the "ally industrial complex" through coming to understand "accomplices not allies."

Senate report on fisheries finds federal government failing First Nations rights-holders.
https://www.aptnnews.ca/national-news/senate-report-on-fisheries-finds-federal-government-failing-first-nations-rights-holders/%3c/
APTN investigates a new report by the Senate Committee on Fisheries and Oceans finding that the federal Department is not living up to its commitments to fully implement First Nations rights-based fisheries as affirmed by the Supreme Court of Canada in 1999.

Teal Jones wins court appeal to extend injunction against Fairy Creek old-growth blockade.
https://www.thestar.com/news/canada/2022/01/30/teal-jones-wins-court-appeal-to-extend-injunction-against-fairy-creek-old-growth-blockade.html%3c/
The Toronto Star investigates the B.C. Court of Appeal's granting Teal-Jones' application to extend a court injunction against the longstanding blockades by the Rainforest Flying Squad in Tree Farm Licence (TFL) 46 near Port Renfrew, B.C. through 26 Sept. 2020.

Films

Falls Around Her. Dir. Darlene Naponse. Pacific Northwest Pictures Inc. 2018.
Is the Crown at War with Us? Dir. Alanis Obomsawin. National Film Board of Canada, 2002.
Kanehsatake: 270 Years of Resistance. Dir. Alanis Obomsawin. National Film Board of Canada, 1993.
The People of the Kattawapiskat River. Dir. Alanis Obomsawin. National Film Board of Canada, 2012.
The Road Forward. Dir. Marie Clements. National Film Board of Canada. 2017.
Sewatokwa'tshera't = The Dish with One Spoon. Dir. Dawn Martin-Hill. Haudenosaunee Confederacy, 2007.
Trick or Treaty? Dir. Alanis Obomsawin. National Film Board of Canada, 2014.

Key Terms

- Gendered colonial violence
- Land-based/water-based cultural practices
- Indigenous sustainable self-determination
- Community resurgence
- The legal billy club

Discussion Questions

1. What is sustainable self-determination? What contemporary examples of it, aside from those discussed by Corntassel and Bryce, can you think of?

2. What is an injuction? How do court injuctions allow the federal government to sidestep and violate its Constitutional obligations to Indigenous peoples? What would be involved in radically transforming the relationship between Indigenous peoples and the state according to Manuel, and how is this different than what is taking place right now?

3. What does the Idle No More Movement stand for, and against? Do you believe it was effective in its goals?

4. Explain what Corntassel and Bryce (Chapter 29) mean by "moving from performance to everyday cultural practices, Indigenous peoples will be recognized by future generations for how they defended and protected their homelands." What does being recognized by future generations for defending and protecting homelands look like to you, and how do you relate to this matter personally?

Activities

Invite an Indigenous representative of a local Indigenous community or organization to speak to the class about contemporary issues faced by the Indigenous community in the area, and how the community has been organizing to address such issues. Next, discuss how non-Indigenous people can best support Indigenous communities in asserting their inherent self-determination.

Cheryl Bryce uses symbolism, such as the bouquets of camas flowers and invasive species cutouts presented in politically significant situations, to "urge people to practice healthier relationships so the land itself can also heal" (ibid., 161). Brainstorm symbolic and artistic expressions that you and your fellow community members could use to express desires to live in ways that demonstrate respect for the health of the Earth and for the health of *all* community members.

Conclusion

In concluding this third edition, we recognize that there have been significant developments in Canadian politics, in particular, since our second edition in 2011. On 19 October 2015, after some nine years of leadership under the rule of Steven Harper, Canadians elected a new liberal government. Prime Minister–elect Justin Trudeau, on election night, reiterated a promise made throughout his campaign. He called for a "renewed nation-to-nation relationship with Indigenous peoples" in Canada. In his own words, he told Canadians that a relationship "that respects rights and honours treaties must be the basis of how we work to close the gap and walk forward together" (*Macleans*, 20 October 2015). Trudeau is now in his third term as Prime Minister of Canada, and while the relationship between Indigenous peoples and the Canadian State has improved somewhat, and some movement has been made in bettering the socioeconomic conditions of Indigenous communities, much still needs to be done.

During his first term in office, Trudeau appointed as Minister of Justice Jody Wilson-Raybould, Canada's first Indigenous federal Justice Minister. He renamed Indian Affairs Canada as the Department of Indigenous and Northern Affairs Canada. He called for an inquiry into Missing and Murdered Indigenous Women and Girls, which released a final report in 2019, followed by an Action Plan in 2021. However, as discussed in Part Six of this text, so far there have been little concrete steps made in addressing the root causes of the gendered violence directed against Indigenous peoples. The current federal government has also promised to mobilize the 94 calls to action by the Truth and Reconciliation Commission and has removed its "objector status" as a nation and has agreed in principle to implement the terms of the United Nations Declaration of the Rights of Indigenous Peoples.

On a moral if not legal basis, these sorts of changes are overdue and furthermore necessary to realize in part the promises for a "renewed relationship" made by Trudeau when he first took office. It has become apparent that the gap between the social conditions of Indigenous and Settler populations still remains alarmingly disparate, in particular in northern and remote communities where news of La Loche and Attawapiskat created public attention (CBC *News*, 8 May 2016a; CBC *News,* 13 April 2016c). While Trudeau has promised to invest billions to deal with poverty, housing, and infrastructure, and to eliminate the long-lasting boil water advisories, many Indigenous communities are still living under such conditions. Just as recently as 20 December 2022, Oneida Nation of the Thames (Lina's own community) had to declare state of emergency amid water shortage (CBC *News*, 20 December 2022c). Indeed, these are issues we addressed in Part Twelve, when connecting environmental injustice with Indigenous peoples' social conditions and Indigenous sovereignty. As we pointed out there, climate change is affecting our water levels; our water is dying, threatening the life of our people. It is urgent that water infrastructure is improved immediately in Indigenous communities; it is unconscionable that many Indigenous peoples still have no access to safe water in a so-called First World country.

In writing this anthology, we are conscious of the enormous complexity of issues facing governments and Indigenous nations committed to changing vast social inequalities. For example, we have hoped to show that it will not be easy through politics alone to change things like poverty, health, and gender violence—issues that have been systemic throughout much of history. We also recognize that a colonial politics of recognition whereby Indigenous peoples are invited into a particular discursive framework continues to be formulated by a Canadian colonial state and has not served Indigenous peoples well. A colonial politics of recognition has been carefully detailed and outlined by Indigenous scholars concerned with Settler colonial state formations (Alfred, 2005;

Coulthard, 2014; Turner, 2006). In summary, we also hope this third edition of the textbook will spur readers to further contemplate and reflect on some of the major conclusions we introduced in the first and second volumes of this textbook, including:

1. That neither Settler colonialism, racism, nor Indigenous peoples are disappearing into the twenty-first century. Despite promising political engagements, interpersonal apathy and everyday racism persists.

2. That the options available for repairing the mistrust and disavowal structuring modern colonial consciousness have already been set out in early historical and nation-to-nation-based agreements, and that a shift has taken place at least politically by Canada's current federal government to recognize these principles.

3. That poverty, economic marginalization, and environmental injustice continue as obstacles as evident and reported in current news events, requiring us to revisit colonial legacies, and—in the first historical instance—the dispossession of lands before fully understanding, repairing, and eradicating them.

4. That Indigenous peoples continue to face serious disparities in educational attainments and health despite ameliorative efforts, the nature of which require us to consider histories of difference-making, antiracist and decolonizing pedagogies and health care approaches. Part of decolonizing education includes a need to validate and affirm Indigenous ways of knowing and doing, which incorporates research methods and ceremonies.

5. That neither institutionalized racism nor Settler colonialism are disappearing, especially as this has been directed toward Indigenous women, men, and nations through the *Indian Act*, even despite recent amendments, a Supreme Court ruling that now recognizes Métis and non-status peoples as "Indians," and the Senate passing an amendment to Bill S3 to eliminate all sexist discriminations in the *Indian Act*, including previous denial of Indian status to children with unstated paternity.

6. That Settler colonial, racialized, and gendered violence (e.g., opposition and backlash to Idle No More, Missing and Murdered Indigenous Women and Girls, Stonechild Inquiry, Ipperwash, Caledonia, Burnt Church, Gustafsen Lake, and Land Back) continues to take place in Canada embodying, in itself, the ongoing physical—and symbolic—removal of Indigenous peoples from their lands into the twenty-first century and the criminalizing of land defenders.

7. That our resistance and resilience as peoples is not disappearing, as is evidenced by the Idle No More movement, the occupation of Indian Affairs in response to reports of suicides at Attawapiskat, the Land Back movement, the Every Child Matters initiatives, and the contributions we continue to make in reformulating academia (see Mihesuah, 1998), the arts, sports, and legal reform in Canada.

Dismantling colonial dominance requires breaking with cycles of oppression founded in the first instance upon histories of racism and sex discrimination. As we have shown, Settler colonialism may seem altogether unrelated to other systems of oppression like racism, sexism, social class exploitation, and even heteronormativity. But Indigenous scholars have nuanced how these systems work together simultaneously to structure distinct kinds of discrimination for Indigenous nations, women, and to a lesser extent in published literature, two-spirited individuals (see Chacaby, 2016). Racialization, sexism, and heteronormativity have quite simply intersected historically to place Indigenous men and women at a disadvantage relative to the state, the justice system, and to each other. As Cannon (2019: 19) writes, "the sexism directed at Indigenous women through the Indian Act belongs collectively to all 'Indians,' women and men. Sexism . . . undermines the collective rights of Indigenous nations . . . Sexism does not belong to women alone—it threatens to define, reduce, and ultimately extinguish the registered Indian population." Put differently, "Indigenous people must collectively face the sexism imposed on our communities by the Canadian state and the racialized injustice that is Indianness" (ibid., 43). We suggest that any meaningful discussions about racism and Indigeneity in Canada need to take these complex interrelationships into account, as they profoundly shape and structure the experiences of Indigenous peoples.

Colonial injustice is racialized injustice. In the first instance, the Indian Act set into motion a way of thinking about identity, governance, and nationhood in racialized terms. It also made compulsory a racialized order of Indian Act governance on Crown lands reserved for Indians. As Indigenous scholars, we believe it is incumbent upon us to revisit these early historical precedents, especially because much of our lives is shaped by them. On the one hand, we agree with scholars who insist that we refuse at every turn the invitation to citizenship (Henderson, 2002), a colonial politics of recognition (Coulthard, 2014), and who reject the fashioning of sovereignty grievances under the guise of racial minority status (Porter, 1999). At the same time, we cannot help but be concerned by a racialized construct of Indianness, largely because it is so fundamentally tied to colonialism in the first instance. For better or worse, Indianness shapes the everyday experience of Indigenous peoples in Canada, but it does not prevent us from naming and then employing a politics of self-recognition and the revitalization of Indigenous governance, cultural, and identity practices (Coulthard, 2014).

Racism cannot fully be understood, nor reconciled, so long as Indigenous peoples are administered as Indians under federal legislation. The word "Indian" is a race-based concept. As Cannon (2019: 55) argues, the category "Indian" needs to be seen for what it is: a strategy on behalf of the settler state to institutionalize a race-based idea that is but one instance in a longstanding refusal on the part of Canada to recognize its nation-to-nation relationship with Indigenous peoples. The category Indian and, for that matter, the accompanying doctrine of discovery, is premised on Indigenous peoples' legal, economic, social, and political nonexistence as nations prior to contact (ibid., 76). Indianness is "predicated in the erasure of Indigenous sovereignty and the declaration of lands as terra nullius (empty of unoccupied)" (ibid., 77). In essence, the origins of Canada as a nation state involved the deployment of racialized categories of difference entrenched in law, politics, and economics now for 146 years since the emergence of the Indian Act of 1876.

Canada's earliest categories of racial difference are contained in the Indian Act (RSC, 1985). This piece of federal legislation remains with us today, and has come to define the relationship between Indigenous nations and Canada, in effect rendering all prior treaty and nation-to-nation agreements with our peoples null and void. We appreciate that current relationships may have become shaped by monetary wealth and its unequal distribution, but we also recognize the spirit of our initial nation-to-nation agreements. Our original agreements were about responsibilities and how to best live amongst one another. We think these prior arrangements set an important historical precedent, and we encourage the current liberal government to rejuvenate and realize a relationship based on original treaty and nation-to-nation principles. Indigenous peoples must be truly self-determining, not only self-governing, and to share in the significant royalties that are derived from the land.

The Indian Act needs to be challenged and was recently challenged on the basis of blatant sex discrimination in what is known as the McIvor case. Although it is now possible as an outcome to this case for the grandchildren of Indian women to be federally recognized as Indians and that the matter of unknown and unstated paternity has finally been resolved after the decision of *Gehl v. the Queen*, we also feel that someone should raise the matter of racialization, or racialized injustice as a constitutional challenge (Cannon, 2019). As mentioned in the Introduction of this anthology: the very first act of colonial injustice in Canada is racialized injustice. It is none other than the process through which Indigenous peoples became Indians for state administrative purposes and for the sake of dispossessing us of the lands that are required for capitalist expansion and exploitation. We have meant to draw attention in this anthology to racialized injustice as the earliest form of colonial dominance in Canada, a matter that can no longer go unnoticed or unchallenged in the law (ibid.).

We have hoped to show that racialized thinking represents a double-edged sword for Indigenous peoples. While we might wish to avoid its usage, Indianness shapes the opportunities and outcomes made available to us by the colonizer. It is also tied to a genocidal project that legally requires our total disappearance as nations. In a material sense, the category Indian rests on a blood quantum logic that, as Kauanui (2008: 34–5) points out, enacts, substantiates, and then disguises the further appropriation of lands. In order to justify the appropriation of Indigenous territories, the colonizer has always to mark the bodies of Indigenous peoples as Indians through policy-making and other symbolic, highly gendered practices of difference making. Blood quantum logic effects the denigration of our genealogical connection to territory or place. It is premised on our dilution, reducing our nations in turn to racial minorities instead of sovereign nations.

However paradoxical it may seem, we cannot help but reconcile histories of racism and racialization in Canada without engaging in precisely the same racialized discourses that produced them. As Anishinabek scholar Dale Turner writes: "It is no secret that for Aboriginal peoples to participate effectively in Canadian legal and political cultures they must engage the normative [liberalist] discourses of the state" (2006: 81). It is furthermore paradoxical that a department concerned with the administration of Indians has become known under a Trudeau administration as Indigenous and Northern Affairs. A name change will mean nothing if it does not challenge the status quo, work in itself toward the devolution of an Indian bureaucracy that stems from the *Indian Act*, or the invitation we face at every turn to deal with Canada as "unequal participants" or as Indians (Coulthard, 2014).

Our colleagues suggest to us that the sociolegal and political contexts that prevent Indigenous nationhood, as well as identification approaches to identity and citizenship, require our intense scrutiny and unwavering political will. Histories of racialization require us as nations to posit Indianness—and at once resist it—in a dual-gestured, combative force against colonial and racialized injustice. This will not be an easy process, as Cannon (2019: 109) explains:

> It is true that racialization has required us as nations and individuals to care about our federal recognition as Indians. It is also true that Indianness, regardless of how meaningful it has become, is a colonial-inspired designation that has always been undesirable to us as sovereign nations.

Despite what is believed in some circles, Indigenous peoples are not at all disappearing. Between 2006 and 2011, the "Aboriginal ancestry population" grew by 20.1 per cent compared with 5.2 per cent for the non-Aboriginal population (Statistics Canada, 2011: 4). Today, some of us are registered as status Indians, while others go federally unrecognized and without reserve lands. More recently, some Métis and nonstatus individuals are able to register as Indians as an outcome to a 2016 Supreme Court ruling (*Daniels v. Canada, Indian Affairs and Northern Development*, 2016). Still others blend effortlessly into decidedly urban, multicultural milieu, invisible to many Canadians as Indigenous peoples because of a politics of authenticity structuring the representation of our everyday lives. Indeed, Indigenous peoples are quite literally rendered invisible and unintelligible, not simply by our own choice or determination, but rather by a highly racialized and structured way of thinking about Indianness as if we were a static or unchanging essence, untouched by modern conveniences or even privileges based on social class, education, and skin colour.

In writing this anthology, we have hoped to show how racism pervades the everyday reality of Indigenous people, from criminal justice to the availability of clean and safe drinking water in reserve communities like Kashechewan Cree Nation (*Globe and Mail*, 28 October 2005) or Oneida Nation of the Thames (CBC *News,* 20 December 2022*),* and also issues involving poverty, mental health, and addictions that are contributing, and indeed, leading to reports of suicide (CBC *News*, 12 April 2016d; CBC *News*, 8 May 2016a; CBC *News*, 17 April 2021g).These realities cannot be represented as stemming alone from what John Steckley (2003: 58–63) and Métis scholar Emma LaRocque (1993: 212) have referred to as a "social problems" or "victim blaming" approach to Indigenous disparities. The reality is that systemic and economic inequalities require real solutions, and we cannot only become visible to Canadians when, and only when, we fit into a social problems category of analysis. These perceptions play themselves out in both the living rooms and classrooms of Canada. More often than not, "statistical outliers," including stories of Indigenous successes, receive limited public attention, or they are rendered invisible or inauthentic.

The tendency to represent Indigenous peoples in these ways concerns us greatly. As we have shown, it is true that Indigenous peoples and majority Canadians experience enormous disparities in education, income, health, and well-being. The statistics have been well documented and—in a somewhat peculiar way—are called rapidly to mind by many individuals in our classrooms. But when issues affecting all Canadians like poverty, racial profiling, suicide, or the availability of clean and safe drinking water become a convenient means of showcasing social problems among Indians, it forces us as the original peoples to contemplate the purpose being served. We are encouraged by recent efforts toward critical reflection and possibly even reconciliation and the resolution of Indigenous disparities that are rooted in social and economic inequality. We also believe these practices of representation must be reconciled, especially as the construction of racialized subjects is—and has been—so fundamental to reproducing racism under contemporary colonialism.

As nations of individuals, Indigenous peoples are determined to maintain our presence and livelihood. Many of us work tirelessly in communities to address the social issues we are currently facing. Collectively, we have resisted, survived, dealt with, and indeed envisioned a way forward, often in the face of adversity. We continue to make steadfast contributions to the arts, sports, academia, and legal reform in Canada. Our communities offer programs that are culturally specific and appropriate, many of them seeking to reclaim and revitalize the language, traditions, and teachings of our people. These successes demonstrate our perseverance and our resistance to colonialism. They are indicative of a widespread resilience and resurgence taking place in our nations to maintain our Indigenous ways of knowing, our stories, and our ways of being. We believe this resurgence is key to securing Settler colonial reparations and to combating racism.

Guswentah, or Two Row Wampum, is exemplary of the kinds of continuity and resurgence we are meaning to highlight. We believe this agreement and other nation-to-nation agreements hold an original set of instructions that are key to showing how Indigenous and Settler populations might secure redress for contemporary injustices like colonialism, heteropatriarchy and racism. The principles embodied in nation-to-nation agreements delineate original partnerships, the maintenance of separate jurisdictions, and a clear commitment to self-determination. Not only do these principles remind us of the unbroken assertion of sovereignty (Mitchell, 1989), they are furthermore useful for revisiting, and rethinking, matters of governance, land grievances, citizenship, criminal justice, education, economics, and the family. In each of these areas, we have witnessed the greatest intrusion of colonial dominance and racism. Settler colonialism has sought to undo the sovereignty of our nations.

Combating Settler colonial racism in Canada does not at all require a reinvention of the proverbial wheel. Instead, it requires a return to original principles and partnerships. In doing so, we start by acknowledging that Indigenous territories cannot be reduced to Indian reserves, governance to Indian Act band councils, or citizenship to Indian status. Reserves, Indian status, and band council governments embody the very kinds of infringement that were, in the very first instance, motivated by racialized thinking. Each of them was an affront to Indigenous jurisdiction and sovereignty. We have shown in this anthology that Indigenous scholars each share in this understanding, albeit differently, and that reconciliation requires the restoration of sovereignty and jurisdiction. Whether it is in calls for Indian control of Indian education, the dismantling of the Indian Act (APTN *News*, 13 April 2016), or even the right to determine our own citizens, reparations start with revisiting principles of autonomy and governance contained in historic arrangements.

In our view, recent calls by the Truth and Reconciliation Commission to engage Settler Canadians in a conversation about shared responsibility, mutual respect, reciprocity, and obligation represent positive steps in a healthier and more equitable future on Turtle Island. Murray Sinclair's reminder that the history of residential schools is a Canadian problem and not simply one facing Indigenous peoples points to the reality that solutions to a Settler colonial past will ultimately befall on all Canadians as well as governments to repair. His call is not dissimilar to Indigenous leaders who, in responding to the government of Canada's apology asked similar questions, in particular: "Words must turn into action, . . . What is it that this government is going to do in the future to help our people?" (Jacobs, 2008: 224).

While we in no way wish to denigrate the apology offered to residential school survivors in June 2008 by the federal government, or the papal visit in July 2022 wherein he apologized for the role of the Catholic church in the Canadian residential schooling system, or the declaration of September 30th as the National Day for Truth and Reconciliation, we are asking how Settler populations in particular might start to engage with the 94 calls to action issued by the TRC in summer 2015 (TRC, 2015). These calls to action include matters involving child welfare, education, language and culture, health, and justice. The matter of justice is in particular significant. Sinclair calls on federal, provincial, and territorial governments to have law schools make a course on Aboriginal people and the law mandatory in Canada. This is significant in light also of the Canadian Deans of Education *Accord on Indigenous Education* (2010) to centre non-Indigenous learners, teachers and calls by administrators in particular to address issues related to the "Non-Indigenous Learner and Indigeneity," and the "build[ing of] student capacity for intercultural understanding, empathy, and mutual respect."

It is incumbent on Canada to look to the lessons learned in other countries that have already sought to reconcile the colonial past where the non-Indigenous learner is concerned. An apology is only restorative, when, as Sara Ahmed (2005: 76) has written of the Australian context, "the shamed other can 'show' that its failure to measure up to a social ideal is temporary." Roger Simon (2013: 136) echoed this call by Ahmed by "asking non-Aboriginal Canadians to work out where they 'fit in' to Aboriginal history, not just where Aboriginal history fits into the history of Canada." How will TRC calls result in educational reform and invite critical Settler engagements in colonial reparations? A few of these calls in particular interest us as Indigenous scholars, especially calls to engage nonwhite populations in anticolonial activism.

In seeking to reconcile colonial pasts, specifically histories of Settler colonialism, racialization, and residential schools, it is necessary for Canadians to relinquish structural advantages acquired through both colonialism and privilege. Canadians cannot simply be asked to "feel good about feeling bad," or as Roger Simon (2013: 133) explains:

> [T]he act of acknowledging victimhood [cannot be] reduced to an affective transaction in which one both recognizes and "feels for" the pain of others, a situation in which there is no need to ask difficult questions that might implicate one's psychic, social and economic investments in the conditions and institutions responsible for the genesis and prolongation of that pain.

Having said that, what does it mean to ask Canadians, especially new Canadians, to take responsibility for colonial injustice in the way that Simon is suggesting? Finding answers to that question needs to be taken seriously. Indeed, a burgeoning scholarship continues to be written since our second edition exploring the scholarly, intellectual, and everyday relationships that exist between Indigenous peoples and racialized populations (D. MacDonald, 2020; Rocke and King, 2020; Saranillio, 2013; Sehdev, 2011; Walia, 2012). The matter of new Canadians being asked to take responsibility for racialized injustice when they are often fleeing violent, racist situations themselves is on the minds, and in the actions, of some of those in charge of pursuing colonial reparations (ibid.). In the Canadian context, we have also witnessed what Pamela Palmater has referred to as "Idle No More 2.0" whereby "a much larger and powerful movement than the last, led by Black and Indigenous peoples and supported by millions of Canadians" is taking place (Macleans, 15 September 2020). Furthermore, migrant peoples have been outwardly speaking about what it means to belong as a non-white Settler in a colonizing Canada (Dhamoon, 2015.; Walia, ibid.).

What sets of challenges and limitations surround the building of anticolonial coalitions between migrant and often racialized communities and Indigenous peoples in both theory and in practice? This question requires ongoing scholarly research and analysis (Amadahy, 2008; see also Land, 2015). Our hope is that recent outcomes will lead to the founding of new partnerships. At best, the building of coalitions in particular stands to open new fields of scholarly research and decolonizing inquiry. We view the following as a set of gestures and activities aimed at critical coalitions building, a process which is sure to open fruitful, decolonizing avenues of research and exploration.

1. Idle No More is a grassroots activist political movement comprised of Indigenous peoples and their non-Indigenous allies initiated in December 2012 to draw attention to Settler colonial, legislative, and treaty rights violations in the Canadian and international contexts. We view Idle No More as a landmark promising development that brought much needed awareness of Indigenous issues and saw non-Indigenous allies joining forces with Indigenous peoples. Since then, we have witnessed other grassroots movements where similar solidarity has occurred, such as support for the Wet'suwet'en peoples in the Westcoast, and rallies on 1 July, Canada's Day, in the last couple of years in recognition of the many children that never returned home from residential schools and of the discoveries of many unmarked mass graves of children who went to those schools.

2. The National Inquiry into Missing and Murdered Indigenous Women and Girls was initiated in December 2015 following a campaign promise made by the current Trudeau government to address an historic issue of colonial violence that had been neglected for over 50 years. In June 2019 the final report of the inquiry was released together with its 231 Cals for Justice. The report found that Indigenous women and girls are more likely to be targets of gendered and sexual violence than other groups in Canada, and for this violence to be rooted in historical colonialism. The Calls for Justice asks for a decolonizing approach to be taken in order to address this epidemic, and for culturally relevant support programs to be adequately funded and delivered across the nation.

3. Harsha Walia (2012, 2013, 2021) has written of border imperialism and the ways in which non-white and migrant Indigenous peoples are invited into a particular version of citizenship and belonging that is inherently state based and colonizing. Like Sharma (2020), she is concerned with the ways in which people become of a place or out of place in white settler colonial societies. Similar to Sunera Thobani (2007: 175) who argues that "state sponsored multiculturalism compels [migrants] to negotiate and comprehend their identities on very narrow grounds . . . foreclosing the possibility of alliances," Walia invites similar questions with respect to challenging

white dominance and global corporate capitalism. We view these discussions as especially productive in drawing attention to borders as a concomitant site of Indigenous genocide, migrant exclusion, and antiblack violence whereby, and as Robyn Maynard (2019: 128) writes, technologies of racism "premised on the social grammar of Black people and nonhumans" and enslaveable were refined (see also Part Four of this volume). We are interested in work that explores the confluence of Settler colonialism and border imperialism (Estes, Yazzie, Denetdale, and Correia, 2021). We wish to centre and explore the possibilities, challenges, and contradictions raised by co-resistances to border imperialism by Black, migrant, and racialized peoples from an Indigenous-centered perspective that refuses the so called "gift" of US-Canadian citizenship, and that illuminates (theoretically and in practice) a more critical, historicized, and decolonizing politics of place, mobility, and political consciousness (Part Four, this volume).

4. Since the occupation of federal offices of the Department of Indigenous and Northern Affairs Canada on 13 April 2016 as reported in our second edition, Black and Indigenous peoples continue to join in solidarity to draw attention to systemic and institutionalized racism, settler colonialism, poverty, and the substandard living conditions and poverty experienced by some of our populations. The "solidarity" to which we are referring is perhaps better defined as a relationship of co-resistance (Simpson, 2017: 211–231; Maynard and Simpson, 2020). We think the building of coalitions between racialized and Indigenous communities such as Black Lives Matter holds enormous potential where shedding light on white supremacy, antiblackness, and our collective experience of Settler colonialism is concerned (see generally King, Navarro, and Smith, 2020). In fact, we concur with Pamela Palmater who writes that "[the] pandemic has shown us all how important it is that we pull together—as grassroots Indigenous peoples, Black Lives Matter and non-Indigenous Canadians—and take care of one another" (Macleans, 15 September 2020). We believe that talking about our differences stands to transform the very way in which we view notions of privilege and disadvantage both theoretically and in practice, offering a much more nuanced and sophisticated understanding about the confluences of race, gender, Settler colonial, and class-based inequality;

5. Lorenzo Veracini (2010) writes of the opportunity to disrupt and even apprehend the history of settler colonial dominance when we start with the basic premise that *Empire* may create settlers but that not all settlers are shaped universally by *Empire*. Clearly, not all migrants are settlers because "settlers are founders of political orders and carry their sovereignty with them, whereas immigrants face a political order that is already constituted" (ibid., 3). Roxanne Dunbar-Ortiz (2021: 20) weighs the important of this matter in US contexts, which we feel carries as much relevance in Canada, writing:

> Immigrants and refugees to the United States do have the option to resist becoming settlers, although in most cases they do not know the history of the United States or the political reality. The US Immigration and Naturalization Services policies based on exclusion make the new immigrant's life precarious, particularly of immigrants of color entering a racial order that renders them suspect already, so they may not want to know the reality or they have a choice and that by default they become settlers.

We recognize the complexity of privilege and disadvantage as this is experienced in relation to other people. We also recognize the significant developments since our second edition textbook with respect to the conversations taking place between Indigenous, Black, racialized, and migrant peoples. We feel some of the most valuable kinds of insight, teaching, and learning will continue to stem from our relationships with each other. These kinds of complexity still need to be addressed in Canada, especially oriented toward the restoration and renewal of respectful relationships.

At worst, working across differences may result in "postures of innocence" (Amadahy and Lawrence, 2009: 105; Fellows and Razack, 1998; Land, 2015), making it difficult or even impossible to develop a new vision of mutual responsibility and coexistence. In reconciling histories of racism and colonial injustice, we feel it will be important to avoid thinking hierarchically about the oppressions between us. This point is made eloquently by Patricia Hill Collins (2003: 332) who writes:

> Once we realize that there are very few pure victims or oppressors, and that each one of us derives . . . penalty and privilege from the multiple systems of oppression that frame our lives, then we will be in a position to see the need for new ways of thought and action . . . [without which we remain] locked in a dangerous dance of competing for attention, resources, and theoretical supremacy.

In contemplating the future of self-determination and colonial reparations, one thing is for certain: racist beliefs and practices continue in Canada despite the last five years of ameliorative efforts to curb their effects. In writing the third edition of this anthology, we have hoped to show how this continues to be so. However, we believe that much can be gained by working across differences, rejuvenating original partnerships and agreements, and endeavouring collectively with all Canadians to combat racism. In the words of Justice Murray Sinclair "The important work of reconciliation is not a one-day affair. As we say, it will take us several generations" (CBC News, 30 September 2022d). These are words that require our tenacity and spirit and determination. The time is now. We cannot afford not to.

Glossary

Acculturation "[P]henomena which result when groups of individuals having different cultures come into continuous first-hand contact, with subsequent changes in the original patterns of either or both groups" (Linton, 1940: 463–4).

Assimilation Defined by Davis Jackson (2002: 74) as "the loss, by an individual, of the markers that served to distinguish him or her as a member of one social group, and the acquisition of traits that allow that person to blend in with, and succeed in, a different social group."

Authenticity A state of being authentic, real, and genuine. Colonial powers have used concepts of authenticity to quantify "Indianness," through, for example, blood quantum. To be recognized as a "real Indian" and therefore to hold Indian status, individuals must fit the qualifications created by the colonizer.

Bill C-3 *The Gender Equity in Indian Registration Act*, popularly known as Bill C-3, came into effect in 31 January 2011 and entitled eligible grandchildren of women who lost status as a result of marrying nonstatus Indian men to be registered as status Indians.

Bill C-31 Bill C-31, *An Act to Amend the Indian Act* became law on 28 June 1985 promising to end over 34 years of blatant sex discrimination directed toward Indigenous women and their male and female children under s.12(1)(b) of the prior *Indian Act* of 1951 (Cannon, 2007).

Bill C-45 An omnibus bill passed through the Canadian Senate on 14 December 2012. It made many changes to several Canadian laws, including removal of protection for waterways, and it infringed on treaty and Indigenous rights. In the fall of 2012, the announcement of the Bill inspired the formation of the Idle No More movement, bringing together Indigenous and non-Indigenous allies to stand up against the Bill and show solidarity with Indigenous peoples.

Blood quantum Descent-based criteria for determining eligibility to membership to a band/nation. The percentage of blood quantum required in order to establish one's Indigeneity, and hence eligibility, varies from band to band (Palmater, 2011).

Border imperialism Border imperialism is characterized by the presumptive "falsehood at once created and then perpetuated by the colonizer to have us believe as Indigenous nations that our movement is between and across nation-states like Canada and the U.S.A. instead of original homelands" (Part Four, this volume), and as Walia (2013: 38) writes, it is characterized by "the entrenchment and reentrenchment of controls against migrants who are displaced as a result of the violences of capitalism and empire, and subsequently forced into precarious labor as a result of state illegalization and systemic social hierarchies."

Chief Theresa Spence The former Chief of the Attawapiskat First Nation in Canada. During her tenure, she became a prominent figure by bringing awareness of the housing and infrastructure crises in her community. Additionally, during the Idle No More movement, she participated in a hunger strike to raise concern about Indigenous issues, and the negative impacts of Bill C-45 on the environment and on Indigenous nations.

Citizenship An assigned social and political designation that applies to individuals and the nation states to which they belong and may hold allegiance. Citizenship is a concept finding its early roots in whiteness, a domain from which enslaved peoples were excluded from historically in not being conceived of as human (Maynard, 2019: 127), it is a social and political designation that is utilized still today by nation states to harden nationalism(s) (Sharma, 2020), to exclude and justify the inhumane treatment of migrants, and to construct Indigenous nations as, for example, "American" or "Canadian" in what amounts to an ahistorical storying of history (see Simpson, 2014: 117–120).

Coming in Defined by Alex Wilson (2008: 197) as the process through which Indigenous peoples "'come in' to an empowered identity that integrates their sexuality, culture, gender and all other aspects of who they understand and know themselves to be."

Colonial imaginary A set of ideas that makes up the colonial narrative. This narrative or imaginary establishes how the colonizer imagines the world and sees own self in it. The colonial imaginary has key racial tropes and root ideas that make sense of and justify the colonial project.

Colonial reparations The process through which amends are made to repair the history and consequences of Settler colonialism which may include, but is not limited to, formal apologies, compensation payments, the return of Indigenous lands and territories, the building of memorials, and so forth (see Hamber, 2006).

Colonial violence In a Canadian context, violence against Indigenous peoples, and women in particular, is "not the result of individual criminal acts (although the acts are indeed criminal and often deeply disturbing) but rather a reflection and function of the longstanding disregard for the lives of the original occupants of the territory, which has served the colonial project since contact" (Lavell-Harvard and Brant, 2016: 3).

Colonialism Defined by Henry and Tator (2006: 348) as: "(1) A process by which a foreign power dominates and exploits an indigenous group by appropriating its land and extracting the wealth from it while using the group as cheap labour. (2) A specific era of European expansion into overseas territories between the sixteenth and twentieth centuries during which European states planted settlements in distant territories and achieved economic, military, political, and cultural hegemony in much of Asia, Africa, and the Americas."

Community resurgence A term referring to Indigenous cultural revitalization and self-determination. As a decolonizing approach, it reconnects Indigenous peoples with their homelands, cultural practices, and restores relationships with their homelands (Corntassel and Bryce, Chapter 29, this volume).

Comprehensive claims policy A Canadian federal policy on Indigenous land claims "based on the assertion of continuing Aboriginal rights and title that are not covered by a treaty or other legal vehicle" (Lawrence, Chapter 15, this volume). As Pasternak (2017: 5) writes: "the Comprehensive Land Claims Policy requires negotiating groups to cede their Aboriginal title and the majority of their territory to the Crown in exchange for 'certainty' about their rights." The CCP requires the "extinguishment of all aboriginal rights and title as a part of a claim settlement" (ibid.: 142).

Critical infrastructure A term used by Spice (Chapter 23, this volume) "to index the interconnected networks of human and other-than-human beings that sustain Indigenus life in mutual relation," a "network [that] stands in stark contrast to the critical insfrastuctures of government and industry—infrastructures that are meant to destroy Indigenous life to make way for capitalist expansion."

Cultural competence The endeavour, typically by service providers (police, courts, health care providers, social workers, teachers, etc.) to acquire knowledge about, or better understand Indigenous peoples' customs cultures and languages (Cannon, 2012; 2018). Under a current regime of cultural competence, Settler populations are not expected to know about, transform, and/or remedy systemic inequities, to realize and nuance their own complicity and responsibility within hierarchies of Settler colonial power, or reconcile a process of identity making that is rooted in the perception of Indigenous inferiority and Settler superiority (ibid.). "Cultural competence" can be understood as a Settler re-enactment of lands appropriation, entitlement, and futurity (ibid.), where the objective is to learn as much as possible about Indigenous peoples leading to "a superficial reading of differences that makes power relations invisible" (Jeffery and Nelson, 2009: 98; also see Razack, 1998).

Cultural fundamentalism St Denis (2004: 36) suggests that "cultural revitalization and restoration" has achieved "fundamentalist status" in having become "the primary goal of those involved in promoting Aboriginal education." Cultural fundamentalism, St Denis (ibid.) writes: "encourages Aboriginal people to assert their authenticity and to accept cultural nationalism and cultural pride as solutions to systemic inequality; ironically, this helps keep racial domination intact."

Cultural revitalization A movement in education and/or policy that "calls for the celebration, affirmation, and revitalization of Indian cultures and peoples" (St Denis, 2004: 35). St Denis outlines the way in which an "adherence to cultural revitalization encourages the valorization of cultural authenticity and cultural purity among aboriginal people [helping] to produce the notion and the structure of a cultural hierarchy" (ibid.: 37).

Cultural safety Originally "a concept used to express an approach to healthcare that recognizes the contemporary conditions of Aboriginal people which result from their post-contact history" (Brascoupé and Waters, 2009; see also Polaschek, 1998). Examples of these conditions include social determinants of health such as poverty, poor water quality, stress, and identity-related issues. Culturally safe services delivery requires the participation of non-Indigenous peoples in terms of knowing about, interrogating, and actively dismantling negative health indicators and outcomes, including histories of racism, Settler colonialism, and a Settler entitlement to lands.

Cultural sensitivity An approach to remedying and/or undertaking services delivery that creates a Self/Other binary where Indigenous peoples are thought there to be helped, tolerated, if not better understood and culturally managed as different and deficit instead of calling on service providers to question their own entitlement to lands and belonging, the meaning of culturally safe services provision, and to work in activist ways to improve disparate and negative social and economic conditions.

Culturalism A concept frequently employed in the context of social life and services delivery "to represent the attribution of minority groups' cultural backgrounds characteristic—including behaviours, traditions, problems, barriers—to their cultural backgrounds" (Jeffery and Nelson, 2009: 92). Jeffery and Nelson (ibid.) define culturalism as "a particular form of essentialism whereby the so-called essential characteristics of a group are attributed to the groups' cultural characteristics, performances and forms of knowledge." As Nelson (2009: 27) writes, culturalism typically "provides ways for professionals to engage with racial difference that do not require a systematic rethinking of institutionalized racism."

Cycle of crime Multiple and interrelated risk factors and symptoms of trauma –such as residential schools, structural racism, and intergenerational trauma- increase the risk of crime within Indigenous families and communities over generations (Monchalin, Chapter 21, this volume).

Dead Indians The "stereotypes and clichés that North America has conjured up out of experience and out of its collective imaginings and fears" that are intent on disappearing both "Live" and "Legal" Indians (King in Chapter 4 in this volume).

Decolonizing research As defined by Johnston, McGregor, and Restoule, in Chapter 19 in this volume, "decolonizing research means designing and carrying out research in ways that honour Indigenous knowledges and communities rather than privilege colonizing institutions, such as the academy."

Democratic racism "[A]n ideology in which two conflicting set of values are made congruent with each other. Commitments to democratic principles such as justice, equality, and fairness conflict but coexist with attitudes and behaviours that include negative feelings about minority groups, differential treatment, and discrimination against them" (Henry and Tator, 2006: 22).

Dispossession   "[T]he forcible and relentless . . . theft of [Indigenous] territories, and the implementation of legislation and policies designed to effect their total disappearance as peoples . . ." (Lawrence, 2002: 23–4).

Doctrine of Discovery   Defined by Lindberg (2010: 94) as "a dogmatic body of shared theories . . . pertaining to the right-fulness and righteousness of settler belief systems and the supremacy of the institutions (legal, constitutional, governmental) that are based on those belief systems. The shared theories have been predicated on a notion of 'first' or 'discovery' as original peoples/Indigenous peoples in their own territories did not share settler theory or understanding or settler legal, economic, or governmental institutions and were deconstructed and non-existing in order to allow for 'rightful' and righteous settlement of Indigenous peoples' lands. The Doctrine has been utilized as a rationale to take Indigenous lands on the basis of Indigenous peoples' constructed and Doctrinally defined deficiencies and inhumanity."

Environmental racism   Refers to "environmental policies, practices, or directives that disproportionately disadvantage individuals, groups, or communities (intentionally or unintentionally) based on race or colour" (Bullard, quoted in Waldron, 2018: 12).

Environmental/water security   A traditional worldview held by Indigenous peoples to commit to sustainable economies wherein accessibility to safe water and protection of Mother Earth are secured.

Failed consent   Refers broadly to any of the purposeful and principled actions employed by Indigenous peoples in their refusal to consent to Settler colonialism's eliminatory logic, including have their lands stolen and territories remade, remapped, and reconfigured, and as Audra Simpson (2016: 238) writes "their lives controlled, and their stories told for them."

Feeling citizenship   In the context of membership to her Mohawk nation, Audra Simpson (Chapter 16, this volume) distinguishes "feeling citizenship" from alternative conceptions of identity that rooted in and stem from laws established by the state. Feeling citizenship refers to "an affective sense of being Mohawk of Kanawà:ke, in spite of the lack of recognition that some might unjustly experience" (ibid.).

Fossil-fuel infrastructure   An economic system concerned with energy wrested from hydrocarbon materials found in the earth's core, profit making, and the destructive environmental practices attached to that profit making.

Gdoo-naaganinaa   A precolonial treaty known as "Our Dish" between Nishnaabeg and Haudenosaunee Confederacies; a symbol and protocol of diplomatic, ecological, and sovereign relationships (Simpson, 2008).

Gendered colonial violence   Violence against Indigenous women must be understood through an intersectional analysis of gender, race, sexuality, and colonialism. "In a nation founded on the suffering and violent oppression of Indigenous peoples generally and the targeting of Indigenous women specifically, it is not surprisingly that racist and sexist beliefs coalesce and harden, which continues to encourage the persecution of our women and to justify a lack of response or concern" (Lavell-Harvard and Brant, 2016: 5).

Gendered violence   Any act of violence directed at a woman due to her gender that can result in physical, sexual, or psychological harm or suffering (United Nations, 1993).

Healing and wellness   Relations referring to the "interconnectivity and relational supports, which enable each person to live a good life, following and applying [Indigenous] laws. . . . When there is an imbalance in a person's life, healing is required" (Tagalik, 2015: 30). Million (2013: 105) suggests that healing is a "prerequisite to [Indigenous] self-determination" requiring colonial reparations and social-structural transformation. She writes furthermore: "The space of our medicalized diagnosis as victims of trauma is not a site wherein self-determination is practiced or defined . . . The site and projects that define and manage our trauma must be seen in light of biopower, and what it produces . . . In order to heal what is imagined as past aggression must be reconciled; this view pictures the state as presently humane and benefic" (ibid.: 150, 156).

Heteronormativity   A concept defined as "the notion that heterosexuality is the only 'natural' orientation" (Schick, 2004: 249).

Heteropatriarchy   The term heteropatriarchy originates in 1980s queer studies literature related to understanding the way that heterosexuality is normalized as a mode of gender oppression (see Mariedaughter, 1986; Penelope, 1986; Trebilcot, 1988). Heteropatriarchy assumes that we will as Indians marry members of the opposite sex (Cannon, 2019). It is also premised on a patrilineal model of descent reckoning common to Europeans in the mid-nineteenth century. Under the patrilineal model, a person's identity is determined through the male line of descent.

Historic/modern treaties   Lawrence (Chapter 15, this volume) distinguishes between historic and modern treaties. The former are agreements between Indigenous nations and the Crown entered into during the eighteenth century wherein "the question of title has never been addressed." The latter "otherwise known as land claims agreements, are negotiated through the comprehensive claims policy which came into existence in 1973 as a result of the *Calder* decision."

Historical trauma   The "cumulative wounds inflicted on First Nations people over their lifetime and across generations, and which often resulted in debilitating social, psychological, and physical conditions" (Valaskakis, Dion Stout, and Guimond, 2009: 4).

Idle No More Movement   An ongoing movement that started in 2012 by four women, as a response to Bill C-45 of the

Conservative federal government. It united Indigenous and non-Indigenous groups worldwide to bring awareness to the systemic injustices suffered by Indigenous nations of Canada.

Imperialism   The domination of another land and people through economic and political control established by violent or coercive force. Edward Said (1994: 9) writes: "(n)either imperialism nor colonialism is a simple act of accumulation and acquisition. Both are supported and perhaps even impelled by impressive ideological formations that include notions that certain territories and people *require* and beseech domination."

Indian   The label "Indian" has been an external descriptor, meaningless to the Indigenous peoples of the Americas prior to colonization. As a common identity, it was imposed on Indigenous populations when Settler governments in North America usurped the right to define Indigenous citizenship, reducing the members of hundreds of extremely different nations, ethnicities, and language to a common raced identity as "Indian" (Lawrence, 2002: 23).

Indian Act   Defined by Henry, Tator, Mattis, and Rees (1998: 130) as "the legislation that has intruded on the lives and cultures of status Indians more than any other law. Though amended repeatedly, the act's fundamental provisions have scarcely changed. They give the state powers that range from defining how one is born or naturalized into 'Indian' status to administering the estate of an Aboriginal person after death . . . the act [sic] gave Parliament control over Indian political structures, landholding patterns, and resource and economic development. It covered almost every important aspect of the daily lives of Aboriginal peoples on reserve. The overall effect was to subject Aboriginal people to the almost unfettered rule of federal bureaucrats. The act [sic] imposed non-Aboriginal forms on traditional governance, land-holding practices, and cultural practices."

Indian Defense League   An Indigenous political movement initiated in 1926 by Chief Clinton Rickard (Tuscarora) and based on the activism of Deskehah (Levi General, Cayuga), the Indian Defense League of America (IDLA) was concerned with the inherent rights of Indigenous peoples including unrestricted border passage between the United States and Canada (see Jolene Rickard, 1995).

Indian Status   A legislative categorization referring to those who are registered and federally recognized under Canada's *Indian Act* and eligible for territorial, provincial, and federal services and programs.

Indigenous knowledge   Indigenous knowledge includes systems of thought, ways of being, ways of knowing, and ways of thinking that are held and developed by Indigenous nations and peoples. There is not one Indigenous knowledge system, but often, Indigenous systems of knowledge hold key similarities rooted philosophical ideas and understandings about humanity and the world.

Indigenous mothering   Lavell-Harvard and Anderson, in Chapter 13, this volume, define Indigenous mothering as

practices based upon empowering traditional roles centred on strength, independence, authority, communal responsibility, and resistance to colonialism.

Indigenous nationhood   A constructed sense of community that predates Settler colonialism. Indigenous nationhood contains a shared language, culture, territory, and principles of kinship relations and political organization (Sunseri, 2011: 36–43).

Indigenous relationality   An Indigenous system of thought that views all human and non-human beings to be interconnected. This conception of relationality leads Indigenous peoples to view themselves as caretakers of Mother Earth and all ecosystems.

Indigenous research   A type of research that employs Indigenous ways of knowing and is closely connected to Indigenous peoples' realities, experiences, traditions, and their empowerment.

Indigenous sustainable self-determination   Refers to "both an individual and community-driven process where evolving indigenous livelihood, food security, community governance, relationships to homelands and the natural world, and ceremonial life can be practiced today" (Corntassel and Bryce, Chapter 29, this volume).

Indigenous-Settler relations   Refers in general to the relationships (historic and contemporary, present and absent) held between Settler and Indigenous populations, including white Settlers, and sometimes, "appellants facing a political order that is already constituted" (Veracini, 2010: 3) or those described by Walia (2013: 126, emphasis in original) as: "Indigenous to their own lands, but often displaced due to Orientalist crusading and corporate plundering . . . thrown into capitalism's pool of labor and, in a cruel twist, violently inserted into the political economy of genocide: *stolen labor on stolen land.*"

Intellectual imperialism   A project whereby Western scientific thought is portrayed as the only legitimate, ultimate truth, and limits the validity of all other non-Western knowledges, including Indigenous ones (Absolon, Chapter 20, this volume).

Institutional racism   "[R]acial discrimination that derives from individuals carrying out the dictates of others who are prejudiced or of a prejudiced society" (Henry and Tator, 2006: 352).

Kinship   Refers in general to the means through which people become linked together socially, whether through the mother's line (as with matrilineal societies), the father's line (as with patrilineal societies), clan-based systems of social organization structured by matrilineal or patrilineal descent; and sometimes, through the division of labour in society itself.

Land-based/water-based cultural practices   Refers to Indigenous practices of self-determination which (re) establish "longstanding, reciprocal relationships with the natural world, as well as by transmitting knowledge and everyday cultural practices to future generations" (Corntassel and Bryce, Chapter 29, this volume).

Legal assimilation Legal assimilation is the word that is used to describe the act of losing legal status of *Indian Act* status in Canada (Cannon, 2007: 38).

Mandaluyong Declaration A statement provided by a group of Indigenous women at the Global Conference on Indigenous Women, Climate Change and REDD in Legend Villas, Philippines. The declaration outlines the negative impacts of environmental injustice on Indigenous communities, in particular women, and proposes a number of actions Indigenous women can take collectively to mitigate such effects.

Matrilocal/matrilineal societies Refers to kinship organization and residence patterns organized through the female line of descent. Women in the vast majority of matrilineal and matrilocal societies hold economic and political power unknown in patriarchal societies.

Métis A Nation or People with specific roots and histories rooted in kinship-based forms of nationalism, peoplehood, and precolonial relationships in Canada (Andersen, 2014: 91).

Missing and Murdered Indigenous Women and Girls (MMIWG) An inquiry commissioned by the government of Canada in 2016 to study the epidemic of violence against Indigenous women and girls in Canada, by analysing its roots and proposing recommendations to address it.

Modern Indigenous leader Defined by Calliou and Wesley-Esquimaux, in Chapter 26 in this volume, as someone who is intelligent, wise, ethical, able to adapt to the constant and rapid changes, and willing to work for the welfare of Indigenous communities.

Multiculturalism Defined by Henry and Tator (2006: 351) as "an ideology that holds that racial, cultural, religious, and linguistic diversity is an integral, beneficial, and necessary part of Canadian society and identity. It is an official policy operating in various social institutions and levels of government, including the federal government." As Porter (1999: 158) suggests, multiculturalism would have us believe that Indigenous peoples ought to be represented and/or dealt with as a component of ethnic diversity—as racialized groups—but never as sovereign Indigenous nations. As a model of education, multiculturalism "is centered on unifying all peoples in the nation-state" (Grande, 2004: 47). Within this model of education, there is very little room to call attention to matters of lands appropriation and dispossession, a truly decolonizing education, or to centre a conversation about Indigenous nationhood and futurity (Cannon, 2018). The effect is also to create the impression that Indigenous peoples are "of culture not mind" (Cote-Meek, 2010).

Nationhood/citizenship/membership Audra Simpson (2014: 27) defines nationhood as "both a traditional and contemporary form of political organization . . . Nationhood is a construct . . . that is a cultural and political "right" and a "good", and a matter of principle rather than procedure." Furthermore, Simpson distinguishes between citizenship and membership

to an Indigenous nation, in particular her Mohawk nation. Membership is an institutional and legal recognition to an Indigenous nation by enlistment to a band. Citizenship is "socially and politically recognized in the everyday life of the community" (Simpson, Chapter 16, this volume).

Nation-building The process of building and maintaining a nation. It can refer to Indigenous nation-building processes following from colonialism, or to the process of colonial nation-building. According to Lawrence (2002), nation-building is central to the maintenance of Settler colonialism. As mythology, it refers to the way in which "Canada maintains its posture of being 'innocent' of racism and genocide" (ibid.: 26).

Patriarchy Refers to the assumption that "heads of state must be male and male voices rightfully dominate public/private spaces" and to "male dominance in personal, political, cultural, and social life, and to patriarchal families where the law of the father prevails" (Code, 2000: 378).

Peoplehood A term referring to Indigenous peoples who find their origins and ethnogenesis not in histories of racialization, but in a distinct constellation of land-based, historical, and pre-colonial relationships. Andersen (Chapter 6, this volume) describes a peoplehood way of thinking about identity, nationhood, and events at once tied to and embodied in the land. He writes of Métis peoplehood: "I'm Métis because I belong (and claim allegiance) to a set of Métis memories, territories, and leaders who challenged and continue to challenge colonial authorities' unitary claims to land and society" (2011: 165).

Politics of recognition A liberal pluralist rights-based strategy premised on Canadian state's recognition of self-determination that does not reflect inherent Indigenous rights and responsibilities to their homelands, or Indigenous cultural practices (Coulthard, 2014).

Race card rhetoric Starblanket and Hunt, in Chapter 22, this volume, define race card rhetoric as "the assumption that individuals who are trying to name or identify prejudice and discrimination are attempting to use their identity as a strategy to gain an advantage, or at the very least, that they are trying to bring the issue of race into contexts where it does not belong. Yet, the very notion of a 'race card' functions as a strategy to contain and discredit efforts to account for the implications of past and present experiences of racism."

Racialization The process by which people are formed into a racial category, and through which racism is justified by representations of these groups. "Sociologists refer to this process, whereby a heterogeneous, linguistically diverse population is singled out for different (and often unequal) treatment in Canada, as racialization" (Li, 1990: 7).

Racism "[T]he assumptions, attitudes, beliefs, and behaviours of individuals as well as the institutional policies, process, and practices that flow from those understandings" (Henry and Tator, 2006: 5).

Recolonization It refers to the current discrimination, marginalization, land destruction and dispossession of Indigenous peoples through globalization and neo-liberalism (McGregor, Chapter 24, this volume).

Reconciliation Defined in the Canadian context by Coulthard (2014) as threefold: (1) "the diversity of individual or collective practices that Indigenous people undertake to re-establish a positive "relation to self" in situations where this relation has been damaged or distorted by some form of symbolic or structural violence" (ibid.: 106–7); (2) "the act of restoring estranged or damaged social and political relationships" (ibid.: 107), and (3) "rendering *consistent* Indigenous assertions of nationhood with the state's unilateral assertion of sovereignty over Native people's lands and populations" (ibid.: emphasis added).

Refusal Audra Simpson (2017: 19) draws ethnographic attention to the ways in which Indigenous life "refused, did not consent to, and still refuses to be folded into" a Settler colonial based approach to recognition politics (i.e. the ruse of consent) defining refusal as an "option for producing –and maintaining –alternative structures of thought, politics and traditions away from and in critical relationship to states."

Relational accountability A central principle of Indigenous research methodologies, whereby Indigenous researchers are expected to be accountable and responsible not only to research participants and communities, but to the lands and all relations (Johnston, McGregor, and Restoule, Chapter 19, this volume).

Relationality A term referring in general to the exchanges taking place historically and at present between Settler–Indigenous and Indigenous–Indigenous populations that relinquishes an exclusively judicial or colonial-based policy way of thinking about these relationships (Andersen, Chapter 6, this volume).

Representation The way in which a person, place, or thing is commonly represented by another.

Residential schooling A colonial system of schooling enforced on Indigenous nations aimed at effecting cultural genocide and assimilation on children, many of whom were forcibly removed and abducted from their families and communities. The residential school experience is characterized by forced removal from families; systemic and ritualized physical and sexual assault; spiritual, psychological, and emotional abuse; and malnutrition, inhumane living conditions, death, and murder.

Restitution Refers to "the return of Indigenous lands and resources and power to determine their uses" (Joseph, 2008: 212). As Joseph (ibid.: 218) writes: "Restitution assumes the continuing co-existence of the harmed and the perpetrator of the harm, although with an altered balance of power. Restitution involves the restoration of what was taken to right the imbalance caused by injustice."

Resurgence "Regeneration of power gives us the strength to continue to fight; restoring connection to each other gives us the social support that is crucial to human fulfillment; reconnection to our own memory roots us in a culture; and reconnection to spirit gives us a strong and whole mind. These are the elements of resurgence" (Alfred, 2005: 256).

Risk factors of crime Social, economic, and political conditions "related to the victimization and incarceration affecting Indigenous peoples . . . The factors include, but are not limited to, high levels of unemployment, low incomes, poverty, overcrowded, disorganized, and substandard living conditions, social exclusion and marginalization, racism and discrimination, lack of cultural identity and pride, alcohol and drug addiction or misuse . . ." (Monchalin, 2016: 146).

Romanticism The representation of noble, innocent, and idealized "Indians." Often romantic colonial images have "Indians" disappearing through their innocence.

Self-government Self-government is based on an a priori concept of governance as defined through Canadian federal policy and the Department of Indian and Northern Development. It is often understood to stand in lesser and inferior relation to self-determination, which refers in general to an inherent set of rights given to Indigenous peoples by the Creator.

Self-government policy Refers to a policy created by the federal government of Canada in response to constitutional changes. Lawrence, in Chapter 15, this volume, states that this policy articulates that "Aboriginal laws and traditional jurisdictions cannot be part of negotiations relating to self-government", ultimately constraining Indigenous rights and title.

Settler colonialism A distinct form of colonialism that is characterized by lands acquisition and dispossession that seeks to destroy and then replace the original Indigenous inhabitants with Settler populations who in the first historical instance and still today are beneficiaries and claim jurisdiction over them and their territories (see Wolfe, 2006).

Settler fragility Refers to a series of reactions and behaviours resulting from any interrogation of Settler colonialism, complicity, and colonial injustices today. Like "white fragility" defined by Robin Diangelo (2018: 103), Settler fragility refers to a reactionary state where even a minimum amount of stress or discomfort "becomes intolerable, triggering a range of defensive moves [including] outward displays of emotions such as anger, fear, and guilt and behaviors such as argumentation, silence, and leaving the stress-inducing situation."

Settler violence A specific form of violence, often genocidal in nature, that occurs in ongoing colonial contexts. It refers to the systemized ideological, political, social, symbolic, spiritual, military, and state violence enacted with impunity by Settlers on Indigenous nations and individuals.

Sexism Refers to "a term coined in the late 1960s to refer to social arrangements, policies, language, and practices enacted by men or women that express a systematic, often institutionalized belief that men are superior, women inferior" (Code, 2000: 441).

Sisters in Spirit A research initiative conducted by the Native Women's Association of Canada on the case of the Missing and Murdered Indigenous Women of Canada.

Social determinants of health Environmental factors linked to Settler colonialism such as poverty, unemployment, educational and housing disparities, unclean water, and nutritional concerns, which all have a profound effect on health (Reading and Waters, 2009: 17).

Sovereignty A term employed by nation-states (e.g. Canada, United States of America, etc) to claim the "highest source of legitimate power for the people", political authority, and jurisdiction over a territory and all the individuals residing as part of the political community therein (Russell, 2021: 10; also see Asch, 2014: 101–2).

Status and nonstatus Indians Individuals of Indigenous heritage are categorized as either status or nonstatus Indians in a process that is commonly understood as federal recognition. As Lawrence (2012) states: "in Canada, historically, there is only one means of recognition of Indianness—to be registered as a status Indian within the meaning of the Indian Act" (2012: 8). Furthermore, "*Individuals* are non-status for a variety of reasons. Either their ancestors once held Indian status but lost it due to certain regulations under the Indian Act, or they never acquired it because their ancestors for various reasons were left off the list of band members developed by Indian agents" (ibid.).

Stereotype Representations created by a dominant group to typecast and classify the "Other." These stereotypical representations, whether "positive" or "negative," are used to justify objectification, control, and oppression by the dominant group (for example, "Native people are lazy"). This hyper-disseminated stereotype works to justify the systematic impoverishment of Indigenous nations by blaming Indigenous people for the economic conditions created by the colonizer.

Structural racism "[I]nequalities rooted in the system-wide operation of a society that exclude[s] substantial numbers of members of particular groups from significant participation in major social institutions" (Henry and Tator, 2006: 352).

Systemic racism While racism is often equated with abhorrent individual prejudice or ignorance, systemic racism is a form of power that controls power relations between dominant and oppressed racial groups. In the case of Canadian colonialism, the manufacturing of the racial group "Indian," occurred alongside the creation of racist political, social, and economic systems used to maintain white Settler dominance and the control of lands.

The legal billy club Refers to the legal action taken by industry and Settler governments to acquire and impose enforcement orders, normally in the from of court injunctions, that in turn allow police, paramilitaries, and armies to criminalize Indigenous land defenders, disavow Aboriginal title, and restore the unilateral assertion of Settler Crown sovereignty and the Doctrine of Discovery (see Manuel, Chapter 30, this volume).

The Other The theoretical term used to refer to the creation of an us/them binary, where normality is understood in the "us" and the abnormality, sub-humanity, or inferiority is understood as belonging to "them"—the Other.

Treaty mythologies Interpretations produced by Settlers and the Canadian state about treaties; such interpretations of treaties negatively impact Indigenous peoples because they ignore the ongoing land dispossession and other effects of Settler colonialism.

Two-Spirit A term describing an Indigenous person whose gender and/or sexuality defies simple either/or binary categorization, who is gay and Indigenous (Gilley, 2006), or who possesses two spirits.

Ukwehuwé In the Onyota'a:ka language (Oneida, People of the Standing Stone) a word used to refer to "original people"; the "first people" or "real people" (also see Hill, 2017: 290).

Unknown and unstated paternity The current Indigenous Affairs and Northern Development Canada's policy in regard to eligibility to Indian Status, whereby the Registrar of Indigenous Affairs denies Indian Status registration to those who lack a father's signature on their birth certificate (Gehl, Chapter 14, in this volume).

Urbanity/Indigeneity binarism The tendency to view Indigenous peoples as either urban- or reserve-based and, in binary fashion, the imaging of both spheres as separate and distinct, with "reservation Indians depicted as the 'real' Natives and urban Indians depicted as hopelessly assimilated and alienated from their cultures" (Smith, 2008: 204; also see Ramirez, 2007).

White Settler society A white Settler society is one that is established through processes of colonialism and genocide effected by Europeans on non-European soil (Razack, 2002: 2–3). "Settler states in the Americas are founded on, and maintained through, policies of direct extermination, displacement, or assimilation" (Lawrence and Dua, 2005: 123).

Wise practices model A model developed by Calliou and Wesley-Esquimaux (Chapter 26, this volume) of Indigenous community development that proposes "locally-appropriate actions, tools, principles, or decisions that contribute significantly to the development of sustainable and equitable conditions."

Bibliography

Acoose, Janice. 1995. *Iskwewak-Kah'Ki Yaw Ni Wahkomakanak: Neither Indian Princesses nor Easy Squaws*. Toronto: Women's Press.

Alfred, Taiaiake (Gerald). 2005. *Wasáse: Indigenous Pathways of Action and Freedom*. Peterborough: Broadview Press.

Alfred, Taiaiake (Gerald). 1995. *Heeding the Voices of Our Ancestors: Kahnawake Mohawk Politics and the Rise of Native Nationalism*. Toronto: Oxford University Press.

Alfred, Taiaiake, and Jeff Corntassel. 2005. "Being Indigenous: Resurgences Against Contemporary Colonialism," *Government and Opposition* 40 (4): 597–614.

Ahmed, Sara. 2005. "The Politics of Bad Feeling," *Australian Critical Race and Whiteness Studies Association Journal* 1: 72–85.

Amadahy, Zainab. 2008. "Listen, Take Direction and Stick Around: A Roundtable on Relationship-Building in Indigenous Solidarity Work," *Briarpatch* June/July: 24–29.

Amadahy, Zainab, and Bonita Lawrence. 2009. "Indigenous Peoples and Black People in Canada: Settlers or Allies?" pp. 105–136 in Arlo Kempf, ed., *Breaching the Colonial Contract: Anti-Colonialism in the US and Canada*. New York: Springer.

Amnesty International. 2014. *Violence against Indigenous Women and Girls in Canada: A Summary of Amnesty International's Concerns and Call to Action*. Available at www.amnesty.ca.

Andersen, Chris. 2011. "'I'm Métis, What's Your Excuse?': On the Optics and the Ethics of Misrecognition of Métis in Canada," *Aboriginal Policy Studies* 1 (2): 161–165.

Andersen, Chris. 2014. *Métis: Race, Recognition, and the Struggle for Indigenous Peoplehood*. Vancouver: UBC Press.

Anderson, Kim. 2000. *A Recognition of Being: Reconstructing Native Womanhood*. Toronto: Second Story Press.

APTN News. 2016. "During suicide debate Justice Minister says it's time for First Nations to shed Indian Act 'shackles'," *APTN News*, 13 April. Available at http://aptn.ca/news/2016/04/13/during-first-nation-suicide-debate-justice-minister-says-its-time-for-first-nations-to-shed-indian-act-shackles/

Asch, Michael. 2014. *On Being Here to Stay: Treaties and Aboriginal Rights in Canada*. Toronto, ON: University of Toronto Press.

Association of Canadian Deans of Education. 2010. *Accord on Indigenous Education*. Association of Canadian Deans of Education. Available at http://www.csse-scee.ca/docs/acde/acde_accord_indigenousresearch_en.pdf.

Bastien, Elizabeth. 2008. "Matrimonial Real Property Solutions," *Canadian Woman Studies* 26 (3 & 4): 90–93.

Bellfy, Phil. 2013. "The Anishnaabeg of Bawating: Indigenous People Look at the Canada-US Border," pp. 199–222 in Kyle Conway and Timothy Pasch, eds, *Beyond the Border: Tensions across the Forty-Ninth Parallel in the Great Plains and Prairies*. McGill-Queens University Press.

Blackstock, Cindy. 2007. "Residential Schools: Did They Really Close or Just Morph into Child Welfare?" *Indigenous Law Journal* 6 (1): 71–78.

Borrows, John. 1997. "Wampum at Niagara: The Royal Proclamation, Canadian Legal History, and Self-Government," pp. 155–172 in Michael Asch, ed., *Aboriginal and Treaty Rights in Canada: Essays on Law, Equality, and Respect for Difference*. Vancouver: UBC Press.

Bourgeois, Robyn. 2015. "Colonial Exploitation: The Canadian State and the Trafficking of Indigenous Women and Girls in Canada," *UCLA Law Review* 62 (6): 1426–1463.

Brascoupé, Simon, and Catherine Waters. 2009. "Cultural Safety: Exploring the Applicability of the Concept of Cultural Safety to Aboriginal Health and Community Wellness," *International Journal of Indigenous Health* 5 (2): 6–41.

Browne, Annette J., and Jo-Ann Fiske. 2001. "First Nations Women's Encounters with Main Stream Health Care Services," *Western Journal of Nursing Research* 23 (2): 126–147.

Canadian Bar Association. 2022. "Reconciling the contradictions in Aboriginal and Indigenous law," *Canadian Bar Association*, 30 September. Available at https://www.nationalmagazine.ca/en-ca/articles/law/in-depth/2022/reconciliation-requires-us-to-reconcile-contradictions-in-our-law

Cannon, Martin J. 2019. *Men, Masculinity, and the Indian Act*. Vancouver: University of British Columbia Press.

Cannon, Martin J. 2018. "Teaching and Learning Reparative Education in Settler Colonial and Post-TRC Canada," *Canadian Journal of Native Education* 40 (1): 164–181.

Cannon, Martin J. 2014. "Race Matters: Sexism, Indigenous Sovereignty, and McIvor," *Canadian Journal of Women and the Law* 26 (1): 23–50.

Cannon, Martin J. 2012. "Changing the Subject in Teacher Education: Centering Indigenous, Diasporic, and Settler Colonial Relations," *Cultural and Pedagogical Inquiry* 4 (2): 21–37.

Cannon, Martin J. 2008. "Revisiting Histories of Gender-Based Exclusion and the New Politics of Indian Identity." A Research Paper for the National Centre for First Nations Governance.

Cannon, Martin J. 2007. "Revisiting Histories of Legal Assimilation, Racialized Injustice, and the Future of Indian Status in Canada," pp. 35–48 in Jerry White, Erik Anderson, Wendy Cornet, and Dan Beavon, eds, *Aboriginal Policy Research: Moving Forward, Making a Difference, Volume V*. Toronto: Thompson Educational Publishing.

Carter, Sarah. 1997. *Capturing Women: The Manipulation of Cultural Imagery in Canada's Prairie West*. McGill-Queen's University Press.

CBC News. 2022a. "Senate committee presents plans for peaceful fishery that sidelines DFO for Indigenous groups," 12 July. Available at https://www.cbc.ca/news/canada/nova-scotia/senate-committee-presents-plan-for-peaceful-fishery-1.6518449

CBC News. 2022b. "July 1 celebrations need to evolve, attendees at Saskatoon Cancel Canada Day event say," *CBC News*, 2 July. Available at https://www.cbc.ca/news/canada/saskatoon/canada-day-celebrations-saskatoon-1.6508752

CBC News. 2022c. "State of emergency declared amid water shortage in Oneida Nation of the Thames," *CBCNews*, 20 December. Available at https://www.cbc.ca/news/canada/london/state-of-emergency-declared-amid-water-shortage-in-oneida-nation-of-the-thames-1.6692141

CBC News. 2022d. "On the National Day for Truth and Reconciliation, Murray Sinclair challenges Canadians to be mindful year-round," *CBC News*, 30 September. Available at https://www.cbc.ca/news/politics/nationa-day-truth-reconciliation-canada-1.6600748

CBC News 2021a. "Racism, prejudice contributed to Joyce Echaquan's death in hospital, Quebec coroner's inquiry concludes," *CBC News*, 1 October. Available at https://www.cbc.ca/news/canada/montreal/joyce-echaquan-systemic-racism-quebec-government-1.6196038

CBC News 2021b. "Why have Indigenous communities been hit harder by the pandemic than the population at large?," *CBC News*, 25 April. Available at https://www.cbc.ca/news/canada/newfoundland-labrador/apocalypse-then-indigenous-covid-1.5997774

CBC News 2021c. "Kanien'kehá:ka teen shares 'coming out' journey with love and support from family," *CBC News*, 21 June. Available at https://www.cbc.ca/news/indigenous/kanien-kehá-ka-teen-journey-pride-month-1.6069871

CBC News 2021d. "Sixties scoop class action settlement to move forward after delays," *CBC News*, 1 February. Available at https://www.cbc.ca/news/indigenous/sixties-scoop-settlement-moves-forward-1.5893774

CBC News 2021e. "MMIWG national action plan criticized by Indigenous leaders in B.C.," *CBC News*, 3 June. Available at https://www.cbc.ca/news/canada/british-columbia/indigenous-leaders-criticize-mmiwg-action-plan-1.6051920

CBC News. 2021f. "Remains of 215 children found buried at former B.C. residential schools, First Nations say," *CBC News*, May 27. Available at https://www.cbc.ca/news/canada/british-columbia/tk-emlúps-te-secwépemc-215-children-former-kamloops-indian-residential-school-1.6043778

CBC News. 2021g. "'We don't want anymore tears': First Nations urge Ottawa to boost mental health spending." *CBC News*. 17 April. Available athttps://www.cbc.ca/news/politics/indigenous-mental-health-resources-federal-budget-2021-1.5989070

CBC News. 2019a. "Indian status could be extended to hundreds of thousands as Bill S-3 provisions come into force," *CBC News*, 15 August. Availabe at https://www.cbc.ca/news/indigenous/bill-s-3-indian-act-sex-discrimination-1.5249008

CBC News. 2017. "Ignored to death: Brian Sinclair's death caused by racism, inquest inadequate, group says," *CBC News*, 18 September. Available at https://www.cbc.ca/news/canada/manitoba/winnipeg-brian-sinclair-report-1.4295996

CBC News. 2016a. "First Nations leaders call for action from Justin Trudeau on Attawapiskat suicide crisis," *CBC News*, 8 May. Available at http://www.cbc.ca/news/canada/sudbury/first-nation-leaders-seek-action-1.3571709

CBC News. 2016b. "Justin Trudeau takes pointed questions from Indigenous youth," *CBC News*, 27 April. Available at http://www.cbc.ca/news/politics/justin-trudeau-indigenous-youth-pointed-questions-1.3555042

CBC News. 2016c. "Idle No More, Black Lives Matter protesters demand action on Attawapiskat suicide crisis," *CBC News*, 13 April. Available at http://www.cbc.ca/news/canada/toronto/protesters-occupy-indigenous-northern-affairs-office-1.3533662

CBC News. 2016d. "Desperation in Attawapiskat, where First Nation leaders fear for the worst," *CBC News*, 12 April. Available at http://www.cbc.ca/news/canada/sudbury/attawapiskat-suicide-emergency-going-forward-1.3531531

CBC News. 2016e. "Wikwemikong Josphine Mandamin honoured for conservation excellence," *CBC News*, 26 February. Available at https://www.cbc.ca/news/canada/thunder-bay/josephine-mandamin-ontario-award-1.3465895

CBC News. 2014. "Stephen Harper's comments on missing, murdered aboriginal women show 'lack of respect'," *CBC News*, 19 December. Available at http://www.cbc.ca/news/indigenous/stephen-harper-s-comments-on-missing-murdered-aboriginal-women-show-lack-of-respect-1.2879154

Chaat Smith, Paul. 2009. *Everything You Know about Indians Is Wrong*. Minneapolis, MN: University of Minnesota Press.

Chacaby, Ma-Nee, and Mary Louisa Plummer. 2016. *A Two-Spirit Journey: The Autobiography of a Lesbian Ojibwa-Cree Elder*. Winnipeg: University of Manitoba Press.

Code, Lorraine. 2000. *Encyclopedia of Feminist Theories*. New York: Routledge.

Collins, Patricia Hill. 2003. "Toward a New Vision," pp. 331–348 in Michael S. Kimmell and Abby L. Ferber, eds, *Privilege: A Reader*. Boulder, CO: Westview Press.

Comack, Elizabeth, and Gillian Balfour. 2004. *The Power to Criminalize: Violence, Inequality and the Law*. Halifax: Fernwood Publishing.

Cote-Meek, Sheila. 2014. *Colonized Classrooms: Racism, Trauma and Resistance in Post-Secondary Education*. Black Point, N.S.: Fernwood Publishing.

Cote-Meek, Sheila. 2010. Exploring the Impact of Ongoing Colonial Violence on Aboriginal Students in the Postsecondary Classroom. PhD Dissertation, University of Toronto.

Coulthard, Glen Sean. 2014. *Red Skin, White Masks: Rejecting the Colonial Politics of Recognition.* Minneapolis: University of Minnesota Press.

CTV News. 2022. "Report urges more re-investigation into deaths of Indigenous people in Thunder Bay, Ont.," *CTV News.* 17 March. Available at https://www.ctvnews.ca/canada/report-urges-more-re-investigations-into-deaths-of-indigenous-people-in-thunder-bay-ont-1.5823592

Davis Jackson, Deborah. 2002. *Our Elders Lived It: American Indian Identity in the City.* DeKalb, IL: Northern Illinois University Press.

Dhamoon, Rita. 2015. "A Feminist Approach to Decolonizing Anti-Racism: Rethinking Transnationalism, Intersectionality, and Settler Colonialism," *Feral Feminisms: Complicities, Connections and Struggles: Critical Transnational Feminist Analysis of Settler Colonialism 4* (Summer): 20–37.

Dion, Susan D. 2009. *Braiding Histories: Learning from Aboriginal Peoples' Experiences and Perspectives.* Vancouver: University of British Columbia Press.

Doxtator, Deborah. 1996. "What Happened to the Iroquois Clans?: A Study of Clans in Three Nineteenth Century Rotinonhsyonni Communities." Unpublished PhD dissertation, University of Western Ontario.

Dunbar-Ortiz, Roxanne. 2021. *Not "A Nation of Immigrants": Settler Colonialism, White Supremacy, and a History of Erasure and Exclusion.* Boston MA: Beacon Press.

Dyck, Noel. 1985. *Indigenous People and the Nation-State: Fourth World Politics in Canada, Australia and Norway.* St. John's NF: Memorial University of Newfoundland.

Estes, Nick, Melanie K. Yazzie, Jennifer Nez Denetdale, and David Correia. 2021. *Red Nation Rising: From Bordertown Violence to Native Liberation.* Oakland, CA: PM Press.

Eversole, Robyn, John-Andrew McNeish, and Alberto D. Cimadamore, eds. 2005. *Indigenous Peoples and Poverty: An International Perspective.* London: Zed Books.

Fellows, Mary Louise, and Sherene Razack. 1998. "The Race to Innocence: Confronting Hierarchical Relations among Women," *Journal of Gender, Race and Justice 1* (2): 335–352.

Financial Post. 2020. "B.C.'s Supreme court rules for $6.6-billion Coastal GasLink pipeline, against Indigenous law," *Financial Post* 2 January. Available at https://financialpost.com/commodities/b-c-s-top-court-rules-for-6-6-billion-coastal-gaslink-pipeline-against-indigenous-law

Fiske, Jo-Anne, and Annette Browne. 2006. "Aboriginal Citizen, Discredited Medical Subject: Paradoxical Constructions of Subjectivity in Health Care Policies," *Policy Sciences 39* (1): 91–111.

Fleras, Augie. 2009. "'Playing the Aboriginal Card': Race or Rights?" pp. 75–78 in Maria Wallis and Augie Fleras, eds, *The Politics of Race in Canada: Readings in Historical Perspectives, Contemporary Realities, and Future Possibilities.* Toronto: Oxford University Press.

Gehl, Lynn. 2022. "The First Peoples Group Report Re: Queen's U and Ardoch," Available at https://www.lynngehl.com/gehl-blogging/the-first-peoples-group-report-re-queens-u-and-ardoch

Gehl, Lynn. 2014. *The Truth That Wampum Tells: My Debwewin on the Algonquin Land Claims Process.* Halifax: Fernwood Publishing.

Gilley, B. J. 2006. *Becoming Two-Spirit: Gay Identity and Social Acceptance in Indian Country.* Lincoln, NB: University of Nebraska Press.

Gilio-Whitaker, Dina. 2019. *As Long as Grass Grows: The Indigenous Fight for Environmental Justice, From Colonization to Standing Rock.* Boston, MA: Beacon Press.

Global News. 2022. "The Pope's tour is over. Here's what some Indigenous Peoples want Canadians to take away," *Global News*, August 5. Available at https://globalnews.ca/news/9037661/pope-tour-over-takeaway-canadians/

Globe and Mail. 2015. "Cindy Gladue was reduced to a body part," *Globe and Mail*, 6 April. Available at https://www.theglobeandmail.com/opinion/reduced-to-a-body-part/article23790508/

Globe and Mail. 2008. "What Dick Pound said was really dumb –and also true," *Globe and Mail.* 25 October. Available at https://www.theglobeandmail.com/news/national/what-dick-pound-said-was-really-dumb—and-also-true/article716641/

Globe and Mail. 2005. "Tainted tap water common on reserves across province," *Globe and Mail.* 25 October. Available at https://www.theglobeandmail.com/news/national/tainted-tap-water-common-on-reserves-across-province/article989010/

Grande, Sandy. 2004. *Red Pedagogy: Native American Social and Political Thought.* New York: Rowman and Littlefield Publishers, Inc.

Green, Joyce, ed. 2007. *Making Space for Indigenous Feminism.* Halifax, NS: Fernwood Publishing/Zed Books.

Green, Joyce, ed. 2006. "From *Stonechild* to Social Cohesion," *Canadian Journal of Political Science 39* (1): 507–527.

Hamber, Brandon. 2006. "Narrowing the Micro and Macro: A Psychological Perspective on Reparations in Societies in Transition," pp. 560–588 in Pablo De Greiff, ed, *The Handbook of Reparations.* New York: Oxford University Press.

Harris, Cheryl I. 1993. "Whiteness as Property," *Harvard Law Review 106* (8): 1707–1791.

Haudenosaunee Confederacy. 1983. "Statement of the Haudenosaunee Concerning the Constitutional Framework and International Position of the Haudenosaunee Confederacy," in *House of Commons Minutes of Proceedings and Evidence of the Special Committee on Indian Self-Government*, Issue # 31, Appendix 36. Ottawa: Queen's Printer.

Hele, Karl. 2015. "An Era's End? Imposing/Opposing Control in the Sault Ste. Marie Borderlands," pp. 47—70 in Ute Lischke, David McNab, and Paul-Emile McNab, eds, *Tecumseh's Vision: Indigenous Sovereignty and Borders since the War of 1812*. Winnipeg, Manitoba: Aboriginal Issues Press.

Henderson, James (Sákéj) Youngblood. 2002. "Sui Generis and Treaty Citizenship," *Citizenship Studies 6* (4): 415–440.

Henry, Frances, and Carol Tator. 2006. *The Colour of Democracy: Racism in Canadian Society*, 3rd edn. Toronto: Thomson Nelson Canada.

Henry, Frances, Carol Tator, Winston Mattis, and Tim Rees. 1998. *The Colour of Democracy: Racism in Canadian Society*, 2nd edn. Toronto: Thomson Nelson Canada.

Hill, Susan M. 2008. "'Travelling Down the River of Life Together in Peace and Friendship Forever': Haudenosaunee Land Ethics and Treaty Arrangements as the Basis for Restructuring the Relationship with the British Crown," pp. 23–45 in Leanne Simpson ed., *Lighting the Eighth Fire: The Liberation, Resurgence, and Protection of Indigenous Nations*. Winnipeg: Arbeiter Ring Publishing.

Hill, Susan M. 2017. *The Clay We Are Made Of: Haudenosaunee Land Tenure on the Grand River*. Winnipeg: University of Manitoba Press.

Indian Act, RSC 1985, c I-5 Available at https://laws-lois. justice.gc.ca/eng/acts/i-5/.

Indigenous Bar Association. 2010. "Position Paper on Bill C-3 – Gender Equity in Indian Registry Act," Submitted to Senate Committee on Human Rights. December 6, 2010. Ottawa: Indigenous Bar Association.

Indigenous Bar Association. 2017. "Bill S-3 An Act to Amend the Indian Act (elimination of sex-based inequities in registration)," April 24 2017. Ottawa: Indigenous Bar Association. http://www.indigenousbar.ca/pdf/ ibc_bill_S-3.pdf.

Ing, Rosalyn. 2006. "Canada's Indian Residential Schools and Their Impacts on Mothering," pp. 157–172 in D. Memee Lavell-Harvard and Jeanette Corbiere Lavell, eds, *"Until Our Hearts Are on the Ground": Aboriginal Mothering, Oppression, Resistance and Rebirth*. Toronto: Demeter Press.

Jacobs, Beverley. 2014. "There has been a war against Indigenous women since colonization: Former NWAC president," *APTN National News*, 23 September.

Jacobs, Beverley. 2008. "Response to Canada's Apology to Residential School Survivors," *Canadian Woman Studies 26* (3 & 4): 223–225.

Jay, Dru Oia. 2014. "What If Natives Stop Subsidizing Canada?" pp. 108–112 in The Kino-nda-niimi Collective, eds, *The Winter We Danced: Voices from the Past, the Future, and the Idle No More Movement*. Winnipeg: Arbeiter Ring Publishing.

Jeffery, Donna, and Jennifer J. Nelson. 2009. "The More Things Change . . .: The Endurance of 'Culturalism' in Social Work and Healthcare," pp. 91–110 in Carol Schick and James McNinch, eds, *"I Thought Pochahontas Was a Movie" Perspectives on Race/Culture Binaries in Education and Service Professions*. Regina: Canadian Plains Research Centre Press.

Johnston, Darlene M. 1986. "The Quest of the Six Nations Confederacy for Self-Determination," *University of Toronto Faculty Law Review 44* (1): 1–32.

Joseph, R.A. 2008. "A Jade Door: Reconciliatory Justice as a Way Forward Citing New Zealand Experience," pp. 205–232 in Marlene Brant Castellano, Linda Archibald and Mike DeGagn, eds, *From Truth to Reconciliation: Transforming the Legacy of Residential Schools*. Ottawa: Aboriginal Healing Foundation.

Kalman, Ian. 2021. *Framing Borders: Principle and Practicality in the Akwesasne Mohawk Territory*. Toronto: University of Toronto Press.

Kauanui, J. Kehaulani. 2008. *Hawaiian Blood! Colonialism and the Politics of Sovereignty and Indigeneity*. Durham, NC: Duke University Press.

Kebaowek First Nations. 2016. "Urgent Message to Pikwakanagan Anishinabe." Available at www.medium. com.

Kelm, Mary-Ellen. 1998. *Colonizing Bodies: Aboriginal Health and Healing in British Columbia, 1900–50*. Vancouver: University of British Columbia Press.

King, Tiffany Lethabo. 2016. "New World Grammars: The 'Unthought' Black Discourses of Conquest," *Theory and Event 19* (4).

King, Tiffany Lethabo, Jenell Navarro, and Andrea Smith, eds. 2020. *Otherwise Worlds: Against Settler Colonialism and Anti-Blackness*. Durham, NC: Duke University Press.

Land, Clare. 2015. *Decolonizing Solidarity: Dilemmas and Directions for Supporters of Indigenous Struggles*. New York: Zed Books.

Landertinger, Laura. 2017. *Child Welfare and the Imperial Management of Childhood in Settler Colonial Canada, 1880s–2000s*. PhD Dissertation, University of Toronto.

LaRocque, Emma. 1993. "Three Conventional Approaches to Native People in Society and in Literature," in Brett Balon and Peter Resch, eds., *Survival of the Imagination: The Mary Donaldson Memorial Lectures*. Regina, SK: Coteau Books.

Lavell-Harvard, Memee, and Jennifer Brant, eds. 2016. *Forever Loved: Exposing the Hidden Crisis of Missing and Murdered Indigenous Women and Girls in Canada*. Bradford, ON: Demeter Press.

Lawrence, Bonita. 2004. *"Real" Indians and Others: Mixed-Blood Urban Native Peoples and Indigenous Nationhood*. Vancouver: UBC Press.

Lawrence, Bonita. 2002. "Rewriting Histories of the Land: Colonization and Indigenous Resistance in Eastern Canada," in S. Razack, ed., *Race, Space, and the Law: Unmapping a White Settler Society*. Toronto: Between the Lines.

Lawrence, Bonita. 2012. *Fractured Homeland: Federal Recognition and Algonquin Identity in Ontario*. Vancouver: UBC Press.

Lawrence, Bonita, and Zainab Amadahy. 2009. "Indigenous Peoples and Black People in Canada: Settlers or Allies?"

pp. 105–136 in Arlo Kempf, ed., *Breaching the Colonial Contract: Anticolonialism in the U.S. and Canada.* Netherlands: Springer.

Lawrence, Bonita, and Ena Dua. 2005. "Decolonizing Antiracism," *Social Justice* 32 (5): 120–143.

Logan McCallum, Mary Jane and Adele Perry. 2018. *Structures of Indifference: An Indigenous Life and Death in a Canadian City.* Winnipeg: University of Manitoba Press.

Lindberg, Tracey. 2010. "The Doctrine of Discovery in Canada," pp. 89–125 in R. J. Miller, J. Ruru, L. Behrendt, & T. Lindberg, eds, *Discovering Indigenous Lands: The Doctrine of Discovery in the English Colonies.* New York: Oxford University Press.

Linton, Ralph. 1940. *Acculturation in Seven American Indian Tribes.* New York: Appleton-Century.

Lovelace, Sandra and Brian Francis. 2022. "First Nations Women, Children Deserve Federal Action to Address Ongoing Indian Act Discrimination." Ottawa: Senate of Canada. Available at https://sencanada.ca/en/sencaplus/opinion/first-nations-women-children-deserve-federal-action-to-address-ongoing-indian-act-discrimination/.

MacDonald, David B. 2020. "Paved with Comfortable Intentions: Moving Beyond Liberal Multiculturalism and Civil Rights Frames on the Road to Transformative Reconciliation," pp. 3–24 in Aimée Craft and Paulette Regan, eds., *Pathways of Reconciliation: Indigenous and Settler Approaches to Implementing the TRC Calls to Action.* Winnipeg: University of Manitoba Press.

Mackey, Eva. 2016. *Unsettled Expectations: Uncertainty, Land and Settler Decolonization.* Halifax: Fernwood Publishing.

Macleans. 2020. "What we are seeing in 2020 is Idle No More 2.0," *Macleans*, 15 September. Available at https://www.macleans.ca/opinion/what-were-seeing-in-2020-is-idle-no-more-2-0/.

Macleans. 2015. "Justin Trudeau, for the record: 'We beat fear with hope,'" *Macleans*, 20 October. Available at http://www.macleans.ca/politics/ottawa/justin-trudeau-for-the-record-we-beat-fear-with-hope/.

Madden, Paula. 2009. *African Nova Scotian–Mi'kmaw Relations.* Halifax: Fernwood Publishing.

Manuel, Arthur and Grand Chief Ronald Derrickson. 2017. *The Reconciliation Manifesto: Recovering the Land Rebuilding the Economy.* Toronto, ON: James Lorimer and Company Ltd., Publishers.

Mariedaughter, Paula. 1986. "Too Butch for Straights, Too Femme for Dykes." Lesbian Ethics 2 (1): 96–100.

Maynard, Robyn. 2019. "Black Life and Death Across the U.S.-Canada Border: Border Violence, Black Fugitive Belonging, and a Turtle Island View of Black Liberation," *Journal of the Critical Ethnic Studies Association* 5 (1–2): 124–151.

Maynard, Robyn and Leanne Betawamosake Simpson. 2020. "Towards Black and Indigenous Futures on Turtle Island: A Conversation," pp. 75–94 in Rodney Diverlus, Sandy Hudson and Syrus Marcus Ware, eds. *Until We Are Free: Reflections on Black Lives Matter in Canada.* Regina: University of Regina Press.

Mihesuah, Devon A., ed. 1998. *Natives and Academics: Research and Writing about American Indians.* Lincoln, NE: University of Nebraska Press.

Million, Dian. 2013. *Therapeutic Nations: Healing in an Age of Indigenous Human Rights.* Phoenix, AZ: University of Arizona Press.

McIvor v. Canada (Registrar, Indian and Northern Affairs). 2007. BCSC 827.

McKittrick, Katherine, ed. 2015. *Sylvia Wynter: On Being Human as Praxis.* Durham, NC: Duke University Press.

Mitchell, Grand Chief Michael. 1989. "Akwesasne: An Unbroken Assertion of Sovereignty," pp. 105–136 in Boyce Richardson, ed., *Drum Beat: Anger and Renewal in Indian Country.* Ottawa: Summerhill Press/The Assembly of First Nations.

Monchalin, Lisa. 2016. *The Colonial Problem: An Indigenous Perspective on Crime and Injustice in Canada.* Toronto: University of Toronto Press.

Montour, Martha. 1987. "Iroquois Women's Rights with Respect to Matrimonial Property on Indian Reserves," *Canadian Native Law Reporter* 4: 1–10.

Monture, Patricia. 2008. "Women's Words: Power, Identity, and Indigenous Sovereignty," *Canadian Woman Studies* 26 (3 & 4): 154–159.

Monture, Patricia. 1999. "Standing against Canadian Law: Naming Omissions of Race, Culture, and Gender," pp. 73–93 in Elizabeth Comack and Karen Busby, eds, *Locating Law: Race/Class/Gender/Sexuality Connections, 2nd edition.* Halifax: Fernwood Publishing.

Monture, Patricia. 1999. *Journeying Forward: Dreaming First Nations Independence.* Halifax, NS: Fernwood Publishing.

Monture, Patricia. 1995. *Thunder in My Soul: A Mohawk Woman Speaks.* Halifax, NS: Fernwood Publishing.

National Inquiry into Missing and Murdered Indigenous Women and Girls. 2019. *Reclaiming Power and Place: the Final Report of the National Inquiry into Missing and Murdered Indigenous Women and Girls.* Ottawa: Government of Canada.

Native Women's Association of Canada. 2015. *Fact Sheet: Violence Against Aboriginal Women.* Available at www.nwac.ca/wp-content/uploads/2015/Fact_Sheet_Violence_Against_Aboriginal_Women.pdf.

Nelson, Jennifer J. 2009. "Lost in Translation: Anti-racism and the Perils of Knowledge," pp. 15–32 in Carol Schick and James McNinch, eds, *"I Thought Pocahontas Was A Movie" Perspectives on Race/Culture Binaries in Education and Service Professions.* Regina: Canadian Plains Research Centre Press.

Obomsawin, Alanis. 2016. *We Can't Make the Same Mistake Twice.* National Film Board.

Palmater, Pamela D. 2011. *Beyond Blood: Rethinking Indigenous Identity.* Saskatoon: Purich Publishing.

Pasternak, Shiri. 2014. "Occupy(ed) Canada: The Political Economy of Indigenous Dispossession," pp. 44–51 in The Kino-nda-niimi Collective, eds, *The Winter We Danced: Voices from the Past, the Future, and the Idle No More Movement.* Winnipeg: Arbeiter Ring Publishing.

Pasternak, Shiri. 2017. *Grounded Authority: The Algonquins of Barriere Lake Against the State*. Minneapolis MN: University of Minnesota Press.

Penelope, Julia. 1986. "Language and the Transformation of Consciousness." *Law & Inequality 4*: 379.

Phung, Malissa. 2011. "Are People of Colour Settlers Too?" pp. 291–298 in Ashok Mathur, Jonathan Dewar, and Mike DeGagné, eds., *Cultivating Canada: Reconciliation through the Lens of Cultural Diversity*. Ottawa: Aboriginal Healing Foundation Research Series.

Polaschek, N.R. 1998. "Cultural Safety: A New Concept in Nursing People of Different Ethnicities," *Journal of Advanced Nursing 27* (3): 452–457.

Porter, Robert B. 1999. "The Demise of the Ongwehoweh and the Rise of the Native Americans: Redressing the Genocidal Act of Forcing American Citizenship upon Indigenous Peoples," *Harvard Black Letter Law Journal 15*: 107–183.

Posluns, M. 2007. *Speaking with Authority: The Emergence of the Vocabulary of First Nations' Self-Government*. New York: Routledge.

Provincial Court of Manitoba. 12 December 2014. *In the Provincial Court of Manitoba in the Matter of The Fatalities Inquiries Act and in the matter of Brian Lloyd Sinclair, Deceased*.

R. v. Desautel. 2021. SCC 17.

Ramirez, Renya. 2007. *Native Hubs: Culture, Community, and Belonging in Silicon Valley and Beyond*. Durham, NC: Duke University Press.

Razack, Sherene H. 2015. *Dying from Improvement: Inquests and Inquiries into Indigenous Deaths in Custody*. Toronto: University of Toronto Press.

Razack, Sherene H. 2002. "Gendered Racial Violence and Spatialized Justice: The Murder of Pamela George," pp. 121–156 in Sherene H. Razack, ed., *Race, Space and the Law: Unmapping a White Settler Society*. Toronto: Between the Lines Press.

Razack, Sherene H. 1998. *Looking White People in the Eye: Gender, Race, and Culture in Courtrooms and Classrooms*. Toronto: University of Toronto Press.

Reid, Gerald F. 2007. "Illegal Alien?: The Immigration Case of Mohawk Ironworker Paul K. Diabo," *Proceedings of the American Philosophical Society 151* (1): 61–78.

Rickard, Jolene. 30 September 1995. "The Indian Defense League of America," *Akwesasne Notes 1* (2): 48–53.

Rifkin, Mark. 2014. *Settler Common Sense: Queerness and Everyday Colonialism in the American Renaissance*. Minneapolis, MN: University of Minnesota Press.

Rocke, Cathy and Regine Uwibereyeho King. 2020. "What Does Reconciliation Mean to Newcomers Post-TRC," pp. 173–188 in Aimée Craft and Paulette Regan, eds., *Pathways of Reconciliation: Indigenous and Settler Approaches to Implementing the TRC Calls to Action*. Winnipeg: University of Manitoba Press.

Russell, Peter H. 2021. *Sovereignty: The Biography of a Claim*. Toronto, ON: University of Toronto Press.

Said, Edward W. 1979. *Orientalism*. New York: Vintage Books.

Saranillio, Dean. 2013. "Why Asian Settler Colonialism Matters: A Thought Piece on Critiques, Debates and Indigenous Difference," *Settler Colonial Studies 3* (3-4): 280–294.

Schick, Carol. 2004. "Disrupting binaries of self and other: Anti-homophic pedagogies for student teachers," pp. 243–254 in J. McNinch and M. Cronin, eds, *I Could Not Speak My Heart: Education and Social Justice for Gay and Lesbian Youth*. Regina: Canadian Plains Research Centre.

Schick, Carol, and Verna St Denis. 2005. "Troubling National Discourses in Anti-racist Curricular Planning," *Canadian Journal of Education 28* (3): 295–317.

Sehdev, Robinder Kaur. 2011. "People of Colour in Treaty," pp. 264–274 in Ashok Mathur, Jonathan Dewar, and Mike DeGagné, eds, *Cultivating Canada: Reconciliation through the Lens of Cultural Diversity*. Ottawa: Aboriginal Healing Foundation Research Series.

Sharma, Nandita. 2020. *Home Rule: National Sovereignty and the Separation of Natives and Migrants*. Durham, NC: Duke University Press.

Simon, Roger. 2013. "Towards a Hopeful Practice of Worrying: The Problematics of Listening and the Educative Responsibilities of Canada's Truth and Reconciliation Commission," pp. 129–142 in Pauline Wakeham and Jennifer Henderson, eds, *Reconciling Canada: Critical Perspectives on the Culture of Redress*. Toronto: University of Toronto Press.

Simpson, Audra. 2017. "The Ruse of Consent and the Anatomy of Refusal: Cases from Indigenous North America and Australia," *Postcolonial Studies 20* (1): 18–33.

Simpson, Audra. 2016. "Consent's Revenge," *Cultural Anthropology 31* (3): 326–333.

Simpson, Audra. 2014. *Mohawk Interruptus: Political Life Across the Borders of Settler States*. Durham, NC: Duke University Press.

Simpson, Audra. 2008. "Subjects of Sovereignty: Indigeneity, the Revenue Rule, and Juridics of Failed Consent," *Law and Contemporary Problems 71*: 191–216.

Simpson, Audra. 1998. "The Empire Laughs Back: Tradition, Power, and Play in the Work of Shelley Niro and Ryan Rice," pp. 48–54 in Doris I. Stambrau, Alexandra V. Roth, and Sylvia S. Kasprycki, eds, *IroquoisArt: Visual Expressions of Contemporary Native American Artists*. Altenstadt, DE: European Review of Native American Studies.

Simpson, Leanne Betasamosake. 2017. *As We Have Always Done: Indigenous Freedom Through Radical Resistance*. Minneapolis, MN: University of Minnesota Press.

Simpson, Leanne Betasamosake. 2014. *Islands of Decolonial Love: Stories and Songs*. Winnipeg, MB: Arbiter Ring Publishing.

Smith, Andrea. 2008. *Native Americans and the Christian Right: The Gendered Politics of Unlikely Alliances*. Durham, NC: Duke University Press.

Smith, Andrea. 2006. "Heteropatriarchy and the Three Pillars of White Supremacy," pp. 66–73 in *Color of*

Violence: The Incite! Anthology. Incite!: Women of Color against Violence. Cambridge, MA: South End Press.

Smith, Andrea. 2005. *Conquest: Sexual Violence and American Indian Genocide.* Cambridge, MA: South End Press.

Statistics Canada. 2011. *Aboriginal Peoples in Canada: First Nations People, Metis and Inuit (National Household Survey).* Statistics Canada. Available at https://www12.statcan.gc.ca/nhs-enm/2011/as-sa/99-011-x/99-011-x2011001-eng.cfm

St Denis, Verna. 2004. "Real Indians: Cultural Revitalization and Fundamentalism in Aboriginal Education," pp. 35–47 in Carol Schick, JoAnn Jaffe, and Aisla M. Watkinson, eds, *Contesting Fundamentalisms.* Halifax, NS: Fernwood Publishing.

St Denis, Verna, and Carol Schick. 2003. "What Makes Anti-racist Pedagogy in Teacher Education Difficult? Three Popular Ideological Assumptions," *The Alberta Journal of Educational Research* 49 (1): 55–69.

Steckley, John. 2003. *Aboriginal Voices and the Politics of Representation in Canadian Introductory Sociology Textbooks.* Toronto: Canadian Scholars Press.

Stevenson, Winona. 1999. "Colonialism and First Nations Women in Canada," pp. 49–80 in Enakshi Dua and Angela Robertson, eds, *Scratching the Surface: Canadian Anti-racist Feminist Thought.* Toronto: Women's Press.

Sunseri, Lina. 2011. *Being Again of One Mind: Oneida Women and the Struggle for Decolonization.* Vancouver: UBC Press.

Sunseri, Lina. 2007. "Indigenous Voice Matters: Claiming Our Space through Decolonising Research," *Junctures* 9: 93–106.

Sunseri, Lina. 2000. "Moving Beyond the Feminism versus the Nationalism Dichotomy: An Anti-colonial Feminist Perspective on Aboriginal Liberation Struggles," *Canadian Woman Studies* 20 (2): 143–148.

Supreme Court of Canada. 14 April 2016. *Daniels v. Canada (Indian Affairs and Northern Development).* Supreme Court of Canada. Available at https://scc-csc.lexum.com/scc-csc/scc-csc/en/item/15858/index.do

Tagalik, Shirley. 2015. "Inuit Knowledge Systems, Elders, and Determinants of Health," pp. 25–32 in Margo Greenwood, Sarah de Leeuw, Nicole Marie Lindsay, and Charlotte Readings, eds, *Determinants of Indigenous Peoples' Health in Canada: Beyond the Social.* Toronto: Canadian Scholars' Press Inc.

The Canadian Press. 2022. "UNDRIP 15 years on: Genuine truth and reconciliation requires legislative reform," *The Canadian Press.* 30 September. Available at https://nationalpost.com/pmn/news-pmn/undrip-15-years-on-genuine-truth-and-reconciliation-requires-legislative-reform.

The Conversation. 2019. "Remembering Neil Stonechild and exposing systemic racism in policing," *The Conversation.* 5 December. Available at https://theconversation.com/remembering-neil-stonechild-and-exposing-systemic-racism-in-policing-128436.

The Kino-nda-niimi Collective, eds. 2014. *The Winter We Danced: Voices from the Past, the Future, and the Idle No More Movement.* Winnipeg: Arbeiter Ring Publishing.

The Star Phoenix. 2019. "Gerald Stanley trial: jury delivers not guilty verdict in death of Colten Boushie," *The Star Phoenix.* 8 February. Available at https://thestarphoenix.com/news/local-news/gerald-stanley-trial-jury-delivers-not-guilty-verdict-in-murder-of-colten-boushie.

The Tyee. 2022. "Overrepresentation of Indigenous women in jails hits record levels in BC," *The Tyee.* 31 May. Available at https://thetyee.ca/News/2022/05/31/Overrepresentation-Indigenous-Women-In-Jail/.

Thielen-Wilson, Leslie. 2014. "Troubling the Path to Decolonization: Indian Residential School Case Law, Genocide, and Settler Illegitimacy," *Canadian Journal of Law and Society* 29 (2): 181–197.

Thobani, Sunera. 2007. *Exalted Subjects: Studies in the Making of Race and Nation in Canada.* Toronto: University of Toronto Press.

Tobias, John L. 1983. "Protection, Civilization, Assimilation: An Outline History of Canada's Indian Policy," pp. 39–55 in Ian A.L. Getty and Antoine S. Lussier, eds, *As Long as the Sun Shines and Water Flows: A Reader in Canadian Native Studies.* Vancouver: UBC Press.

Trask, Haunani-Kay. "The Color of Violence." (pgs. 81–87) in INCITE! Women of Color Against Racism (eds.) *Color of Violence: The INCITE! Anthology.* Cambridge, MA: South End Press, 2006.

Trebilcot, Joyce. 1988. "Dyke Methods or Principles for the Discovery/Creation of the Withstanding*." *Hypatia* 3(2): 1–14.

Truth and Reconciliation Commission of Canada. 2015. *Honouring the Truth, Reconciling for the Future: Summary of the Final Report of the Truth and Reconciliation Commission of Canada.*

Turner, Dale. 2006. *This Is Not a Peace Pipe: Towards a Critical Indigenous Philosophy.* Toronto: University of Toronto Press.

University of British Columbia, Faculty of Arts 2022. "How Indigenous Communities have battled COVID-19." UBC Faculty of Arts 5 April. Available at https://www.arts.ubc.ca/news/how-indigenous-communities-have-battled-covid-19/

United Nations. 2007. *United Nations Declaration on the Rights of Indigenous Peoples.* Available at http://www.un.org/esa/socdev/unpfi/en/declaration.html.

United Nations. 1993. *United Nations Declaration on the Elimination of Violence against Women.* Available at https://www.ohchr.org/en/instruments-mechanisms/instruments/declaration-elimination-violence-against-women.

Valaskakis, Gail Guthrie, Madeleine Dion Stout, and Eric Guimond, eds. 2009. *Restoring the Balance: First Nations Women, Community, and Culture.* Winnipeg: University of Manitoba Press.

Veracini, Lorenzo. 2010. *Settler Colonialism: A Theoretical Overview.* New York: Palgrave Macmilan.

Venne, Sharon Helen. 1981. *Indian Acts and Amendments 1868–1975: An Indexed Collection.* Saskatoon, SK: University of Saskatchewan, Native Law Centre.

Voyageur, Cora, and Brian Calliou. 2003. "Aboriginal Economic Development and the Struggle for

Self-Government," pp. 121–144 in Les Samuelson and Wayne Anthony, eds, *Power and Resistance: Critical Thinking about Canadian Social Issues*, Third Edition. Halifax: Fernwood Publishing.

Waldron, Ingrid R.G. 2018. *There's Something in the Water: Environmental Racism in Indigenous and Black Communities*. Black Point, N.S.: Fernwood Publishing.

Walia, Harsha. 2021. *Border and Rule: Global Migration, Capitalism and the Rise of Racist Nationalism*. Chicago, Ill: Haymarket Books.

Walia, Harsha. 2013. *Undoing Border Imperialism*. Oakland, CA: AK Press and the Institute for Anarchist Studies.

Walia, Harsha. 2012. "Decolonizing Together: Moving Beyond a Politics of Solidarity toward a Practice of Decolonization," *Briarpatch* Jan/Feb: 27–30.

Wallis, Maria, and Augie Fleras, eds. 2009. *The Politics of Race in Canada: Readings in Historical Perspectives,* *Contemporary Realities, and Future Possibilities*. Toronto: Oxford University Press.

Williams, Paul, and Curtis Nelson. 1995. *Kaswantha*. Ottawa: Royal Commission on Aboriginal Peoples [paper no. 88a].

Wilson, Alex. 2008. "N'tacimowin inna nah': Our Coming In Stories." *Canadian Woman Studies 26* (3/4): 193–199.

Winnipeg Sun. 2018. "Tina Fontaine Murder Case Never Had a Chance," *Winnipeg Sun*. 22 February. Available at https://winnipegsun.com/opinion/columnists/tina-fontaine-murder-case-never-had-a-chance.

Wolfe, Patrick. 2006. "Settler Colonialism and the Elimination of the Native," *Journal of Genocide Research* 8 (4): 387–409.

Wotherspoon, Terry L., and Vic Satzewich. 1993. *First Nations: Race, Class and Gender Relations*. Toronto: Nelson.